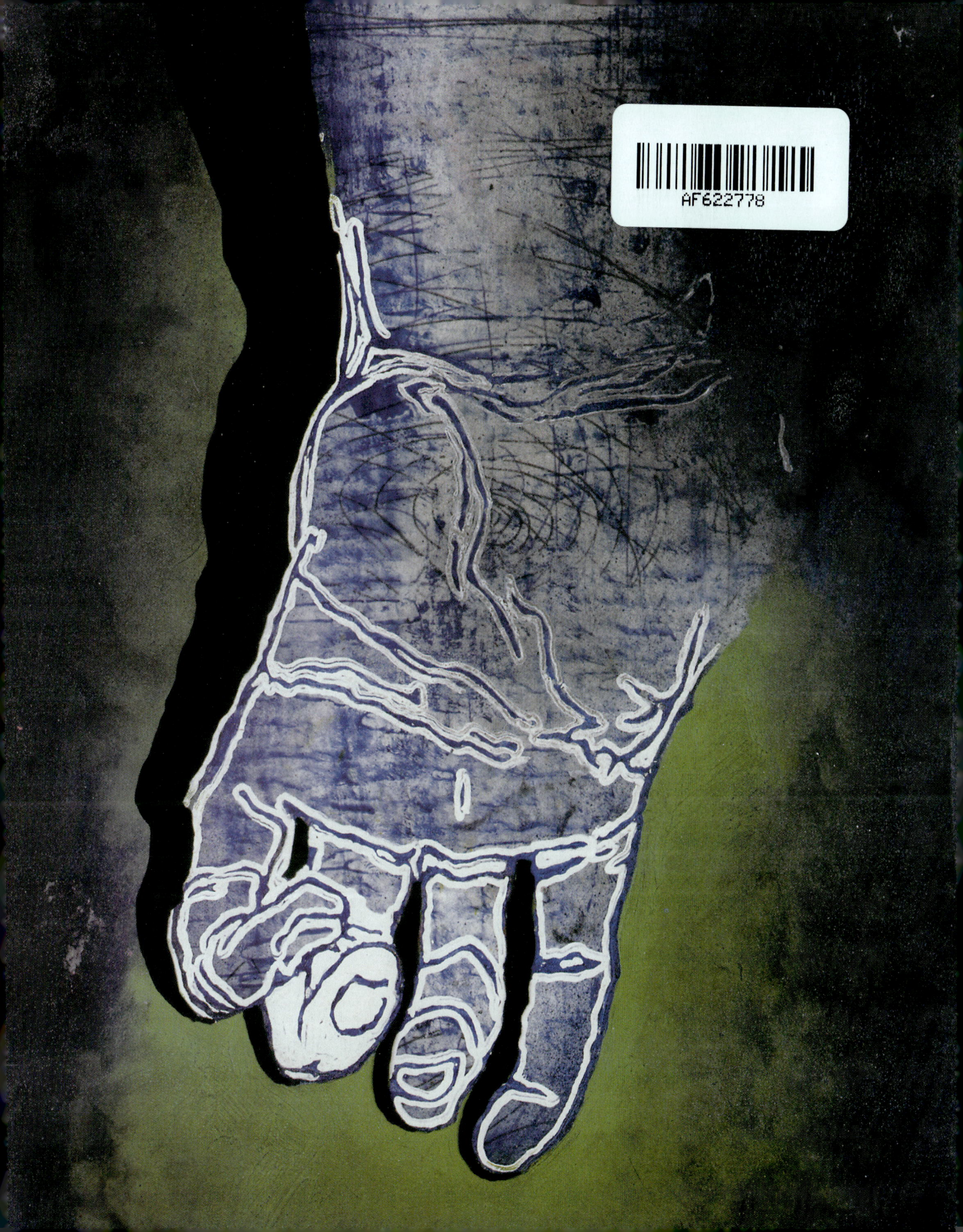

DIE PARKETT-REIHE MIT GEGENWARTSKÜNSTLERN / THE PARKETT SERIES WITH CONTEMPORARY ARTISTS

Book Series with contemporary artists in English and German, published three times a year. Each volume is created in collaboration with artists, who contribute an original work specially made for the readers of Parkett. The works are reproduced in the regular edition and available in a limited and signed Special Edition.

Buchreihe mit Gegenwartskünstlern in deutscher und englischer Sprache, erscheint dreimal im Jahr. Jeder Band entsteht mit Künstlern oder Künstlerinnen, die eigens für die Leser von Parkett einen Originalbeitrag gestalten. Diese Werke sind in der gesamten Auflage abgebildet und zusätzlich in einer limitierten und signierten Vorzugsausgabe erhältlich.

PARKETT NR. 73 ENTSTEHT IN COLLABORATION MIT • **ELLEN GALLAGHER, PAUL McCARTHY, ANRI SALA** • WILL BE COLLABORATING ON PARKETT NO. 73

JAHRESABONNEMENT (DREI NUMMERN) / ANNUAL SUBSCRIPTION (THREE ISSUES) SFR. 116.– (SCHWEIZ), € 78 (D), € 82 (ÜBRIGES EUROPA), US$ 80 (USA AND CANADA ONLY)

ZWEI- UND DREIJAHRESABONNEMENTPREISE SIEHE GELBE BESTELLKARTE IM HEFT / FOR TWO & THREE YEAR RATES, PLEASE CONSULT YELLOW ORDER FORM.

Zürichsee Druckereien AG (Stäfa) Satz, Litho, Druck / Copy, Printing, Color Separations

PARKETT-VERLAG AG ZÜRICH DECEMBER 2004 PRINTED IN SWITZERLAND ISBN 3-907582-32-2 ISSN 0256-0917

Special thanks to Vivien Bittencourt, Vincent Katz, and Barbara Carneglia, Galleria Emi Fontana, Milano.

Cover / Umschlag: RICHARD PRINCE, SURGICAL NURSE, 2002, ink-jet print and acrylic on canvas, 58 x 36", detail / 147,3 x 91,4 cm.
Cover flap / Umschlagklappe: MONICA BONVICINI, STAIRWAY TO HELL, 2003, installation; RED ON PARKING LOT, 1999, digital print.
Page / Seite 1 & back cover / Rückseite: URS FISCHER, SCENES FROM AN OLD INTERNAL BACKDROP, 2000, mixed media on paper, & DAYLIGHT PILLOW, 2004, installation, detail view / Teilansicht. *(All images slightly cropped / Alle Bilder leicht beschnitten.)*

PARKETT Zürich New York

Bice Curiger Chefredaktorin / Editor-in-Chief; **Jacqueline Burckhardt** Redaktorin / Senior Editor; **Cay Sophie Rabinowitz** Redaktorin USA / Senior Editor US; **Suzanne Schmidt** Textredaktion und Produktion / Editing and Production; **Hanna Koller · Simone Eggstein** Graphik / Design, **Trix Wetter** Graphisches Konzept / Founding Designer (–2001); **Catherine Schelbert** Englisches Lektorat / Editorial Assistant for English; **Claudia Meneghini Nevzadi** Korrektorat / Proof Reading

Beatrice Fässler Vorzugsausgaben, Inserate / Special Editions, Advertising; **Nicole Stotzer** Buchvertrieb, Administration / Distribution, Administration; **Mathias Arnold** Abonnemente / Subscriptions; **Jeremy Sigler** Redaktionsassistenz USA / Assistant Editor US; **Monika Condrea** Vorzugsausgaben, Inserate und Abonnemente USA / Special Editions, Advertising, and Subscriptions US; **Charlotte Marra** Praktikantin USA / Intern US; **Adrian Koerfer** Deutsche Verlagsvertretung / German Representative

Jacqueline Burckhardt – Bice Curiger – Dieter von Graffenried Herausgeber / Parkett Board;
Jacqueline Burckhardt – Bice Curiger – Dieter von Graffenried – Walter Keller – Peter Blum Gründer / Founders

Dieter von Graffenried Verleger / Publisher

www.parkettart.com

PARKETT-VERLAG AG, QUELLENSTRASSE 27, CH-8031 ZÜRICH, TEL. 41-1-271 81 40, FAX 41-1-272 43 01
PARKETT, NEW YORK, 155 AV. OF THE AMERICAS, N.Y. 10013, PHONE (212) 673-2660, FAX (212) 271-0704

EDITORIAL

Einst war sie ein beliebtes Schlagwort, die Rede von den «individuellen Mythologien». Monica Bonvicini, Alex Katz, Richard Prince und Urs Fischer machen in ihrer Arbeit deutlich, wie fliessend der Austausch von kollektiv und individuell, von Subkultur, Hochkultur und Mainstream in der heutigen Zeit geworden ist. Aber sie zeigen auch auf, dass Mythen an ganz unerwarteten Orten anzutreffen sind und künstlerisch verstärkt werden können.

Wie die Voraussetzungen in der Kunst sich verändert haben, zeigt gerade auch Boris Groys im letzten der drei zu Ehren des 20-Jahre-Parkett-Jubiläums erschienenen Essays zum Thema «(IM)MATERIAL?». Groys stellt eine «Retechnisierung» der Kunst fest, welche material- und arbeitsintensiv ist. Diese sei ironischerweise gerade durch die scheinbar immaterielle Computer- und Videokunst ausgelöst worden. Groys interessiert sich auch für den Weg, den der Mythos der immateriell sich äussernden künstlerischen Entscheidungen seit dem Duchampschen Readymade durchschritten hat.

Urs Fischer, der das Dasein als Künstler durch Anspielungen an seine «Atelierexistenz» in umwerfend griffigen, sozusagen folkloristischen Bildern spürbar macht, zeigt uns etwa Stühle, die den Geist von Bruce Nauman beschwören: Stühle, die eisenschwere, materialisierte Schatten werfen. Auch Fischers Edition für Parkett, die plastische Darstellung der Hand eines Zauberers, die gerade ein Kaninchen aus dem Zylinder hervorholt, gebärdet sich, als wäre der von Groys umschriebene Mythos der künstlerischen Schöpfung in einer breit wirkenden Kraft materiell und bildhaft geworden.

Gerade die Editionen scheinen in dieser Ausgabe untereinander besonders gut zu kommunizieren. Richard Prince greift in seiner Photoauflage für Parkett das mythische Ereignis einer ganzen Epoche auf: Woodstock. Dazu berichtet er in einem kleinen Text, wie er 1969 dem legendären Konzert mit nur noch einem einzigen Bild in der Kamera beiwohnte. Jetzt, 35 Jahre später, entschied sich Prince, dieses eine Photo als Parkettedition zu veröffentlichen und zu verbreiten. Somit überlagert sich der Mythos Woodstock mit der persönlichen Erzählung eines Künstlers, der selber Teil jener Kultur geworden ist, die er und seine spezifische Generation geprägt hat (eindrücklich dargestellt im Text seines Freundes Dike Blair, S. 103).

Auch Monica Bonvicini und Alex Katz greifen in ihren Editionen auf frühere, mittlerweile ikonisch gewordene Werke zurück. So ist es Duchamps Multiple COIN DE CHASTETÉ (1954), ein Bronzekeil in Dentalmasse, übrigens Duchamps Hochzeitsgeschenk an seine Frau Teeny, das Monica Bonvicini in ihrem Objekt DRILL 4 CHASTITY zitiert, wiederbelebt und neu interpretiert. Als «Metafetische» bezeichnet Juliane Rebentisch (S. 23) die Objekte von Monica Bonvicini. Was aber, wenn nun in einem solchen nichts weniger als einer der Urfetische des grossen Erotikers der Avantgarde aufscheint? Es entsteht eine Potenzierung der bildhaften Verschränkung von Geschlecht und Kunstobjekt: als veredelter Minischraubbohrer, der sich zur Ruhe gelegt hat.

Alex Katz' Bild seines Hundes Sunny, SUNNY (1971), ist eines seiner bekanntesten Werke. Nun schuf er ein Cutout in Metall, auf welches das gemalte Motiv im Siebdruckverfahren übertragen wurde. Als würde der Hund uns aus der Tiefe der Zeit aus dem Bild entgegenspringen.

Parkett ist ein Instrument zur Auseinandersetzung mit und Verbreitung von Kunst. Besonders freut es uns, zum Abschluss des extensiv gefeierten Jubiläumsjahres einen solch sinnigen Strauss von Äusserungen künstlerischer Selbstreflexion präsentieren zu können.

Die Herausgeber von Parkett möchten den Künstlerinnen und Künstlern, aber auch den Autorinnen und Autoren ganz herzlich danken für ihre in diesem Jubeljahr geschaffenen speziellen Beiträge, die so sprühend sind, dass wir darin eine Bestätigung unserer Jugend erkennen wollen. Auch den Leserinnen und Lesern danken wir in der Hoffnung, dass sie uns noch lange auf unserem Weg begleiten werden.

EDITORIAL MATERIAL MYTHS

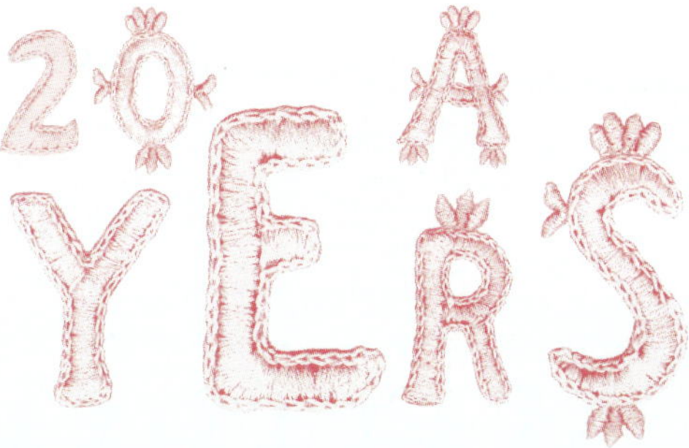

It used to be a much-debated topic with a buzzword all its own: individual mythologies. The works of Monica Bonvicini, Alex Katz, Richard Prince, and Urs Fischer unmistakably demonstrate how fluid the exchange between collective and individual, between subculture, elitist culture and mainstream has become. But these artists also show that myths may be found and artistically enhanced in the most unexpected places.

In the last of the three essays on the subject of "(IM)MATERIAL?" commissioned in honor of Parkett's 20-year anniversary, Boris Groys examines just how much the premises of art have changed. He observes that art has undergone a "retechnization" which is both material and work intensive–a development paradoxically sparked by supposedly immaterial computer and video art. Groys is also interested in how the myth of immaterially formed artistic decisions has evolved since Duchamp's readymade.

In stunningly trenchant, folklorically embroidered images, Urs Fischer makes the life of the artist tangible through allusions to his "studio existence." He creates chairs that conjure up the spirit of Bruce Nauman and cast materialized shadows which are as heavy as iron. In his Edition for Parkett, a sculptural rendition of a magician's hand pulling a rabbit out of a top hat, it seems as if far-reaching forces have charmed the myth of artistic creation, discussed by Groys, into material and visual form.

The Editions seem to communicate with each other especially well in this issue of Parkett. Richard Prince's photo edition evokes the mythic event that has come to represent an entire epoch: Woodstock. He has appended a short text describing how and why he attended that legendary concert in 1969 with only one exposure in his camera. Now, 35 years later, Prince has decided to print and present this photograph to the readers of Parkett. A personal story is thus superimposed on the myth of Woodstock by an artist who has become part of that very culture which he and his specific generation shaped (impressively described in the essay by his friend Dike Blair, p. 96).

The Editions of Monica Bonvicini and Alex Katz also make reference to earlier and now iconic works. In DRILL 4 CHASTITY, Monica Bonvicini revives and reinterprets Duchamp's multiple, WEDGE OF CHASTITY (1954), a bronze wedge in dental plastic, which he gave his wife Teeny as a wedding present. Juliane Rebentisch (p. 27) speaks of Monica Bonvicini's "meta-fetishistic objects." But what happens when such an object resonates with one of the ur-fetishes of that great eroticist of the avant-garde? The visual blend of sex and art object acquires an undeniable potency as a refined miniature drill that has laid itself to rest.

Alex Katz's picture of his dog, SUNNY (1971), is one of his best-known works. He has now created a metal cutout onto which the motif has been silkscreened–as if the dog were jumping towards us out of the picture and the depths of time.

Parkett has set itself the goal of analyzing and disseminating art. We are especially pleased, at the end of this extensively celebrated anniversary year, to be able to present such a sharp-witted bouquet of artistic self-reflection.

The editors of Parkett wish to extend very special thanks to all the artists and writers whose contributions, created especially for us during this anniversary year, manifest such effervescence that we cannot help reading them as a confirmation of our youth. We thank our readers as well and hope that they will continue to take part in our venture for many years to come.

BICE CURIGER

MATTHEW BUCKINGHAM

ANSELM FRANKE

When asked about his relation to history, Matthew Buckingham paraphrases William Faulkner's observation that "history is not what was, history is what is."[1] Buckingham says that becoming a historian could have been his occupation, had it not been art. All of his work since the early nineties depicts historical subjects. This shows his concern for the kind of history Walter Benjamin envisioned in his "Theses on the Philosophy of History," which is an account of the past that acknowledges the "barbarism" of violent ruptures, selective recollection, and the willful obliteration of those aspects of history which fail to conform to the viewpoint of the victors who write it.

The question that underlies much of Buckingham's work is: What makes a story? The genres and technologies that he uses and reflects on in his installations frame that very question, as they are themselves technologies of memory. The question then becomes immanent to the aesthetic system in which it is being asked. It is important to note, however, that he extends this systematic reflection onto all components of his installations, including that which is easily forgotten, especially when pertaining to film. Cinematic space, for example, is normally designed to make the viewer forget his or her surroundings. Consequently, Buckingham starts the outline of his film-installation, SITUATION LEADING TO A STORY (1999), by describing the installation. Before speaking about the actual content of the projected images and the installation's sound, he describes two adjoining spaces, one containing the 16mm projector (which projects the image through one small opening and into another, and is constructed in such a way that the viewer can approach the projector first) and the projection. The projected image is not centered on the wall, and the voice-over is heard broadcasted in both parts of the installation. The films shown are four amateur home movies made in the twenties that Buckingham found on the street in

ANSELM FRANKE is a critic and the curator of KW Institute for Contemporary Art in Berlin. He lectures and publishes widely in Europe and the Americas, and contributes to magazines such as *Cabinet* and *Archis*.

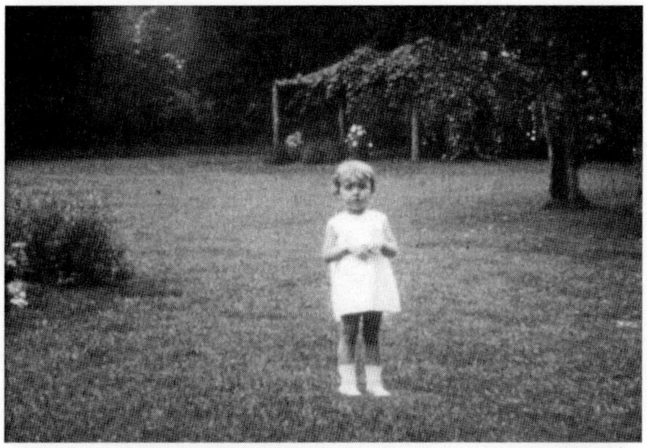

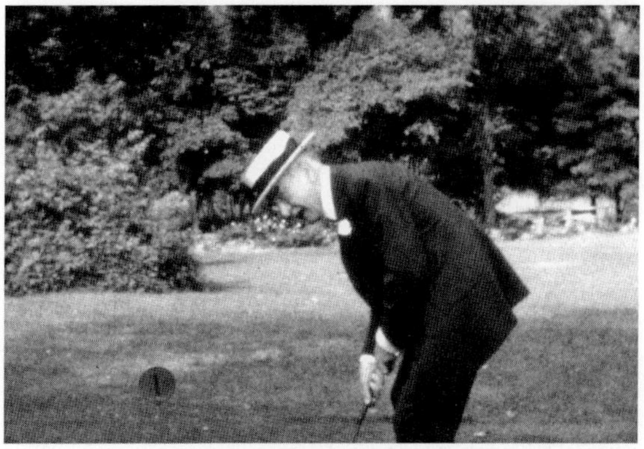

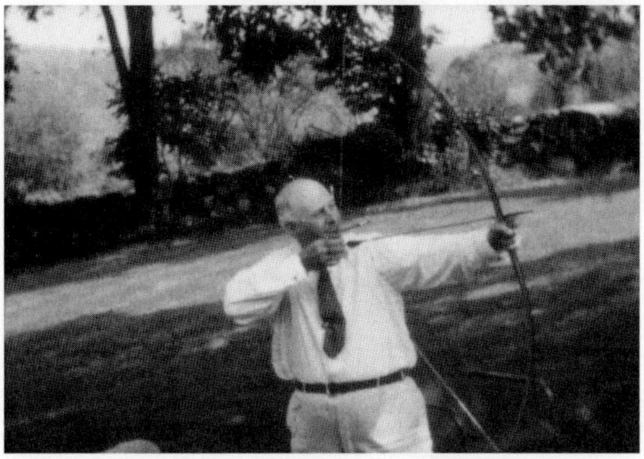

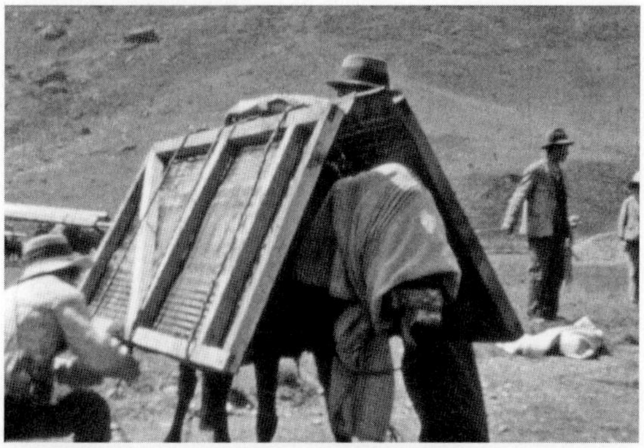

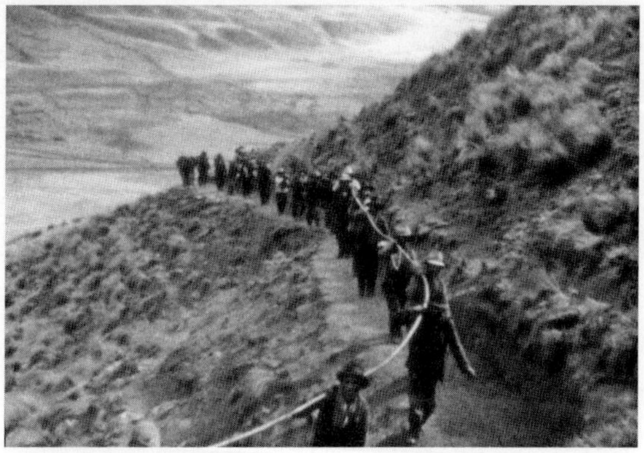

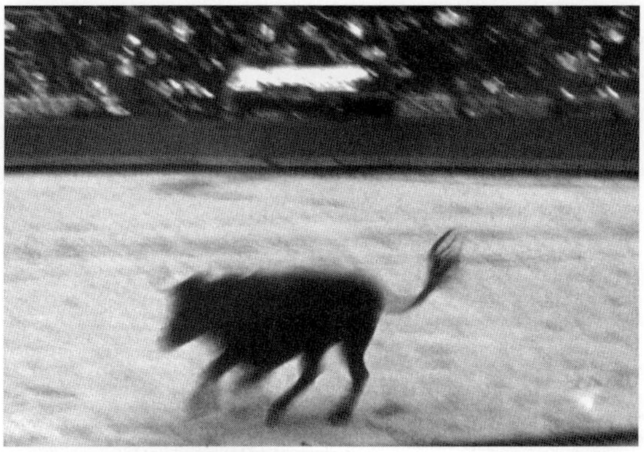

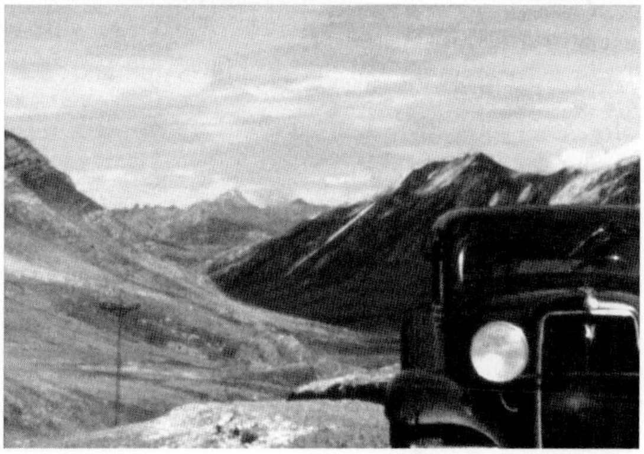

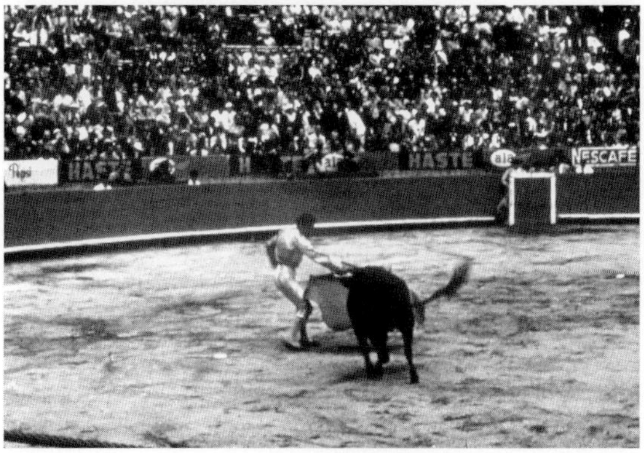

MATTHEW BUCKINGHAM, SITUATION LEADING TO A STORY, 1999, *film stills* / SITUATION, DIE ZU EINER GESCHICHTE FÜHRT, *Filmszenen.*

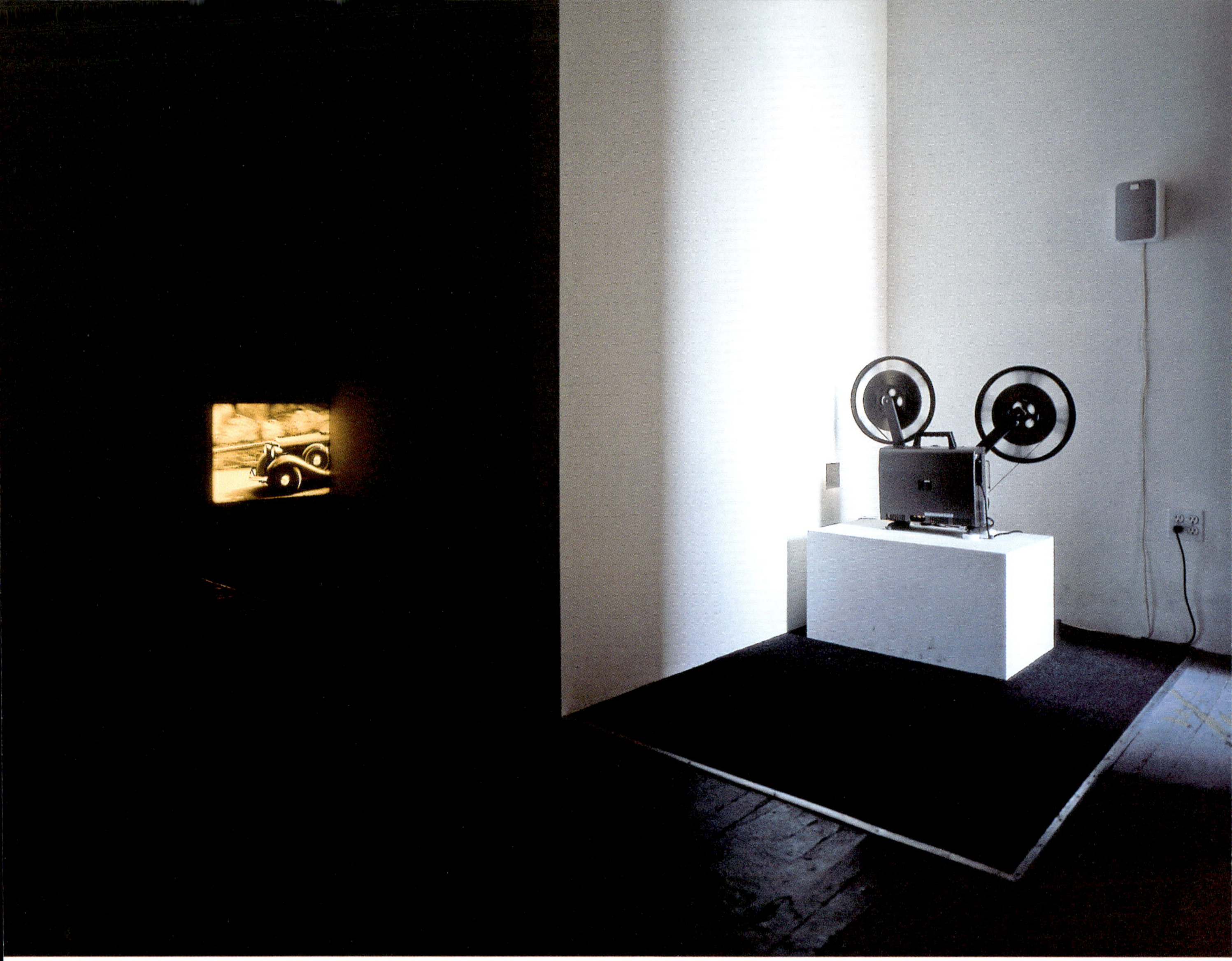

MATTHEW BUCKINGHAM, SITUATION LEADING TO A STORY, 1999, film installation, 21 minutes of 16mm black-and-white film, sound, P.S. 1, New York / SITUATION, DIE ZU EINER GESCHICHTE FÜHRT, Filminstallation, 21 Minuten 16-mm-Schwarzweissfilm mit Ton.

New York: the first shows the members of a wealthy American family in their garden, the second is a documentary about the expansion of a copper mine in Peru, the third shows the same family from the first film, this time supervising construction at their house, and the fourth shows scenes from a bullfight in Mexico or Spain. The small opening in the wall, through which the image is projected, creates a voyeuristic setting. This reflects the fact that these are private movies and that they were not meant to be watched by anybody outside the family. All four films are silent, and except for the second, have no narrative or story. As such, they provoke interpretation; they become screens themselves on which fantasies about the past are inevitably projected. What primarily integrates the four films is the voice-over spoken by Buckingham himself, in which Buckingham tells the story of how he found these films, as well as what he was able to determine about their origins, and the information they include. But the voice-over also has sections like the following:

Narrative is a chain of events in cause and effect relationship occurring in time and space. The plot of a narrative is selected from the events of a story, which, in turn, have been selected from experience, ordering time and erasing contingency. But in home-movies a minute is really a minute, there is no condensation or ordering of time, no selection of plot from story, just a few hyper-quotidian moments; banal activities performed only because there is a camera there recording them. The family playing lawn games and walking in gardens displays a familiar awkwardness, the self-consciousness of constituting one's self in the process of posing for a movie that has no story.

Another of Buckingham's works with the same type of voice-over reminds me of the narrative strategies used in the essay-films of Chris Marker, in which images are played off words with great virtuosity, rotating between their interior and exterior meanings, their personal and discursive resonances—words used as a means to describe the capacity for involvement in what one sees. But Buckingham mentions another origin of the voice-over. It is in the early days of Japanese cinema when films were still silent and when the narration of the actor's voices was left to the prowess of the so-called Benshi, or film narrator. Screening silent films with Benshi commentary (especially in the case of foreign movies) and narration was the norm in Japan until the introduction of sound-film, at which time it became itself an art form, a sort of theatrical appropriation of the inherently mechanical process of recording and screening. Considering that in the cinema we are normally "asked to mistake the structure of somebody else's mind for our own,"[2] the voice-over represents, as well, a cinematic strategy to reflect, or resist, this take-over. Buckingham by means of his installation is engaged with this question of the active or passive involvement of both the filmmaker and the spectator. Take for example, A MAN OF THE CROWD (2003), where he projects an image on a two-way mirror so that it not only gets doubled, but includes the reflection of the viewer as well. In this re-enactment of Edgar Allan Poe's short story *The Man of the Crowd* from 1840 (an investigative story about the impossibility of deciphering a man's identity on the basis of his appearance and behavior), Buckingham restages the story in Vienna, the town that would now appear to be an ideal setting for what Walter Benjamin has called the nineteenth century's obsession with history.

One could situate Matthew Buckingham's work in the tradition of "investigative art," the practice that turns artists into detectives who search for clues to specific contexts, histories, or events. They become interrogators of reality or fiction, or collectors of the material evidence of a story that has been lost in the past, or that has yet to be written. The romantic Edgar Allan Poe was among the first authors to develop in his novels the figure of the private detective. This figure introduced a radical, rational consciousness characterized by a universal suspicion, and the methodological tools needed to mount an investigation. This established a permanent paranoia of the gestures of the enlightenment, suspicion of the potential crime that, by then, became ubiquitous in the normality of the everyday. The detective has since experienced a triumphant procession through the genres of narrative art and mass media. Boris Groys recently declared him to be "the hero of culture" *par excellence* in his book *Unter Verdacht* (Under Suspicion).[3] But Buckingham's use of investigative narratives does not refer to a "crime," whether it be real, imagined, or immanent to all media—the crime, in other words, of hiding what one presents. Nor does he have an interest in questioning the narratives' actual potency in representing reality—his work is not about the deconstruction of narrative structures, nor is it about a structuralist critique of visual or narrative regimes. He arranges narratives and images according to their resonance, and their presence or absence in time—their potency to c r e a t e and to f r a m e what, only later, becomes referred to as reality. In trying to find a term that would provide an accurate framework for these qualities, I came across the concept of the "imaginative horizon," a term coined by Vincent Crapanzano,[4] which describes the boundaries of the imagination that separate the here and now from what lies beyond, in time and space. This is what Buckingham's works really are: journeys along the imaginative horizon, where edges

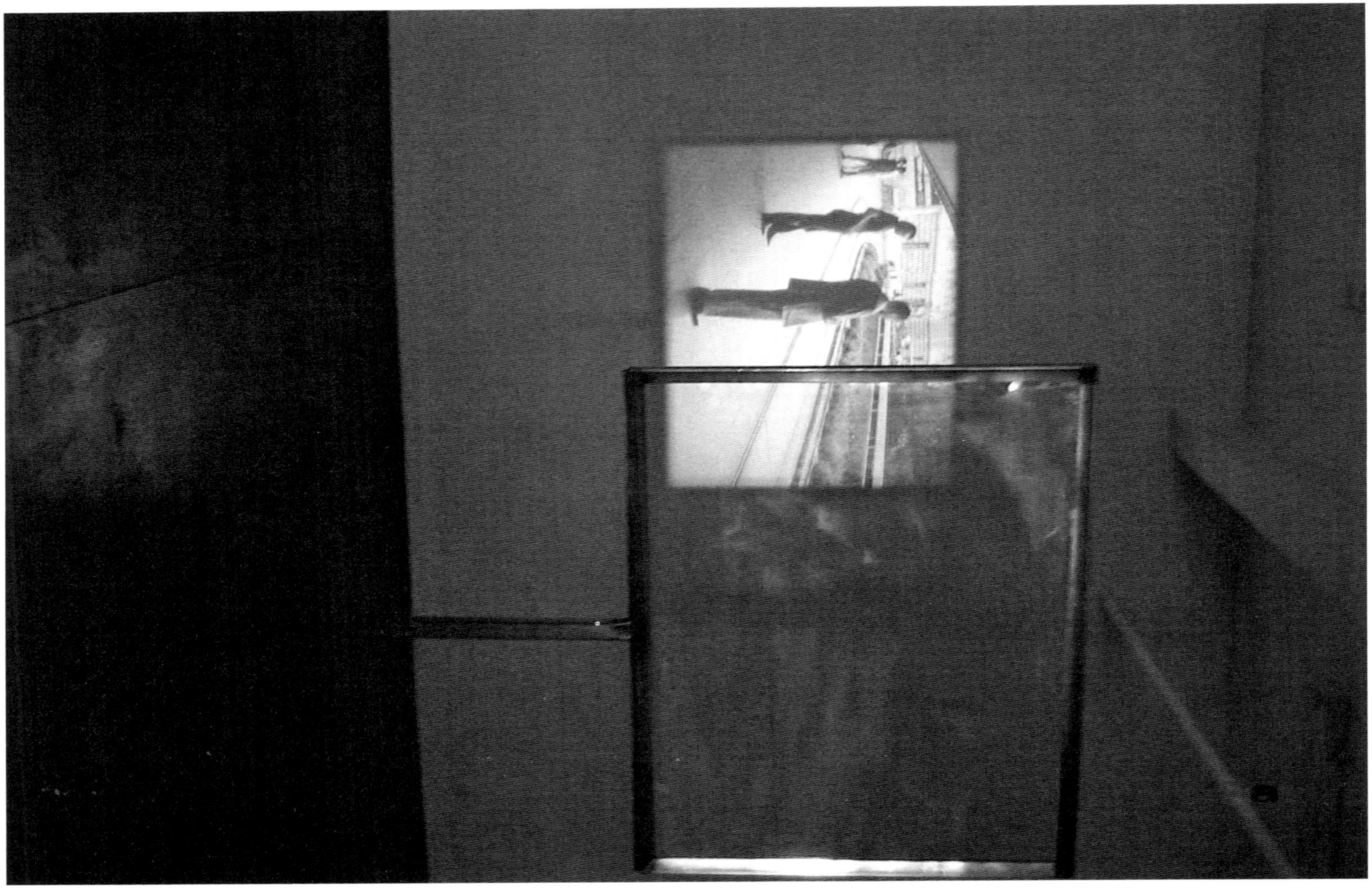

MATTHEW BUCKINGHAM, A MAN OF THE CROWD, 2003, film installation, 16mm black-and-white film with sound, 20-minute loop, installation view Murray Guy Gallery, New York / EIN MASSENMENSCH, Filminstallation, 20 Minuten 16-mm-Schwarzweissfilm mit Ton. (ALL PHOTOS: MURRAY GUY GALLERY, NEW YORK)

and demarcations constitute reality as the presence of the past in the present.

One of Buckingham's recent works is MUHHEAKANTUCK, EVERYTHING HAS A NAME (2003/2004), a film installation with a 16mm projection and a voice-over examining the "brief but disastrous" European colonialization of the Hudson Valley. MUHHEAKANTUCK, EVERYTHING HAS A NAME shows an aerial view of the Hudson River shot from a helicopter, starting in Manhattan, flying upriver, and returning after about twenty minutes. The image is slightly colored with a patina that connotes a sense of alienation. The moving image of the Hudson River is itself like a running stream, thus duplicating the river's tide. It is an image of great perspectival depth, with its horizon creeping by, the river passing a bit faster, and accelerating as it nears the camera. Speed, though, can only be imagined; it has no actual visual reference; it exists only as an abstraction. The voice-over, while narrating the history of the colonialization of the area, contains numerous comments on the bird's-eye view—the "dream of hovering ascent," of detachment, of objectivity, of the cartographer's gaze. The piece is about the "writing" of space, just like the writing of history—it juxtaposes mapping and narration as two complementary means of representation. The voice-over says:

... Muhheakantuck, the river that flows in two directions. The people who named it this called themselves the Lenape, or Leni-Lenape, meaning people, or common people, or real people. Europeans translated this name as "we the people."... We understand the world through our experience, and our experience of other people's experience. Writing substitutes the eye for the ear. Writing substitutes the hand for the mouth. Colonizing language also colonizes memory and imagination.

The streams of images and words both manage to evoke a dream-like, hypnotic trance. This blurs the boundaries of factuality and fiction up to the point of complete indistinguishability releasing a paradoxical experience of the historical "real," which recreates its subject in the imagination of the here and now. This "stream" is not a montage in the classical sense but rather what the psychologist William James described in 1890 as the "stream of consciousness"[5]—something that, in Buckingham's work, becomes identical with the streaming of time and the structuring of a journey along the imaginative horizon. In his work, there is both an "it speaks," and an "I am speaking," a plurality (of identities, meanings) in negotiation with a singularity bare of all attributes other than that of consciousness, moving between proximity and distance, attraction and repulsion, subjection and objection.

The fiction of history is to imagine the real. History makes reality desirable. It has the illusion of "speaking itself" as if it simply happened.

The "it speaks" is the archive of the past—its signs and symbols, its collective knowledge and experiences, its imposed order on all meanings and subjects. The "discourse" of the past is not enunciated by the mind; it enunciates itself within the mind, structuring the horizons of the imagination. It thus gives everything its name and location in time and space. The formal gesture that structures Matthew Buckingham's streaming environments of consciousness and reflection is that of a panorama, of the imagination's horizon, which becomes the ultimate site of agency, language, images, meanings, and ideologies. These landscapes of the known, the unknown, and the unknowable are what we experience when looking at his work.

1) The often quoted passage from William Faulkner's *Requiem for a Nun* actually reads: "The past is never dead. It's not even past." (Act I, Scene III.)

2) Lev Manovich, *The Language of the New Media* (Cambridge: MIT Press, 2001).

3) Boris Groys, *Unter Verdacht. Eine Phänomenologie der Medien* (Munich: Carl Hanser Verlag, 2000), p. 226.

4) See Vincent Crapanzano, *Imaginative Horizons: An Essay in Literary-Philosophical Anthropology* (Chicago: University of Chicago Press, 2003).

5) William James, "The Stream of Consciousness," in *Principles of Psychology* (New York: Holt, 1890), chapter XI.

MATTHEW BUCKINGHAM

ANSELM FRANKE

Fragt man Matthew Buckingham nach seinem Verhältnis zur Geschichte, so zitiert er William Faulkner dahingehend, dass Geschichte nicht das sei, was war, sondern das, was ist.[1] Buckingham meint, dass er möglicherweise Historiker geworden wäre, wenn er sich nicht für die Kunst entschieden hätte. Alle seine Werke seit den frühen 90er Jahren greifen geschichtliche Themen auf und zeugen von seinem Interesse für die Art von Geschichte, die Walter Benjamin in seinen Thesen «Über den Begriff der Geschichte» im Visier hatte: ein Bericht über die Vergangenheit, der dem Barbarischen gewaltsamer Umstürze, der selektiven Erinnerung und der bewussten Unterschlagung jener Aspekte der Geschichte Rechnung trägt, die nicht zur Perspektive der Sieger passen, die diese Geschichte schreiben.

Die Frage, die vielen von Buckinghams Werken zugrunde liegt, ist: Was macht eine Geschichte oder Erzählung aus? Und auf dieselbe Frage laufen auch die Genres und Techniken hinaus, die er in seinen Installationen verwendet und reflektiert, da sie ja selbst Erinnerungstechniken sind. Die Frage wird so zu einer dem ästhetischen System, in dem sie gestellt wird, immanenten. Es ist jedoch wichtig festzuhalten, dass Buckingham diese systematische Reflexion auf alle Komponenten seiner Installationen ausdehnt, etwas, was gern vergessen wird, besonders wenn es um den Film geht. Der filmische Raum, zum Beispiel, ist gewöhnlich daraufhin angelegt, dass die Betrachter oder Betrachterinnen ihre Umgebung vergessen. Folgerichtig beginnt Buckingham den Entwurf seiner Film-Installation, SITUATION LEADING TO A STORY (Situation, die zu einer Geschichte führt, 1999), damit, dass er die Installation beschreibt; noch bevor er über den eigentlichen Inhalt der projizierten Bilder und den Sound zur Installation spricht, schildert er die zwei aneinander grenzenden Räume, von denen der eine den 16-mm-Projektor beherbergt (der das Bild durch eine kleine Öffnung in den anderen projiziert und so eingerichtet ist, dass der Betrachter zuerst den Projektor anschauen kann), der andere die Projektion. Letztere ist nicht in der Mitte der Wand und die Stimmen aus dem Off sind in beiden Räumen zu hören. Gezeigt werden vier Amateurfilme aus den 20er Jahren, die Buckingham in New York auf der Strasse gefunden hat: Der

ANSELM FRANKE ist Kunstkritiker und Kurator der Kunst-Werke, Berlin. Er lehrt und publiziert in Europa, Nord- und Südamerika und schreibt für Zeitschriften wie *Cabinet* und *Archis*.

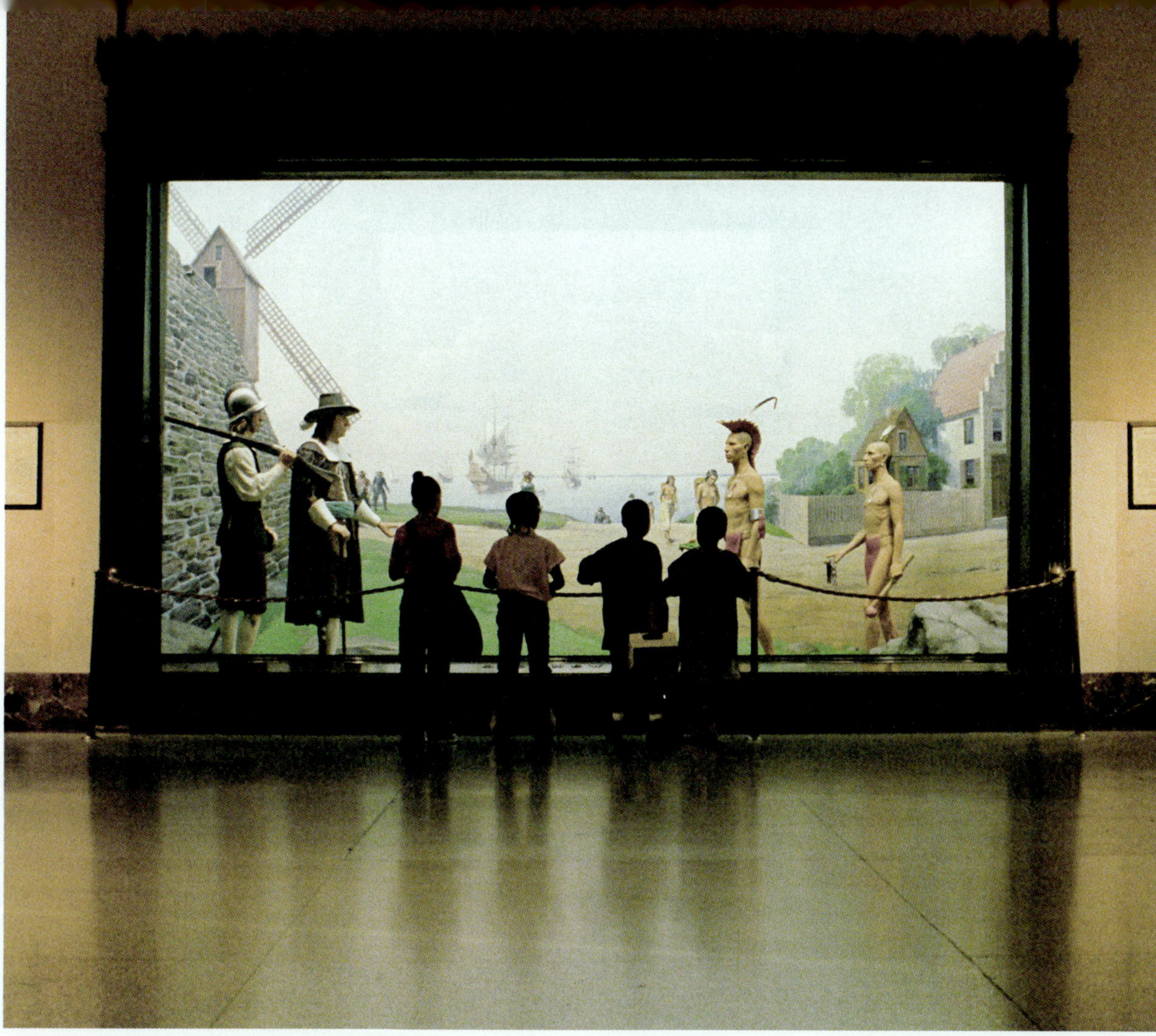

MATTHEW BUCKINGHAM, NEW AMSTERDAM, 2003, C-print, 10 x 11" / 25,4 x 30 cm.

erste zeigt eine wohlhabende amerikanische Familie in ihrem Garten, der zweite ist ein Dokumentarfilm über die Expansion einer Kupfermine in Peru, der dritte zeigt wieder die Familie aus dem zweiten Film, wie sie bauliche Massnahmen an ihrem Haus überwacht, und der vierte zeigt Szenen eines Stierkampfes in Mexiko oder Spanien. Die kleine Wandöffnung, durch die das Bild projiziert wird, schafft eine voyeuristische Situation. Das entspricht der Tatsache, dass es sich hier um private Filme handelt, die nicht dafür gedacht waren, je von jemandem ausserhalb der Familie gesehen zu werden. Alle vier Filme sind stumm und ausser dem zweiten hat keiner eine Handlung oder erzählt eine Geschichte. Sie provozieren uns also zur Interpretation und werden selbst zu Projektionsflächen, auf die wir unweigerlich unsere Phantasievorstellungen über die Vergangenheit projizieren. Was die vier Filme zu einem Ganzen macht, ist der von Buckingham selbst gesprochene Begleittext, in dem Buckingham erzählt, wie er die Filme gefunden hat, was er über ihre Herkunft herausgefunden hat und welche Informationen sie uns liefern. Aber im Text finden sich auch Passagen wie diese:

Eine Erzählung ist eine Kette von Ereignissen, die in einem Verhältnis von Ursache und Wirkung stehen und in Zeit und Raum stattfinden. Die Handlung der Erzählung besteht aus ausgewählten Ereignissen einer Geschichte, die

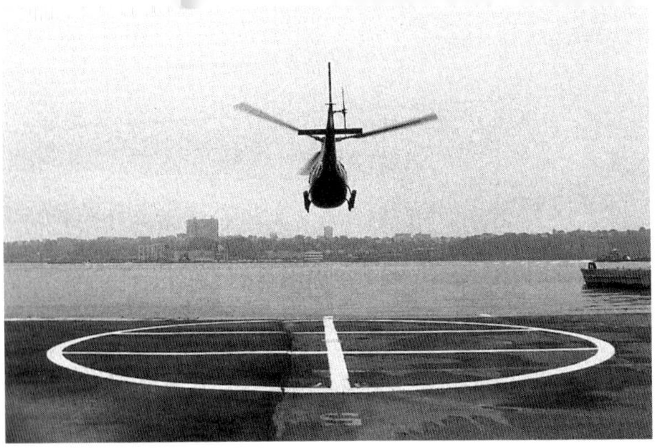

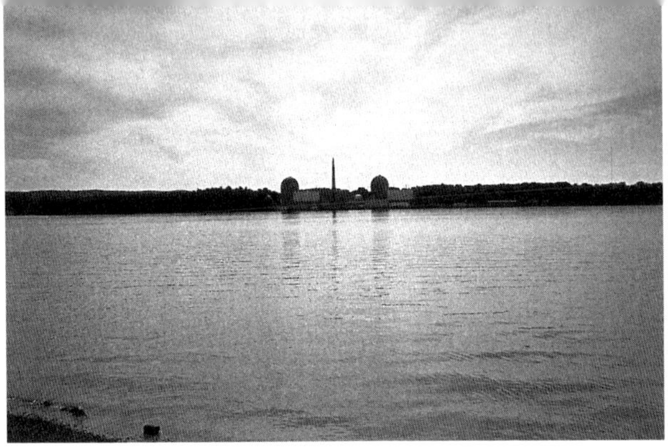

MATTHEW BUCKINGHAM, MUHHEAKANTUCK – EVERYTHING HAS A NAME, 2003, film installation, 16mm black-and-white film with sound, 40-minute loop. The images shown here are photographic editions which are part of the project / ALLES HAT EINEN NAMEN, Filminstallation, 40 Minuten 16-mm-Schwarzweissfilm mit Ton; die hier gezeigten Bilder sind Photoeditionen, die mit zum Projekt gehören.

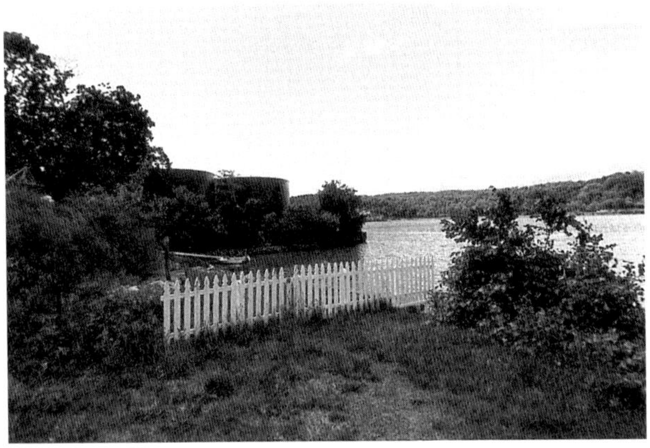

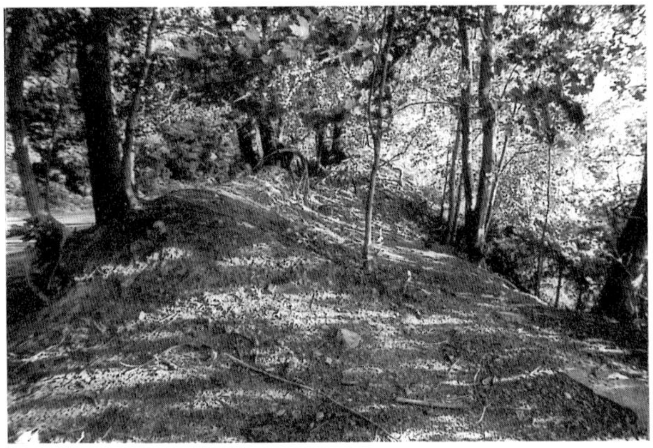

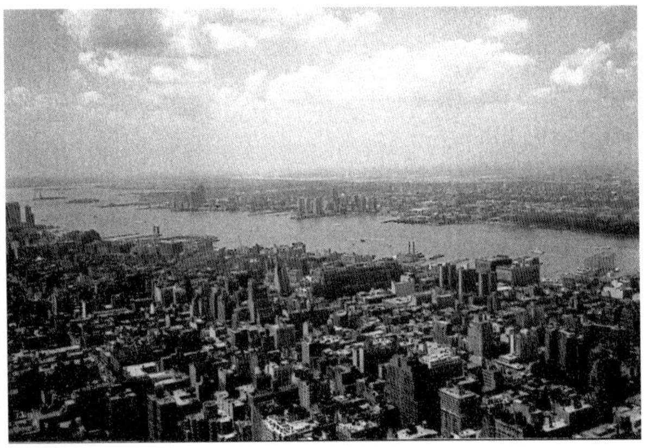

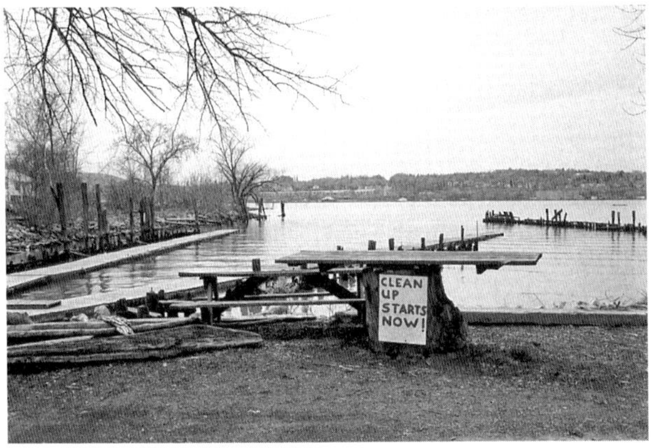

wiederum auf Erfahrungen beruhen und unter Ausschaltung des Zufalls in eine zeitliche Ordnung gebracht wurden. Aber in Amateurfilmen ist eine Minute wirklich eine Minute, da gibt es keine Verdichtung oder Strukturierung von Zeit, kein Auswählen einer Episode aus einer Geschichte, nur ein paar hyperalltägliche Momente; banale Tätigkeiten, die nur ausgeführt werden, weil eine Kamera da ist, die sie festhalten soll. Die Familie, die Rasenspiele spielt und in Gärten herumspaziert, wirkt auf eine vertraute Art befangen, es ist die Befangenheit der Selbstdarstellung, wenn man für einen Film ohne Handlung posieren muss.

Eine andere Arbeit von Buckingham, die mit derselben Art Stimme aus dem Off operiert, erinnerte mich an die narrativen Strategien in den Filmessays von Chris Marker – der Bilder mit Worten in Beziehung setzt und mit grosser Virtuosität zwischen ihrer einfachen und verborgenen Bedeutung, ihren persönlichen und diskursiven Konnotationen hin und her pendelt, und die Worte dazu verwendet, die Fähigkeit zur Teilnahme an dem, was man sieht, zu beschreiben. Doch Buckingham erwähnt noch einen anderen Ursprung der Stimme aus dem Off, und zwar aus den Anfängen des japanischen Kinos, als die Filme noch stumm waren und die Sprechakte der Schauspieler der Tüchtigkeit eines sogenannten Benshi oder Filmerzählers anvertraut wurden. Das Abspielen von Stummfilmen begleitet vom Kommentar (insbesondere bei ausländischen Filmen) oder der Erzählung eines Benshi war in Japan bis zur Einführung des Tonfilms die Norm; später wurde es zu einer eigenen Kunstform, einer Art theatralischer Appropriation des an sich mechanischen Prozesses von Aufzeichnung und Projektion. Angesichts der Tatsache, dass wir im Kino gewöhnlich dazu angehalten werden, die Vorstellungswelt eines anderen für unsere eigene zu halten,[2)] ist die Stimme aus dem Off unter anderem auch eine filmische Strategie, um diese «Überwältigung» zu reflektieren und ihr zu widerstehen. Buckingham spricht in seinen Installationen diese Frage der aktiven oder passiven Rolle des Filmemachers und Zuschauers an. So etwa in A MAN OF THE CROWD (Ein Massenmensch, 2003), wo er ein Bild so auf einen Einwegspiegel projiziert, dass es nicht nur verdoppelt wird, sondern auch noch das Spiegelbild des Betrachters in sich aufnimmt. In dieser Reinszenierung von Edgar Allan Poes Kurzgeschichte *Der Massenmensch* aus dem Jahr 1840 (einer Detektivgeschichte über die Unmöglichkeit, die Identität eines Menschen aus seiner Erscheinung und seinem Verhalten abzulesen) verlegt Buckingham die Geschichte nach Wien und damit in eine Stadt, die einen idealen Hintergrund dafür abgibt, was Walter Benjamin als Geschichtsbesessenheit des neunzehnten Jahrhunderts bezeichnete.

Matthew Buckinghams Werk liesse sich in der Tradition der «Spurensicherung» ansiedeln, einer Kunstrichtung, die Künstler in Detektive verwandelt, die nach Indizien für spezifische Kontexte, Geschichten oder Ereignisse suchen und dabei Realität und Fiktion gleichermassen hinterfragen, oder materielle Beweise für eine Geschichte zusammentragen, die sich in der Vergangenheit verloren hat oder erst noch geschrieben werden muss. Der Romantiker Edgar Allan Poe hat als einer der ersten die Gestalt des Privatdetektivs in seinen Romanen entwickelt. Mit dieser Figur wurde ein radikal rationales Bewusstsein eingeführt, dem grundsätzlich alles verdächtig war, das aber auch die notwendigen wissenschaftlichen Aufklärungsmethoden beherrschte. Daraus ergab sich ein paranoides Beharren auf den Aufklärungsmassnahmen gegen das potenzielle Verbrechen, das inzwischen zu einem allgegenwärtigen Element des normalen Alltags geworden war. Seither hat der Privatdetektiv seinen Triumphzug durch alle Genres der Erzählkunst und der Massenmedien angetreten. Erst kürzlich hat ihn Boris Groys – in seinem Buch *Unter Verdacht* – zum «eigentlichen Helden der medialen Kultur» erklärt.[3)] Doch Buckinghams Verwendung des Detektivischen setzt kein «Verbrechen» voraus, weder ein reales noch ein fiktives, und auch nicht das allen Medien immanente, nämlich: zu verschleiern, was man zeigt. Er hat auch keinerlei Interesse daran, in Zweifel zu ziehen, dass die Erzählung Wirklichkeit zu repräsentieren vermag; in seinem Werk geht es weder um die Dekonstruktion narrativer Strukturen noch um eine strukturalistische Kritik bestehender visueller oder narrativer Systeme. Er ordnet Geschichten und Bilder nach ihrer Resonanz, ihrer Gegenwart oder Abwesenheit in der Zeit – entsprechend ihrem Vermögen etwas zu erzeugen und auszudrücken, was erst später als Realität aufgenommen werden wird. Auf der Suche nach einer passenden systematischen Beschreibung dieser Eigenschaften bin ich auf den von Vincent Crapanzano geprägten Begriff des «imaginativen Horizonts»[4)] gestossen, der die Grenzen der Vorstellungskraft beschreibt, welche das Hier und Jetzt von dem trennen, was sich zeitlich und räumlich jenseits davon befindet. Und Buckinghams Arbeiten sind eigentlich genau dies: Reisen entlang des imaginären Horizonts, wo Ränder und Grenzlinien Wirklichkeit erstehen lassen als Gegenwart der Vergangenheit in der Gegenwart.

Eine von Buckinghams neueren Arbeiten ist MUHHEAKANTUCK, EVERYTHING HAS A NAME (Muhheakantuck, alles hat einen Namen, 2003/2004). Die Filminstallation besteht aus einer 16-mm-Projektion und einem gesprochenen Kommentar, der die «kurze, aber verheerende» Phase der Kolonisierung des Hudson Valley durch die Europäer unter die Lupe nimmt. MUHHEAKANTUCK... zeigt eine Luftansicht des Hudson aus einem Helikopter, der in Manhattan startet, flussaufwärts fliegt und nach etwa zwanzig Minuten wieder zurückkommt. Die Bilder sind leicht getönt mit einer verfremdenden Patina. Das bewegte Bild des Hudson wirkt selbst wie ein fliessender Strom und verdoppelt so das Strömen des Flusses. Das Bild hat eine grossartige Tiefenperspektive mit dem langsam wandernden Horizont, dem etwas rascher vorbeiströmenden Fluss, der immer schneller wird, je näher er der Kamera kommt. Die Geschwindigkeit muss man sich jedoch vorstellen, es gibt keinen sichtbaren Referenten im Bild, sie existiert lediglich als Abstraktion. Der gesprochene Kommentar, der die Geschichte der kolonialistischen Besiedlung der Gegend erzählt, enthält zahlreiche Anspielungen auf die Vogelperspektive – er spricht vom «Traum des schwebenden Aufsteigens», von Losgelöstsein, Objektivität, vom Blick des Kartographen. Die Arbeit handelt ebenso vom «Schreiben» des Raumes wie von der Geschichtsschreibung; sie stellt Kartographie und Erzählung einander gegenüber als zwei sich ergänzende Darstellungsmethoden. Der Kommentar lautet:

... Muhheakantuck, der Fluss, der in zwei Richtungen fliesst. Die Menschen, die ihn so nannten, waren die Lenape oder Leni-Lenape, was so viel bedeutet wie Volk oder gewöhnliche Menschen oder wirkliche Menschen. Die Europäer übersetzten diesen Namen als «Wir, das Volk» (...) Wir verstehen die Welt aufgrund unserer Erfahrung und aufgrund dessen, was wir über die Erfahrung anderer in Erfahrung gebracht haben. Die Schrift setzt das Auge an die Stelle des Ohrs. Die Schrift setzt die Hand an die Stelle des Mundes. Die Kolonisierung der Sprache kolonisiert auch die Erinnerung und die Phantasie.

Die strömenden Bilder und Worte versetzen uns in eine träumerisch hypnotische Stimmung. Dies lässt die Grenzen zwischen Fakten und Fiktion bis zur völligen Ununterscheidbarkeit verschwimmen, wodurch eine paradoxe Erfahrung der historischen «Realität» möglich wird, die ihren Gegenstand in der Phantasie hier und jetzt neu erschafft. Dieser «Strom» ist keine Montage im klassischen Sinn, sondern entspricht eher dem, was der Psychologe William James 1890 als «Bewusstseinsstrom»[5] beschrieb: etwas, was in Buckinghams Arbeiten identisch ist mit dem Zeitstrom und dem, was einer Reise entlang des imaginativen Horizonts Struktur verleiht. In seinem Werk gibt es beides, das «es spricht» und das «ich spreche»: eine Vielfalt (von Identitäten, Bedeutungen) im Widerstreit mit einer Singularität bar jeden Attributes ausser demjenigen, ein Bewusstsein zu haben und sich zwischen Nähe und Distanz, Anziehung und Abstossung, Unterwerfung und Widerstand hin und her zu bewegen.

Die Fiktion der Geschichte ist die Idee der Wirklichkeit. Geschichte macht Wirklichkeit begehrenswert, weil sie die Illusion erzeugt «für sich selbst zu sprechen», als habe sie sich einfach ereignet.

Das «es spricht» ist das Archiv der Vergangenheit – deren Zeichen und Symbole, deren kollektives Wissen und kollektive Erfahrung, deren allen Bedeutungen und Themen auferlegte Ordnung. Der Diskurs der Vergangenheit wird nicht vom Bewusstsein geführt; er führt sich selbst innerhalb des Bewusstseins und formt dabei den Horizont unserer Vorstellungskraft. So weist er jedem Ding seinen Namen und seinen Ort in Zeit und Raum zu. Die formale Gebärde, die Matthew Buckinghams «strömende» Bewusstseins- und Reflexionslandschaften prägt, ist jene des Panoramas, des Vorstellungshorizonts, der die letzte Basis für Vermittlung, Sprache, Bilder, Meinungen und Ideologien bildet. Was wir erleben, wenn wir sein Werk betrachten, sind eben diese Landschaften aus Bekanntem, Unbekanntem und nicht Wissbarem.

(Übersetzung: Suzanne Schmidt)

1) Wohl eine Anspielung auf das berühmte Zitat: «Die Vergangenheit ist nicht tot, sie ist nicht einmal vergangen», in: William Faulkner, *Requiem für eine Nonne,* 1. Akt, 3. Szene.

2) Vgl. dazu: Lev Manovich, *The Language of the New Media* (Cambridge, Mass.: MIT Press, 2001).

3) Boris Groys, *Unter Verdacht. Eine Phänomenologie der Medien,* Carl Hanser Verlag, München 2000, S. 226.

4) Vgl. Vincent Crapanzano, *Imaginative Horizons: an Essay in Literary-Philosophical Anthropology,* University of Chicago Press, Chicago 2003.

5) William James «The Stream of Consciousness», in: *Principles of Psychology,* Holt, New York 1890, Kapitel XI.

20 YEARS OF PARKETT

PART III / TEIL III

(IM)MATERIAL?

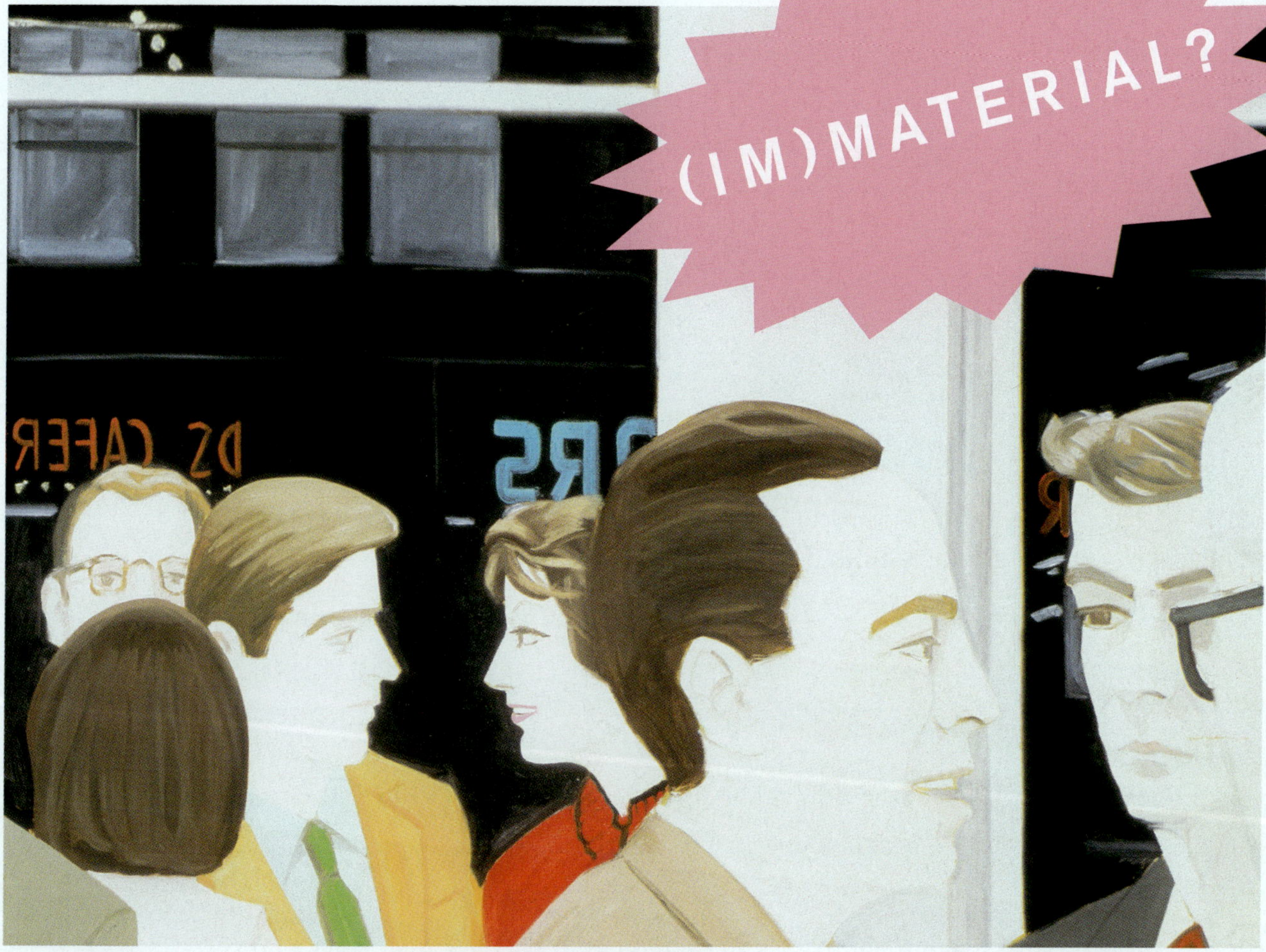

THE THIRD OF THREE ESSAYS ON THE WHYS AND WHEREFORES OF MATERIAL IN CONTEMPORARY ART, IN CELEBRATION OF PARKETT'S 20TH ANNIVERSARY /

DER DRITTE VON DREI ESSAYS ZUM MATERIALBEGRIFF IN DER GEGENWARTSKUNST ANLÄSSLICH DES 20-JÄHRIGEN JUBILÄUMS VON PARKETT

WITH A SPECIAL COLLABORATION BY / MIT EINER EXTRA-COLLABORATION VON

ALEX KATZ

AND ARTISTS' PAGES / UND KÜNSTLERBEITRÄGEN

Cover page / Umschlagseite: ALEX KATZ, COCKTAIL PARTY, 1965, 76 x 96", detail / 193 x 243,8 cm, Ausschnitt.

INHALT

DIE RETECHNISIERUNG DER KUNST

BORIS GROYS

Zunächst einmal eine Geschichte aus dem Leben. Ich habe einmal einen Direktor einer provinziellen deutschen Kunsthalle ganz beiläufig gefragt, ob er in seiner Kunsthalle Video- oder Netzkunst zeigt. Daraufhin hat er geantwortet, dass er leider keine immaterielle Kunst zeigen könne, weil die Geräte, die man dazu bräuchte, zu schwer und sowohl sie selbst als auch ihre Benutzung zu teuer seien – so müsse er seine Ausstellungsaktivitäten leider auf die traditionelle Kunst begrenzen, da die Leinwand im Sinne des Materialaufwands viel günstiger sei. Aber eigentlich weiss ja auch jeder Schriftsteller, dass es viel weniger kostet und körperlich weniger anstrengend ist, «materiell» mit dem Stift zu schreiben als «immateriell» mit dem Computer. Was kann also einen Schriftsteller dazu bewegen, zu behaupten, die Kunst sei heutzutage immateriell geworden – im Sinne einer Erlösung von der körperlichen Arbeit? Auf diese Behauptung stösst man aber immer wieder bei der Lektüre einschlägiger Publikationen.

Nun führte die künstlerische Avantgarde in der Tat einen erbitterten Kampf gegen das Kunsthandwerk – und somit, wenn man will, gegen die Materialität der Kunst. Den Höhepunkt dieses Kampfes stellt bekanntlich das Readymade-Verfahren dar, das von Duchamp initiiert wurde. Dieses Verfahren wird üblicherweise als eine rein immaterielle Operation interpretiert, die darin besteht, einem beliebigen Objekt Kunststatus zu verleihen. Ein Künstler, der mit Readymades operiert, arbeitet nicht am Material, er benötigt auch nicht viel Zeit um Readymades zu produzieren: Die Entscheidung ein Objekt zu Kunst zu erklären ist augenblicklich. Die Produktion wird hier durch Selektion ersetzt. Der Künstler hört auf, ein Arbeiter zu sein – er wird stattdessen zum Konsumenten. Es handelt sich hier um einen quasi paradiesischen Zustand, in dem Produktion und Konsum identisch werden. Man kann Suppen kochen, Süssigkeiten verteilen, Konversationen führen, Haare schneiden – alles wird zur Kunst. Der Sieg des Immateriellen scheint gesichert zu sein. Der Geist weht frei durch die Kunsträume – befreit vom Gefängnis des Körperlichen, des Materiellen. Der Schweissgeruch der harten Arbeit, der gerade bei der Annäherung an die Meisterwerke der klassischen Kunst deutlich zu spüren ist, verschwindet – und wird ersetzt durch das vornehme, angenehme, herrschaftliche Parfum der Immaterialität.

Ist es aber wirklich so? Nicht ganz, wie mir scheint. Damit das Readymade-Verfahren gelingen kann, muss es innerhalb des Kunstsystems praktiziert werden. Die blosse Erklärung eines beliebigen Gegenstandes zu Kunst reicht nicht aus – diese Erklärung muss zusätzlich dokumentiert werden, damit sie als solche für den Künstler selbst und für andere Geltung bekommen kann. Eine Erklärung muss einen Zeugen haben, um Gültigkeit zu erlangen. Man kann nur dann ernsthaft über die Immaterialität sprechen, wenn man die Existenz Gottes oder anderer Götter akzeptiert, die als immaterielle Zeugen einer einsamen, nicht materiell dokumentierten Entscheidung fungieren können. Doch heute können wir nicht einmal glauben, dass der Mensch selbst als Zeuge seiner eigenen Entscheidungen dienen kann, denn auch die immaterielle menschliche Subjektivität ist inzwischen unglaubwürdig geworden. Die Entscheidung über den Kunststatus eines Objekts braucht also einen realen, wenn man so will, materiellen Zeugen, um überhaupt getroffen werden zu können. Der heutige Kunstbetrieb funktioniert wie ein solcher Zeuge. Seine Funktion besteht darin, die Entscheidungen der Künstler zu dokumentieren – und andere über diese Entscheidungen zu informieren. Diese Funktion ist durchaus materiell – und extrem arbeitsintensiv. Es werden immer grössere Museen und Kunsthallen gebaut, es werden immer dickere Kataloge publiziert, es wird immer mehr organisiert, kommuniziert, auf Tonband aufgenommen, gefilmt und ausgestellt. Und es wird dementsprechend mehr und mehr gearbeitet – auch seitens des Künstlers. Inzwischen verwendet der Künstler mehr Arbeit und Energie, um seine immateriellen künstlerischen Entscheidungen zu dokumentieren, als frühere Künstler für ihre handwerklichen Erzeugnisse verwendet haben. Und noch einmal: Dieser Dokumentationsvorgang ist nichts Äusserliches in Bezug auf künstlerische Entscheidungen, sondern er bietet erst die Möglichkeit, solche Entscheidungen überhaupt zu treffen.

Die Duchampschen Readymades geben das Versprechen einer einzigen «realen Utopie», die sich mit dem Versprechen des Kommunismus messen kann und somit scheinbar eine wirksame Alternative zum Marxismus bietet: eine Erlösung von der Arbeit durch Entdeckung einer verborgenen Kunst- und somit auch Geldpräsenz im Armen, Niedrigen, Alltäglichen, Gescheiterten, Konkurrenzunfähigen. Aber die marxistische Kritik am Warenfetischismus bleibt auch für die Readymades relevant. Es bereitet nämlich keine grossen Schwierigkeiten zu erkennen, wie die Aneignung des durch Arbeit produzierten Mehrwerts im Falle der Readymade-Kunst funktioniert. Seit den Zeiten der Avantgarde wird die Kunstpraxis oft beschrieben als Transgression, Überschreitung und Tabuverletzung, so dass der Eindruck entstehen mag, dass es sich dabei um einen Weg aus den Kunstinstitutionen heraus ins Offene, ins Andere handelt. Doch die Überschreitung funktioniert hier im Dienste der Inklusion: Die heutige Kunst will nicht exklusiv, sondern inklusiv sein – und jede Überschreitung der Grenzen der Kunst erweitert das Netzwerk der Kunst, macht dieses Netzwerk noch inklusiver. Das Netzwerk der Kunst braucht allerdings eine materielle Infrastruktur, eine materielle Basis. Hier handelt es sich nicht mehr um «ideelle» Grenzen des Normativen, Wertvollen und Tradierten, deren Überschreitung als «Tabuverletzung» gelten dürfte, sondern um ganz reale, «materielle» Grenzen von Museen, Kunsthallen, Kunstvereinen und so weiter. Diese Grenzen sind nicht bloss von ästhetischen Normen oder Vorurteilen bestimmt, sondern vielmehr von der Bauindustrie errichtet. Jede Zunahme der Inklusion in der Kunst impliziert also eine Zunahme der anonymen, physischen Arbeit beim weiteren Aufbau von Kunsträumen. Die gleiche, durchaus materielle Arbeit wird notwendig, um Kataloge, Filme und sonstige Dokumentationen zu produzieren – weswegen es am Ende letzlich keine Rolle spielt, ob die Kunst innerhalb oder ausserhalb der etablierten Kunsträume stattfindet. Der Kunstwert, den der Künstler einem beliebigen Gegenstand, einem beliebigen Raum oder einem beliebigen Vorgang zuschreibt, wird zunächst einmal durch die anonyme nicht-künstlerische Arbeit von Bauarbeitern, Technikern, Putzpersonal und so weiter produziert – und erst danach vom Künstler angeeignet. Diese Tatsache wird meistens durch den Diskurs verdeckt, der die heutige avancierte Kunst als Kritik der Kunstinstitutionen interpretiert. Aber diese Kritik führt letztendlich zur Erweiterung dieser Institutionen – um eine immer grössere Inklusivität zu erreichen.

Nun kann man aber sagen, dass eine einzelne künstlerische Entscheidung als solche trotzdem als immateriell gelten darf – unabhängig von ihrer faktischen Dokumentation und Realisierung. Und man kann weiter sagen, dass die Kunst dann immateriell ist, wenn sich das Kunstwerk als eine Reihe von explizit formulierten künstlerischen Entscheidungen und Anweisungen präsentiert, die dazu dienen, Installationen und Objekte aufzubauen, Performances aufzuführen oder Ereignisse zu organisieren. Das Immaterielle bedeutet in diesem Fall weniger das Nicht-Materielle als vielmehr das Transparente, Rationale, Nachvollziehbare. Die Magie der künstlerischen Kreation, die einmalig wirkt und vom Körper des Künstlers untrennbar ist, wird hier durch ein explizites, wiederholbares Programm zur Herstellung von Kunst ersetzt. Eben diese Unabhängigkeit der Kunst vom Körper des Künstlers wird gern als Immaterialität bezeichnet: Die Befreiung vom individuellen, kreativen Körper zugunsten eines transparenten, intersubjektiven, immateriellen Programms. Vor allem bietet das Zeitalter des Digitalen anscheinend die Möglichkeit, so etwas wie eine digitale Seele zu schaffen, die von ihren Verkörperungen – von ihren materiellen Inkarnationen in der jeweiligen Hardware – weitgehend unabhängig bleibt. Diese digitale Seele begibt sich somit auf eine Seelenwanderung vom Körper eines Menschen (eines Künstlers) zum Computerkörper – und von einem Computerkörper zum anderen. Dabei handelt es sich anscheinend um eine solche Seelenwanderung, welche die Identität der Seele im Grossen und Ganzen intakt lässt. Diese neoplatonische Vision von digitalen Seelen auf der Suche nach ihren materiellen Hardware-Inkarnationen beherrscht weitgehend die Imagination unserer Gegenwart, denn der digitale Code 0/1 präsentiert sich auf den ersten Blick als Vollendung des Duchampschen Traums von der Identität zwischen Kreation und Selektion, Produktion und Konsum.

Allerdings kann eine solche Seelenwanderung schon deswegen nicht gelingen, weil der technische Fortschritt ständig neue Körper schafft, die zu den alten Seelen nicht mehr richtig passen. Gerade das digitale Zeitalter demonstriert de facto die extreme Abhängigkeit der Software von der Hardware – der Seele vom Körper. Programme lassen sich nicht ohne Weiteres vom Menschen auf den Computer und von einer Computergeneration zur anderen übertragen – dazu braucht es viel Übertragungsarbeit. So beginnt der Künstler, genauso fleissig am Computer zu arbeiten, wie er früher etwa fleissig gemalt hat. Aus heutiger Perspektive präsentiert sich die von der historischen Avantgarde vollzogene Enttechnisierung der Kunst zunehmend als Vorbereitung einer neuen Phase ihrer radikalen Retechnisierung. Die alten Techniken der Zeichnung, der Malerei und der Bildhauerei wurden von der Avantgarde abgeschafft – oder vielmehr in ihrer Bedeutung relativiert. Doch nach einer Phase der Befreiung von der Technik hat nun eine Phase der Retechnisierung der Kunst eingesetzt – und zwar unter Verwendung der neuen digitalen Techniken der Bildproduktion und -distribution. Der Künstler ist erneut zu einem Techniker, zu einem Spezialisten, zu einem Produzenten geworden. Programmierung und Digitalisierung bedeuten Arbeit ohne Ende. Die heutigen «virtuellen» Bilder verbreiten einen noch stärkeren Schweissgeruch als die traditionellen Meisterwerke. Die kurzen avantgardistischen Ferien der fröhlichen Immaterialität sind längst vorbei. Der Kunst steht ein neuer, langer Arbeitsalltag bevor.

BORIS GROYS
ist Professor für Philosophie und Medientheorie an der Hochschule für Gestaltung Karlsruhe.

THE RETECHNIZATION OF ART

BORIS GROYS

To begin with, a story from life. I once casually asked the director of a provincial German Kunsthalle if he presented video or net art at his institution. He told me that he couldn't show any immaterial art because the equipment it required was too heavy, and both purchasing and using it were too expensive—so, unfortunately, he had to restrict his exhibition activities to traditional paintings on canvas which is much less costly. And, indeed, as every writer knows, it's much less expensive and much less strenuous to write "materially" with a pen than "immaterially" with a computer. So what makes a writer claim that art has become immaterial today—in the sense of no longer being physical work? It is a claim that keeps cropping up in art publications.
The artistic avant-garde did indeed fight an embittered battle against arts & crafts—and therefore, if you will, against the materiality of art. The battle famously culminated in the readymade, a procedure initiated by Duchamp. The procedure is conventionally interpreted as a purely immaterial operation that consists of bestowing artistic status on any object of choice. The artist who operates with readymades does not work on materials; nor does it take much time to produce a readymade. The decision to call an object a work of art is instantaneous. Production is replaced by selection. The artist stops being a laborer—and is, instead, a consumer. This is almost a paradisiacal condition, in which production and consumption become identical. You can cook soup, hand out candies, conduct conversations, cut somebody's hair—it is all art. The victory of immateriality has apparently been secured. Spirits waft freely through the spaces of art, liberated from the prison of physicality or materiality. The sweaty smell of hard work, so unmistakable on studying the masterpieces of classical art, has disappeared—giving way to the refined, agreeable, stately scent of immateriality.
But is that really true? Not quite. For the readymade procedure to succeed, it has to be practiced within the art system. Merely declaring an object to be a work of art will not do—the declaration must be documented so that it can acquire value both for the artist himself and for others. A declaration requires a witness to establish its validity. The condition of immateriality is given only if we accept the existence of God or other gods, who can function as immaterial witnesses of a lonely, non-materially documented decision. But today we are not even sure anymore whether people can serve as plausible witnesses to their own decisions because immaterial human subjectivity has become implausible as well. It is therefore impossible to make a decision on the status of an object as a work of art without a real "material" witness. The art trade today functions as just such a witness. Its function consists of documenting the decisions artists make, and informing others about these decisions; it is a function that is definitely material—and extremely labor-intensive. The art world is building larger and larger museums and kunsthalles; catalogues are getting thicker and thicker; more and more is being organized, communicated, taped, filmed, and exhibited. That means more and more work is being done—by artists as well. They are investing more work and energy in documenting their immaterial artistic decisions than their colleagues of old once did in their handcrafted output. To repeat: the process of documentation is not an external record of artistic decisions, it is intrinsic to the decision-making process itself: no decision without documentation.
Duchamp's readymades offer the promise of one single "real utopia," which can measure up to the promise of communism and would seem to provide an effective alternative to Marx-

ism: deliverance from drudgery through the discovery of a hidden artistic and therefore monetary presence in things that are poor, lowly, mundane, in the failure to be competitive, and in failure itself. But the Marxist critique of commodity fetishism applies to readymades as well. It does not require a great effort to understand how the appropriation of added value produced by work functions in readymade art. Since the days of the avant-garde, artistic practice has often been described as transgression, infringement, and the breaking of taboos, which creates the impression that it has walked out of art institutions, out into the open and to otherness. But stepping across borders has proven to be inclusive: art today does not want to be exclusive; it wants to be inclusive—every border that is crossed expands the network of art; it makes the network even more inclusive. It is a network that requires a material infrastructure, a material basis. We are not talking about "ideal" boundaries of norms, values, and conventions, whose transgression might be considered as a "breaking of taboos," but rather about the real, material boundaries of museums, kunsthalles, and other art establishments. Their boundaries are not merely defined by aesthetic norms or preconceived ideas but even more so by the construction industry. Every increase in the inclusiveness of art also implies an increase in the anonymous, physical work required to construct more art spaces. The same obviously material work also goes into producing catalogues, films, and other forms of documentation—for which reason it ultimately makes no difference whether art takes place inside or outside of established venues. The art value, which the artist assigns to any given object, any given space, or any given process, is essentially the product of anonymous, non-artistic work performed by construction workers, technicians, cleaning staff, etc.—and only then appropriated by the artist. This fact is generally eclipsed by discourse that interprets today's advanced art as critiquing art institutions, but actually such criticism expands those institutions—in order to achieve ever-expanding inclusiveness.

Nonetheless, one can still consider a single artistic decision as immaterial, regardless of its factual documentation and realization. And one can also say that art is immaterial when the work of art is presented as a series of explicitly formulated artistic decisions and instructions required to construct installations and objects, to produce performances, or to organize events. In this case, immateriality does not mean the non-material but rather something transparent, rational, and comprehensible. The magic of artistic creation, whose effect is unique and which is inseparable from the body of the artist, is replaced by an explicit, repeatable program for the manufacture of art. It is precisely the independence of art from the body of the artist that is often designated as immateriality: the liberation from the individual, creative body in favor of a transparent, intersubjective, immaterial program. The age of digital technology apparently offers the opportunity to create something like a digital soul that remains largely independent of its embodiments—its material incarnations in the relevant hardware. The digital soul embarks on a spiritual journey from the body of a human being (an artist) to the body of the computer—and from one computer body to another. And the journey apparently leaves the identity of the soul largely intact. This Neoplatonic vision of digital souls seeking their material hardware incarnations has captured the contemporary imagination, for the digital code 0/1 would seem at first sight to be the consummation of the Duchampian dream of the identity of creation and selection, production and consumption.

A closer look reveals, however, that the journey cannot succeed because technological progress is constantly creating new bodies that no longer match the old souls. The digital age has demonstrated de facto the extreme dependence of software on hardware—of the soul on the body. Programs cannot always be transferred, as a matter of course, from people to the computer and from one computer generation to another—a great deal of hard work and readjustment is required. So artists have begun working as diligently at their computers as they used to work at, say, painting. In hindsight, the historical avant-garde's de-technization of art actually set the stage for a new phase of radical retechnization. The avant-garde abolished or rather relativized the meaning of the old techniques of drawing, painting, and sculpture. Emancipation from technique has now been succeeded by retechnization that exploits the new digital techniques of pictorial production and distribution. The artist has once again become a technician, a specialist, a producer. Programming and digitalization means work without end. Today's "virtual" images exude an even stronger smell of sweat than the traditional masterworks. The brief avant-garde vacation to cheerful immateriality has been over for ages. Today art confronts a new, much longer daily grind.

Translation: Catherine Schelbert

BORIS GROYS

is a professor of philosophy and media theory at the Hochschule für Gestaltung Karlsruhe.

Special Collaboration

A L E X K A T Z

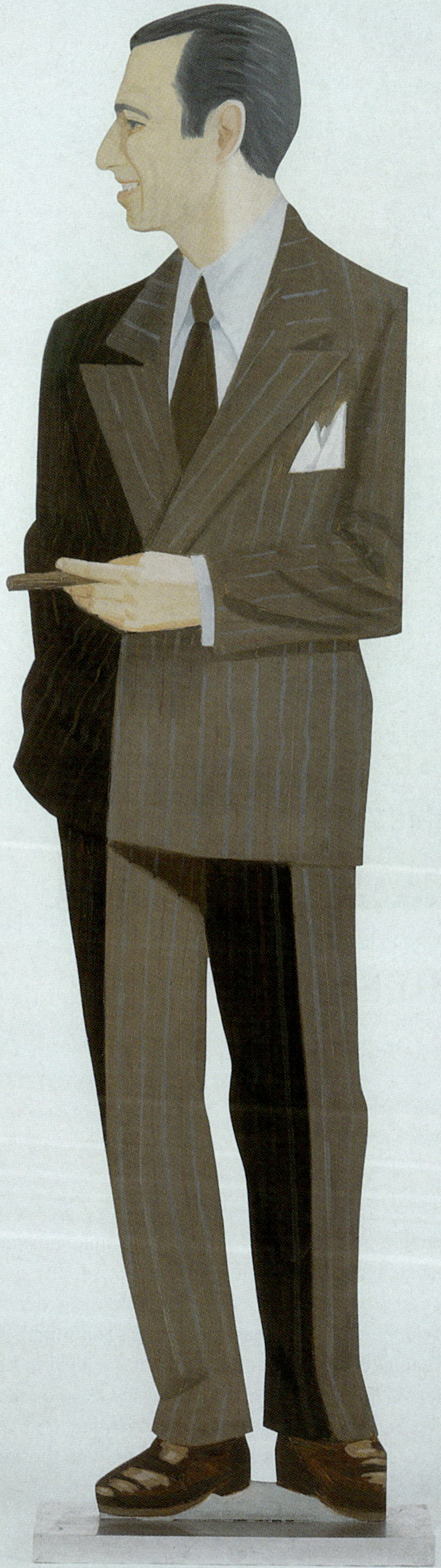

ALEX KATZ, CUTOUT ALEX, 1968, oil on aluminum, front view, 71 1/8 x 18 3/4" / Öl auf Aluminium, Frontansicht, 180,7 x 47,6 cm. (PHOTO: OREN SLOR)

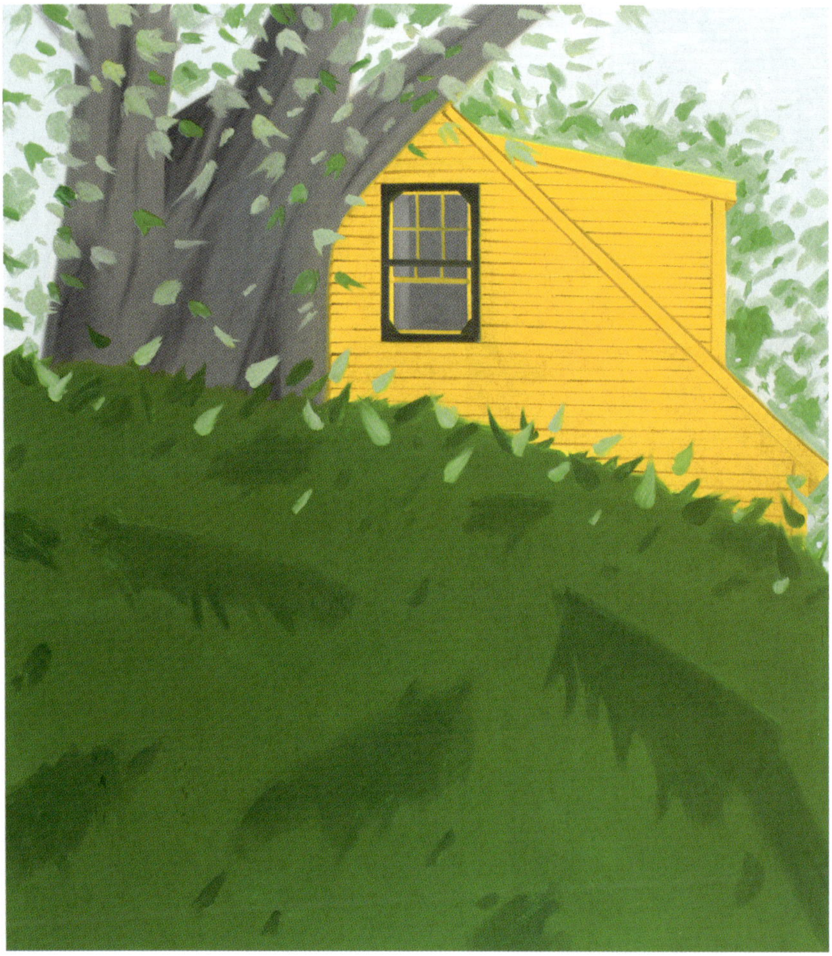

ALEX KATZ, YELLOW HOUSE, 2004, oil on canvas, 77 x 69" / GELBES HAUS, Öl auf Leinwand, 195,6 x 175,3 cm. (PHOTO: KERRY RYAN McFATE / PACE WILDENSTEIN, NEW YORK)

LIKE A QUARTER MILE RACE

A CONVERSATION

ENA SWANSEA & ALEX KATZ

ENA SWANSEA: During the time you have been a painter, there have been seismic movements in the means of transmission, in all areas perhaps, but, clearly, with image transmission, money, market transmissions, and critical discourse—we have popped out of the membrane that held us in, and into the immaterial ozone of the digital world. Our experience of space changes as we spend more time in this immaterial environment, checking our email, and whatnot; and so shifting back and forth between the virtual and the material world is fluid and reflexive. It is as if our hidden inner life has not changed; only the gadgets, which have moved part of that life out of tangible things, have changed. Painting is transmitted in an intimate, optical way, unlike what is received from a glowing screen. With the resonance of

history behind it, painting is in a unique position to reflect these shifts, and the resulting difference in the atmosphere of the culture.
ALEX KATZ: That's not a question. *(laughter)*
ES: Yes it is. *(laughter)*
AK: Our culture has been inundated with images of graphic information, and it changes the way the world looks. Each artist has to deal with that, and, in many ways, its transferal to a painting is more difficult than to another medium. The tradition of painting is both a help and a hindrance to dealing with the immediate world.
ES: Do you think that there's a hidden pressure on painting to be more graphic? Robert Storr talked about "graphic painting" having this kind of currency now. Do you think that painters feel that they have to step out into this swirl of different forms of images and compete?
AK: Painting is malleable. It's up to each artist to adjust it to his temperament. There are interesting artists who choose not to make a real contemporary painting, and that seems valid to them. If you deal with the contemporary landscape, so to speak, you have to make some adjustments to the graphic. It's easy, it's something you can use, and something you're in conflict with. I don't see anything wrong with graphic art per se. It's like, who does it?
ES: Who does it?
AK: Yeah, just because there's bad art around doesn't make the idea bad.
ES: One time you said, "If you really break your ass on a painting, any truck driver can see it." Everybody understands painting, and this open access gives freedom to the painter. It allows paintings a possibility of being a means of transmission for the not known.
AK: I don't know whether painting, per se, is any more communicable than other forms of visual art; perhaps it's even a little less so, because of techniques. We've gone through a time period when artists were making paintings for a very small audience, and now they're making paintings for a much larger audience. I like art that is like Shakespeare and Blake, rather than Joyce or Pound. I like the idea of painting being structured in levels. Edwin Denby once said, when he wrote for the Tribune, "I like to write something that the man on the street can read and understand and get something from, but all of my friends have to read it twice." *(laughter)* There's always a sentence in there that's real complicated and the general public will miss it, and his friends will pick up on it. That's my idea of what a painting should be.
ES: So one of your paintings exists on a number of levels at one time.
AK: Absolutely, it's supposed to. You want to make a complicated object, not an obscure object.
ES: Do you think the complication comes directly from your subconscious, or do you build it in?
AK: You get an idea or conception of what you think art should be.

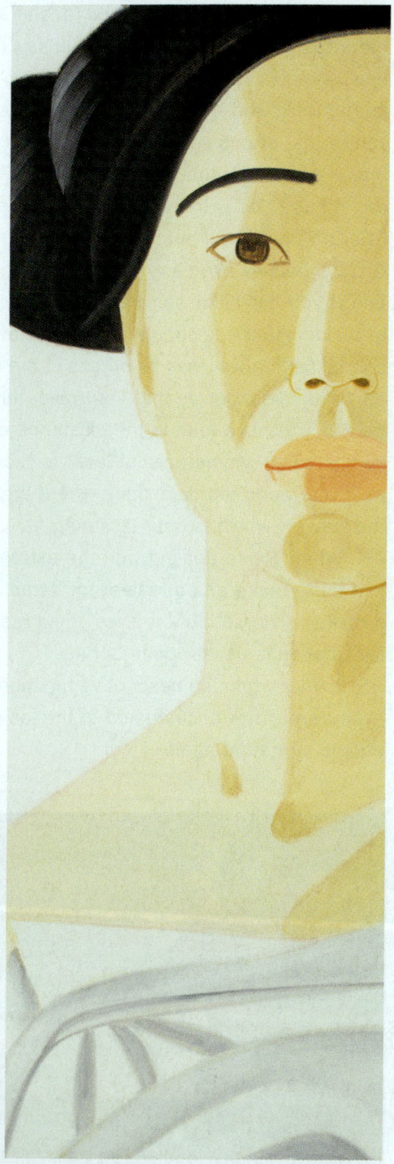

ALEX KATZ, MARIKO, 2004, oil on canvas, 96 x 33½" / Öl auf Leinwand, 243,8 x 85,1 cm. (PHOTO: ELLEN LABENSKI / PACE WILDENSTEIN, NEW YORK)

It's kind of complicated how you receive it, because you receive a lot of it from just thinking about it, and other things pop into it. So, I would say, how you arrive at a conceptual basis is as intuitive as anything else, and how you direct that conception to a material object is complicated, because you try, and it fails, and you try, and it's off, and you try this, and you try that, and it works, finally, something works, and you've just stumbled your way into it. A lot of the process of painting is going from one part of your brain—the conceptual part, which is intuitive, but a different type—to the part that's almost unconscious, and it has to do with taste—what you like and what you don't like.

ES: And that's built in to the back of your head.

AK: It's built in. We carry that from birth. When you're born there are some things you like, and some things you don't like; some things stay with you and others are acquired. It's quite a complicated system of building, but you should always pay attention to your taste.

ES: Taste, in a way, has its origins in the subconscious, where paintings come from, and there seems to be some passageway that you travel through, leading what is not known out onto the canvas. For instance, you have faith in the existence of irregular features in a portrait of someone who, in the flesh, seems quite symmetrical, at least to those who are not you. And yet, your image asserts itself as real, as if you found the flash point where the image arrives, not just in the eye, but in the nervous system of the viewer—which is not reassuring.

AK: When you're dealing with the external world, it's far too much to comprehend intellectually, so you just try to make an equivalent for its appearance. Making it literal doesn't make it better; a lot of times it makes it worse. So if it gives you a feeling of what you want, that's good enough, because literal representation is usually quite boring.

ES: In your work, the descriptive function always seems to have something *off* about it. It is as if your eyes never grew accustomed to the look of this world, of manufactured objects, the social practices of people, of nature itself.

ALEX KATZ, ORANGE SUNSET 1, 2004, oil on canvas, 103 x 240" / ORANGER SONNENUNTERGANG 1, Öl auf Leinwand, 261,6 x 609,6 cm. (PHOTO: OREN SLOR)

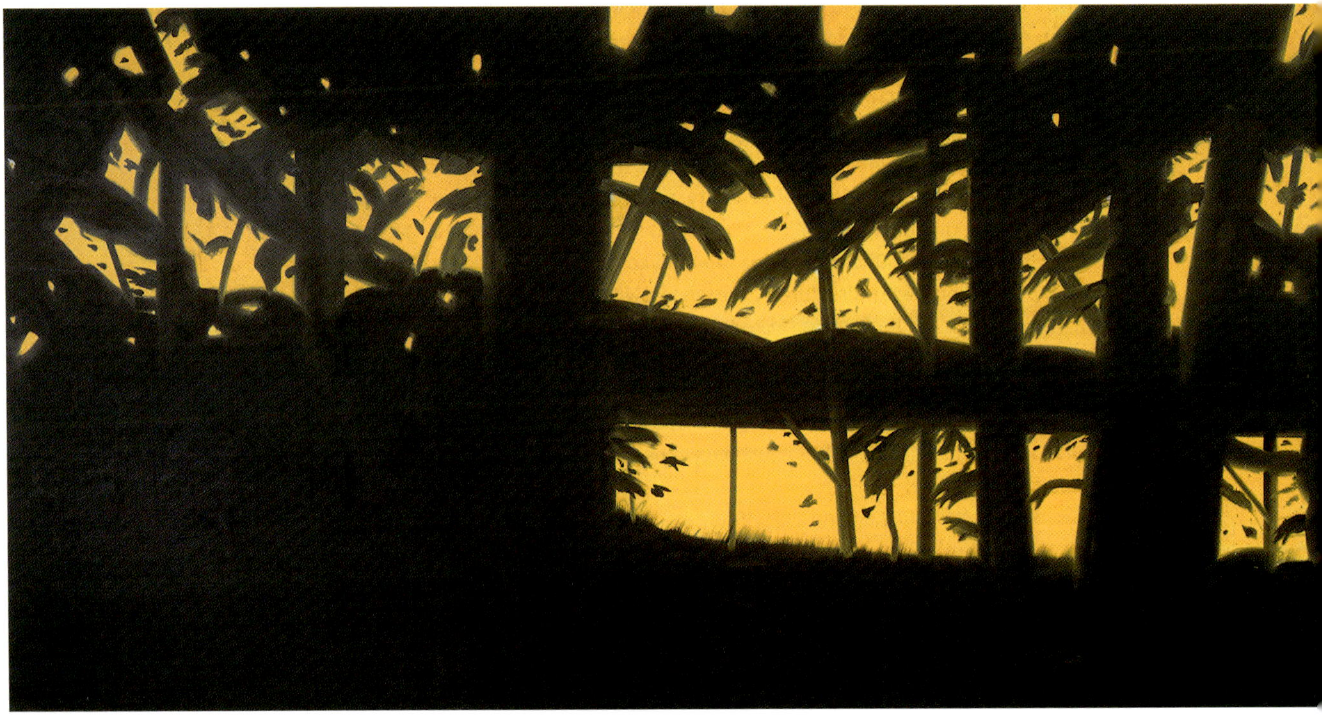

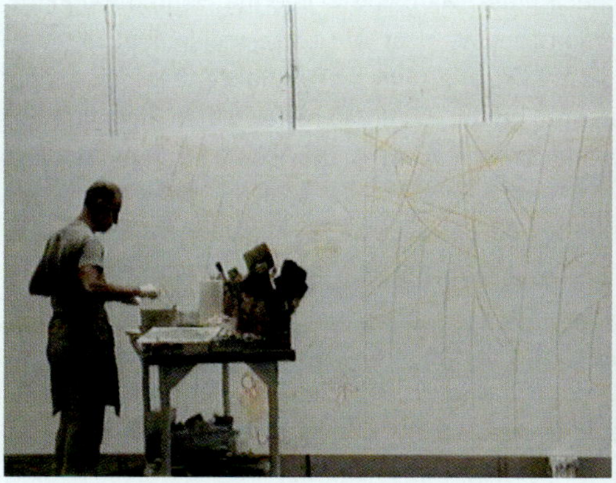

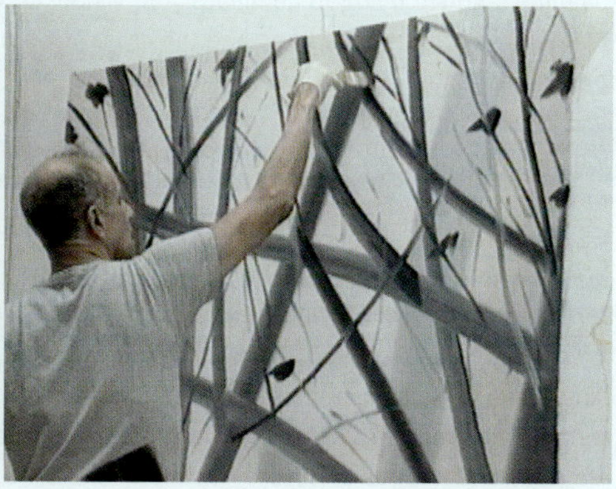

Alex Katz in his studio / bei der Arbeit im Atelier. Video stills from / aus: ALEX KATZ FIVE HOURS, 1996, directed by Vivien Bittencourt & Vincent Katz.

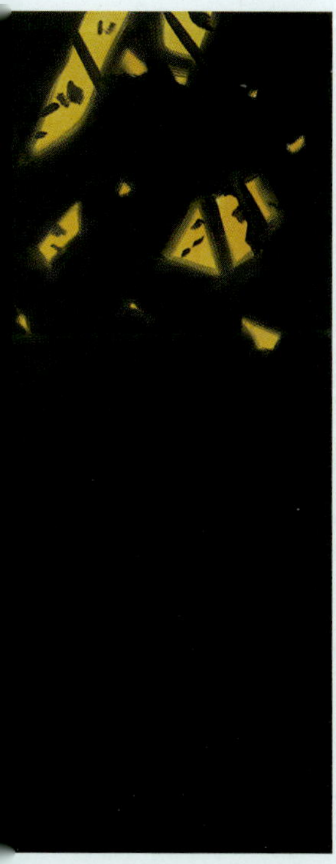

AK: Sometimes I try to squeeze too many things into a painting at once, and then it gets kind of irregular. I can make a precise drawing and there's no problem, but when I get into a painting, there's the life of the painting—the life of the colors, the life of the image, and the life of the subject—and I try to squeeze all these things together, and the edges break, and things go irregular, and if it looks okay, I say, fine. I just go with that; I really trust the unconscious motor which paints it. If it doesn't look good, I'll fix it... or try to. *(laughter)*

ES: In all of these areas, which you contemplate over decades, things never seem to settle down, and move out of being weird. I never knew, for instance, that a rock, formed before humans roamed the earth, or a twenty-three-year-old human hand, was weird looking until you painted it. *(laughter)*
AK: What can I say? What's weird to some people is natural to others.
ES: Where does that navigation system that you have come from?
AK: Some people, when they see my paintings, think they don't look real. It's like Indian miniatures that don't look real; then, all of a sudden, one day, bingo! They're very real! You try to make a way of seeing things you haven't seen before, and it can be quite abrasive because, on one hand, you're faced with information that leads you to believe this is something you've seen before, and, in other ways, it's an idea of making something you haven't seen before. If you haven't seen it before, your mind doesn't properly collate the information that's in front of you. So, I don't think of my things as weird, I think that some of my audience is not ready to accept what I've done.
ES: After a while, looking at your paintings, and then looking at the world that corresponded to them, I noticed it was a two-way street.
AK: What do you mean?
ES: Stuff in reality started to look like your paintings.

AK: That's the idea. The idea is to show you a new way of looking at things. I'm trying to make a new painting, and I'm trying to dominate your vision. In other words, I want you to see the world through my painting, so the irregular hand and the cross-eyed person become okay. Of course, you look at all those old paintings, and they're cross-eyed and irregular, but they're in a form that you accept as being logical. If that's logical, then my paintings are illogical; and I've gotten more bad reviews than any other living artist, at this point. *(laughter)* They can't see the world through my eyes; they see it through the eyes of Michelangelo or something.
ES: Franz West, in his conversation with Bice Curiger about these topics (in *Parkett* 70), said that experience with LSD and reading Wittgenstein taught him that everything lives. So, looking at all your pictures, what about you? Did anything teach you that?
AK: No, but I found things that were on similar wavelengths. In the early fifties, there was Bebop and Abstract Expressionism; they were both using open, non-linear forms, and that was very interesting. In the late fifties and sixties there were poets like Frank O'Hara, Kenneth Koch, and John Ashbery, who were making images that were not linear. There was just ... bang! One image and then another. It was a way of dismissing content and form, or changing what the ideas of form and content were; and that's where I was looking. I was thinking, I can't be totally nuts if these guys are doing it too.
ES: Does your work change in the way it looks to you across time?
AK: Definitely. There are some paintings that I thought were really good—and they're usually harmonious paintings (they're perfectly done)—and a lot of them become less interesting. Some of the stranger ones settle and become more palatable. Some of my paintings, I have a hard time with. When I walk away from one of those, I know it's the best I can do. Generally, when I go into new areas, I can't control the paintings the way I would like to, and they feel rough and hard to take, and I don't like them because they're a little rough. Twenty years later, some of them seem to have a little more energy. I also think the way I look at the paintings determines, to an extent, the way other people look at the paintings. I make a painting, and if it's an extended painting, I don't really know what I did, fully. I know I got the paint on it all right, but I really don't understand the whole thing. People explain it to me every ten or twenty years—they look at the paintings differently. What they're looking at is more real than what I'm looking at, and I learn through them about my paintings.
ES: Does that mean that you're becoming them, in the sense of Auden, in that poem about Yeats, who said that he became his admirers? Are you becoming your admirers?
AK: Well, I sure listen to them. Take the painting LAWN PARTY (1965); it's really an abrasive picture. When I had the retrospective at the Whitney (1986), I decided not to put it in because it was so abrasive. Then I had a retrospective in Buenos Aires (1998), and there I put it in, and I realized it was perfectly okay with the rest of the work. That was an interesting transition because it was a time I didn't have other people talking about it—my own viewpoint changed. I do think we change in time, and the pictures change. Actually, oil paintings do change. They have a freshness, and then they mellow out. A really good oil painting gets better in five years; it sort of pulls together. My paintings have the tendency to be a little apart. A painting of mine—a good painting—in five or ten years looks a little more together. They age well if they're right, and that's one of the things about oil. It takes a long, long time for an oil painting to dry.
ES: In addition to what's going on with the object, you have said that paintings are moving in time, and maybe there's something about the immaterial aspects of the painting that congeal as time passes, and this is something that you have said photography lacks. In a sense, photography remains static and paintings always move.
AK: Photography is basically past-tense art, and if it's any good, painting is present-tense art. You look at an old painting—it is like it's still in the present tense, fresco particularly, because it doesn't have oil.
ES: And what about your paintings? I mean... I haven't made so many. But the way they look to me, as I've made more, begins to shift, and I'm not sure why. So, in your case, you've made like fifty thousand

paintings. *(laughter)* Do they change in your eyes as they pass across the whole arc of the body of work that you've made?
AK: Painting is a passage through time, and generally, you try to stay in the present tense, try something that will give you a kick, so that you're continually reduced to ineptness, in a sense, of not being able to deal with what you're trying to do. That is what I concentrate on. The past is the past; the paintings look good or they don't look good.
ES: I'm thinking about time.
AK: The painting is supposed to be an instantaneous action. You get this flash, and if it's any good, it doesn't go away. An old painting is the same as a new painting if it has had that sense of being in the present tense. It's sort of like style. You *know* when something had a lot of style. Rubens always did flashy paintings. He had that energy. It's a matter of energy.

ES: You're a high-speed moving guy. You have a particular sense of time. Do you think that making paintings has helped you have a grip on time?
AK: No. The only way I can adjust to the whole thing is by making paintings. It can occupy me. I can go in a room for six hours and be completely occupied with putting paint on a canvas, which is terrific. It's very interesting getting paint on a canvas.
ES: That's where you're most able to tolerate present time. If you go for a run or go to a cocktail party it's like maximum eighteen minutes and you're gone, and you're done.
AK: In the paintings, you get inside the whole being. When you're running, you're inside your whole being too, but it's not as engaging as painting. Painting is fully engaging. You drift the way you do when you run or swim, but there's a lot of tension in making a painting. I always thought of painting as running a quarter mile race. It's a blast from the start, and you float, and you go into rigor mortis—the rigs—and the body stiffens up, and you try to get through it somehow. You have to put something into a painting that you don't have to put in other things
ES: A part of your self?
AK: A part of your self. That's really a big strain, a huge strain. I don't think a photographer gets that kind of a kick, that kind of strain. That's one of the things you need in order to paint, and one of the things you hold in common with other painters—that *that* person went through *that* thing in *that* painting. That's why I have respect for other painters who go through that. There are some painters who don't do anything, but a good painter goes through that.

ENA SWANSEA
is a painter who lives and works in New York.

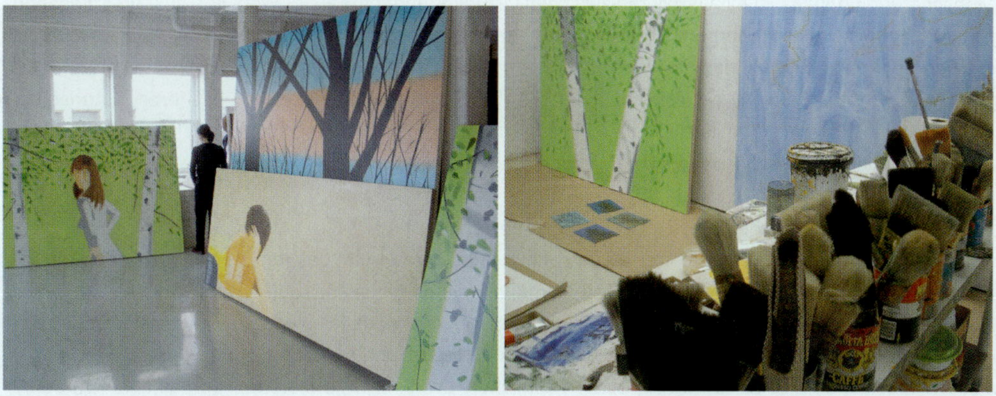

In Alex Katz's studio / im Atelier von Alex Katz.
(PHOTOS: VIVIEN BITTENCOURT, 2004)

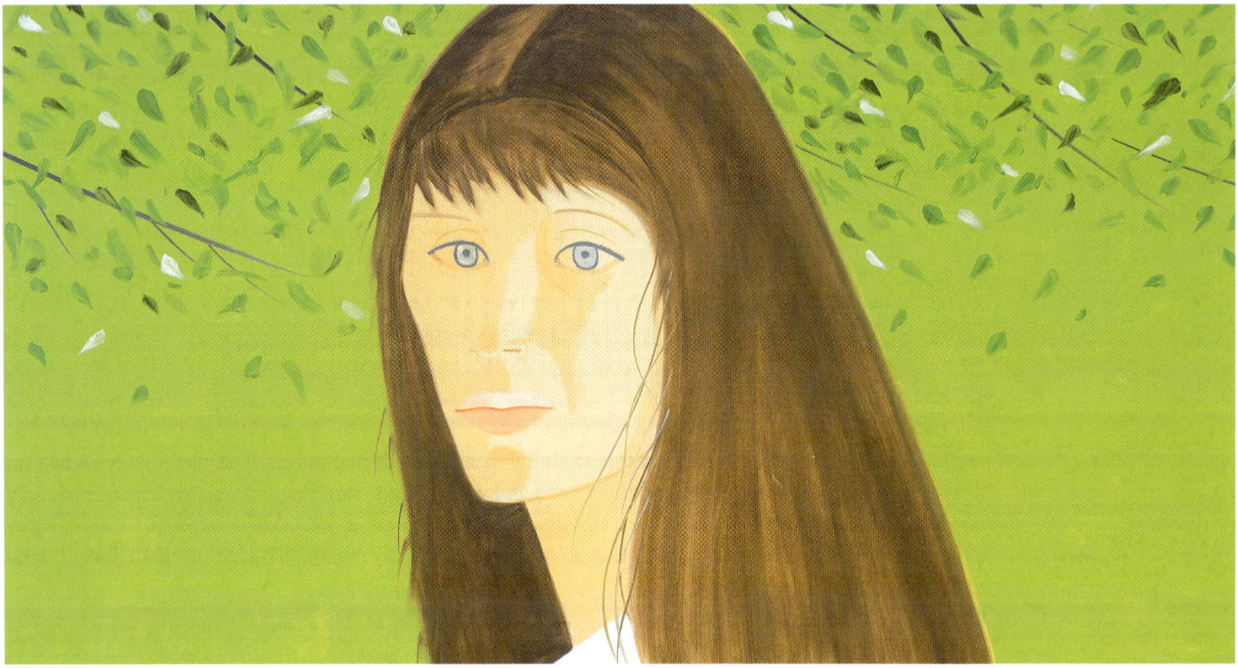

ALEX KATZ, KYM, 2004, oil on canvas, 96 x 120" / Öl auf Leinwand, 243,8 x 304,8 cm. (PHOTO: OREN SLOR)

WIE EIN 400-METER-LAUF

ENA SWANSEA IM GESPRÄCH MIT ALEX KATZ

ENA SWANSEA: In deinem Leben als Maler hat es im Bereich der Kommunikationsmittel gewaltige Umwälzungen gegeben, in allen anderen Bereichen wahrscheinlich auch, doch mit der Übertragung auf der Ebene von Bildern, Geld, Märkten und kritischem Diskurs haben wir den Kokon, in dem wir steckten, gesprengt und atmen nun die dünne Luft der digitalen Welt. Unsere Erfahrung des Raumes verändert sich mit der Zeit, die wir in der virtuellen Sphäre verbringen, wo wir unsere E-Mails lesen und alles Mögliche erledigen; es ist ein Oszillieren zwischen virtueller und materieller Welt, das äusserst fliessend und reflexiv ist. Unser verborgenes Innenleben scheint sich nicht verändert zu haben, nur die Technik, die den konkreten Dingen dabei etwas von diesem Leben entzogen hat. Anders als ein Bild auf dem leuchtenden Bildschirm vermittelt sich Malerei auf eine intime, optische Art. Mit ihrer historischen Resonanz im Rücken ist die Malerei in einer einzigartigen Position, diese Umwälzungen und die sich daraus ergebenden atmosphärischen Veränderungen unserer Kultur zu reflektieren.
ALEX KATZ: Das ist keine Frage. *(lacht)*
ES: Doch, ist es. *(lacht ebenfalls)*
AK: Unsere Kultur ist von einer Bilderflut überschwemmt worden und das hat die Welt verändert. Jeder Künstler muss sich damit auseinander setzen, und in vielerlei Hinsicht ist die Umsetzung dieser Tatsache in einem gemalten Bild schwieriger als in einem anderen Medium. Die Tradition der Malerei ist zugleich eine Hilfe und ein Hindernis bei dieser Auseinandersetzung mit dem Unmittelbaren.
ES: Glaubst du, es gibt so etwas wie einen heimlichen Druck auf die Malerei, «graphischer» zu sein?

Robert Storr liess sich darüber aus, dass «graphische Malerei» im Augenblick hoch im Kurs sei. Glaubst du, dass die Maler sich gedrängt fühlen, sich in diesen Wirbel unterschiedlicher Bildformen hinauszuwagen um mitzuhalten?
AK: Malerei ist gefügig. Jeder Künstler kann sie seinem Temperament anpassen. Es gibt sehr interessante Künstler, die keine brandaktuellen Bilder machen wollen und das auch überzeugt vertreten. Lässt man sich aber auf die zeitgenössische Landschaft ein, muss man das Graphische schon mit einbeziehen. Das ist einfach; man kann es benutzen und kommt auch in Konflikt damit. Es spricht auch nichts gegen die graphische Kunst als solche. Die Frage ist: Wer macht sie?
ES: Wer macht sie?
AK: Ja, nur weil es schlechte Bilder gibt, heisst das noch lange nicht, dass auch die Idee falsch ist.
ES: Du hast einmal gesagt: «Wenn man sich wirklich ins Zeug legt, kann das jeder LKW-Fahrer sehen.» Jeder versteht Malerei, und diese leichte Zugänglichkeit bedeutet Freiheit für den Maler. Bilder können so eine Mittlerfunktion für das Nichtbekannte übernehmen.
AK: Ich weiss nicht, ob Malerei an sich leichter kommunizierbar ist als andere Formen visueller Kunst; vielleicht ist es auf Grund der Techniken sogar etwas schwieriger. Es gab einmal eine Zeit, in der Künstler nur für einen sehr kleinen Kreis gemalt haben. Inzwischen hat sich dieser Kreis enorm erweitert. Ich mag Kunst in der Art von Shakespeare und Blake jedenfalls lieber als von Joyce und Pound. Mir gefällt die Idee von Bildern, die auf mehreren Ebenen funktionieren. Als Edwin Denby für die *Tribune* schrieb, meinte er einmal: «Ich schreibe gern so, dass der Mann von der Strasse es lesen, verstehen und auch etwas damit anfangen kann, aber all meine Freunde es zweimal lesen müssen.» *(Lachen)* Man stösst bei ihm immer auf einen Satz, dessen Komplexität dem Durchschnittsleser entgeht, seinen Freunden aber sofort ins Auge springt.
Das entspricht genau meiner Vorstellung von einem guten Bild.
ES: Ein Bild von dir existiert also auf verschiedenen Ebenen gleichzeitig?
AK: Absolut, zumindest ist das meine Absicht. Ich möchte etwas Komplexes, aber nichts Obskures produzieren.
ES: Kommt die Komplexität direkt aus deinem Unterbewusstsein, oder baust du sie gezielt ein?
AK: Man hat eine bestimmte Vorstellung oder einen Begriff davon, wie Kunst sein sollte. Wie man sie erfährt, ist einigermassen kompliziert, denn vieles erkennt man erst beim Nachdenken darüber, und da funken noch ganz andere Sachen dazwischen. Ich glaube, dass man eine konzeptuelle Grundlage auf ebenso intuitive Weise findet wie alles andere. Und wie man sein Konzept auf den konkreten Gegenstand überträgt, ist eine komplizierte Angelegenheit. Man versucht es, der Versuch missglückt, man versucht es erneut, und der Versuch missglückt wieder, dann probiert man dies und jenes aus und schliesslich klappt es; irgendetwas klappt immer und man ist einfach hineingestolpert. Ein grosser Teil des malerischen Prozesses besteht in einer Bewegung von einer Gehirnhälfte – jener des begrifflichen Denkens, die auch intuitiv ist, nur auf andere Art – zur anderen, die unbewusster funktioniert, und hat mit Geschmack zu tun, mit dem, was man mag und was nicht.
ES: Und das steckt im Hinterkopf.
AK: Das ist mit eingebaut. Wir kommen damit zur Welt. Von Geburt an gibt es Dinge, die wir mögen, und Dinge, die wir nicht mögen; manches bleibt so, anderes erwirbt man dazu. Unser Geschmack ist ein ziemlich kompliziertes Gebilde, aber man sollte sich immer auf ihn verlassen.
ES: Der Geschmack hat also seine Wurzeln irgendwie im Unterbewussten, wo auch die Bilder herkommen: Es scheint da eine Art Durchgang zu geben, den du benützt, um noch nicht Bewusstes auf die Leinwand zu schleusen. Zum Beispiel vertraust du den Unregelmässigkeiten in einem Porträt, auch bei einem Gesicht, das, zumindest in den Augen anderer, sehr ebenmässig ist. Und doch behauptet sich dein Bild als Realität, als hättest du den Reaktionspunkt gefunden, an dem das Bild wirklich ankommt, weniger im Auge als im Nervensystem des Betrachters – was eher verstörend ist.
AK: Beschäftigt man sich mit der konkreten Welt der Dinge, so lässt sich das intellektuell einfach nicht

ALEX KATZ, TWO BUILDINGS, 2002, oil on canvas, 125 x 92" / ZWEI GEBÄUDE, Öl auf Leinwand, 317,5 x 233,7 cm.
(PHOTO: KERRY RYAN McFATE / PACE WILDENSTEIN, NEW YORK)

bewältigen, deshalb versucht man eine Entsprechung für die Phänomene zu finden. Eine Eins-zu-eins-Wiedergabe hilft einem dabei nicht weiter, häufig wird dadurch alles nur noch schlimmer. Wenn es aber ein Gefühl dessen vermittelt, was man zeigen will, ist das schon was, denn die blosse Wiedergabe ist meist ziemlich langweilig.

ES: In deinen Arbeiten wirkt das Deskriptive immer irgendwie etwas schräg. Es ist, als hätte sich dein Auge nie so richtig an den Anblick dieser Welt gewöhnt, weder an ihre Artefakte, die gesellschaftlichen Gepflogenheiten der Menschen, noch an die Natur selbst.

AK: Manchmal versuche ich, zu viele Dinge auf einmal in einem Bild unterzubringen, und dann wird es irgendwie schräg. Ich kann eine ganz genaue Zeichnung machen, das ist überhaupt kein Problem, wenn ich mich aber aufs Malen einlasse, dann kommt das Eigenleben des Bildes ins Spiel – das Leben der Farben, das Leben des Gemalten, das Leben des Sujets. Ich versuche all diese Dinge unter einen Hut zu bringen, wobei häufig die Ränder aufbrechen und die ursprüngliche Ordnung durcheinander gerät. Wenn es gut aussieht, sage ich mir, okay, dann machen wir das so; ich habe wirklich Vertrauen in den unbewussten Motor, der da malt. Sieht es nicht gut aus, bring ich es wieder in Ordnung ... oder versuche es zumindest. *(lacht)*

ES: In all diesen Themenbereichen, mit denen du dich schon seit Jahrzehnten befasst, scheinen die Dinge nie zur Ruhe zu kommen oder ihre Merkwürdigkeit abzulegen. Zum Beispiel ist mir, bevor du das gemalt hast, noch nie aufgefallen, wie seltsam ein Felsbrocken aussehen kann, der geformt wurde, bevor es Menschen auf der Erde gab; oder auch eine dreiundzwanzigjährige menschliche Hand.

AK: Was soll ich sagen? Was manchen seltsam erscheint, finden andere ganz normal.

ES: Du musst über ein ganz besonderes Navigationssystem verfügen.

AK: Manchmal finden Leute, die meine Bilder sehen, dass sie nichts mit der Wirklichkeit zu tun haben. Das ist wie bei indischen Miniaturen, die überhaupt nicht wirklichkeitsnah erscheinen, bis sie dann plötzlich eines Tages, bingo, absolut real sind. Man sucht einen Weg, die Dinge neu zu sehen, Dinge zu sehen, die man noch nie gesehen hat, was ziemlich zermürbend sein kann, denn einerseits sieht man sich Informationen gegenüber, die einen verführen zu glauben, es handle sich um etwas, was man schon gesehen hat, aber andererseits ist die Idee ja gerade, etwas machen zu wollen, was man noch nie zuvor so gesehen hat. Hat man etwas noch nie zuvor gesehen, kann der Verstand die Information, die er vorfindet, nicht richtig aufnehmen. Ich halte meine Sachen also keineswegs für merkwürdig. Ich glaube vielmehr, dass mein Publikum zum Teil noch nicht bereit ist, zu akzeptieren, was ich gemacht habe.

ES: Nachdem ich deine Bilder eine Weile betrachtet habe und dann den ihnen entsprechenden Teil der Welt, fiel mir auf, dass es keine Einbahnstrasse ist.

AK: Wie meinst du das?

ES: Dass reale Dinge plötzlich wie auf deinen Bildern auszusehen begannen.

AK: Genau darauf will ich hinaus. Es geht mir darum, eine neue Art des Sehens aufzuzeigen. Ich versuche ein neues Bild zu machen und euch meine Sichtweise aufzuzwingen. Mit anderen Worten, ich möchte, dass ihr die Welt durch meine Malerei seht, so dass die deformierte Hand und der schielende Mensch schliesslich ihre Richtigkeit haben. Sieht man nämlich auf alten Bildern Schielende und Missgestaltete, akzeptiert man dies als formal folgerichtig. Im Vergleich dazu, sind meine Bilder dann unlogisch. Bis heute habe ich mehr Verrisse bekommen als irgendein anderer lebender Künstler. *(lacht)* Die Leute können die Welt nicht mit meinen Augen sehen; sie sehen sie mit den Augen von Michelangelo oder wem auch immer.

ES: Franz West hat in seinem Gespräch mit Bice Curiger, bei dem es auch um diese Fragen ging, gesagt, er habe dank LSD und Wittgenstein erkannt, dass alles lebt. Angesichts deiner Bilder frage ich mich, wie das bei dir ist. Hast du eine ähnliche Erfahrung gemacht?

AK: Nein, aber ich bin auf Dinge mit ähnlicher Wellenlänge gestossen. Anfang der 50er Jahre gab es den Bebop und den Abstrakten Expressionismus; beide arbeiteten mit offenen, nicht linearen Formen und das war extrem spannend. Ende der 50er und in den 60er Jahren waren es dann Dichter wie Frank

O'Hara, Kenneth Koch, und John Ashbery, die nicht lineare Bilder schufen. Das ging Schlag auf Schlag: ein Bild und dann das nächste. Begriffe wie Inhalt und Form hatten ausgedient oder ihre Bedeutung war dabei, sich zu ändern. Daran hab ich mich orientiert und mir gedacht, völlig durchgedreht könne ich ja nicht sein, wenn diese Leute dasselbe taten.

ES: Hat sich dein Werk für dich im Lauf der Zeit verändert?

AK: Na klar. Es gibt einige Bilder, die ich für wirklich gut gehalten habe – meist harmonische, perfekt gemalte Bilder –, und viele davon werden zunehmend weniger interessant. Dagegen sind die etwas seltsameren Bilder gereift und annehmbarer geworden. Mit manchen Bildern hab ich grosse Schwierigkeiten. Wenn ich da jeweils die Waffen strecke, weiss ich, dass es die beste Lösung ist. Im Allgemeinen habe ich, wenn ich mich auf Neuland begebe, die Bilder nicht so unter Kontrolle, wie ich es gerne möchte: Ich empfinde sie als unfertig und schwer auszuhalten und deshalb gefallen sie mir auch nicht. Zwanzig Jahre später scheint dann in einigen dieser Bilder mehr Energie zu stecken. Ich glaube auch, dass meine Art die Bilder zu sehen ein Stück weit die Sichtweise anderer beeinflusst. Ich male also ein Bild, und wenn es sehr komplex ist, weiss ich nicht mehr so genau, was ich im Detail getan habe. Natürlich weiss ich, dass ich die Farbe aufgetragen habe, aber verstehen tu ich das Ganze nicht wirklich. Alle zehn oder zwanzig Jahre gibt es Leute, die es mir erklären – aber andere sehen die Bilder anders. Was sie sehen, ist realer, als was ich sehe, und durch sie lerne ich meine Bilder erst richtig kennen.

ES: Heisst das, dass du mit ihren Augen siehst, wie in Audens Gedicht über Yeats, in dem er schreibt, dass dieser eins wurde mit seinen Bewunderern? Gilt das auch für dich?

AK: Nun, zumindest höre ich ihnen gut zu. Im Fall von LAWN PARTY (Rasenparty, 1965), einem wirklich irritierenden Bild, war es so, dass ich es 1986 bei meiner Retrospektive im Whitney Museum nicht ausstellte, eben weil es so abweisend wirkt. Ein paar Jahre später in Buenos Aires (1998) habe ich es dann gezeigt. Ich hatte begriffen, dass es sehr gut zu den übrigen Arbeiten passte. Das war ein interessanter Umschwung, denn damals gab es niemanden, der mit mir darüber gesprochen hätte: Mein eigener Blickwinkel hatte sich verändert. Ich bin überzeugt, dass wir uns mit der Zeit ändern, und die Bilder auch. Das gilt insbesondere für Ölbilder. Zuerst haben sie diese Frische und später reifen sie dann aus. Ein gutes Ölbild wird in fünf Jahren noch besser sein; es wird irgendwie kohärenter. Meine Bilder haben die Tendenz, etwas inkohärent zu wirken. Ein gutes Bild von mir wirkt nach fünf oder zehn Jahren einheitlicher. Sie altern gut, wenn sie gelungen sind, das ist eine der Besonderheiten von Öl. Ein Ölbild braucht einfach sehr lange, bis es trocken ist.

ES: Zu diesen objektiven Veränderungen kommt noch hinzu, dass Bilder sich, wie du sagst, in der Zeit bewegen, und vielleicht gibt es immaterielle Aspekte, die erst mit der Zeit quasi gerinnen und greifbar werden; etwas, was es, wie du gesagt hast, in der Photographie nicht gibt. Diese bleibt gewissermassen immer statisch, während gemalte Bilder immer in Bewegung sind.

AK: Photographie ist im Grunde eine Kunst der Vergangenheit, während Malerei, sofern sie was taugt, eine Kunst der Gegenwart ist. Wenn man ein altes Bild anschaut, so wirkt es immer noch absolut gegenwärtig, besonders die Freskomalerei, weil dabei kein Öl verwendet wird.

ES: Und wie ist das bei deinen Bildern? Ich meine, ich habe selbst noch nicht so viele gemalt. Aber auch die scheinen sich je länger je mehr irgendwie zu verändern, und ich weiss nicht genau, warum. Bei dir ist es ja so, dass du ungefähr fünfzigtausend Bilder gemalt hast. *(lacht)* Verändern sich diese Bilder auch in deinen Augen, wenn du dem Bogen folgst, den dein Werk beschreibt?

AK: Malerei ist eine Bewegung in der Zeit und im Allgemeinen versucht man in der Gegenwart zu bleiben. Man versucht etwas, was einem einen Kick verschafft, so dass man laufend mit der eigenen Unzulänglichkeit konfrontiert ist und mit dem, was man machen will, nicht zu Rande kommt. Darauf konzentriere ich mich. Die Vergangenheit ist Vergangenheit; die Bilder schauen entweder gut aus oder eben nicht.

ES: Und die Zeit?

AK: Das Bild soll eine Art Blitzaktion sein. Man hat diesen Flash, und wenn er etwas taugt, verflüchtigt er sich auch nicht. Ein altes Bild unterscheidet sich nicht von einem neuen, wenn es dieses Gefühl von

Gegenwart vermittelt. Ähnlich wie der Stil. Man weiss einfach, dass etwas Stil hat. Rubens malte immer aus diesem Flash heraus. Er besass die nötige Energie. Es ist eine Frage der Energie.

ES: Du hast ein atemberaubendes Tempo. Und du hast ein ganz besonderes Zeitgefühl. Hat dir das Malen geholfen, die Zeit in den Griff zu bekommen?

AK: Nein. Ich kann das Ganze nur in den Griff bekommen, indem ich male. Es hält mich in Atem. Ich kann sechs Stunden lang in einem Raum Farbe auf die Leinwand auftragen und es absorbiert mich vollkommen, eine tolle Sache. Es ist sehr spannend, Farbe auf die Leinwand aufzutragen..

ES: Und so erträgst du die Gegenwart am besten. Beim Joggen oder auf einer Cocktailparty bist du höchstens etwa achtzehn Minuten mit von der Partie, dann bist du weg und erledigt.

AK: Beim Malen fühlt man sich ganz seiend. Das kann auch beim Joggen der Fall sein, aber es nimmt einen weniger in Anspruch. Das Malen absorbiert einen ganz. Man lässt sich treiben, ähnlich wie beim Joggen oder Schwimmen, aber das Malen eines Bildes ist mit enormer Anspannung verbunden. Für mich war Malen immer so etwas wie ein 400-Meter-Rennen. Man startet sofort voll durch, man driftet, man ist übersäuert, der Körper versteift sich total – Rigor mortis – und man versucht es irgendwie zu überstehen. In ein Bild muss man etwas legen, was man in andere Dinge nicht hineinzulegen braucht.

ES: Einen Teil seiner selbst?

AK: Einen Teil seiner selbst. Und das ist eine Riesenanstrengung, das zehrt. Ich glaube nicht, dass ein Photograph diese Erfahrung macht, diesen Kick, diese Anstrengung erlebt. Das ist eines der Dinge, die man braucht, um malen zu können, und etwas, was einen mit anderen Malern verbindet – dass nämlich d i e s e Person mit d i e s e m Bild d a durch musste. Ich hab deshalb auch grossen Respekt vor jedem Maler, der sich darauf einlässt. Es gibt auch welche, die nichts dergleichen tun, aber ein guter Maler muss da durch.

Übersetzung: Uta Goridis

ENA SWANSEA
ist Malerin. Sie lebt und arbeitet in New York.

Alex Katz in his studio / bei der Arbeit im Atelier.
Video stills from / aus: ALEX KATZ FIVE HOURS, 1996, directed by Vivien Bittencourt & Vincent Katz.

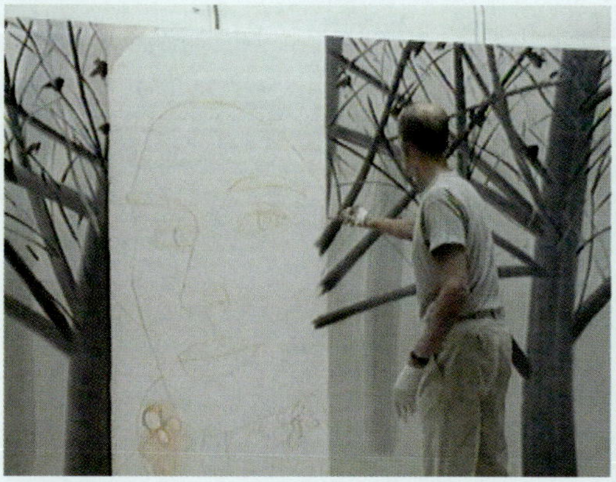

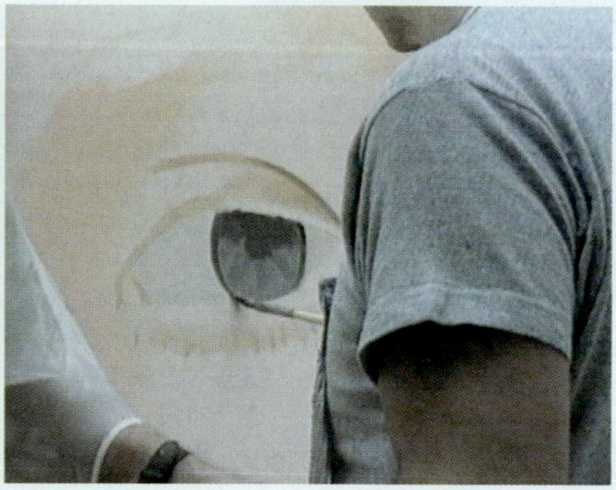

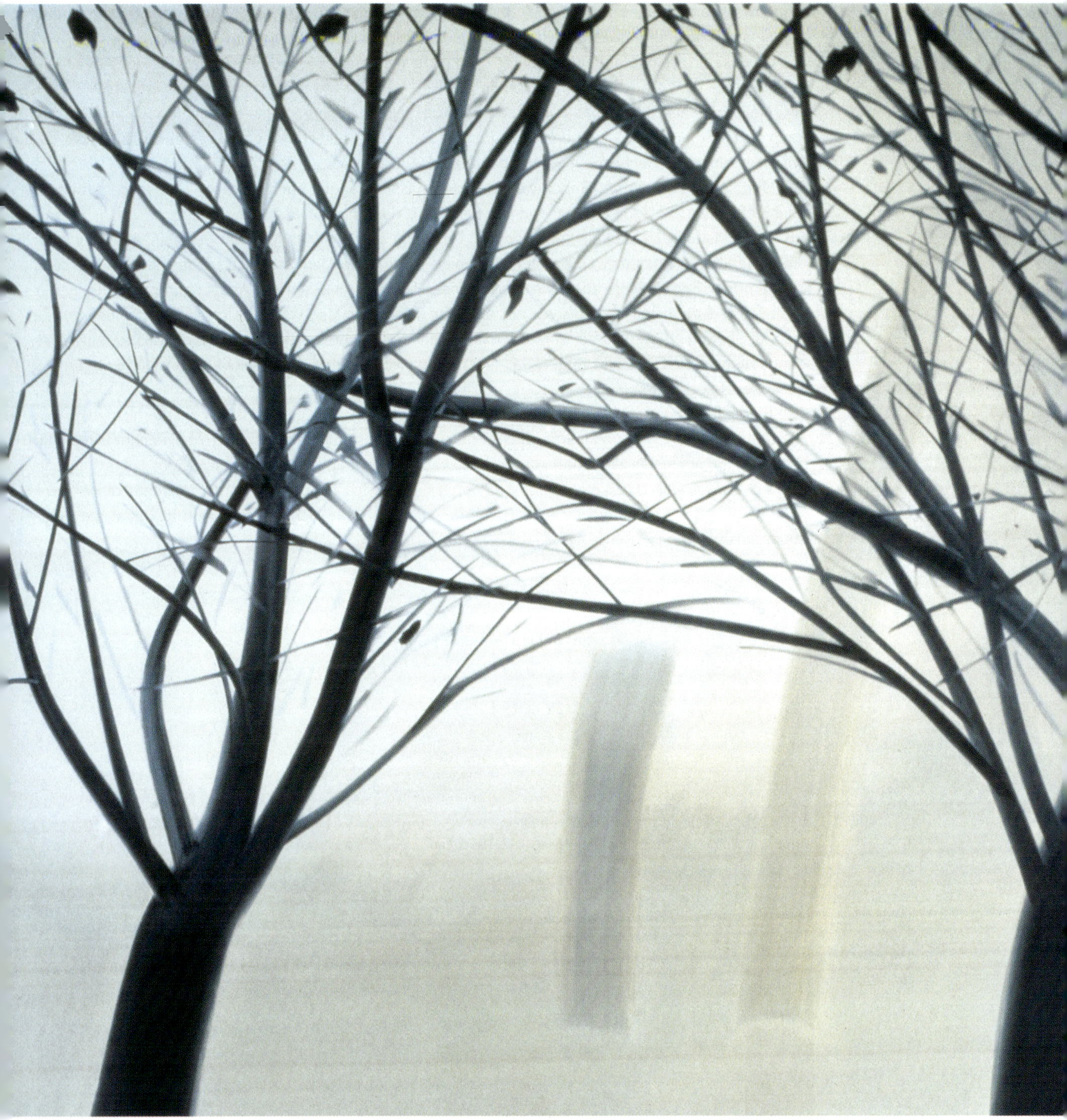

ALEX KATZ, WINTER LANDSCAPE, 1993, oil on canvas, 132 x 240" (destroyed in warehouse fire) / WINTERLANDSCHAFT, Öl auf Leinwand, 335,3 x 609,6 cm (wurde beim Brand eines Lagerhauses zerstört).

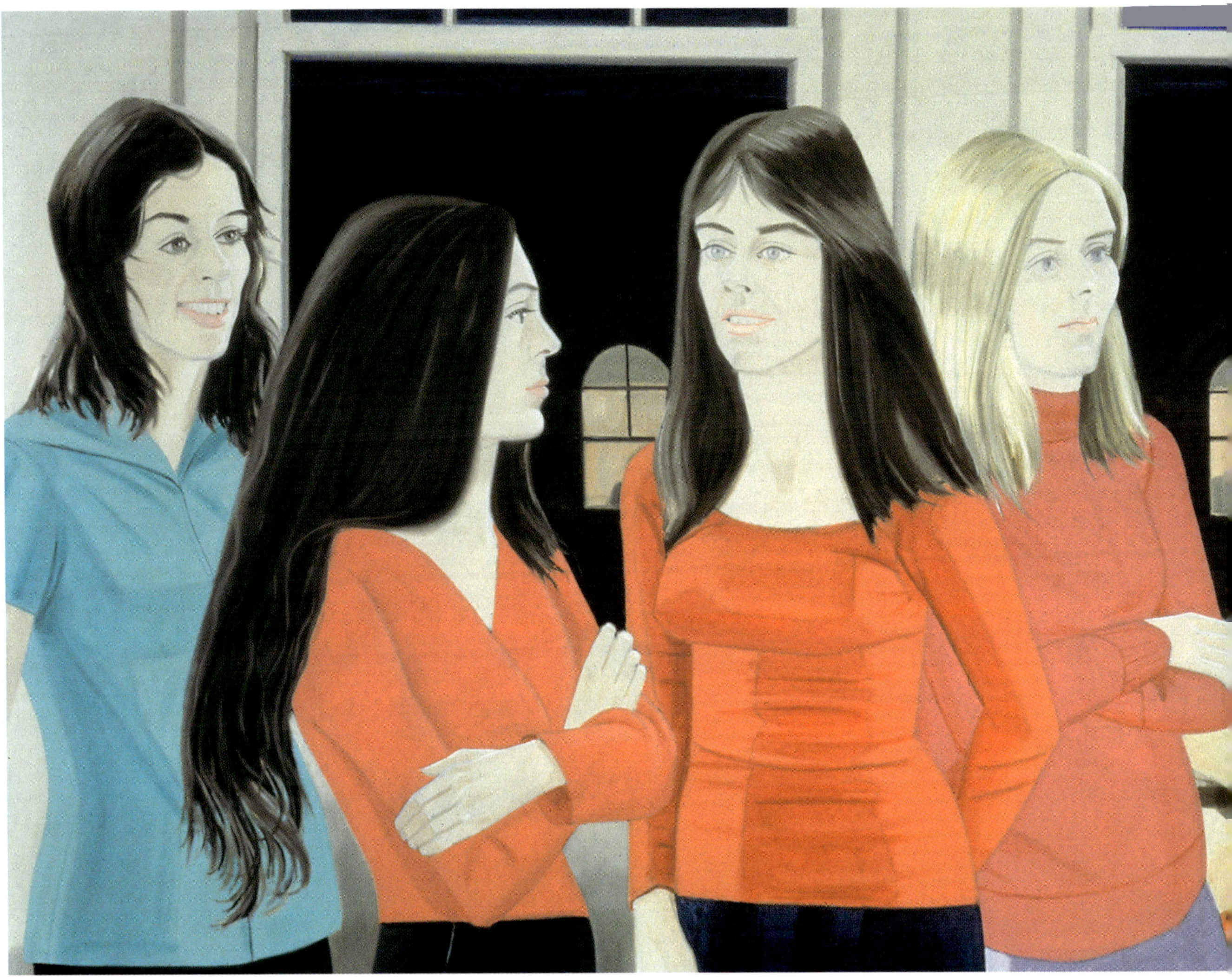

IT'S ALL ABOUT CLOTHES AND HAIRCUTS!

BRUCE HAINLEY & ALEX KATZ IN CONVERSATION

BRUCE HAINLEY: I wanted to ask you about the book cover you did for James Schuyler years ago, as a way of linking you and your work with light, immediacy, and the world that's around us.
ALEX KATZ: I think the upside-down boat on the shore is like a beautiful thing that's slightly depressed. The imagery is just like his poems. I thought the font was ultra-chic, which relates to his taste.
BH: I associate you with ultra-chic, too.
AK: Jimmy was the most tasty of his time. He was John Ashbery's reader. I think his colloquialisms are the most refined. His poem about milk basically has no subject matter yet it's beautifully ordinary. It's not

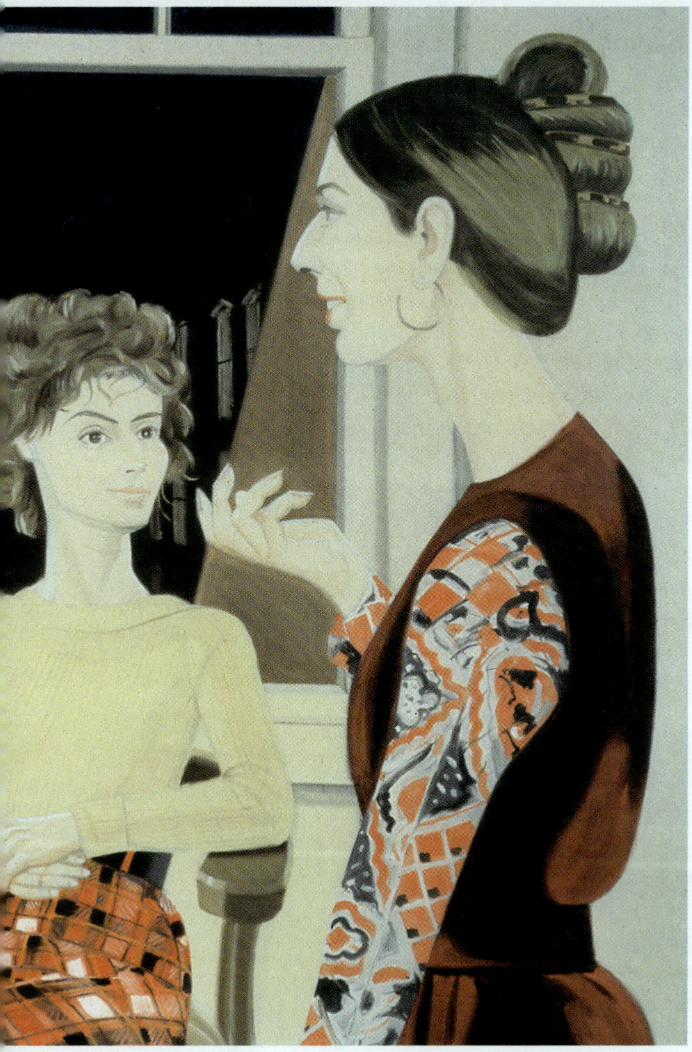

ALEX KATZ, FEBRUARY, 5:30 PM, 1972, oil on canvas, 72 x 144" / FEBRUAR, 5 UHR 30 NACHMITTAGS, Öl auf Leinwand, 182,9 x 365,8 cm. (PHOTO: OREN SLOR)

really light. Schuyler's about plainness—not light—and fantastic taste.

BH: Schuyler lived with the Fairfield Porters for many years. I associate you with Fairfield Porter. I'm interested in that you both remained figurative painters when it was highly unfashionable. I always thought of his work—and very much your work—in terms of the supposed, easy separation between representation and nonrepresentation, figuration and abstraction.

AK: In the day, I just didn't like the generalizations, I didn't feel comfortable with any of them, but there are differences. Abstraction—when it's interesting—is about interesting generalities; figuration is interesting when it's about specific things. The more intelligent painters were all painting abstract at that time—and Fairfield, he liked the good painters. We all liked abstract painting, but Fairfield especially liked de Kooning because he was painting figuratively. I first saw Fairfield's paintings at the Stable Annual. They looked like a Coke ad. I thought that was terrific. There was something mysterious about it because it sort of looked like a dead old painting. It had dead tones in it, dead color tones, which interested me. He could paint on a painting day after day and the whole thing stayed alive. Porter's banal subject matter is amazing—very natural because it wasn't abstract or artificial. He was completely civilized and tasty when most of the stuff around seemed like Hicksville.

BH: In a project like the one you did recently for *W,* when you did the portraits of Martha Stewart and others, what kind of specificity were you looking to achieve?

AK: They're all recognizable. Everyone pretty much looks like the real person. That's being specific. What's realistic is giving the viewer enough information so that his brain can fill in the rest. That's realistic painting. What happens is people get convinced by the form that something's realistic, but then when you move into another form you have problems because t h e y a l r e a d y t h i n k that the Rembrandt looks realistic and think that what I'm doing looks like sign painting. If you put everything in, it becomes naturalistic. You may be able to recognize it, but it's out of the realm of perception. Perception is when you get the whole thing without necessarily seeing the pieces. That's what's interesting to me. What you see is a variable. People think of it as a fixed thing—but I doubt it.

BH: I want to ask you about the painting of the Skye Terrier, SUNNY (1971). Was it your Skye Terrier?

AK: Oh yeah, he was. Quite a dog.

BH: It's such a great painting. Do you think it may trump a lot of the portraits you've done of people?

AK: It's certainly one of the most popular paintings I ever did. There was something about the idea of painting a three-foot red tongue. I did four of them for that series, which was difficult because the dog was moving. I actually have the first sketch here. *(Alex leaves room and returns with the small painting.)*

I was lying in the grass facing Sunny when I painted it, just looking straightforward at him, thinking how the dog panting in the grass didn't seem to have any form. Then I looked at the painting, and it did have form. Marlborough Gallery put it on the back cover of *Artforum. (laughter)* The magazine was really uptight about it.

BH: I was looking at the cutout painting when I came in. Could you talk about that moment when you began cutting out the figure from the canvas?

AK: In the fifities I did more experimenting than now, and I destroyed a lot of paintings, maybe over a thousand. I knew that painting open and direct was the way I wanted to paint. When you don't know what you're doing, you tend to make a lot of messes. I just threw them away. But in one painting that started out with a few people, I couldn't get the background to work. Every so often, I could pull one out, but basically, if I had to go work on it twice it would just get worse, and worse, and worse, and wind up looking like a piece of junk. But the people in that painting, they weren't so bad, so I decided to just cut them out. That's how it started. Then, all of a sudden, I was left with this weird object. They had been life-size in the canvas, but were only so big once you cut them out. So the whole thing with scale and size became intriguing.

BH: The first time I saw the Frank O'Hara cutout it gave the weirdest sensation of catching this person out of the corner of my eye. And flipping around ...

AK: It looks like a real person. Then you come up to it and find its only 7/8 ths ... Edwin Denby wrote that exact thing in an article on me—about catching the figure out of the corner of his eye, walking up and realizing he was fooled. Perception of size is a variable. In a Giacometti, the little figures, they look small, but actually he thinks of them as being off in the distance. The Etruscans also did that. There's a big disparity between measurements and what you see. Close-ups in movies are "life-size"—and then there's Mt. Rushmore.

BH: Do you paint every day? Do you paint at different times a day?

AK: I work seven days a week. Right now, I'm stuck waiting for things to dry before I can paint again. So the next couple days are off. I fool around with different lights—nighttime and daytime and twilight. Sometimes there's only fifteen minutes of a specific light to get it right for a study. When I do the finished paintings, I do them in daylight; usually I start at about ten in the morning.

BH: When you did the night series, how did that come about?

AK: With the nights in backgrounds of paintings from the sixties, like COCKTAIL PARTY (1965), I was just looking out the window and painted. When we moved here, I looked out the window and it took twenty years to get to that night painting. One day I just went to the window and looked out, and I got it. The only question was should it be eleven or twelve feet square. So I made a sketch and made the painting. It was just hot—it really was. I had never painted anything like it. A couple years later, when I looked at COCKTAIL PARTY, I realized that it wasn't as muscular as the subject matter of the night painting. At first I couldn't do another one. Sometimes you can keep doing them, and people will like them, but you'll be wasting your time, essentially. But one night I saw another one, and this was a better painting than the first one—it was more proficient. I want all my paintings to have that kind of proficiency. The figure paintings are just now getting to be more fluid than the ones I did in the seventies and eighties.

BH: Do you have a favorite cocktail?

AK: I like to drink vodka 'cause you know where you are. Two glasses, that's enough for me. If I have a third glass, I'll regret it.

BH: In David Salle's movie, *Search and Destroy*, there's a scene played against one of your paintings. I've never seen a painting used in a film with such gusto, but I think your painting ends up trumping the film. How do you think of your paintings in relationship to the cinematic?

AK: I get as much from the cinema as from the old masters. It started in the sixties. I used to go to movies every day after work. I'd just walk in and have a seat. Meanwhile, I'm looking at the way they're breaking up the frame. I want to make a painting that looks new. At the time, there was this idea of rep-

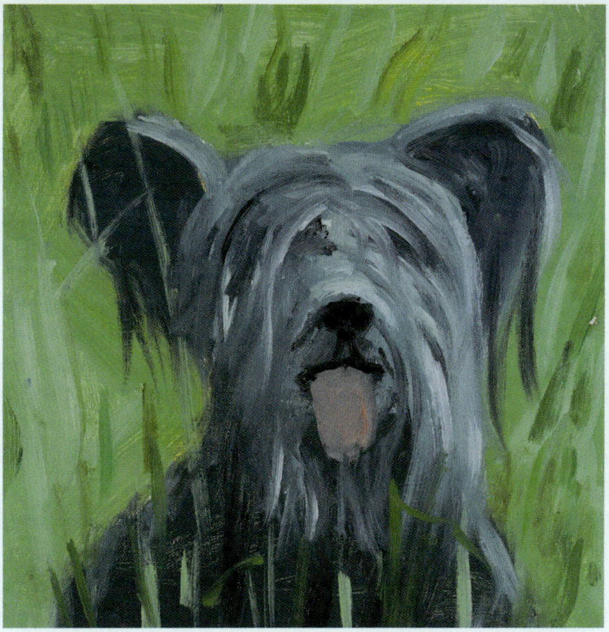

ALEX KATZ, SUNNY, 1971, oil on board, 12 x 12" / Öl auf Malkarton, 30,5 x 30,5 cm.
(PHOTO: OREN SLOR)

resentational painting being passé and dead, and the cinema gave me a lot of new visuals. *The Winter* series, with the big snow paintings and Ada, for example, were taken from a Russian movie. I went to Film Forum a lot because they showed movies from other places. In this Russian film, I was interested in the people walking through the woods. I thought, what a great theme! In film, there are always such great visuals and trends and styles.

BH: I thought that about Soderbergh's remake of *Ocean's Eleven*: I liked watching it because Brad Pitt and George Clooney wore their suits so well. It was the only thing that interested me …

AK: That's plenty! My parents used to come back from a movie and say Rosalind Russell wears her clothes great. Take *Collateral.* The best thing about the movie was that the guy can wear his collar open and look good. It's really hard to do. I thought that was pretty sensational. People say they don't like Tom Cruise, and, I say, he can't be that bad if he can pull off that open collar like that.

BH: That's one of the great things about the career of Cary Grant. He knew how to wear a jacket.

AK: He had a suit body, for one thing, and perfect grooming. I think our culture is dedicated to that: clothes and grooming. Hairstyles and clothes mark our social separations. The Presidential election has to do with the clothes and the haircuts. They have to look good in a suit and all want to look good without a jacket on.

BH: With their sleeves rolled up. *(laughter)* Do you have a favorite suit? Bespoke or off-the-rack?

AK: The smoothest off-the-rack suit, a Cerruti, I can, like, pour into. Perfect fit. I've also had suits made to order. When I grew up, there were artists on the block and ballplayers. My father had this fantastic body for a ballplayer—a body for violence, like a Roman gladiator—and I didn't have it. I've always regretted it … But one guy who I was out playing ball with one day said, "Alex, you were built for suits. I'd rather have your build than your father's any day." *(laughter)*

BRUCE HAINLEY
is a writer who lives in Los Angeles. His collaboration with John Waters, *Art—A Sex Book*, appeared from Thames & Hudson in late 2003.

AUF TENÜ UND HAARSCHNITT KOMMT ES AN!

BRUCE HAINLEY & ALEX KATZ IM GESPRÄCH

BRUCE HAINLEY: Ich würde gerne mit dir über diesen Buchumschlag sprechen, den du vor Jahren für James Schuyler gemacht hast, und so dich und dein Werk mit dem Licht, dem Unmittelbaren und der Welt, die uns umgibt, in Verbindung bringen.

ALEX KATZ: Für mich ist dieses umgekehrte Boot am Strand ein sehr hübsches Bild mit einer leicht melancholischen Note. Genau wie seine Gedichte. Auch die Schrift war ultraschick und entspricht seinem guten Geschmack.

BH: Ultraschick verbinde ich auch mit dir.

AK: Jimmy war damals der Mann mit dem besten Geschmack. Er war ein begeisterter Leser von John Ashbery. Seine umgangssprachlichen Wendungen sind ausgesprochen raffiniert. Sein Gedicht über Milch hat gar kein eigentliches Thema und trotzdem wirkt es so wunderbar alltäglich. Aber nicht wirklich leicht. Charakteristisch für Schuyler sind die einfachen – nicht die leichten – Dinge und eine phantastische Stilsicherheit.

BH: Schuyler hat viele Jahre bei den Fairfield Porters gelebt. Fairfield Porter assoziiere ich auch mit dir. Interessant finde ich, dass ihr beide weiterhin figurativ gearbeitet habt, als dies als völlig überholt galt. Ich habe sein Werk – und zum grossen Teil auch deines – immer im Licht der angeblich einfachen Unterscheidung zwischen «gegenständlich» und «gegenstandslos», «figurativ» und «abstrakt» betrachtet.

AK: Diese Verallgemeinerungen mochte ich damals nicht. Es war mir bei keiner von ihnen wohl, doch muss man auch da unterscheiden. In der guten abstrakten Kunst geht es um interessante allgemeine Qualitäten; die figurative Malerei ist hingegen nur dann interessant, wenn sie sich mit spezifischen Dingen beschäftigt. Damals malten alle intelligenteren Maler abstrakt – für Fairfield zählten aber nur die guten Maler. Wir alle liebten die abstrakte Malerei, doch Fairfield begeisterte sich vor allem für de Kooning, weil er figurativ malte. Ich sah Fairfields Bilder erstmals an der regelmässigen Jahresausstellung. Sie wirkten wie eine Cola-Reklame. Ich fand das toll. Sie hatten etwas Mysteriöses, und zwar, weil sie toten alten Bildern glichen. Diese stumpfen Töne, diese stumpfen Farbnuancen reizten mich. Er konnte tagelang an einem Bild malen und trotzdem blieb es lebendig. Porters banale Themen wirken erstaunlich – und absolut natürlich, weil sie weder abstrakt noch gekünstelt sind. Er war einfach durch und durch kultiviert und stilsicher, während fast alles andere dort irgendwie «provinziell» wirkte.

BH: Was genau wolltest du im Rahmen deines Projekts für das Modejournal *W* erreichen, für das du Martha Stewart und andere porträtiert hast?

AK: Man kann sie alle erkennen. Jede sieht mehr oder weniger so aus wie in Wirklichkeit. Das verstehe ich unter genau sein. Ein realistisches Bild gibt dem Betrachter genügend Informationen, dass sein Hirn den Rest ergänzen kann. Das ist realistische Malerei. Gewöhnlich ist es so, dass die Form die Leute dazu bringt, etwas für realistisch zu halten. Sobald man jedoch die Form wechselt, wird das problematisch, weil die Leute von vornherein schon denken, dass Rembrandt realistisch ist und dass das, was ich mache, wie Reklamemalerei aussieht. Fügt man alle Details hinzu, wird das Ganze naturalistisch. Man kann es vielleicht gerade noch erkennen, doch es liegt schon ausserhalb unseres Wahrnehmungsvermögens. Wahrnehmung bedeutet das Ganze zu erfassen, ohne unbedingt jede Einzelheit zu sehen. Darauf kommt es mir an. Was man sieht, ist eine Variable. Doch die Leute halten es für etwas Feststehendes – was ich fragwürdig finde.

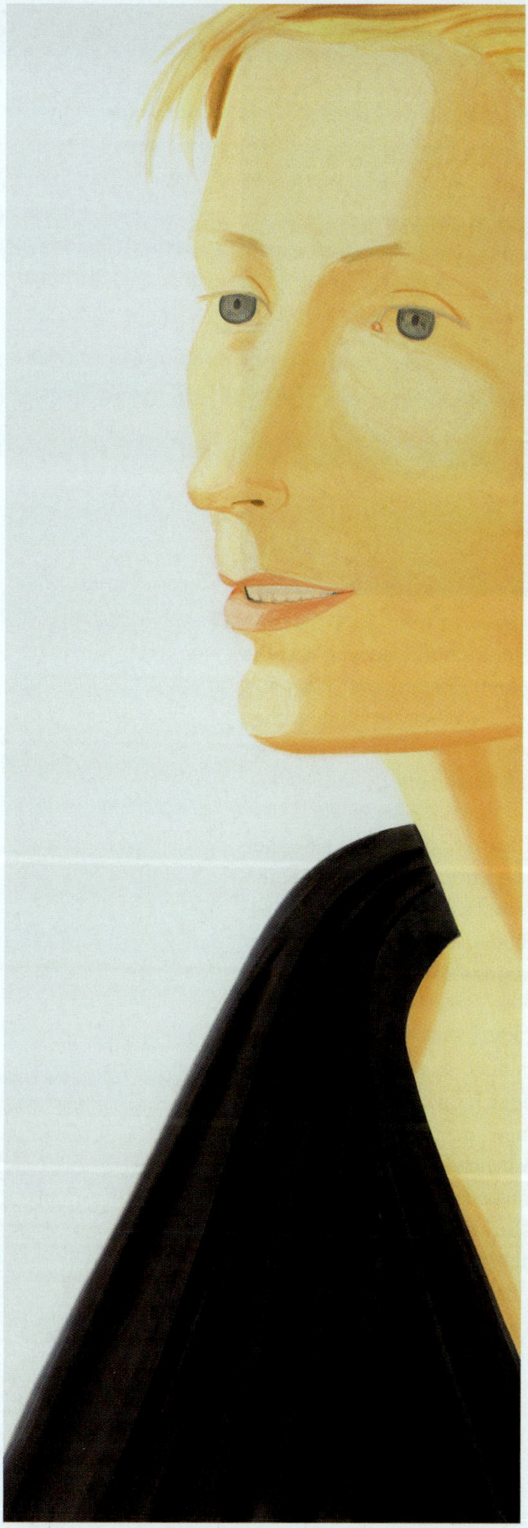

ALEX KATZ, TILDA, 2004, oil on canvas, 96 x 33 1/2" /
Öl auf Leinwand, 243,8 x 85,1 cm.
(PHOTO: ELLEN LABENSKI / PACE WILDENSTEIN, NEW YORK)

BH: Ich möchte dich etwas fragen zum Bild des Skyeterriers SUNNY (1971). War das dein Hund?

AK: Oh ja. Das war er. Ein tolles Tier.

BH: Es ist ein grossartiges Bild. Glaubst du, dass es womöglich besser ist als manches menschliche Porträt, das du gemacht hast?

AK: Bestimmt ist es eines meiner beliebtesten Bilder. Der Gedanke, eine neunzig Zentimeter lange rote Zunge zu malen, hatte schon was. Ich habe vier Bilder für diese Serie gemalt, und das war nicht einfach, denn der Hund bewegte sich ständig. Die erste Skizze müsste übrigens hier irgendwo sein. *(Alex verlässt den Raum und kommt mit dem kleinen Bild zurück.)* Ich lag direkt vor Sunny im Gras, als ich es malte; ich schaute ihn unentwegt an und dachte, dass dieser im Gras hechelnde Hund überhaupt keine Form zu haben schien. Dann schaute ich auf das Bild, und es hatte durchaus eine Form. Die Marlborough Gallery hat es auf der hinteren Umschlagseite von *Artforum* platziert. *(Lachen)* Die Zeitschrift wurde echt nervös deswegen.

BH: Beim Hereinkommen ist mir das Cutout aufgefallen. Kannst du etwas darüber sagen, wie es war, als du begonnen hast die Figur aus der Leinwand herauszulösen?

AK: In den 50er Jahren habe ich mehr herumexperimentiert als heute, und dabei zerstörte ich eine Menge Bilder, vielleicht über tausend. Ich wusste, dass ich offen und direkt malen wollte. Wenn man aber nicht wirklich weiss, was man tut, produziert man viel Schrott. Ich habe das dann einfach weggeworfen. Doch bei einem Bild mit mehreren Figuren bekam ich einfach den Hintergrund nicht hin. Manchmal liess sich das noch beheben, meist wurde es aber, wenn ich ein zweites Mal darüber ging, nur noch schlimmer und schliesslich ganz unbrauchbar. Doch die Leute auf dem Bild waren gar nicht so schlecht, also beschloss ich sie auszuschneiden. So hat das angefangen. Und dann sah ich mich plötzlich mit diesem komischen Objekt konfrontiert. Auf der Leinwand hatten die Figuren ihre natürliche Grösse gehabt, aber ausgeschnitten waren sie nur noch so und so gross. Auf diese Weise begann das spannende Spiel mit den Grössenverhältnissen.

BH: Als ich zum ersten Mal das Cutout von Frank O'Hara sah, war das ganz merkwürdig, so als sei diese Person zufällig in mein Blickfeld geraten. Und als ich mich umdrehte, …

AK: Sie sieht richtig lebendig aus. Kommt man aber näher, merkt man, dass sie nur etwa sieben Achtel ihrer natürlichen Grösse hat … Edwin Denby beschrieb genau dies in einem Artikel – wie er die Figur aus

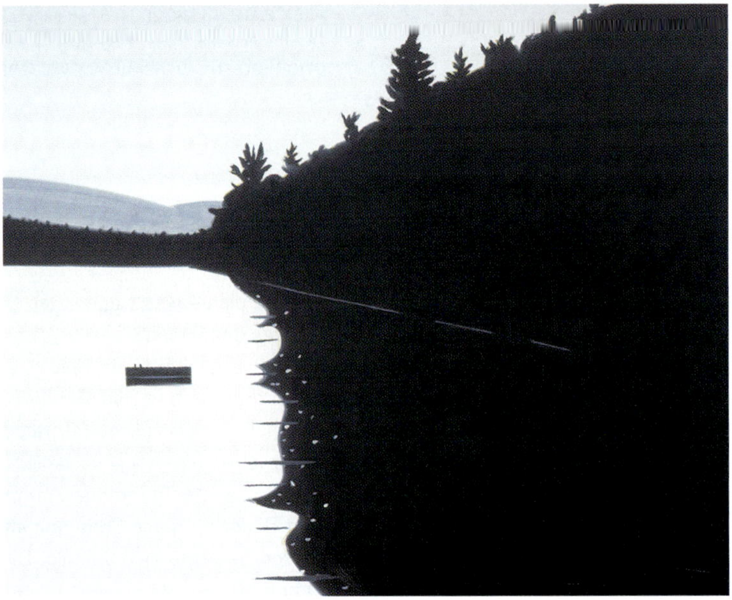

6:30 PM, 2004, oil on canvas, 96 x 120" /
6 UHR 30 ABENDS, Öl auf Leinwand, 243,8 x 304,8 cm.
(PHOTO: OREN SLOR)

dem Augenwinkel heraus erfasste, näher kam und entdeckte, dass es eine optische Täuschung war. Die Wahrnehmung der Grösse ist relativ. Bei einem Giacometti sehen die kleinen Figuren zwar klein aus, doch sind sie für ihn nur weit weg. Die Etrusker sind auch so vorgegangen. Zwischen den eigentlichen Massen und dem, was man sieht, besteht ein Riesenunterschied. Grossaufnahmen im Kino sind «lebensgross», daneben gibt es aber auch die monumentalen Köpfe am Mount Rushmore .

BH: Arbeitest du jeden Tag? Malst du zu unterschiedlichen Zeiten?

AK: Ich arbeite sieben Tage die Woche. Im Augenblick muss ich darauf warten, dass die Leinwände trocknen, bevor ich weitermachen kann. Die nächsten paar Tage hab ich also frei. Ich spiele mit unterschiedlichen Lichtverhältnissen herum: Tag, Nacht und Dämmerung. Manchmal kann man bei einem bestimmten Licht nur eine Viertelstunde lang arbeiten, das reicht für eine Studie. Die eigentlichen Bilder mache ich dann bei Tageslicht; gewöhnlich fang ich etwa um zehn Uhr morgens an.

BH: Wie kam die Nachtserie zustande?

AK: Bei den Nachthintergründen der Bilder aus den 60er Jahren, wie COCKTAIL PARTY (1965), schaute ich einfach aus dem Fenster und malte. Als wir hierher zogen, schaute ich auch aus dem Fenster, aber es dauerte zwanzig Jahre, bis dieses Nachtbild dabei herauskam. Eines Tages ging ich zum Fenster und schaute hinaus, und das war's dann. Die Frage war nur noch, ob es 335 oder 365 Zentimeter im Quadrat messen sollte. Ich machte also eine Skizze und malte das Bild. Es war richtig geil. Ich hatte noch nie so etwas gemacht. Als ich mir ein paar Jahre später COCKTAIL PARTY anschaute, bemerkte ich, dass es thematisch nicht so stark war wie das Nachtbild. Zunächst konnte ich kein weiteres Bild malen. Manchmal kann man zwar weitermachen und die Leute sind begeistert, aber im Grunde ist es Zeitverschwendung. Doch eines Nachts sah ich dann wieder ein anderes, eines, das besser war als das erste – sehr viel gekonnter. Ich will, dass alle meine Bilder diese Kunstfertigkeit aufweisen. Die Bilder mit den Figuren beginnen mir jetzt allmählich etwas flüssiger von der Hand zu gehen als die, die ich in den 70er und 80er Jahren gemacht habe.

BH: Hast du einen Lieblingscocktail?

AK: Am liebsten trinke ich Wodka, da weiss man, was man hat. Zwei Gläser reichen mir. Ein drittes bereue ich gewöhnlich.

BH: In David Salles Film *Search and Destroy* gibt es eine Szene, die vor einem deiner Bilder spielt. Ich habe noch nie zuvor gesehen, dass ein Bild in einem Film so lustvoll eingesetzt wurde, eigentlich toppt das Bild den Film. Welche Beziehung besteht zwischen deinen Bildern und dem Kino?

AK: Das Kino ist für mich ebenso inspirierend wie die alten Meister. Es begann in den 60er Jahren. Damals ging ich jeden Tag nach der Arbeit ins Kino. Ich spazierte einfach rein und setzte mich in einen Sessel. Heute schaue ich mir an, wie die Strukturen aufgebrochen werden. Ich möchte ein Bild malen, das neu wirkt. Zu jener Zeit war gegenständliche Malerei total aus der Mode, passé, tot, und das Kino hat mir neues Bildmaterial geliefert. Die Winterserie mit den grossen Schneebildern und Ada stammen zum Beispiel aus einem russischen Film. Ich ging oft ins Filmforum, weil dort Filme aus anderen Ländern gezeigt wurden. In jenem russischen Film faszinierten mich die Leute, die zu Fuss in den Wäldern unterwegs waren. Ich dachte, was für ein Thema! Im Film gibt es immer grossartige Bildmotive und Trends und Stile.

BH: Das dachte ich auch, als ich Søderberghs Remake von *Ocean's Eleven* sah. Es war wirklich ein Vergnügen, sich das anzuschauen, denn Brad Pitt und George Clooney sahen in ihren Anzügen einfach umwerfend aus. Eigentlich hat mich nur das interessiert …

AK: Das reicht vollkommen! Meine Eltern kamen jeweils aus dem Kino und meinten, Rosalind Russel mache in ihren Roben eine gute Figur. Nimm zum Beispiel Collateral. Das Beste am ganzen Film ist, dass der Typ sein Hemd offen tragen kann und gut dabei aussieht. Das ist wirklich nicht einfach. Ich fand das sensationell. Wenn die Leute sagen, sie könnten Tom Cruise nicht leiden, sag ich nur, einer, der mit offenem Hemdkragen so fabelhaft aussieht, kann so schlecht nicht sein.

BH: Das ist auch eines der Glanzlichter von Cary Grants Karriere. Er wusste, wie man ein Jackett trägt.

AK: Er hatte die Figur für einen Anzug und eine gepflegte Erscheinung. In unserer Kultur sind zwei Sachen enorm wichtig: Kleidung und gepflegtes Aussehen. Frisur und Kleidung kennzeichnen die sozialen Unterschiede. Auch die Präsidentschaftswahl steht und fällt mit dem richtigen Tenü und Haarschnitt. Die Kandidaten müssen einfach einen Anzug tragen können, dabei haben sie nur den Ehrgeiz, auch ohne Jackett gut auszusehen.

BH: Und mit hochgekrempelten Ärmeln. *(Lachen)* Hast du einen Lieblingsanzug? Massgeschneidert oder von der Stange?

AK: Einen sehr eleganten von der Stange, einen Cerruti, der sitzt wie angegossen, einfach perfekt. Ich hab mir aber auch schon Anzüge schneidern lassen. In meiner Jugend gab es in unserem Viertel Künstler und Basketballspieler. Und mein Vater hatte diese tolle Figur eines Basketballspielers – ein Körper mit echtem Gewaltpotenzial, wie ein römischer Gladiator. Zu meinem Leidwesen hatte ich das nicht … Aber einer der Burschen, mit denen ich Ball spielte, sagte eines Tages zu mir: «Alex, du bist der Typ für Anzüge, ich hätte viel lieber deine Statur als die deines Vaters.» *(Lachen)*

Übersetzung: Uta Goridis

Alex Katz in his studio / bei der Arbeit im Atelier.
Video stills from / aus: ALEX KATZ FIVE HOURS, 1996, directed by Vivien Bittencourt & Vincent Katz.

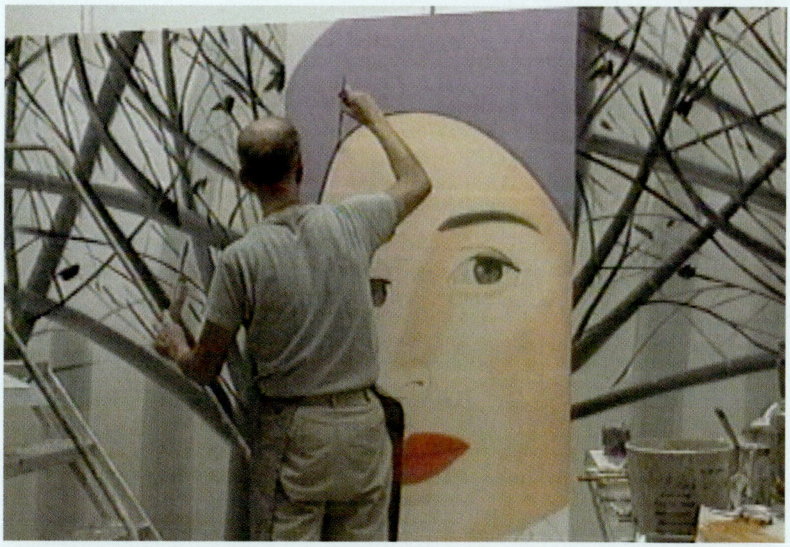

BRUCE HAINLEY
ist Schriftsteller und lebt in Los Angeles. Zusammen mit John Waters publizierte er den Band *Art – A Sex Book* (Thames & Hudson, 2003).

ANNIVERSARY EDITION FOR PARKETT

ALEX KATZ

SUNNY, 2004

Silkscreen on aluminum, 5 1/8 x 5 7/8 x 2"

Printed by Atelier für Siebdruck Lorenz Boegli, Zürich.

Edition of 70/XXX, signed and numbered.

Siebdruck auf Aluminium, 13 x 15 x 5 cm.

Druck; Atelier für Siebdruck Lorenz Boegli, Zürich.

Auflage: 70/XXX, signiert und nummeriert.

PHOTO: MANCIA/BODMER, FBM-STUDIO, ZÜRICH

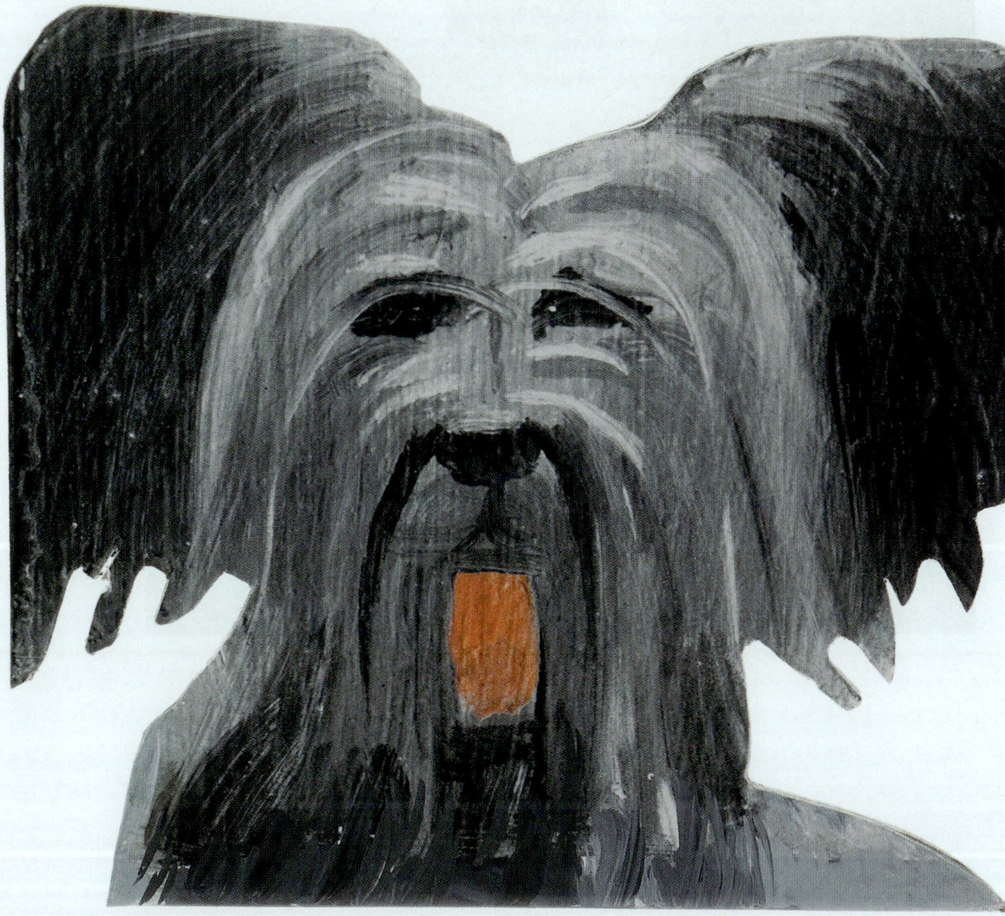

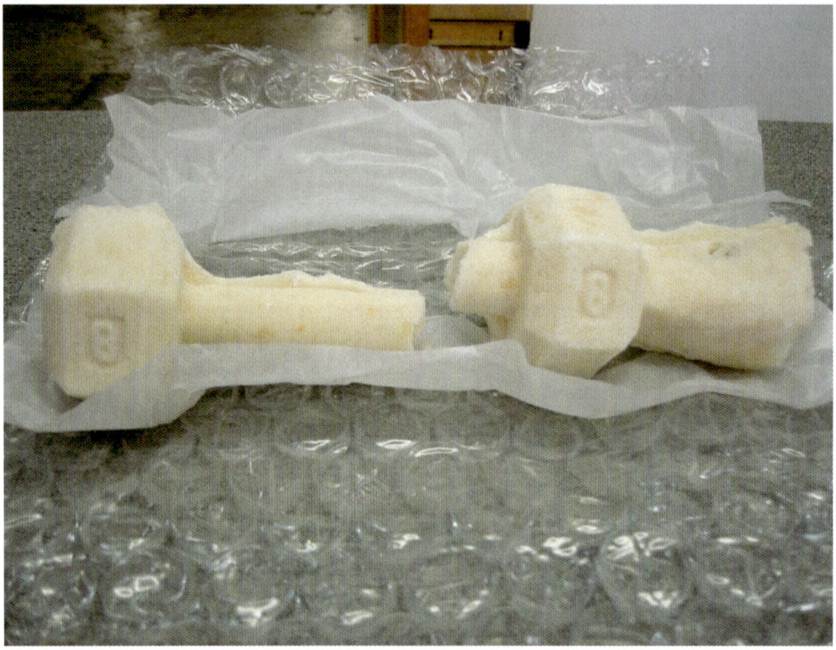

MATTHEW BARNEY, 2004

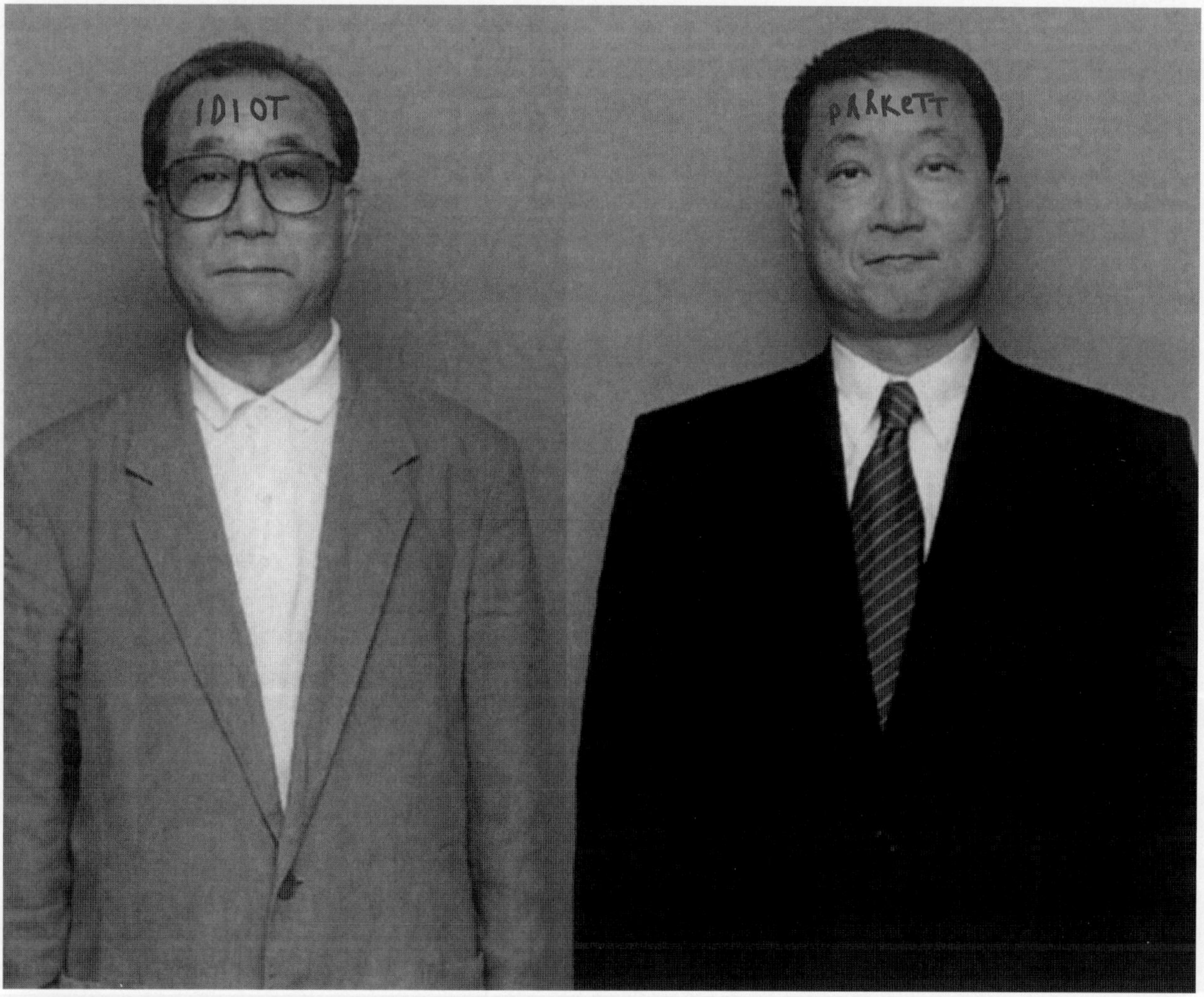

MAURIZIO CATTELAN, 2004

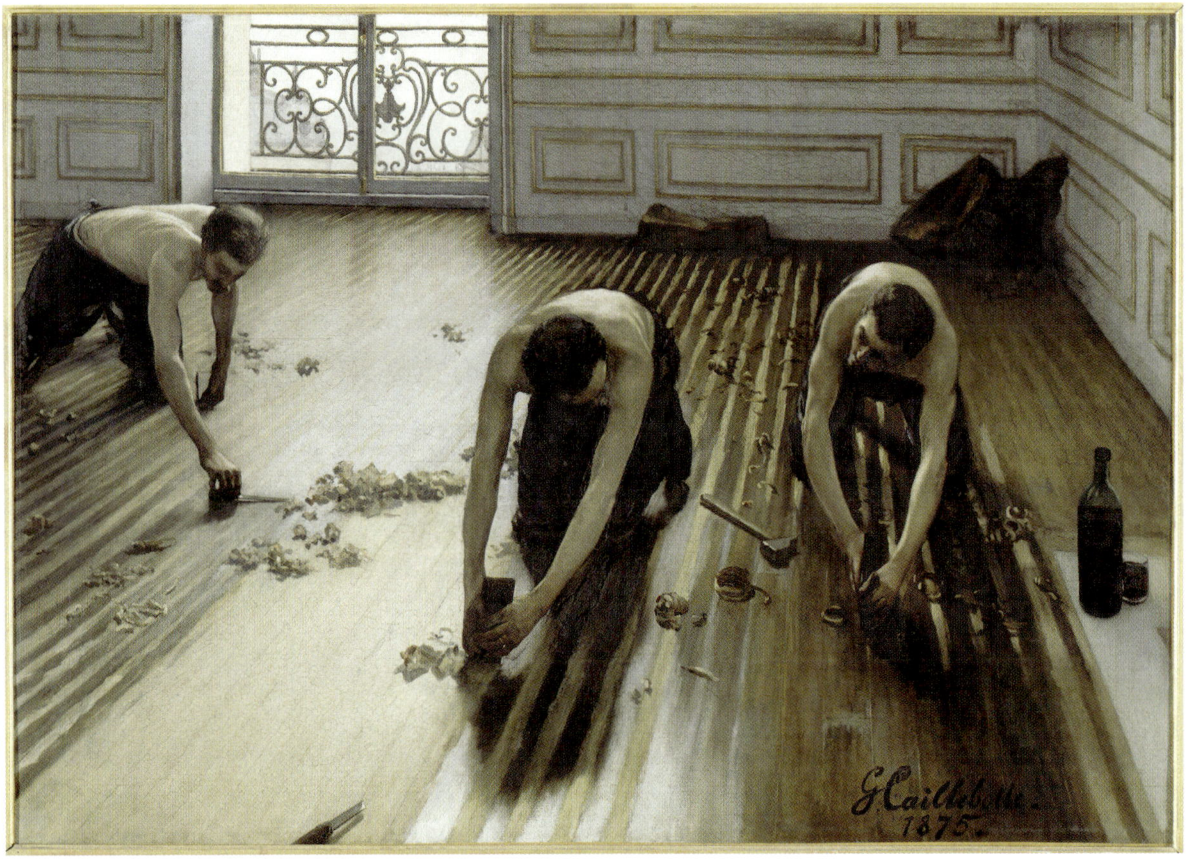

GUSTAVE CAILLEBOTTE (1848–1894),
RABOTEURS DE PARQUET, 1875, MUSÉE D'ORSAY, PARIS.
(PHOTO: RMN / HERVÉ LEWANDOWSKI)

The railroad he died in was nearly dead too. The big trains left town in the sixties, taking the neighborhood with them. The apartment, looking out on the rusting girders of the abandoned El, had taken it personally. Unfolding sullenly through a line of mean and tilting doorways, its essential emptiness was unredeemed by a scattered collection of small objects that seemed to have no common point of reference. Plastic flowers and Japanese dolls mingled with single gloves and castings of body parts in rooms whose crumbling crown moldings and sloping, splintered floors were coated in a gritty crust of chocolate brown paint. It had the exact emotional temperature of a bitterly resentful relative confined to a distant and unforgiving institution that you never visit.

The apartment didn't want to feel that way but it did. The feeling gave it a way to keep going, to protect a tiny, irrational flame of hope that someone would come and rescue it some day. And now one of the detectives was paying far more attention to the exposures and the number of rooms than to what looked like the residue of a hoarding disorder but wasn't.

"This could be fixed up nice…it's got good light," he muttered.

The apartment felt faint. Could it be Him?

"For Christ's sake, Mike, it's a dump. Can we pay a little less attention to your Bob Vila fantasies, somebody just died here."

The other detective snapped her notebook shut and walked a little further into the gloom.

The apartment did not like her.

"I've got to live somewhere," he mumbled, "So maybe it needs a little work. I've got a right to live somewhere, don't I? You don't see three exposures every day, I've been looking for four months, maybe I could get in on the ground floor here."

Now, the apartment thought, now is the time to show him something special.

And Mike said, "Holy shit, just look at that."

Hoping he might have noticed something related to actual police work, Anna turned her head. They had arrived in the kitchen. Never an underachiever, in its loneliness, the apartment had set a new benchmark for squalor there. It too was filled with the strange hodgepodge of esoteric artifacts. But there was one thing, right there on the grease stained wall that was all too familiar. A diagram, last witnessed in blood at the scene of several murders: each more grotesque, more 'artistic' than the last.

Suddenly her heart was pounding. She was sweating and surely the world itself was sinking and rising with her hopes, because this feeling was why she had become a detective and this feeling was why she had stopped being a homicide detective. It all flooded back. The spiraling logic and terror of her final case, the case they called 'the wheel', for its circular and endless motion, the case that had become an unsolvable trap, its stains forever fresh.

She had quit, cold turkey, transferred out to missing persons and accidentals but now here it was; right up in her fucking grill. It had sought her out and she could feel the warm and poisonous orchid of the bad need blossoming inside her. She needed to back out, now, and she needed some backup, some serious fucking backup.

But Mike was on his knees, tugging at the decaying linoleum.

"Just look at these floors; is that parquet?"

MATTHEW RITCHIE, 2004

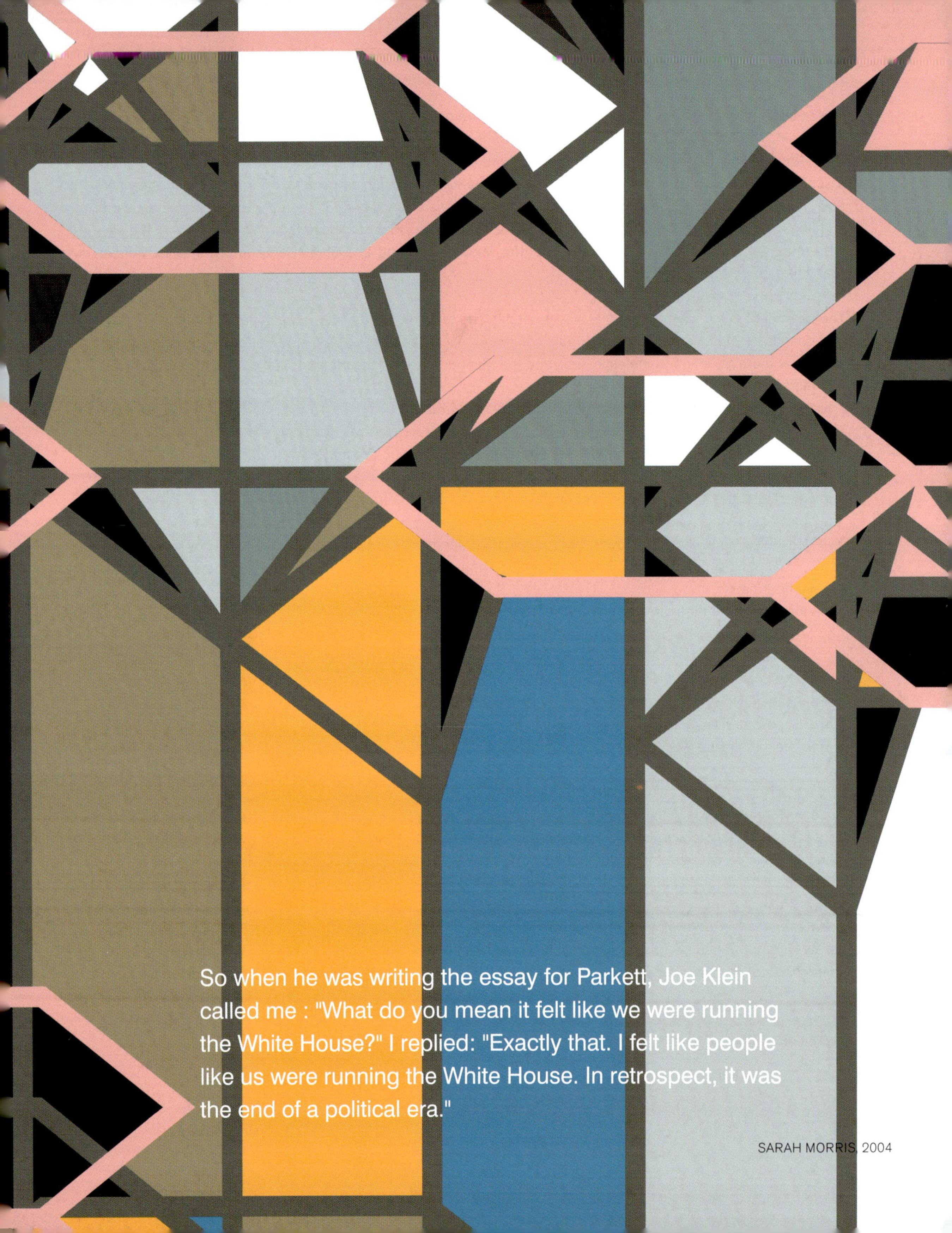

So when he was writing the essay for Parkett, Joe Klein called me : "What do you mean it felt like we were running the White House?" I replied: "Exactly that. I felt like people like us were running the White House. In retrospect, it was the end of a political era."

SARAH MORRIS, 2004

Monica Bonvicini

born 1965 in Venice, Italy, lives and works in Berlin and Los Angeles / geboren 1965 in Venedig, lebt und arbeitet in Berlin und Los Angeles.

Richard Prince

born 1949 in the Panama Canal Zone, lives and works in Upstate New York / geboren 1949 in der Panamakanalzone, lebt und arbeitet in Upstate New York.

Urs Fischer

geboren 1973 in Zürich, lebt und arbeitet in Los Angeles, Zürich und Berlin / born 1973 in Zurich, lives and works in Los Angeles, Zurich, and Berlin.

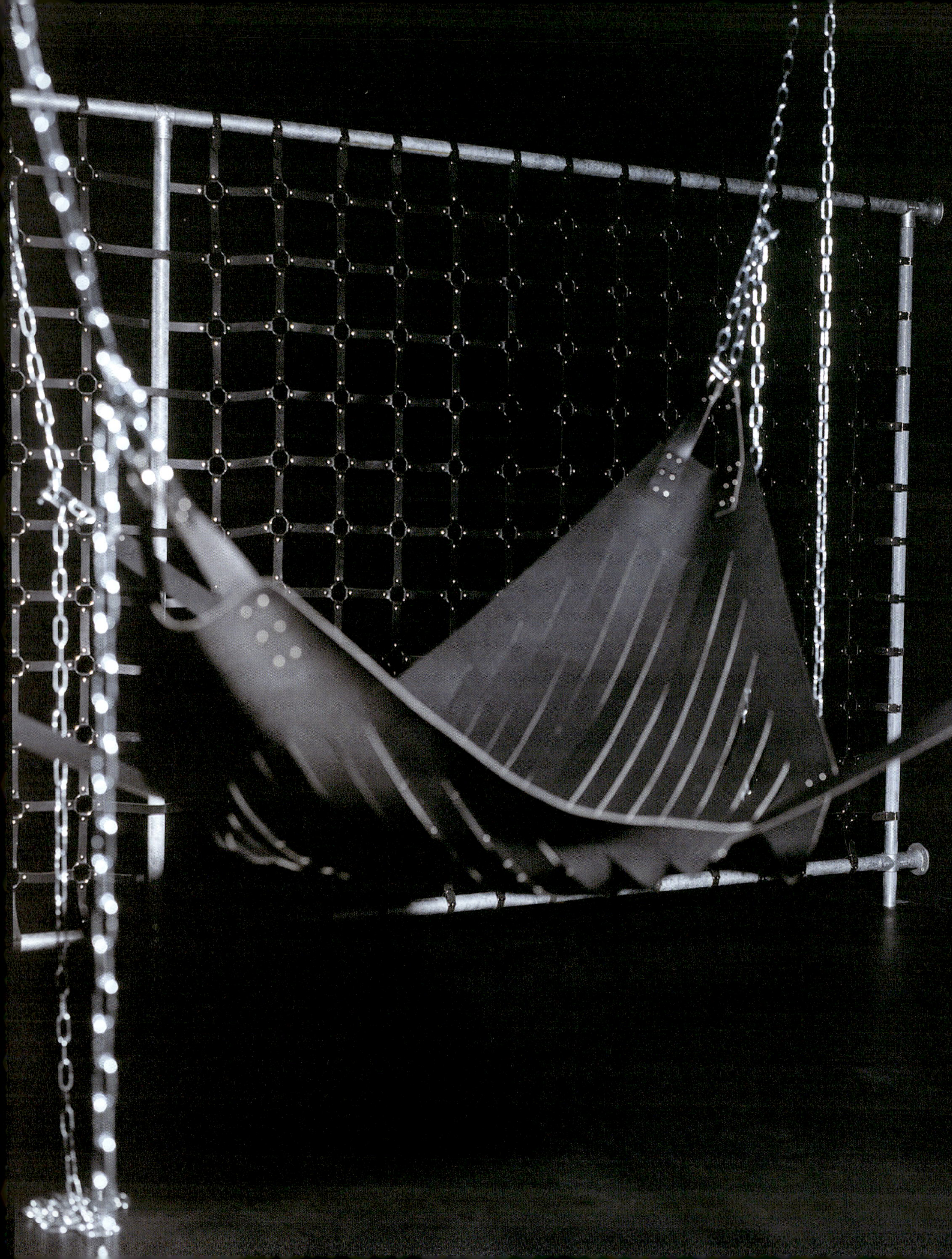

MONICA BONVICINI, BLACK, 2002, installation, Aarhus Kunstmuseum, Denmark.

MONICA BONVICINI

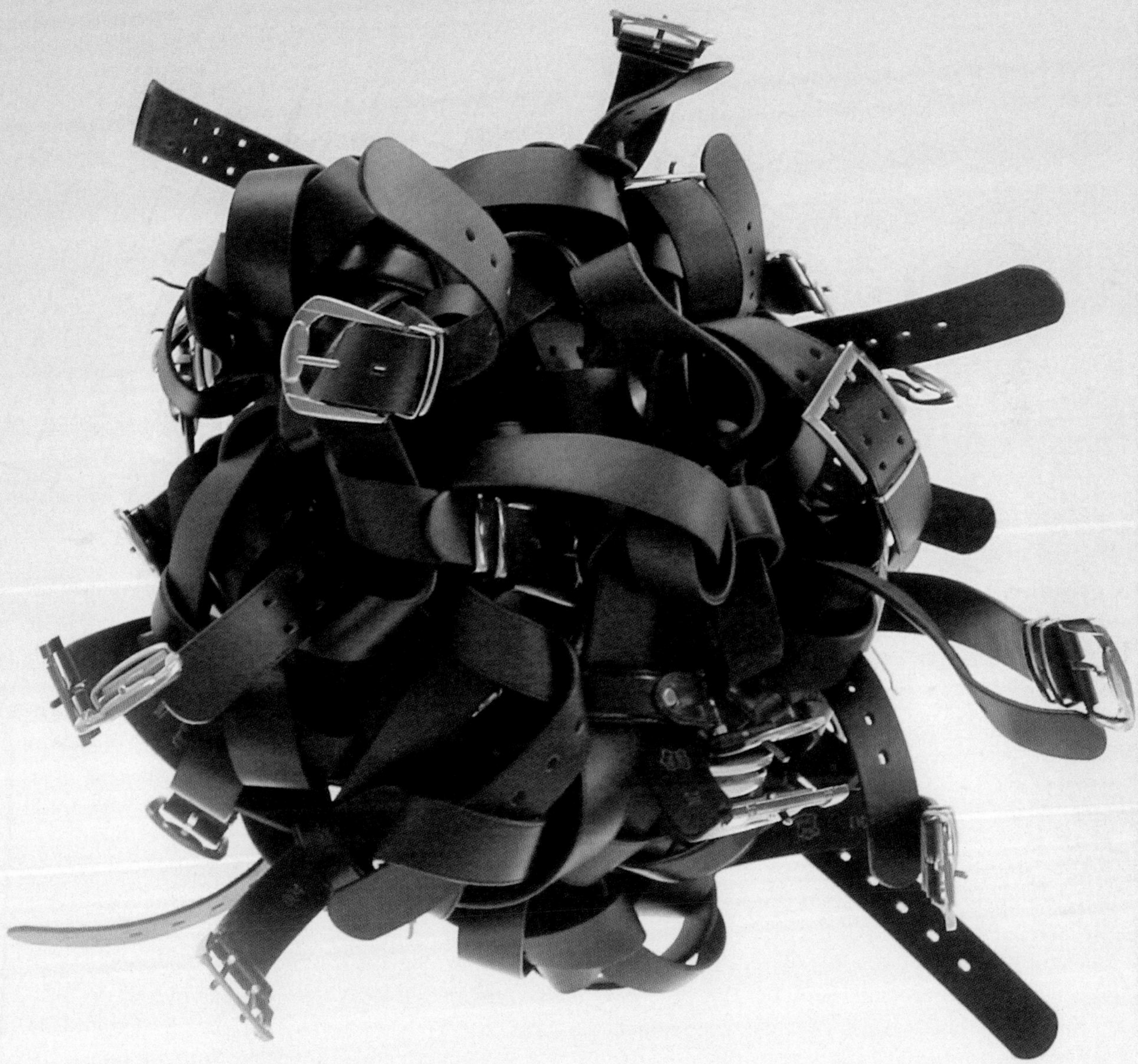

MONICA BONVICINI, BELTED THROUGH, 2003, men's leather belts, diameter ca. 27 1/2" / Lederne Herrengürtel, Durchmesser ca. 70 cm.

JULIANE REBENTISCH

Monica Bonvicinis FETISCHkunst

Man will sie wirklich gerne anfassen, besitzen auch. Das feine schwarze Leder liegt schön straff an, sie sind perfekt verschnürt; mit äusserster Sorgfalt ist das gemacht worden. G e i l. Erstaunlich, wie gut das funktioniert: die Sexualisierung zum Beispiel eines einfachen Holzhammers mit der Holzhammermethode, durch eine Fetisch-Lederbespannung. Ein typischer Bonvicini-Witz, abgründig in seiner Buchstäblichkeit. Dazu ein paar Thesen:

1 Der Fetischismus ist nach Freud ja bekanntlich die männliche Perversion *par excellence.* Der Fetisch ersetzt den bei der Mutter vermissten Penis. Lässt man die ganze komplizierte Sache mit der Kastrationsdrohung einmal beiseite, so kann man abkürzend sagen, dass der Mann im Fetisch letztlich nichts anderes als den Phallus, das Zeichen männlicher Macht, verehrt. Monica Bonvicinis Fetischwerkzeuge, das wäre eine erste Lesart, karikieren das narzisstische Moment im männlichen Fetischismus, nicht diesen selbst. Sie handeln nämlich ganz offensichtlich nicht vom Penisersatz, sondern von dessen symbolischer Überhöhung. Entsprechend hat Bonvicini mit den Werkzeugen Objekte ausgewählt, die den Penis des Mannes symbolisch verdoppeln oder verlängern, statt solche, die – wie der Frauenfuss oder -schuh bei Freud – den fehlenden des sogenannten «Weibes» ersetzen. Ersetzt wird der Penis indes hier ebenfalls durch den Phallus. Ein erster Herrenwitz für Feministinnen und Schwule ergibt sich denn auch bereits durch die offensichtliche Diskrepanz zwischen Phallus und Penis. Was vermag schon der echte Bauarbeiter gegen das Versprechen seines in Leder verpackten Schlagbohrers?

2 Doch gehen die in ihrer Phallizität drastischen Schlagbohrer, Kettensägen, Hämmer und so weiter nicht in der Karikatur männlicher Potenzinszenierungen auf. Sie funktionieren als Lederobjekte zu gut, sind zu ernsthaft sexy, um wirklich in die Welt eines *Tom-of-Finland*-Comics zu passen. Darin liegt übrigens generell der ästhetische Witz von Bonvicinis Witzen: dass sie sich in keiner nahe liegenden Pointe erschöpfen. So wirken einige der Objekte, vor allem die Bohrer-Variationen (BLIND SHOT, 2004), im Kontext ihrer Installation durchaus gewalttätig, bedrohlich geradezu. Wenn man es nur entsprechend hält, kann offenbar jedes Werkzeug zur Waffe wer-

---

JULIANE REBENTISCH ist Wissenschaftliche Mitarbeiterin an der Fakultät für Kulturwissenschaften der Europa-Universität Viadrina in Frankfurt an der Oder und lebt in Berlin.

den. Andere, vor allem die kleineren Werkzeuge, sehen wiederum gar nicht unbedingt nur phallisch aus. Vielmehr erinnert deren Fetischlook durch die Schnürung auch an Korsetts; sie wirken gleichsam verkleidet und verweisen so überdies auf den Zusammenhang zwischen Fetischismus und Maskerade, der zuweilen unter dem Stichwort eines «weiblichen Fetischismus» diskutiert wurde.[1)] Nicht zufällig ist das Leder, das Bonvicini hier verwendet hat, weich wie Handschuhleder; tatsächlich verkehren sich diese Werkzeugobjekte im Prozess der Betrachtung ständig in ihrer sexuellen Konnotation – wie ein Handschuh, den man wendet. Es sind, so gesehen, eigentümlich «queere» Objekte. Das tut ihrem Fetischcharakter keinen Abbruch; nach Freud halten Fetische, die «aus Gegensätzen doppelt geknüpft» wurden, sogar besonders gut.[2)] Aber sie rücken damit tendenziell auch weiter aus der Reichweite der Freudschen Psychoanalyse hinaus und in die jener Theorien hinein, die – gegen die psychoanalytischen Begriffe von «männlich» und «weiblich» – den Anteil von Maskerade, Performanz und Bedeutungszuschreibung im sozialen Spektakel der fortlaufenden Fabrikation von Geschlechtsidentitäten betonen. Letztlich exponieren aber auch die anderen, grösseren Fetischobjekte den Phallus als Bühnenrequisit, als zu installierendes Ding, das seine Bedeutung durch eine performative Praxis erhält, in der wir, die interpretierenden Zuschauer, nicht die geringste Rolle spielen.

3 Andererseits funktionieren diese Objekte, ob man sie nun psychoanalytisch oder psychoanalysekritisch wendet, nicht wirklich als sexuelle Fetische; dafür sind sie als Objekte zu ausgedacht, zu sehr Konzeptkunst. Von einem «Mangel an Sinnlichkeit», den man nicht müde wird dieser immer wieder vorzuhalten, kann hier zwar keine Rede sein, doch blendet man in keinem Moment aus, dass der Fetischismus im Medium der Kunst zitiert wird. Es handelt sich deutlich um Kunstfetische, um Fetische zweiter Ordnung. Interessanterweise leitet sich bereits das Wort Fetisch aus dem portugiesischen *feitiço* (künstlich, kunstvoll hergestellt) ab, und dieses wie-

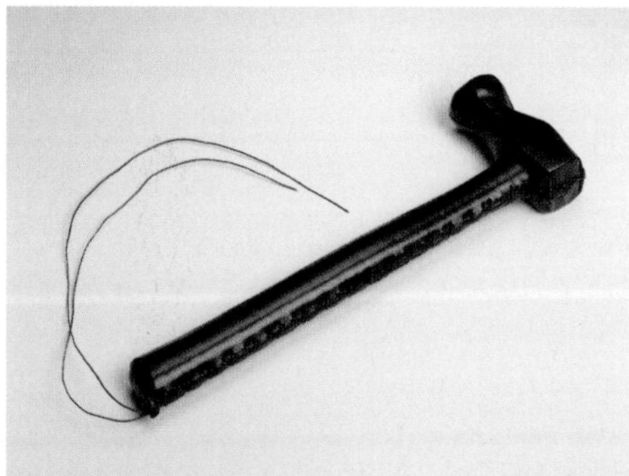

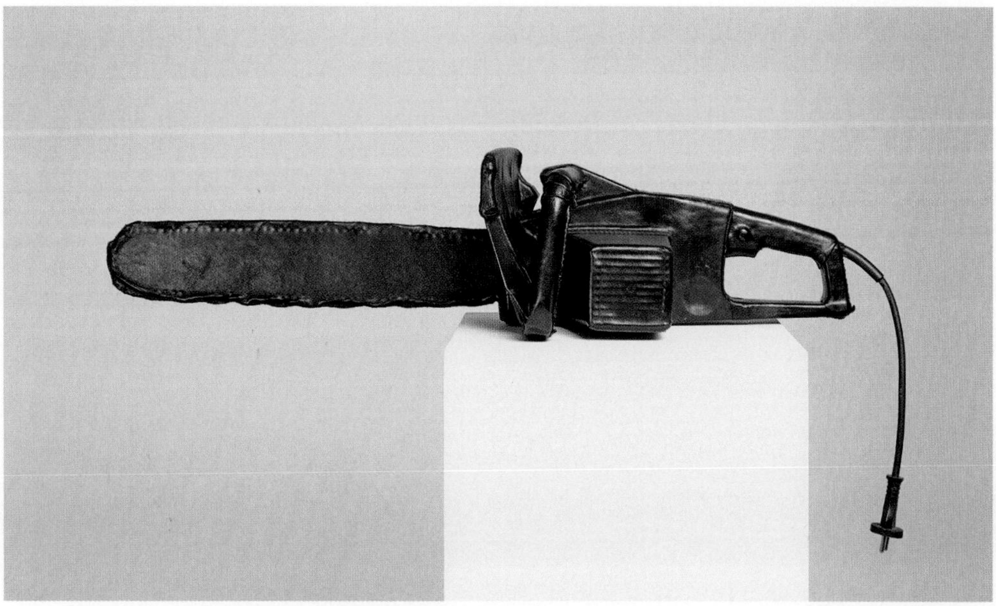

Top / Oben: MONICA BONVICINI, LEATHERHAMMER 1, 2004, leather-covered hammer, 11 13/16 x 3 15/16" / lederüberzogener Hammer, 30 x 10 cm.
Bottom / Unten: MONICA BONVICINI, UNTITLED, 2004, leather-covered chainsaw, 36 1/4 x 9 7/8 x 8 5/8" / lederüberzogene Kettensäge, 92 x 25 x 22 cm.

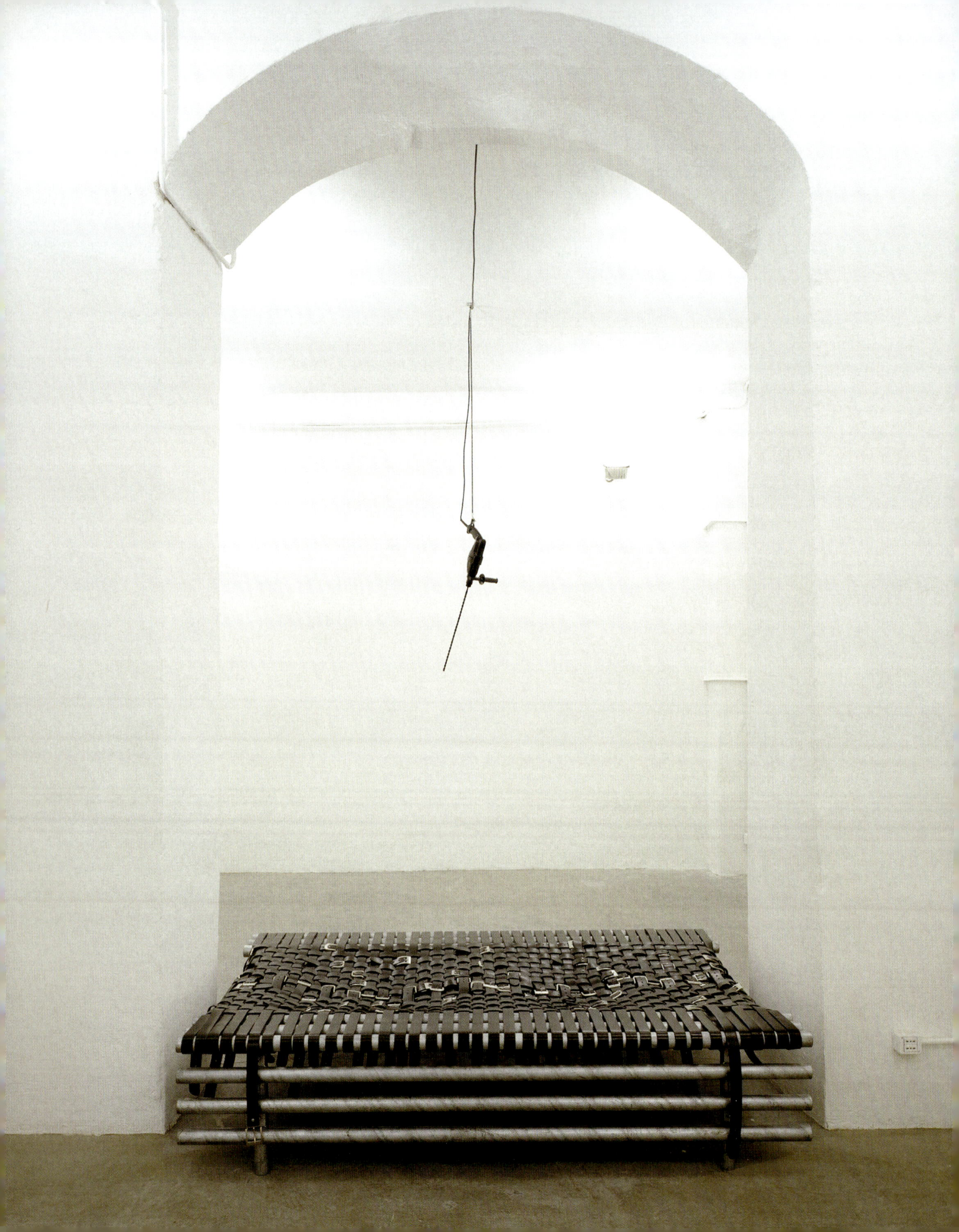

MONICA BONVICINI, BLIND SHOT, 2004, drill, black spray paint, timer, bench, galvanized steel, and black leather belts, bench measurements 18 1/8 x 52 x 78 3/4" / Bohrmaschine, schwarze Sprühfarbe, Timer, Bank, verzinkter Stahl und schwarze Ledergurte, Bankmasse: 46 x 132 x 200 cm.

derum aus dem lateinischen *facere* (machen) oder *facticius* (künstlich hergestellt).[3] Bonvicinis metafetischistische Objekte verweisen, das wäre eine dritte These, nicht nur auf die performative Herstellung der Geschlechter, sondern auch auf die Herstellung, das Machen von Kunst, und zwar zunächst ihrer eigenen. In diesem Zusammenhang erhält die Fetischisierung von Werkzeugen freilich eine ganz andere Bedeutung. Werkzeuge braucht man wohl generell zur Konstruktion von Kunst an irgendeiner Stelle, insbesondere aber braucht man sie für die Herstellung solcher im weitesten Sinne skulpturalen Werke, wie man sie von dieser Künstlerin kennt. Allerdings kann man Werkzeuge, das zeigt ebenfalls ein Blick auf ihr Œuvre, auch zur Destruktion benutzen. In einer nach einem Ausspruch von Le Corbusier betitelten Installation, I BELIEVE IN THE SKIN OF THINGS AS IN THAT OF WOMEN (Ich glaube an die Haut der Dinge wie an jene der Frauen, 1999), sah es beispielsweise an einigen Stellen aus, als sei jemand mit einem Hammer Amok gelaufen; und zwar, so konnte man meinen, gegen die fetischistische Gleichsetzung der Frau mit dem Ding ebenso wie gegen den latent in den glatten Oberflächen der modernistischen Architektur eingelagerten Heterosexismus. Entsprechend ist auch Glas (der modernistische Baustoff schlechthin) immer wieder ein bevorzugtes Objekt für Bonvicinis gesetzten Vandalismus. Nachdem sie mit dem Hammer bearbeitet worden sind, sehen die Glasflächen bezeichnenderweise oft aus, als habe jemand darauf geschossen. Wenn nun Bonvicini ausgerechnet unter anderem einer Reihe von Hämmern eine Haut aus Leder anlegt, so könnte dies auch als ironisch radikalfeministische Antwort auf den Glaubenssatz von Le Corbusier verstanden werden: Diese Fetische schlagen zurück. (In dieser Vorstellung kehrt auch ein Element von Slapstick oder clownesker Verzweiflungskomik aus Bonvicinis Video HAUSFRAU SWINGING (1997) wieder, für das sie einer ansonsten nackten Darstellerin das Modell eines Einfamilienhauses über den Kopf zog und diese damit wiederholt gegen eine Wand wanken liess.)

4 Aber eine solche «feministische» Lesart betonte doch zu sehr das destruktive Moment in Bonvicinis modernismuskritischen Installationen. Offensichtlich geht es ihr nämlich nicht einfach um einen Akt der Befreiung durch das Kaputtmachen dessen, was kaputt macht. Dafür ist sie selbst zu sehr an den Oberflächen der modernistischen Architektur interessiert, zu sehr davon geprägt, zu sehr Fan davon auch. So sehen ja beispielsweise die mit dem Hammer bearbeiteten Glasflächen mit ihren spinnwebartigen Strukturen selbst ausserordentlich gut aus; sie verbleiben in der modernistischen Logik, die sie attackieren. Für eine blosse Ästhetisierung des ursprünglich destruktiven Aktes sollte man deshalb die dekorativen Effekte ihrer Arbeiten nicht halten. Eher hat man es hier recht buchstäblich mit dekonstruktiven Interventionen zu tun. Der modernistischen Raumordnung werden Risse und Brüche beigefügt, um sie unserer Gewöhnung zu entfremden und für eine Reflexion auf die mit ihr verbundene soziale Praxis freizusetzen, nicht um sie ganz zu verwerfen. Insofern zielt die Destruktion hier gewissermassen auf ein konstruktives Moment: Es geht um eine Distanzierung von den Vorgaben der Väter, um sich deren Welt potenziell neu, anders aneignen zu können. Eben dies ist aber, wenn man es so abstrakt formuliert, ein zentrales Moment in a l l e r künstlerischen Produktion. Bei Bonvicini wird es allerdings explizit thematisch. In gewisser Hinsicht steht sie damit auch in der Tradition jener Künstlerinnen (und es sind vornehmlich Künstlerinnen gewesen), die den Zusammenhang zwischen der sogenannten «Einflussangst»[4] und dem (männlichen) Mythos von der künstlerischen Originalität aufgedeckt haben. An die Stelle einer verleugnenden Negation des Einflusses von Vorläuferfiguren haben sie die ausgestellte Aneignung von deren Prinzipien gesetzt. Doch lässt bekanntermassen auch die Appropriationskunst ihre Vorlagen nicht intakt – ebenso wenig wie die Ideologie des Originals, die ihnen unterliegt. Negation, das ist Bonvicinis Einsatz, ist somit auch hier die Bedingung der künstlerischen Handlungsfähigkeit; sie ist der Motor auch noch der selbstkritischsten Kreativität. In einer jüngeren Zusammenarbeit mit Sam Durant scheint Bonvicini den für künstlerisches Arbeiten konstitutiven Knoten aus Destruktion und Konstruktion, Determination und Freiheit, Differenz und Wiederholung selbst zu inszenieren. In dem Performance-Video BREAK IT / FIX IT (Machs kaputt / flicks 2003) zerstören die beiden zunächst eine Holz-

MONICA BONVICINI, HAUSFRAU SWINGING, 1997, drywall panels, impregnated wood, white paint, monitor, color video, $80^{11}/_{16}$ x 59 x $17^{1}/_{2}$". (Top: installation view; bottom: video still) / Rigipsplatten, imprägniertes Holz, weisse Farbe, Monitor, Farbvideo, 205 x 150 x 44,5 cm. (Oben: Installation; unten: Videostill)

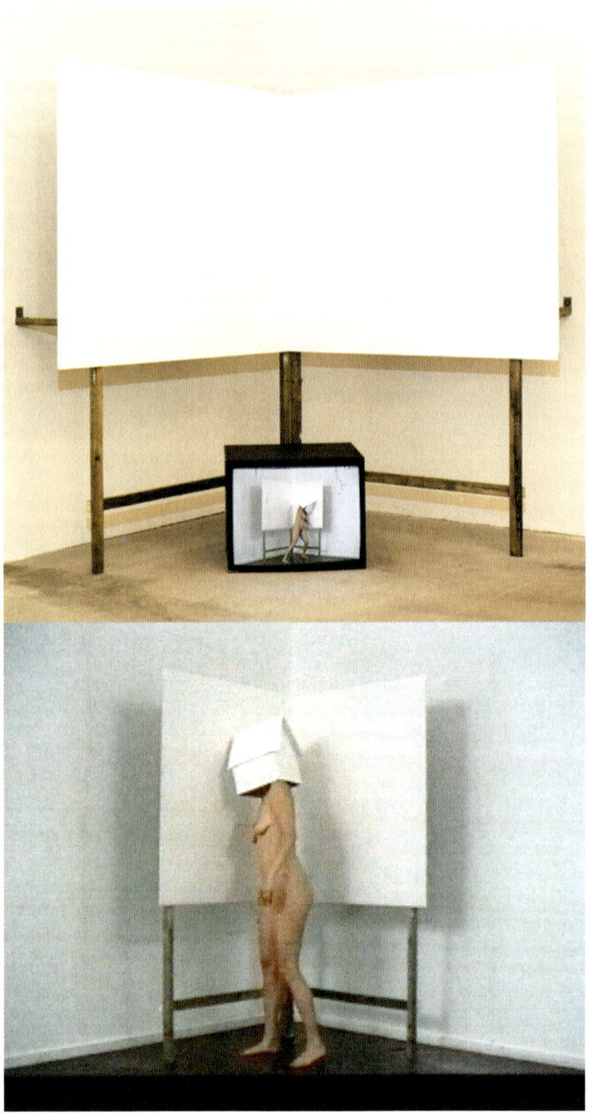

skulptur, die – noch ein im doppelten Sinne unheimlich buchstäblicher Witz – aus einem dreidimensionalen Schriftzug des Wortes «ANGST» besteht; hinterher zimmern sie aus deren sinnfälligen Trümmern etwas sehr Ähnliches und doch ganz Anderes: das Wort «FEAR». Werkzeug, um endlich aufs Thema zurückzukommen, ist in beiden Teilen des Videos im Einsatz. Anders als dieses ist das Fetischwerkzeug hingegen aus solchen praktischen Gebrauchskontexten herausgelöst. Eben deshalb vermag seine Bedeutung auch zwischen destruktiver und konstruktiver Funktion zu changieren. Es wird so, das ist die vierte These, zu etwas wie einem Emblem künstlerischer Produktion überhaupt.

5 Das Ausser-Gebrauch-Sein markiert generell den Gegensatz des Kunstfetischs zum gewöhnlichen Ding. Nirgends könnte das deutlicher werden als am Beispiel von Werkzeug. Werkzeuge sind nämlich das Paradigma für das, was bei Heidegger allgemein «Zeug» heisst: jene alltäglichen Dinge, von denen wir ständig umgeben sind und mit denen wir praktisch umgehen. Das Zeug im Sinne Heideggers ist bestimmt durch das Wozu und Wofür unserer alltäglichen Praxis; es ist dienlich für, brauchbar für, wird verwendet oder benutzt oder gemacht für etwas.[5] Bonvicinis Fetischobjekte stellen dagegen nichts mehr her. Darin erweisen sie sich auch als weitläufige Verwandte jener kontextfrei inszenierten Werkzeuge, die Walker Evans in einer bekannten Photoserie zu Ausstellungsstücken gemacht hat. (*The Beauties of the Common Tool* / Die Schönheiten des gemeinen Werkzeugs, 1955) Wie bei gewöhnlichen Fetischen ist es nämlich auch im Falle der Kunstfetische gerade ihr Ausser-Gebrauch-Sein, das einer Art von abgründigem Mehrwert stattgibt. Insofern stellen Bonvicinis Fetischwerkzeuge aus, dass die Bewegung der Kunstwerke, wie Derrida einmal gesagt hat, über die Fetischisierung verläuft. Wenn auch nicht eigentlich über diese selbst, so doch über deren Bedingung: die Entfremdung der Dinge aus ihrem gewöhnlichen Gebrauchskontext.[6] Anders jedoch als echte Fetische sind Bonvicinis Kunstfetische auch kein Mittel mehr zu irgendeinem sexuellen Zweck. Ihr perverser Mehrwert ist derjenige der Kunst: Sie produzieren einen (übrigens auch jede Liste abzählbarer Thesen sprengenden) Exzess möglicher Bedeutungen, gerade weil sie dem Raum der Produktion, dem Raum der Zwecke, enthoben sind.

6 Nun hat der Fetisch, das ist bekannt, auch noch eine weitere theoretische Konnotation. THE FETISHISM OF COMMODITY (Der Warenfetischismus, 2002) heisst eine von Bonvicinis neueren Installationen. Im

Blick auf deren S/M-Ästhetik funktioniert der Titel hier zunächst durchaus wieder als Kalauer: So, als sexuellen, hat sich Marx (denn der überlegte sich seine Sache ja vor Freud) den Fetischismus natürlich nicht vorgestellt. Auf den zweiten Blick lässt die Szene jedoch sowohl für eine Kritik an der allgegenwärtigen Fetischisierung der Sexualität in der Warengesellschaft interpretativen Raum als auch für die weniger düstere Einsicht, dass der einzig gangbare und gar nicht mal so unattraktive Ausweg aus diesem Zustand vermutlich eben der sexuelle Fetischismus ist – und nicht die ideologische Rückkehr zu einer vermeintlich ursprünglichen, nicht entfremdeten Sexualität. Jenseits dieses semantischen Feldes und seiner diversen Ausläufer lässt sich der Titel aber, und darum geht es mir hier, auch als Provokation hinsichtlich des unter ihm gezeigten Kunstwerks verstehen. Man kann dies in vielerlei Hinsicht heisse Kunstwerk erwerben; es ist käuflich wie alle Kunst. Aber man wird seiner als Kunst kaum habhaft werden, indem man es besitzt. Denn der eigentümliche Mehrwert, der auch aus Werkzeugen Werke der Kunst zu machen vermag, sitzt nicht verdinglicht in den Objekten selbst (oder in deren kunstvoller Verpackung). Vielmehr erzeugt er sich einzig in den semantisch exzessiven Verstehensvollzügen, zu denen sie uns provozieren. Dies ist schliesslich der skandalöse Witz der Kunst selbst: dass sie zum Besitz, zur geistigen und materiellen Aneignung herausfordert und dass doch das, was sie zur Kunst macht, eben gerade nicht in Form von Erkenntnis oder Konsum angeeignet, sondern nur immer wieder neu erfahren werden kann. Eben deshalb ist Kunst vielleicht der ultimative Fetisch.

1) Vgl. den Sammelband *Weiblichkeit als Maskerade,* hrsg. von Liliane Weissberg, S. Fischer Verlag, Frankfurt am Main 1994.
2) Sigmund Freud, «Fetischismus», in: ders., *Studienausgabe,* Bd. III, S. Fischer Verlag, Frankfurt am Main 1975, S. 379–388, hier: S. 387.
3) Vgl. Liliane Weissberg, «Gedanken zur ‹Weiblichkeit›. Eine Einführung», in: *Weiblichkeit als Maskerade,* vgl. Anm. 1, S. 14.
4) Vgl. Harold Bloom, *Einflussangst. Eine Theorie der Dichtung,* Verlag Stroemfeld Roter Stern, Frankfurt am Main/Basel 1995.
5) Vgl. Martin Heidegger, *Sein und Zeit,* Niemeyer Verlag, Tübingen 1957, S. 68 ff.
6) Vgl. Jacques Derrida, «Restitutionen. Von der Wahrheit nach Mass», in: ders., *Die Wahrheit in der Malerei,* Passagen Verlag, Wien 1992, S. 301–442, hier: S. 401.

MONICA BONVICINI, BLIND SHOT, 2004, installation view with CAGED TOOLS Nos. 1, 2, 3, and 4; metal grids, power tools (hammer drill, stone saw, mixer, and chain saw), black leather, black leather belts, brick bases, 94 1/2 x 39 7/16 x 39 7/16" each / Ansicht der EINGESPERRTEN WERKZEUGE Nr. 1, 2, 3 und 4; Gitter, Elektrowerkzeuge (Schlagbohrer, Steinsäge, Mixer und Kettensäge), schwarzes Leder, schwarze Ledergurte, gemauerte Backsteinsockel, je 240 x 100 x 100 cm.

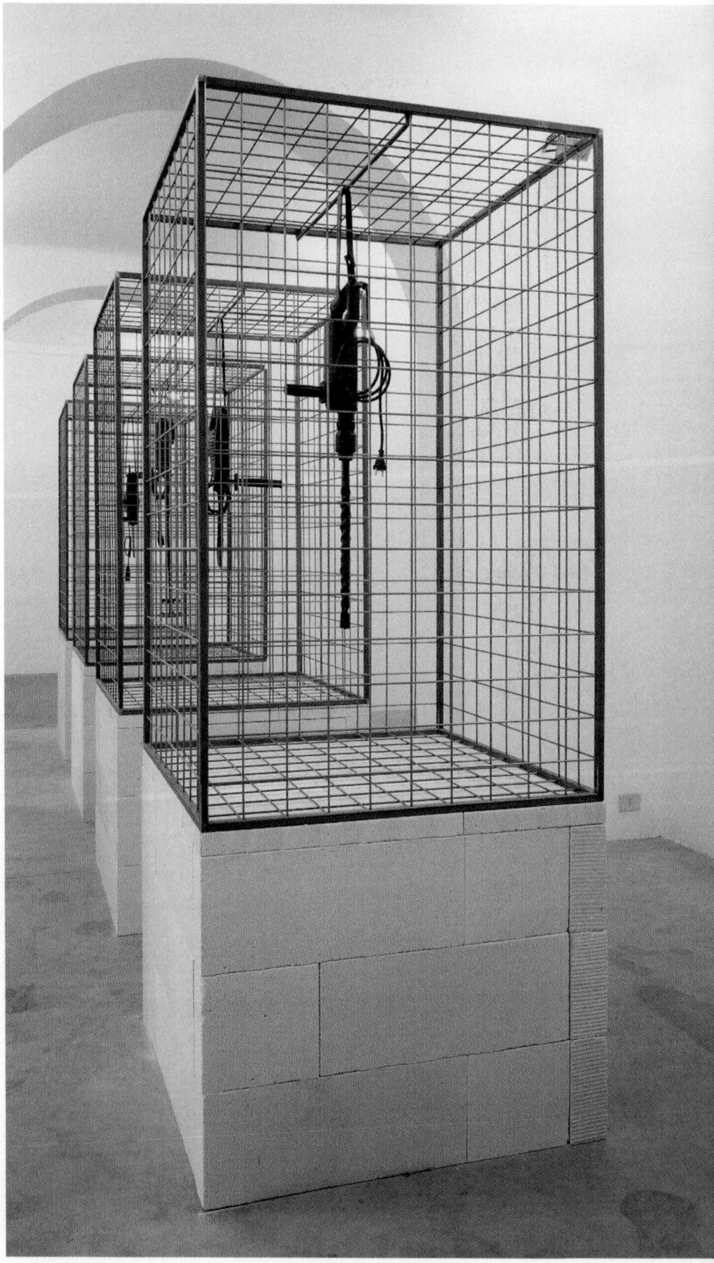

JULIANE REBENTISCH

Monica Bonvicini's FETISH art

One would really like to touch them, and own them too. Covered in a snug-fitting sheath of smooth black leather and laced up perfectly, they have been made with infinite care. Hot. It's amazing how well it works, the sledgehammer tactic of a fetishistic leather skin sexualizing (for instance) a common mallet. It is a typical Bonvicini joke, limit-defying in its literalness. Here are a few exploratory theses.

1 As we know since Freud, fetishism is the male perversion par excellence. The fetish replaces the mother's absent penis. Leaving aside the tangled issue of the castration threat, what a man ultimately idolizes in the fetish, elliptically speaking, is simply the phallus, the symbol of male strength and power. Hence, Monica Bonvicini's fetish tools could be read as a caricature of male fetishism's narcissistic moment, not male fetishism itself; for these works are not about replacing the penis but about its symbolic enhancement. Correspondingly, Bonvicini's chosen objects are all tools that symbolically reduplicate or elongate the male penis, and not those—such as a woman's foot or shoe—that replace the penis that "woman" lacks. Here, too, the phallus replaces the penis, and a good chauvinist joke for feminists and gays might start with this obvious distinction between phallus and penis: What's a real-life construction worker compared to the promise of his leather-sheathed percussion drill?

2 But the drastically phallic percussion drills, chain saws, hammers, and so on do not simply caricature displays of male potency. They are far too good as leather objects, far too sexy to belong to a Tom of Finland comic world. And this is the general aesthetic humor of Bonvicini's jokes: they go beyond any ready-to-hand punch line. In their respective installations, some of the objects, especially the drill variations (BLIND SHOT, 2004), seem downright violent, even menacing. Evidently every tool can become a weapon, depending on how one holds it. Other objects, in particular the smaller implements, don't necessarily look only phallic. The fetish look of their lacing is reminiscent of a corset; they seem to be costumed. Thus they also bring out the link between fetishism and masquerade sometimes referred to as "female fetishism."[1] It is no accident that the leather Bonvicini uses in these pieces is as supple as glove leather. While viewing her tool-objects, we find their sexual connotation constantly alternating—like a glove being turned inside out. They are, in this light, curiously queer objects. Not that this diminishes their fetish character. According to Freud, fetishes that are "constructed out of two opposing ideas" are "capable of great tenacity."[2] But that interpretation does tend to remove them from the reach of Freudian psychoanalysis with its emphasis on the male/female dichotomy, and instead stresses the role

JULIANE REBENTISCH is research associate at the Faculty of Cultural Sciences, European University Viadrina, Frankfurt (Oder), and lives in Berlin.

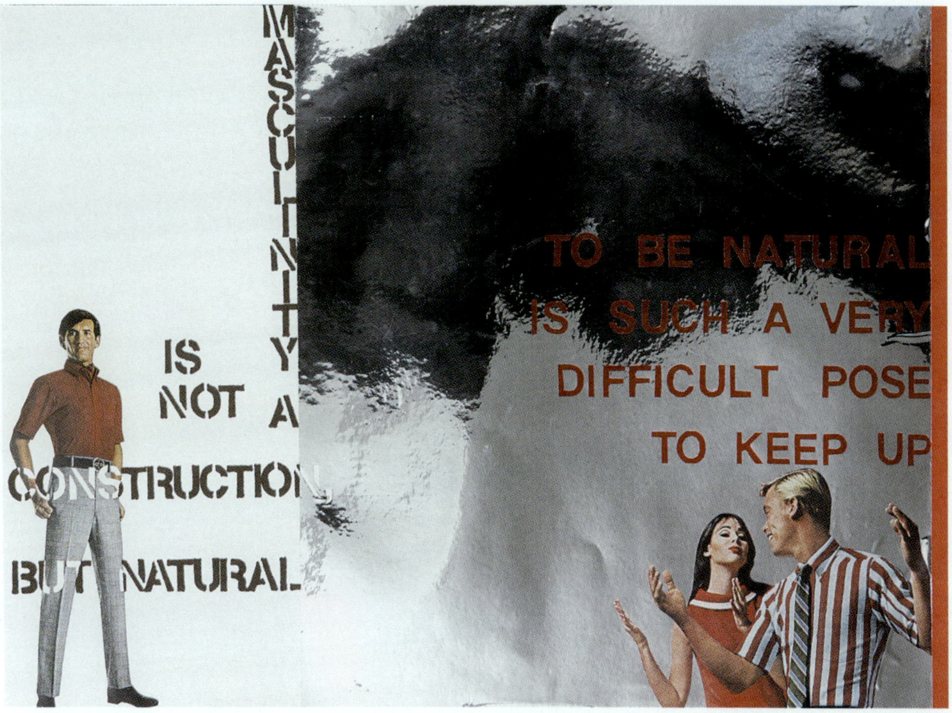

MONICA BONVICINI, ETERNALE, 2000, drawing from the eponymous series, 24 3/8 x 32 1/4" / Zeichnung aus der gleichnamigen Serie, 62 x 82 cm.

of masquerade, performance, and meaning ascription in the social spectacle of ongoing gender identity construction. Ultimately, however, even the other, bigger fetish objects present the phallus as a stage prop, as an object in need of installation whose significance depends on a performative praxis where we, the interpreting viewers, play no role at all.

3 On the other hand, whether understood as espousing or eschewing psychoanalysis, Bonvicini's objects don't really function as sexual fetishes. They are too constructed as objects, ostensibly existing as Conceptual Art. True, the lack of sensuality, which people never tire of laying at Conceptual Art's door, is not in evidence here. But not for a moment does one forget that fetishism is being cited through the medium of art. These are clearly art fetishes; they are fetishes once removed. Interestingly enough, the word "fetish" derives from the Portuguese *feitiço* (artificial, made artfully), which itself comes from the Latin *facere* (to make) or *facticius* (made artificially).[3)] Bonvicini's meta-fetishistic objects—my third thesis—refer not only to the performative construction of gender, but also to the construction, the making, of art, first and foremost her own. In this context, of course, the fetishization of tools assumes a very different meaning. Tools are generally required for the construction of art, and, in particular, for the production of such broadly speaking sculptural works as this artist produces. As a glance at her oeuvre confirms, though, tools can also be used to destroy. Various points of her installation titled after Le Corbusier's dictum I BELIEVE IN THE SKIN OF THINGS AS IN THAT OF WOMEN (1999) look as if someone had run amok with a hammer. This amounts to a protest as much against, one might suspect, the fetishizing identification of woman with thing, as against the heterosexism latent in modernist architecture's sleek surfaces. Not surprisingly, glass, the modernist building material par excellence, is a frequent target of Bonvicini's tempered vandalism. After being worked over with a hammer the glass surfaces often look as if someone had shot at them. And when Bonvicini fits a leather skin on hammers, of all things, one might see this as an ironic, radical feminist reply to Le Corbusier's credo: these fetishes strike back. (This interpretation con-

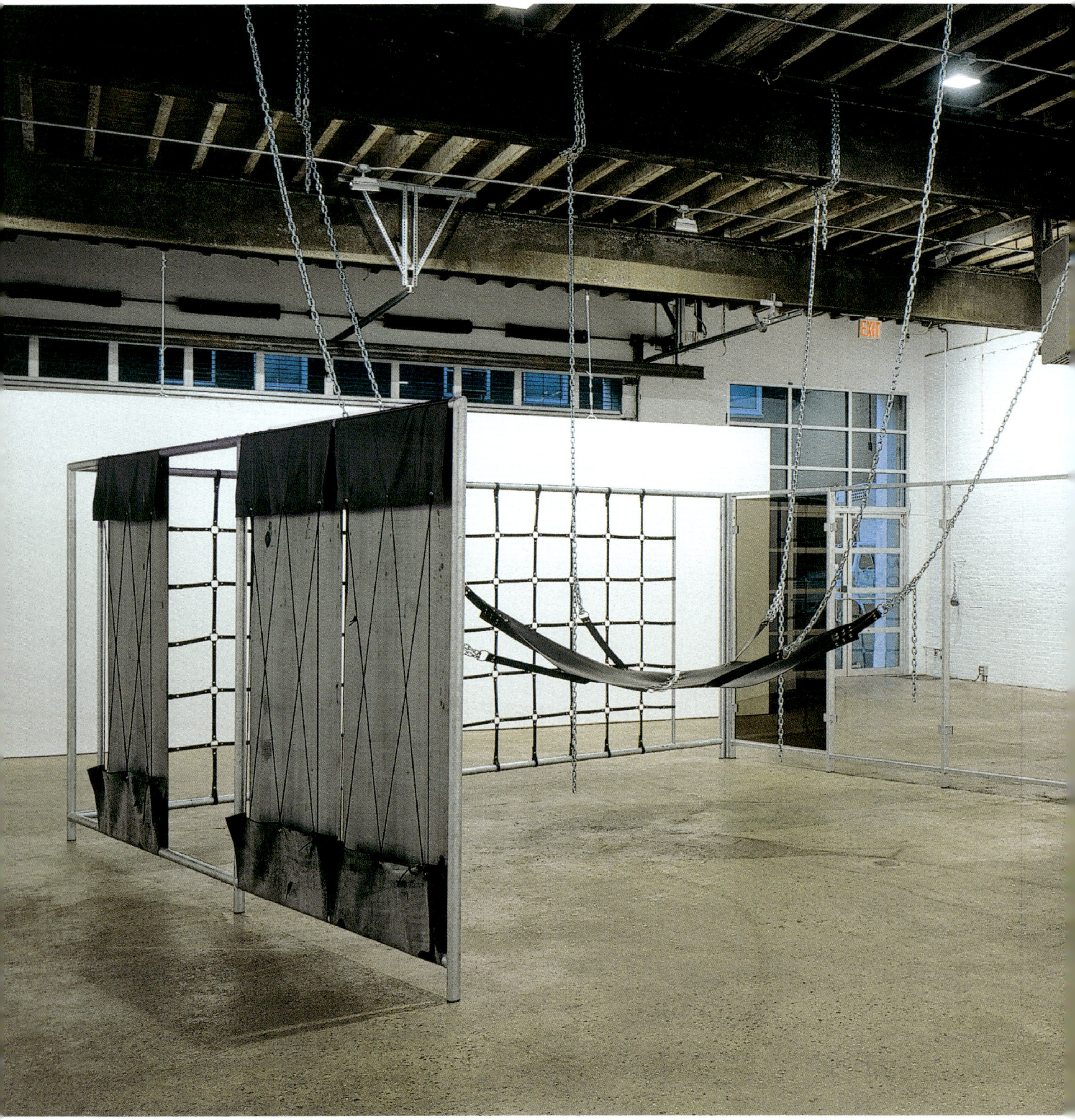
EXIT

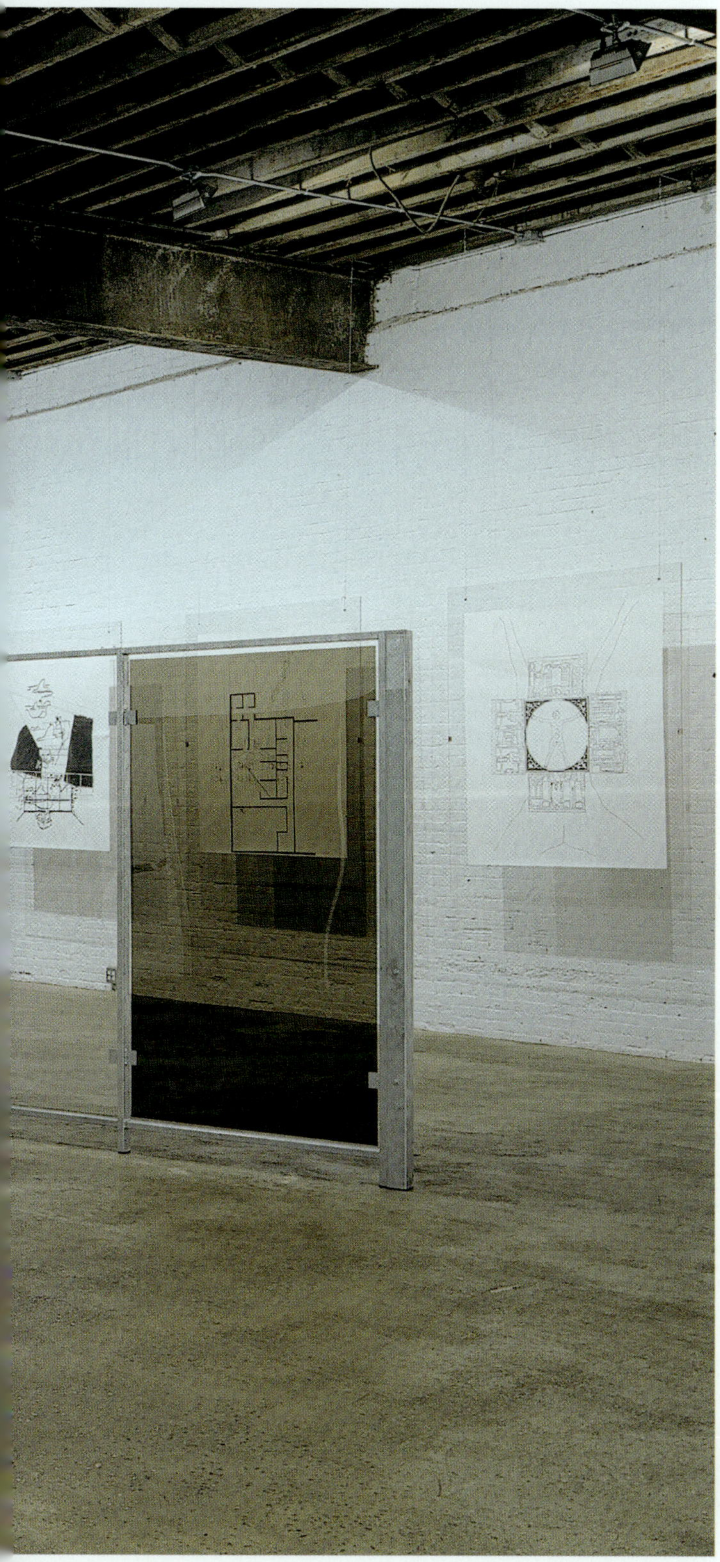

tains an element of the slapstick or zany black comedy of Bonvicini's video HAUSFRAU SWINGING (1997), in which a nude woman with a cardboard house pulled over her head repeatedly bangs her head and house against a wall.)

4 However, such a "feminist" reading overemphasizes the destructive moment in Bonvicini's modernist-critical installations. Clearly the liberating act of wrecking what itself wrecks is not her sole aim. She is much too interested in, influenced by, and, in fact, enamored of modernist architecture and its surfaces. After all, her vandalized glass surfaces with their cobweb-like reticulations are vastly appealing and they remain within the modernist logic which they attack. Not that one should therefore see such decorative effects in her work as a mere aestheticization of the original destructive act: her deconstructive interventions are extremely literal. Cracks and fractures inflicted on the modernist spatial order do not subvert it, but rather defamiliarize it so that we can consider the social praxis in which it is embedded. Destruction therefore has constructive consequences: This enables the canonical forms to become alienated in order to appropriate their progenitors' world in potentially new, different ways. That approach, when formulated in such abstract terms, is central to all artistic production. However, Bonvicini thematizes it explicitly. In some sense this also places her in that tradition of women artists (for they are primarily women artists) who have exposed the link between the "anxiety of influence"[4)] and the (male) myth of artistic originality. Instead of negating their precursors' influence by denial, they overtly appropriate their principles—though we all know that not even Appropriation Art leaves its materials intact, any more than it does the underlying ideology. Negation, for Bonvicini, is here the precondition of artistic activity. It drives even the most self-critical creativity. In a recent collaboration with Sam Durant, Bonvicini seems to be acting out this very nexus—destruction/construction, constraint/freedom, difference/

MONICA BONVICINI, THE FETISHISM OF COMMODITY, 2002, galvanized steel, leather, chains, Plexiglas, latex, 81 7/8 x 196 7/8 x 174 3/4" / verzinkter Stahl, Leder, Ketten, Plexiglas, Latex, ca. 208 x 500 x 444 cm.

repetition—at the heart of artistic work. In the performance video BREAK IT / FIX IT (2003) the two artists first shatter a wooden sculpture—profoundly uncanny in its form as a literally double joke—consisting of a three-dimensional model of the word "angst," only to reassemble its pieces to form something very similar but entirely different: the word "fear." Tools, to come back to the point at last, are used in both parts of the video. But being fetish tools, they have been detached from their practical, utilitarian contexts. It is in virtue of this that they can oscillate between destructive and constructive connotations. The fetish tool—this is the fourth thesis—becomes almost emblematic of artistic production per se.

5 What in general distinguishes the art fetish from ordinary objects is that it exists outside the sphere of use. This is especially clear in the case of tools. Tools are the paradigm of what Heidegger refers to generically as "equipment" *(Zeug),* the everyday objects that are constantly around us and that we put to various uses. Equipment, in Heidegger's sense, is defined by the aims and ends of everyday practical concerns. Equipment is serviceable for or useful for; it is employed or used or made for something.[5)] But Bonvicini's fetish objects produce noth-ing. As such they can be seen as distant relatives of the tools Walker Evans detached from their surroundings and staged as exhibits in his well-known portfolio *The Beauties of the Common Tool* (1955). Like ordinary fetishes, the art fetish does not inhabit the sphere of use, which confers on it a kind of boundless surplus value. To this extent Bonvicini's fetish tools illustrate that the movement of works of art, as Derrida once put it, proceeds via fetishization—not necessarily fetishization itself, but the premise upon which it is based, namely the alienation of things from their regular utilitarian contexts.[6)] Unlike genuine fetishes, however, those made by Bonvicini are no longer means toward a sexual end. Their perverse surplus value is that of art. They generate an excess of possible meanings—even more than covered by any number of theses—precisely because they exist outside the spheres of production and of ends.

6 Fetishism has a further and familiar theoretical connotation. THE FETISHISM OF COMMODITY (2002) is the title of one of Bonvicini's more recent installations. Given the S/M aesthetic of the installation, its title seems at first like another rather corny joke: Marx was around long before Freud and obviously didn't envisage fetishism in this, sexual, sense. Upon closer examination, one soon realizes that the piece can be read not only as a critique of the ubiquitous fetishization of sexuality in our consumer society but that there is also room for an interpretation not quite so bleak, namely that the only possible (and not entirely unattractive) way out of the situation is probably sexual fetishism itself rather than an ideological return to some supposedly primordial, unalienated sexuality. But aside from this semantic field and its outposts—and this is what interests me here—the title is also a provocation, given the work of art that it names. The work—a *hot* piece in many ways—can be acquired. Like all art, it can be bought. But owning it will hardly help one to possess it *as art*. For the surplus value that can turn tools into works of art does not exist reified in things themselves (or in their artistic packaging). On the contrary, it comes into being only because the work of art provokes semantic and hermeneutic excess. This, ultimately, is the scandalous joke of all art. It makes one want to possess it, to appropriate it intellectually and materially; and yet the very quality that makes art cannot be appropriated, either as knowledge or as a commodity, but only experienced over and over again in new ways. Precisely this makes art perhaps the ultimate fetish.

(Translation: Christopher Jenkin-Jones)

1) See *Weiblichkeit als Maskerade,* ed. Liliane Weissberg (Frankfurt am Main: S. Fischer Verlag, 1994).

2) Sigmund Freud, "Fetishism," *Int. J. Psychoanal., 9* (1928), pp. 161 ff, trans. Joan Riviere. (A different translation of the article is reprinted in the standard edition of Sigmund Freud's *Psychological Works,* Vol. 21.)

3) See Liliane Weissberg, "Gedanken zur 'Weiblichkeit': Eine Einführung," in op. cit. note 1, p. 14.

4) See Harold Bloom, *The Anxiety of Influence: A Theory of Poetry* (New York: Oxford University Press Inc., 1997).

5) See Martin Heidegger, *Being and Time,* trans. J. Macquarrie and E. Robinson (Oxford: Blackwell, 1967), pp. 99–100.

6) See Jacques Derrida, *The Truth in Painting,* trans. G. Bennington and I. McLeod (Chicago: University of Chicago Press, 1987), p. 332.

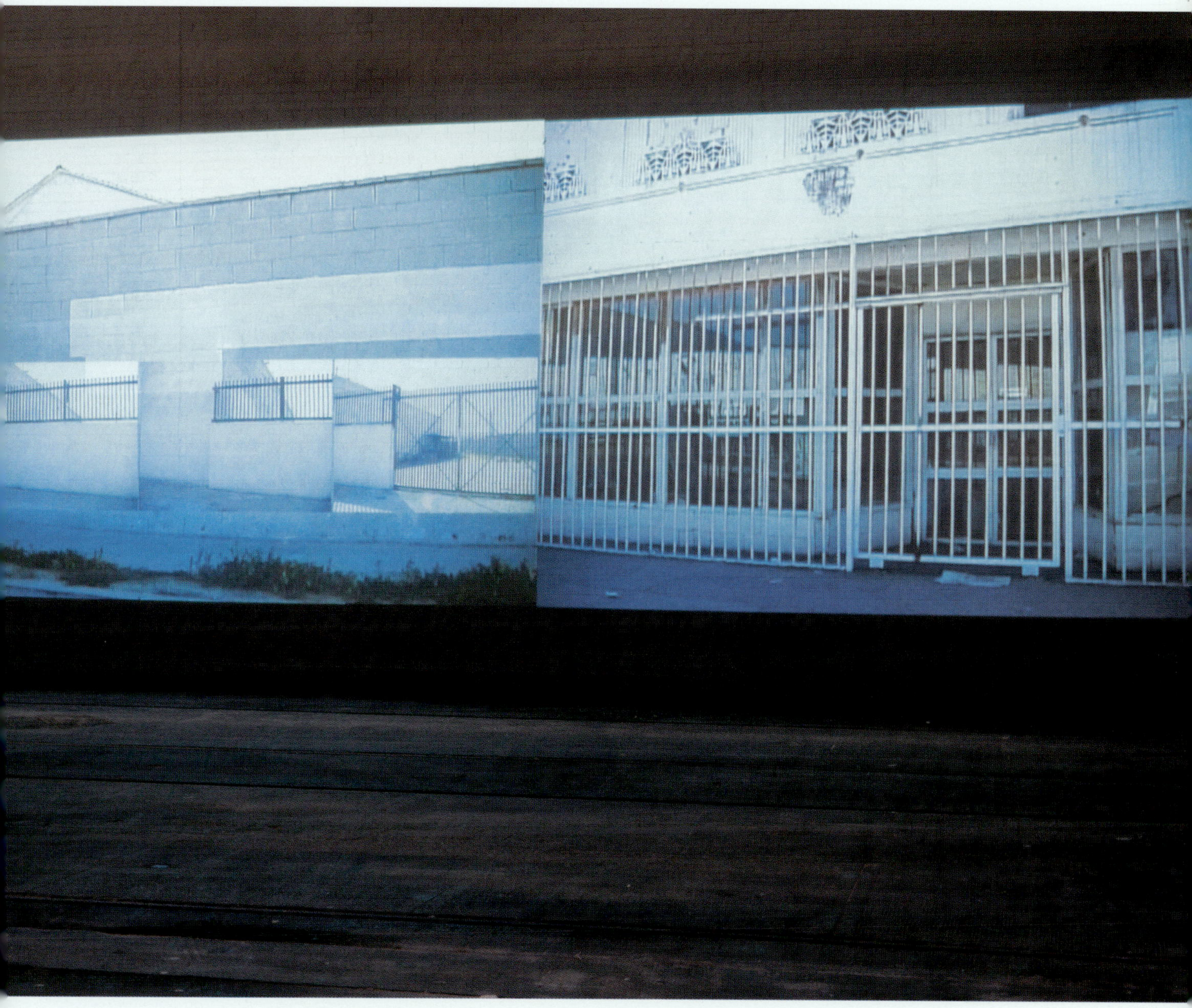

MONICA BONVICINI, SHOTGUN, 2003, multi-channel DVD projection, loop of 10 min. 29 sec., sound, installation view, Tramway, Glasgow, dimensions variable / Mehrkanal-DVD-Projektion, Endlosschleife von 10 Min. 29 Sek., Ton, Grösse der Installation variabel.

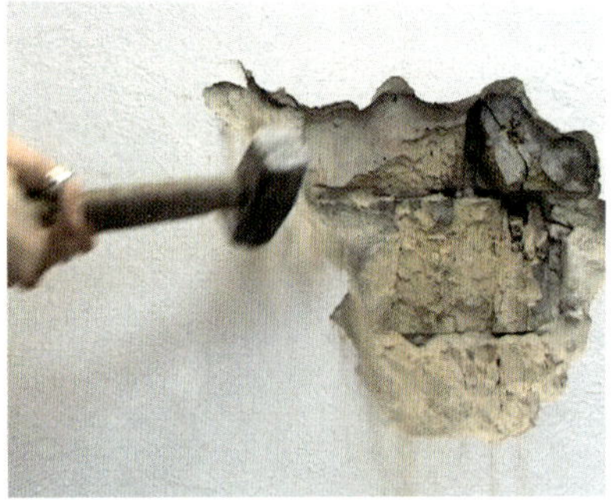

CRASH COURSE IN ARCHITECTURAL MATTER

Expressed in a more general way, the life of forms gives definition to what may be termed "psychological landscapes," without which the essential genius of the environments would be opaque and elusive for all those who share them. Greece, for instance, exists as a geographical basis for certain ideas about man, but the landscape of Doric art, or rather Doric art as landscape, created a Greece without which the real Greece is a merely great luminous desert. Again, the landscape of Gothic art, or rather Gothic art as landscape, created a France and a French humanity that no one could foresee: outlines of the horizon, silhouettes of cities—a poetry, in short, that arose from Gothic art, and not from geology or from Capetian institutions.[1)]

LARS LERUP

If architecture can be said to have a formal geography with, say, classicism at its center, then it can also be said to have a psychological landscape. As Henri Focillon suggests, such a landscape may have national origins and extent. For example, in the US, the single-family house occupies the psychological center, one characterized by variously gendered spaces (with their dark, carefully denied closets of shame) draped in an all-encompassing quotidian life. While in Italy (Monica Bonvicini's birthplace), it may be the piazza, with its public theater, that occupies the psychological center. Whether "home" or "piazza," however, all architecturally-bound space is confining.

The psychological landscape may be visualized as a flat, roughly circular disk, with a wobbly outer edge moving at a dizzying speed around a calcified, almost motionless, center. At

---

LARS LERUP is a writer living in Stockholm and Houston.

MONICA BONVICINI, HAMMERING OUT (AN OLD ARGUMENT), 1998, DVD, 60-minute video color projection / DVD, 60 Minuten Farbvideoprojektion.

the outer fringes, architecture's hegemony loses its grip; art, psychosis, mayhem, and phobias help to increase speed and turbulence there. Agents operating at the center are confined to the most mundane and predictable behavior, while those speeding along the outer edge may establish their own rules. Some perceive that along this edge, architecture is the enemy, the villain, an obstacle to liberty and freedom, while at the center, architecture rests in the embrace of the familiar. Yet, nowhere in this psychological domain can the unwilling escape Michel Foucault's "disciplinary mechanisms," which assert that the apparent freedom at the edge is, in fact, mere illusion.

Monica Bonvicini has stated: "There is something basic to architecture that I sometimes miss in art."[2] If this "basic" character is presumed to be architecture's practicality—its sheltering necessity—then it is not unlike painting, which at one time had to have a frame—gilded, to boot. However, Bonvicini works as an artist with and in architecture to bring architecture into the non-basic realm of art (the conceptual and non-pragmatic). In the psychological landscape where Bonvicini has chosen, at least in part, to perform her art, the shadow of the "basic" in architecture is cast across the landscape's approximate circularity. Yet, centrifugal forces at the edge, if nothing else, have scrambled the "basic" so that, at the turbulent edge, what's commonly up may be down, or perhaps sideways. But, since architecture and art are still in the real world, gravity prevails, however discombobulated it may be.

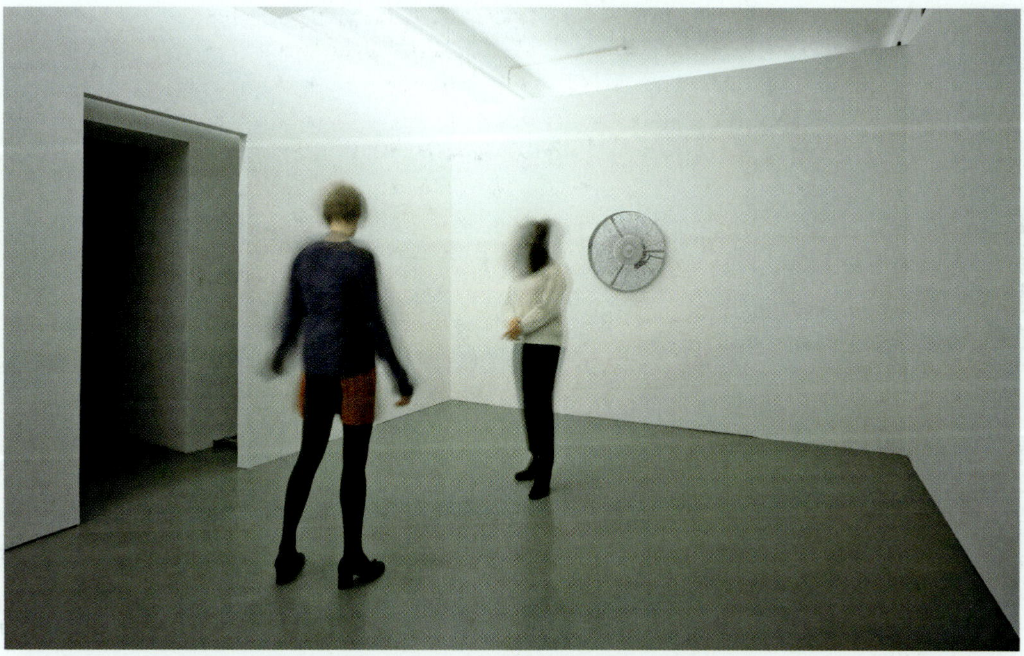

MONICA BONVICINI, A VIOLENT, TROPICAL, CYCLONIC PIECE OF ART HAVING WIND SPEEDS OF OR IN EXCESS OF 75 MPH, 1998, aluminum studs, drywall panels, white paint, 2 axial fans, 137 3/4 x 236 1/4 x 157 1/2" / Aluminiumstützen, Rigipsplatten, weisse Farbe, 2 Axialventilatoren, 350 x 600 x 400 cm.

Bonvicini is clearly aware of this architectural shadow as she careens along the outer edge of the constructed psychological landscape. Thus she describes an early childhood recollection in an interview with Andrea Bowers:

My parents' house had a huge hedge around the garden. They loved it because it provided privacy, but I didn't like it because I wasn't able to see what was happening outside on the street. I remember that if I was nervous or angry, my father used to tell me to run across the garden and crash into the hedge. I did that a lot—it was a nice feeling.[3]

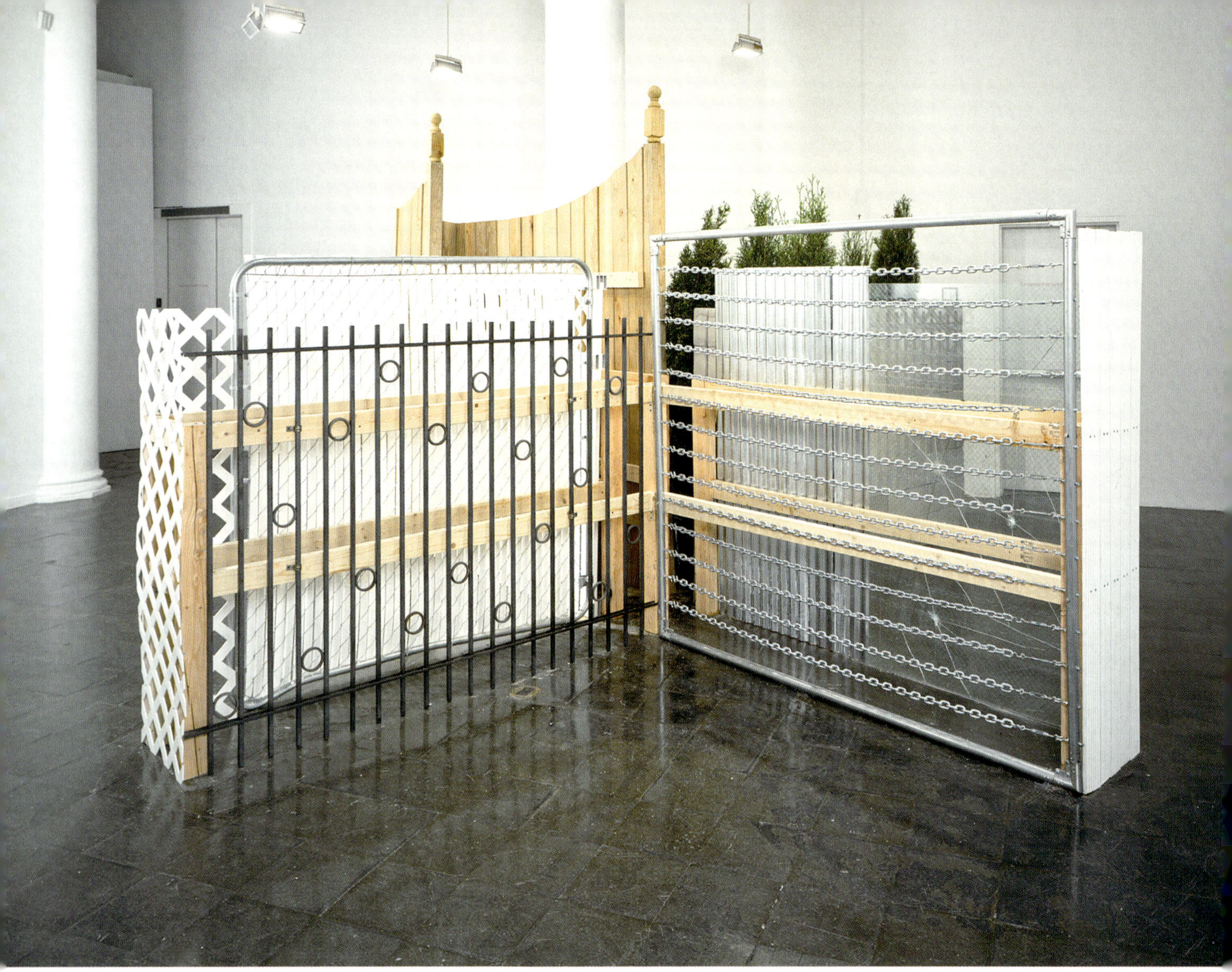

MONICA BONVICINI, TURNING WALLS, NEW YORK, 2003, wood, galvanized steel, chains, vinyl fence, concrete bricks, aluminum panel, broken safety glass, plants, installation for "Living Inside the Grid," The New Museum, New York, ca. 98 1/2 x 275 1/2 x 236 1/4" / Holz, galvanisierter Stahl, Vinylzaun, Bausteine, Aluminium, gesprungenes Sicherheitsglas, Pflanzen, ca. 250 x 700 x 600 cm.

Seeing this as a premature experience of the basic confines of architecture leads us to the more concrete examples expressed in Bonvicini's later projects. But let me first engage the h e d g e - c r a s h i n g.

Falling recklessly into a hedge, supported by an intricate jumble of clipped branches feathered with leaves, though a wonderful feeling, is not as dramatic a gesture as Yves Klein's famous leap, photographed by Harry Shunk, and captioned: "The Painter of Space Hurls Himself into the Void!" But both are equally architectonic. Bonvicini throws herself inside and into architectural matter—literally, i n s i d e t h e w a l l, while Klein leaps into architectural s p a c e—marked by the rapidly approaching Parisian street. However, there is one great difference: Klein's leap was staged. There is another similarity in how Klein's and Bonvicini's work is designed to instill in viewers the sense of an extreme experience, be it fear, pleasure, or even pain.

This "diving into," despite inevitable resistance, recurs in Bonvicini's A VIOLENT, TROPICAL, CYCLONIC PIECE OF ART HAVING WIND SPEEDS OF OR IN EXCESS OF 75 MILES PER HOUR (1998) and HAUSFRAU SWINGING (1997). Since phenomenological meaning comes about through usage, throwing oneself into various densities of matter asks a most basic question: What is matter? And more particularly, what is architectural matter? Or more precisely, why is architecture so confining, and indeed literally repulsive—particularly here at the edge of the psychological landscape?

If architecture is anything with a ceiling greater than eight feet, does fascist architecture exist? No. Does sexist architecture exist? No. However, fascist space does exist, as well as sexist, gendered, and liberated space. How is that possible? Because all spatial meaning comes about in use. It is not inherent in the built matter, but a social construction—a product of the collusion between people and buildings. People motivate space. (Abu Ghraib, we are told today, is now a "good" prison, while just months ago it was hell.) We also know, through Bonvicini's spatial installations, I BELIEVE IN THE SKIN OF THINGS AS IN THAT OF WOMEN (1999) and STONEWALL 3 (2002), that space resists bodily assaults; it hurts when you pound a wall with your fist, though perhaps less so in HAMMERING OUT (AN OLD ARGUMENT) (1998).

Bonvicini's persistent questioning of architectural resistance is an important process that, in the end, does not aim to, or need to, find an answer. These questions can only be approached by throwing oneself into the stream of meaning. Philosophers such as Gianni Vattimo from Torino have argued beautifully that there may be no way to overcome *(Aufhebung)* this fundamental obstacle; we can only get used to it *(Verwindung)*—as if learning to accept a lingering cold or a weak thought *(pensiere debole)*. Bonvicini seems unwilling to merely "get used to it" as her work demonstrates (always with resistance at its center) that at least you can try. I suspect that Bonvicini does not like this weak approach, but prefers the crash course.

TURNING WALLS (2001) may be Bonvicini's most emblematic approach to the fundamental question of access to architectural matter. One is led to walk around this pinwheel of inaccessible walled-in perpetuity—no access, no answers, just a menu of obstacles. The artist's preparatory drawings, made by attaching paper clips and safety pins to a white background, may well serve as the genetic code of architectural resistance. Long chains of interlocking paper clips form a loose grid. These are then clasped together with safety pins that serve as locks, suggesting that inside architectural matter (in this case a woven wall, as in Gottfried Semper's analogy between *Wand* and *Gewand* that he discussed in an 1856 lecture in Zurich), a lock (or glue) always holds wall assemblies together, whether steel in a concrete wall, or mortar in a brick wall. It is hard to know what is what: without bricks we wouldn't have a wall, despite all the mortar in the world. And the same goes for paper clips and safety pins.

1) Henri Focillon, *The Life of Forms in Art,* trans. George Kubler (Cambridge, MA: Zone Books with MIT Press, 1992), p. 61.
2) Monica Bonvicini, *Scream & Shake,* (Grenoble: Le Magasin, 2001; Berlin: Kunst-Werke, 2002; New York: P.S. 1 Contemporary Art Center/Museum of Modern Art, 2002), p. 33.
3) Ibid. p. 33.

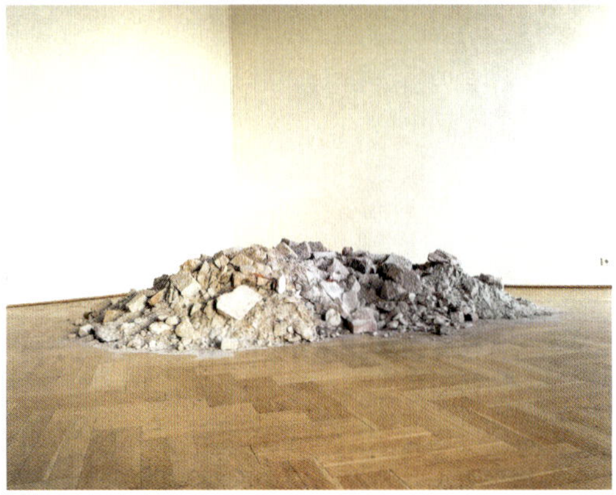

CRASH-KURS IN ARCHITEKTONISCHER MATERIE

Allgemeiner gesagt: das Leben der Formen prägt psychologische Landschaften, ohne die die schöpferische Kraft des Ortes undurchsichtig und unfassbar wäre für alle jene, welche daran teilhaben. Griechenland existiert als geographische Basis einer bestimmten Idee des Menschen; aber die Landschaft der dorischen Kunst, oder vielmehr die dorische Kunst als Landschaft hat ein eigenes Griechenland geschaffen, ohne das das Griechenland der Natur nur eine lichtvolle Wüste ist; die gotische Landschaft oder vielmehr die gotische Kunst als Landschaft hat ein nie dagewesenes Frankreich geschaffen, eine französische Humanität, Horizontlinien, Städtesilhouetten, kurz gesagt eine Poetik, die aus ihr hervorgeht und nicht aus der Geologie oder den Einrichtungen der Capetinger.[1)]

LARS LERUP

Wenn man in Bezug auf Architektur von einer formalen Geographie sprechen kann, in deren Zentrum, sagen wir, der Klassizismus steht, so kann man auch von einer psychologischen Landschaft sprechen. Wie Henri Focillon andeutet, kann eine solche Landschaft national begründet und begrenzt sein. In den Vereinigten Staaten, zum Beispiel, besetzt das Einfamilienhaus mit seinen unterschiedlich definierten Räumen (und deren dunklen, sorgsam verborgenen Schamkabinetten) das psychologische Zentrum. In Italien dagegen (wo Monica Bonvicini geboren wurde) ist es vielleicht die Piazza, ein öffentlicher Schauplatz. Aber ob «Zuhause» oder «Piazza», jeder architektonisch definierte Raum setzt Grenzen.

Die psychologische Landschaft kann man sich als eine flache, mehr oder weniger runde Scheibe vorstellen, deren wabbelnder Rand sich in Schwindel erregendem Tempo um das sklerotische, fast reglose Zentrum dreht. In den äusseren Bezirken greift das straffe Regime

LARS LERUP lebt und schreibt in Stockholm und Houston, Texas.

MONICA BONVICINI, 2 TONNEN ALTE NATIONALGALERIE, 1998, *Bauschutt der Fassade der alten Nationalgalerie Berlin, Grösse variabel / rubble from the façade of the old Berlin National Gallery, dimensions variable.*

der Architektur nicht mehr; Kunst, Psychose, Chaos und Phobien steigern dort zusätzlich das turbulente Tempo. Die Akteure im Zentrum sind dazu verdammt, sich mit dem ganz Banalen und Vorhersagbaren zu begnügen, während jene, die am äusseren Rand dahinjagen, ihre eigenen Regeln aufstellen können. Manche sehen es so, dass die Architektur am Rand als etwas Feindliches gilt, als Übeltäter und Hindernis für jede Art von Freiheit, während die Architektur im Zentrum als etwas Bewährtes und Vertrautes nicht angefochten wird. Doch nirgendwo innerhalb dieser psychologischen Zone entgeht das Widerstrebende letztlich Michel Foucaults «disziplinarischen Mechanismen», das heisst, die scheinbare Freiheit am Rand ist in Wahrheit eine Illusion.

Monica Bonvicini meinte einmal: «Die Architektur hat etwas Grundlegendes, das ich in der Kunst manchmal vermisse.»[2] Angenommen dieses «Grundlegende» ist ihre praktische Seite – ihre Geborgenheit verleihende Notwendigkeit –, so ist sie gar nicht so verschieden von der Malerei, die früher ohne (vergoldeten) Rahmen zu nichts taugte. Wie dem auch sei, Bonvicini arbeitet als Künstlerin mit und in der Architektur, um diese in den alles andere als grundlegenden Bereich der Kunst (also das Konzeptuelle und nicht Pragmatische schlechthin) einzubringen. In der psychologischen Region, in der Bonvicini – zumindest teilweise – ihre Kunst ausübt, wirft sich der Schatten des «Grundlegenden» der Architektur quer über die annähernd kreisförmige Landschaft. Doch das «Grundlegende» ist, wenn nicht durch etwas anderes, so doch von den Zentrifugalkräften am Rand, durcheinander gewirbelt worden, so dass am wirbelnden Rand das, was gewöhnlich oben ist, sich nun unten oder auf der Seite befindet. Doch da Architektur und Kunst nach wie vor Teil der wirklichen Welt sind, bleibt die Gravitation, wie durcheinander gewirbelt auch immer, in Kraft.

Während sie sich schwankend am äusseren Rand dieser konstruierten psychologischen Landschaft entlangbewegt, ist sich Bonvicini dieses a r c h i t e k t o n i s c h e n S c h a t t e n s offensichtlich bewusst. Das deutet zumindest eine frühe Kindheitserinnerung an, von der sie im Interview mit Andrea Bowers erzählt:

Der Garten um das Haus meiner Eltern war von einer grossen Hecke umgeben. Sie liebten diese Hecke, weil sie ihre Privatsphäre schützte, mir war sie gar nicht recht, weil ich nicht sehen konnte, was draussen auf der Strasse vor sich ging. Ich erinnere mich, wenn ich nervös oder zornig war, riet mir mein Vater, quer durch den Garten und in die Hecke hineinzulaufen. Das habe ich oft gemacht. War ein gutes Gefühl…[3]

Versteht man dies als frühe Erfahrung der grundlegenden Einschränkung durch Architektur, so führt uns das zu den handfesteren Beispielen in Bonvicinis späteren Arbeiten. Aber wenden wir uns zuerst diesem I n - d i e - H e c k e - L a u f e n zu.

MONICA BONVICINI, DRAWING FOR ANXIETY ATTACK (No. 7), 2003, *collage and mixed media on paper, 16 1/8 x 69 11/16" / Collage und Mischtechnik auf Papier, 41 x 177 cm.*

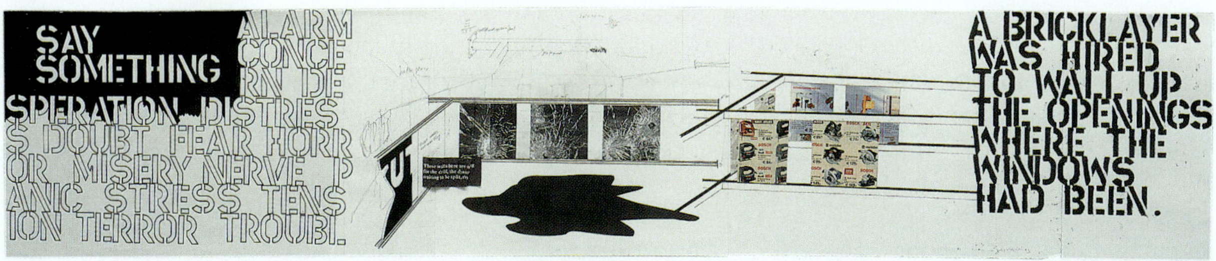

Sich ungebremst in eine Hecke fallen zu lassen und von einem Gewirr gestutzter und mit Blättern versehener Äste getragen zu werden, mag ein wunderbares Gefühl sein, ist als Geste jedoch nicht so dramatisch wie der von Harry Shunk photographierte, berühmte Sprung von Yves Klein mit dem Kommentar: «Der Maler des Raums schleudert sich selbst ins Leere!» Dennoch sind beide gleichermassen architektonisch. Bonvicini wirft sich in die architektonische Materie hinein – im wahrsten Sinne des Wortes in die Wand hinein. Wogegen Klein in den architektonischen Raum hineinspringt, was an der sich rasch nähernden Pariser Strasse zu erkennen ist. Dennoch gibt es einen grossen Unterschied: Kleins Sprung war inszeniert. Eine Ähnlichkeit zwischen beiden wiederum liegt darin, dass sowohl Klein wie Bonvicini es darauf angelegt haben, dem Betrachter das Gefühl einer extremen Erfahrung zu vermitteln, sei es Furcht, Freude oder auch Schmerz.

Diesem «Eintauchen» trotz unvermeidlicher Widerstände begegnen wir auch in Bonvicinis Arbeit A VIOLENT, TROPICAL, CYCLONIC PIECE OF ART HAVING WIND SPEEDS OF OR IN EXCESS OF 75 MILES PER HOUR (Ein heftiges, tropisches, zyklonisches Kunstwerk mit Windgeschwindigkeiten von 75 Meilen oder mehr pro Stunde, 1998) oder in HAUSFRAU SWINGING (1997). Da phänomenologische Bedeutung durch Praxis zustande kommt, wirft dieses Sich-in-unterschiedlich-dichte-Materien-Stürzen eine fundamentale Frage auf: Was ist Materie? Und spezifischer: Was ist architektonische Materie? Oder genauer: Weshalb ist Architektur so einschränkend, ja buchstäblich abstossend – insbesondere hier, am Rande der psychologischen Landschaft?

Wenn alles, dessen Decke höher als 240 Zentimeter ist, Architektur sein soll, gibt es dann faschistische Architektur? Nein. Gibt es sexistische Architektur? Nein. Aber es gibt den faschistischen Raum und auch den sexistischen, geschlechtsspezifischen und befreiten Raum. Wie ist das möglich? Dadurch, dass jegliche Bedeutung des Raums erst durch seine Nutzung entsteht. Sie ist kein Element der baulichen Materie, sondern eine soziale Konstruktion – ein Produkt des Aufeinandertreffens von Menschen und Gebäuden. Die Menschen machen den Raum. (Abu Ghraib, so erzählt man uns heute, ist jetzt ein «gutes» Gefängnis, obwohl es vor einigen Monaten noch die Hölle war.) In Bonvicinis Rauminstallationen I BELIEVE IN THE SKIN OF THINGS AS IN THAT OF WOMEN (Ich glaube an die Haut der Dinge wie an jene der Frauen, 1999) und STONEWALL 3 (2002) haben wir auch gesehen, dass der Raum dem Ansturm des Körpers widersteht; es tut weh, wenn man mit der Faust auf eine Wand schlägt, auch wenn das in HAMMERING OUT (AN OLD ARGUMENT) / (EINEN ALTEN STREIT) AUSBÜGELN (1998) nicht so sehr der Fall zu sein scheint.

Bonvicinis beharrliche Infragestellung des architektonischen Widerstandes ist ein wichtiger Prozess, der am Ende gar nicht auf eine Antwort aus ist oder sein muss. Diese Fragen kann man nur angehen, wenn man sich selbst in den Bedeutungsstrom stürzt. Philosophen wie Gianni Vattimo aus Turin haben wunderbar dargelegt, dass es vielleicht nicht möglich ist, dieses grundlegende Hindernis zu überwinden oder «aufzuheben»; wir können uns nur daran gewöhnen, es «verwinden» – wie man sich an eine drohende Erkältung oder einen nicht wirklich tragfähigen Gedanken *(pensiere debole)* gewöhnt. Bonvicini scheint sich nicht einfach «daran gewöhnen» zu wollen, zumindest demonstriert ihre Arbeit (in deren Zentrum es immer um Widerstand geht), dass alles immer einen Versuch wert ist. Vermutlich kann Bonvicini mit der Resignation nichts anfangen, sondern zieht es vor, auf Kollisionskurs zu gehen.

TURNING WALLS (Drehwände, 2001) ist vielleicht Bonvicinis rätselhafteste Annäherung an die Grundfrage nach dem Zugang zur architektonischen Materie. Man wird dazu gebracht, um dieses Windrad aus unzugänglich eingemauerter Ewigkeit herumzugehen – kein

MONICA BONVICINI, STAIRWAY TO HELL, 2003, steel stairs, chains, broken safety glass, spot lights, installation for "poetic Justice" 8th International Istanbul Biennale, detail view, all over size: 334 5/8 x 141 3/4 x 157" / Stahltreppe, Ketten, gesprungenes Sicherheitsglas, Scheinwerfer, Teilansicht, insgesamt 850 x 360 x 400 cm.

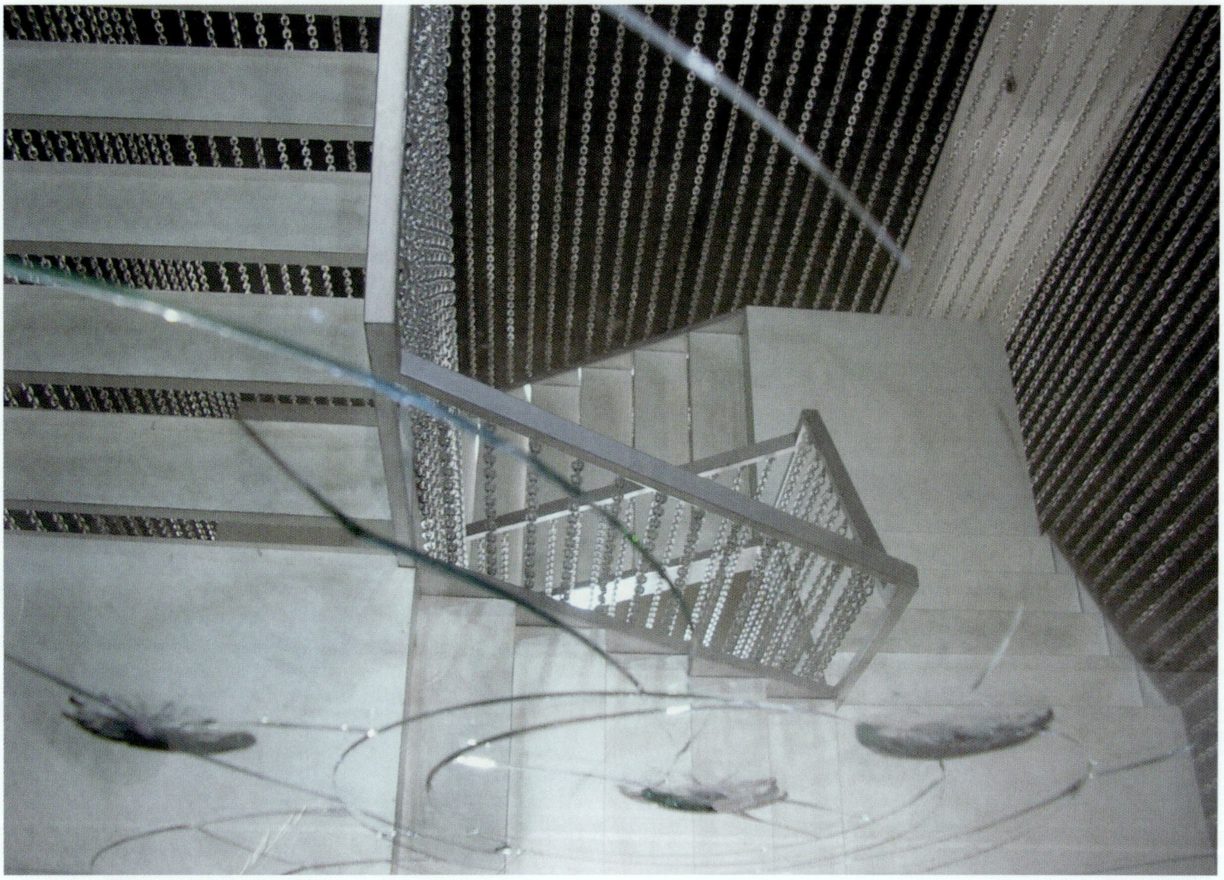

Zugang, keine Antworten, nur Hindernisse sind im Angebot. Bonvicinis vorbereitende Zeichnungen mit Büroklammern und Sicherheitsnadeln auf weissem Hintergrund könnten als genetischer Code des architektonischen Widerstandes verstanden werden. Lange Ketten ineinander verhakter Büroklammern ergeben übereinander gelegt ein loses Gitter. Mit Sicherheitsnadeln, die zur Fixierung dienen, werden diese Ketten dann aneinander und am Hintergrund befestigt, wie um anzudeuten, dass im Inneren der architektonischen Materie (in diesem Fall eine gewobene «Wand» entsprechend Gottfried Sempers Vergleich zwischen «Wand» und «Gewand» in seiner Zürcher Vorlesung von 1856) immer ein Sicherungselement (oder ein Klebstoff) die Bestandteile der Wand zusammenhält, sei es die Armierung bei einer Betonwand oder der Mörtel bei einer Backsteinwand. Es ist schwer zu sehen, was eigentlich was ist: Ohne Backsteine entsteht keine Wand, selbst mit allem Mörtel der Welt nicht. Und dasselbe gilt für Heftklammern und Sicherheitsnadeln.

(Übersetzung: Suzanne Schmidt)

1) Henri Focillon, *Das Leben der Formen,* aus dem Franz. übers. v. Gritta Baerlocher, Francke Verlag, Bern 1954, S. 31.

2) Monica Bonvicini, *Scream & Shake,* Le Magasin Grenoble / Kunst-Werke Berlin / P.S.1 Contemporary Art Center MoMA, New York 2001/2002, S. 36.

3) Ebenda.

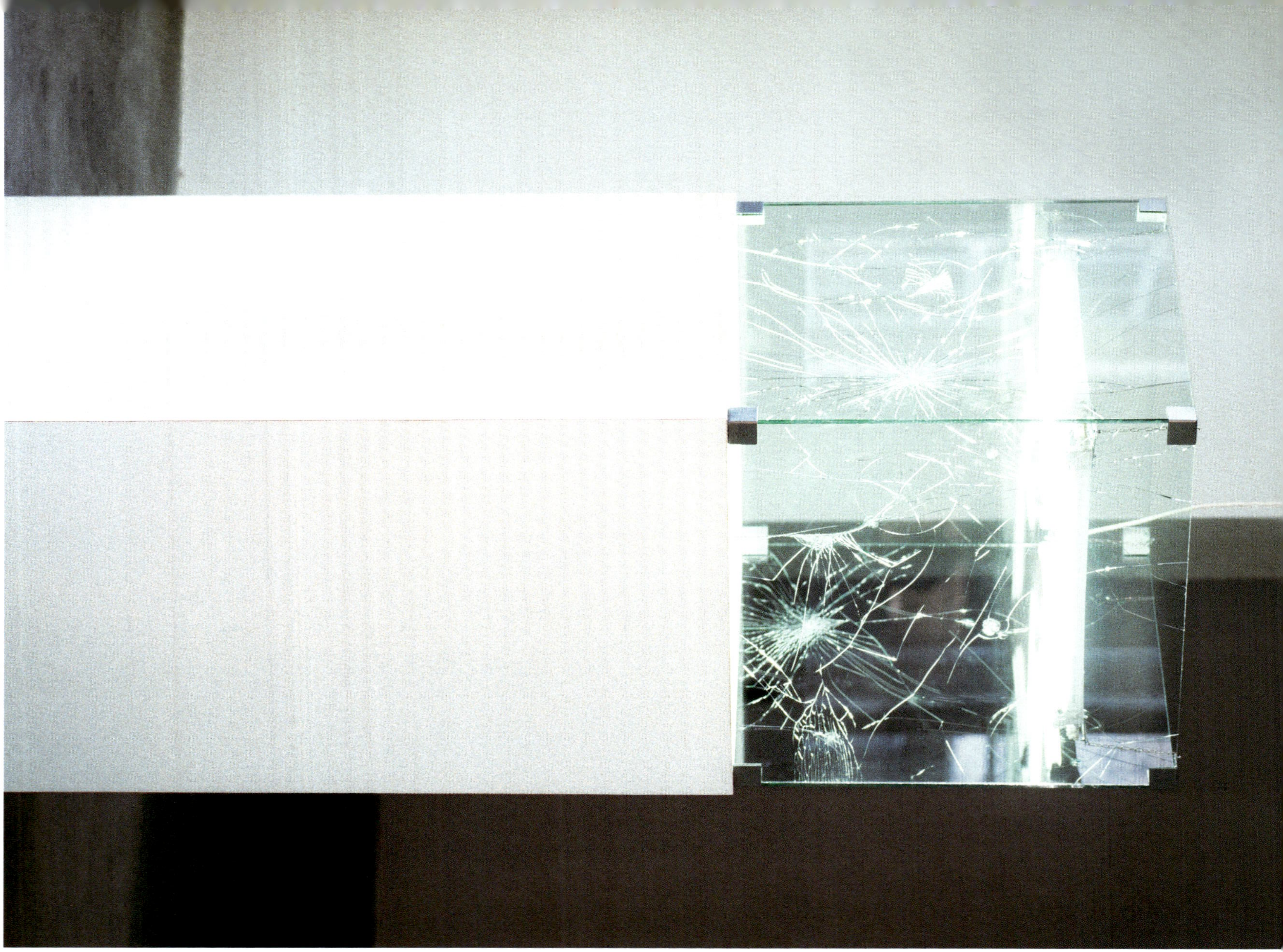

MONICA BONVICINI, *WHITE*, 2003, *fluorescent lights, broken safety glass, aluminum corners, base. Glass cube: 26 x 26 x 26"; base:* $46^{1}/_{16}$ *x* $27^{1}/_{8}$ *x* $27^{1}/_{8}$*" / Leuchtstoffröhren, gesprungenes Sicherheitsglas, Aluminiumecken, Sockel. Glaskubus: 66 x 66 x 66 cm; Sockel: 117 x 69 x 69 cm.*

MONICA BONVICINI, *DON'T MISS A SEC*, 2003/2004, *detail view, two-way mirror structure, stainless-steel toilet unit, concrete floor, aluminum, fluorescent lights, Art Basel 2004,* $98^{7}/_{16}$ *x* $55^{1}/_{8}$ *x* $74^{13}/_{16}$*" / Teilansicht, Einwegspiegelkabine, Edelstahl-WC, Betonboden, Aluminium, Leuchtstoffröhren, 250 x 140 x 190 cm.*

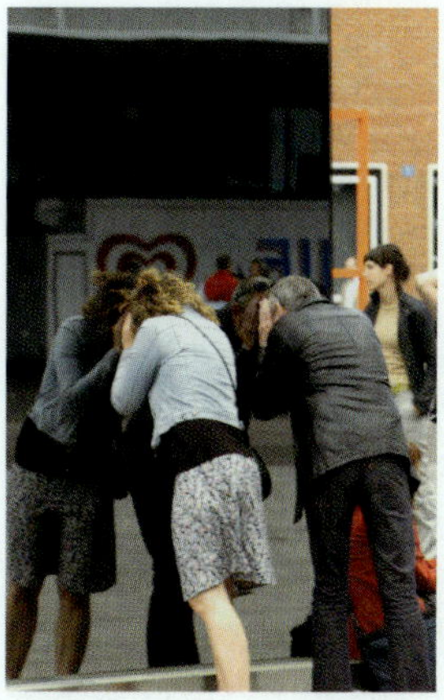

JÖRG HEISER

Geheimnisse des Satzbaus

Architecture is the ultimate erotic act, carry it to excess, schreibt Bernard Tschumi in einem seiner *Advertisements for Architecture* (1976).[1] *A window is a man, it stands upright,* insistierte der Architekt Auguste Perret im Streit mit seinem Schüler Le Corbusier um horizontale versus vertikale Fenster.[2] *Shotgun* (Gewehr) heisst ein Pilz, der auf verrottendem Holz wächst und sich auf Wänden besonders aggressiv festsetzt. *Add elegance to your property,*[3] lautet der Slogan einer kalifornischen Firma für Gartenzäune.

Bonmots, Titel und Slogans wie diese sind für Monica Bonvicini nicht in erster Linie Verweis auf eine Quelle, ein Hinweispfeil nach draussen (*fishing for references* und damit *for compliments*), sondern – in entgegengesetzter Richtung – herangeschafftes Material, hineingekarrt in die skulpturale Produktion wie Schnäppchen aus dem Zitate-Baumarkt. Sie sind Rohstoff, so wie Rihgips, Ziegel, Stahl, Pressspan oder Glas. Sie fühlen sich auf eine bestimmte Weise an, haben bestimmte Eigenschaften der Verarbeitbarkeit, sind geschmeidig, grob oder zerbrechen leicht.

Architecture is the ultimate erotic act, carry it to excess, steht in schwarzen Grossbuchstaben auf der weissen Wand. Der Satz ist ein Witz; er klingt widersinnig, denkt man an die logistische und praktische Widerspenstigkeit des «Akts» des Bauens. Aber genau deshalb wohl muss Tschumi in Superlativen formulieren: «ultimativ», «Exzess», eine rhetorische Beschwörung von Übermut, kühnem Wagnis, radikaler Subjektivität, Hemmungslosigkeit, Schamlosigkeit. Es ist superernst gemeint. Und nun kommt der entscheidende Dreh bei Bonvicini: Sie behandelt die kühne rhetorische Behauptung als konkrete, praktische Handlungsanweisung. Sie nimmt sie beim Wort. Sie sprüht sie nicht in verspielter Hip-Hop-Graffiti-Ästhetik, sondern in der schnellen, schnörkellosen Handschrift politischer Kampfparolen an die Wand. In der Installation im Migros Museum Zürich (2003) platzierte sie direkt davor die Arbeit STONEWALL 3 (2003): eine frei stehende Konstruktion aus galvanisierten Stahlrohren, in denen Ketten zu grossen quadratischen Maschen verknotet sind, dazwischen gebrochenes Sicherheitsglas, ebenfalls in die Rohre eingepasst. Das Ganze sieht aus wie eine Mischung aus Trainingsparcours für Guerillakämpfer und sadomasochistischem Klettergerüst. «Stonewall» ist eine symbolisch höchst aufgeladene Vokabel der Schwulenbewegung: So hiess die Bar in Lower Manhattan, vor deren Tür sich 1969 Schwule erstmals militant gegen eine diskriminierende Polizeirazzia wehrten. Als Rethorik schien der «ultimate erotic act» nichts anderes als eine architektonische Penetrationsphantasie, die sich hinein in den urbanen Raum bohrt, ohne sich

---

JÖRG HEISER ist Redaktor der Kunstzeitschrift *Frieze* und lebt in Berlin.

um dessen administrative Restriktionen und praktische Grenzen zu scheren. Bezogen auf diese konkrete gebaute Struktur aber geht es nun einerseits um «wirklichen» sexuellen Exzess, um deviante, zu Zeiten von «Stonewall» ausdrücklich illegale Sexpraktiken, andererseits um libidinös besetzte Militanz.

Bonvicini bezieht die männerdominierte Sphäre der Stararchitekten nicht auf die Sphäre männlich-schwulen Sadomasochismus, um einfach Homosozialität mit Homosexualität gleichzusetzen. Vielmehr geht es darum, diese Homosozialität mit genau jenen libidinösen Implikationen zu konfrontieren, die sie in dem Masse verdrängt, in dem sie sich der Akzeptanz ihrer überwiegend heterosexuellen, konservativen, männlichen Auftraggeber aus Politik und Wirtschaft versichert. Bernard Tschumis Beschwörung des Erotischen ist angesichts dessen nur die Flucht nach vorn, die abstrakt und leer bleibt. Und diese leere Abstraktion wird komisch, bildet man sie konkret ab. MIES CORNER (2002) ist eine im rechten Winkel frei stehende Konstruktion aus Stahl, in deren linken Flügel drehbare vertikale Jalousie-Blätter eingepasst sind, während sich im rechten eine grossformatige Tuschzeichnung unter Plexiglas befindet. Diese funktioniert ähnlich brutal direkt wie die berühmten *Bringing the war home*-Collagen Martha Roslers (Den Krieg mit nach Hause bringen, 1967–72): nur dass diesmal nicht Opfer des Vietnamkriegs in die sorgsam designte bürgerliche Wohnwelt zurückgebracht werden, sondern drei schwule Protagonisten eines komplizierten Sadomaso-Fetischspiels in den Barcelona-Pavillon mit seinem höchst kostbaren Marmor, von dem vier verschiedene Sorten verwendet wurden (römischer Travertin, grüner Alpenmarmor, griechisch-antiker grüner Marmor und goldener Onyx aus dem Atlasgebirge). Bei einer zunächst besonders nüchtern anmutenden Konstruktion entpuppt sich das Material als versteckter Fetisch, dessen Ausgesuchtheit sich dem Kennerauge erschliesst wie ein sexueller Code (die Jalousienblätter in Bonvicinis Arbeit erscheinen selbst wiederum als Code für dieses entkörperlichte «Kennerauge»).

Eine gemeinsam mit Sam Durant gemachte Zeichnung offenbart eine weitere libidinöse Implikation der Homosozialität, jene der infantilen Regression: Drei Herren sitzen in Abendgarderobe am Dinner-Tisch, mit leicht gezwungenem Lächeln für den Schnappschuss (SANDBOX, 2003); vor ihnen sind die Hände eines Architekten beim Zeichnen einmontiert. Über den Köpfen der drei – es sind Peter Eisenman, Philip Johnson und Frank O. Gehry – prangt der Satz: *Why should they play in my sandbox if they don't want me to play in theirs?*[4] Es ist, als denke einer der drei das gerade. Architektur, besonders jene von Stararchitekten wie diesen, geht immer mit einer mehr oder weniger kolossalen Geltendmachung von Erhabenheit einher. Die Sandkastenspieler sind immerhin diejenigen, die das Guggenheim Bilbao (Gehry), das Denkmal für die ermordeten Juden Europas (Eisenman) und das Seagram-Building (Johnson mit Mies van der Rohe) erbaut haben. Kindlicher Narzissmus, eifersüchtige Konkurrenz und gute Miene zum bösen Spiel verschränken sich vor diesem Hintergrund zu einer Beschreibung, die zwischen Selbstironie und trotzigem Ernst schwankt.

Doch bei aller Koketterie mit dem Sandkasten bleibt ein Ewigkeitsanspruch der Architektur, dem sich in der Moderne nur wenige – etwa der Brite Cedric Price mit seiner ausdrücklichen Apologie des Abrissunternehmens – widersetzten. «Break it/Fix it» hiess die Ausstellung, die Bonvicini und Durant zusammen in der Wiener Secession 2003 bestritten, in deren Zusammenhang auch die genannte Zeichnung entstand. Im gleichnamigen Video (2003) wird das Errichten und Einreissen am Wort-als-Skulptur durchgespielt: Wir sehen die beiden Künstler aus der Perspektive der Überwachungskamera, wie sie um ein hölzernes ANGST von der Grösse eines Autos herumstreichen wie Katzen um den heissen Brei. Harte Schnitte suggerieren das Vergehen langer, gedehnter Zeit, bis sie diverse mehr oder weniger geeignete Werkzeuge zum Einreissen der Holzkonstruktion zum Einsatz bringen – nur um daraus (weitere harte Schnitte machen es möglich) wieder unversehens ein FEAR von gleicher Grösse entstehen zu lassen. Aus dem Ewigkeitsanspruch wird also in der Heimatstadt Freuds – vor allem aber im gnadenlosen Loop des Videoschnitts – der *Circulus vitiosus* der Angstneurose.

Die Strategie des wörtlichen Übersetzens verbindet sich also mit der des Errichtens und Einreissens in einem. Eine Arbeit von 1999 ist benannt nach

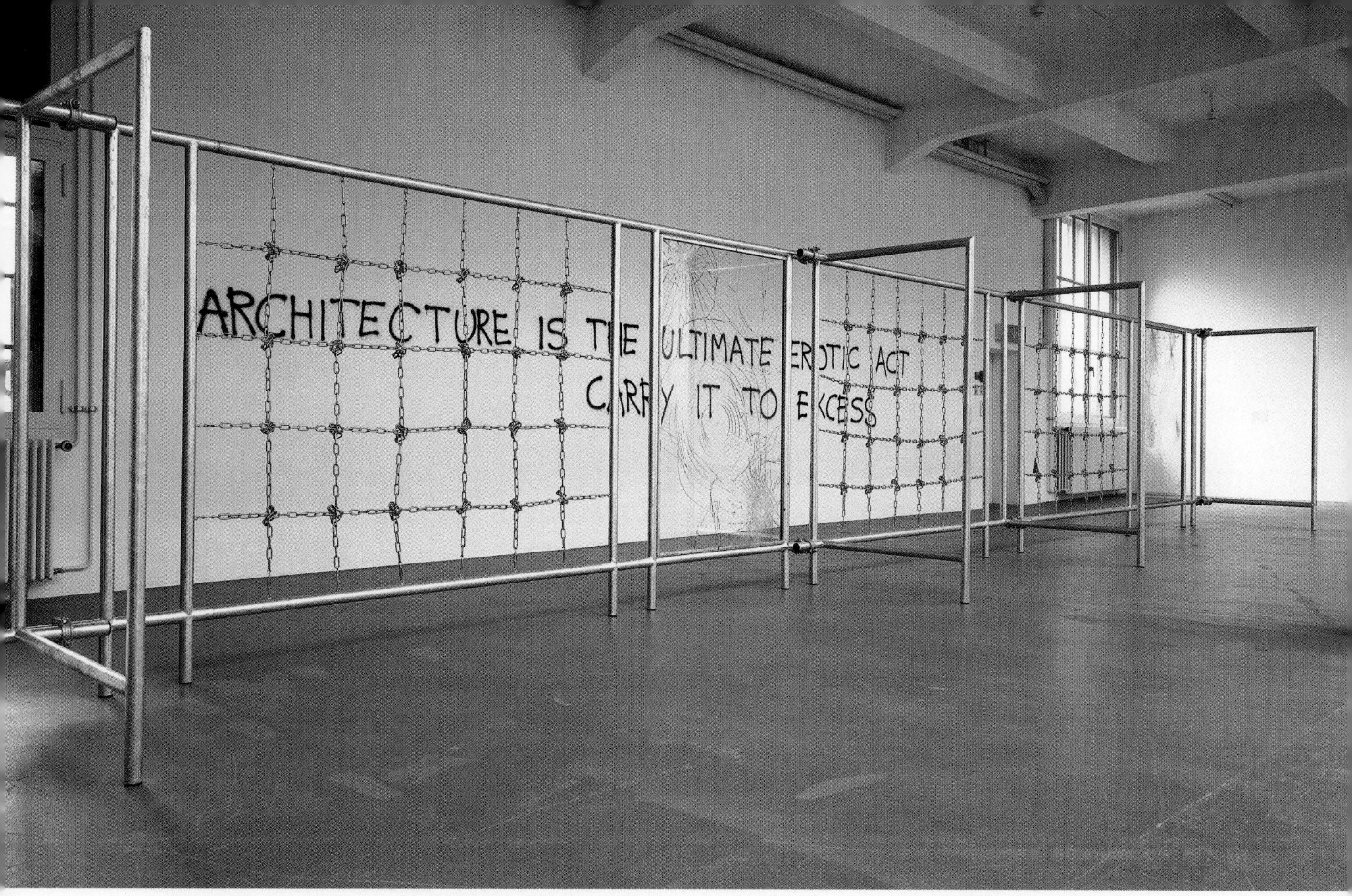

MONICA BONVICINI, STONEWALL 3, 2002, galvanized steel, chains, broken safety glass, installation Kunsthalle Zürich, 78¾ x 484¼ x 39⁷⁄₁₆" / verzinkter Stahl, Ketten, gesprungenes Sicherheitsglas, 200 x 1230 x 100 cm.

einem denkwürdigen Zitat über Fassaden von Le Corbusier: I BELIEVE IN THE SKIN OF THINGS AS IN THAT OF WOMEN (Ich glaube an die Haut der Dinge wie an jene der Frauen). Bonvicini stellt die Behauptung auf und reisst sie gleich wieder ein: eine raumartige Schachtel aus Rigipsplatten, an manchen Stellen eingetreten wie ein vandalisiertes öffentliches Klo, mit dreckigen Sprüchen draufgekritzelt. Der ehrwürdige Auguste Perret hatte mit seinem Schüler Le Corbusier über horizontale versus vertikale Fenster gestritten und wird zitiert mit den Worten, *a window is a man, it stands upright,* begleitet von der Karikatur eines knollennasigen Männchens, das mit einer Hand salutiert und mit der anderen an seiner Erektion rumfummelt. Perret hatte «natürlich» mit *man* den aufrecht gehenden Menschen ganz universal gemeint – und doch, implizit, in der befehlsartigen Formulierung, auch den salutierenden, strammstehenden soldatischen Mann, dem Bonvicini nur noch seine Spind- und Latrinenkarikatur verpassen muss, um ihn zum Vorschein zu bringen. Errichten und Erektion..., aber lassen wir das.

DON'T MISS A SEC (2003) mutet minimalistisch opak an und bewegt sich doch im gleichen Dreieck von Fensterblicken, Fassadenhaut und Klospruch-Humor. Der Titel spielt auf den Modus des Sehens und Gesehenwerdens an – nur keine wichtige Begegnung mit einem Semiprominenten verpassen! Die so betitelte Aussenskulptur war vor der Tate Britain platziert, wo alljährlich der Turner Prize unter grosser Medienanteilnahme ausgelobt wird, und vor der Kunstmesse Basel, einem der Haupttermine der inter-

MONICA BONVICINI, DON'T MISS A SEC, 2003/2004, interior and exterior view; two-way mirror structure, stainless-steel toilet unit, concrete floor, aluminum, fluorescent lights, Art Basel 2004, $98\,{}^{7}/_{16}$ *x* $55\,{}^{1}/_{8}$ *x* $74\,{}^{13}/_{16}$*" /*
Innen- und Aussenansicht; Einwegspiegelkabine, Edelstahl-WC, Betonboden, Aluminium, Leuchtstoffröhren, 250 x 140 x 190 cm.

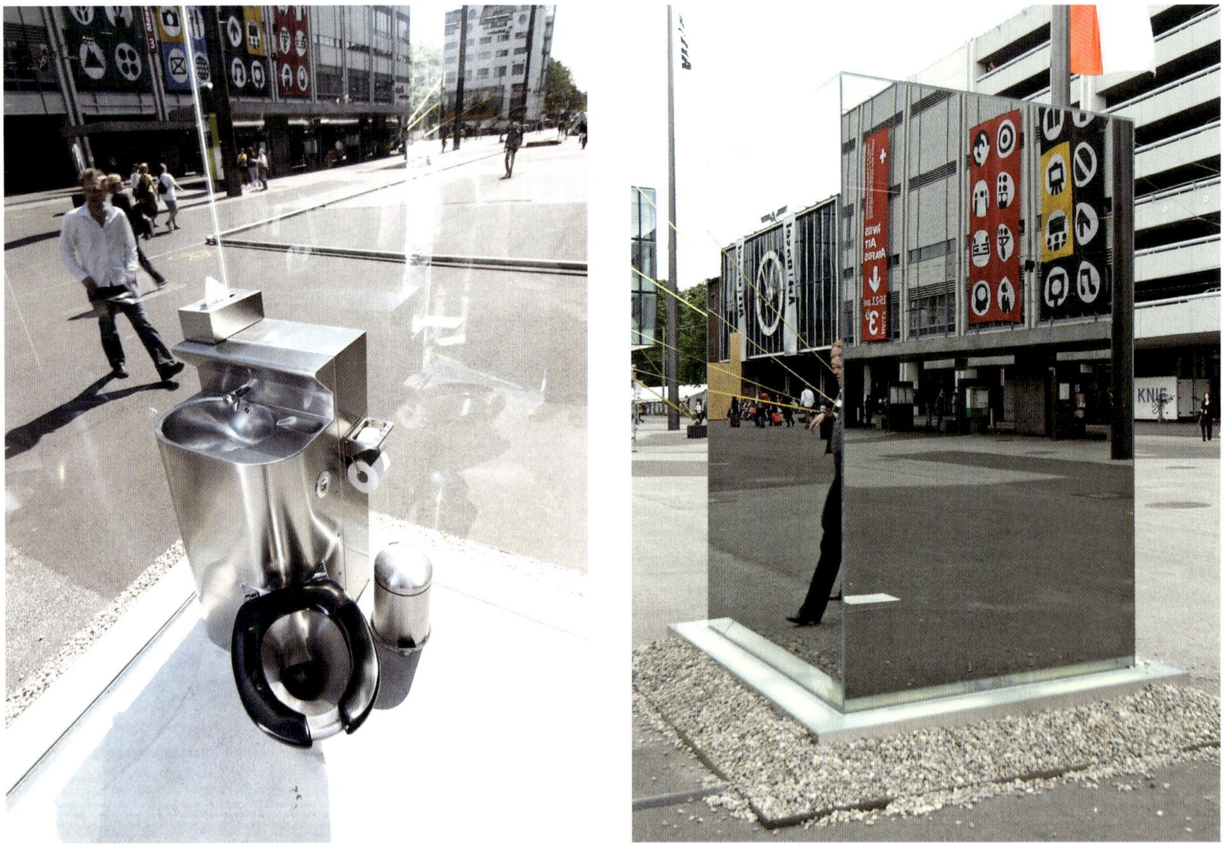

nationalen Kunstwelt. Das Objekt weckt zunächst nicht die Assoziation einer öffentlichen Toilette, es handelt sich um einen rundum verspiegelten, mehr als mannshohen Kubus. Doch wenn man die minimalistisch eingepasste Tür öffnet, erscheint ein voll funktionstüchtiges WC. Und es wird klar, dass man durch die Spiegelflächen hindurch rundum nach draussen blicken kann. So wird die Pointe des Titels offenbar: *Don't Miss a Sec* (Keine Sekunde verpassen), selbst auf dem Klo noch – sehen und nicht gesehen werden. Man weiss zwar, dass man von aussen unsichtbar ist und fühlt sich doch als Exhibitionist: ein absurder Exhibitionismus ohne Zeugen, der zwischen Unbehagen und Angstlust verharrt.

Man könnte nun in diesem Zusammenhang nach der architektonischen Entsprechung der Kastrationsangst forschen – und würde vielleicht mit Bonvicini bei SHOTGUN landen (2003). Wir sehen eine Autofahrt entlang verschlossenen, menschenleeren Ladenfronten und umzäunten Parkplätzen anonymer

Strassenzüge in Los Angeles, zerstückelt und multipliziert in der Loop-Hölle des Videoschnitts. Dazu ertönt wie aus dem Autostereosystem eine Trouvaille des Talkradio; wir hören einen jovialen Seelsorger für verzweifelte Heimwerker, der selten um Lösungen verlegen scheint, wenn es darum geht, dringende Probleme mit Bohrern und Abflussrohren zu lösen. Doch nun gerät er selbst in Verzweiflung, als eine Anruferin den Pilz beschreibt, der aus dem Holzmulch in ihrem Garten kommt und Sporen abschiesst, die bereits Risse in ihrer Hauswand verursacht haben: «Wenn der Pilz aus dem Mulch kommt, Sie werden keine Freude haben an meiner Antwort, dann ist es der *Shotgun*-Pilz, und das ist kein Scherz, den werden Sie nicht mehr los... Ich habe keine Ahnung....»

Das angstbesetzte Absichern gegen Invasionen durch *Shotgun*-Pilze, böse Einbrecher oder gesellschaftliche Konkurrenten bringt sprechende Stilblüten hervor. Ein kalifornischer Werbeslogan für Gartenzäune – *add elegance to your property* – wird bei Bonvicini zum spöttischen Graffito ADD ELEGANCE TO YOUR POVERTY (Ergänzen Sie Ihre Armut durch Eleganz, 2002) – zusammen mit einem stilisierten Gartenzaun ist es in Schwarz auf eine weisse Wand gesprüht. Als ich Bonvicini um einen Beitrag zur Ausstellung «Funky Lessons» (Berlin, Büro Friedrich, 2004) bat, konzipierte sie die Arbeit als räumlichen Eingriff neu, als eine Art Werbeplakatwand, die den Zugang zu den Ausstellungsräumen des Büro Friedrich zu verwehren scheint. Die Arbeit lässt sich als genereller Kommentar zum Zusammenhang von Sicherheitswahn und sozialem Status lesen, nimmt zugleich aber neue Bedeutungen an im lokalen Zusammenhang, in dem sie erscheint. Im Berlin der Gegenwart muss man unweigerlich an die Diskrepanz zwischen Erwartung und Realität denken, was die wirtschaftliche Prosperität der neuen Hauptstadt angeht, und an die Erosion der Sozialleistungen, während die Stadt zugleich von den Superreichen als trashig prickelndes Umfeld entdeckt wird, wo Luxus – anders als in München oder Sankt Moritz – noch auffällt.

Bei Bonvicinis Beitrag zur Istanbul Biennale 2003 ging es nicht darum, den Zugang zu verwehren, sondern ihn zu ermöglichen. Eine frei schwebende Stahltreppe verband den Skulpturenteil der Ausstellung mit der Sektion Videoinstallationen. Sie wurde nur von Kettensträngen zwischen Decke und Boden gehalten; der obere Zugang war von gebrochenem Sicherheitsglas umrahmt. Man fragte sich, ob man sich dieser Konstruktion überhaupt anvertrauen wollte (von Architekten skeptisch beurteilt, erwies sie sich allerdings als erstaunlich stabil). Led Zeppelins «Stairway to Heaven» war eines der Lieder, das nach den Anschlägen des 11. September eine Zeit lang von amerikanischen Radiosendern auf den Index gesetzt wurde. Und nun, als STAIRWAY TO HELL, führt der Weg immer nur vom Skulpturenfriedhof zum Videopurgatorium und wieder zurück.

Der Titel realisiert sich bei Bonvicini als konkrete praktische Entsprechung oder als absurde Allegorie. So oder so werden Sprache und Gebautes in direkten, ruppigen Akten zu- und übereinander gelegt wie Protagonisten einer choreographierten Pornoszene. Zitatfetzen und stummes Material verwandeln sich einander an: Es ist, als würden Wörter und Sätze sich materialisieren und auf der Wand, im Staub, zu Buchstabenbrocken erstarrt physisch präsent werden und als würde umgekehrt das Gebaute sich vollsaugen mit Syntax und Signifikation. Das Unbewusste sei strukturiert wie eine Sprache, heisst es bekanntlich bei Lacan; das Gebaute auch, könnte man mit Bonvicini anfügen, und dass die Struktur des einen nicht ohne die des anderen zu verstehen ist: Übersetzungen sind also gefragt. Diese lesen sich bei Bonvicini aber nicht als säuberliche Gebrauchsanweisung, sondern als dreckiger Witz.

1) «Architektur ist der ultimative erotische Akt, treibt ihn auf die Spitze...» Vgl. Bernard Tschumi, *Architectural Manifestoes*, (London: Architectural Association, 1979), Ausstellungskatalog, unpaginiert, oder: derselbe, *Architecture and Disjunction*, MIT Press, Cambridge, MA, 1998, S. 75.

2) «Ein Fenster ist ein Mensch und steht aufrecht.» Von der Künstlerin zitiert nach: Le Corbusier, «Précisions sur un état présent de l'architecture et de l'urbanisme» (1930), englisch zitiert in B. Columina, «The Split Wall: Domestic Voyeurism», chapter in *Sexuality and Space*, Architectural Press, Princeton 1992, S. 113.

3) «Ergänzen Sie Ihren Besitz durch Eleganz.»

4) «Warum sollen die in meinem Sandkasten spielen, wenn sie mich nicht in ihrem spielen lassen wollen?»

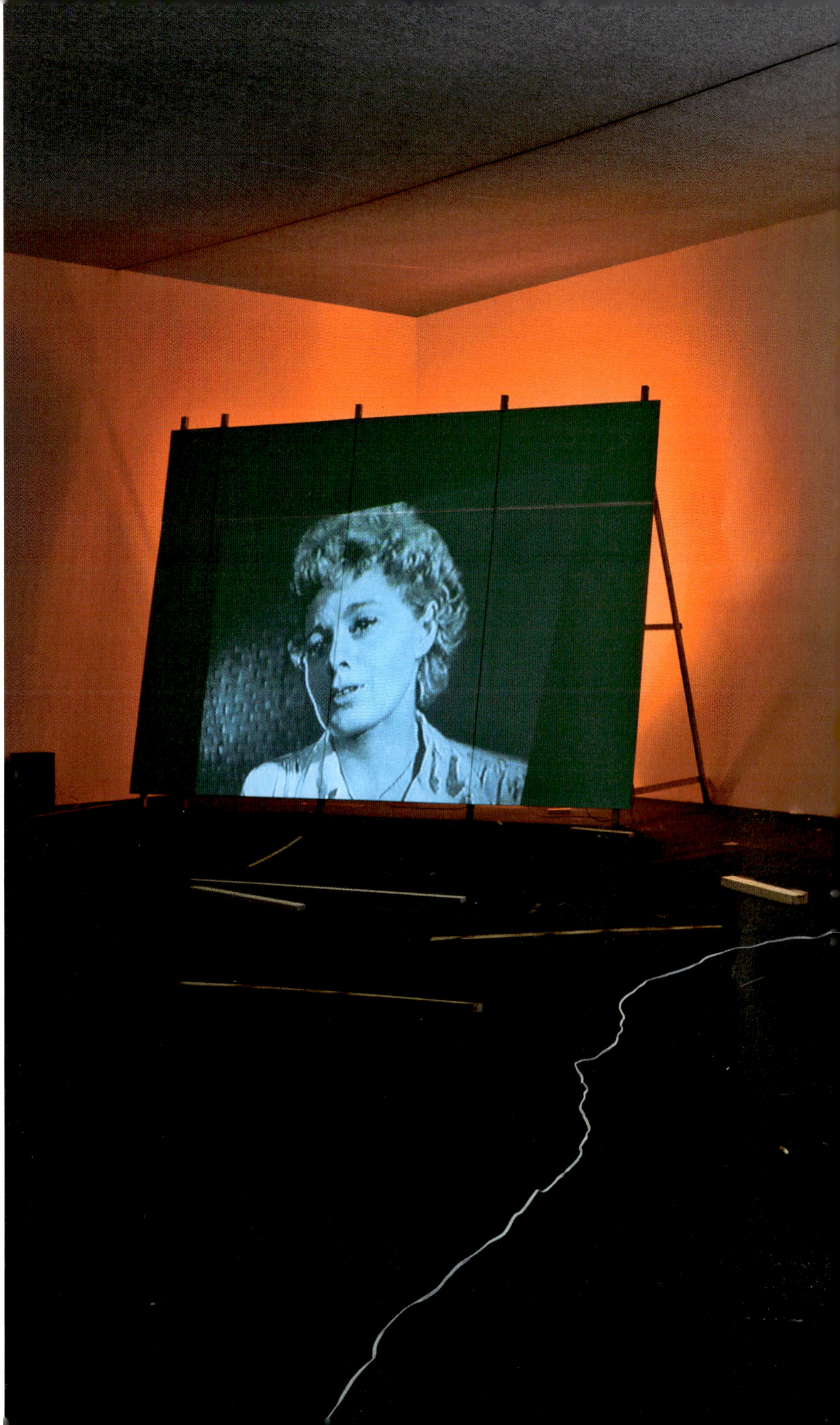

MONICA BONVICINI, DESTROY SHE SAID, 1998, double 60-minute color-video projection, DVD, stereo sound, 2 drywall screens, wooden structures, white paint, sound system, dimensions variable, installation at De Appel, Amsterdam / doppelte 60-minütige Farbvideoprojektion, DVD, Stereoton, 2 Rigips-Projektionswände, Holzgerüst, weisse Farbe, Lautsprecheranlage, Grösse variabel.

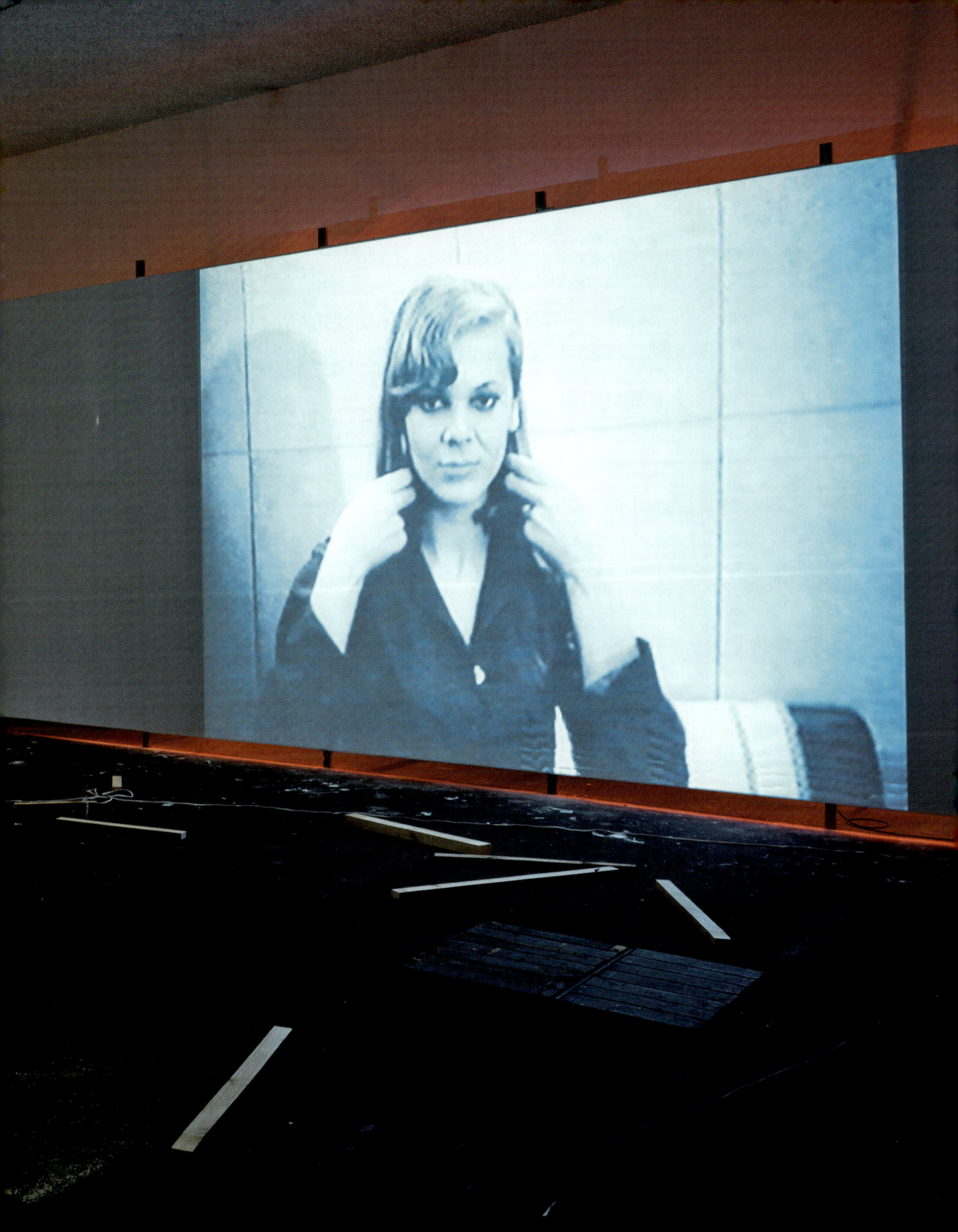

Monica Bonvicini

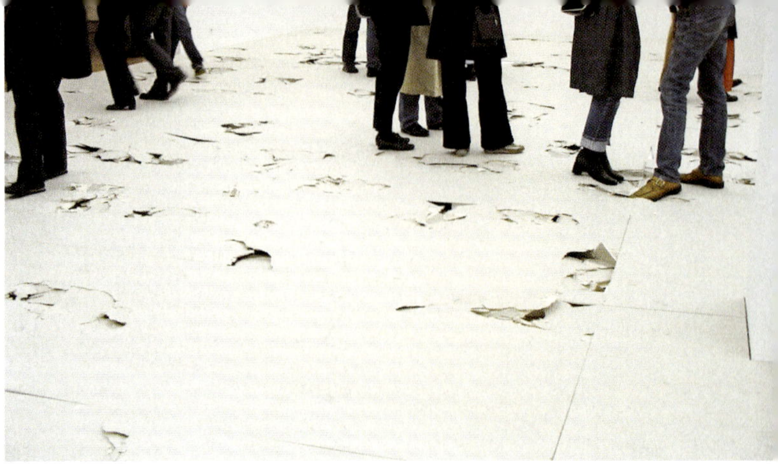

MONICA BONVICINI, PLASTERED, 1998, drywall panels and styrofoam, dimensions variable, installation for "Quobo," Hamburger Hauptbahnhof / Rigipsplatten und Styropor, Grösse variabel.

Secrets of Sentence Building

JÖRG HEISER

"Architecture is the ultimate erotic act, carry it to excess," wrote Bernard Tschumi in one of his *Advertisements for Architecture* (1976).[1] "A window is a man, it stands upright," as Auguste Perret insisted in a dispute with his pupil Le Corbusier about horizontal versus vertical windows.[2] "Shotgun" is a type of fungus that grows on rotten wood and takes particularly aggressive hold of walls. "Add elegance to your property" is the slogan of a Californian firm for their garden fences.

In Monica Bonvicini's hands, catch phrases, names, and slogans like these are not primarily references to another source, pointers to the outside world (fishing for references and hence for compliments), but—on the contrary—specially procured building materials, carted into the sculptural production like bargains from Home Depot. They are her raw materials—plasterboard, tiles, steel, chipboard, and glass. They have a particular feel; they have distinct qualities when it comes to handling them; they can be smooth, rough, or fragile.

JÖRG HEISER is co-editor of the art journal *Frieze* and lives in Berlin.

"Architecture is the ultimate erotic act, carry it to excess" is written in large black letters on the white wall. The sentence is a joke; it sounds nonsensical considering the logistical and practical intractability of the "act" of building. But it's precisely because of this that Tschumi has to resort to superlatives: "ultimate," "excess." A rhetorical invocation of wantonness, dauntless audacity, radical subjectivity, abandon, shamelessness. The intention is utterly serious. Which brings us to the crucial twist in Bonvicini's work: she treats the bold rhetorical statement as a concrete, practical instruction to the user. She takes it at its word. She doesn't spray it onto the wall in imitation of the playful aesthetic of hip-hop graffiti but chooses instead the swift, unembellished hand-writing of political battle cries. In the installation in the Migros Museum Zürich (2003) she placed the work STONEWALL 3 (2003) directly in front of it: a free-standing construction made of galvanized steel pipes, with chains inside them knotted into huge stitches, interspersed by broken security glass, also fitted into the pipes. The whole thing looks like a combined obstacle course for guerrilla fighters and sadomasochistic climbing frame. "Stonewall" has a

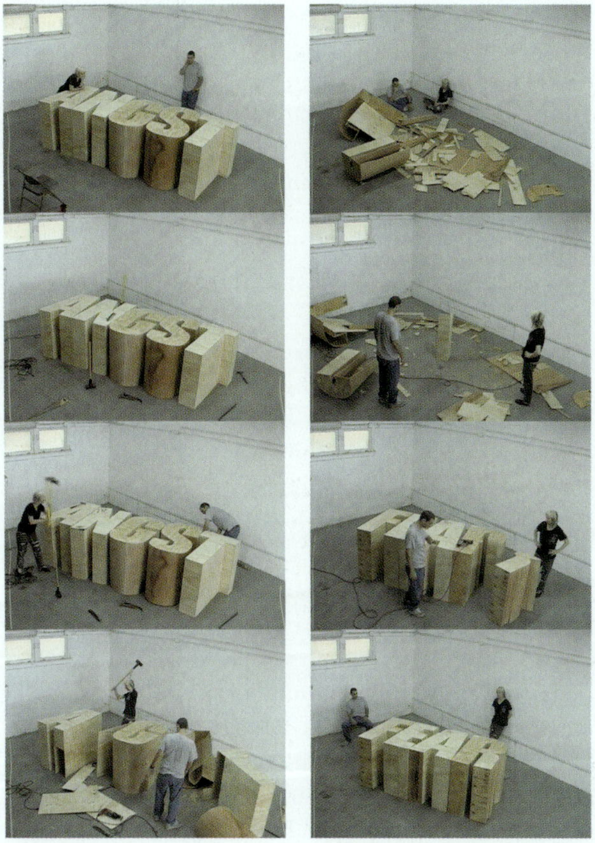

MONICA BONVICINI & SAM DURANT, BREAK IT FIX IT, 2003, stills from the 11 min. 10 sec. color video, part of the eponymous installation at Vienna Secession / Szenen aus dem 11 Min. 10 Sek. langen Farbvideo, Teil der gleichnamigen Installation in der Wiener Sezession.

highly charged symbolic meaning for the gay community; it was the name of the bar in Lower Manhattan where militant gays first went out into the street and stood up (in 1969) against a discriminatory police raid. In terms of the rhetoric, the "ultimate erotic act" seemed to be nothing less than an architectural penetration fantasy, boring into the urban sprawl without paying heed to its administrative constraints or practical limits. On one hand, in the context of this physically present, built structure it is about "real" sexual excess—about supposedly deviant sexual practices that were specifically illegal in the days of New York's Stonewall—on the other hand, it is about libido-laden militancy.

Bonvicini doesn't relate the male-dominated world of star architects to the world of gay male sadomasochism merely in order to equate homosociality with homosexuality. On the contrary, the point is to confront this homosociality with precisely those libidinous implications it suppresses in direct proportion to the extent that it seeks to secure the acceptance of its predominantly heterosexual, conservative, male clients in politics and business. In that sense, Bernard Tschumi's reference to the erotic act is about seizing the bull by the horns, but in a manner that remains abstract and empty. And any concrete illustration of this empty abstraction soon becomes comical. MIES CORNER (2002) is a free-standing, right-angled steel construction, with rotating vertical strips in its left wing and a large-format ink drawing under Plexiglas in the right wing. The latter operates with a brutal directness reminiscent of Martha Rosler's famous *Bringing the war home* collages (1967–72): only that this time it is not victims of the Vietnam War transferred into a painstakingly designed bourgeois domestic world, but the three gay protagonists of a complicated SM fetish game who are transported into the Barcelona Pavilion with its immensely precious, four different kinds of marble (Roman travertine, green Alpine marble, ancient Greek green marble, and golden onyx from the Atlas mountains). While the construction seems sober in the extreme, the material turns out to be a secret fetish, whose exclusivity is legible—like a sexual code—to the eye of the insider (the vertical slatted blind in Bonvicini's piece looks like a code for the disembodied "insider's eye").

A drawing made together with Sam Durant reveals yet another libidinous implication of homosociality, in this case concerning infantile regression: Three men in tuxedos are sitting at a dinner table, with mildly contrived smiles for the camera (SANDBOX, 2003); in front of them the hands of an architect engaged in the act of drawing have been added. Above the heads of the three—Peter Eisenman, Philip Johnson und Frank O. Gehry—we see the words "Why should they play in my sandbox if they don't want me to play in theirs?" as though we were reading the

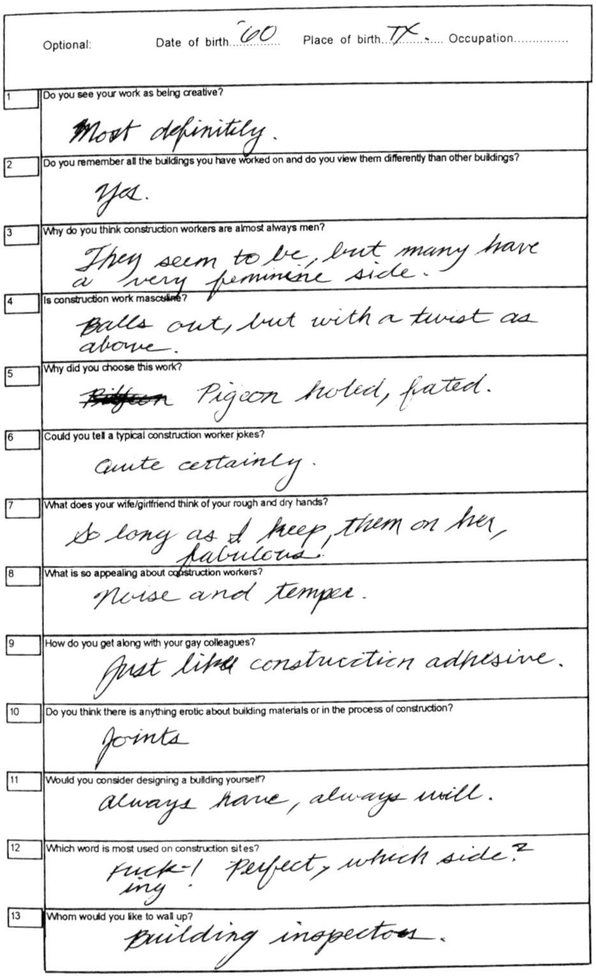

Optional: Date of birth '60 Place of birth TX. Occupation

1 Do you see your work as being creative?
Most definitely.

2 Do you remember all the buildings you have worked on and do you view them differently than other buildings?
Yes.

3 Why do you think construction workers are almost always men?
They seem to be, but many have a very feminine side.

4 Is construction work masculine?
Balls out, but with a twist as above.

5 Why did you choose this work?
~~Pidgeon~~ Pigeon holed, fated.

6 Could you tell a typical construction worker jokes?
Quite certainly.

7 What does your wife/girlfriend think of your rough and dry hands?
So long as I keep them on her, fabulous!

8 What is so appealing about construction workers?
Noise and temper.

9 How do you get along with your gay colleagues?
Just like construction adhesive.

10 Do you think there is anything erotic about building materials or in the process of construction?
Joints

11 Would you consider designing a building yourself?
Always have, always will.

12 Which word is most used on construction sites?
Fuck-ing! Perfect, which side?

13 Whom would you like to wall up?
Building inspectors.

mind of one of the three. Architecture, particularly by star architects such as these, always comes with a more or less colossal assertion of the sublime. After all, the sandbox players are responsible for the Bilbao Guggenheim Museum (Gehry), the Memorial to the Murdered Jews of Europe (Eisenman), and the Seagram Building (Johnson with Mies van der Rohe). Childlike narcissism, jealous rivalry, and putting a good face on things all combine against this background to arrive at a contention that veers between self-irony and stubborn solemnity.

But despite this flirtation with the sandbox there are still architecture's claims to immortality, which few Modernists have dared confront—the British architect Cedric Price being one such, with his explicit apology for demolition work. "Break it/Fix it" was the name of the exhibition that Bonvicini and Durant put on together in the Vienna Secession in 2003, for which they made SANDBOX. In a video of the same name (2003), the erection and demolition of the word-as-sculpture is played out: we see the two artists as though through a security camera, prowling round a wooden ANGST (Fear), beating around the proverbial bush. Abrupt editing suggests the passage of long stretches of time, until they set about destroying the wooden construction with a variety of more or less suitable tools—only to find (more abrupt cuts come to their assistance) that by mistake they have formed the word FEAR in exactly the same size. In Freud's native city, the claims to immortality—above all through the relentless loop of the video clip—turn into the *circulus vitiosus* of neurotic anxiety.

The strategy of literal translation is thus linked to the erection/demolition process. A work from 1999 is named after the memorable quote about façades by Le Corbusier: I BELIEVE IN THE SKIN OF THINGS AS IN THAT OF WOMEN. Bonvicini sets up the statement only to demolish it again: a room-like box made from plasterboard, kicked in here and there like a vandalized public toilet, with dirty comments scribbled on it. The venerable Auguste Perret had a dispute with his student, Le Corbusier, concerning horizontal versus vertical windows, and is cited with the words "a window is a man, it stands upright," accompanied by a caricature of a little man with a bulbous nose, saluting with one hand and fumbling with his erection with the other. Perret's "man" was "of course" a reference to biped human beings in general—yet, by implication, the peremptory formulation also refers to a soldierly figure, saluting and standing to attention, with Bonvicini only needing to sketch him in like a locker-room caricature, to bring him out. Two kinds of erection... let's not go there.

DON'T MISS A SEC (2003) seems obscure, in a rather Minimalist way, yet it operates in the same triangle of views from windows, the skins of façades, and toilet graffiti humor. The title is a play on the fact of seeing and being seen—make sure not to miss that important encounter with some minor celebrity! This outdoor sculpture was placed outside Tate

Britain, where the Turner Prize is awarded each year amidst a media frenzy of sorts, and outside at the Art Fair in Basel, one of the main dates in the diaries of the international art world. At first sight DON'T MISS A SEC—an all-round mirror cube, taller than a man—doesn't inspire thoughts of public toilets. Only when you open the virtually concealed door, you find a fully-functioning toilet and that you can see out on all sides through the reflective walls. So now the point of the title is obvious: Don't Miss a Sec, not even when you go to the toilet—seeing but not being seen. Although occupants know they are invisible from the outside, nevertheless they feel like exhibitionists: an absurd exhibitionism without witnesses, located somewhere between discomfiture and the thrill of fear.

In this connection one might want to explore the architectural equivalent of the fear of castration—and might well end up at Bonvicini's SHOTGUN (2003). We are on a car journey past closed, deserted shop fronts and fenced-in parking lots in an anonymous Los Angeles neighborhood, dissected and multiplied by the loop-hell of a video clip. At the same time a snippet of talk radio is heard, as though from stereo speakers inside the car; we hear a jovial agony uncle for despairing would-be home improvers, who rarely seems stuck for an answer when it comes to solving urgent problems with drills and waste-pipes. But now even he despairs, when a woman calls and describes the mold forming on the wooden mulch in her garden which releases spores that have already caused cracks to open up in the wall of her house:

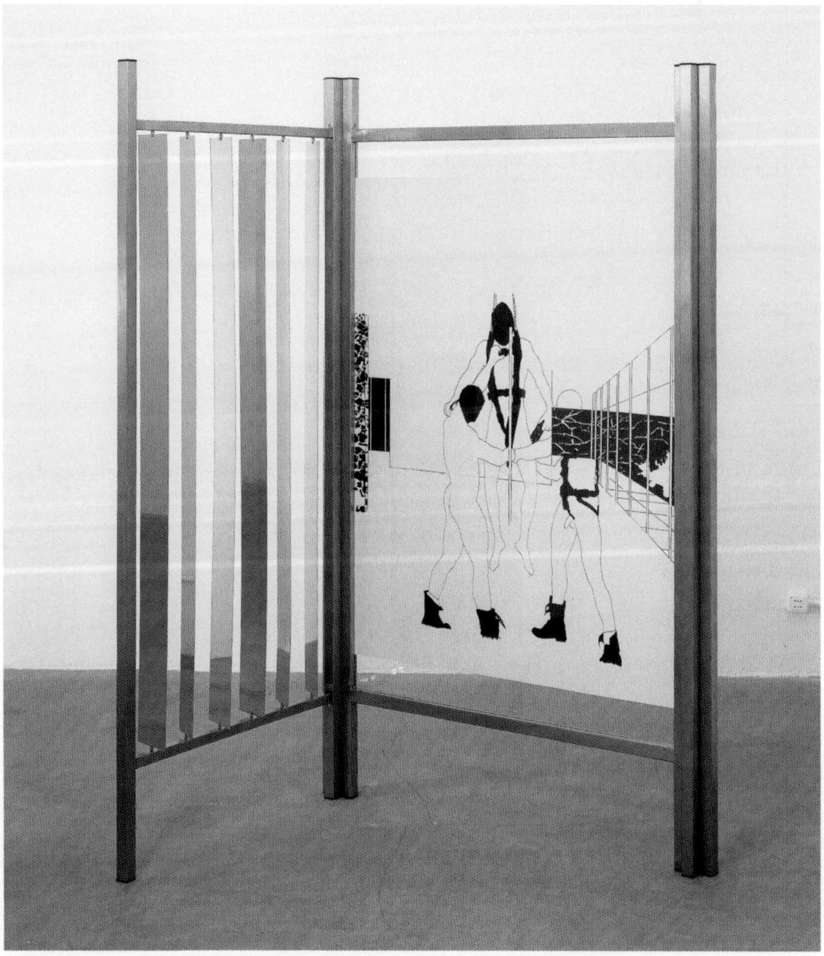

MONICA BONVICINI, MIES CORNER, 2002, stainless-steel structure, Plexiglas, and drawing on paper, paint marker, 2 panels of 89 x 51 3/16" and 89 x 39 7/16" / Edelstahlgerüst, Plexiglas und Zeichnung auf Papier, 2 Tafeln von 226 x 130 cm bzw. 226 x 100 cm.

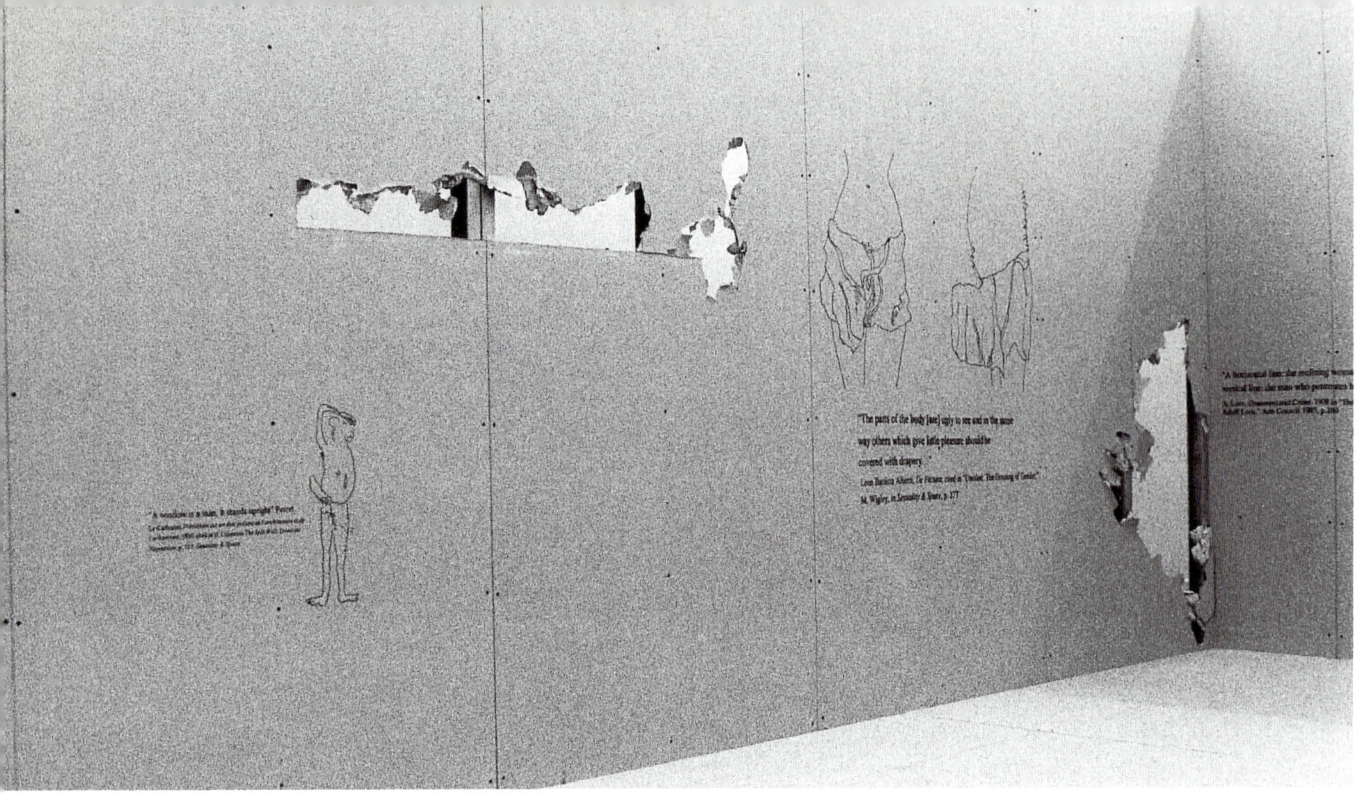

MONICA BONVICINI, I BELIEVE IN THE SKIN OF THINGS AS IN THAT OF WOMEN, 1999, drywall panels, aluminum studs, wood panels, graphite, dimensions variable, installation for the solo show "Scream & Shake," Le Magazin, Grenoble / Rigipsplatten, Aluminiumstützen, Holzplatten, Graphit, Grösse variabel.

"If the fungus is from the mulch, you not gonna like my answer, it's called shotgun fungus, I'm dead serious, you can't get it off... I have no idea."

Anxiety-ridden precautions against shotgun fungus, malevolent burglars, or social rivals spawn eloquent gaffes. A Californian adline for garden fences—add elegance to your property—is turned by Bonvicini into a mocking graffito, ADD ELEGANCE TO YOUR POVERTY (2002)—sprayed (with a stylized garden fence) in black onto a white wall. When I asked Bonvicini for a work for the exhibition "Funky Lessons" (Berlin, Büro Friedrich, 2004), she reworked this piece as a spatial intervention, as a wall of billboards, so to speak, apparently blocking access to the exhibition spaces at the Büro Friedrich. This piece can be read as a commentary on the connection between social status and the mania for security, although it also takes on other meanings in the local situation where it is being shown. In present-day Berlin one cannot help thinking of the discrepancy between expectations and reality as far as the finan-

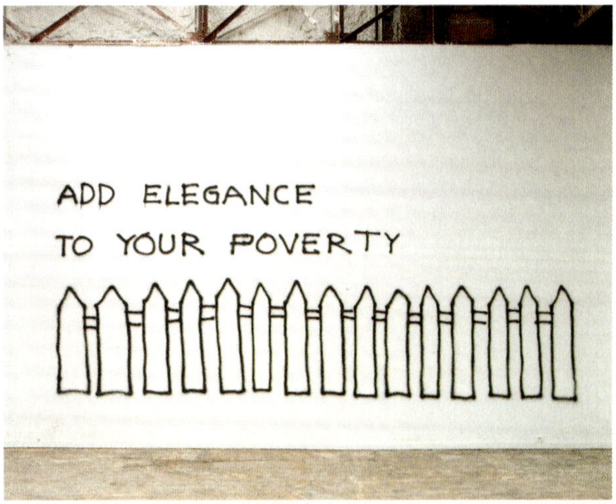

MONICA BONVICINI, ADD ELEGANCE TO YOUR POVERTY, 2002, graffiti, black spray paint, dimensions variable, Palais de Tokyo, Paris / Graffiti, schwarze Sprühfarbe, Grösse variabel.

cial prosperity of the new capital city is concerned; equally one's thoughts turn to the erosion of social services at the same time as the city is discovered by the super-rich as a trashily enticing playground where luxury—unlike in Munich or St Moritz—still stands out.

In Bonvicini's contribution to the Istanbul Biennial 2003, the point was not to prevent access but to open it up. A free-floating flight of steps connected the sculpture section of the exhibition with the video installations section. It was suspended between the ceiling and the floor on chains; the upper access was framed in broken security glass. One's first response was to wonder whether one should entrust oneself to this construction (viewed with skepticism by architects, it turned out to be astonishingly stable). After the attacks of 9/11, Led Zeppelin's "Stairway to Heaven" was one of the songs that American radio stations temporarily put on the Index. And now, as STAIRWAY TO HELL, the path only ever leads from the sculpture cemetery to the video purgatory and back again.

For Bonvicini titles are concrete, practical equivalents or absurd allegories. One way or another, language and built structures are positioned next to and on top of each other, abruptly engaging in blatant acts like the protagonists in a choreographed porn scenario. Fractured quotes and voiceless material mutually transform: it is as though words and sentences were materializing, developing a physical presence on the wall, in the dust, rigidified into fragmented letters; it is as though built structures were, in return, soaking up syntax and signification. As Lacan has said, the subconscious is structured like a language; and, one might add in Bonvicini's case, so too is the built structure, and the structure of one cannot be understood without the other: so translations are needed. Although in Bonvicini's work, these never read as simple users' instructions but as dirty jokes.

(Translation: Fiona Elliott)

1) See also Bernard Tschumi, *Architectural Manifestoes,* (London: Architectural Association, 1979), exh. cat., n.p. (first published by Artists' Space, New York, 1978), and *Architecture and Disjunction* (Cambridge, MA: MIT Press, 1998), p. 75.

2) Quotation by the artist after Le Corbusier, "Précisions sur un état présent de l'architecture et de l'urbanisme" (1930), cited in B. Columina, "The Split Wall: Domestic Voyeurism," chapter in *Sexuality and Space* (Princeton: Architectural Press, 1992), p. 113.

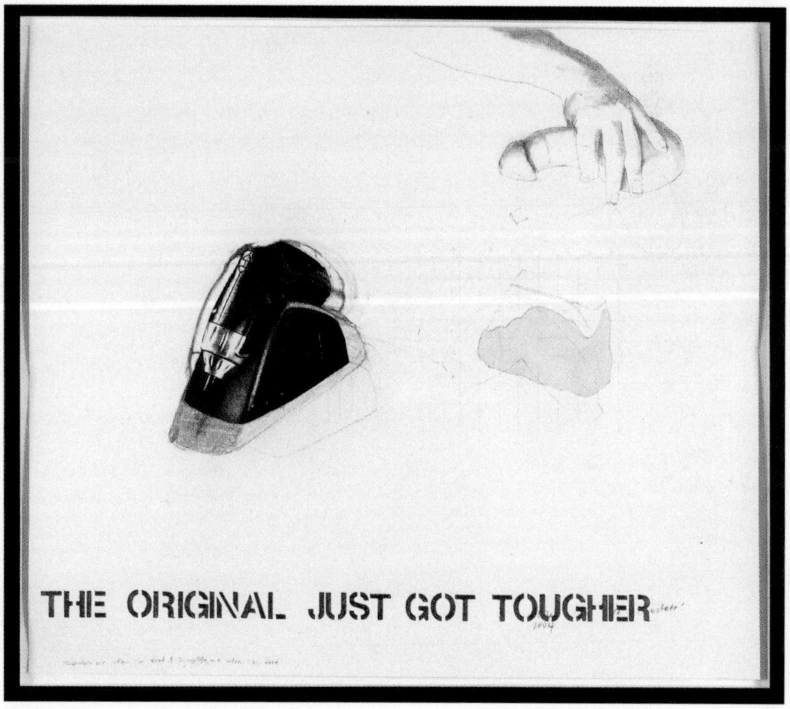

MONICA BONVICINI, BLIND SHOT: DUCHAMP'S DICK, 2004, drawing and collage on paper, framed 25 3/16 x 29 1/8" / Zeichnung und Collage auf Papier, gerahmt 64 x 74 cm.

Edition for Parkett

MONICA BONVICINI
DRILL 4 CHASTITY, 2004

2-part cast, bronze and resin, $4\,^1/_8$ x $5\,^7/_8$ x $3\,^1/_2$".
Edition of 35 / XX, signed and numbered.

2-teiliger Guss, Bronze und Kunstharz, 10,5 x 15 x 9 cm.
Auflage: 35 / XX, signiert und nummeriert.

(PHOTO: UWE BOEK, BERLIN)

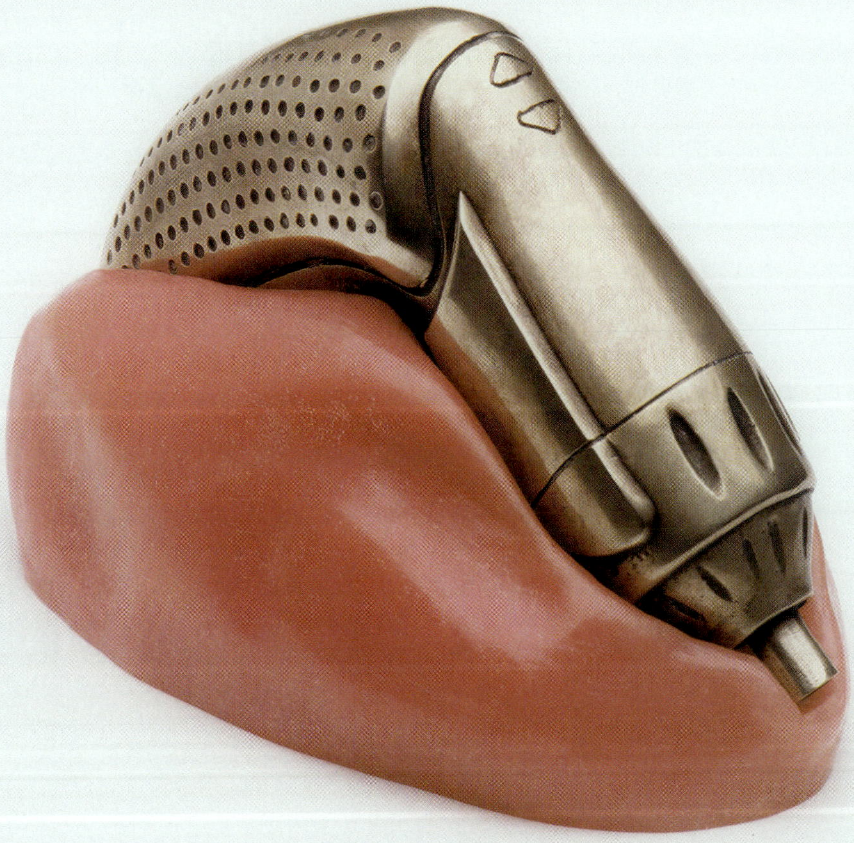

URS FISCHER

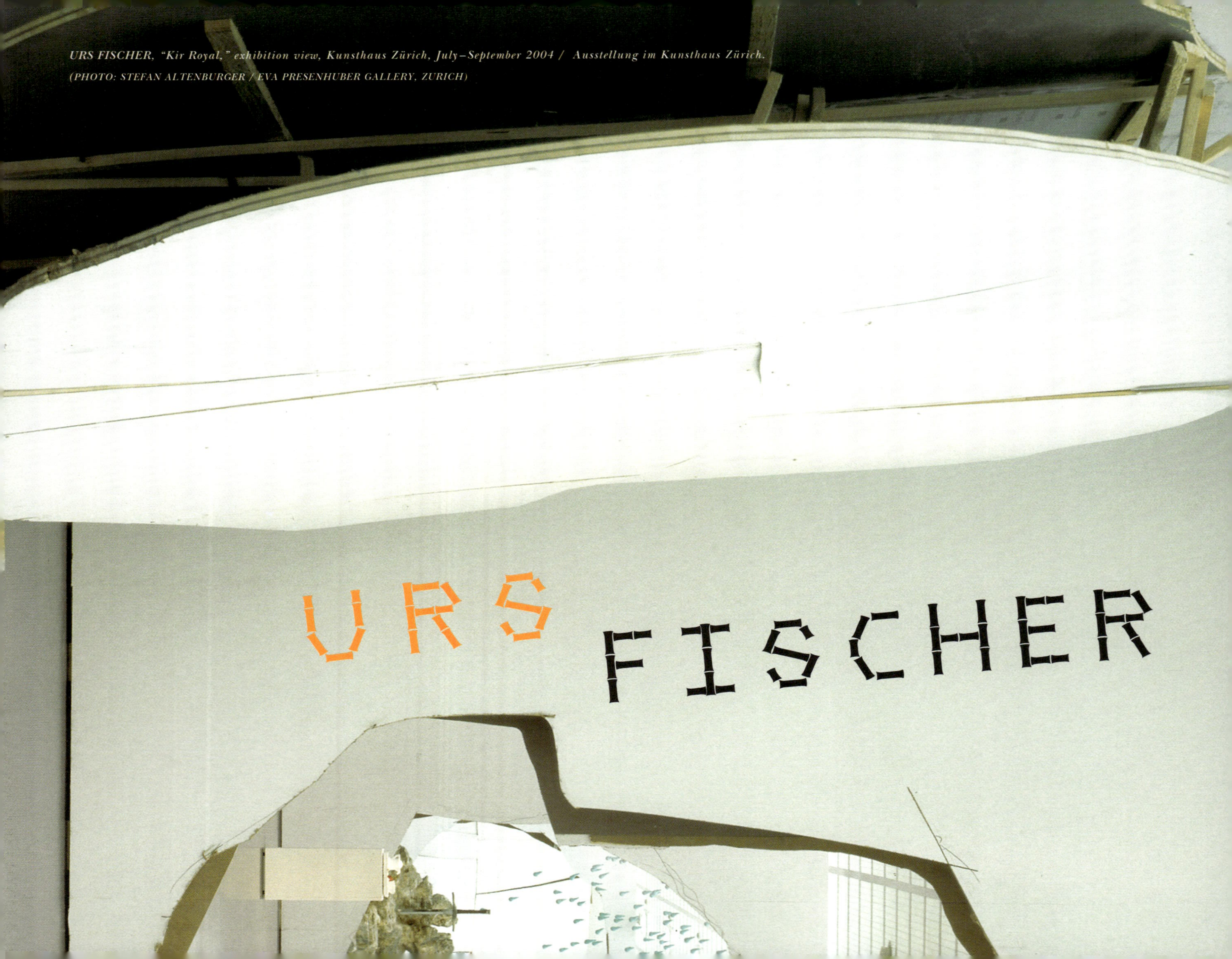

URS FISCHER, "Kir Royal," exhibition view, Kunsthaus Zürich, July–September 2004 / Ausstellung im Kunsthaus Zürich.
(PHOTO: STEFAN ALTENBURGER / EVA PRESENHUBER GALLERY, ZURICH)

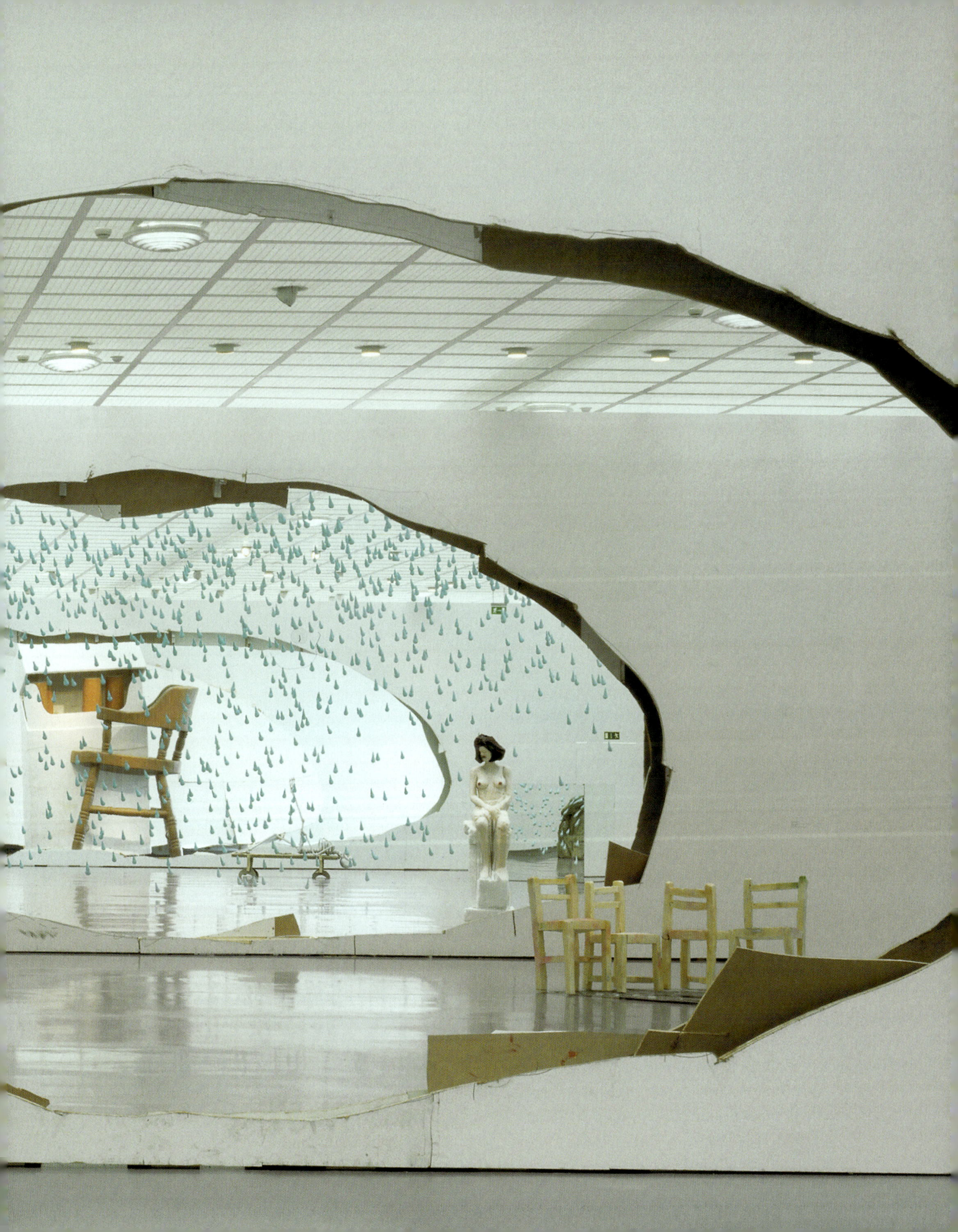

Postcard from America

Down the Rabbit-Hole in Zürich

BRENDA RICHARDSON

Disconnected by time and distance, I'm still thinking about Urs Fischer's exhibition-installation, invitingly titled "Kir Royal," at the Kunsthaus Zürich. (When I saw the show, I hadn't anticipated writing about it, hence took no notes; I write here from the perspective of memory alone.) I arrived in Zürich on the morning of August 4 after an overnight flight from Baltimore via Atlanta and a couple of hours later walked from my nearby hotel to the Kunsthaus. Unfamiliar with Fischer's work (having missed his show last year at Gavin Brown's Enterprise in New York), I didn't know what to expect. I was certainly beguiled by the teaser image on the banner in front of the museum: a pair of bare feet and ankles, insouciantly crossed, in a relaxed and somehow jaunty pose. Clearly male. Hard to say how so much could be read into a scant fragment of human limbs—each leg cleanly chopped off at the lower shin—but so it was.

Entering the exhibition space, I was drawn toward a female wax figure, seated on the floor, somewhat smaller than life-size and casually painted rather like a slightly lewd china doll. The figure was embedded with two or three burning candles and she was in the slow process of molten-wax disfigurement. In a show that had been open for about a month, she was still entirely recognizable (as a painted lady), though somewhat marbleized and shriveled. Rivulets had pooled decorative patterns of splashed wax on the floor around the figure's perimeter. She was very appealing, very pretty, and both sad and funny at the same time. Most startling, however, was the very fact of the burning candles. Perhaps an open flame in a public museum doesn't startle the general visitor. But for an American career museum professional, the burning candles were a disorienting show-stopper. There was just a brief moment when I wondered

BRENDA RICHARDSON was Curator of Modern Painting and Sculpture at The Baltimore Museum of Art from 1975 to 1998 (and at the Berkeley Art Museum for ten years before that). She is now an independent art writer who is currently working on major Robert Gober and Richard Tuttle projects.

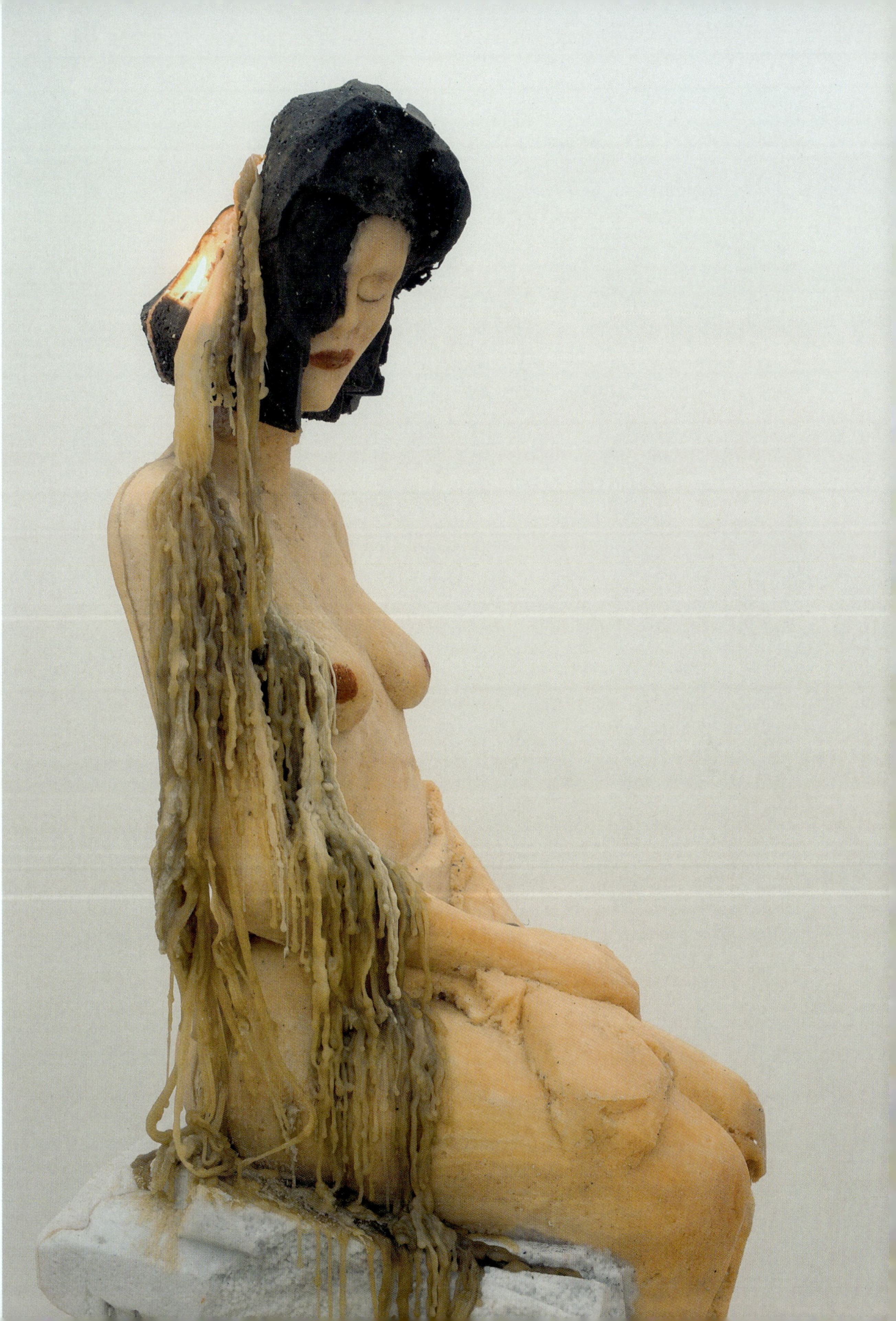

URS FISCHER, WHAT IF THE PHONE RINGS, 2003, wax, pigment, wick, one of 3 figures, exhibition copy, $78^3/_4$ x $21^1/_4$ x $18^1/_8$" / Wachs, Pigmente, Docht, eine von drei Figuren, Ausstellungskopie, 200 x 54 x 46 cm. (ALL PHOTOS: STEFAN ALTENBURGER / EVA PRESENHUBER GALLERY, ZURICH, UNLESS OTHERWISE INDICATED)

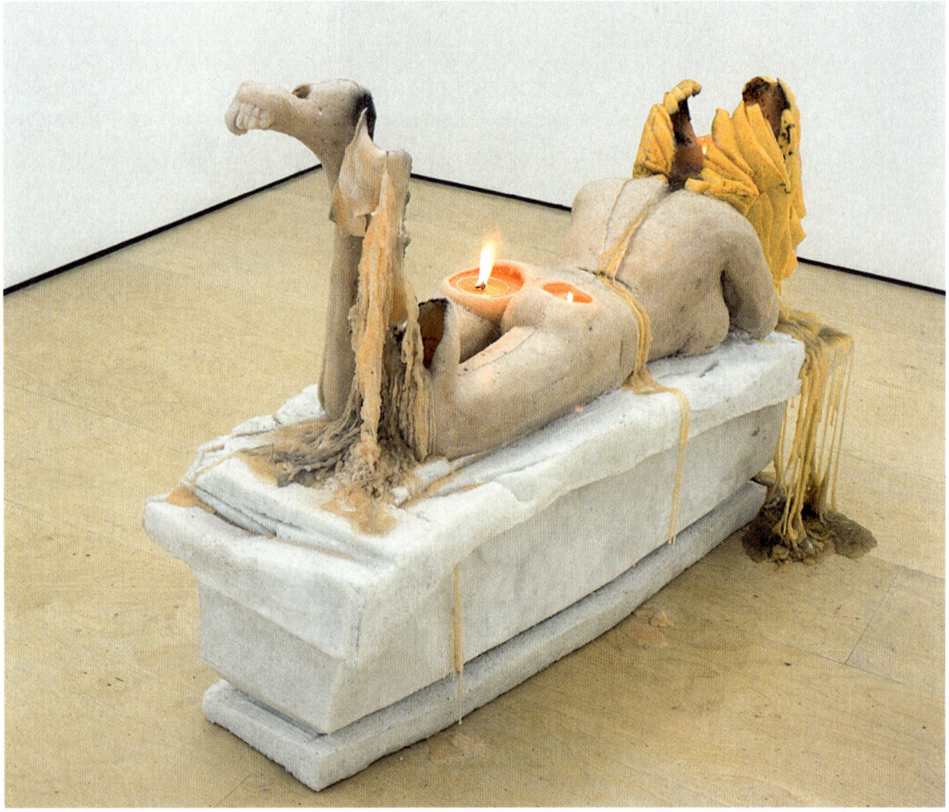

URS FISCHER, WHAT IF THE PHONE RINGS, 2003, wax, pigment, wick, one of 3 figures, $41^{3}/_{4}$ x $55^{7}/_{8}$ x $18^{1}/_{8}$" / Wachs, Pigmente, Docht, eine von drei Figuren, 106 x 142 x 46 cm.

where I was. Indoors? Outdoors? In a public museum? (In the U.S. an open flame would most likely not be permitted at all. But if it were allowed, one might expect to see trained personnel with fire extinguishing gear posted next to the piece!)

My first overall impression was a blur of color and varied form—large paintings on the walls, small sculpture on pedestals, a second burning-candle wax figure, a maze-like structure of conjoined upright slabs of whitened aluminum in vaguely architectural configuration (drolly called PEANUTS IN COMPARISON, 2004). I was having trouble bringing into focus what this artist might be up to. When I looked ahead, space opened onto space. I saw a sequence of gigantic openings—irregular, rough-edged, more or less kidney-bean-shaped cut-outs—in the still more gigantic floor-to-ceiling walls that presumably once defined the museum's galleries. The effect was extraordinarily disorienting. (I began to wonder if I was more jet-lagged than I realized.) It felt almost like a house of mirrors. Was that r e a l l y a sequence of room-size openings? Or was it an illusion somehow created of reflected images? The Kunsthaus exhibition space is very big, perhaps sixty feet across, probably sixteen feet high, and maybe as much as sixty-five yards to the far end wall. I spotted a mirrored cube about five feet square, sitting on the floor, its reflections further confounding one's spatial orientation.

I walked directly ahead into a shower of oversize azure raindrops (or teardrops?). Moving under and through the "cloud" of these suspended drops, I could see my reflection in the mirrored cube across the way. In size and color (and charm) the raindrops were pure animation in effect. I was reminded a bit of the magical experience of stepping into Yayoi Kusama's 2002 room of lights and mirrors, FIREFLIES ON THE WATER. The wonder is that Fischer is able to evoke childlike surprise and delight with such an elementary vocabulary: the piece, sweetly called HORSES DREAM OF HORSES (2004), consists only of painted plaster and some nylon thread. (It occurs to me that the title may incline more toward the erotic than the sweet, in which case the overhead drops may allude to a shower of fluid more potent than rain or tears.)

Moving toward the first cut-away wall, and seeing its revealed construction, I understood that these walls were not original to the Kunsthaus gallery space at all. The artist and crew had built the walls *in situ* in order to cut them away. Jagged edges marked the progress of the saw cutting through the drywall. To gain access to each space, visitors had to step gingerly across the wall's ragged drywall edges and wood-beam construction, a maneuver not entirely without hazard for the less than nimble. Evidence of the workers' presence remained in nooks and crannies—a crumpled sweatshirt, a beer bottle, tools, sawdust. Cut-out segments of the walls had been put to good use. Some were joined together to make an affecting abstract sculptural backdrop. Others had been structurally latticed to create a free-standing prow-shaped "wall" on the back side of which were displayed several dozen small paintings and drawings, each presented in a humble, self-consciously hand-crafted frame.

A monumental (as in Oldenburg) sculpture composed of a "wood" chair embracing a ghost cigarette carton, probably fifteen feet high, anchored this last room. The most prominent architectural feature of the space is the enormous second-floor window wall with which the Kunsthaus fronts its site on Heimplatz. I glimpsed something in the window and as I moved closer I realized that it was the exhibition banner's pair of feet (styrofoam carved and painted in trompe l'oeil style to simulate the aged marble of a classical fragment). Suspended from the high ceiling by a long nylon line, the heels rested lightly on the window ledge, subject to barely perceptible movement from air currents. The "missing man" (the figure who belongs to these feet) could be intuited as sitting at ease in the big chair, having a smoke, legs stretched out across the room, feet propped at a comfortable angle, surveying the street scene. Well, except the chair has its back to the window...

"Curiouser and curiouser!"cried Alice (she was so much surprised that for the moment she quite forgot how to speak good English). "Now I'm opening out like the largest telescope that ever was! Good-bye, feet!" (for when she looked down at her feet, they seemed to be almost out of sight, they were getting so far off). "Oh, my poor little feet, I wonder who will put on your shoes and stockings for you now, dears? I'm sure I shan't be able! I shall be a great deal too far off to trouble myself about you: you must manage the best way you can; but I must be kind to them," thought Alice, "or perhaps they won't walk the way I want to go! Let me see. I'll give them a new pair of boots every Christmas."

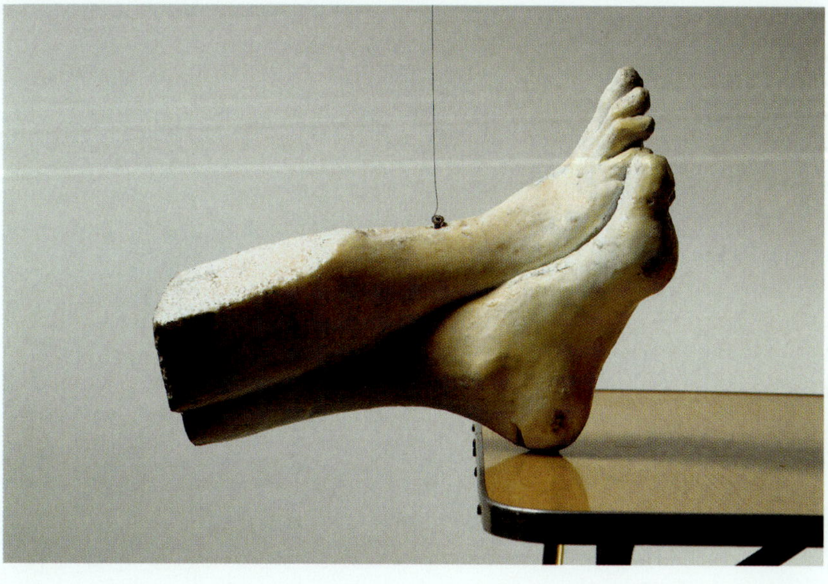

URS FISCHER, SEPTEMBER SONG, 2002, styrofoam, glue, paint, screw, felt-tip pen, 9 x 23 5/8 x 3 15/16" / Styropor, Leim, Farbe, Draht, Schraube, Filzstift, 23 x 60 x 10 cm.

And she went on planning to herself how she would manage it. "They must go by the carrier," she thought; "and how funny it'll seem, sending presents to one's own feet! And how odd the directions will look!

Alice's Right Foot, Esq.
Hearthrug,
near the Fender,
(with Alice's love).

Oh dear, what nonsense I'm talking!"[1)]

There was much more to see. An enchanting skeleton, seemingly doing exercises for a bad back (which is, after all, a very funny idea!), sprinkled with sawdust and reclining on a small, primitively handmade wooden bench… Excalibur waiting for its Lancelot… a carousel-like sculpture of chairs, some "real" (sculpted), some "missing" (cut-out shapes), some "reflected," altogether a work of shadows and mirrors and disjunctions of scale… a perfect miniature tea set on a pedestal… more chairs and human limbs (Nauman's presence was tangible)… large paintings that nodded respectfully to Polke and Disney and Artschwager, among others, and yet bespoke a lively and provocative identity entirely unique…

Wow! What a show! A real tour de force. I didn't want to leave. And when I did, finally, I left knowing that I had encountered an artist of mad ambition whose work—revelatory with inspired conjunctions and dazzling invention, the product of incredibly demanding labor carried out in a spirit of play—casts a spell of fairy-tale enchantment. That initial blur of form and color had cohered, step by step as one walked through the space, into a visually engaging and intellectually complex presentation of stunning integrity. The exhibition included a selection of discrete works dating from the last three years and yet, at the same time, comprised a convincingly unitary "installation piece" that stood memorably on its own as a resonant work of art. And those feet in the window? Back on the street, I looked up and saw them flaunting their soles in my direction. Fischer laid claim to exterior and interior and made it all art for as far as the eye could see.

1) Lewis Carroll, *Alice's Adventures in Wonderland,* beginning of chapter II, "The Pool of Tears."

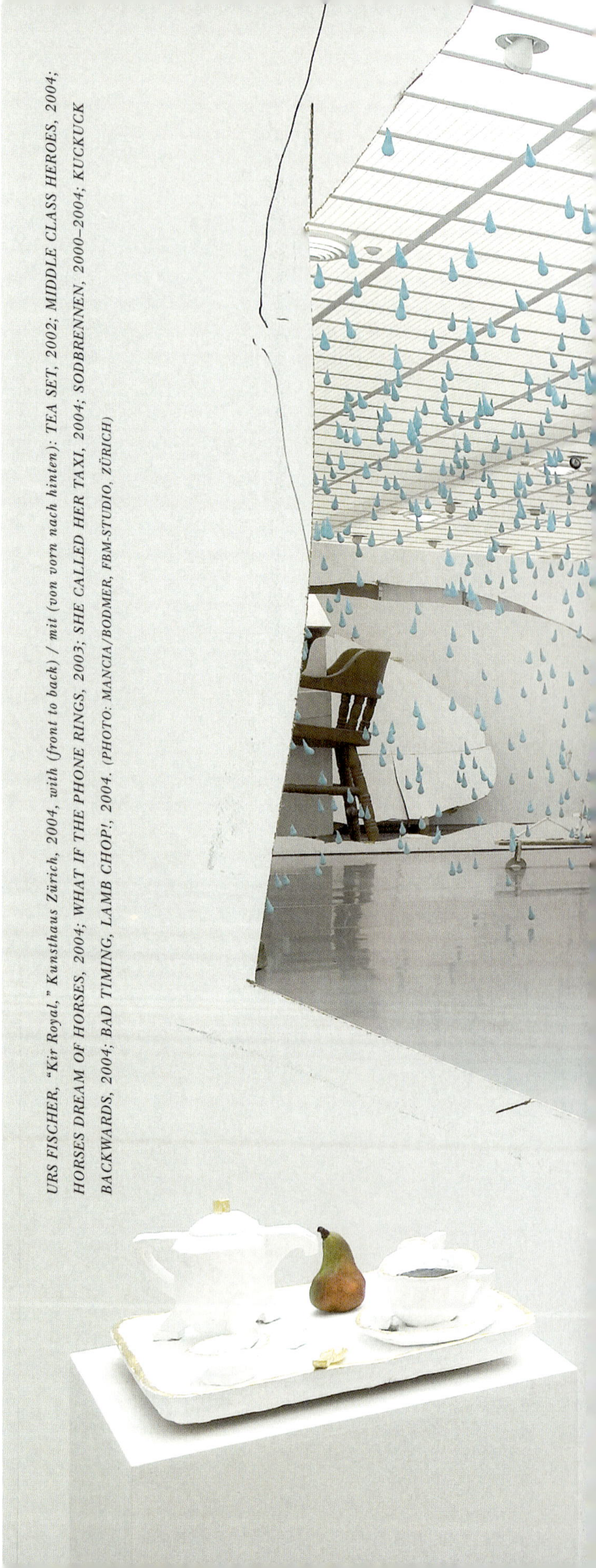

URS FISCHER, "Kir Royal," Kunsthaus Zürich, 2004, with (front to back) / mit (von vorn nach hinten): TEA SET, 2002; MIDDLE CLASS HEROES, 2004; HORSES DREAM OF HORSES, 2004; WHAT IF THE PHONE RINGS, 2003; SHE CALLED HER TAXI, 2004; SODBRENNEN, 2000–2004; KUCKUCK BACKWARDS, 2004; BAD TIMING, LAMB CHOP!, 2004. (PHOTO: MANCIA/BODMER, FBM-STUDIO, ZÜRICH)

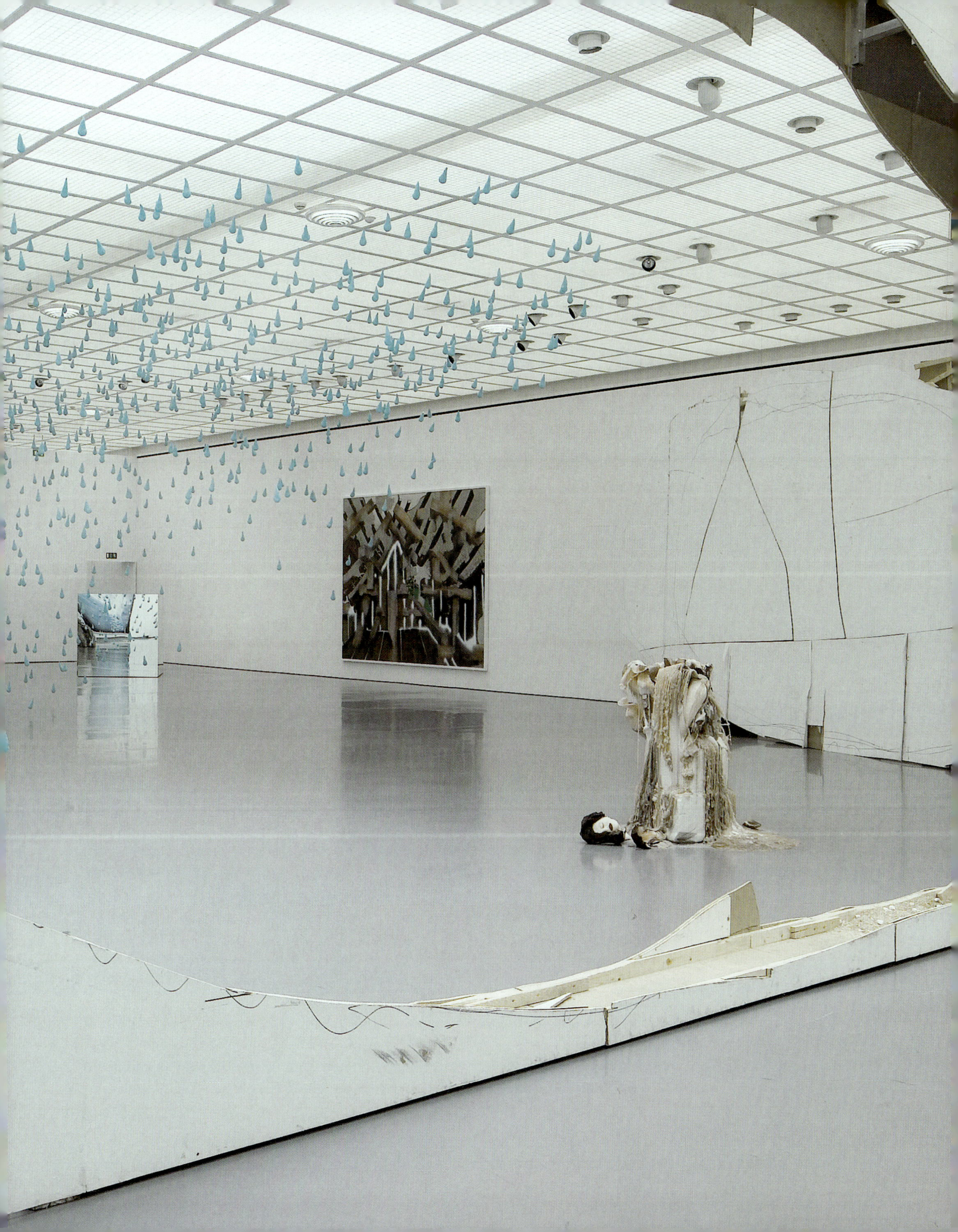

Postkarte aus Amerika

Hinab ins Kaninchen-loch in Zürich

BRENDA RICHARDSON

Obwohl ich zeitlich und räumlich mittlerweile weit davon entfernt bin, denke ich noch immer über Urs Fischers Ausstellungsinstallation mit dem einladenden Titel «Kir Royal» im Kunsthaus Zürich nach. (Als ich mir die Ausstellung anschaute, dachte ich noch nicht daran, darüber zu schreiben, und machte mir deshalb keine Notizen; ich verlasse mich hier also ganz auf mein Gedächtnis.) Nach einem Nachtflug von Baltimore via Atlanta war ich am Morgen des 4. August in Zürich gelandet. Wenige Stunden später spazierte ich zu Fuss vom nahe gelegenen Hotel zum Kunsthaus. Ich kannte Fischers Werk noch nicht – seine letztjährige Ausstellung bei Gavin Brown in New York hatte ich verpasst – und hatte daher keine Ahnung, was mich erwartete. Natürlich war ich entzückt vom Aufmacherbild auf dem Werbetransparent vor dem Kunsthaus: ein paar nackte Füsse und Fussgelenke, unbekümmert gekreuzt in einer entspannten, etwas lässigen Pose. Unverkennbar männlich. Schwer zu sagen, wie man so viel aus einem derart minimalen Fragment menschlicher Gliedmassen ablesen kann – beide Beine waren am unteren Schienbein abgehackt –, aber so war es.

Als ich den Ausstellungsraum betrat, wurde ich von einer weiblichen Wachsfigur angezogen, die auf dem Boden sass, etwas kleiner als lebensgross und salopp bemalt wie eine leicht obszöne Porzellanpuppe. In der Figur brannten zwei oder drei Kerzendochte und durch das Schmelzen des Wachses war sie in einem langsamen Entstellungs- und Auflösungsprozess begriffen. Die Ausstellung war seit rund einem Monat geöffnet und die Figur war noch immer gut (als bemalte Dame) zu erkennen, wenn auch inzwischen etwas gesprenkelt und geschrumpft.

BRENDA RICHARDSON war von 1975 bis 1998 Kuratorin für Moderne Malerei und Skulptur am Baltimore Museum of Art (und war davor zehn Jahre am Berkeley Art Museum). Heute ist sie freie Kunstpublizistin und arbeitet an umfangreichen Projekten zu Robert Gober und Richard Tuttle.

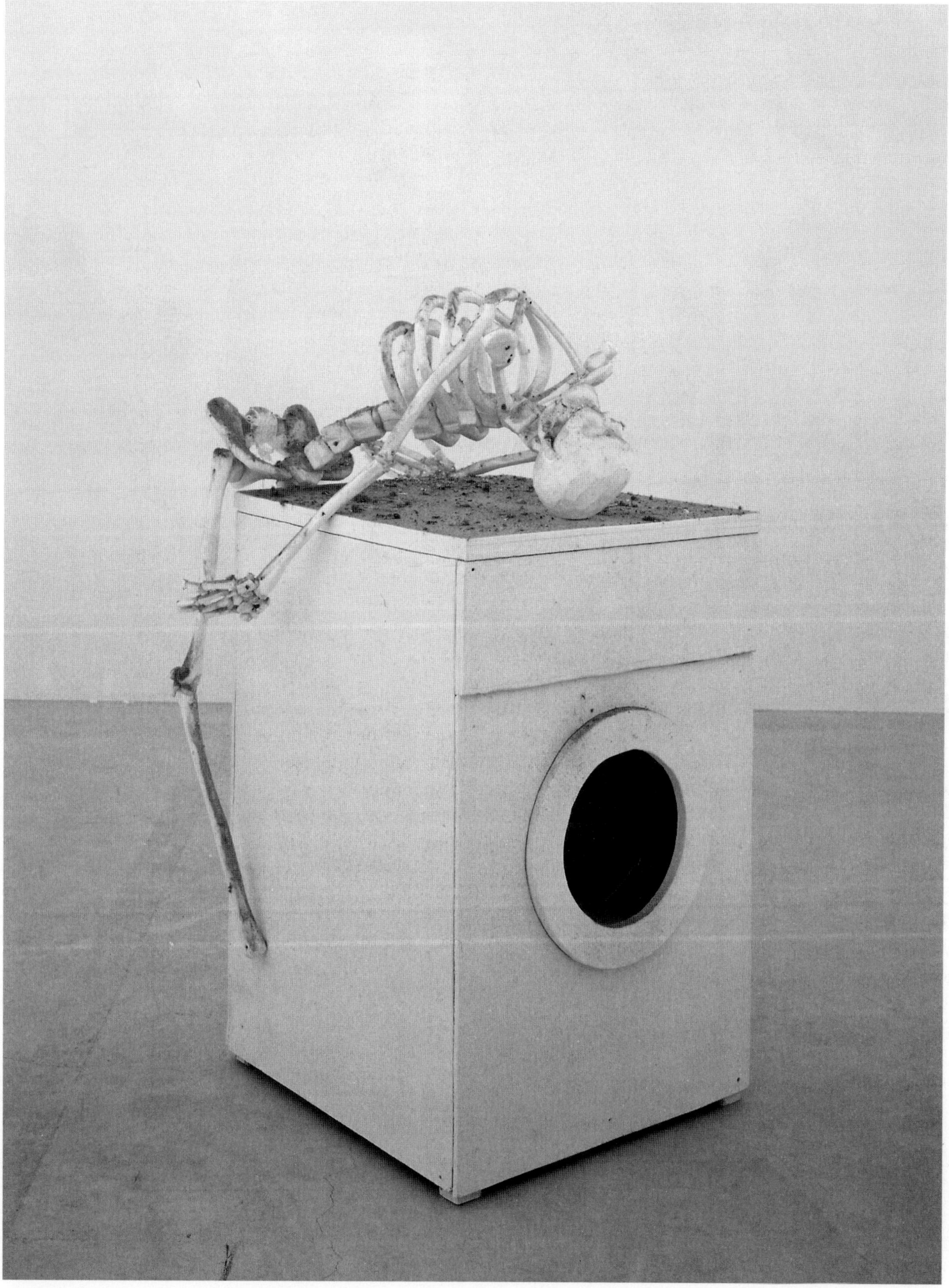

URS FISCHER, ONE MORE CARROT BEFORE I BRUSH MY TEETH, 2001, mixed media, 51 9/16 x 31 7/8 x 38 3/16" / diverse Materialien, 131 x 81 x 97 cm.

Wachsbächlein waren im Umkreis der Figur zu dekorativen Lachen und Mustern geronnen. Sie wirkte sehr ansprechend und hübsch, traurig und lustig zugleich. Am meisten irritierten mich jedoch die tatsächlich brennenden Kerzen: Vielleicht wirkt eine offene Flamme auf das normale Publikum nicht weiter alarmierend, aber auf eine Fachfrau mit amerikanischer Museumskarriere wirkten die brennenden Kerzen sensationell und verstörend. Einen Moment lang fragte ich mich, wo ich eigentlich war. Drinnen? Im Freien? In einem öffentlichen Museum? (In den USA würde eine offene Flamme mit grösster Wahrscheinlichkeit gar nicht erlaubt. Und wenn doch, müsste man darauf gefasst sein, dass speziell ausgebildetes Personal mit Feuerlöschern neben dem Werk postiert würde!)

Mein erster Gesamteindruck war der eines bunten Gewirrs aus Farben und Formen – grosse Bilder an den Wänden, kleine Skulpturen auf Sockeln, eine zweite brennende Wachsfigur, ein labyrinthartiges Gebilde aus rechtwinklig aneinander gefügten aufrechten weisslich bemalten Aluminiumplatten in

URS FISCHER, "Kir Royal," Kunsthaus Zürich: PEANUTS IN COMPARISON, 2004, wood, aluminum, silicon, acrylic paint, dimensions variable / Holz, Aluminium, Silikon, Acrylfarbe, Grösse variabel.

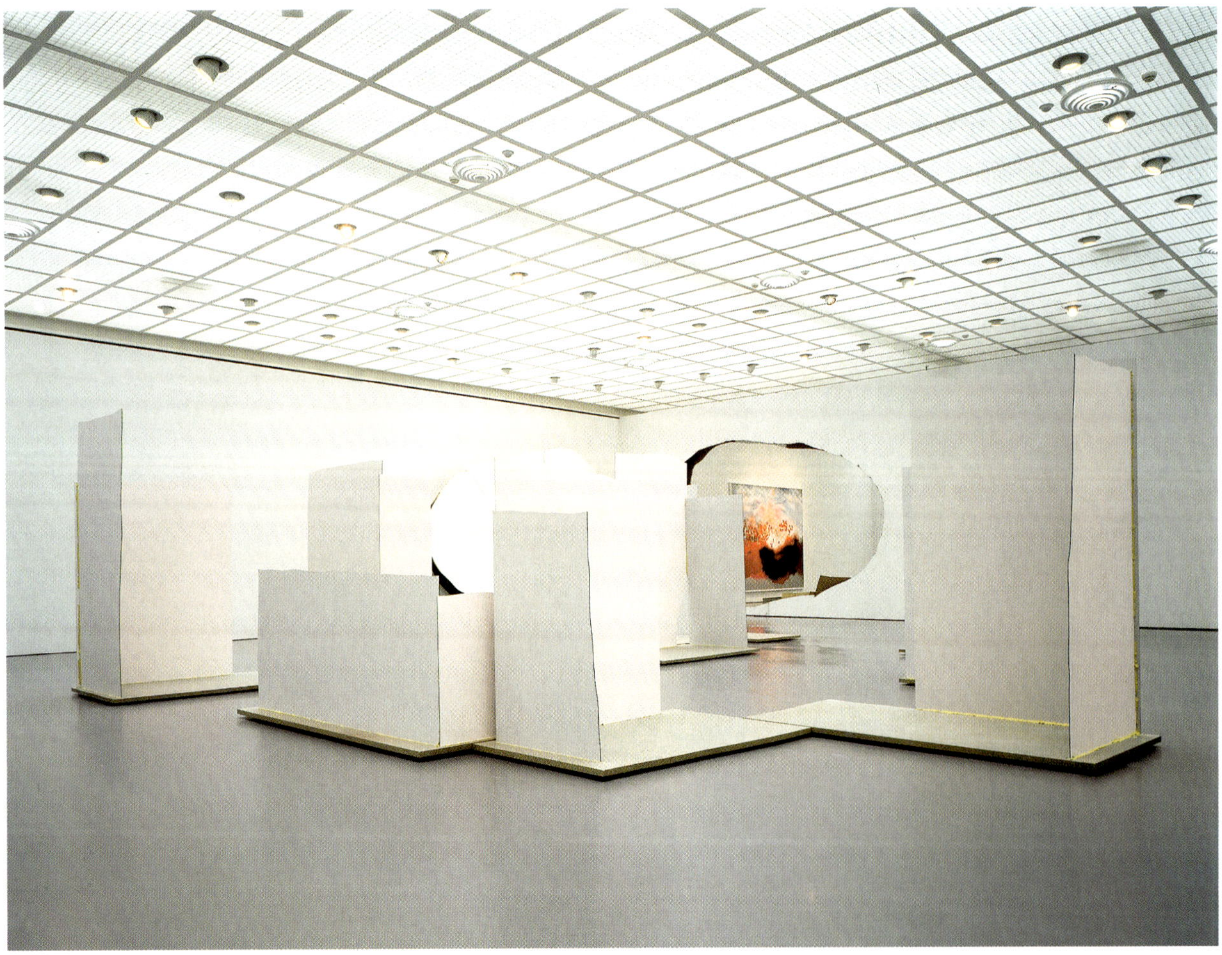

vage architektonischer Anordnung – mit dem drolligen Namen PEANUTS IN COMPARISON (2004). Ich konnte mir zunächst nicht zusammenreimen, was dieser Künstler wohl im Sinn haben mochte. Wenn ich nach vorne schaute, öffnete sich Raum auf Raum. Ich erblickte eine Folge gigantischer Öffnungen – unregelmässig, rau, mehr oder weniger saubohnenförmig ausgesägt – in den noch grösseren, vom Boden bis zur Decke reichenden Wänden, die wohl ursprünglich die Ausstellungsräume des Mu-seums voneinander getrennt hatten. Die Wirkung war extrem verwirrend (ich begann mich ernsthaft zu fragen, ob ich wohl stärker unter Jetlag litt, als ich dachte). Es war beinah wie in einem Spiegelkabinett. War das wirklich eine Reihe von Öffnungen in Raumgrösse? Oder war es nur eine optische Täuschung durch reflektierte Bilder? Der Ausstellungsraum des Kunsthauses ist sehr gross, etwa achtzehn Meter breit, knapp fünf Meter hoch und sicher sechzig Meter lang bis zur hinteren Stirnwand. Weiter hinten entdeckte ich einen verspiegelten Kubus von etwa 150 Zentimeter Kantenlänge; er stand auf dem Boden und seine Reflexionen brachten die eigene räumliche Wahrnehmung noch zusätzlich durcheinander.

Ich ging geradeaus weiter, direkt in einen Schauer aus übergrossen hellblauen Regentropfen hinein, dabei konnte ich mein eigenes Spiegelbild in dem Spiegelkubus vorne rechts erkennen. In Grösse und Farbe (und Zauberhaftigkeit) waren die Regentropfen das pure Leben in Aktion. Ich fühlte mich ein bisschen an die magische Erfahrung beim Betreten von Yayoi Kusamas Raum aus Lichtern und Spiegeln, FIREFLIES ON THE WATER (Glühwürmchen auf dem Wasser, 2002) erinnert. Das Wunderbare ist, dass Fischer mit einem derart elementaren Vokabular so viel kindliche Überraschung und Freude hervorzurufen vermag – in diesem konkreten Fall, der Arbeit HORSES DREAM OF HORSES (Pferde träumen von Pferden, 2004), mit etwas bemaltem Gips und Nylonfaden. (Mir fällt ein, dass der Titel wohl eher zum Erotischen als zum Sentimentalen tendiert und demnach die Tropfen über unseren Köpfen vielleicht eine potentere Flüssigkeit als Regen oder Tränen meinen.) Als ich mich der ersten herausgeschnittenen Wand näherte und sah, woraus sie bestand, begriff ich, dass diese Wände überhaupt nichts mit dem ursprünglichen Ausstellungsraum des Kunsthauses zu tun hatten. Der Künstler und seine Mitarbeiter hatten die Wände an Ort und Stelle eingefügt, um sie anschliessend aufbrechen zu können. Die gezackten Ränder zeugten noch vom Durchsägen der Spanwand. Um in die verschiedenen Raumteile zu gelangen, mussten die Besucher behutsam über die rauen Ränder der herausgesägten Spanplatten- und Holzträgerkonstruktion steigen, ein Manöver, das nicht mehr ganz so Gelenkige eher abenteuerlich anmuten mochte. In den Ecken und Ritzen waren noch Spuren der Arbeiter zu sehen – ein zerknüllter Pulli, eine Bierflasche, Werkzeuge, Sägespäne. Die herausgesägten Segmente wurden aufs Beste genutzt: Einmal waren sie zu einem skulpturähnlichen Bühnenhintergrund zusammengestellt. Einmal dienten sie als Raumteiler, so dass eine abgewinkelte Wand entstand, auf deren Rückseite mehrere Dutzend kleine Bilder und Zeichnungen hingen, jeweils in einfachen, bewusst unbeholfen von Hand gefertigten Rahmen.

URS FISCHER, "Kir Royal," Kunsthaus Zürich, with / mit: KUCKUCK BACKWARDS; MIDDLE CLASS HEROES; BAD TIMING, LAMP CHOP!, all 2004.

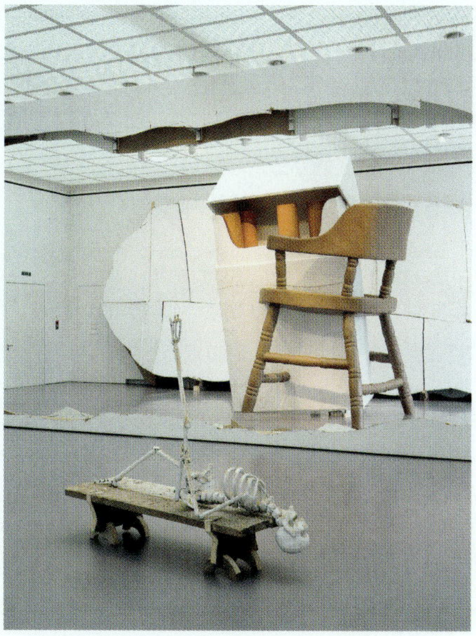

Eine (im Sinn von Oldenburg) monumentale Skulptur aus einem Stuhl, der eine geisterhafte Zigarettenpackung umschliesst, insgesamt rund viereinhalb Meter hoch, bildete den Angelpunkt im hintersten Raum. Das hervorstechendste architektonische Merkmal dieses Raums im zweiten Stock des Kunsthauses ist die riesige dem Heimplatz zugewandte Fensterfront. Ich bemerkte etwas im Fenster und als ich näher ging, erkannte ich, dass es sich um dasselbe Fusspaar handelte, das ich auf dem Ausstellungstransparent gesehen hatte (in Styropor geschnitzt und in *Trompe-l'œil*-Manier bemalt, um den verwitterten Marmor eines Fragments aus der klassischen Antike zu suggerieren): an einem Nylonfaden hing es von der Decke, die Fersen leicht auf die Fensterbrüstung gestützt, kaum wahrnehmbar sich im Luftzug bewegend. Den «fehlenden Mann» (die zu den Füssen gehörende Figur) konnte man sich bequem in dem grossen Stuhl sitzend vorstellen, wie er – rauchend, die Beine quer durch den Raum gestreckt, die Füsse bequem aufgestützt – die Szene draussen überblickt. Nur stand der Stuhl mit dem Rücken zum Fenster...

«Ülkiger und ülkiger!» rief Alice (und in ihrer Überraschung entging ihr, dass man das eigentlich gar nicht sagen kann); «jetzt schiebe ich mich auseinander wie das längste Fernrohr, das es jemals gegeben hat! Lebt wohl, Füsse!» (denn als sie nach unten sah, waren ihre Füsse schon kaum mehr in Sicht, so weit versanken sie in der Tiefe). «Ihr armen kleinen Füsse, wer wird euch jetzt wohl Schuhe und Strümpfe anziehen? Ich jedenfalls kann das bestimmt nicht mehr! Ich bin bald viel zu weit fort, als dass ich mich um euch noch kümmern könnte; ihr müsst eben sehen, wie ihr allein zurechtkommt – aber ich muss sie freundlich behandeln», dachte Alice, «sonst gehen sie vielleicht nicht mehr dahin, wohin ich will! Ich habs schon: sie sollen von mir jedes Jahr zu Weihnachten ein Paar neue Stiefel haben.»

Und dann legte sie sich zurecht, wie sie das anfangen würde. «Sie müssen per Boten gesandt werden», dachte sie; «und wie sonderbar das sein wird, Geschenke an die eigenen Füsse zu verschicken! wie seltsam sich die Adresse ausnehmen wird:

An S. Wohlgeb.
Den Rechten Fuss von Alice
Teppich beim Ofenschirm
Mit bestem Gruss!

Ach was rede ich für ungereimtes Zeug!»[1)]

Es gab aber noch viel mehr zu sehen: Ein entzückendes Skelett, das offenbar Rückenübungen machte (immerhin ein ziemlich witziger Einfall!), mit Sägespänen übersät auf einer kleinen primitiv gezimmerten Holzbank liegend... Excalibur, das auf seinen Lanzelot wartete... eine karussellartige Skulptur aus Stühlen, einige «real» (modelliert), andere «abwesend» (scherenschnittartige Umrisse), oder «reflektiert»; alles in allem eine Arbeit der Schatten, Reflexionen und verrückten Massstäbe... ferner ein perfektes Miniatur-Teeservice samt Tablett auf einem Sockel... noch mehr Stühle und menschliche Gliedmassen (Naumans Präsenz war mit Händen zu greifen)... grosse Gemälde, respektvolle Reverenzen an Polke, Disney, Artschwager und andere, die dennoch von einer ganz eigenen lebendigen und provokativen Identität kündeten...

Wow, was für eine Ausstellung! Ein echtes Bravourstück. Ich wollte gar nicht mehr weggehen. Und als ich schliesslich doch ging, wusste ich, dass ich einem Künstler begegnet war, der sich ein wahnsinnig ehrgeiziges Ziel gesteckt hatte und dessen Werk uns mit seinem märchenhaften Zauber in Bann schlägt: Dank seinen inspirierten Verknüpfungen und verblüffenden Einfällen wirkt es äusserst erhellend. Und auch wenn die Ausführung spielerisch leicht daherkommt, steckt dahinter eine unglaublich anspruchsvolle Arbeit. Das anfänglich wahrgenommene Wirrwarr aus Form und Farbe hat sich beim Durchqueren des Raums Schritt für Schritt in eine visuell attraktive und intellektuell komplexe Präsentation von überwältigender Integrität verwandelt. Die Ausstellung setzte sich aus einer Auswahl von Einzelwerken aus den letzten drei Jahren zusammen und überzeugte dennoch als einheitliche Installation, die in ihrer Vielschichtigkeit eindrücklich in sich zu bestehen vermochte. Und jene Füsse im Fenster? Wieder auf der Strasse unten schaute ich hinauf und sah, wie sie mir die Sohlen entgegenstreckten. Fischer hat den Aussen- und Innenraum für sich beansprucht und alles zu Kunst gemacht, so weit das Auge reichte.

(Übersetzung: Suzanne Schmidt)

1) Lewis Carroll, *Alice im Wunderland,* Anfang des 2. Kapitels, «Der Tränenteich», übers. v. Christian Enzensberger, Insel Verlag, Frankfurt am Main 1963.

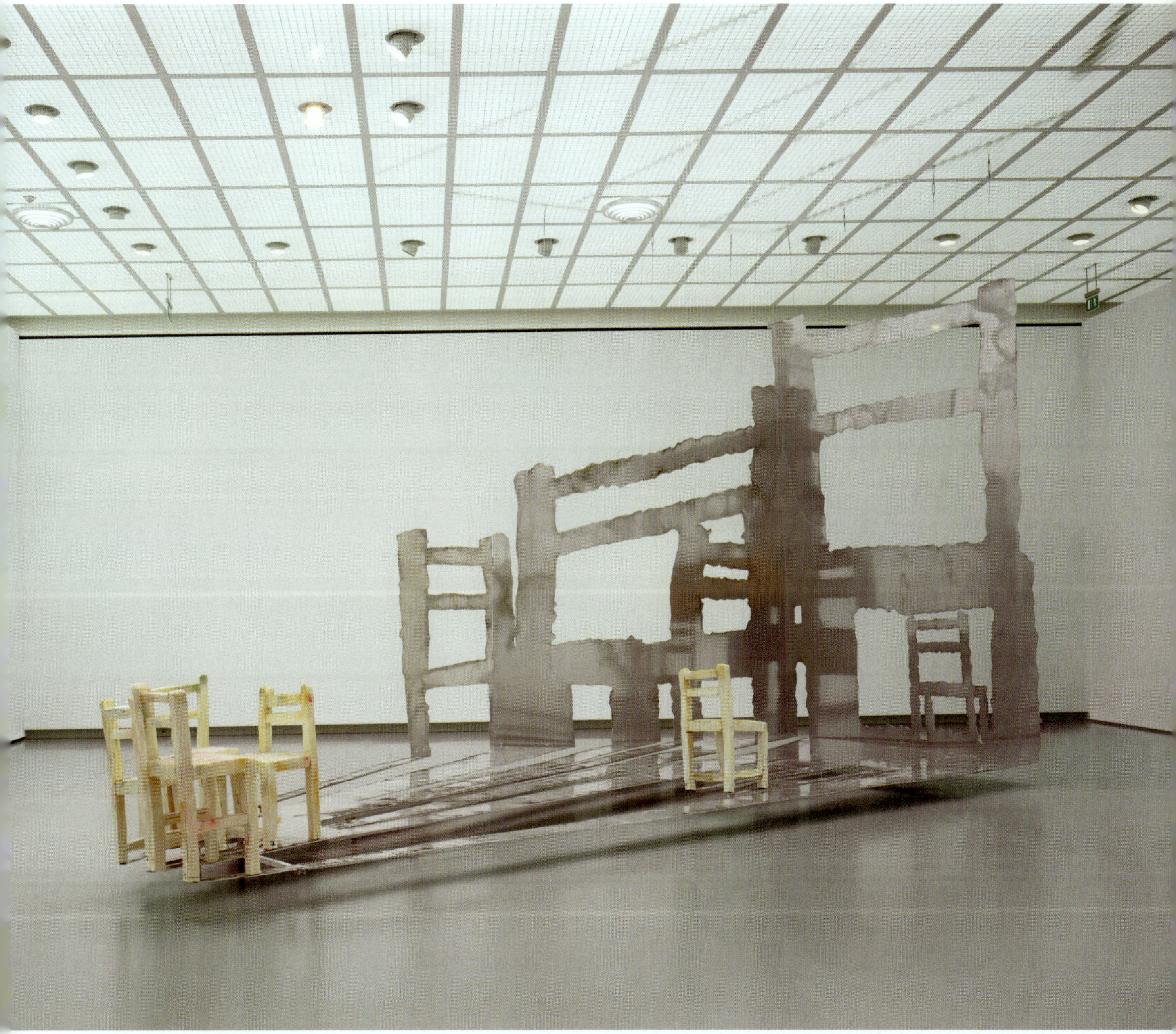

URS FISCHER, MEMORIES OF A BLANK MIND, 2004, Kunsthaus Zürich, aluminum, steel rope, 2K-polyurethane, wood, marker, screws, 157 1/2 x 236 1/4"/ Aluminium, Stahlseil, 2K-Polyurethan, Holz, Lackstift, Schrauben, 400 x 600 x 600 cm.

«wollte gerade musik anstellen aber sie läuft schon»

BEATRIX RUF

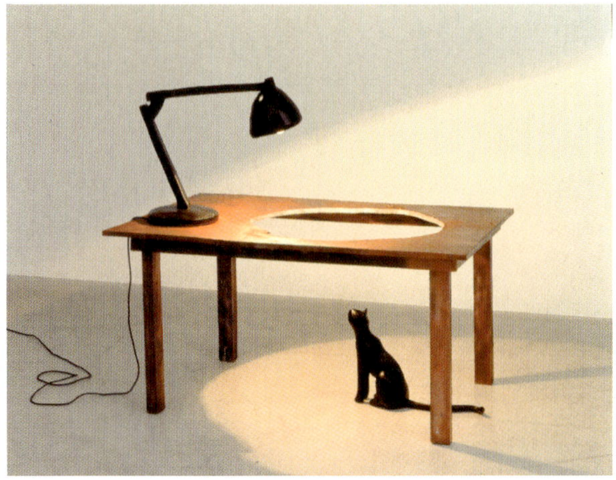

URS FISCHER, DAYLIGHT PILLOW, 2004, aluminum, acrylic paint, light bulb / Aluminium, Acrylfarbe, Glühbirne.

Unser Leben mit den Formen und Ingredienzien, die wir für uns erfunden haben, tritt eigensinnig auf. Bei Urs Fischer, dessen künstlerisches Schaffen in allen erdenklichen Erscheinungsformen um die Dinge des Lebens kreist, heisst das vor allem, dass wir uns in einem fortdauernden und immer wieder wechselnden Dialog mit diesen Dingen und unseren und ihren Bedingungen befinden. Eigensinnig, wie die Dinge sind, sind sie irgendwie immer schon da, werden gerade im Auftauchen erwischt, oder aber sie haben sich schon wieder verändert, gerade, wenn wir sie endlich realisiert haben. Urs Fischers Zitat, «wollte gerade musik anstellen aber sie läuft schon»,[1] formuliert deutlich und auch vielfältig paradox die Beziehung des Subjektes zu seiner Umgebung: Unsere Sehnsüchte, Wunschvorstellungen, Handlungen, Entscheidungen, Vorgehensweisen, Aktionen sind geprägt von einer nie ganz aufschlüsselbaren zeitlichen Abfolge von Ursachen und Wirkungen. Urs Fischers Werke zeigen uns Wirklichkeit aus zahlreichen Schichten bestehend, deren zeitliche wie materielle Aktualisierungen transitorisch als «Realität» erscheinen mögen. In seinen Werken ist diese temporäre Realität immer Potenzialität, Merkwürdigkeit und Widerspruch, überraschende Wendung und autonomes Gegenüber.

Die Vorwegnahme möglicher Szenarien und Konstruktionen für potenzielle Realisierungen des noch nicht Anwesenden sind irgendwie immer zentral im Werk Fischers: Eine Wirklichkeit ist schon eingetreten, wir haben es nur noch nicht gemerkt, und sie muss uns leider immer wieder darauf hinweisen, dass wir nicht genau zusehen, hinhören, mitdenken und mitfühlen: «wollte gerade musik anstellen aber sie läuft schon...» Idealerweise fällt das, was wir erhoffen, erahnen, ins Reale zwingen wollten, ins Lot mit unserem Begehren und unseren Aktionen, wahrscheinlicher aber ist, dass die Überraschung über den Einklang alles schon wieder verändert hat.

In der Arbeit DAYLIGHT PILLOW (Tageskissen, 2004) sehen wir eine Katze unter einem Tisch sitzen und herausfordernd in Richtung eines Lampenlichts schauen. Offensichtlich ist hier das richtige Verhält-

BEATRIX RUF ist Direktorin der Kunsthalle Zürich.

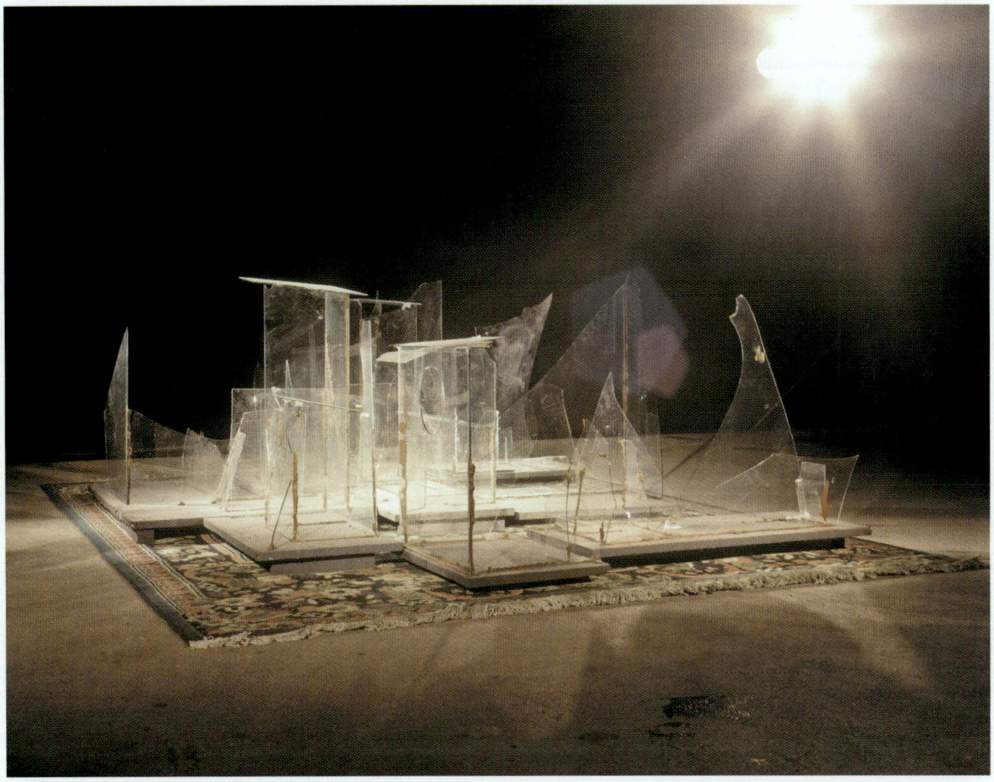

URS FISCHER, GLASKATZEN – MÜLLEIMER DER HOFFNUNG, 1999, wood, glass, silicon, acrylic, on a carpet of 151 9/16 x 105 7/8" / Holz, Glas, Silikon, Acryl, auf einem Teppich von 385 x 269 cm.

nis zwischen Begehren, Aktion und Ereignis hergestellt. Sie hat es auf das Licht abgesehen, ganz offensichtlich, dieses Licht ist ihres und sie zwingt der Tischplatte ein grosses klaffendes Loch ab, so dass sie voll im Lampenlicht sitzen und Wärme, Helligkeit und die ungebrochene Aufmerksamkeit der Lampe gleichzeitig geniessen kann. Absicht, Wille, Offenheit, Direktheit des Wollens – eins sein mit seinen Wünschen und die Realität ist mit uns? Immer wieder sind es die Katzen, die dies im Werk des Künstlers realisieren können: in häuslichen Szenerien herumlungernd, fordernd auf Kühlschränken oder vor Backöfen hockend (MR. FLOSKY, 2001–2002) oder im Mimikry einen Stöckelschuh harmlos aussehen lassend (SKYLINE, 2002) und so fort.

Urs Fischer arbeitet mit allen künstlerischen Mitteln und in allen Medien. Motivisch und thematisch bekanntes «Material» der Kunstgeschichte wie Stillleben, Porträts, Akte, Landschaften, Interieurs finden ihre Umsetzungen sowohl in Plastiken, Objekten, collagierten Bildern, Gemälden, Computerzeichnungen, Installationen und Photographien, und immer wieder gibt es auch Texte. Medien- und stilübergreifend wird die «Handschrift» des Künstlers Urs Fischer sichtbar in der individuellen und immer wiederkehrenden Qualität seines Umgangs mit Materialien und Medien, der geprägt ist von Prozessen und Transformation. Fischer scheint beständig im Dialog zu stehen mit den je spezifischen Verhaltensweisen der verschiedenen Dinge der Welt. Seine Befragung von Strukturen, Beziehungen, Konstellationen und Wirkungsmechanismen der Kunst wie der Realität bleibt ein offener Dialog, dessen ebenso offene Plots potenziert werden in der Rezeption des Publikums.

Urs Fischers «Bilder» sind in einen intimen Kontakt mit der Welt verwickelt. Und da der Moment der Aktualisierung von Realitäts-Dingen ein immer wieder anderer ist, scheint es nur logisch und folgerichtig, dass in Fischers Werk ikonographische Elemente in immer wieder neuen Spielarten wiederkehren, so dass eigentliche Serien entstehen: weibliche Schönheiten, Katzen, Tische, Bänke, Stühle, Vasen, Kerzenständer, Zigarettenschachteln, Feuerzeuge, Früchteschalen, Tee- und Kaffeesets, Kühlschränke, Gläser, Regale – Gegenstände mit Schatten, ihrem erzählerischen Gegenüber; Stühle und ihre gebrochenen Doubles; Stühle, Tische und anderes Alltagszeugs mit ihren Schatten; Skelette in lasziv erotischen oder komischen Situationen; Objekte und Skulpturen in Materialprozesse verstrickt oder durch undefinierbare Materialduschen zur Unbeweglichkeit erstarrt. Die Vergänglichkeit des einen und die Präsenz des anderen – alles bei Urs Fischer ist materiellen wie inhaltlichen Mutationen und Variationen ausgesetzt. Das gilt zum Beispiel auch für die frühe Plastik FAULES FUNDAMENT (1998), in der eine Backsteinmauer auf einem modernden Fundament mit dem Prozess des organischen Verfalls ihre Geometrie aufgeben muss, oder für die Damen-Wachskerzengruppe WHAT IF THE PHONE RINGS (2003), deren Schönheiten und Charaktere im Ausstellungsverlauf vor sich hinschmelzen.

Fischers Arbeiten sind nicht nur Formen und Bilder, sondern auch Erzählungen von der Begegnung kollektiver Übereinkünfte mit der Wirklichkeit individueller Erfahrungswelten und damit auch der Metamorphose des Bekannten zum Unheimlichen, zum Unbehagen und zum Surrealen. Wie die wiederkehrenden Skelette direkter zeigen, sind sie aber auch *Vanitas*-Bilder, welche die Angreifbarkeit der materiellen Erscheinungsform in einen zeitgenössischen und vor allem entmythologisierenden Diskurs mit unseren Auffassungen verwickeln.

Neben den Objekten und Bildern, die als Protagonisten eines grösseren Handlungszusammenhangs Urs Fischers Kunstkosmos bevölkern, hat der Künstler immer wieder auch Raumsituationen geschaffen, die als abstrahierte Innenräume einer möglichen Erzählung die ganze Breite seines Umgangs mit Materialisierungen und Fiktionalisierungen durchspielen: In der Arbeit DR. KATZELBERG (ZIVILISATIONSRUINE) (1999) spielt Fischer mit der permanenten Reorganisation des Sehens. Aus Spiegelflächen zusammengesetzte Katzen spiegeln sich in Räumen aus Spiegeln und binden den umgebenden Raum in einem unendlichen Brechen, Widerspiegeln und Ablenken. Die Arbeit GLASKATZEN – MÜLLEIMER DER HOFFNUNG (1999) dagegen ist eine offene Raumfolge aus Glaswänden, die gefährlich instabil wirken und eine fiktive Ordnung eines ebenso fiktiven Innenlebens beschreiben. Teppichbodenfragmente brechen das Verhältnis zu dieser «durchsichtigen» Ordnung, in dem sie unangemessene Realitätsebenen einführen und eine unangenehme Heimeligkeit ausbreiten.

Auch GLASKATZENSEX – TRANSPARENT TALE (2000) besteht als Raumsituation aus Glasscheiben, die aggressiv beleuchtet, eine vergangene Szene heraufbeschwören: Staub liegt auf den Scheiben, und Silikonfetzen hängen wie abgezogene Häute über ihnen. In der Arbeit THE MEMBRANE (2000) ist der Raum nur noch durch eine offene Struktur von Holzrahmen und den Spanplattenboden definiert; Materialität als Leerstelle, in der wie durch zu grosse Hitze geschmolzene Fragmente roten Materials über den Raumangaben hängen. Noch abstrakter wird die Materialität des Raumes in der Arbeit PEANUTS IN COMPARISON aus dem Jahr 2004. Die Raumlandschaft aus Aluminium ist mit einem beinahe undefinierbaren Farbanstrich behandelt, der die eigentliche Materialität der Installation kippen lässt und die labyrinthische Raumfolge in ein hybrides Objekt zwischen Minimal Art und Sciencefictionset verwandelt.

Von Beginn an spielt der Grad der An- oder Abwesenheit realisierter oder initiierter Fiktionalisierungen im Werk des Künstlers eine wichtige Rolle: Objekte, Skulpturen und Installationen, die sich durch Materialdeformationen, Verfall oder Auflösung auszeichnen, ihren narrativen Gehalt als Live-Act vorführen und eine Geschichte in der Zeit entfalten, stehen neben Objekten, deren Formatwechsel oder Oberflächengestaltung, Verdoppelung oder Schattenbildung Fiktionen erzeugen. Diese sind Fischers Zeichnungen, Collagen, Computerbildern oder auch Texten näher, die immer schon fiktionalisierte Formulierungen als Transformations- und Surrealisierungsprozesse des Künstlers verkörpert haben.

URS FISCHER, A RUIN LOOKING GOOD AT DAWN, 2003,
Iris print, 18 1/8 x 15 1/8" / Irisdruck, 46 x 38,3 cm.

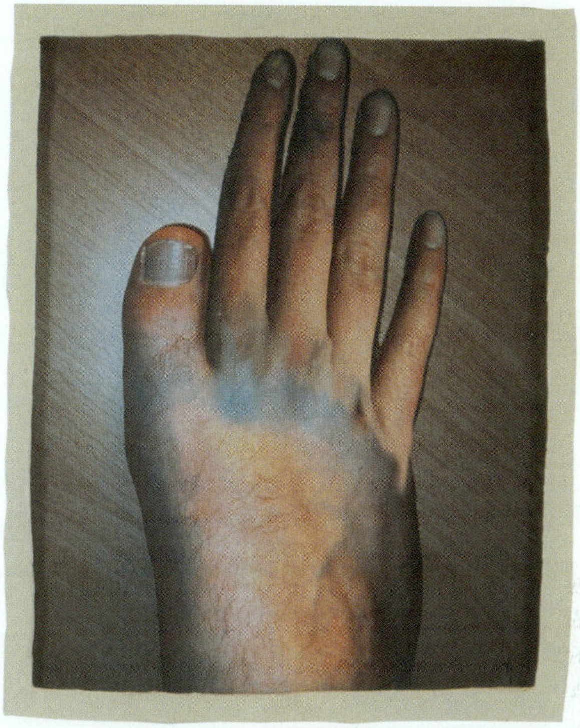

Zunehmend verbindet Fischer die beiden Zustandsformen von Fiktionalisierungen in seinen Arbeiten und Ausstellungsinstallationen. So etwa, wenn er für die Ausstellungen in der Galerie Gavin Brown's Enterprise in New York und im Kunsthaus Zürich Wände mit einer grossen zeichnerischen Geste aufschneidet und Durchblicke schafft, welche die räumliche Anordnung von Objekten, Skulpturen und Bildern in ein noch grösseres Bild fassten. Dass man beim Abschreiten der Ausstellung dann in den Raum dieses Zwei- wie Dreidimensionalität und Perspektiven verwirrenden Bildes tritt, ist ebenso irritierend, wie selbst Teil dieses von Urs Fischer erzeugten Bildes zu sein.

Im Moment scheint es, dass der Künstler mehr daran interessiert ist, seine individuellen Geschichten als Einschreibungen in die Materialien und Oberflächen seiner Objekte zu realisieren, als daran, die Materialien als Performer von Narrationen für seine Objekte zu verwenden. Das zeigen etwa die «Pop»-artigen Vergrösserungen der Arbeit STALAGMITES OF LOVE (2004) oder auch die Experimente, von denen Fischer im Zusammenhang mit zukünftigen Ausstellungen berichtet, bei denen er Objekte gegen ihre Materialität agieren lassen möchte (Wie stark muss eine Schnur sein, damit ein massiver Ballon an ihr schweben kann?).

Wirklichkeits-, aber auch Zeitüberlappungen sind zentral in den narrativen Konstruktionen Fischers. Und das eingangs erwähnte Zitat, «wollte gerade musik anstellen aber sie läuft schon», bringt auch zum Ausdruck, dass sich Wirklichkeit immer in parallelen Ebenen wahrnehmen lässt, geprägt durch subjektive Wahrnehmung und objektiv Vorhandenes, die sich wechselseitig «verändern». In seinen neuesten Collagebildern experimentiert der Künstler zusehends mit einer Gleichzeitigkeit und Gleichwertigkeit dieser Realitätsschichten, zum Beispiel in der Arbeit: BIRDS SING, RAIN FALLS (2004), die aus zwei sich ineinander schiebenden Bildebenen entsteht. Einem grossen Tropfen gleich trieft eine von Grafitti-Elementen geprägte Bildfläche in eine Boden-Asphaltfläche. Malerisches und Photographisches hybridisieren sich sowohl auf der ikonographischen wie medialen Ebene dieses Bildes, und der im Fallen gestoppte Tropfen, der im oberen Bereich des Bildes hängt, hat bereits eine Tropfspur in der Asphaltfläche hinterlassen. Fällt er? Steigt er auf? Findet beides gleichzeitig statt, gibt es ein Davor oder Danach? Beinhaltet das eine das andere? Vielleicht hilft dabei ein weiteres Zitat des Künstlers: «nicht vergessen: der arsch klebt am stuhl durch gravitation.»[2]

1) Urs Fischer, «Auszüge aus: Soulkebab, Bing Crosby – Meine Grossmutter, Hello Vanity, Die Warten am Tisch, Slobodan, Fools, Boxiwoxi (Random Selection / Unedited)», in: *Kir Royal,* Ausstellungskatalog, Kunsthaus Zürich, JRP Ringier Verlag, Zürich 2004, S. 167–230, hier: 180.
«anstellen»: Schweizer Dialekt für «einschalten».
2) Ebenda, S. 171.

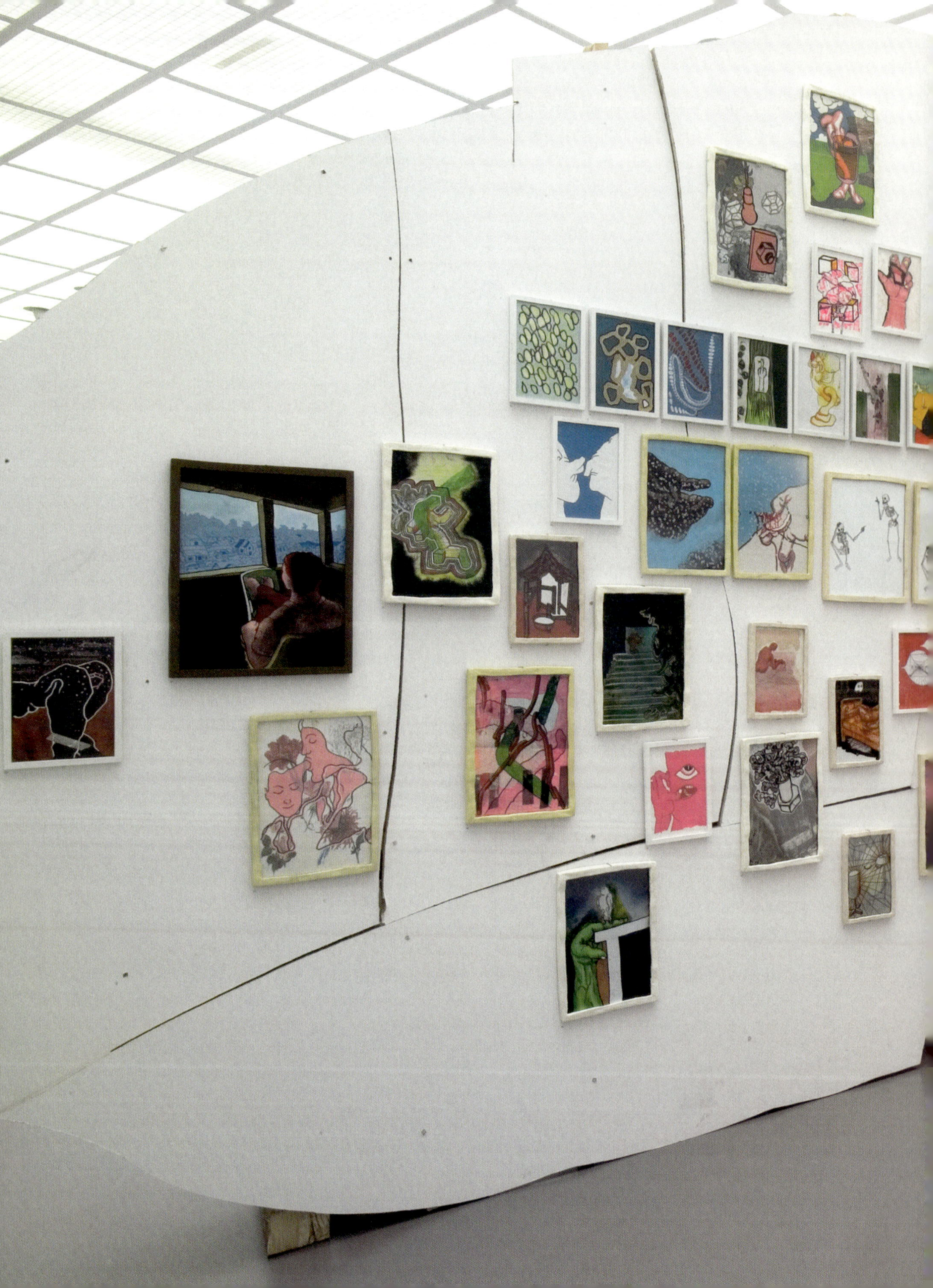

URS FISCHER, *"Kir Royal," Kunsthaus Zürich, 2004: MIDDLE CLASS HEROES and drawings by the artist / und Zeichnungen des Künstlers. (PHOTO: MANCIA/BODMER, FBM-STUDIO, ZÜRICH)*

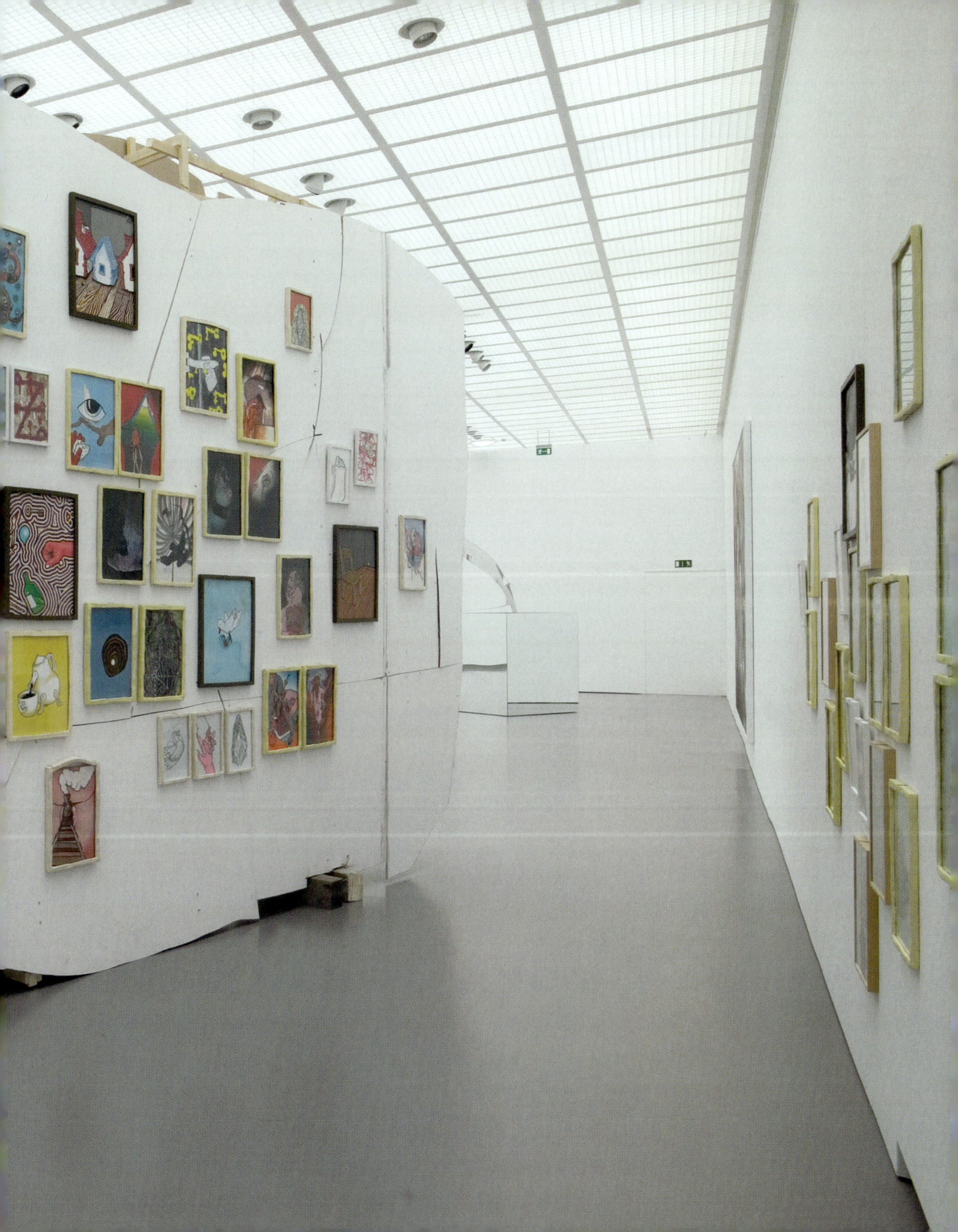

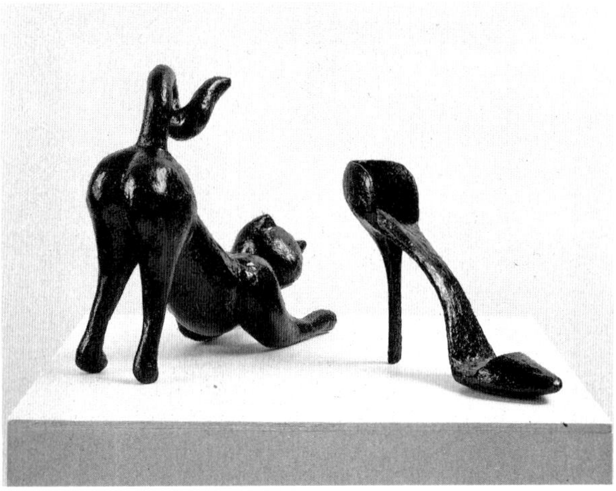

URS FISCHER, SKYLINE, 2002, styrofoam, ink, acrylic, wire, 11 x 17 1/2 x 19 1/4" / Styropor, Tinte, Acryl, Draht, 28 x 44,5 x 49 cm.

"wanted to turn the music on but it was already playing"

BEATRIX RUF

Given the forms and ingredients that we have invented for ourselves, life has acquired a willful appearance. In dealing with Urs Fischer, whose artistic output circles the things of life in every conceivable shape, we are drawn into a continuing and forever changing dialogue with just those things, with their status and ours. And being willful, they are always there somehow, caught in the act of cropping up, or already in the process of changing the moment we realize they are there. Fischer's statement, "wanted to turn the music on but it was already playing,"[1)] unmistakably expresses the complex and paradoxical relationship between a subject and its environment. Our longings and desires, the way we act and behave, the decisions we make and how we proceed—these all are determined by a succession of causes and effects that we can never fully comprehend. Urs Fischer's work reveals a world that consists of multiple layers, rendered temporally and materially in what may be described as a transitory "reality." In his works, he informs this temporary reality with potentiality, oddity, and contradiction, with surprising turns and an autonomous other.

Anticipating possible scenarios and making constructions for potential realizations of something that is not yet present are both somehow always central to Fischer's practice: a reality has already taken place, we just haven't noticed it yet and, unfortunately, it is always reminding us that we are not very good at watching, listening, understanding, and empathizing: "wanted to turn the music on but it was already playing." Ideally, whatever we hope for, anticipate, or try to press into reality will be aligned with our desires and our actions; it is more likely, however, that our surprise at the consonance has already changed everything.

In DAYLIGHT PILLOW (2004), a cat sitting under a table is gazing provocatively toward the light of a lamp. The right relationship of desire, action, and event has clearly been established. The cat is after the light; the light obviously and incontestably belongs to her. She coerces the tabletop into obliging with a gigantic gaping hole so that she can sit in the

BEATRIX RUF is the director of the Kunsthalle Zürich.

unobstructed light of the lamp, enjoying its warmth, brightness, and undivided attention. Purpose, will, openness, directness of desire—need we only be at one with our desires for reality to be with us? In Fischer's work, it's always cats that serve as the medium of that message: lolling about in domestic scenarios, insistently squatting on refrigerators or in front of ovens (MR. FLOSKY, 2001–2002), or mimicking and hence making a stiletto shoe look harmless (SKYLINE, 2002).

Urs Fischer works with all the tools of the fine arts and in every medium. He translates the familiar "material" of art history—its motifs and subject matter, its still lifes, portraits, nudes, landscapes, and interiors—not only into sculptures, objects, collages, paintings, computer drawings, installations, and photographs, but into texts as well. Regardless of medium, regardless of style, the artist's "signature" is visible in the individual and consistently recurring quality of his procedural and transformative treatment of materials and media. Fischer seems to be conversing with the distinctive modes of behavior specific to each of the different things of the world. His investigations of the structures, relations, configurations, and consequences of both art and reality remain an open-ended dialogue, with an equally open-ended plot, magnified and enhanced through the response of the public.

Urs Fischer's "pictures" are intimately involved with the world, and since implementing the things of reality is never the same in Fischer's oeuvre, it is only logical that iconographic elements reappear in a host of new and different variations. Such repetition might essentially be read as work in series: female beauties, cats, tables, benches, chairs, vases, candlesticks, cigarette packages, lighters, fruit bowls, tea and coffee sets, refrigerators, glasses, and shelves. Then there are objects with shadows, with a narrative other; chairs and their broken doubles; chairs, tables, and other items of daily use with their shadows; skeletons in lasciviously erotic or funny situations; objects and sculptures entangled in physical processes or petrified and rigid in indefinable torrents of material. The transience of the one and the presence of the other—everything in Fischer's oeuvre is subjected to material and substantial mutations and variations. Take, for instance, the early sculpture, FAULES FUNDAMENT (1998), in which a brick wall on

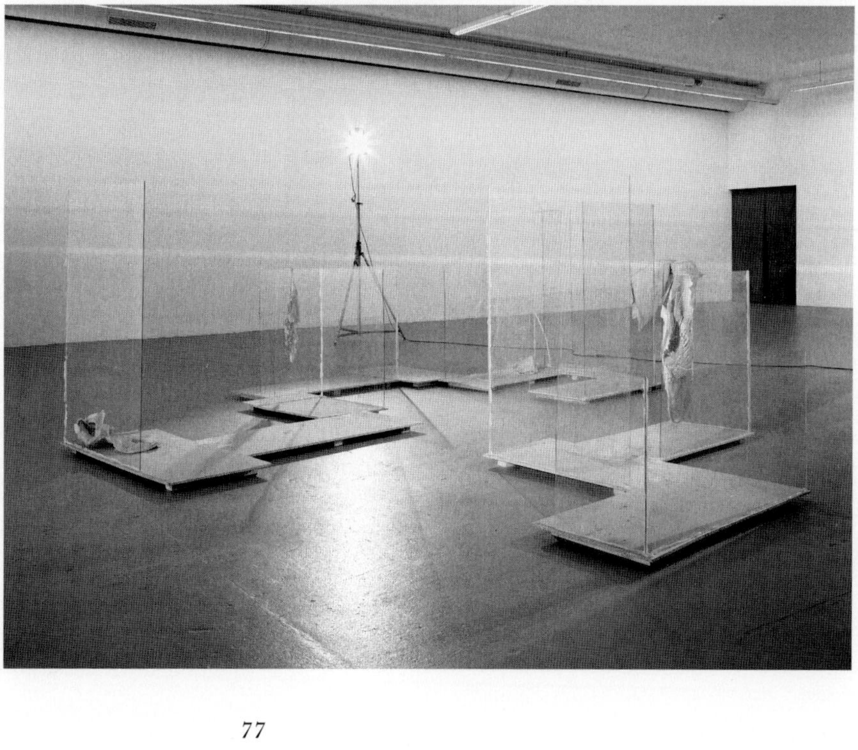

URS FISCHER, GLASKATZENSEX – TRANSPARENT TALE, 2000, mixed media, Migros Museum für Gegenwartskunst, Zürich, 62 1/4 x 220 1/2 x 236 1/4" / diverse Materialien, 158 x 560 x 600 cm.

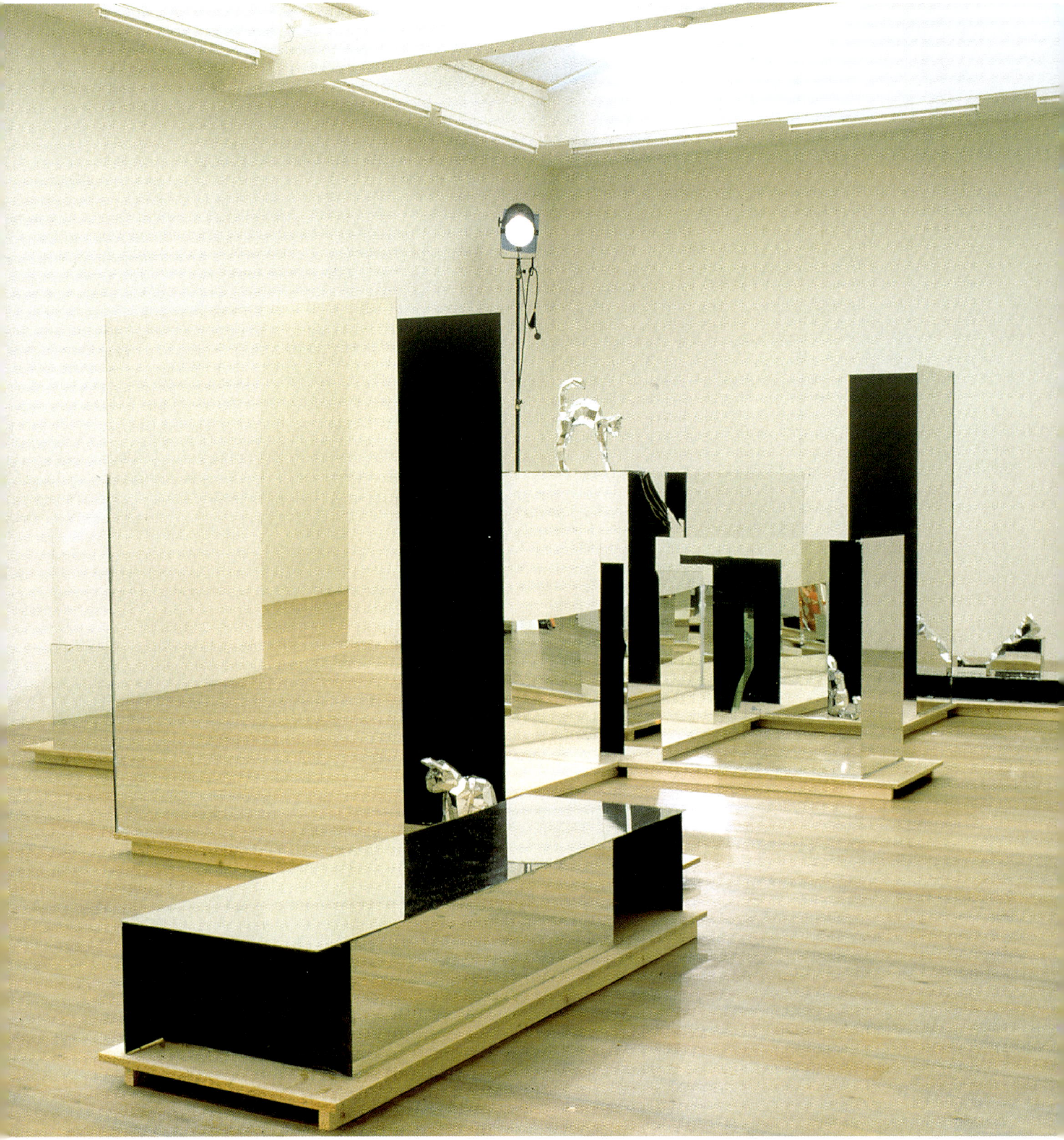

URS FISCHER, DR. KATZELBERG (ZIVILISATIONSRUINE), 1999, mirror, silicon, wood, styrofoam, spotlights, 82 11/16 x 196 7/8 x 137 13/16" / Spiegel, Silikon, Holz, Styropor, Scheinwerfer, 210 x 500 x 350 cm.

a rotting foundation is forced by the process of organic decay to abandon its geometry, or the wax-candle women in WHAT IF THE PHONE RINGS (2003), whose beauty and character melt away in the course of the exhibition.

Fischer's works are not only shapes and images but also narratives of encounters with collective agreement on the reality of individual worlds of experience; they therefore also embody the metamorphosis of the known into the uncanny, the weird, and the surreal. However, as shown explicitly by his recurring skeletons, they are also *vanitas* images, which embroil the vulnerability of material forms of appearance in a contemporary and above all demythologizing discourse with our conceptions.

In addition to objects and pictures, which function as the protagonists that inhabit the larger context of his artistic universe, Urs Fischer regularly creates situations in space, abstract interiors of a potential narrative in which he runs the entire gamut of materialization and fictionalization. In DR. KATZELBERG (ZIVILISATIONSRUINE) (1999), Fischer plays with the permanent reorganization of vision. Cats made out of mirrored surfaces are mirrored in a room of mirrors, turning the space of the room into infinite refraction, mirroring, and diffraction. In contrast, GLASKATZEN MÜLLEIMER DER HOFFNUNG (1999) is a series of rooms with glass walls that look precariously fragile and describe a fictional order of an equally fictional inner life. Fragments of carpeting rupture our relationship to that "transparent" order by introducing inappropriate levels of reality and dispensing an unpleasant coziness.

Another installation, GLASKATZENSEX–TRANSPARENT TALE (2000), consists of aggressively illuminated panes of glass and conjures a scene of the past: the glass is covered with dust, and bits of silicon are draped over them like pieces of cast-off skin. In THE MEMBRANE (2000), the room is defined only by a loose structure of wooden frames and a plywood floor; materiality is a void, hung with scraps of a red substance that looks as if extreme heat had melted it. The reality of the room is even more abstract in PEANUTS IN COMPARISON (2004). The aluminum landscape of this piece is coated with an almost indefinable layer of paint, essentially undermining the materiality of the installation and transforming the labyrinthine sequence of rooms into a hybrid object between minimal art and science fiction stage set.

Defining the presence or absence of realized or initiated fictionalizations has always played an important role in Urs Fischer's work. Objects, sculptures, and installations are subjected to material deformation, decay, or dissolution and display their narrative content as a live act, as a story that unfolds in time. In other objects, fictions are generated through a change of format or redesigned surfaces, through duplication or the casting of shadows. The

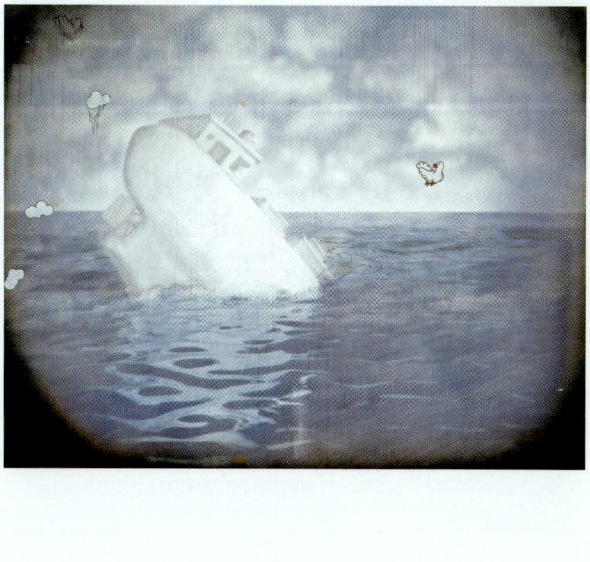

URS FISCHER, STALAGMITES OF LOVE, 2004, acrylic, marker, and UV ink-jet print on aluminum, 108 5/8 x 140 1/8" / Acryl, Lackstift und UV-Inkjetdruck auf Aluminium, 276 x 356 cm.

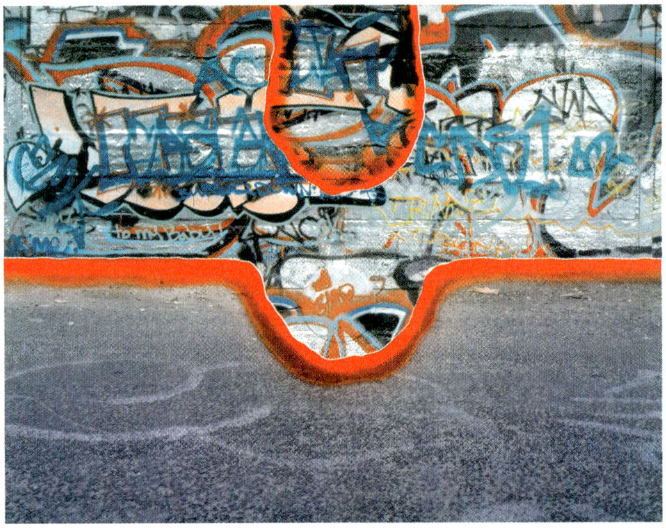

URS FISCHER, BIRDS SING, RAIN FALLS, 2004, acrylic, marker, and UV-ink-jet print on aluminum, 108 5/8 x 140 1/8" / Acryl, Lackstift und UV-Inkjetdruck auf Aluminium, 276 x 356 cm.

latter are closer to Fischer's drawings, collages, computer pictures, and texts, which have always embodied fictionalized formulations of the processes enlisted to achieve transformation and surrealization.

Increasingly, Fischer has begun to unite the two forms of fictionalization in his individual works as well as his installations. In his exhibitions at Gavin Brown's enterprise in New York and at the Kunsthaus Zürich, he cut through walls with a draftsman's sweeping gesture, creating views that place the spatial arrangement of objects, sculptures, and pictures in an even larger framework. Walking through the exhibition and being drawn into a bewildering space of two and three dimensions and unsettling perspectives is quite as disconcerting as finding oneself part of the picture that Fischer has generated.

Currently, the artist seems to be more interested in rendering his stories as inscriptions in the materials and surfaces of his objects—as in the pop-like enlargements of STALAGMITES OF LOVE (2004) or experiments envisioned for future exhibitions, in which the artist wants to test his materials (How strong does a rope have to be in order to suspend a gigantic balloon from it?)—than in using the materials as performers of narratives for his objects.

Overlapping realities and times are central to Urs Fischer's narrative constructions. And his above-quoted remark, "wanted to turn the music on but it was already playing," also indicates that reality can always be perceived in parallel worlds, under the mutually modifying influence of subjective perception and objective existence. In his latest collages, the artist has begun experimenting with the simultaneity and equivalence of these layers of reality, as in the work, BIRDS SING, RAIN FALLS (2004), which emerges in the process of two visual layers overlapping. Like a huge globule, a picture plane covered with graffiti drips onto an asphalt floor. This hybrid of painting and photography takes place in both the iconographic and mediated levels of the picture, and the globule caught in mid-air, hanging in the upper part of the picture, has already left a dripping trail on the asphalt. Is it falling? Is it climbing? Is it doing both at once, is there a before or an after? Does the one contain the other? Another comment made by the artist may give us some insight, "don't forget: gravity makes your ass stick to the chair."[2]

(Translation: Catherine Schelbert)

1) Urs Fischer, "Excerpts from: Soulkebab, Bing Crosby – Meine Grossmutter, Hello Vanity, Die Warten am Tisch, Slobodan, Fools, Boxiwoxi (Random Selection / Unedited)," in *Kir Royal,* exh. cat., Kunsthaus Zürich / JRP Ringier Verlag, Zürich, 2004, pp. 167–230, here: 180.
2) Ibid., p. 171.

URS FISCHER, THE MEMBRANE (HALF FULL, HALF EMPTY), 2000, mixed media, ca. 236 1/4 x 118 1/8 x 118 1/8" / diverse Materialien, ca. 600 x 300 x 300 cm.

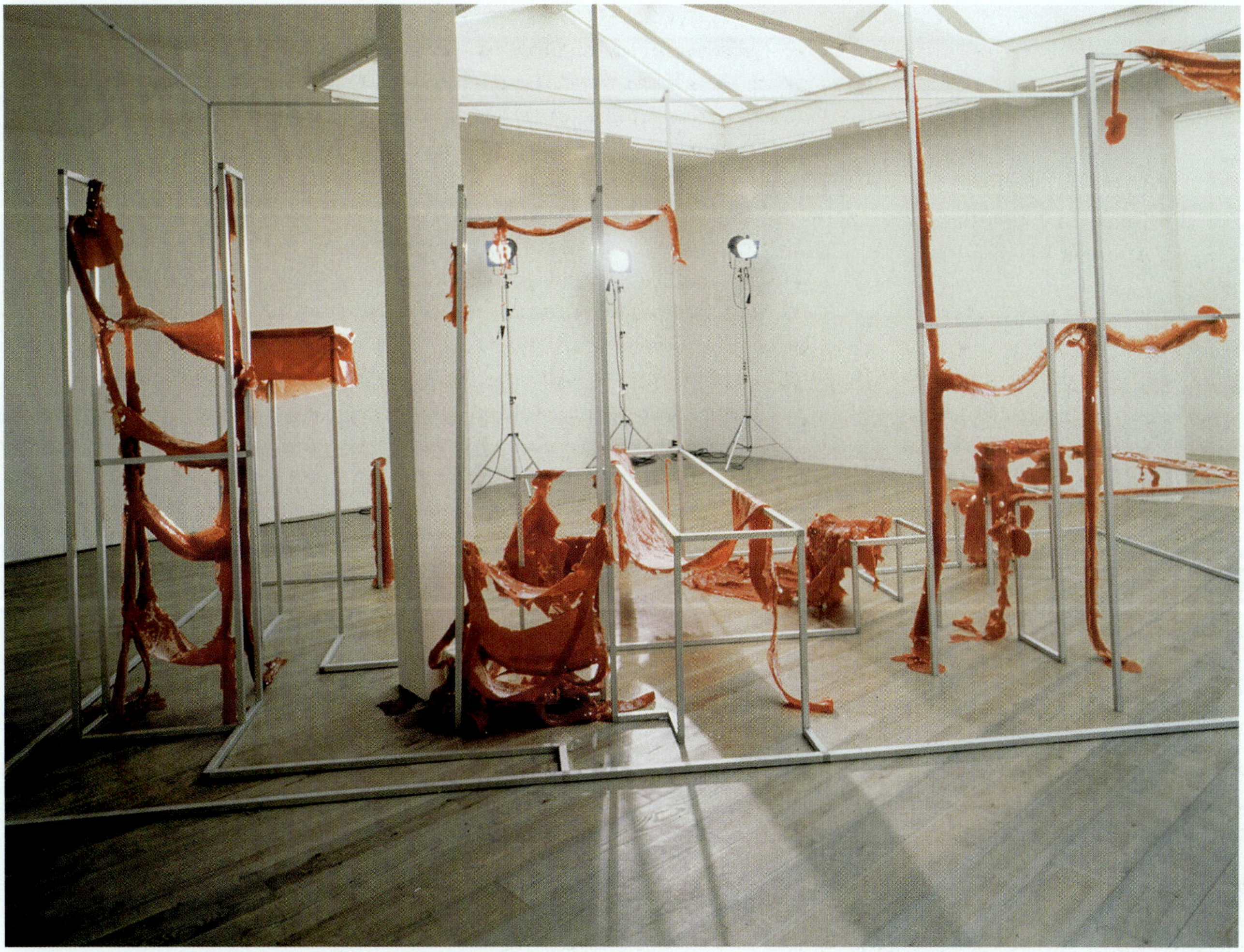

GARDEN of Earthly HATES

BENJAMIN WEISSMAN

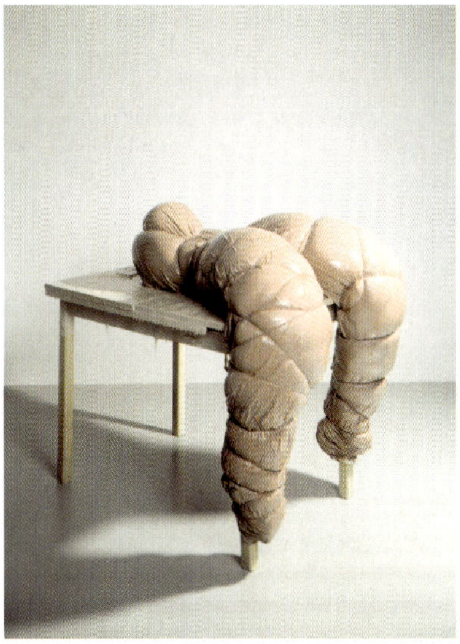

URS FISCHER, TABLE WITH, 1995–2001, mixed media, $41\,^{3}/_{4}$ x $48\,^{7}/_{16}$ x $38\,^{9}/_{16}$" / diverse Materialien, 106 x 123 x 98 cm.

I hate bouncers at strip clubs who tell me they'll break my hands if I *do that again.* I abhor them, frankly, and please, take note of the imprecise nature of the phrase, *do that again,* and the fact that I am a pianist with fine long fingers, which can only be taken to mean that I am expected *to do that;* management is sending out a vague invitation via a warning but it's more of an encouragement, or a dare, and dares have always pulled the man of true conviction and multiple interests toward the brightest lights. Sometimes I have to shake my head like a cat in order to reorient myself before I fall into a mental ditch, or an emotional hole in the road, and amazingly enough the head rattling works because the soft steamed brain-cauliflower actually vibrates against the inside of my skull bone and the miracle of forgetting, clean up, and remembrance follows automatically and sets me back on a slightly different path which is just what I had in mind. Some men believe that the best thing a man could do under those circumstances, after he's been warned *not to do something,* would be *to not do that again* but rather to remain perfectly still, or to do *something entirely different,* something *never before conceived,* a brand new act. Instead of doing that which caused bouncer meat to take notice (I repeat the phrase, *I will not abide by your coercive control,* over and over again, for that is not how I see the so-called land of the free, I abhor your form of government, America, I'm just letting you know, I'm giving notice) you do something else because it wouldn't be fair to count the new thing as *that again* because they're different actions. If, for example, one were to accidentally graze the back of the left hand, possibly just the second knuckle where my

BENJAMIN WEISSMAN is the author of *Headless* (Akashic Books, 2004) and *Dear Dead Person* (Serpent's Tale, 1994). He teaches fiction writing in the graduate program at Otis College of Art.

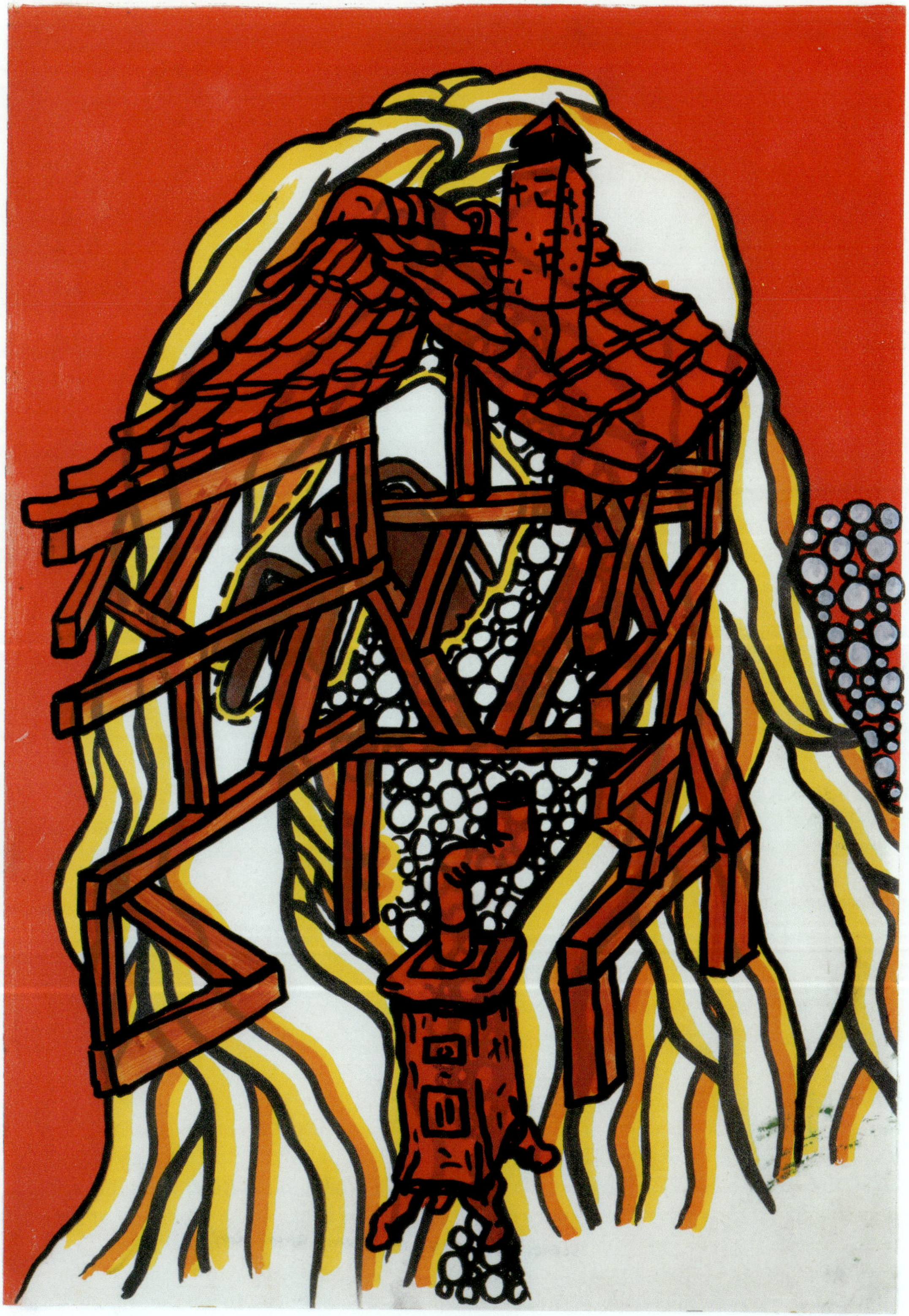

URS FISCHER, SCENES FROM THE INTERNAL BACKDROP (part 1 of 5), 2000, mixed media on paper, framed by the artist, 16 1/2 x 11 1/2" / Mischtechnik auf Papier, vom Künstler gerahmt, 42 x 29,3 cm.

Left / Links: URS FISCHER, STUHL FÜR EINEN GEIST: THOMAS, 2003, sand-cast aluminum, paint, varnish, wire, 27 1/2 x 16 1/2 x 40 1/2" / 70 x 42 x 103 cm. Right / Rechts: STUHL FÜR EINEN GEIST: URS, 2003, Aluminium-Sandguss, Farbe, Firnis, Draht, 71 x 74 x 102 cm / 28 x 29 1/8 x 40 1/8".

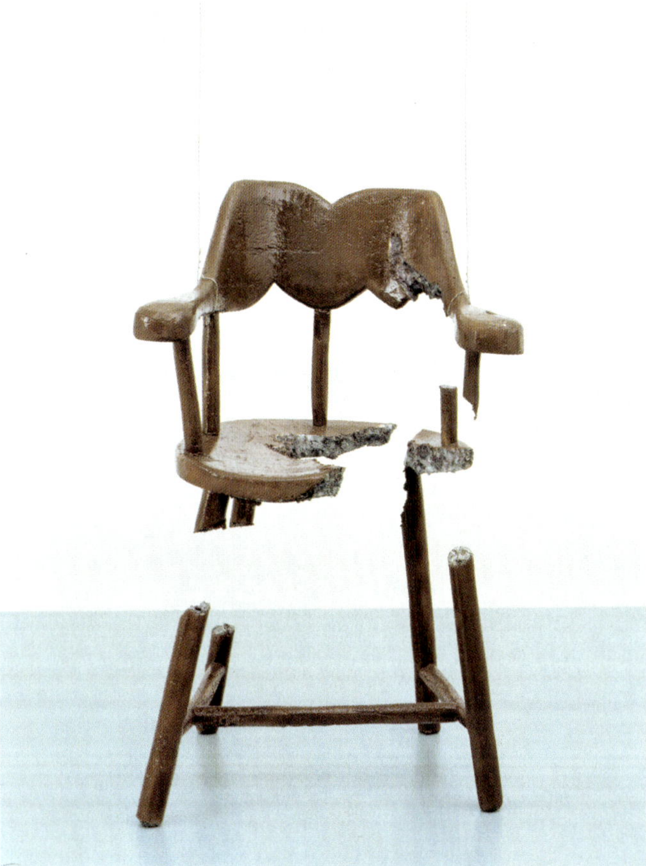

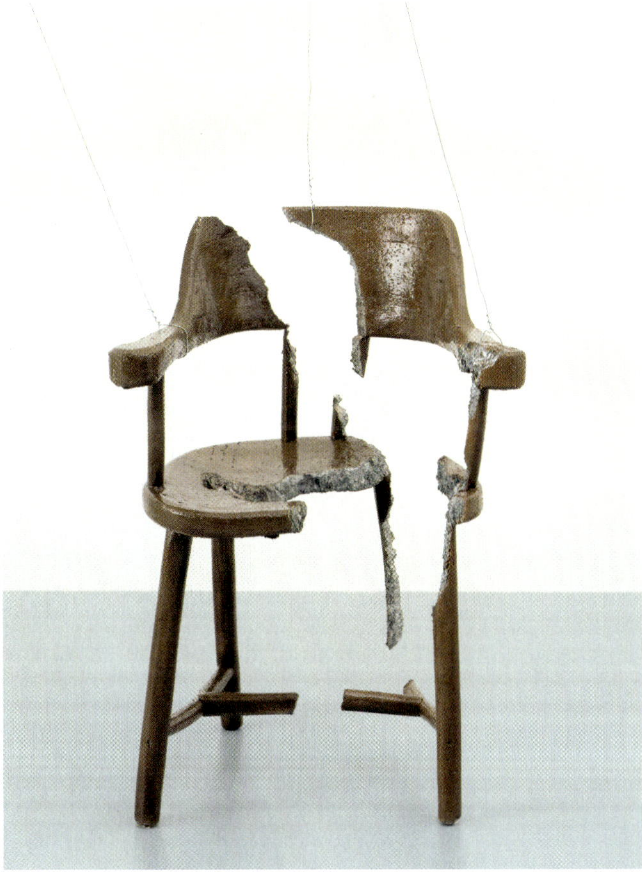

thick college ring resides, on a bikini top that guards the greater bosom area of a female performer, which is what occurred during the first episode (my crime against humanity), then perhaps I should up the ante to something much greater like squeezing both ass cheeks, pulling them apart and twisting them like valves on war ships and finally jamming my nose straight into the crack and reciting sonnets from memory in that position. I speak for all men when I say, we'd just like to know the rules, unfortunately Bouncerballs will not invite me to the back room for a private consultation where we get comfortable in leather chairs and unlock leather bound volumes and peruse the official rulebooks on conduct unbecoming, behavior that resembles pig sty antics, and converse about the ambiguities and nuances of English and its Latin, Dutch, or German origins. Even though I'm a big fan of repetitious acts, I pose the question, why would I want to *do that again* when there are many new things to try and I am here to expand my horizons, broaden the hues of my bow of rain, show the cashier, who greets me with caring facial features that curl up and a truly sincere *hello* and a deeply felt and exceedingly unnecessary *enjoy the show* pleasantry, as well as the fellow responsible for spinning the tunes that connect to the core of who I am and affect my future, DJ Smoke, who points a smooth trigger finger in my general direction before every Olivia Newton-John song,

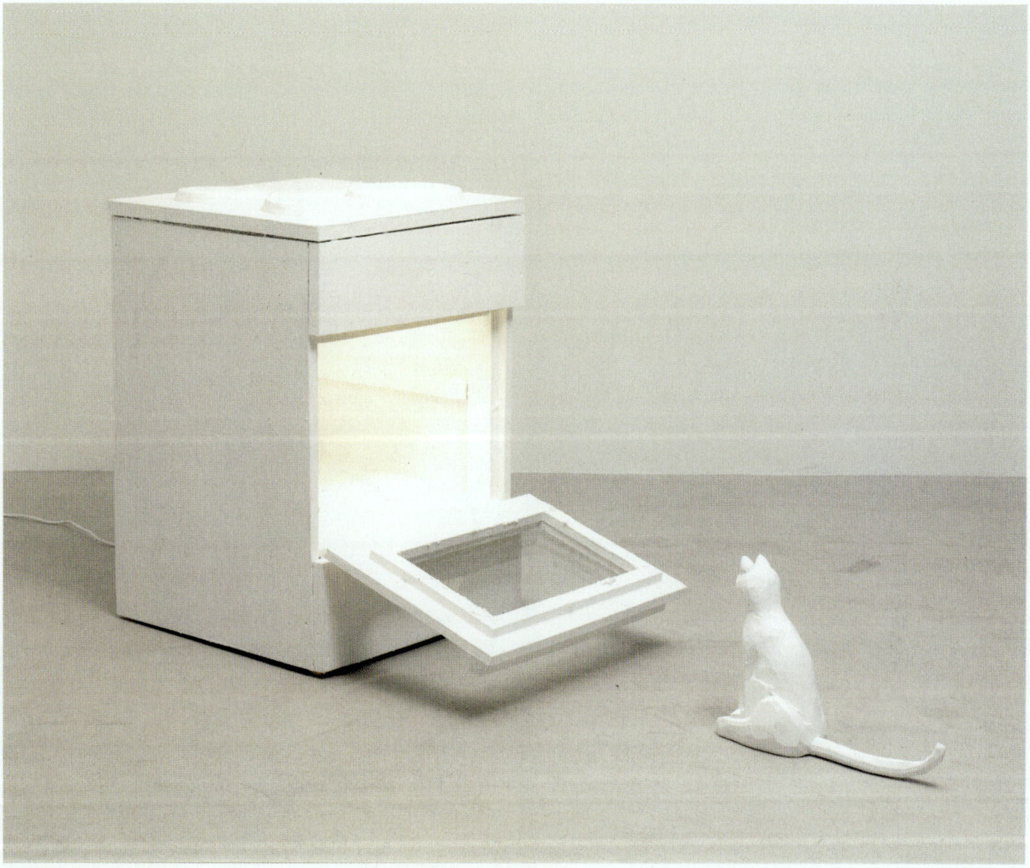

URS FISCHER, MR. FLOSKY, 2001/2002, mixed media, stove 38 3/4 x 41 3/8 x 23 1/4"; cat 13 3/16 x 18 1/8 x 5 11/16" / diverse Materialien, Ofen 98,5 x 105 x 59 cm; Katze 33,5 x 46 x 14,5 cm.

that I am not only grateful, but also a man with discrete charms and hidden recesses of brilliance? Olivia is from down under and that's what I'm talking about, going into the vivid moments of one's life, snorkeling around a hottie's camisole and tremendous frontage overhang. But first another suave sip, and another, and perhaps a huge gulp just to show anyone watching me that alcohol doesn't really change my demeanor. There are many ways to show real appreciation, to stand out and be friendly, and there comes a time in an audience member's life when applause and a folded five after a three song set just won't do, when a heart felt message spoken via "Body Talk" to a lovely lady is the only poetry that cuts through the bullshit, that says I appreciate the fine art of burlesque—I am a man of intelligence, I understand that a feather boa is not just a fluffy scarf, I don't come here strictly for the snatch. My *assessment* (let me pause on that word and point out that I've chosen it because it's a word that denotes thinking, that the first three letters conjure the buttocks), my *ass*essment of talent takes into account a number of factors, the principle one being a register of intelligence in the face area of the disrobing damsel. The serious performer will level an ambiguous glaze at you, not simply a gaze, but a glaze that is hard and shiny and porcelain like, hands on hips, like she's saying *bring it, old man,* or maybe an inquiring *what are you doing inches from my platform,* or *why are you wearing sweatpants at 1:45 A.M.?*, or *how many warm Pepsis can one human drink in a five hour period?*, all good questions that deserve answers, and then perhaps something a little more intellectual regarding the sum of an isosceles triangle equaling the square root of Sappho's dildo. I used to work at

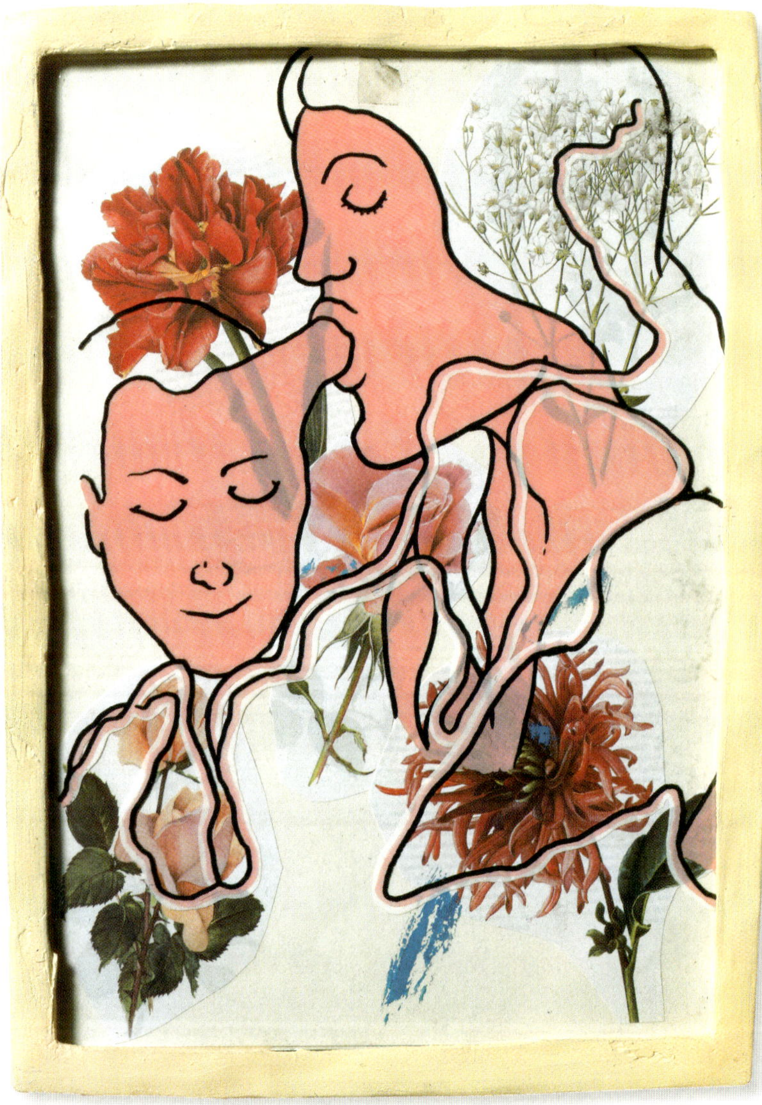

URS FISCHER, DENKST DU AUCH SO VIEL AN DICH WIE ICH, 2001, Mischtechnik auf Papier, vom Künstler gerahmt, 42 x 29,3 cm / mixed media on paper, framed by the artist, 16 1/2 x 11 1/2".

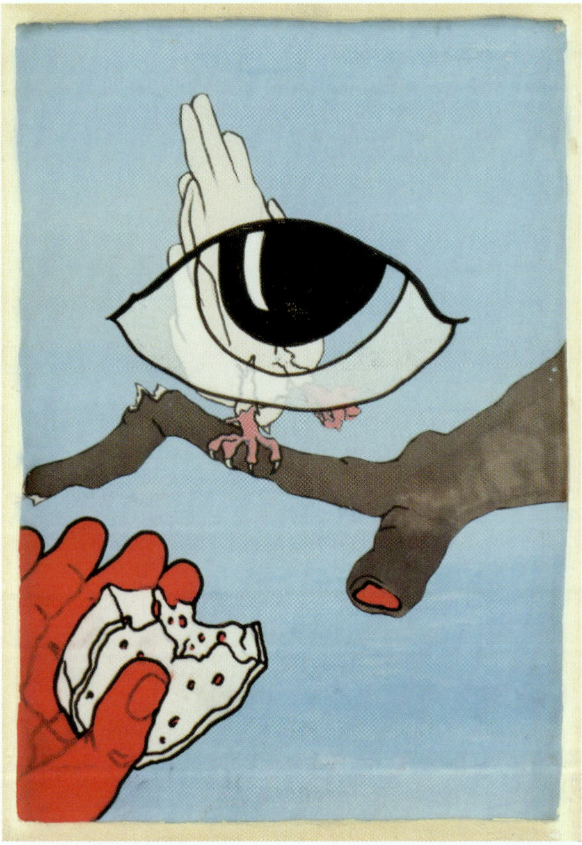

URS FISCHER, WAS IST DER BESTE SATZ DEN DU JE GEHÖRT HAST?, 2001, Teil 1 einer Serie von 2 Zeichnungen, Mischtechnik auf Papier, vom Künstler gerahmt, je 42 x 29,3 cm / part 1 of a series of 2 drawings, mixed media on paper, framed by the artist, 16 1/2 x 11 1/2" each.

Jumbo's so I know what it's like to play securityman, to roll out the muscle and drop whoever's interfering with the overall harmony of the room. Not intending to brag, but back in the day I lived to bend back fingers and drive my knee through the sternum of a misbehaving gent, I once inspired a frat boy to cough up a third of his heart. I told him *you better pick up that red filet before some starving rodent snatches that potential food source and eats it.* That's what I said to the guy who was doubled over after I'd let him know that my rock hard anatomy came from the secular order of old American wood sheds and we don't take kindly to insolence. But now that I'm on the civilian end of things I feel shallow just offering the dancers who live to entertain me petty cash. The ladies have made personal requests to know my inner thoughts because they have expressed their intimate urges and longings through their intricate routines involving air kisses, pole swirls, pelvic grinds, and frontal melvins. What to do in response to all those messages? My answer would be that it goes beyond our pecuniary structuring system, to a deeper plane. God watches people but Jesus is the king that likes to touch. Aren't we all trying to live up to the master? I assumed that Live Nude Girls was a place for free thought and open expression. I also took each of the three capital X's on the marquee seriously. Like one X meant naked body, two, a glimpse into the gashes of Eve, and the third capital X was loud kick ass music like Zeppelin to get this party started right, so don't fucking arrest me, I don't even have a home.

I also hate motion detectors, silent alarms, guns that misfire, bullets with names on them, dull blades, parole officers, ATF pricks with their stylish windbreakers (secretly jealous, I want one of those so badly), leg irons, plastic cuffs, metal detectors, support groups, soft ball leagues, skim milk, svelte umpires (—as terrible as a skinny Santa—chubby is what I want and trust), dogs dressed up to look like Mickey Rooney, *Pappas & Beer* bumper stickers, *The Hollywood Squares,* golf shoes, tuxedo tee shirts, shawls, satin bed sheets, waterbeds, backgammon, the male voice amplified, group discussions, table bunting, floral arrangement, get well cards, disparaging remarks about canned peas, paying for sex, the word nougat, the Denver Nuggets, the city of Denver, the entire state of Colorado, dull knives, the word credo, miniature chairs, sticky table tops, Playmates who insist that their fantasy man groom *down there,* empty tank trailers that jiggle on the highway, seagulls that steal Cheetos, all those pigeons who found me in the dead of night and pinched out a white load onto my head like I was the only target worth nailing, curled up like a baby in Echo Park.

EIN GARTEN irdischer HASSGEFÜHLE

BENJAMIN WEISSMAN

Ich hasse Rausschmeisser in Striplokalen, die damit drohen, mir die Hand zu brechen, wenn ich *das nochmal tue.* Ich verabscheue sie, ehrlich gesagt, und bitte darum, die Ungenauigkeit des Ausdrucks *nochmal tun* zu beachten sowie die Tatsache, dass ich ein Pianist mit langen feinen Fingern bin, was nur bedeuten kann, dass man von mir erwartet, genau *das zu tun;* die Geschäftsleitung spricht eine vage Einladung in Form einer Warnung aus, aber eigentlich ist es eher eine Ermutigung oder Herausforderung zu einer Mutprobe, und Mutproben haben Männer von wahrer Überzeugung und vielfachen Interessen schon immer zu Höchstem beflügelt. Manchmal muss ich den Kopf schütteln wie eine Katze, um mich neu zu orientieren, bevor ich in einen geistigen Graben falle oder in ein emotionales Schlagloch. Und erstaunlicherweise hilft dieses Kopfschütteln, weil der weich gedämpfte Hirnblumenkohl sich tatsächlich an der Innenseite des Schädels reibt, was automatisch das Wunder des Vergessens, Aufräumens und Erinnerns zur Folge hat und mich auf eine leicht andere Spur zurückführt, genau was ich im Sinn hatte. Manche Männer glauben, das Beste, was ein Mann tun könne, wenn er gewarnt wird *etwas nicht zu tun,* sei, *es nicht wieder zu tun,* sondern vollkommen reglos zu verharren oder *etwas ganz anderes* zu tun, etwas *noch nie Dagewesenes,* eine völlig neue Handlung. Statt dasselbe zu tun, was die Aufmerksamkeit dieses Muskelpakets von Rausschmeisser erregt hat (ich wiederhole den Satz, *Ich werde mich mit eurem Zwangsregime nicht abfinden,* immer und immer wieder, denn das entspricht nicht meiner Auffassung vom sogenannten Land der Freiheit, ich verabscheue deine Regierungsform, Amerika, das möchte ich dich wissen lassen und tue es hiermit kund), tut man also etwas anderes, denn es wäre nicht fair, dieses Neue als *nochmal das* zu betrachten, da es sich um verschiedene Dinge handelt. Würde man zum Beispiel mit dem linken Handrücken, möglicherweise exakt mit dem zweiten Fingerknöchel, wo mein massiver College-Ring thront, das Bikinioberteil, welches mehr oder weniger die Busenregion einer Tänzerin bedeckt, streifen, und dies wäre die erste Episode (meines Verbrechens gegen die Menschlichkeit), dann sollte ich danach wohl etwas viel

BENJAMIN WEISSMAN ist der Autor von *Headless* (Akashic Books, 2004) und *Dear Dead Person* (Serpent's Tale, 1994). Er lehrt literarisches Schreiben im Rahmen des Graduiertenprogramms am Otis College of Art and Design, Los Angeles.

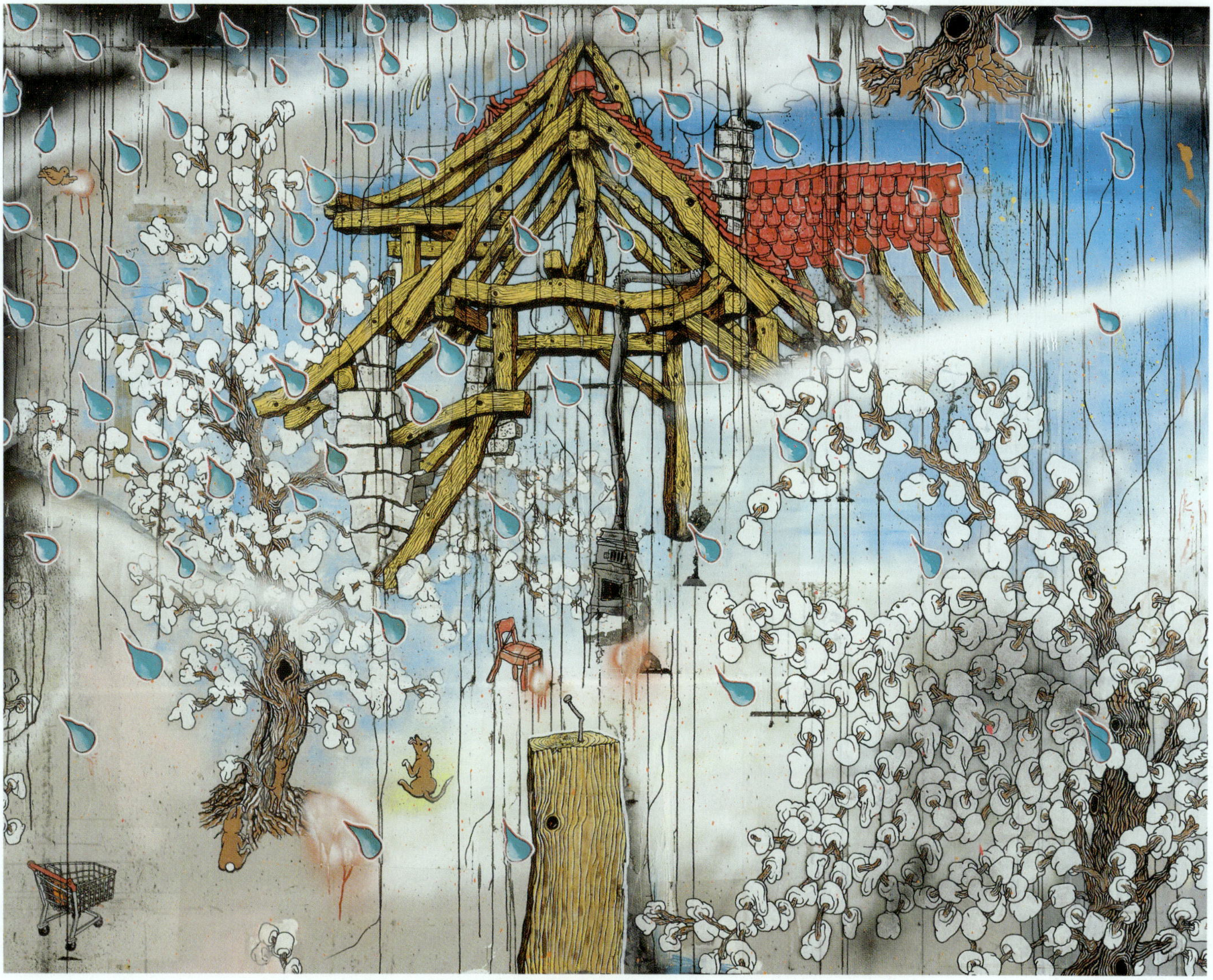

URS FISCHER, THE TRICK IS TO KEEP BREATHING, 2001, mixed media on wood, 86 3/8 x 110 5/8" / Mischtechnik auf Holz, 219,5 x 281 cm.

(ALL PHOTOS: STEFAN ALTENBURGER / EVA PRESENHUBER GALLERY, ZURICH, UNLESS OTHERWISE INDICATED)

Schwerwiegenderes tun, etwa beide Pobacken packen, sie auseinander ziehen, wie Schiffsventile aufdrehen und schliesslich meine Nase in den Spalt stecken und in dieser Stellung frei aus dem Gedächtnis ein paar Sonette deklamieren. Ich spreche für alle Männer, wenn ich sage, wir würden einfach gern die Regeln kennen, denn leider wird mich Mister Muskelpaket nicht zu einer vertraulichen Besprechung ins Hinterzimmer bitten, um in bequemen Ledersesseln ledergebundene Wälzer aufzuschlagen oder offizielle Regelbücher über unangebrachtes Benehmen und schweinische Mätzchen durchzublättern, geschweige denn die Zweideutigkeiten und Nuancen der englischen Sprache und deren Ursprünge im Lateinischen, Niederländischen oder Deutschen zu diskutieren. Obwohl ich ein grosser Anhänger von Wiederholungen bin, stelle ich die Frage, weshalb ich *das nochmal* tun sollte, wo es doch so viele neue Dinge auszuprobieren gibt und ich hier bin um meinen Horizont zu erweitern, neue Farben an meinem Regenbogen zu entdecken, aber auch um der Kassierin, die mich wohlwollend begrüsst, ihre Mundwinkel zu einem aufrichtigen *Hallo* verzieht und mir ein tief empfundenes, wenn auch ausgesprochen unnötiges, augenzwinkerndes *Viel Vergnügen!* hinterherflötet, sowie dem Typen, der die Musik abspielt, die mich im Innersten berührt und meine Zukunft in neue Bahnen lenkt, DJ Smoke, der vor jedem Olivia-Newton-John-Song seinen glatten Abzugsfinger mehr oder weniger genau auf mich richtet, zu zeigen, dass ich nicht nur dankbar bin, sondern auch ein Mann von diskretem Charme und ungeahnten verborgenen Vorzügen? Olivia kommt aus *Down under* und davon rede ich doch die ganze Zeit: sich auf die lebendigen Momente des eigenen Lebens einzulassen und um das Mieder und den voluminösen Frontumhang einer heissen Braut herumzuschnorcheln. Aber zunächst noch einen süssen Schluck, und noch einen und dann vielleicht einen langen Zug, um jedem, der zusieht, zu zeigen, dass Alkohol mein Verhalten überhaupt nicht beeinflusst. Es gibt viele Möglichkeiten seine ehrliche Wertschätzung zu zeigen und durch Freundlichkeit aufzufallen, und früher oder später kommt für jeden Zuschauer der Zeitpunkt, wo Beifall und ein gefalteter Fünfdollarschein nach einem Auftritt mit drei Songs nicht mehr genügen; dann ist eine von Herzen kommende, via Körpersprache an eine schöne Dame gerichtete Botschaft die einzige Poesie, die das allgemeine Gesülze noch durchbrechen kann und so viel heisst wie: «Ich weiss die schöne Kunst des Varieté zu schätzen – ich bin ein Mann von Welt und weiss, dass eine Federboa mehr ist als ein flauschiger Schal, ich komme nicht bloss der Fotzen wegen her.» Meine Wertschätzung des Talents berücksichtigt mehrere Faktoren, wobei Anzeichen von Intelligenz im Gesicht der sich ausziehenden Dame eine entscheidende Rolle spielen. Eine seriöse Tänzerin wird dir einen zwiespältig glasigen Blick zuwerfen, nicht irgendeinen Blick, sondern einen glasharten, leuchtenden, porzellanartigen Blick, die Hände auf den Hüften, als ob sie sagen wollte, *Zeig, was du drauf hast, Alter,* oder vielleicht auch, als ob sie fragen wollte, *Was tust du dort so nah an meiner Bühne?* oder *Warum läufst du bloss um 1 Uhr 45 früh in Trainerhosen rum?* oder *Wie viele warme Pepsis kann ein Mensch in fünf Stunden trinken?* Das sind alles gute Fragen, die eine Antwort verdienen und danach vielleicht eine etwas intellektuellere Erläuterung der Tatsache, dass die Summe eines gleichschenkligen Dreiecks gleich der Quadratwurzel von Sapphos

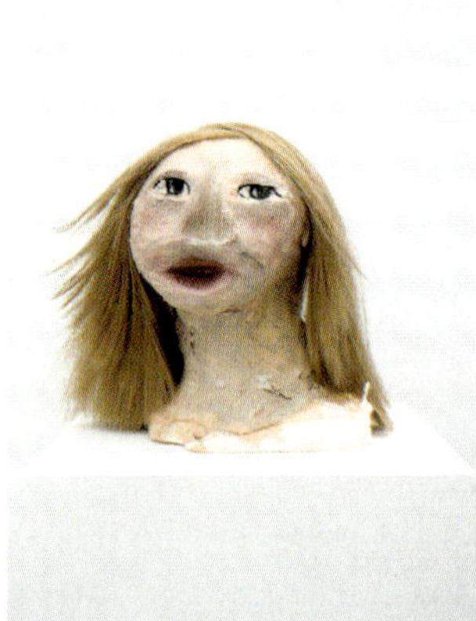

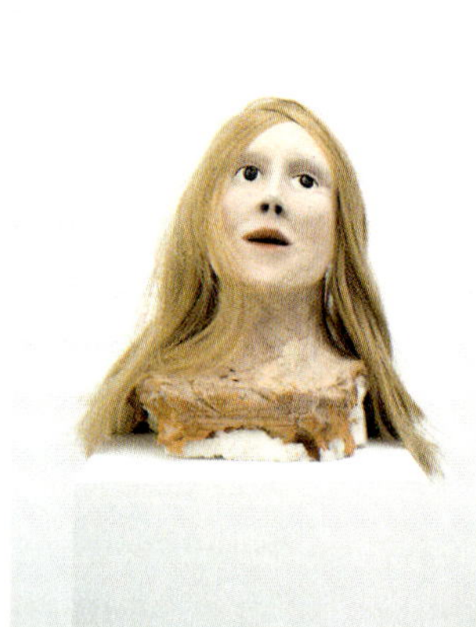

Left / Links: URS FISCHER, NAPOLEON, MISUNDERSTOOD, 2001, styrofoam, stearin, oil paint, wig hair, pigment, 10 5/8 x 11 13/16 x 9 1/2" / 27 x 30 x 24 cm.
Right / Rechts: NAPOLEON, IS THERE SOMETHING YOU DIDN'T TELL ME, 2001, Styropor, Stearin, Ölfarbe, Perückenhaar, Pigmente, 27 x 23 x 31 cm / 10 5/8 x 9 x 12 1/4".

Dildo ist. Ich habe früher bei Jumbo gearbeitet und weiss deshalb, was es heisst, den Aufpasser zu spielen. Ich will nicht angeben, aber zu jener Zeit lebte ich dafür, Finger zu brechen und mein Knie in die Weichteile von Typen schnellen zu lassen, die sich schlecht benahmen. Einmal brachte ich das Mitglied einer Gang dazu, einen Drittel seines Herzens auszukotzen. Ich sagte ihm, *Lies dieses rote Filet lieber auf, bevor ein hungriger Nager es als potenzielle Futterquelle ausfindig macht und auffrisst.* Das sagte ich zu dem Typen, der zusammengeklappt war, nachdem ich ihn hatte wissen lassen, dass ich meine steinharte Anatomie der Tatsache verdanke, dass ich zu dem bodenständigen altamerikanischen Club gehöre, der die Tradition des Hinter-den-Holzschuppen-Gehens pflegt, und dass wir keine Frechheiten duldeten.[1)] Aber jetzt, da ich auf der zivilisierten Seite stehe, fühlt es sich schal an, den Damen, die für mich tanzen, bloss schnödes Kleingeld anzubieten. Die Damen müssen persönliche Nachforschungen angestellt haben, um meine geheimsten Gedanken kennen zu lernen, denn sie haben in ihren ausgeklügelten Nummern ihre intimen Begierden und Wünsche zum Ausdruck gebracht, mit Küssen in die Luft, wilden Drehungen an der Stange, mahlenden Beckenbewegungen und wiederholt frontal dargebotenen Einblicken in ihre Intimzonen. Was tun als Reaktion auf diese geballten Botschaften? Meine Antwort wäre, dass das unser pekuniäres Ordnungssystem sprengt und in eine tiefere Ebene vorstösst. Gott beobachtet die Menschen, aber Jesus ist der König, der sie gern anfasst. Und versuchen wir nicht alle unserem Herrn nachzuleben? Ich hatte angenommen, dass *Live Nude Girls* ein Ort der freien Gedanken und des freien Ausdrucks wäre. Ich habe auch jedes der drei kapitalen X auf der Markise am Eingang ernst genommen und dachte, das erste X stehe für den nackten Körper, das zweite für den Blick in Evas Spalten und das dritte für laute, aufreizende Musik wie Zeppelin, damit die Party auch richtig in Fahrt kommt, also untersteht euch, mich zu verhaften, ich habe nicht einmal ein Zuhause.

Ich hasse auch Bewegungsdetektoren, lautlose Alarmanlagen, Gewehre, die danebenschiessen, Kugeln mit Namen drauf, stumpfe Klingen, Bewährungshelfer, die Alkohol-Tabak-Schusswaffen-Ärsche mit ihren modischen Windbreaker-Jacken (heimlich eifersüchtig, wünsche ich mir sehnlichst genau so eine), Fusseisen, Plastikhandschellen, Metalldetektoren, Fanclubs, Softball-Ligen, Magermilch, schlanke Schiedsrichter (genauso schlimm wie dürre Weihnachtsmänner – nur auf die Pummeligen ist Verlass), auf Mickey Rooney getrimmte Hunde, *Pappas & Beer*-Heckkleber, das TV-Gewinnspiel *Hollywood Squares,* Golfschuhe, Tuxedo-T-Shirts, Schals, Satinbettwäsche, Wasserbetten, Backgammon, die elektronisch verstärkte männliche Stimme, Gruppengespräche, Tischerücken, Blumenarrangements, Karten mit Genesungswünschen, abschätzige Bemerkungen über Büchsenerbsen, bezahlten Sex, das Wort Nougat, die Denver Nuggets, die Stadt Denver, den ganzen Staat Colorado, stumpfe Messer, das Wort Credo, Miniaturstühle, klebrige Tischplatten, Betthäschen, die darauf bestehen, dass die Männer ihrer Träume *da unten* für ihr Wohl sorgen, leere Tankwagenanhänger, die auf der Autobahn schlingern, Chips stibitzende Seemöwen, all diese Tauben, die mich mitten in der Nacht ausfindig gemacht und meinen Kopf mit ihrer weissen Ladung bekleckert haben, als sei ich – zusammengekauert wie ein Baby im Echo Park liegend – das einzig lohnende Ziel weit und breit.

(Übersetzung: Suzanne Schmidt)

1) Im Original: *from the worldly order of the old American wood sheds.* Das Amerikanische *to take someone behind the woodshed* (mit jemandem hinter den Holzschuppen gehen) bedeutet *sich mit jemandem schlagen, jemanden tüchtig verhauen,* ferner dann auch: *jemanden im sportlichen Wettkampf vernichtend schlagen, einen Kantersieg erringen.*

Edition for Parkett

URS FISCHER
SIGH, SIGH, SHERLOCK! 2004

Fiberglass reinforced plaster cast, partially painted,

36 1/4 x 12 5/8 x 12 5/8".

Cast by Kunstgiesserei Felix Lehner, St. Gall, Switzerland.

Edition of 45 / XXV, signed and numbered.

Glasfaserverstärkter Hartformgips, teilweise bemalt,

92 x 32 x 32 cm.

Guss: Kunstgiesserei Felix Lehner, St. Gallen.

Auflage: 45 / XXV, signiert und nummeriert.

(PHOTO: MANCIA / BODMER, FBM-STUDIO, ZÜRICH)

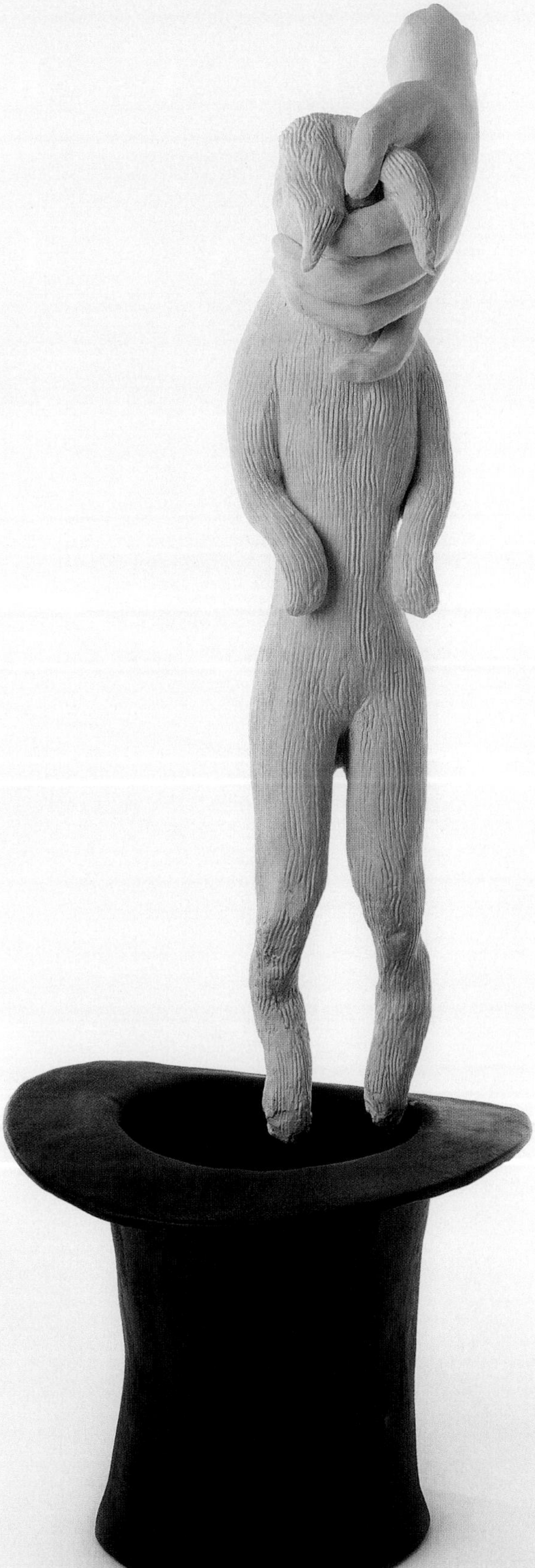

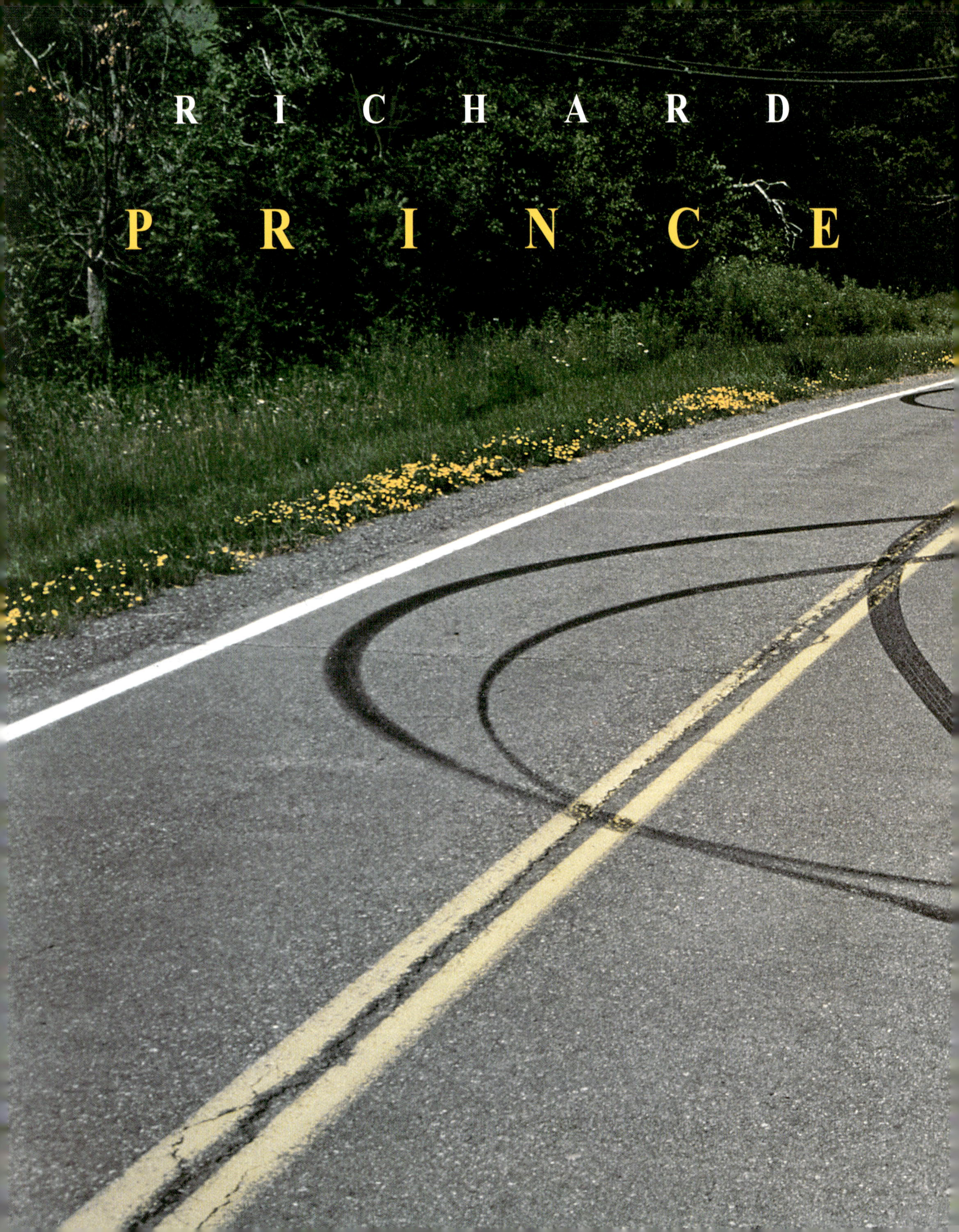
R I C H A R D
P R I N C E

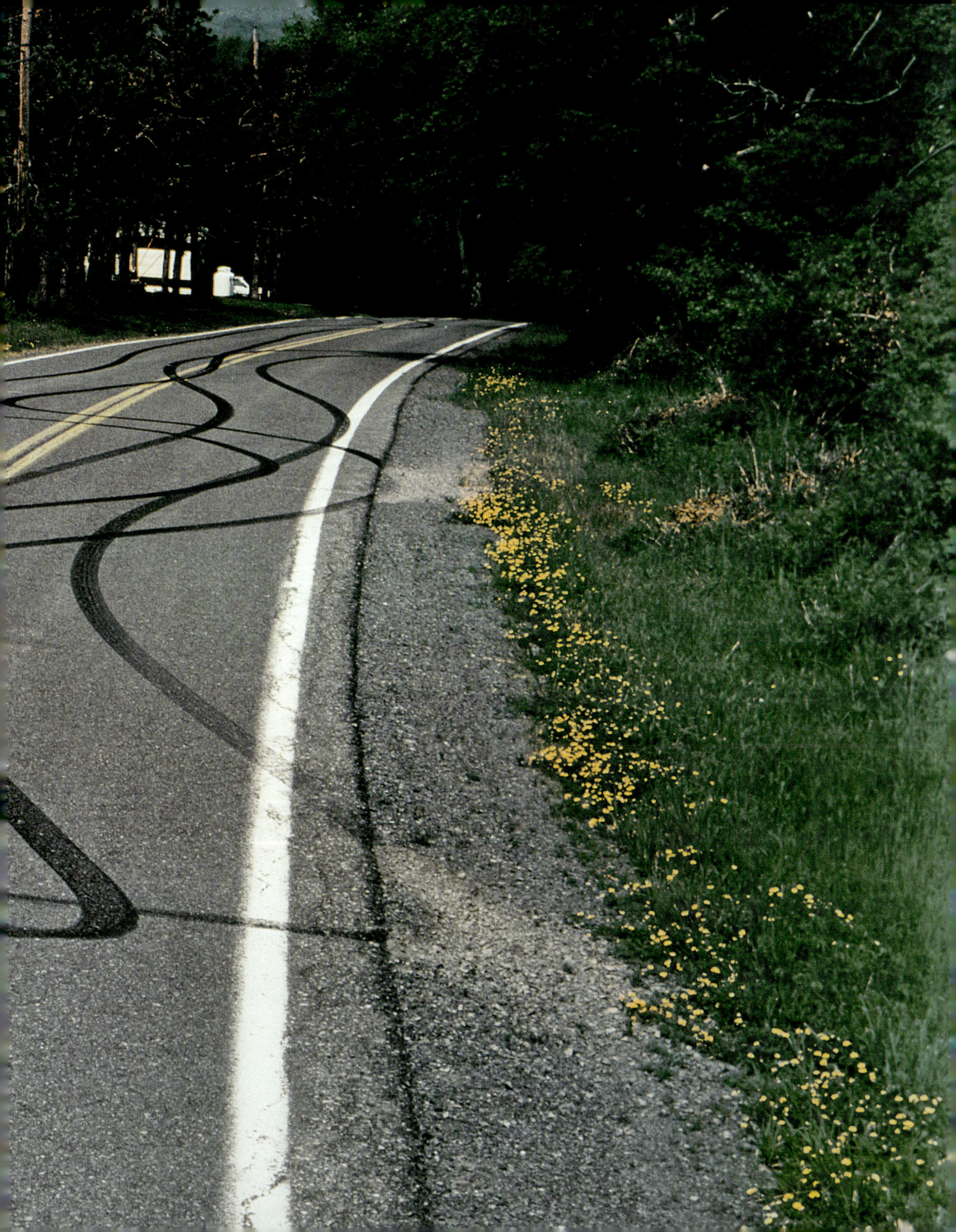

A Reflection or Two

DIKE BLAIR

I used to consider discussions of Richard Prince's work in terms of appropriation, those surrounding issues of originality, to be stupid because they made secondary the best part: the work's dark poetry and saturated eroticism. But perhaps I was wrong, or not entirely right. After visiting him recently, I began to think more about appropriation in terms of ownership. The root *propos* (property) does resonate with his work. He o w n s things in all senses of the word, and I've come to see that as really essential; but let me return to this idea later.

I think I first met Richard at the Mudd Club in 1978. I remember sharing a table with mutual friends on the second floor. We were all young artists at the time working on our stuff, playing at our identities, trying to get a leg up, a break, and a drink ticket. I asked Richard about his work and where I might see it. Richard was drunk and mumbled a few times about how he mostly showed in Europe, implying he was pretty big there. He wasn't, though I bought it—a Princeian bluff that later would become familiar at the poker table (often involving my stack of chips getting shorter). And, at the time, I thought he was a little bit of a jerk.

Not long after that first meeting, I visited Richard's show at Artists Space of still life re-photographs of luxury pen sets and watches. I remember VO liquor ads and models' head triptychs, and most vividly, I remember being stunned by the recognition of some-

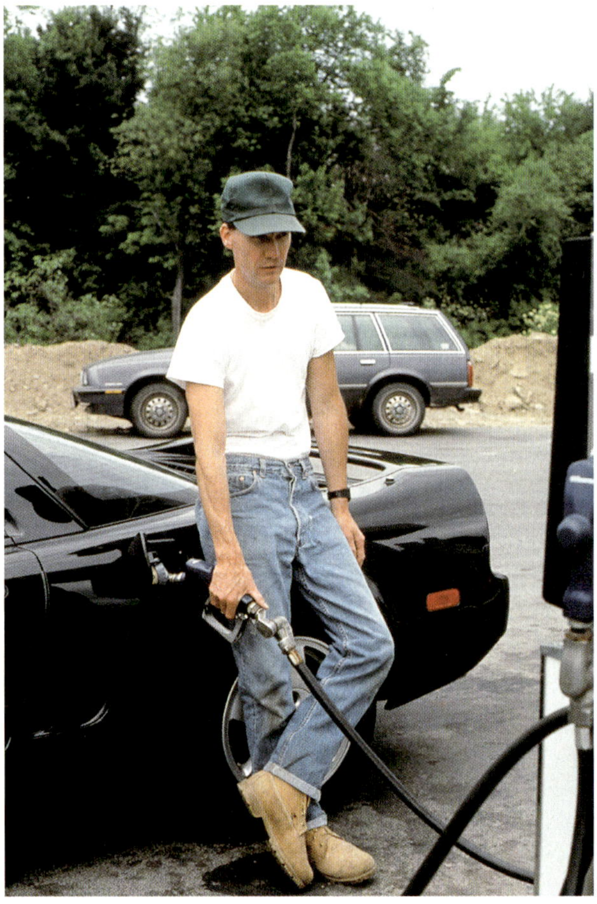

RICHARD PRINCE, PORTRAIT, 1991, Ektacolor photograph.

Page/Seite 94/95: RICHARD PRINCE, UPSTATE, 1995–1999, Ektacolor photograph, 40 x 60" / 101,6 x 152,4 cm.

DIKE BLAIR is an artist who lives in New York City.

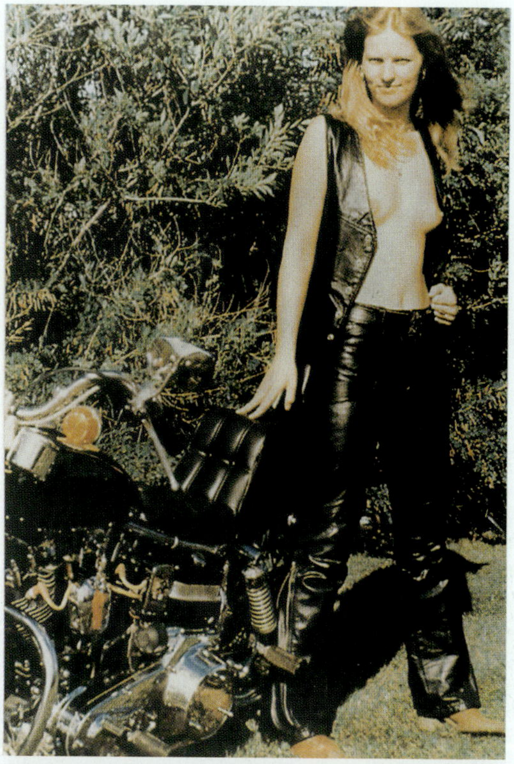

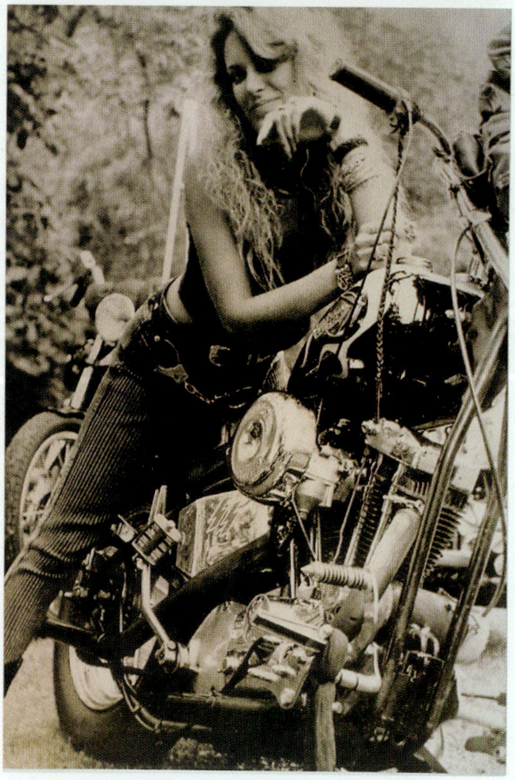

Top/Oben: RICHARD PRINCE, UNTITLED (GIRLFRIEND), 1993, Ektacolor print, 64 x 44" / 162,6 x 111,8 cm.
Bottom/Unten: UNTITLED (GIRLFRIEND), 1993, Ektacolor print, 74 1/2 x 50" / 189,2 x 127 cm.

thing deeply intelligent, erotic, poetic, new, and important. That the work was appropriated seemed beside the point... already, appropriation was very much in the air. It was more a matter of *what* was being appropriated—subjects that had already been heavily processed and heavily mediated, and then reprocessed and further reflected upon. The luxurious, artistic work of the subject and the perfection of the image were all in the service of a tony dream that Richard craftily shanghaied and placed behind glass, darkly. Implicit in his vision was the role of artist as off-screen actor/editor/director/producer; and while this too was in the air, I was yet to have seen it so concisely (yet mysteriously) manifested in framed objects on a gallery wall. Jerk or not, I wanted to know this guy better. We exchanged studio visits, and became friends.

Richard's studio apartment on East 12th Street was organized in the same manner as his later environments. Some surfaces got the treatment, others were left exposed—an aesthetic that became highly distilled in his later house projects. His interior was precise, framed, strictly rectilinear, and black and white, except for the yellow Kodak supply boxes slotted around the kitchen that served as his portfolios. His desk was neat, and on it there was always a lightbox with a grid of slides. Later, that grid would come to be the basis for the *Gangs*. When you visited his studio, there'd be a few clues to how his works were made: *where* or *how* the early *New Yorker* joke paintings were drawn, or the magazines re-photo-

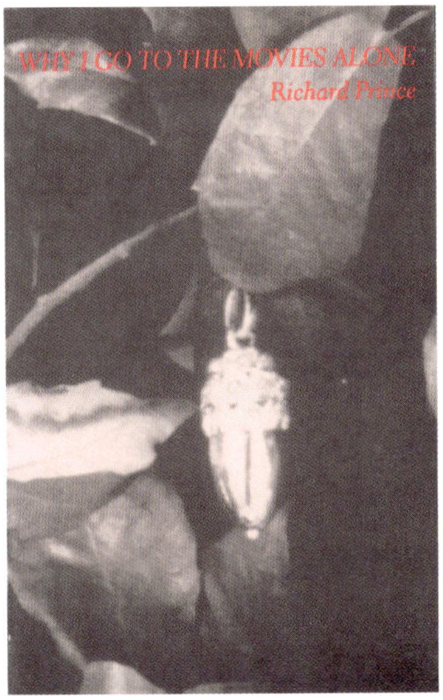

RICHARD PRINCE, WHY I GO TO THE MOVIES ALONE, front cover of the reprint by Barbara Gladstone Gallery, New York, 1995 / Titelseite des 1995 neu aufgelegten Buches.

graphed. He'd organize our visits by removing pictures from their boxes and placing them on his bed or on the Formica board, which covered the kitchen tub. He'd then carefully place them back in their boxes. I think he had lots of visitors, and practiced his act—his patter and timing—on me before doing it for the critics and paying customers. In retrospect, I see that Richard's art—his apartment, the pictures, the books, the patter—was all there in the beginning. And it wasn't long before he really was big in Europe.

In the early eighties, Richard and I would drink martinis at Paul's Lounge on 3rd Avenue and 10th Street. Paul's was kind of a New Jersey wannabe mob place, incongruously plopped in the East Village. It had pressed white tablecloths and sculpted napkins, satellite, an early projection TV, a black stucco ceiling peppered with glitter, and, occasionally, Joey Ramone, hunching over the bar cradling a drink. We'd talk about books (Richard was the most literate artist I knew) and movies, make up fictitious band names, and engage in art and girl talk. Mostly, I was the listener, the sounding board for Richard's semi-true stories and wonky memes. Often I'd wonder what the fuck he was talking about, and then, a month or a year or two later, one of his phrases or counterintuitive aphorisms, would boomerang out of the noosphere, hit me in the back of my head, and begin to make perfect sense.

Even after his fourth Martini, Richard was still working on his act; a lot of the bar talk was about trying out the sound and surface of words and ideas. He was test-driving his titles and catch phrases all the while, and constructing his idea of a cool persona—working out things like whether "Headliner" sounded cooler than "Entertainer," or vice versa. What I didn't realize about Richard, at the time, was the sheer intensity of his inner world, or that he was busy writing *Why I Go to the Movies Alone.* Richard isn't so much secretive as canny about timing—he's something of a social and artistic stripper, knowing what to c o n c e a l, and when and how to r e v e a l. I recently reread *Why I Go to the Movies Alone* and saw that—like his apartment, like his Artists Space show—it was all there from the beginning. His semi-opaque, noir, beat, blurb-styled fiction is an effective lexicon; I'd note that he's honed his writing over the years, and it may be the most underappreciated part of his act.

Most everything Richard does is calculated to reflect another of his practices. Every medium and every theme is supported by, and in turn supports, another body of work. *Gangs* and *Jokes* and *Books* and *Collections* and *Cowboys* and *Sunsets* and *Houses* and *Hoods* and *Planters* all reflect, and enhance, each other. At times, he collates his images in picture books—the first was *Inside World,* which served as the title of a catalogue for a group show (with the same title) that Richard participated in at Kent Gallery. These picture books are probably my favorite of his books because they are where Richard creates and curates himself. He never wanted his work to be dependent on art world powers-that-be. He never allowed himself to be owned by friendly critics ("crickets," as he'd often call them at Paul's Lounge) or curators. He would do that for himself—he would own himself—and the books were one way to accomplish this. Inside the covers he scrambles re-photographed and original snaps (often pictures documenting his own work) and creates his "real" artist's life. Though Richard's life is certainly glamorous, the version of his life depicted in his books is only as true as is any particular photograph. What is true of these photographs is their beauty, and his pacing and pairing of imagery syncs, which he does with perfection and a profound love of all bound paper. (I've observed how Richard's hands take on a particular grace when he handles his rare books and magazines.)

When I visited Richard last summer, not much had changed. In the twenty-five years I've known him, he's gone from bathtub in the kitchen to swimming pool in the yard. But prosperity always seemed to be in the cards. Richard is proprietary in a big way and I now see this trait as an essential aspect of his art. His practice has a lot to do with his self-reflexive orchestration of ownership. He owns concretely. He owns the stuff of his (and our culture's) dreams—houses, rare books, and cars—and he turns that stuff into art by hijacking their images. He acquired all that he has by taking aesthetic possession. His work, by employing a canny approach to the mediated image, takes abstract ownership of a type of imagery that deals with desire and consumption.

Richard told me that all he wants to do these days is collect. But he needs to keep making his art to finance his collecting. Most everything Richard says about his work is expressed with a somewhat Warholian ambivalence—there is the joke, and then there is the truth inside the joke. Like Warhol, Richard's craft can seem superficial and ironic; and it is. But as much as he extols the "sent-away-for" aesthetic, he remains a painter of refined and detached sensuality, as he keeps his hand in the surface of at least some of his making. But, most certainly, some aspect of col-

RICHARD PRINCE, FIRST HOUSE, 1993, mixed media installation, detail / Teilansicht.

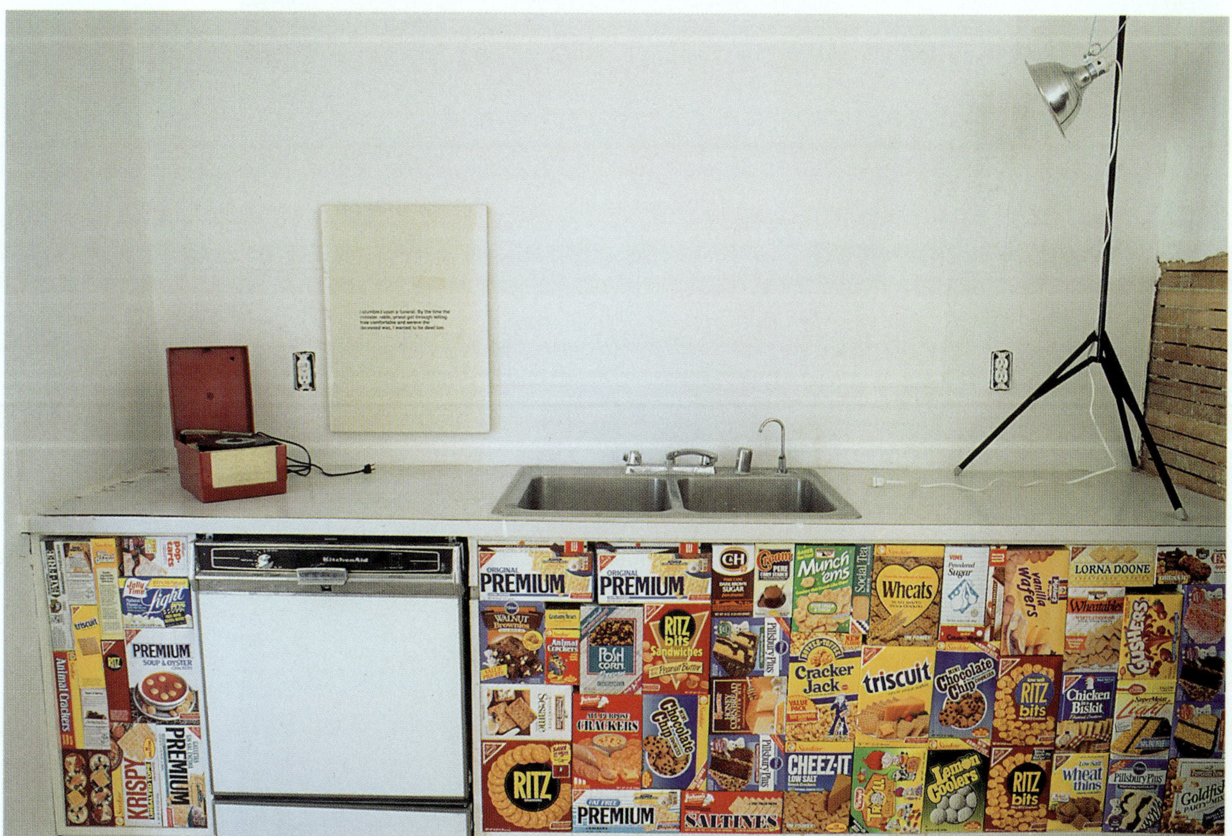

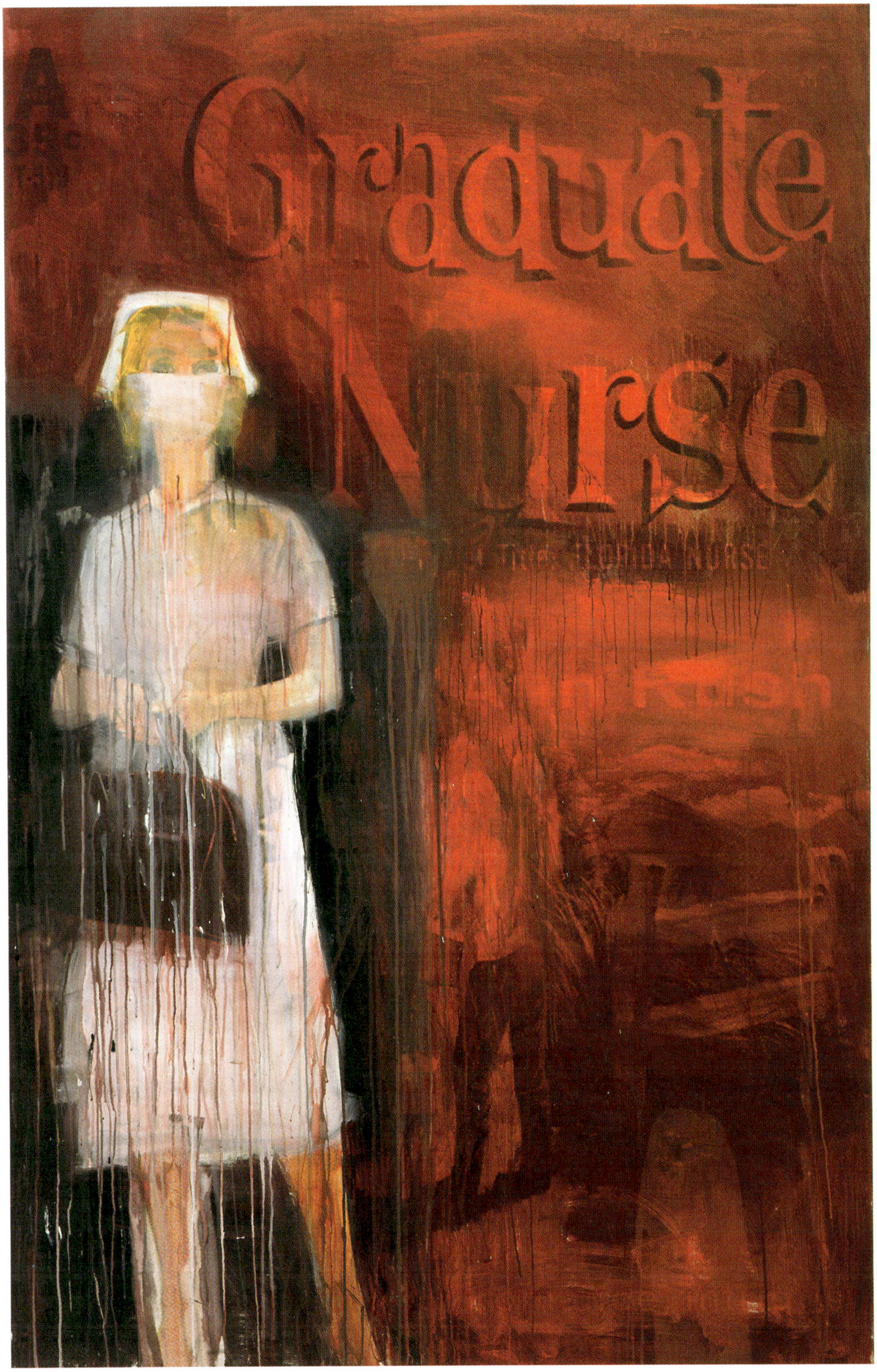

RICHARD PRINCE, GRADUATE NURSE, 2002, ink-jet print and acrylic on canvas, 89 x 52" / DIPLOMKRANKENSCHWESTER, Inkjet-Print und Acryl auf Leinwand, 226,1 x 132,1 cm.

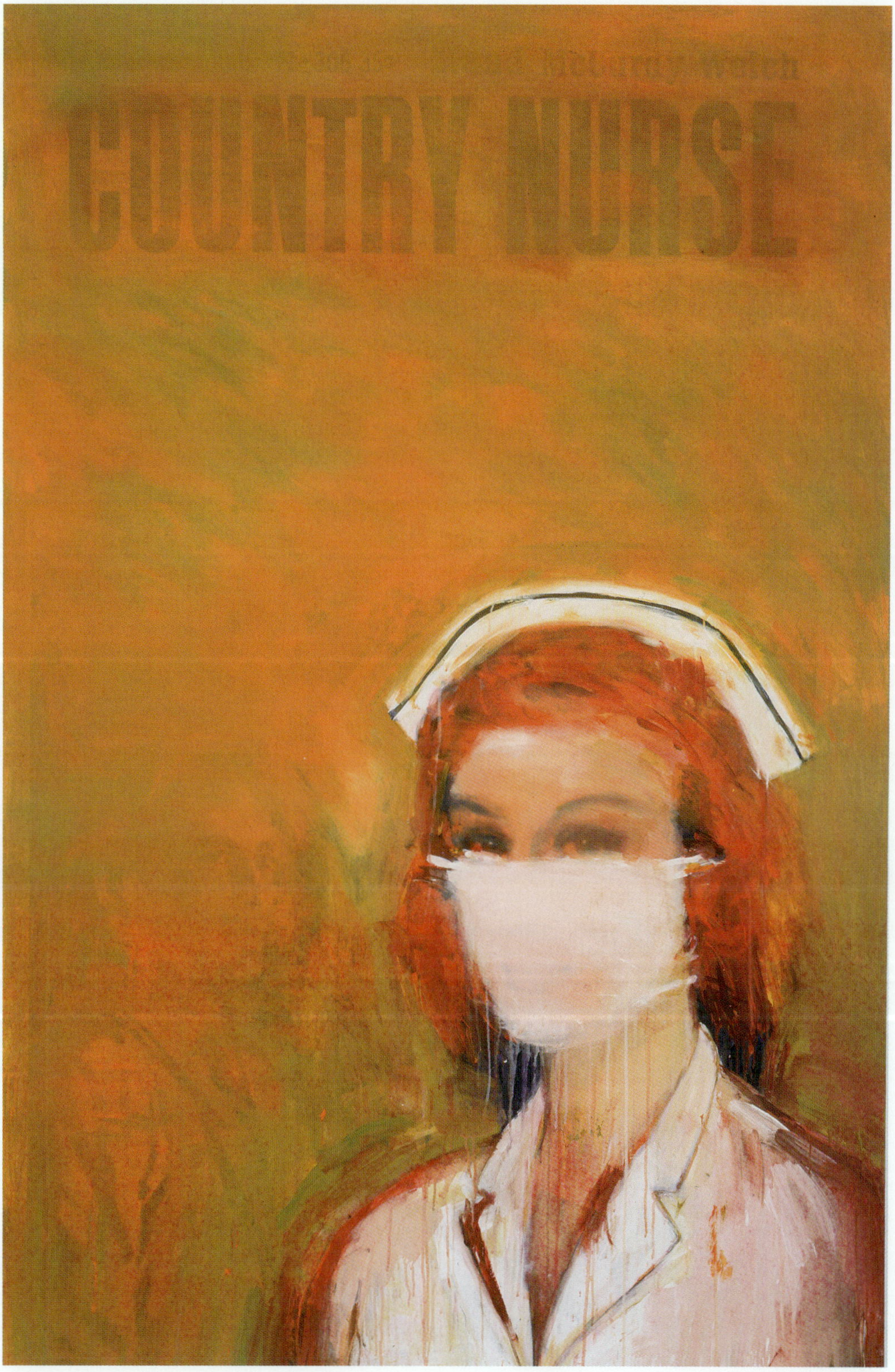

RICHARD PRINCE, COUNTRY NURSE, 2003, ink-jet print and acrylic on canvas, 79 3/4 x 52 1/4" /
LANDKRANKENSCHWESTER, Inkjet-Print und Acryl auf Leinwand, 202,6 x 132,7 cm.

lecting has always been at the root of everything he's done, and collecting means owning. In Richard's studio, for example, there is a stunning library of first edition books and pulp ephemera. Over the years, I've watched him build this collection—the original criteria for the collection being that all books, at one time or another, had to have been adapted to film. His ambition, it would seem, is to collect, collate, and display in such a unique, ambitious, and intelligent manner that multiple literary domains get slightly bent through a Princeian lens. When most people who know Richard's work see an "original," unappropriated Marlboro cowboy, they experience his power to superimpose himself on images he didn't author. Like the barely visible reflection of an image on the glass under which it is framed, Richard Prince, the artist, is overlaid on the iconic cowboy. Imagine the same sensation of superimposition when seeing a copy of Nabokov's *Lolita* or Kerouac's *On the Road*. I must confess, I find the prospect a little bit scary, and that reminds me that all of Richard's best work has always scared me a bit.

To a greater extent than previous generations, and less than later ones, our generation found self-definition through our cultural artifacts: the posters on our walls, our record albums, and the magazines arranged on our tables. To some degree, that kind of store-bought identity is what Richard's art has always been about. Now that Richard's artifacts have been part of the culture for a couple of decades, in ever-expanding ripples of context, he can re-appropriate his own work and replay himself into art history. These days, he spends no small amount of studio time arranging his own work in configurations that may spark new images and meanings—new ways of projecting himself into the culture, with the purpose of being able to read his own reflection. It seems like a convoluted way to try to see oneself, but, come to think of it, that kind of transference is what most artists do—minus a brilliant reflection or two.

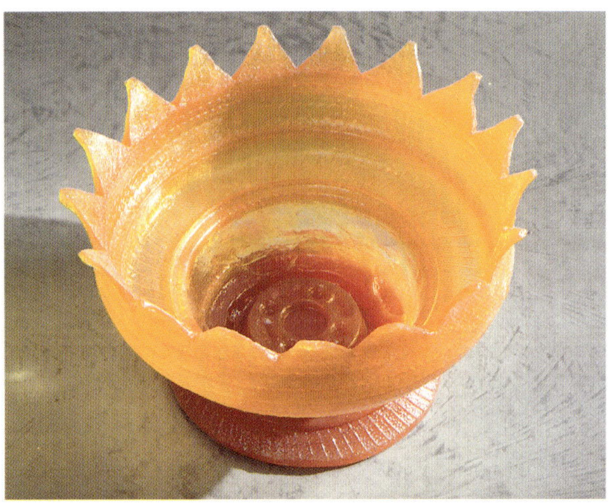

RICHARD PRINCE, UNTITLED (FLOWER TIRE), 1999, polyurethane cast, 13 1/2 x 23 x 23" / OHNE TITEL (BLUMEN-AUTOREIFEN), Polyurethan-Guss, 35 x 58 x 58 cm.

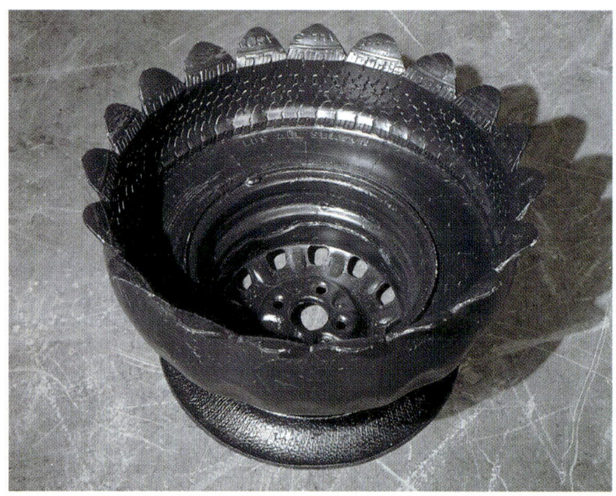

RICHARD PRINCE, UNTITLED (FLOWER PLANTER), 1999, tire and paint, 26 x 15 x 15" / OHNE TITEL (BLUMENTOPF), Autoreifen und Farbe, 91,5 x 38 x 38 cm.

Die eine oder andere Reflexion

DIKE BLAIR

Diskussionen des Werks von Richard Prince, die vor allem das Appropriative, die originellen Begleitumstände, in den Vordergrund rücken, habe ich immer für dumm gehalten, weil sie das Beste – seine dunkle Poesie und erotische Fülle – sekundär erscheinen lassen. Aber vielleicht habe ich mich geirrt oder war zumindest nicht hundertprozentig im Recht. Nach meinem jüngsten Besuch bei Richard begann ich etwas gründlicher über Appropriation im Zusammenhang mit Besitz nachzudenken. Die Wortwurzel *propos* (des englischen Worts *property*, Eigentum) hallt uns überall aus seinem Werk entgegen. Die Dinge sind ihm in jedem Sinn des Wortes e i g e n und inzwischen habe ich begriffen, dass dies von ganz entscheidender Bedeutung ist; aber lassen Sie mich später darauf zurückkommen.

Ich glaube, ich bin Richard Prince 1978 zum ersten Mal begegnet, und zwar im Mudd Club. Ich erinnere mich, dass wir mit gemeinsamen Freunden an einem Tisch im ersten Stock sassen. Damals waren wir alle junge Künstler, die mit unserer eigenen Arbeit beschäftigt waren und unsere Individualität auslebten, wir versuchten Fuss zu fassen, warteten auf den Durchbruch oder wenigstens einen Gratisdrink. Ich fragte Richard nach seiner Arbeit und wo ich sie sehen könne. Richard war betrunken und murmelte mehrmals, dass er vor allem in Europa ausstelle, wobei er andeutete, dass er dort ziemlich erfolgreich wäre. Das war durchaus nicht der Fall, obwohl ich es ihm abnahm – ein Princescher Bluff, wie ich ihn später noch oft am Pokertisch hören sollte (meist dann, wenn meine Chips arg am Schwinden waren).

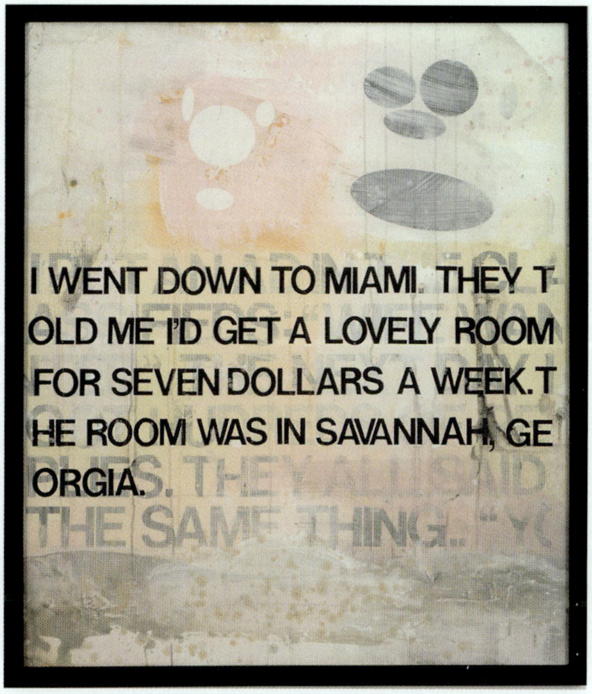

RICHARD PRINCE, UNTITLED, 2001, acrylic and silkscreen on gatorboard, $50^{1}/_{2}$ x $45^{5}/_{8}$" / OHNE TITEL, Acryl und Siebdruck auf Gator Board, 128 x 116 cm.

DIKE BLAIR ist Künstler und lebt in New York.

Damals dachte ich, bei ihm sei wohl eine Schraube locker.

Nicht lange nach dieser ersten Begegnung schaute ich mir im Artists Space Richards Ausstellung seiner photographischen Stillleben mit Luxusfüllern und -uhren an. Ich erinnere mich an Anzeigen für edle Spirituosen mit dem Prädikat VO (very old), an Triptychen mit Köpfen von Models, aber am lebhaftesten ist die Erinnerung an die überraschende Erkenntnis, dass dies alles hochintelligent, erotisch, poetisch, neu und bedeutend war. Dass es sich um Appropriationen handelte, war nicht der springende Punkt…, die Appropriation lag bereits spürbar in der Luft. Es ging vielmehr darum, w a s und w i e hier appropriiert wurde, nämlich Gegenstände, die bereits stark bearbeitet und vielfach vermittelt waren und dann erneut bearbeitet und reflektiert wurden. Die üppige, kunstvolle Arbeit des Subjekts und die Perfektion des Bildes standen ganz im Dienst eines schicken Traums, den Richard sich kunstfertig unter den Nagel riss und hinter dunkles Glas bannte. Zu seiner Vision des Künstlers gehörte auch die Rolle des selbst nicht in Erscheinung tretenden Akteurs, Herausgebers, Regisseurs und Produzenten; und obwohl auch dieses Rollenverständnis damals in der Luft lag, hatte ich es noch nie so klar (und dennoch geheimnisvoll) in Form gerahmter Objekte an der Wand einer Galerie umgesetzt gesehen. Schraube locker oder nicht, diesen Typen wollte ich näher kennen lernen. Also besuchten wir uns gegenseitig in unseren Ateliers und wurden Freunde.

Richards Atelierwohnung an der 12th Street East war gleich ausgestattet wie seine späteren Environments. Manche Flächen waren bearbeitet, andere roh belassen – eine Ästhetik, die Prince in seinen späteren Hausprojekten in stark verfeinerter Form einsetzen sollte. Seine Inneneinrichtung war präzise, konsequent, strikt geometrisch und schwarzweiss, mit Ausnahme der flachen gelben Kodakschachteln, die überall in der Küche verstaut waren und ihm als Werkmappen dienten. Sein Arbeitstisch war aufgeräumt und darauf stand immer ein Leuchtpult mit rasterartig angeordneten Dias. Daraus entwickelten sich später seine *Gangs*. Bei Besuchen in seinem Atelier gab es immer Anhaltspunkte für die Entstehungsweise seiner Arbeiten; dafür, w o oder w i e die frühen *New Yorker*-Witzzeichnungen entstanden oder die abphotographierten Zeitschriften. Die Besuche verliefen jeweils so, dass er Bilder aus den Schachteln hervorholte und auf dem Bett ausbreitete oder auch auf der MDF-Abdeckplatte über dem Schüttstein. Danach legte er sie wieder sorgfältig in ihre jeweiligen Schachteln zurück. Ich glaube, er hatte sehr viele Besucher und probierte diesen Akt der Präsentation – Text und richtiges Timing – an mir aus, bevor er ihn vor Kritikern und potenziellen Käufern anwandte. Im Rückblick sehe ich, dass Richards Kunst – seine Wohnung, seine Bilder, seine Bücher, sein Jargon – von Anfang an da war. Und es sollte nicht mehr lange dauern, bis er in Europa wirklich gross herauskam.

In den frühen 80er Jahren tranken wir beide unsere Martinis jeweils in Paul's Lounge an der Ecke 3rd Avenue, 10th Street. Paul's war eine Art New-Jersey-Möchtegern-Insider-Treffpunkt, der nicht recht ins East Village passen wollte. Es gab gebügelte weisse Tischtücher und kunstvoll gefaltete Servietten, Satellitenfernsehen, eines der ersten Fernsehgeräte mit Bildprojektion, eine schwarze, mit Glitter übersäte Stuckdecke, und hin und wieder hing Joey Ramone an der Bar und nahm sich einen zur Brust. Wir sprachen über Bücher (Richard war der belesenste Künstler, den ich kannte) und Filme, erfanden fiktive Namen für Musikbands und liessen uns über Kunst und Frauen aus. Meistens war ich Zuhörer und Testperson für Richards halbwahre Geschichten und wackelige Entwürfe. Häufig fragte ich mich, wovon er verdammtnochmal redete, aber dann, einen Monat oder ein, zwei Jahre später, schoss einer seiner Sätze oder jeglicher Intuition zuwiderlaufenden Aphorismen wie ein Bumerang aus der Noosphäre heraus direkt in meinen Hinterkopf und machte plötzlich Sinn.

Selbst nach seinem vierten Martini feilt Richard noch immer an seinem Auftritt; in den meisten dieser Bargespräche ging es darum, den Klang und die Oberflächenbeschaffenheit von Worten und Ideen zu testen. Er textete laufend seine Werktitel und Kernsätze und arbeitete an seiner Idee einer coolen Persönlichkeit; es konnte darum gehen, ob *Headliner* (Schlagzeilenschreiber) cooler klänge als *Entertainer* (Unterhaltungskünstler) oder umgekehrt. Was ich

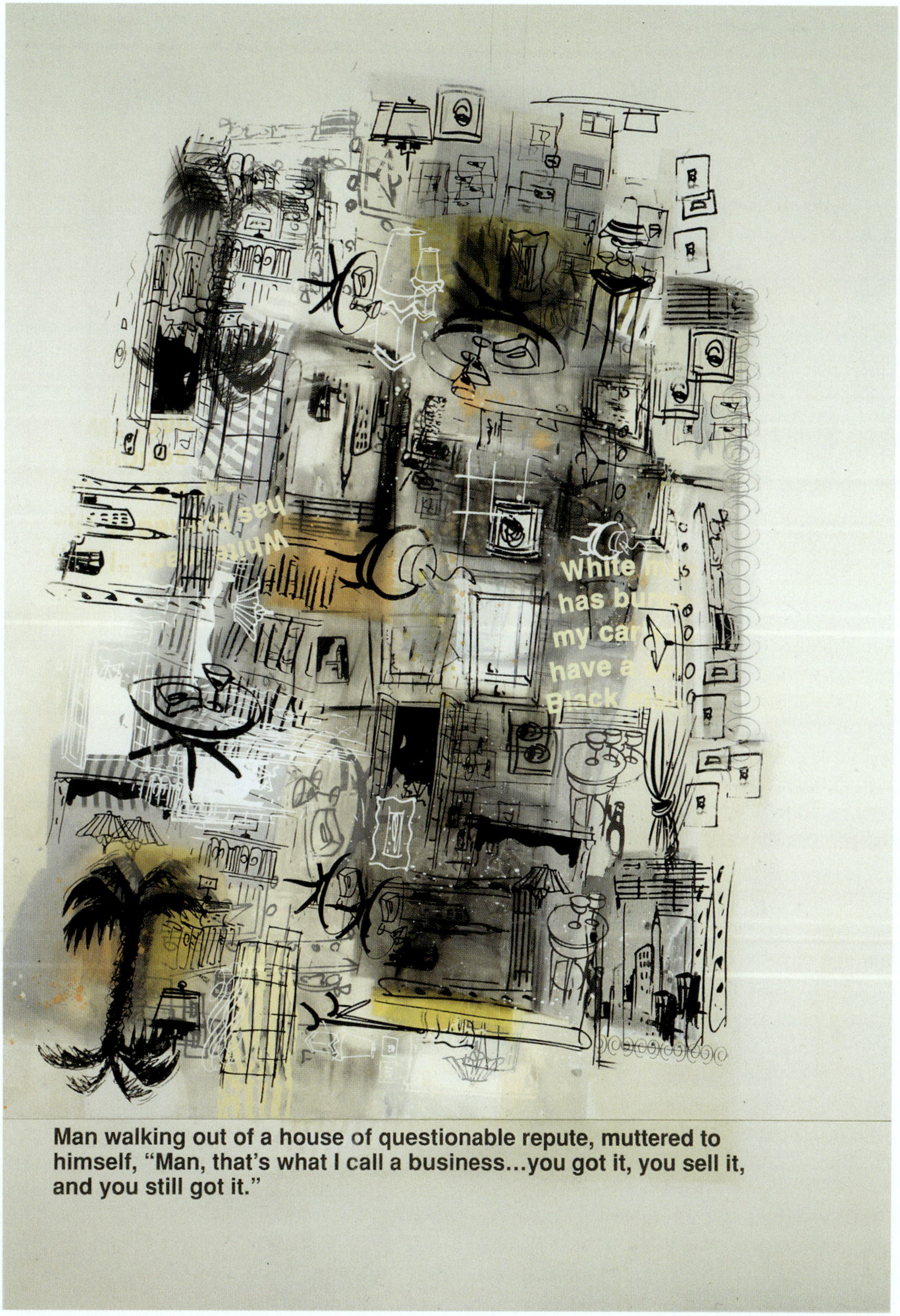

RICHARD PRINCE, THE LITERATURE RACK, 1994, acrylic and silkscreen on canvas, 136 x 96" /
DIE LITERATURABLAGE, Acryl und Siebdruck auf Leinwand, 345,4 x 243,8 cm.

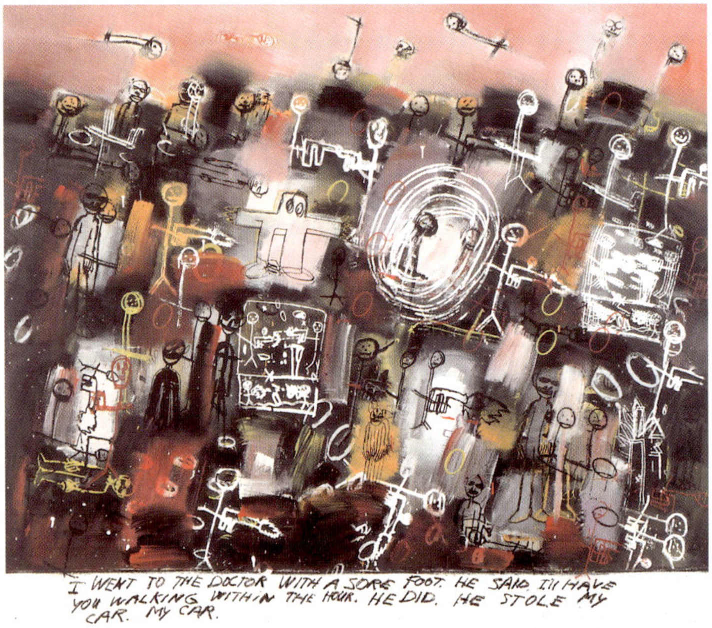

RICHARD PRINCE, MY CAR, 1998, acrylic, silkscreen and Conte Crayon on canvas, 79 x 75" / MEIN AUTO, Acryl, Siebdruck und Conté-Stift auf Leinwand, 200,7 x 190,5 cm.

damals nicht bemerkte, war die schiere Intensität von Richards Innenwelt, und auch nicht, dass er dabei war, *Why I Go to the Movies Alone* (Warum ich allein ins Kino gehe) zu schreiben. Dabei ist Richard nicht eigentlich verschlossen, sondern nur gerissen, was das richtige Timing angeht: Er ist eine Art ebenso geselliger wie kunstvoller Stripper, der genau weiss, was es zu verbergen gilt und was er wann und wie enthüllen muss. Ich habe *Why I Go to the Movies Alone* erst kürzlich wieder gelesen und begriffen, dass – wie in seiner Wohnung und in seiner Ausstellung bei Artists Space – auch da alles von Anfang an vorhanden war. Seine teils undurchsichtige, düstere, resignierte, sprechblasenartige Literatur stellt ein ergiebiges Lexikon dar; ich möchte festhalten, dass er seine Art zu schreiben im Lauf der Jahre immer mehr verfeinert hat; und vielleicht ist dies der am meisten unterschätzte Teil seiner Darbietung.

Beinah alles, was Richard tut, ist darauf angelegt, eine seiner anderen Tätigkeiten zu reflektieren. Jedes Medium und jedes Thema wird von einem anderen Element seines Werks gestützt beziehungsweise stützt seinerseits wiederum ein anderes Element. *Gangs* und *Jokes* (Witze) und *Books* (Bücher) und *Collections* (Sammlungen) und *Cowboys* und *Sunsets* (Sonnenuntergänge) und *Houses* (Häuser) und *Hoods* (Kühlerhauben) und *Planters* (Pflanzgefässe): sie alle reflektieren und ergänzen einander. Manchmal versammelt er seine Bilder in Bildbänden – der erste war *Inside World* (Innere Welt). So lautete auch der Titel (und Katalogtitel) einer Gruppenausstellung in der Kent Gallery, an der Richard teilnahm. Diese Bildbände sind mir vielleicht die liebsten unter Richards Büchern, weil Richard sich darin selbst erschafft und sein eigener Kurator ist. Er wollte nie, dass sein Werk von den Machtverhältnissen in der Kunstwelt abhängig würde. Er liess sich auch von wohlwollenden Kritikern (*crickets,* Grillen, wie er sie in Paul's Lounge oft nannte) oder Kuratoren nie vereinnahmen. Das besorgte er selbst – er interpretiert und gehört sich selbst – und die Bücher waren ein Weg, dies zu erreichen. Zwischen den Buchdeckeln kombiniert er abphotographierte mit echten Schnappschüssen (oft Bilder, die seine eigene Arbeit dokumentieren) und erschafft so sein «wahres» Künstlerleben. Richards Leben ist ohne Zweifel glamourös, doch die Version, die man in seinen Büchern abgebildet sieht, ist nicht wahrer als irgendeine andere Photographie. Das Wahre an diesen Photos ist ihre Schönheit sowie der Rhythmus und die Kombination und Synchronisation der Bildeinheiten; das macht er absolut perfekt und mit einer tiefen Liebe zum Buch als solchem. (Ich habe beobachtet, dass seine Hände sich besonders grazil bewegen, wenn er seine seltenen Bücher und Zeitschriften hervornimmt und anschaut.)

Als ich Richard im letzten Sommer besuchte, hatte sich nicht viel verändert. In den fünfundzwanzig Jahren, seit ich ihn kenne, hat sich zwar die Badewanne in der Küche zum Swimmingpool im Garten gemausert. Aber der Wohlstand schien von jeher in seinen Sternen zu stehen. Richard ist auf eine grossartige Weise Besitz ergreifend und ich betrachte diesen Zug heute als wesentlichen Aspekt seiner Kunst. Seine Kunst hat viel mit seiner selbstreflektierenden Orchestrierung von Eigentum zu tun. Er eignet sich Dinge ganz konkret an. Er ist Eigentümer des Stoffs seiner Träume (und der Träume unserer Kultur) – Häuser, seltene Bücher, Autos –, und er verwandelt diesen Stoff in Kunst, indem er dessen Bilder kidnappt. Alles, was er hat, hat er dadurch erworben, dass er es ästhetisch in Besitz nahm. Seine Arbeit ergreift durch ihren raffinierten Umgang mit dem vermittelten Bild auf abstrakte Weise Besitz von einer Bildsprache, die von Begehren und Konsum handelt.

Richard erzählte mir, dass er heute eigentlich nur noch sammeln möchte. Doch er muss weiterhin Kunst machen, um seine Sammlertätigkeit zu finanzieren. Fast alles, was Richard über seine Arbeit sagt, kommt in einer an Warhol erinnernden Ambivalenz daher – es ist immer der Witz und die Wahrheit, die darin steckt. Wie im Fall von Warhol kann auch Richards Kunst oberflächlich und ironisch anmuten; und sie ist dies auch. Doch wie vehement er auch jede «weit hergeholte» Ästhetik austreibt, er bleibt ein Maler von feiner, kühler Sinnlichkeit, jedenfalls dort, wo seine Hand noch am Erscheinungsbild seiner Arbeit beteiligt bleibt. Aber an der Wurzel von allem, was er gemacht hat, lag immer ein sammlerischer Aspekt und sammeln heisst besitzen. In Richards Atelier findet sich zum Beispiel eine beeindruckende Bibliothek von Erstausgaben diverser Bücher und Schundliteratur. Über die Jahre habe ich zugeschaut, wie er diese Sammlung aufgebaut hat, deren ursprüngliches Kriterium war, dass jedes Buch irgendwann verfilmt worden sein musste. Es scheint, dass er darauf aus ist, Dinge auf eine so einmalige, anspruchsvolle und intelligente Weise zu sammeln, zusammenzutragen und auch zu präsentieren, dass verschiedene Bereiche der Literatur durch die Princesche Linse leicht verzerrt werden. Die meisten Leute, die mit Richards Werk vertraut sind, erleben seine Macht sich über Bilder zu legen, die nicht von ihm sind, immer wieder, wenn sie einen «originalen», nicht appropriierten Marlboro-Cowboy sehen. Wie die kaum sichtbare Reflexion eines Bildes auf dem Glas, hinter dem es gerahmt ist, legt sich der Künstler Richard Prince über die Cowboy-Ikone. Man stelle sich das gleiche Überlagerungserlebnis vor beim Anblick einer Ausgabe von Nabokovs *Lolita* oder Kerouacs *On the Road.* Ich gestehe, diese Aussicht macht mir ein bisschen Angst, und dabei fällt mir ein, dass mir alle seine wirklich guten Arbeiten schon immer Angst eingejagt haben.

Mehr als frühere Generationen und weniger als spätere hat sich unsere Generation durch ihre kulturellen Erzeugnisse definiert: die Plakate an unseren Wänden, unsere Plattenalben und die Zeitschriften auf unseren Tischen. Bis zu einem gewissen Grad ist es in Richards Kunst schon immer um diese Art im Laden gekaufter Identität gegangen. Nun, da Richards Arbeiten selbst seit etlichen Jahrzehnten Teil dieser Kultur sind und ihren Kontext fortwährend erweitert haben, kann er auf sein eigenes Werk zurückgreifen, um es sich erneut anzueignen und sich erneut in die Kunstgeschichte einzubringen. Er kann sich selbst sammeln und jede Ausstellung, an der er beteiligt war; er kann jedes Buch, in dem er vorkommt, von neuem in Besitz nehmen und jedes Haus, in dem er gewohnt hat, was dann ebenso Teil dieser Sammlung wird. In diesen Tagen verbringt er einen guten Anteil seiner Zeit im Atelier damit, seine eigenen Arbeiten so neu zu ordnen, dass daraus neue Bilder und Bedeutungen entstehen – neue Weisen sich in die Kultur zu projizieren, um seine eigene Reflexion erkennen zu können. Es erscheint wie ein verschlungener Versuch, sich selbst zu sehen, doch wenn man darüber nachdenkt, ist diese Übertragung genau das, was die meisten Künstler tun – abzüglich der einen oder anderen brillanten Reflexion.

(Übersetzung: Suzanne Schmidt)

HOW I LEARNED TO STOP WORRYING AND LOVE THE JOKE (PAINTING)

DOUGLAS FOGLE

My paintings are about working up a routine, going on the road and crossing into Laos.[1)]

Saigon, shit. I'm still only in Saigon.[2)]

Can a joke be a painting? More to the point, can a painting be a joke? Richard Prince has spent the better part of the last two decades trying to answer these questions, engaging in a voyage to the center of painting's very own heart of darkness. Starting his journey in 1987, Prince broadened his aesthetic strategies beyond the realm of photographic appropriation and into the body, if not the soul, of painterly expression. As he moved in this painterly direction, was Prince the equivalent of Marlon Brando's Kurtz in Francis Ford Coppola's 1979 film *Apocalypse Now,* disappearing up river into Cambodia in an attempt to take post war painting practices to their excessive logical conclusions? Or was he more akin to Martin Sheen's Captain Willard, setting out on a classified recon mission with orders to exterminate painting with extreme prejudice? In the end, perhaps he is more like the comedian Bob Hope singing his theme song "Thanks for the Memories" on a USO tour in Saigon because at the core of his painting agenda rests the repetitious, twisted structural logic of the joke, a staple of old school stand up comedy.

His painterly antecedents are wide ranging, including more traditional practitioners of the medium such as Willem De Kooning, Barnett Newman, Cy Twombly, Robert Rauschenberg, and Andy Warhol, as well as "painters-in-the-expanded-field" such as the comedians Lenny Bruce and Richard Pryor, who would give any action painter a run for his money with their "all over" verbal techniques. As one of Prince's jokes reads across the surface of a painting, "I put an ad in a swinger's magazine and my parents answered it." These are his parents and swing with them he does as he appropriates historical references to his own ends. In some works, monochromatic color field paintings are disrupted by the graphic stenciling of a joke on their surfaces. Newman's "zips" are converted into running punch lines of text transforming the sublime into the ridiculous. Pop-like techniques of appropriation are deployed to transfer fragments of cartoons from magazines like *The New Yorker* to the surface of his canvases sometimes with their accompanying jokes and often times, more dissonantly,

DOUGLAS FOGLE is Associate Curator of Visual Arts at the Walker Art Center in Minneapolis.

RICHARD PRINCE, *SO WHAT ELSE IS NEW,* 1988, *acrylic and silkscreen on canvas, 56 x 48"* / *WAS GIBTS SONST NOCH FÜR NEUIGKEITEN, Acryl und Siebdruck auf Leinwand, 142,2 x 122 cm.* (Zwei Frauen treffen sich am Strand in Miami. Sagt die eine: «Und, was gibts Neues?» Sagt die andere: «Du wirst es nicht glauben! Ich war heut morgen beim Arzt, er hat mich untersucht, und weisst du, was er sagt? Er sagt, ich würde mich allmählich in einen Mann verwandeln.» «Und gibts sonst noch was Neues?»)
(PHOTO: SQUIDDS & NUNNS/BARBARA GLADSTONE GALLERY, NEW YORK)

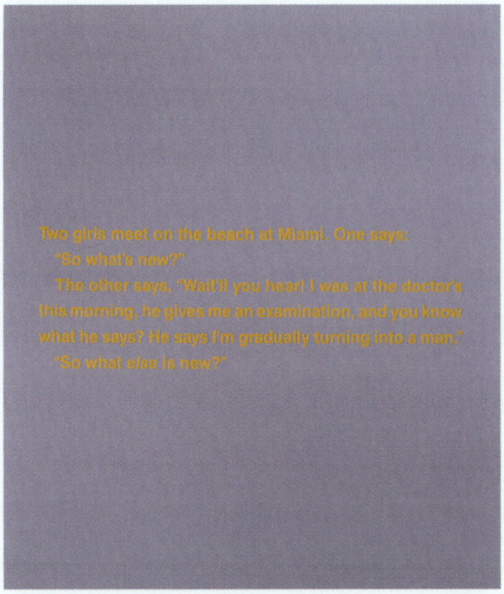

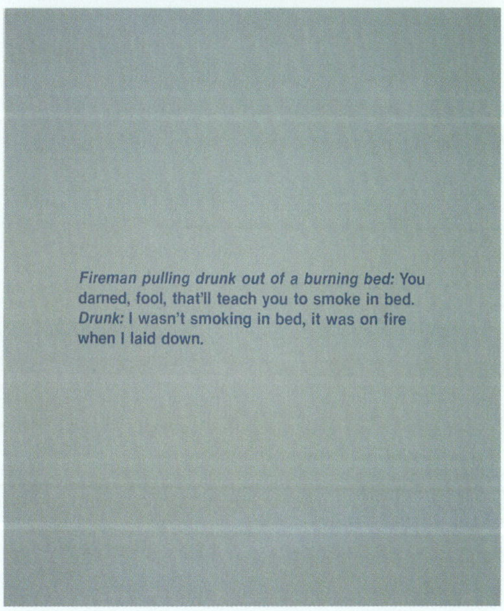

RICHARD PRINCE, FIREMAN AND A DRUNK, 1988, silkscreen and acrylic on canvas, 56 x 48" / FEUERWEHRMANN UND EIN BETRUNKENER, Siebdruck und Acryl auf Leinwand, 142,2 x 122 cm. (Feuerwehrmann, während er den Betrunkenen aus dem brennenden Bett zieht: «Du verdammter Idiot, das wird dich lehren, im Bett zu rauchen.» Betrunkener: «Ich hab nicht im Bett geraucht, es brannte schon, als ich mich hinlegte.») *(PHOTO: LARRY LAMÉ/BARBARA GLADSTONE GALLERY, NEW YORK)*

with the wrong joke. These works move from clean, hard-edged surfaces to messy, gesturally layered palimpsests where archaeological fragments of cartoons and punch lines hover between the poles of nonsense and intelligibility.

At the core of all these painterly ghosts, hovering on the surface of Prince's works, are his appropriated jokes. There are jokes about drinking such as "I eat politics and sleep politics, but I never d r i n k politics." There are jokes about relationships as with this classic joke from the pantheon of Borscht-belt humor: "I met my first girl, her name was Sally. Was that a girl, was that a girl. That's what people keep asking." And of course there is the classic defining joke of Prince's aesthetic project, the joke to end all jokes. "I went to a psychiatrist. He said 'Tell me everything.' I did, and now he's doing my act." Prince's use of the joke, repeated over and over again on his canvases, mixed and matched with the wrong images or no images at all, starts me wondering if it doesn't reveal some dissonance, some dark secret about the American psyche. History repeats itself, said Karl Marx. The first time as tragedy and the second time as farce. Prince's joke paintings offer us another kind of history painting, one that reveals a history that stutters.

As I write this there is a lot of stuttering going on as the U.S. presidential returns are coming in on the television. It looks like it is going to be mourning in America all over again. A joke painting to end all joke paintings. Maybe it's time to get out of Nam on the last chopper at the fall of Saigon before we get to relive our very own *Apocalypse Now Redux.* This might be best summed up by one of Prince's jokes, which goes like this: A traveling salesman's car broke down one evening on a lonely road and he asked at the only farm house in sight, "Can you put me up for the nite?" "I reckon I can," said the farmer. "But you'll have to share the room with my young son." "How about that!" gasped the salesman. "I'm in the wrong joke." Cue the music. Watch as Slim Pickens' bronco rides a nuclear bomb into a mushroom cloud sunset at the end of Stanley Kubrick's film *Dr. Strangelove.* The bomb has the words "HI THERE" written on it. Now that's a good joke. Thanks for the memories Richard.

1) Richard Prince, "Guns and Poses," *Artforum,* October 2004, p. 143.
2) Martin Sheen as Captain Willard in Francis Ford Coppola's *Apocalypse Now* (1979).

WIE ICH LERNTE, DEN (GEMALTEN) WITZ ZU LIEBEN

DOUGLAS FOGLE

Meine Bilder handeln davon, eine Nummer zu entwickeln, loszufahren, und die Grenze nach Laos zu überqueren.[1)]

Saigon, verdammte Scheisse. Ich bin immer noch in Saigon.[2)]

Kann ein Witz Malerei sein? Oder genauer, kann ein Gemälde ein Witz sein? Richard Prince hat einen guten Teil der letzten zwei Jahrzehnte mit der Beantwortung dieser beiden Fragen verbracht und dabei eine Reise mitten ins Herz der Finsternis der Malerei unternommen. Seit 1988, dem Beginn dieser Reise, hat Prince seine ästhetischen Strategien weit über die Grenzen photographischer Appropriation hinaus, bis in die Substanz und vielleicht sogar die Seele des malerischen Ausdrucks erweitert. Aber entspricht Prince' malerischer Feldzug demjenigen von Marlon Brandos General Kurtz – in Francis Ford Coppolas Film *Apocalypse Now* (1979) – flussaufwärts Richtung Kambodscha, im Versuch die Nachkriegsmalerei zu ihrer letzten logischen Konsequenz zu führen? Oder ist er näher bei Martin Sheens Captain Willard und seinem streng geheimen Erkundungsflug, mit dem Auftrag, die Malerei mit Hilfe extremer Vorurteile auszulöschen? Letztlich ähnelt er wohl doch eher dem Komödianten Bob Hope, der sein Lied «Thanks for the Memories» vor den Soldaten in Saigon singt, denn im Zentrum von Prince' malerischer Strategie liegt die auf Wiederholung basierende, perverse strukturelle Logik des Witzes, ein Standardelement der klassischen Stand-Up-Comedy.

Zu Prince' Vorgängern in der Malerei zählen traditionellere Künstler, wie Willem de Kooning, Barnett Newman, Cy Twombly, Robert Rauschenberg und Andy Warhol, aber auch «Maler im weiteren Sinn», wie die Komiker Lenny Bruce und Richard Pryor, die mit ihrer verbalen «*All-Over*-Technik» jedem Vertreter des *Action Painting* die Schau stehlen. Dies sind seine Eltern, und wie ein Witz auf einem seiner Bilder verkündet, «Ich habe in einer *Swinger*-Zeitschrift eine Anzeige aufgegeben und meine Eltern haben geantwortet», so swingt Prince mit ihnen, indem er die historischen Referenzen für seine Zwecke reklamiert. In einigen Werken stören schablonenhaft aufgetragene Witze die Oberfläche monochromer Farbfeldmalerei. Newmans *zips* werden zur Pointe und das Erhabene verkehrt sich ins Lächerliche. Mithilfe der Aneignungsstrategien des Pop werden Cartoons aus Zeitschriften wie *The New Yorker* auf die Oberfläche von Leinwänden übertragen, manchmal mit den dazugehörigen

DOUGLAS FOGLE ist Associate Curator of Visual Arts am Walker Art Center in Minneapolis.

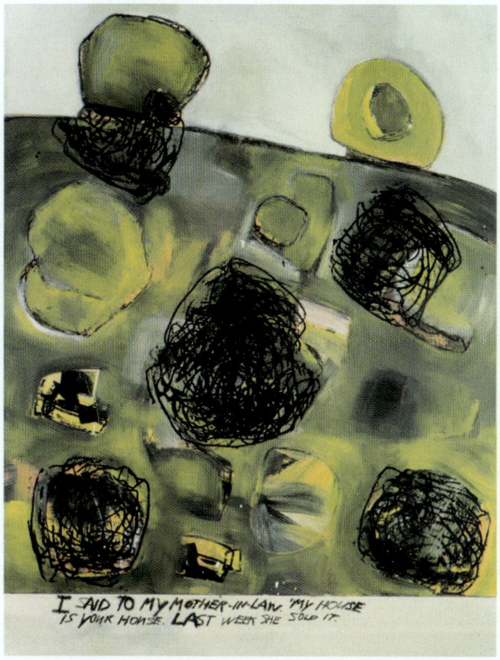

RICHARD PRINCE, TARANTULA, 1997, acrylic, silkscreen, and oilstick on canvas, 62¼ x 48" / Acryl, Siebdruck und Ölstift auf Leinwand, 158,1 x 121,9 cm.

Bildunterschriften, aber öfter, noch schriller, mit einem falschen Scherz. Diese Bilder reichen von klaren, harten Oberflächen bis zu chaotischen, gestisch mehrschichtigen Palimpsesten, in denen archäologische Fragmente von Cartoons und Wortpointen zwischen Unsinn und Verständlichkeit schillern.

Den Kern all dieser Gespenster der Malereigeschichte bilden die auf der Oberfläche von Prince' Arbeiten schwimmenden, von anderswo übernommenen Witze. Diese handeln vom Trinken wie in: «Ich esse Politik und schlafe Politik, aber niemals t r i n k e ich Politik.» Sie handeln von Beziehungen, zum Beispiel in diesem Klassiker aus dem Pantheon des Conférencier-Humors: «Meine erste Freundin hiess Sally. Mensch, war das ein Mädchen, war das ein Mädchen. Das haben mich die Leute gefragt.» Und dann ist da natürlich der Witz, der Prince' ästhetisches Projekt umreisst, der Witz am Ende aller Witze: «Ich war beim Psychiater. Er sagte: ‹Erzähl mir alles.› Das hab ich getan, und jetzt macht er meinen Job.» Die Witze tauchen immer wieder auf seinen Leinwänden auf, manchmal allein, manchmal in Verbindung mit den falschen Bildern, und ich frage mich, ob Prince' Gebrauch dieser Witze nicht auf eine Dissonanz hinweist, auf ein dunkles Geheimnis der amerikanischen Seele. Geschichte ereigne sich zweimal, sagte Marx, das erste Mal als Tragödie, das zweite Mal als Farce.[3)] Prince' gemalte Witze bieten uns eine neue Art von Historienmalerei, eine, die aufzeigt, dass die Geschichte stottert.

Während ich diese Zeilen schreibe, bringt das Fernsehen die ersten Ergebnisse der amerikanischen Präsidentschaftswahlen: Das Stottern ist in vollem Gang. Es sieht ganz danach aus, dass in Amerika wieder einmal Trauer angesagt ist. Ein gemalter Witz als Ende aller Witzgemälde. Vielleicht ist es an der Zeit, den letzten Hubschrauber aus Vietnam zu nehmen, vor dem Fall von Saigon und bevor wir unsere ganz persönliche Version von *Apocalypse Now Redux* erleben. Vielleicht lässt sich dies am besten in einem Witz von Richard Prince zusammenfassen, er geht ungefähr so: «Eines Abends hat ein Handlungsreisender eine Autopanne auf einer abgelegenen Strasse und fragt beim einzigen Bauernhaus weit und breit: ‹Können Sie mich für die Nacht unterbringen?› ‹Ich denke schon›, sagt der Farmer, ‹aber Sie müssen sich das Bett mit meinem kleinen Sohn teilen.› ‹Was sagt man dazu›, sagt der Handlungsreisende, ‹ich bin im falschen Witz!›.» Musikeinblendung. Schnitt zu Slim Pickens, wie er am Ende von Stanley Kubricks Film *Dr. Seltsam oder wie ich lernte, die Bombe zu lieben* (1963) auf einer Atombombe in einen pilzwolkigen Sonnenuntergang reitet. Auf der Bombe stehen die Worte *HI THERE* geschrieben. Endlich mal ein guter Witz. Danke für die Erinnerungen, Richard.

(Übersetzung: Christian Rattemeyer)

1) Richard Prince, «Guns and Poses», *Artforum*, Oktober 2004, S. 143.

2) Martin Sheen als Captain Willard in Francis Ford Coppolas Film *Apocalypse Now* (1979).

3) Genauer: «Hegel bemerkte irgendwo, dass alle grossen weltgeschichtlichen Tatsachen und Personen sich sozusagen zweimal ereignen. Er hat vergessen, hinzuzufügen: das eine Mal als Tragödie, das andere Mal als Farce.» Karl Marx, in: «Der achtzehnte Brumaire des Louis Napoleon», erstmals veröffentlicht in: *Die Revolution. Eine Zeitschrift in zwanglosen Heften,* New York 1852. Erstes Heft.

Richard Prince's
SECOND HOUSE

ALISON M. GINGERAS

THE DRIVE UPSTATE

The northeast corner of Albany County is home to Rensselaerville, a tiny hamlet (population 1,915) situated approximately 130 miles from New York City. Driving north along the West Side Highway of Manhattan, the trip to Rensselaerville takes about three hours—provided that you have bypassed the city's gridlock as well as the suburban sprawl that radiates around New York.

The Hudson River runs parallel to the main highway for the majority of this upstate journey; this otherwise banal geographical detail is replete with symbolic importance. Since its exploration by Henry Hudson in the early 1600s, this majestic waterway has played a vital role in the history and mythology of the US. Not only was the Hudson a strategic military-economic artery since Revolutionary War times, its natural beauty fueled the imagination of the Hudson River Valley School. Today the Hudson River acts as a socio-economic frontier—bifurcating the hinterlands of Upstate New York into two categories: "the haves" and "haves-much-less." The more picturesque eastern bank is home to numerous wealthy, elegant villages (for example: Rhinebeck, Spencertown) while the shabbier, distinctly working class towns dot the Hudson's more mountainous west side. The region around Rensselaerville falls into the latter category.

This upstate class-divide becomes particularly apparent upon exiting the main highway to access the smaller, local roads. The winding path to Rensselaerville traverses an eerie, yet familiar, landscape. Slowly a partial portrait of the residents of Albany county emerges: every few miles a slightly dilapidated, single story house pops up on the side of the road; there are pick-up trucks with National Rifle Association bumper stickers; Christian Churches (from born-again sects to Episcopalians) adorn the tops of every-other hill; above-ground swimming pools are covered in black plastic for the winter; there are overgrown farm fields, odd little factories, gas stations, and diners; cars in various states of disrepair are slowly rusting on front lawns; a lone basketball hoop on an empty playground lets out a silent cry of melancholy.

For anyone familiar with Richard Prince's *Upstate* photographs (1995–1999), driving to Rensselaerville will provoke a riveting sense of déjà vu. While not documentary in intent, Prince's images convey the psychic as well as physical ambience of these rural, working class communities in decline. With a deceptively simple, formal economy, Prince's *Upstate* im-

ALISON M. GINGERAS is a curator and writer living in Paris and New York.

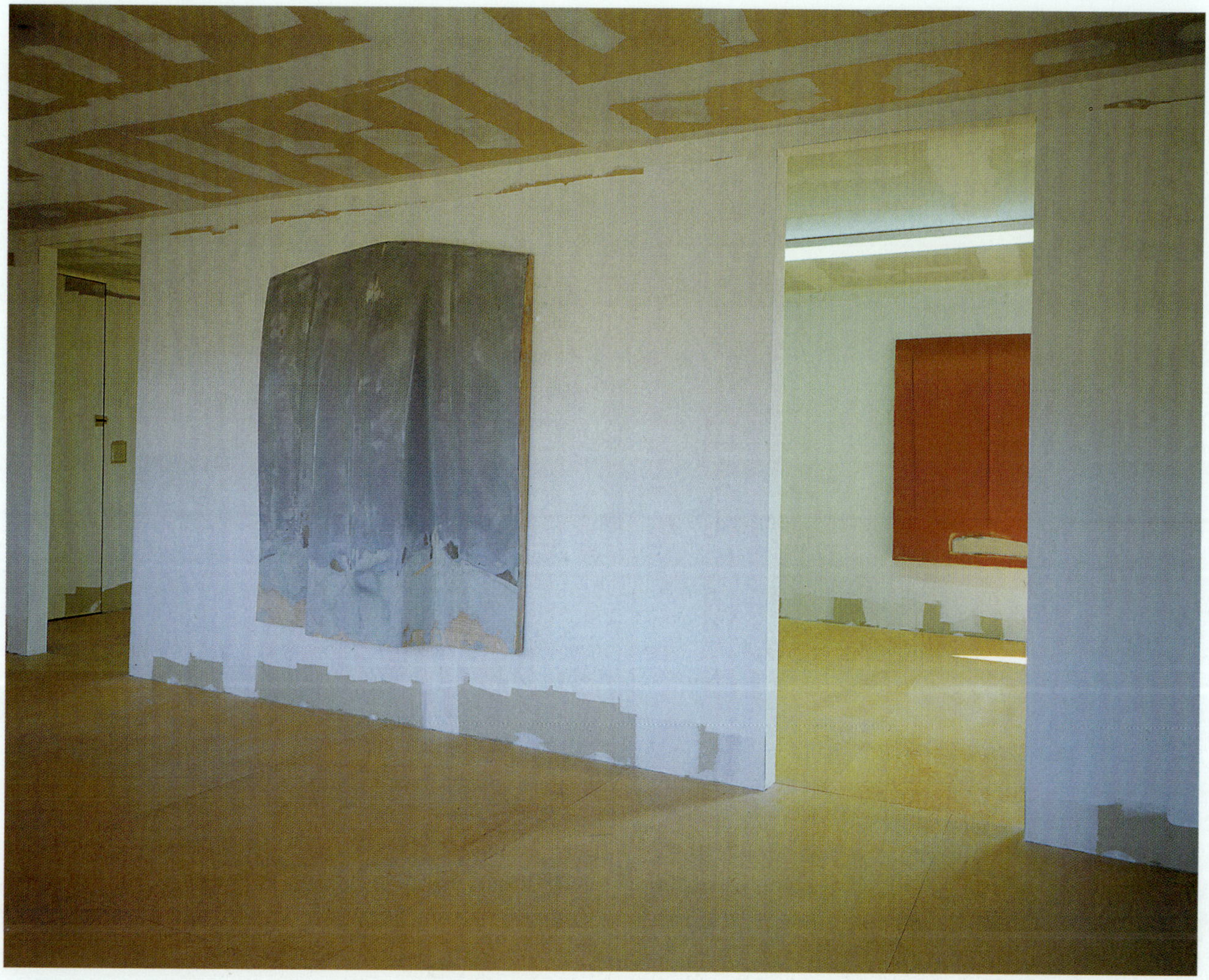

RICHARD PRINCE, SECOND HOUSE, November 2003. (PHOTO: DAVID REGEN/BARBARA GLADSTONE GALLERY, NEW YORK)

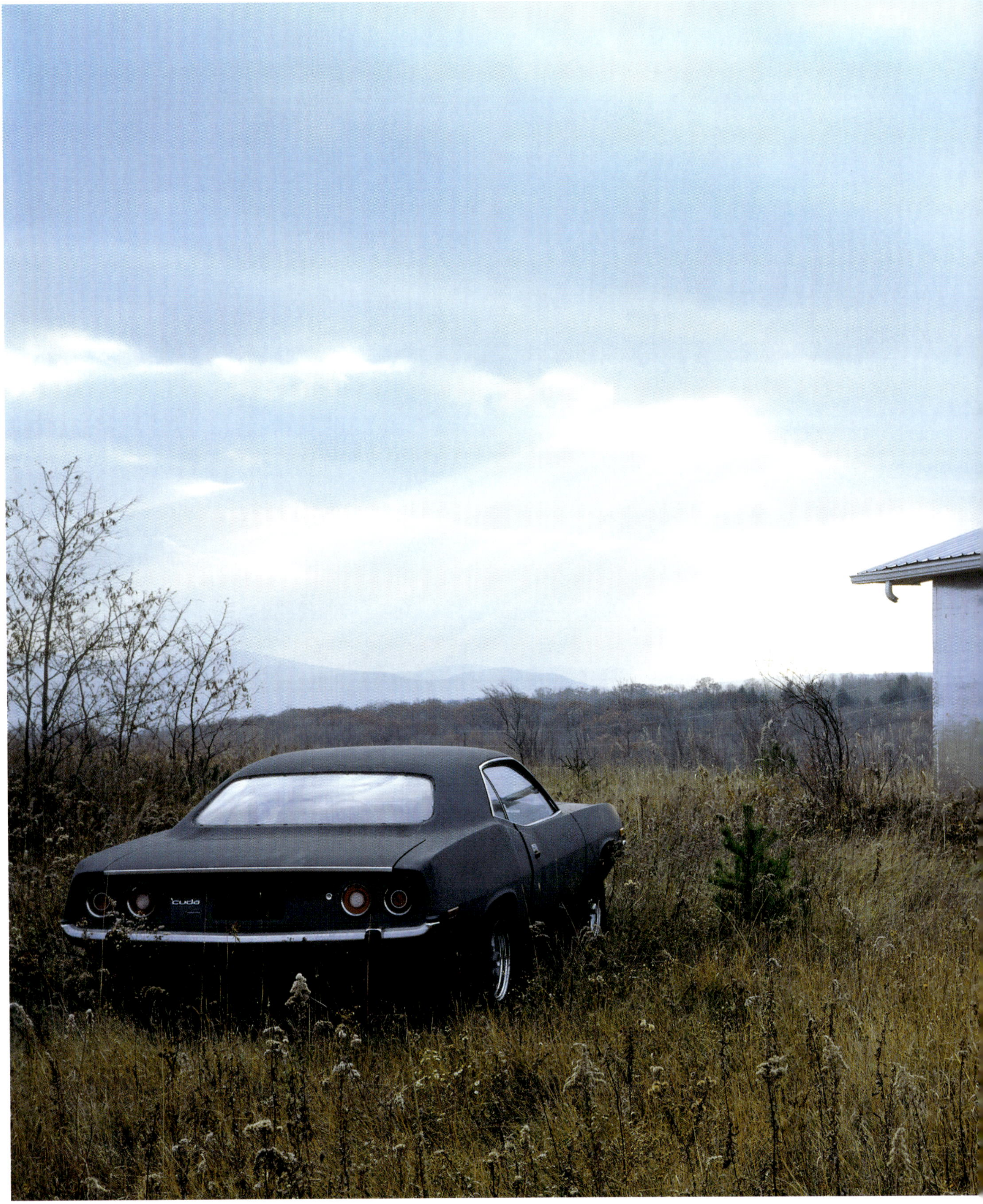
'cuda

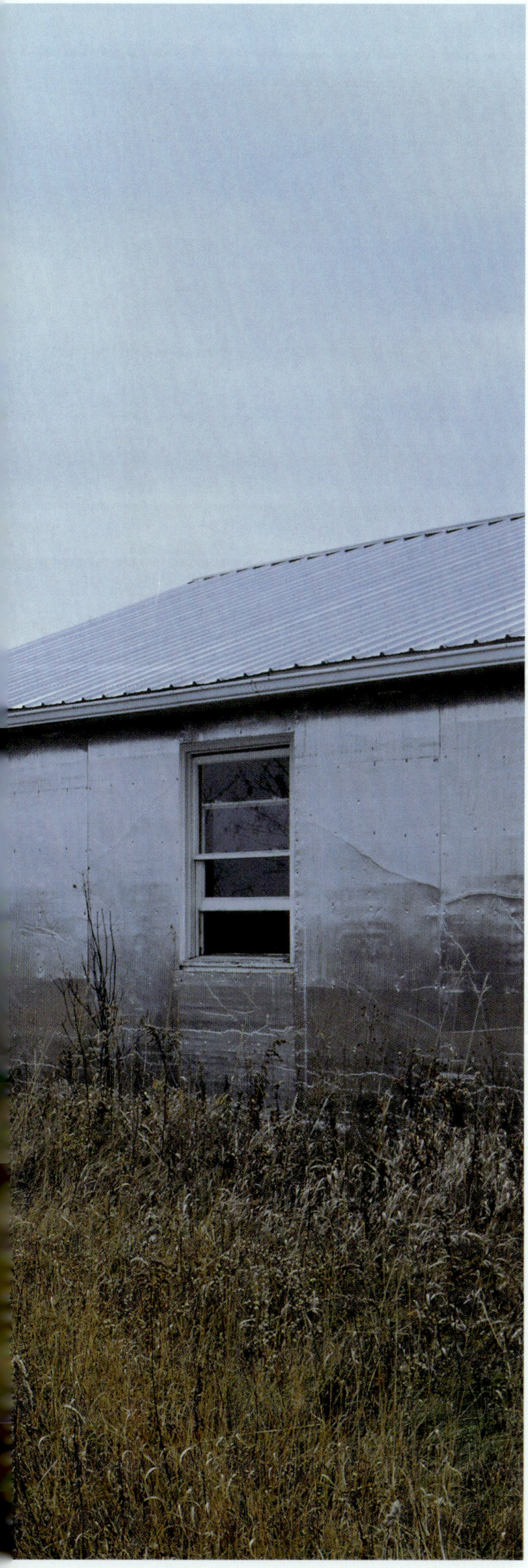

RICHARD PRINCE, SECOND HOUSE, November 2003. (PHOTO: DAVID REGEN/BARBARA GLADSTONE GALLERY, NEW YORK)

ages subtly conjure the libidinous impulses and dark permutations of pop culture that lie below the surface of towns that one encounters while driving off the highway.

THE HOUSE ON THE HILL

Nestled on a hill on the outskirts of Rensselaerville, Richard Prince's SECOND HOUSE (2001–2004) might at first be understood as a prolongation of his *Upstate* investigations. SECOND HOUSE is perfectly camouflaged in its surroundings—at first glance, it appears to be an utterly ordinary single story ranch house. Yet when approaching it from the long hillside driveway, the overgrown grass strategically obscures the identity of who or what lies within. Like so many other domestic buildings in the area, SECOND HOUSE looks kind of decrepit or unfinished (passersby must wonder: did the owner run out of money and abandon construction?). Its façade is missing—only a thin, silvery skin made of insulation panels covers the exterior. An abandoned 1973 Dodge Barracuda is parked out back, quietly rusting in the tall grass; an inside-out tire planter adorns the completely un-landscaped front yard.

The inside seems as unfinished as the outside. The walls and ceilings are partially painted, leaving the spackled drywall joints visible in many spots. Plywood sheets cover the floors. Exposed fluorescent tubes provide an even, cold light in the five rooms of the house. While the rawness of the interior décor suggests an uninhabited space, SECOND HOUSE is far from empty. The objects and images sheltered within its walls mirror the landscape outside: it's pure Americana (that has been "stolen," cropped, and edited by Richard Prince).

A series of Prince's *Car Hood* (1989–1990) sculptures hangs on the walls of the main room—fiberglass and wood reproductions of the hoods of seventies muscle cars. Like Prince's *Cowboys* (1980–2000) these car bodies evoke a mechanical universe of machismo, speed, romance, and danger (à la Monty Hellman's 1971 film, *Two Lane Blacktop*). A basketball backboard that serves as a table is in the middle of the adjacent room; several carefully selected books have been placed on top. Taken from Prince's own legendary collection of first edition and rare books, titles such as *Hippy Hi* and *Woodstock,* as well as some counterculture ephemera, make reference to another faded chapter of Upstate New York's history. The walls are decorated with photographs of cult idols—a T-shirt painting of Jimi Hendrix and a painting of Sid Vicious framed in the style of Prince's *Untitled (Publicities)* series. On the floor in yet another room, there is an orange tire planter sculpture made of resin that is filled with SECOND HOUSE key chains (like the ones you get for free in the gas station down the road) as well as a concrete highway barrier sculpture. A small glass vitrine is built into the adjoining wall—inside there are two necklaces: one is made of several hundred multicolored plastic tags (the kind used to re-seal packages of white bread), and the other is made of hotel card keys. When you examine the contents in each room, SECOND HOUSE provides a succinct, domestically scaled overview of the material—formal and thematic—parameters of Prince's practice.

Richard Prince is not the first artist to create an architectural or environmental envelope to display his oeuvre.[1)] Yet unlike El Lissitzky's CABINET OF ABSTRACTION (1927) or Donald Judd's Minimalist compound in Marfa, Texas, Richard Prince is neither invested in utopian experimentation, self-aggrandizement, nor the preservation of the purity of an artistic/ideological vision. SECOND HOUSE is an anti-monument. It has been painstakingly crafted to be almost impossible to find—to nearly disappear into the landscape. From its calculated look of unfinishedness to its location in a remote corner of Albany County, Prince designed SECOND HOUSE as a vehicle to further perpetuate the aura of mystery and anonymity that already surrounds him.

The trek to find SECOND HOUSE operates in a very similar way to one of Prince's earliest projects, SPIRITUAL AMERICA (1983). Finding it is like falling victim to a carefully choreographed accident. When Prince rented a storefront gallery on the Lower East Side of Manhattan in 1983, it was like setting a trap for an unaware audience. The gallery contained nothing but a receptionist's desk and a single work of art in a gilt frame—a soft-core pornographic image of the child star, Brooke Shields. Knowing that Shields' fully nude, prepubescent body would be

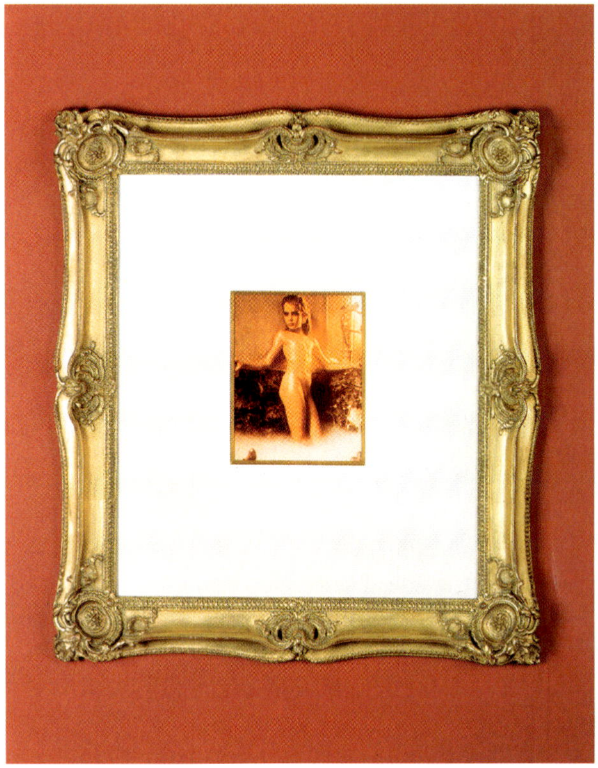

RICHARD PRINCE, BROOKE SHIELDS (SPIRITUAL AMERICA), 1983, Ektacolor photograph, 24 x 20" / 61 x 50,8 cm.

sure to provoke controversy, Prince hired a receptionist (who didn't even know Prince was the mastermind behind the gallery) and promptly left town. "It was only by word of mouth, gossip, rumor, innuendo, and largely unsubstantiated reports that visitors to the show even realized that there was any connection between the Spiritual America Gallery and Richard Prince. For the duration of the exhibition, Prince couldn't be found in New York. Stories circulated downtown that he had gone underground. Or moved to the West Coast..."[2)] Frustrating the public's thirst for putting a face on such a juicy stunt, SPIRITUAL AMERICA helped give birth to Prince's mysterious persona. SECOND HOUSE prolongs that mystery.

SECOND HOUSE: SOME OF ME, SOME OF YOU. MOST OF ME, NONE OF YOU.

Interviewer: *Does your art come from an autobiographical source?*

Richard Prince: *It's all just like me. And it's all what I like. If you like it, I'll call it mine. But you can't say it's all mine. Some of me, some of you. Most of me, none of you. It's like when they ask me where I'm from—I say, "not from any place really."* [3)]

Most people have no idea who Richard Prince is. This is not for a lack of notoriety or esteem by his peers. Hiding in plain sight, Prince has cultivated an identity that is shrouded in a web of tantalizing clues, shadowy images, false leads, carefully constructed rumors, and pseudonyms. He rarely answers questions in the first person. In interviews, as well as in his own writings, he prefers to invert conventional grammar or even use the third person in order to avoid the classical construction of self-expression. When he does use the pronoun "I," he expressly empties out the content so that it sounds like a pastiche of appropriated texts or an amalgamation of banal clichés. His photographic images operate in a similar way to his self-presentation. No matter if they are appropriations of existing images from magazines or original photographs, they share an authorless, artless quality. In terms of subject matter—a pantheon of biker chicks, cowboys, and flash-in-the-pan celebrities, to name but a few—his choice is highly charged, yet completely empty. It is nearly impossible to detangle his artistic production and the construction of his furtive persona. The lack of any credible biographical information invites the viewer to speculate: who is the r e a l Richard Prince?

Visiting SECOND HOUSE does not help to answer that question. Perhaps it is because it's the wrong question to ask. Like a chameleon, Prince continues to master the language of his surroundings: the vernacular architecture of Albany County, and the icons and clichés that make up the fabric of the local history (from the failed utopian moment of Woodstock to the badges of working class decline). Using the anonymity provided by these vernacular forms to cover his tracks, Prince deflects questions about his own identity back onto the collective body. Visiting SECOND HOUSE does not provide any conclusions about the Americana it conjures. Instead, it forces the viewer to contemplate the clichés, to consider overlooked banalities, and to appreciate underestimated beauty. For many, the temptation is to read SECOND HOUSE as a shrine to the disappearance of many different Americas—the dystopia of the working class, the momentary countercultural utopias of the sixties, or the subcultures of bikers and cowboys. Richard Prince's work is undeniably a b o u t America, but it is also about something more. To borrow Prince's own dry, enigmatic remarks, "[it is] some of me, some of you. Most of me, none of you."

1) In fact, SECOND HOUSE is not Prince's first project that was conceived as an "environment" for the display of his work. FIRST HOUSE operated in a similar manner to his current project—only it was located in a residential neighborhood of West Hollywood in April 1993. This temporary installation transformed a typical LA bungalow into a gallery for the domestic display of his photographs, paintings, drawings, and works directly painted onto the walls.

The mise-en-scène of his own work is also evident in the numerous photographs he takes of his own works and collections in his studio and house. For some recent examples, see his artist book *American English* (2003) or his website: www.richardprinceart.com

2) Rosetta Brooks, "Spiritual America: No Holds Barred," in Lisa Phillips, *Richard Prince* (New York: Whitney Museum of American Art, 1992), pp. 87–88.

3) Interview with Richard Prince, "Like a Beautiful Scar on your Head," *Modern Painters*, Special American Issue, Autumn 2002, Volume 15, Number 3, pp. 68–75.

Richard Prince'
SECOND HOUSE

ALISON M. GINGERAS

DIE FAHRT NACH NORDEN

In der Nordostecke von Albany liegt Rensselaerville, ein winziger Weiler mit 1915 Einwohnern, etwa zweihundert Kilometer von New York City entfernt. Fährt man auf dem West Side Highway von Manhattan nach Norden, dauert die Fahrt nach Rensselaerville rund drei Stunden, vorausgesetzt man hat den Stau in der Stadt und die ausgedehnten Vorortssiedlungen New Yorks bereits hinter sich gelassen.

Der Hudson fliesst während der ganzen Reise nach Norden meist parallel zur Hauptverkehrsachse; diese an sich banale geographische Tatsache ist von grosser symbolischer Bedeutung. Denn seit ihrer Erforschung durch Henry Hudson im frühen sechzehnten Jahrhundert spielte die majestätische Wasserstrasse eine wichtige Rolle für die Geschichte und den Mythos der USA. Der Hudson war nicht nur seit den Revolutionskriegen eine strategisch wichtige, militärische und ökonomische Lebensader, nein, seine Naturschönheiten beflügelten auch die Phantasie der Maler der *Hudson River Valley*-Schule. Heute markiert der Hudson eine sozioökonomische Grenze und trennt das Hinterland von Uptstate New York in zwei Kategorien: «die Besitzenden» und «die sehr viel weniger Besitzenden». Das malerische Ostufer beherbergt viele reiche, gediegene Städtchen (etwa Rhinebeck oder Spencertown), während das etwas hügeligere Westufer mit sichtlich schäbigeren Ortschaften übersät ist, in denen die Arbeiterklasse wohnt. Die Gegend um Rensselaerville gehört in die zweite Kategorie.

Dieser Klassenunterschied im Norden des Staates New York wird besonders augenfällig, wenn man die Autobahn verlässt und auf die kleineren Nebenstrassen gelangt. Der verschlungene Weg nach Rensselaerville durchquert eine gespenstische und dennoch vertraute Landschaft. Allmählich bekommt man ein ungefähres Bild der Einwohner von Albany: alle paar Kilometer taucht ein etwas heruntergekommenes, einstöckiges Haus am Strassenrand auf; Pick-ups mit Aufklebern der *National Rifle Association* stehen herum; auf jedem zweiten Hügel thront eine Kirche (von Wiedergeborenen-Sekten bis zu den Episkopalen); nicht im Boden eingelassene Swimmingpools sind zum Überwintern in schwarze Plastikfolie gepackt; man sieht überwucherte Felder, seltsame, kleine Fabriken, Tankstellen und Diners; Autos in diversen Stadien des Verfalls rosten auf dem Rasen vor sich hin; und ein einsamer Basketballkorb auf einem verlassenen Spielfeld schreit stumm auf vor Melancholie.

Für jeden, der Richard Prince' *Upstate*-Photos (1995–1999) kennt, wird die Fahrt nach Rensselaerville zum überwältigenden *Déjà-vu*-Erlebnis. Obwohl

ALISON M. GINGERAS ist Kuratorin und Publizistin. Sie lebt in Paris und New York.

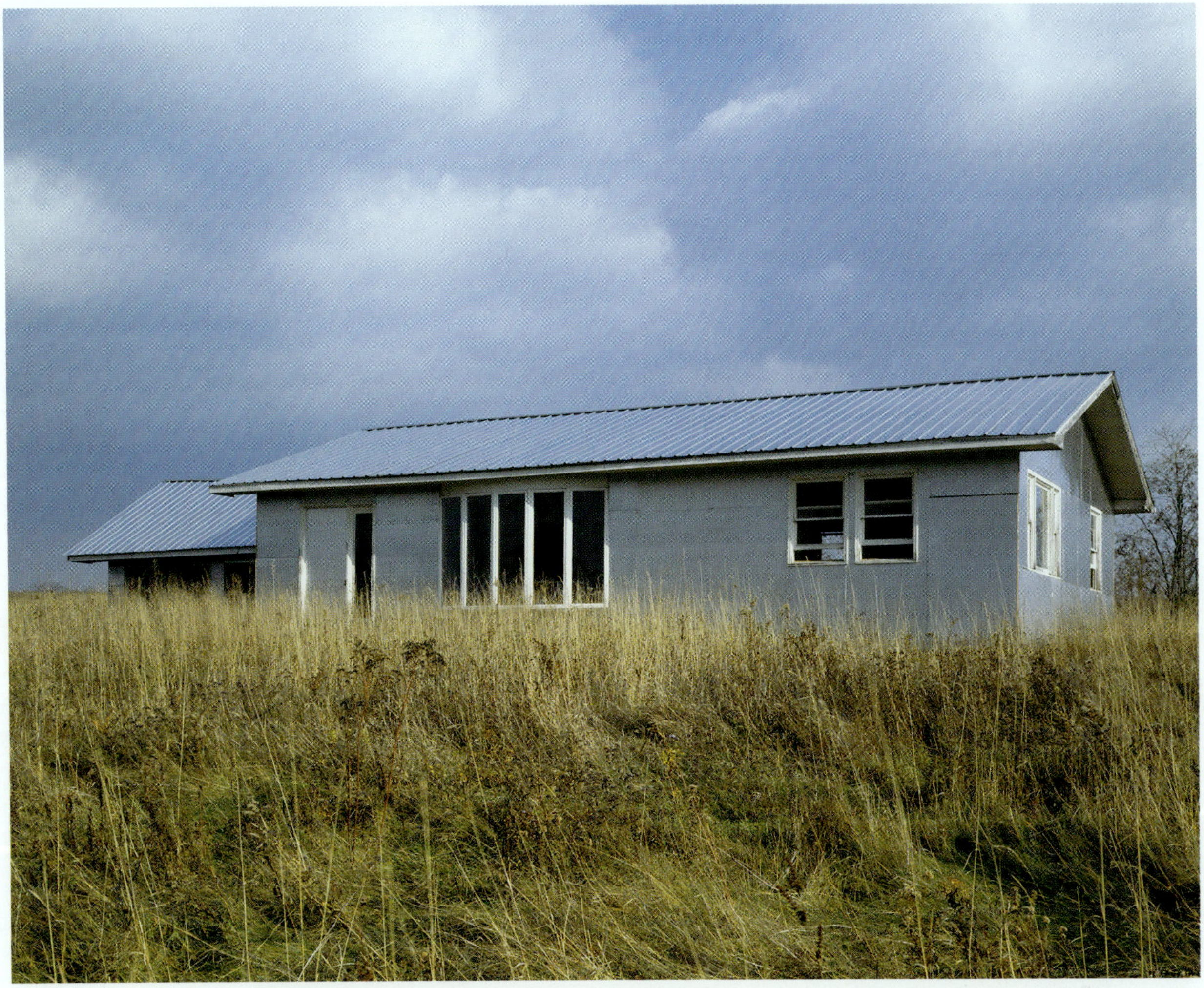

RICHARD PRINCE, SECOND HOUSE, November 2003.
(PHOTO: DAVID REGEN/BARBARA GLADSTONE GALLERY, NEW YORK)

die Bilder von Prince keinerlei dokumentarische Absicht verfolgen, vermitteln sie exakt die psychische und physische Atmosphäre dieser heruntergekommenen ländlichen Arbeitergemeinden. Mit irreführend simpler formaler Ökonomie machen sie auf subtile Weise die triebhaften Impulse und düsteren Variationen der Popkultur sichtbar, die unter der Oberfläche dieser Ortschaften neben der Autobahn schlummern.

DAS HAUS AUF DEM HÜGEL

An der Peripherie von Rensselaerville an einen Hügel gekuschelt könnte Richard Prince' SECOND HOUSE zunächst als Fortsetzung seiner *Upstate*-Erforschung verstanden werden. SECOND HOUSE verschmilzt perfekt mit seiner Umgebung – auf den ersten Blick scheint es ein ganz gewöhnliches einstöckiges Landhaus zu sein. Doch wenn man sich auf der langen hangseitigen Zufahrt nähert, verbirgt das

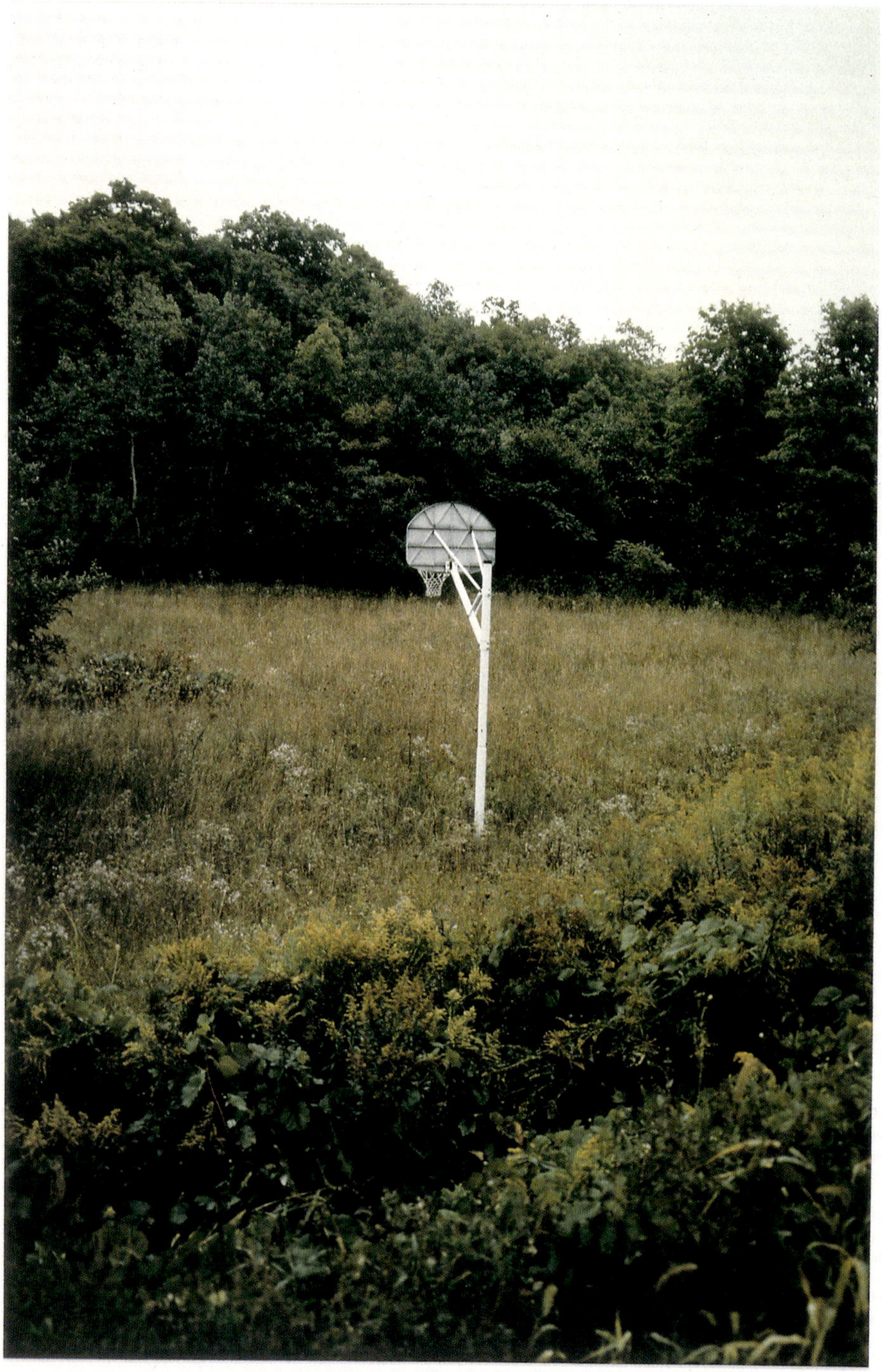

RICHARD PRINCE, UPSTATE, 1995–1999, Ektacolor print, 60 x 40"; framed 69 x 49" / 152,4 x 101,6 cm; gerahmt 175,3 x 124,5 cm.

ungemähte Gras, was wirklich dahinter steckt. Wie so viele andere Wohngebäude in der Gegend wirkt SECOND HOUSE irgendwie baufällig oder unfertig. (Leute, die zufällig vorbeikommen, werden wohl denken, dass dem Besitzer das Geld während des Bauens ausgegangen sei.) Die Fassade fehlt – nur eine dünne silberne Haut aus Isolationsplatten bedeckt die Aussenwand. Hinter dem Haus steht ein verlassener Dodge Barracuda aus dem Jahr 1973 und rostet im hohen Gras still vor sich hin; ein Pflanzgefäss aus einem umgestülpten Autoreifen schmückt den sonst überhaupt nicht gestalteten Platz vor dem Haus.

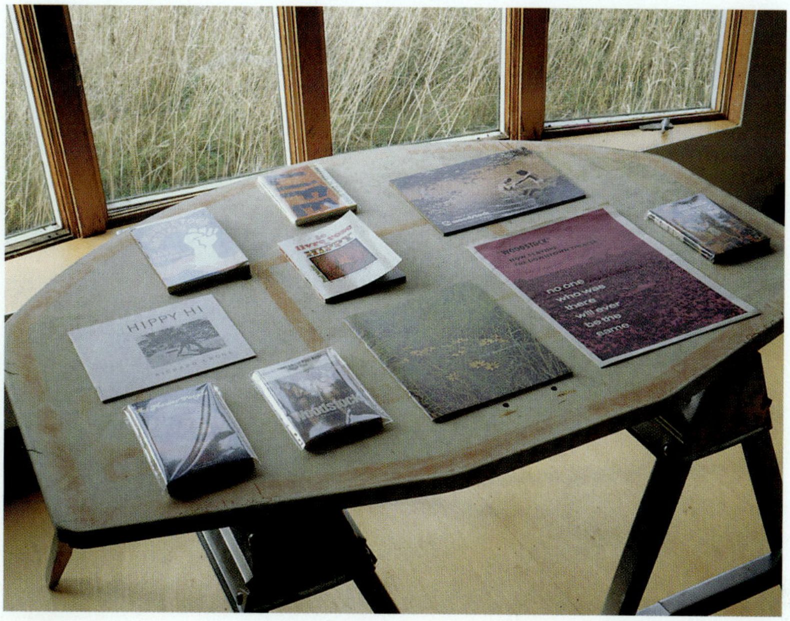

RICHARD PRINCE, SECOND HOUSE, November 2003, installation inside the house, a selection of Woodstock memorabilia displayed on a basketball backboard / Woodstock-Memorabilien auf Basketballkorbrückwand im Innern des Hauses.

Innen wirkt das Ganze ebenso unfertig wie aussen. Die Wände und Decken sind teilweise gestrichen, so dass an vielen Stellen die verleimten Fugen der Fertigwandelemente zu erkennen sind. Der Boden ist mit Furnierholzplatten bedeckt. Nackte Neonröhren liefern in allen fünf Räumen des Hauses ein gleichmässig kaltes Licht. Und obwohl der rohe Zustand der Innenausstattung vermuten lässt, dass das Haus nicht bewohnt wird, ist SECOND HOUSE alles andere als leer. Die Gegenstände und Bilder im Innern spiegeln die Landschaft draussen wider: Es sind reine Amerikana (von Richard Prince «zusammengestohlen», beschnitten und herausgegeben).

Eine Serie der *Car Hood*-Skulpturen des Künstlers hängt an den Wänden des zentralen Raums – Fiberglas- und Holzreproduktionen von Kultauto-Kühlerhauben aus den 70er Jahren. Wie Prince' *Cowboys* beschwören auch die Autoteile ein mechanisches Universum von Machismo, Tempo, Abenteuer und Gefahr (im Stil von Monty Hellmans Film *Two Lane Blacktop,* 1971). Im Zimmer nebenan dient eine Basketballkorb-Rückwand als Tisch; darauf liegen ein paar sorgfältig ausgewählte Bücher; sie stammen aus Prince' eigener legendärer Sammlung von Erstausgaben und seltenen Büchern, wie zum Beispiel *Hippy Hi* und *Woodstock,* aber es sind auch Raritäten aus der Untergrundkultur darunter – Anspielungen auf ein weiteres vergangenes Kapitel der Geschichte von Upstate-New York. Die Wände sind mit Photos von Kultidolen dekoriert – ein gemaltes T-Shirt-Porträt von Jimi Hendrix und ein ebenfalls gemaltes Porträt von Sid Vicious, beide gerahmt wie die Bilder in Prince' Serie *Untitled (Publicities).* In einem weiteren Zimmer steht eine orange Autoreifen-Pflanzgefäss-Skulptur aus Kunstharz auf dem Boden, gefüllt mit SECOND HOUSE-Schlüsselanhängern (denselben, die man an der nächsten Tankstelle gratis bekommt), sowie die Betonskulptur einer Strassensperre. In der angrenzenden Wand ist eine kleine Glasvitrine eingelassen, darin befinden sich zwei Halsketten: die eine besteht aus mehreren hundert kleinen bunten Plastikklammern (jene zum Wiederverschliessen angebrochener Toastbrotpackungen), die andere aus Plastikkarten-Hotelschlüsseln. Insgesamt bietet SECOND HOUSE einen lakonischen, der häuslichen Domäne angepassten Überblick über die materiellen – formalen und thematischen – Parameter von Prince' Arbeitsweise.

Richard Prince ist nicht der erste Künstler, der sich einen architektonischen Rahmen schafft, um sein Werk zu präsentieren.[1] Aber anders als El Lissitzkys ABSTRAKTES KABINETT (1927) oder Donald Judds minimalistische Fabriklandschaft in Marfa, Texas, geht es Richard Prince weder um utopische Experimente noch um Selbstdarstellung, noch um das unverfälschte Bewahren einer künstlerisch-ideologischen Vision. SECOND-HOUSE ist ein Anti-Monument und wurde mit grosser Sorgfalt so errichtet, dass man es kaum findet, ja, es verschwindet fast ganz in der Landschaft. Vom bewusst erzeugten «unfertigen» Aussehen bis zur Lage in einem entlegenen Winkel von Albany hat Prince SECOND HOUSE so konzipiert, dass es die geheimnisumwitterte und anonyme Aura, die ihn umgibt, weitervermittelt.

Die Reise zu SECOND HOUSE funktioniert ähnlich wie bei einem seiner ersten Projekte, SPIRITUAL AMERICA (Spirituelles Amerika, 1983). Sucht man es auf, so ist es, als ob man einem sorgsam inszenierten Unfall zum Opfer fiele. Als Prince 1983 eine Galerie mit Schaufensterfront auf Manhattans Lower East Side mietete, war das wie eine Falle für ein ahnungsloses Publikum. In der Galerie war nichts, ausser einem Empfangstresen und einem einzigen Kunstwerk, einer Softporno-Aufnahme des Kinderstars Brooke Shields in vergoldetem Rahmen. Im Wissen darum, dass Shields' vollkommen nackter, vorpubertärer Körper mit Sicherheit empörte Reaktionen auslösen würde, stellte Prince eine Empfangsdame an (die nicht einmal wusste, dass er es war, der hinter der Galerie stand) und verliess die Stadt. «Nur durch Mundpropaganda, Klatsch, Gerüchte, Andeutungen und unbestätigte Berichte hörten die Galeriebesucher davon, dass möglicherweise eine Verbindung zwischen der Spiritual America Gallery und Richard Prince bestand. Während der ganzen Dauer der Ausstellung blieb Prince in New York unauffindbar. In der Szene kursierten Gerüchte, dass er in den Untergrund gegangen sei. Oder an die Westküste gezogen ...»[2] Dank diesem Akt, dem Publikum zu verweigern, mit der saftigen Geschichte auch ein Gesicht verbinden zu können, wirkte SPIRITUAL AMERICA bei der Entstehung von Prince' geheimnisumwitterter Aura kräftig mit. SECOND HOUSE pflegt dieses Mysterium weiter.

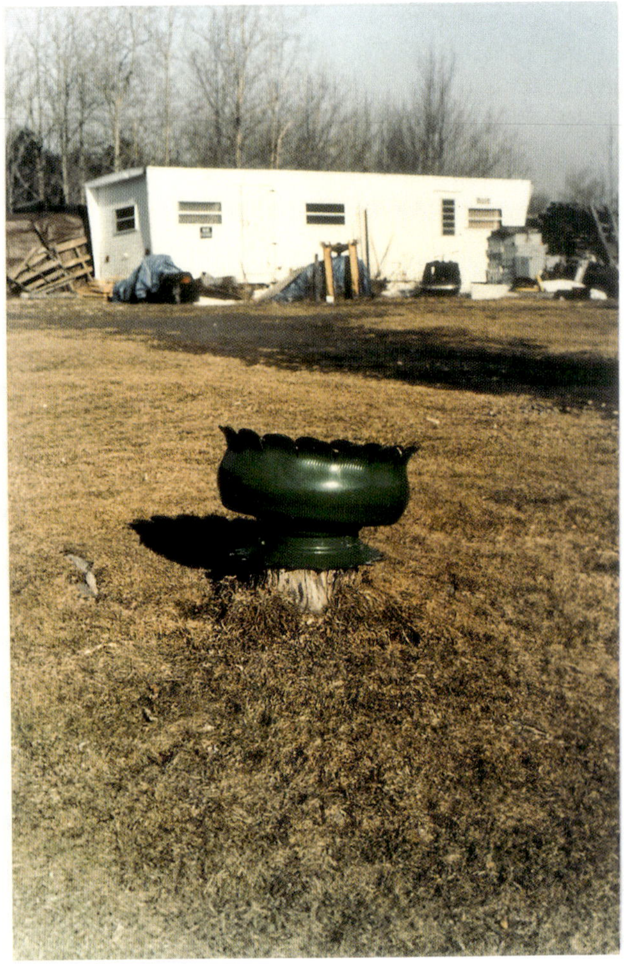

RICHARD PRINCE, UPSTATE, 1995–1999, Ektacolor print, 60 x 40"; framed 69 x 49" / 152,4 x 101,6 cm; gerahmt 175,3 x 124,5 cm.

SECOND HOUSE: MANCHES VON MIR, MANCHES VON DIR. FAST ALLES VON MIR, NICHTS VON DIR.

Interviewer: *Ist deine Kunst autobiographischen Ursprungs?*

Richard Prince: *Sie ist einfach wie ich. Und alles, was ich mag. Wenn du es magst, werde ich sagen, es sei mein. Aber man kann nicht sagen, es ist alles mein. Manches von mir, manches von dir. Fast alles von mir, nichts von dir. Es ist, wie wenn man mich fragt, woher ich komme – ich sage: «Eigentlich von keinem bestimmten Ort.»*[3]

Die meisten haben keine Ahnung, wer Richard Prince ist. Und zwar nicht, weil er unter seinesgleichen zu wenig berüchtigt oder geachtet wäre. Indem er sich, selbst wenn man ihn sieht, versteckt, hat Prince sich eine Identität geschaffen, die hinter einem Schleier verlockender Hinweise, Schattenbilder, falscher Fährten, sorgfältig konstruierter Gerüchte und Pseudonyme verborgen bleibt. Fragen beantwortet er selten in der ersten Person. In Interviews, aber auch in seinen eigenen Texten, verkehrt er gern die konventionelle Grammatik oder benützt die dritte Person, um die klassische Konstruktion des Selbstausdrucks zu umgehen. Und wenn er das Pronomen «Ich» benützt, so beraubt er es absichtlich jeglichen Inhalts, so dass es wie eine Montage aus übernommenen Texten klingt oder wie eine Ansammlung banaler Klischees. Seine photographischen Bilder funktionieren ähnlich im Hinblick auf seine Selbstdarstellung. Egal ob es sich um Appropriationen bestehender Bilder aus Magazinen oder um Originalphotos handelt, sie haben immer dieselbe autor- und kunstlose Qualität. Und auch was seine Wahl der Sujets angeht – ein Tempel für Motorradbräute, Cowboys, irgendwelche Fünfzehn-Minuten-Prominenz, um nur einige zu nennen –, sie sind immer extrem aufgeladen und zugleich völlig leer. Es ist fast unmöglich, seine künstlerische Produktion und die Konstruktion seiner schwer fassbaren Identität auseinander zu dröseln. Das Fehlen jeder glaubwürdigen biographischen Information lädt den Betrachter zum Spekulieren ein: Wer ist der echte Richard Prince?

Ein Besuch von SECOND HOUSE trägt nichts zur Beantwortung dieser Frage bei. Wahrscheinlich, weil es die falsche Frage ist. Wie ein Chamäleon fährt Prince fort, die Sprache seiner Umgebung zu übernehmen: die lokaltypische Architektur von Albany County und all die Ikonen und Klischees, die der Stoff der lokalen Geschichte hergibt (vom fehlgeschlagenen utopischen Moment von Woodstock bis zu den Merkmalen des Niedergangs der Arbeiterklasse). Indem Prince die Anonymität dieser volkstümlichen Elemente benützt, um seine eigene Spur zu verwischen, lenkt er Fragen zu seiner eigenen Identität zurück auf jene des Kollektivs. Ein Besuch von SECOND HOUSE liefert keinerlei Schlussfolgerungen über die Amerikana, die es beschwört. Stattdessen zwingt es den Betrachter dazu, Klischees bewusst wahrzunehmen, bisher unbemerkte Banalitäten zu beachten und unterschätzte Schönheiten zu würdigen. Viele mögen versucht sein, in SECOND HOUSE einen Schrein verschiedener verschwundener Amerikas zu sehen: die Schieflage der Arbeiterklasse, die kurzlebigen Utopien der Gegenkultur in den 60er Jahren, oder die Subkulturen der Motorradbanden und Cowboys. Richard Prince' Werk handelt unverkennbar von Amerika, aber es geht auch noch um etwas anderes. In einer von Prince' eigenen trockenen, rätselhaften Formulierungen ausgedrückt: um «manches von mir, manches von dir. Fast alles von mir, nichts von dir».

(Übersetzung: Suzanne Schmidt)

1) Tatsächlich ist SECOND HOUSE nicht das erste Projekt von Prince, das als «Environment» für sein eigenes Werk konzipiert ist. FIRST HOUSE (April 1993) funktionierte ganz ähnlich, nur war es in einem Wohngebiet von West-Hollywood gelegen. Die vorübergehende Installation verwandelte einen typischen L.A.-Bungalow in eine Galerie zur häuslichen Präsentation seiner Photographien, Bilder, Zeichnungen und direkt auf die Wände gemalten Werke.

Die Inszenierung der eigenen Werke wird auch anhand der zahlreichen Photographien deutlich, die er von den eigenen Arbeiten und seiner Sammlung in seinem Atelier und Wohnhaus macht. Neuere Beispiele finden sich etwa in seinem Künstlerbuch *American English* (2003) oder auf seiner Website: www.richardprinceart.com

2) Rosetta Brooks, «Spiritual America: No holds Barred», in: Lisa Phillips, *Richard Prince,* Whitney Museum of American Art, New York 1992, S. 87–88.

3) Interview mit Richard Prince, «Like a Beautiful Scar on your Head», *Modern Painters,* Special American Issue (Herbst 2002), Bd. 15, Nr. 3., S. 68–75.

Richard Prince: A Reader

VINCENT PÉCOIL

Richard Prince's books and catalogues abound with photographs depicting stacks of books and shelves filled with novels, biographies, and catalogues. The books are in carefully studied piles like his photographs, which he used to present in groups called "gangs." By thus exhibiting his own interior—in the domestic, as well as the psychological sense (his *Inside World,* to quote the title of one of his books)—by making his interior publicly known, Prince's attitude is comparable to those celebrities who open the doors of their mansions to journalists' cameras, as in the MTV show where pop stars offer guided tours through their homes—from the garage to the kitchen, to the living room and the bedroom, to invariably their favorite room: the secret, intimate one. In Prince's case, that room would undoubtedly be the library, more so even than the studio—supposing that the two are not one and the same; he declared in an interview that his "art supply store is a magazine store."[1] Prince's last book, *Good Life,* shows images of the good life as it is seen and circulated in a variety of interior decoration books. The images that are reproduced are from books about "Easy Living" or "Living the Modern Way" (two common interior decoration titles).[2] Generally, interior decoration books are quasi-fictions; they are images of interiors that no one actually owns—probably no one you know, at least. The library presented in Prince's books constitutes a third place, almost as real as his first and second place.

Describing his move to Los Angeles in a 1988 book, Prince enumerated his first acquisitions after moving in: "Books for the house, first buys: ..." which was followed by a full page of bibliographical references, including Don DeLillo, Harry Crews, a beauty advice book, a book on the Auschwitz trials, a signed copy of a Buckminster Fuller book, a biography of Elvis, porn books, Walter Tevis, Bruce Nauman, and others.[3] Prince's other catalogues also include many kinds of books: collections of jokes; photography books (Helmut Newton, Larry Clark, etc.); science-fiction books (*Planet of the Apes, Fahrenheit 451,* and works by Philip K. Dick and J.G. Ballard, who are both well represented); Thomas Pynchon, Gore Vidal; old novels and pulp fiction from the fifties and sixties, whose cover illustrations were presumably a determining factor in their purchase; *Blasted Allegories,* a collection of writing by artists, with a reproduction of one of Prince's *Cowboy* re-photographs; a near exhaustive collection of the different editions of Nabokov's *Lolita*; and a few classics of American counterculture: Beat writers, collections of poetry, and biographies of pop singers, and, last but not least, a number of writings by Prince himself, such as the recently published *Man* catalogue.

An article by Prince entitled "Bringing It All Back Home" describes his compulsive collector's mania. The article initially appeared in *Art in America* in September 1988 and was recently reprinted in *American English.*[4] In it Prince details the manifestations of his bibliophilia. The *Art in America* article showed for the first time a photograph of part of his library—a practice he would repeat from then on in various other publications. In Prince's art, collecting is content in its own right: "collecting" he says, "has become more a part of the work."[5] This is manifestly true in the

VINCENT PÉCOIL is a critic and curator who lives in Dijon, France.

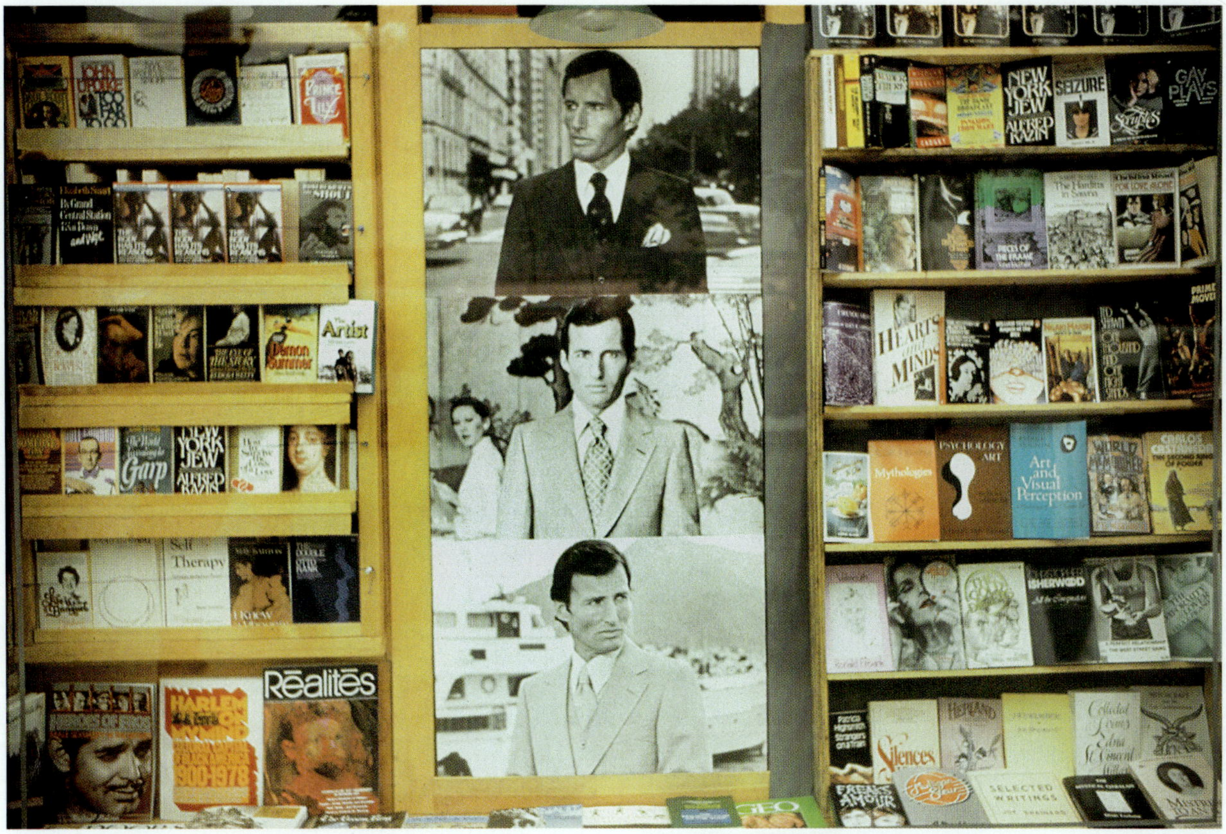

RICHARD PRINCE, window installation at 3 Lives & Co. Bookstore, New York, 1979 / Schaufensterinstallation in der New Yorker Buchhandlung 3 Lives & Co.

last pieces from the *8x10* series, and other related works, which seem like fodder for the obsessions of art collectors (to say nothing of autograph, photography, book, and pin collectors). In fact, many of Prince's publications seem to be similarly conceived as instant collectors' items. The first pamphlet he edited was published in three versions with three different titles *(Menthol Pictures, Menthol Wars,* and *War Pictures)* while the content of the book was identical in all three, a process which brings to mind the records and magazines that are released in several versions with different covers for each. Similarly, there are two versions of Prince's 1997 photography book, *4x4*: a Japanese edition and an American one (the Japanese version being of course the more desirable, as is the case with CD imports). *American English* takes as its subject this double origin: it depicts the American and the English editions of various books, side by side. Prince's own books are also published in limited editions, along with signed editions.

Prince has written numerous texts, fragments, and narratives. His stories, such as *Why I Go To The Movies Alone,* are plot-less; they present themselves as a series of transcriptions of experiences had by various anonymous characters (though the characters can often be identified as Prince). The narrative becomes a kind of flattening, where just about everything becomes reduced to an image.[6] Almost every description is about a character's visual perception, and whatever thoughts such perceptions inspire. The only action consists of the act of watching (movies, television, people), and, less frequently, listening (to

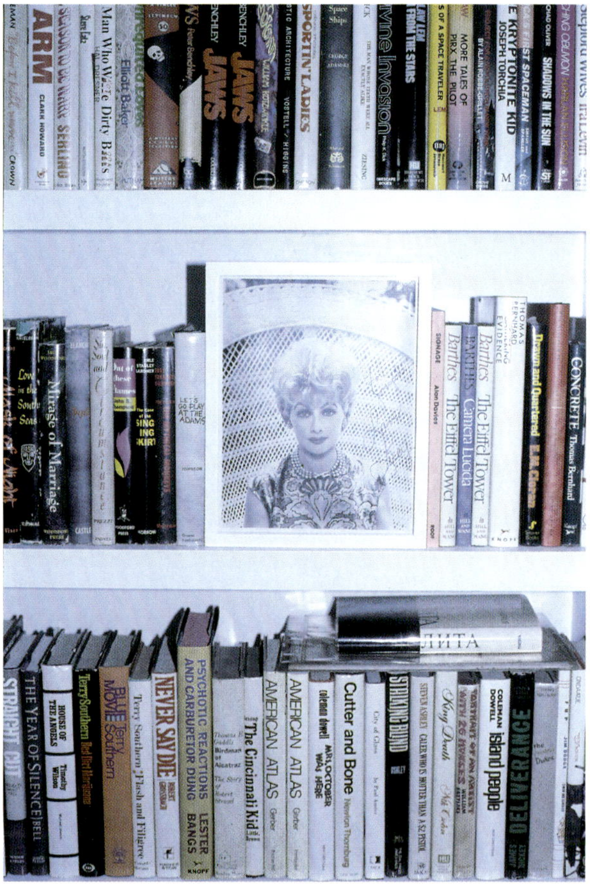

RICHARD PRINCE, Ektacolor photograph of the artist's library / Photo der Bibliothek des Künstlers.

music or to conversations). It's as if "the ways of the world are set in type like maybe someone composed them on a copy terminal and then flashed the whole thing on a screen to see if everything would fit..."[7] The title of one of Prince's photography books, *Adult Comedy Action Drama,* is based on the categories used in video stores, which in the book subsume all dimensions of existence, every event of daily life.

"They (books, videos) change me...," Prince says. "I like having the lives of these things around me. I like having lives I can go in and out of when I'm alone."[8] As autobiographical as any of Prince's stories may be, the true subject of his books is not the character (the "I" or, in this case, the "he"), but rather the image he inhabits and the lives he borrows—in other words, the process through which fiction becomes realized, or becomes real. The same mechanism of projection is what fuels the adolescent desire to possess posters of famous people: "I always thought the choosing of a personality was in itself some kind of expression," Prince says. "It was enough. All my friends did it. We put them on our walls, in our bedroom. I've just kept doing it."[9] Prince has talked many times about the fascination he had as an adolescent for the pictures of artists like Pollock or Kline, more than for their paintings as such. These portrait-images have always existed for him on the same level as those of rock stars or other celebrities. In *Adult Comedy Action Drama,* juxtaposing the iconic photograph of Pollock taken from the cover of the *Evergreen Review* with an image of Captain America taken from the cover of an issue of *Marvel* (caption: "Our Man of The Year"—pick your hero...), Prince wittily suggests this equivalence.[10] Recently, in regard to a photograph of Kline in his studio, Prince told Jeff Rian about the need he felt at the time "to be in the picture." "I think you're alive in the picture," Prince said. "You're more alive in the picture than outside the picture. At least you go on living in the picture after you've died outside it... Is what we are in pictures almost real? Maybe it's become the 'most' real thing."[11]

Prince uses the phrase "social science fiction" to describe his art, claiming it to be another way of describing a kind of art that studies the effects of the media: "Applying the physical facts of the environment upon people."[12] He asserts that it is a way of working and a science concerned with "sounding or looking like fiction, but being about nonfiction." This is just like the images and stories used, about which we may wonder whether they are, as Prince would say, "almost real," or "almost fake." This art, or "social science fiction," takes as its object a variety of already existing images—"already out," as Prince would say—as well as, already uttered phrases. This "already out" language is the point of departure for Prince's activity as a writer, which could better be described as a practice of rewriting. The already uttered phrases that form the material of his books may come from other books, but also from grocery lists, personal ads, movie summaries, the back of videotape covers, as well as from various kinds of magazines: *Muscle Cars, People, American Photographer, Harper's Bazaar, Playboy, Vanity Fair, Hustler, Popular Science, Sports Illustrated,* and so on—raw material from which Prince excerpts jokes, titles, subtitles, tables of contents, headlines, and captions. A title from one of the books in his collection, *Steal This Book,* by Abbie Hoffman, could describe Prince's project; it is a revolutionary survival manual that serves as a guide how to free things (or how to steal them). The titles of some of Prince's catalogues, like *Spiritual America* for example, were themselves "stolen"; other books, like *Inside World,* are described as "compiled by Richard Prince." Prince applies this rewriting principle to himself as well, inserting passages from his own writings, almost verbatim, in various books, interviews, or articles. A large number of passages from *Why I Go To The Movies Alone* had been published with individual titles before the book, and were published again later, either on their own, or within other articles.

One of the oft-rewritten passages appearing in many books and short texts describes the thoughts of a character in a movie theater: "His own desires had very little to do with what came from himself because what he put out (at least in part) had already been out. His way to make it new was to make it again, and making it again was enough for him, and certainly, personally speaking, almost him."[13] Before being a theoretical decision or a literary or artistic stance—taking position against the idea of an author—Prince's attitude is a mental predisposition, a personal inclination. "I was not working against authorship," Prince explains. "I was just dealing with a sort of personal crisis… It is hard to feel like yourself anyway. This has to do with the time in which I grew up. It has to do with my own experience. What I did was in a way biographical. It was not so much about the death of the author it was more about establishing a new life for the author."[14] Prince's work manifests authority, or at least its signs do (the signature). But the author himself is missing. The author is no longer the "I" or "He" of the modern novel, but an "Almost Him" or an "Almost Her"[15]—a spy in someone else's body, as Burroughs would say; a case where no one knows who is spying on whom anymore, the spectator or the writer, the observer or the observed. Prince's father might have taught him long ago "that the position of the observer itself affects the behavior of electrons or the fundamental particles that are being observed."[16] But that memory itself is subject to caution.

(Translation from the French: Anthony Allen)

1) David Robbins, *The Camera Believes Everything* (Stuttgart, 1988), p. 36.
2) Richard Prince, *Good Life* (East Hampton, NY: Glenn Horowitz Bookseller, 2003).
3) Richard Prince, *Untitled Artist's Book* (New York: Barbara Gladstone Gallery, 1988), p. 22.
4) Richard Prince, *American English* (Cologne: Verlag der Buchhandlung Walther Koenig / London: Sadie Coles HQ, 2003).
5) "In the Picture," Interview with Jeffrey Rian, in Rosetta Brooks, Jeff Rian, Luc Sante (eds.), *Richard Prince* (London: Phaidon, 2003), p. 20.
6) See also Brian Wallis, "Mindless Pleasure: Richard Prince's Fictions", *Parkett* 6, 1985, p. 61.
7) Richard Prince, "The Ways of the World," unpublished manuscript, 1981, reproduced in *Man* (Zürich: JRP Ringier, 2004), p. 75.
8) Richard Prince, "Bringing It All Back Home," in *American English* (Cologne: Verlag der Buchhandlung Walther Koenig / London: Sadie Coles HQ, 2003), p. 6, first published in *Art in America* 76 (September 1988).
9) Interview with David Robbins, op. cit. (note 1), p. 46. Regarding the posters, see also Richard Prince, "Anyone Who Is Anyone," *Parkett* 6, 1985, p. 67ff.
10) Richard Prince, *Adult Comedy Action Drama* (Zurich/New York: Scalo, 1995), pp. 224–5.
11) Interview with Jeff Rian, op. cit. (note 5), p. 16.
12) "Extra-ordinary," in Richard Prince, *Spiritual America* (Valencia: IVAM / New York: Aperture Books, 1989), pp. 9–11.
13) *Why I Go To The Movies Alone;* "The Velvet Wall," p. 63; "The Counterfeit Memory," p. 57. This passage is also repeated word for word in Richard Prince, *Pamphlet* (Villeurbanne: Le Nouveau Musée, 1983), p. 24.
14) "But how real is my art, that is the question: Richard Prince interviewed by Noemi Smolik," in *Richard Prince: Photographs, 1977–1993* (Hannover: Kestner-Gesellschaft, 1994), p. 28.
15) *Why I Go To The Movies Alone* (New York: Barbara Gladstone Gallery, 1995), p. 63.
16) "Extra-ordinary," op. cit. (note 12), p. 11.

Der Leser Richard Prince

VINCENT PÉCOIL

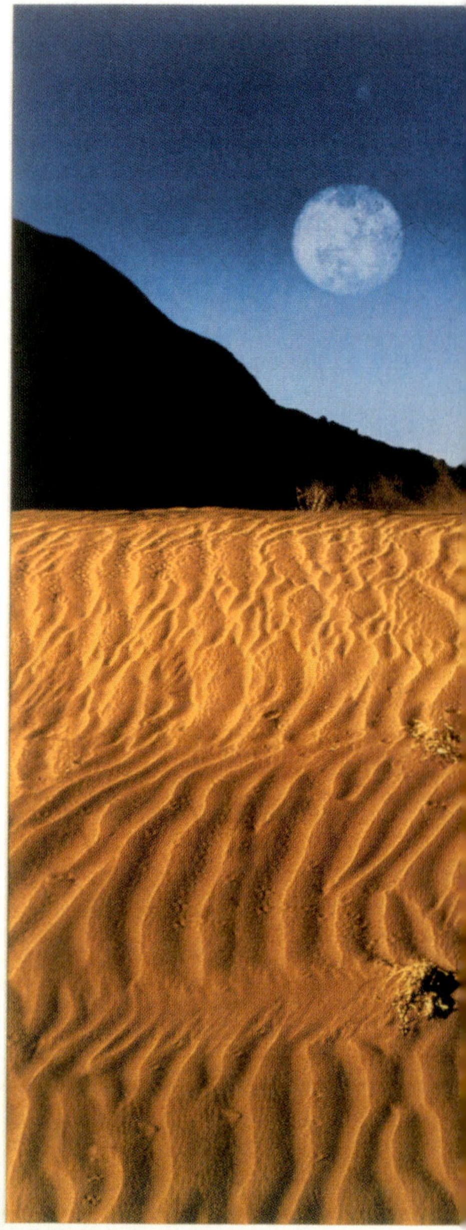

Die Bücher und Kataloge von Richard Prince sind randvoll mit Photographien von Bücherstapeln oder Regalen voller Romane, Biographien und Kataloge. Die Stapel sind sorgfältig und mit Bedacht arrangiert, so wie früher seine zu *Gangs* gruppierten Photos. Indem er in seinen Büchern sein eigenes Inneres oder Interieur zu erkennen gibt – im häuslichen, aber auch im psychologischen Sinn, man denke nur an den Titel seines Buches *Inside World* (Innenwelt) – und öffentlich macht, tut er etwas Ähnliches wie jene «Persönlichkeiten», die ihre Häuser den Kameras von Journalisten zugänglich machen, etwa in der Sendung auf MTV, wo Musiker und Musikerinnen eine Führung durch ihr Heim veranstalten, von der Garage über die Küche bis zum Wohn- und Schlafzimmer, wobei die Führung immer in ihrem geheimen, ganz privaten Lieblingszimmer endet. Bei Prince wäre dieses Zimmer mit Sicherheit die Bibliothek, noch vor dem Atelier – umso mehr, als Prince einmal, um jede Verwechslung auszuschliessen, während eines Interviews erklärt hat, dass sein Kunst-Vorratslager aus Zeitschriften bestehe.[1] Das neuste seiner Bücher zeigt Bilder des «Guten Lebens», wie es in gewissen Innendekorationsbänden propagiert wird. Die Bilder der im Band *Good Life*[2] reproduzierten Bücher zeigen das *Easy Living* oder die moderne

VINCENT PÉCOIL ist Kunstkritiker und Kurator und lebt in Dijon.

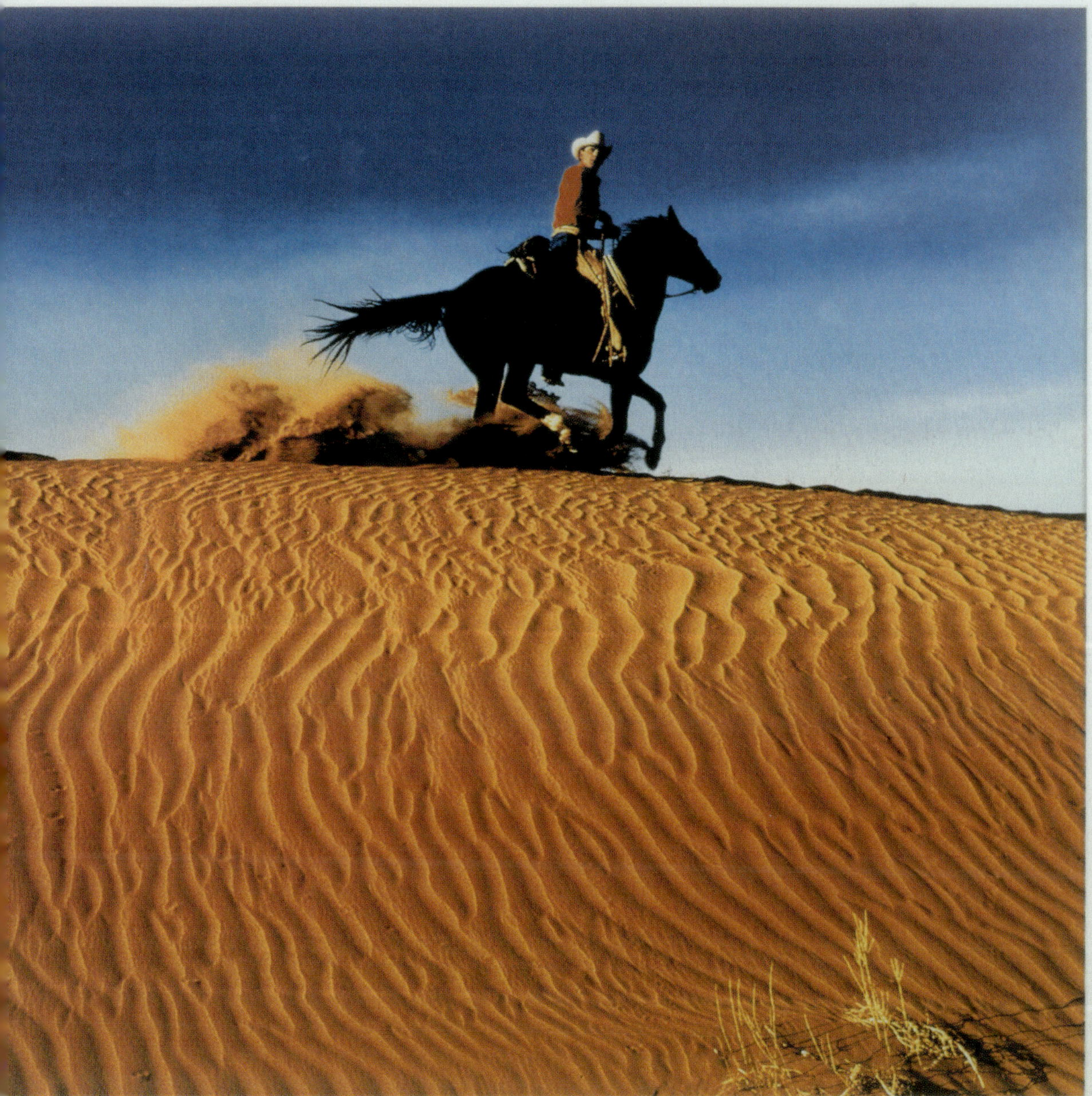

RICHARD PRINCE, UNTITLED (COWBOY), 1997, Ektacolor print, 49 3/4 x 76"; framed 61 1/8 x 88 1/8" / 126,4 x 193 cm; gerahmt 155,3 x 223,8 cm.

Lebensart, *Living the Modern Way* (zwei Titelbeispiele solcher Publikationen). Im Allgemeinen sind diese Innendekorationsbücher reine Fiktion. Es sind Bilder einer Innenarchitektur, über die kein Mensch wirklich verfügt. Jedenfalls kaum jemand, den man persönlich kennt. Die in den Büchern von Prince vorgestellte Bibliothek ist quasi ein dritter Ort, der beinah so real ist wie sein erster und zweiter Ort.

In einem Buch aus dem Jahr 1988 zählt Prince in der Beschreibung seiner Installation in Los Angeles seine ersten Neuerwerbungen nach dem Umzug auf: «Bücher für das Haus; zuerst gekauft: ...» Dann folgt eine ganze Seite mit bibliographischen Angaben, darunter auch: Don DeLillo, Harry Crews, ein Buch mit Schönheitstipps, ein anderes über den Auschwitz-Prozess, ein Buch mit einer Widmung von Buckminster Fuller, eine Elvis-Biographie, Pornobücher, Walter Tevis, Bruce Nauman ...[3] Auch in den übrigen Katalogen von Prince sind ausführlich alle möglichen Bücher aufgelistet: Witzsammlungen; Photobände (Helmut Newton, Larry Clark ...); Sciencefiction (*Planet der Affen, Fahrenheit 451,* aber auch Titel von Philip K. Dick oder J. G. Ballard, die beide besonders breiten Raum einnehmen); Thomas Pynchon, Gore Vidal; alte Krimis oder Kioskromane der 50er und 60er Jahre, bei denen anzunehmen ist, dass die Illustration auf dem Umschlag den Ausschlag zum Kauf gegeben hat. Ferner *Blasted Allegories,* eine Sammlung von Künstlerschriften, die mit abphotographierten Bildern aus seiner Serie *Cowboy* illustriert ist; eine fast vollständige Sammlung der verschiedenen Ausgaben von Nabokovs *Lolita*; und auch einige Klassiker der amerikanischen Gegenkultur: Schriftsteller der Beatgeneration und einige Schriften von Prince selbst, etwa im erst jüngst publizierten Katalog *Man.*

Es gibt einen Artikel von Prince, der sich mit dieser zwanghaften Manie befasst. Es handelt sich um «Bringing it All Back Home», erstmals veröffentlicht im September 1988 in *Art in America* und später erneut abgedruckt in *American English*[4]; Richard Prince geht darin detailliert auf seine Bibliophilie ein. Der Artikel in *Art in America* war erstmals mit einer Teilansicht seiner Bibliothek illustriert – etwas, was er in der Folge in verschiedenen Publikationen wieder aufnehmen sollte. Die Sammlung und das Sammeln ist ein in sich geschlossenes inhaltliches Element der Kunst von Richard Prince: «Das Sammeln ist mehr und mehr zum Bestandteil des Werks geworden», meint er selbst.[5] Das trifft ganz offensichtlich für seine letzten Arbeiten der Serie *8x10* und ihnen verwandte Arbeiten zu, die geradezu auf besessene Sammler zugeschnitten sind, und zwar nicht nur auf Kunstsammler, sondern auch auf Leute, die sich für Autographen, Photographien, Bücher und Abzeichen interessieren. Tatsächlich werden viele von Prince' Publikationen selbst auch als Sammelobjekte wahrgenommen, sobald sie erschienen sind. Die erste Broschüre, die er herausgab, erschien in einer Auflage von drei Exemplaren mit drei verschiedenen Titeln *(Menthol Pictures, Menthol Wars, War Pictures)*, obwohl der Inhalt jedes Mal derselbe war. Dieses Vorgehen erinnert an Schallplatten oder Zeitschriften, die in verschiedenen Versionen erscheinen, jedes Mal mit einer anderen Plattenhülle oder einem anderen Umschlag. Auch von *4x4*, einem Photoband aus dem Jahr 1997, gibt es zwei Versionen: eine amerikanische Ausgabe und eine japanische (wobei natürlich die aus Japan importierte Version wie bei den Platten die begehrteste ist). *American English* thematisiert diesen doppelten Ursprung jedes Originals, indem es jeweils die amerikanische und die britische Ausgabe diverser Bücher einander gegenüberstellt. Im Übrigen sind auch seine eigenen Bücher gewöhnlich limitierte Auflagen, die von einer signierten Edition begleitet werden.

Prince hat auch einige Texte, Fragmente oder Erzählungen geschrieben. Die Geschichten von Prince, etwa *Why I Go to the Movies Alone,* sind frei von komplizierten Verwicklungen und präsentieren sich als Abfolge von Erlebnisberichten verschiedener anonymer Personen (in denen jedoch oft Prince zu erkennen ist). Die Erzählung dieser Erlebnisse ist stark vereinfachend und reduziert sich meist auf ein Bild.[6] Fast jede Beschreibung ist die einer visuellen Wahrnehmung oder der Gefühle, welche diese beim Protagonisten auslöst. Tatsächlich beschränkt sich die Handlung auf das Sehen (von Filmen, Fernsehen oder Menschen), manchmal kommt noch das Hören (von Platten, Gesprächen) hinzu. Wie wenn «der Lauf der Welt als Text gesetzt wäre, als hätte jemand ihn auf einem Redaktionscomputer entworfen und dann das Ganze auf einem Bildschirm sichtbar gemacht,

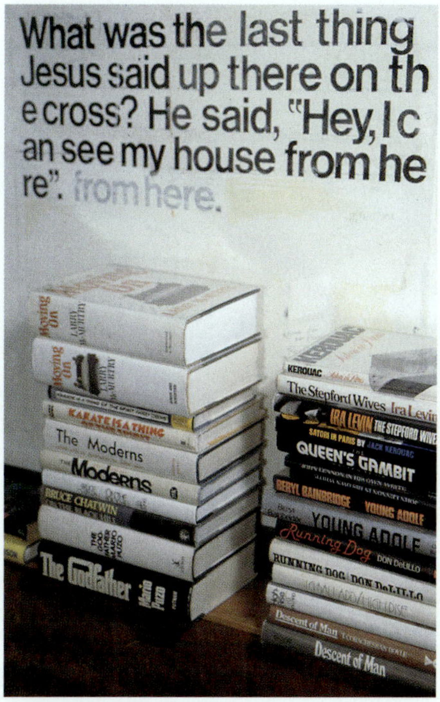

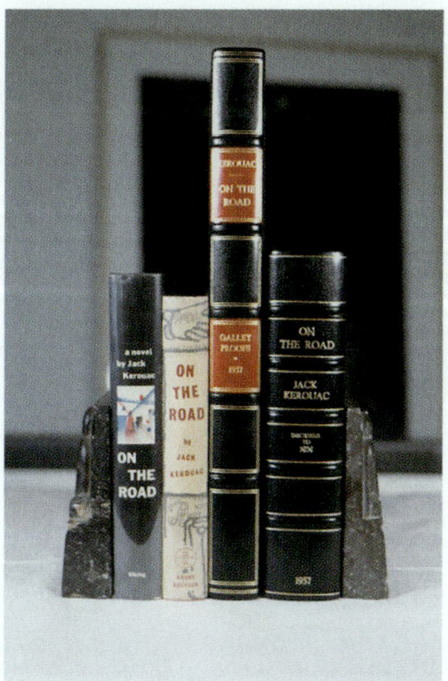

RICHARD PRINCE, Ektacolor photographs of the artist's library / Photos der Bibliothek des Künstlers.

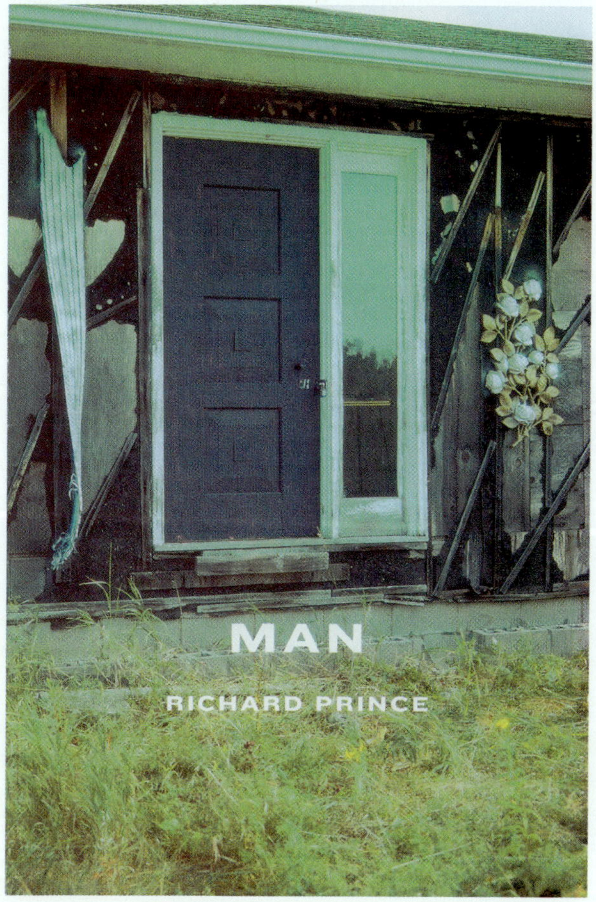

RICHARD PRINCE, MAN, 2004, cover page of the artist's book published on the occasion of the exhibition at Galerie Eva Presenhuber, Zürich / Cover des zur Zürcher Ausstellung im Sommer 2004 erschienenen Künstlerbuches.

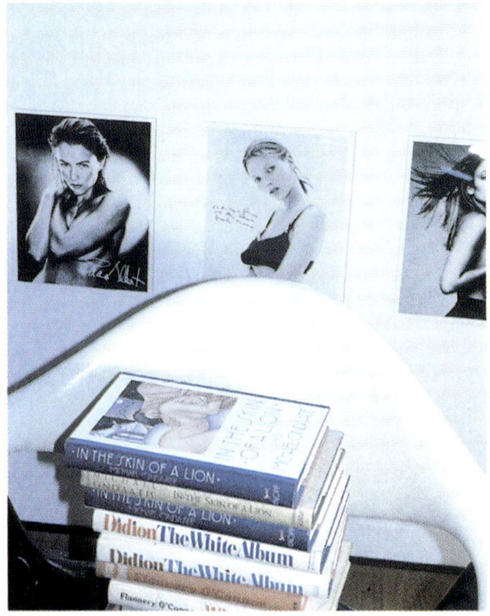

RICHARD PRINCE, Ektacolor photograph of the artist's library / in der Bibliothek des Künstlers.

um zu sehen, ob alles passt...»[7] Ein Leben auf dem Bildschirm: Einer der Photobände des Künstlers, *Adult Comedy Action Drama,* hat seinen Titel der in Videoclubs gebräuchlichen Klassifikation entlehnt: Kategorien, die im Buch von Prince alle Dimensionen der Existenz und alle Ereignisse des täglichen Lebens erfassen.

«Sie (die Bücher und Videokassetten) verändern mich. (...) Ich habe das Leben dieser Dinge gern um mich. Wenn ich allein bin, mag ich es, diese Leben zur Verfügung zu haben, in die ich schlüpfen und die ich jederzeit wieder aufgeben kann.»[8] Wie autobiographisch ein Bericht auch sein mag, das wahre «Thema» seiner Bücher ist nicht die Person (das «Ich» oder allenfalls auch ein «Er»), sondern immer das Bild, das diese Person durchdringt, die Biographien, in die sie vorübergehend schlüpft. Mit anderen Worten, der Prozess, in dem sich die Fiktion realisiert, verkörpert sich selbst und wird Wirklichkeit. Es ist derselbe Projektionsmechanismus, der dem Wunsch des Pubertierenden zugrunde liegt, sich mit Plakaten berühmter Stars zu umgeben: «Ich war schon immer der Ansicht, dass die Wahl einer bestimmten Persönlichkeit an sich schon eine Form von Ausdruck ist. Es genügte bereits. Alle meine Freunde taten das. Wir tapezierten unsere Schlafzimmerwände mit ihnen. Ich habe einfach nie damit aufgehört.»[9] Prince hat immer wieder auf die grosse Faszination hingewiesen, welche Abbildungen von Künstlern wie Pollock oder Kline in seiner Jugend auf ihn ausgeübt haben; sie waren noch wichtiger als die Werke selbst. Ihre Abbilder werden auf dieselbe Ebene gestellt wie jene von Rockstars oder anderen Berühmtheiten. Dass in *Adult Comedy Action Drama* das Photo von Pollock auf dem Cover der *Evergreen Review* neben einer Ausgabe von *Marvel* erscheint, deren Titelbild Captain America ziert (mit dem Hinweis: «Unser Mann des Jahres» – jedem sein eigener Held), ist ein humorvoller Hinweis auf diese Äquivalenz.[10] Im Zusammenhang mit dem Photo von Kline in seinem Atelier hat Prince kürzlich gegenüber Jeff Rian auch über das Bedürfnis, selbst mit im Bild zu sein, gesprochen, das er seinerzeit verspürt hatte. «Ich glaube, man lebt im Bild. Man ist lebendiger im Bild als ausserhalb des Bildes. Zumindest lebt man im Bild weiter, nachdem man ausserhalb gestorben ist (...). Ist das, was wir in Bildern sind, beinah Realität? Vielleicht ist es zum Realsten überhaupt geworden.»[11]

Prince hat den Begriff *social science fiction* zur Charakterisierung seiner Kunst verwendet, eine andere Bezeichnung für eine Kunst, welche die Auswirkungen der Medien untersucht: «Eine Anwendung physischer Tatsachen der Umwelt auf die Menschen.»[12] Eine Arbeit und eine Wissenschaft, die darum bemüht ist, «wie Fiktion zu klingen und auszusehen, jedoch vom Nicht-Fiktiven handelt», genau wie die Bilder und Berichte, die ihren Stoff ausmachen und von denen man sich fragen kann, ob sie «fast Realität» oder «fast Täuschung» sind. Diese Kunst oder *social science fiction* hat ein Ensemble bereits vorhandener Bilder zum Gegenstand – *already out,* wie Prince sagt –, aber auch Dinge, die bereits gesagt sind. Diese «schon veröffentlichte» Sprache bildet den Ausgangspunkt seiner schriftstellerischen Tätigkeit und definiert diese als ein Neu- oder Wiederschreiben von Bestehendem. Unter den Äusserungen, die den Stoff seiner Bücher ausmachen, wird man ebenso andere Bücher finden wie Einkaufslisten, Kleinanzeigen, Filmzusammenfassungen auf Videokassettenhüllen, oder auch allerlei Zeitschriften – *Muscle Cars, People, American Photographer, Harper's Bazaar, Playboy, Vanity Fair, Hustler, Popular Science, Sports Illustrated,* um nur einige zu nennen –, denen er die Witze, Titel oder Untertitel, Zusammenfassungen, Lead-Texte einzelner Artikel oder Bildlegenden entnimmt. Ein Titel aus seiner Sammlung könnte als Programm dienen: *Steal this Book* (Stiehl dieses Buch) von Abbie Hoffman, ein Überlebenshandbuch für Revolutionäre, eigentlich aber eine Anleitung wie man «gratis» zu Dingen kommt (beziehungsweise sie stiehlt). Manche Kataloge von Prince haben ihrerseits von anderen «gestohlene» Titel, etwa *Spiritual America.* Andere Bücher, wie *Inside World,* präsentieren sich als von Richard Prince «kompilierte» Bücher. Doch Prince wendet dieses Prinzip des Wiederaufgreifens in erster Linie auf sich selber an, indem er Passagen aus den in seinen verschiedenen Büchern, Interviews und Artikeln verstreuten, eigenen Schriften kaum verändert wieder aufnimmt. Zahlreiche Passagen von *Why I Go To The Movies Alone* waren schon früher unter verschiedenen Titeln publiziert worden und wurden es später erneut, einzeln oder im Rahmen anderer Artikel.

Eine dieser in Büchern und kurzen Texten unablässig wieder aufgenommenen Passagen beschreibt die Gedanken einer Person, die im Kino sitzt: «Seine eigenen Wünsche hatten nicht viel mit dem zu tun, was von ihm selbst kam, denn was immer er äusserte, war (zumindest teilweise) bereits geäussert worden. Sein Mittel, es neu erscheinen zu lassen, war, e s w i e d e r z u t u n ; es wieder zu tun, war ihm genug und war mit Sicherheit, persönlich betrachtet, f a s t er selbst.»[13] Lange bevor dieses Gefühl zur theoretischen Haltung oder zur literarischen und künstlerischen Richtung wird, die sich gegen die Idee des Autors wendet, ist es aus einer Laune des Denkens, einer persönlichen Neigung zu erklären. «Ich wandte mich nicht gegen die Urheberschaft als solche», erläutert Prince, «ich steckte gerade in einer Art persönlicher Krise. (...) Es ist sowieso schwierig, sich als man selbst zu fühlen. Das hat mit der Zeit zu tun, in der ich aufwuchs. Es hängt mit meinen eigenen Erfahrungen zusammen. Was ich tat, war in gewisser Weise biographisch. Es ging weniger um den Tod des Autors als darum, ein neues Leben für den Autor zu begründen.»[14] In der Arbeit von Richard Prince ist die Autorität immer präsent oder zumindest deren Zeichen (ihre Signatur), aber der Autor selbst ist abhanden gekommen. Der Autor ist nicht mehr das «Ich» oder «Er» des modernen Romans, sondern ein «Beinahe-Er» *(almost him)* oder eine «Beinahe-Sie» *(almost her).*[15] Ein Spion im Körper eines anderen, würde Burroughs sagen, wobei niemand mehr weiss, wer wen ausspioniert, weder vom Zuschauer noch vom Schriftsteller, noch vom Beobachter oder Beobachteten. Etwas, was ihm sein Vater schon früh beigebracht habe, sei, «dass die Position des Beobachters das Verhalten von Elektronen oder beobachteten Elementarteilchen beeinflusst».[16] Aber selbst diese Erinnerung ist mit Vorsicht zu geniessen.

(Übersetzung aus dem Französischen: Suzanne Schmidt)

1) David Robbins, *The Camera Believes Everything / Die Kamera glaubt alles,* dt./engl., Edition Schwarz, Stuttgart 1988, S. 36. Erstmals publiziert in *Aperture* 100, 1985.

2) Richard Prince, *Good Life,* Glenn Horowitz Bookseller, East Hampton, NY, 2003.

3) Richard Prince, *Untitled Artist's Book,* Barbara Gladstone Gallery, New York 1988.

4) Richard Prince, *American English,* Sadie Coles HQ, London / Verlag der Buchhandlung Walther König, Köln 2003.

5) Jeffrey Rian, «In the Picture», Interview mit Richard Prince, in: Rosetta Brooks, Jeff Rian, Luc Sante (Hrsg.), *Richard Prince,* Phaidon, London 2003, S. 6–25, hier: 20.

6) Vgl. dazu: Brian Wallis, «Freuden der Geistlosigkeit. Zu den Kurzgeschichten von Richard Prince», *Parkett* 6, 1985, S. 71.

7) Richard Prince, «The Ways of the World», unpubliziertes Manuskript, 1981, abgedruckt in: Richard Prince, *Man,* JRP Ringier, Zürich 2004, S. 75.

8) Richard Prince, «Bringing It All Back Home», in: *American English,* Verlag der Buchhandlung Walther Koenig, Köln / Sadie Coles HQ, London 2003, S. 6; zuerst erschienen in *Art in America* Nr. 76, September 1988.

9) Interview mit David Robbins, in: op. cit. (Anm. 1), S. 46. Was die Plakate angeht, vgl. auch: Richard Prince, «Jeder ist Einer», *Parkett* 6, 1985, S. 73–76.

10) Richard Prince, *Adult Comedy Action Drama,* Scalo Verlag, Zürich/New York 1995, S. 224–225.

11) Interview mit Jeff Rian, op. cit. (Anm. 5), S. 16 (hier aus dem Engl. übers.).

12) «Extra-ordinary», in: Richard Prince, *Spiritual America,* IVAM, Valencia / Aperture Books, New York 1989, S. 9–11.

13) *Why I Go To The Movies Alone;* «The Velvet Wall», S. 63; «The Counterfeit Memory», S. 57. Die Stelle ist auch wörtlich zitiert in: Richard Prince, *Pamphlet,* Le Nouveau Musée, Villeurbanne 1983, S. 24 (hier aus dem Engl. übersetzt).

14) «But how real is my art, that is the question: Richard Prince interviewed by Noemi Smolik», in: *Richard Prince: Photographs, 1977–1993,* Kestner-Gesellschaft, Hannover 1994, S. 28 (hier aus dem Engl. übersetzt).

15) Richard Prince, *Why I Go To The Movies Alone,* Barbara Gladstone Gallery, New York 1995, S. 63.

16) «Extra-ordinary», op. cit. (Anm. 12), S. 11 (hier aus dem Engl. übersetzt).

Edition for Parkett

RICHARD PRINCE
IT'S A FREE CONCERT FROM NOW ON, 2004

Ektacolor Print, paper size 30 x 40", image size 30 x 33 1/2".
Edition of 66 / XXVI, signed and numbered.

Farbphotographie, Blattformat: 76,2 x 101,6 cm; Bildformat: 76,2 x 85,1 cm.
Auflage: 66 / XXVI, signiert und nummeriert.

Woodstock 1969. I took this picture Friday evening around seven thirty. I had just turned nineteen. It was the only picture I took that weekend. I had gone to Woodstock with only one exposure in my camera. I thought I could buy film in the nearest town. Not knowing what I was getting into, I thought I could get out of it. You know, "come and go."
"Coming" was hard enough (it took six hours to travel the last twenty miles), and "leaving" was impossible. Anyway, realizing I was there to stay, I decided not to save my only exposure but rather get rid of it as fast as I could. So I just stood up, whirled around and (click) took it. – Richard Prince

Woodstock 1969. Ich knipste dieses Bild am Freitagabend, etwa um halb sieben. Ich war eben neunzehn geworden. Es ist das einzige Photo, das ich an diesem Wochenende gemacht habe. Ich war mit nur noch einer Aufnahme in der Kamera nach Woodstock gekommen. Ich dachte, ich könnte mir im nächsten Ort neuen Film kaufen. Da ich keine Ahnung hatte, worauf ich mich da einliess, meinte ich, ich könnte zwischendurch weggehen. «Kommen und gehen» eben.
Das «Kommen» war schon schwierig genug (für die letzten dreissig Kilometer brauchte man sechs Stunden), «gehen» war völlig unmöglich. Wie auch immer, als mir klar wurde, dass ich bleiben musste, beschloss ich, mein einziges Bild nicht aufzusparen, sondern es so schnell wie möglich zu verbraten. Also stand ich auf, drehte mich kurz um und (klick) drückte ab. - Richard Prince

(PHOTO: MANCIA / BODMER, FBM-STUDIO, ZÜRICH)

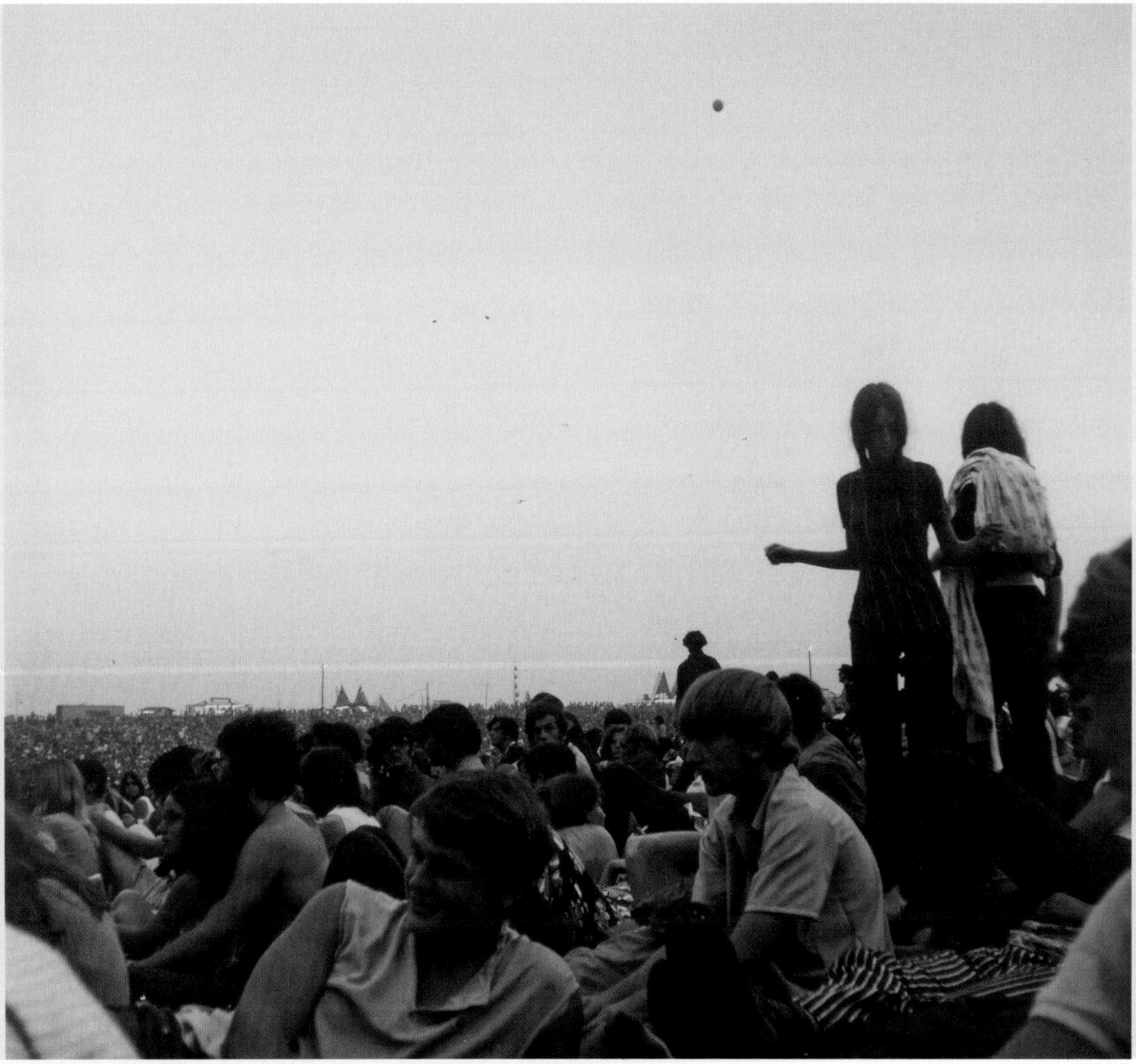

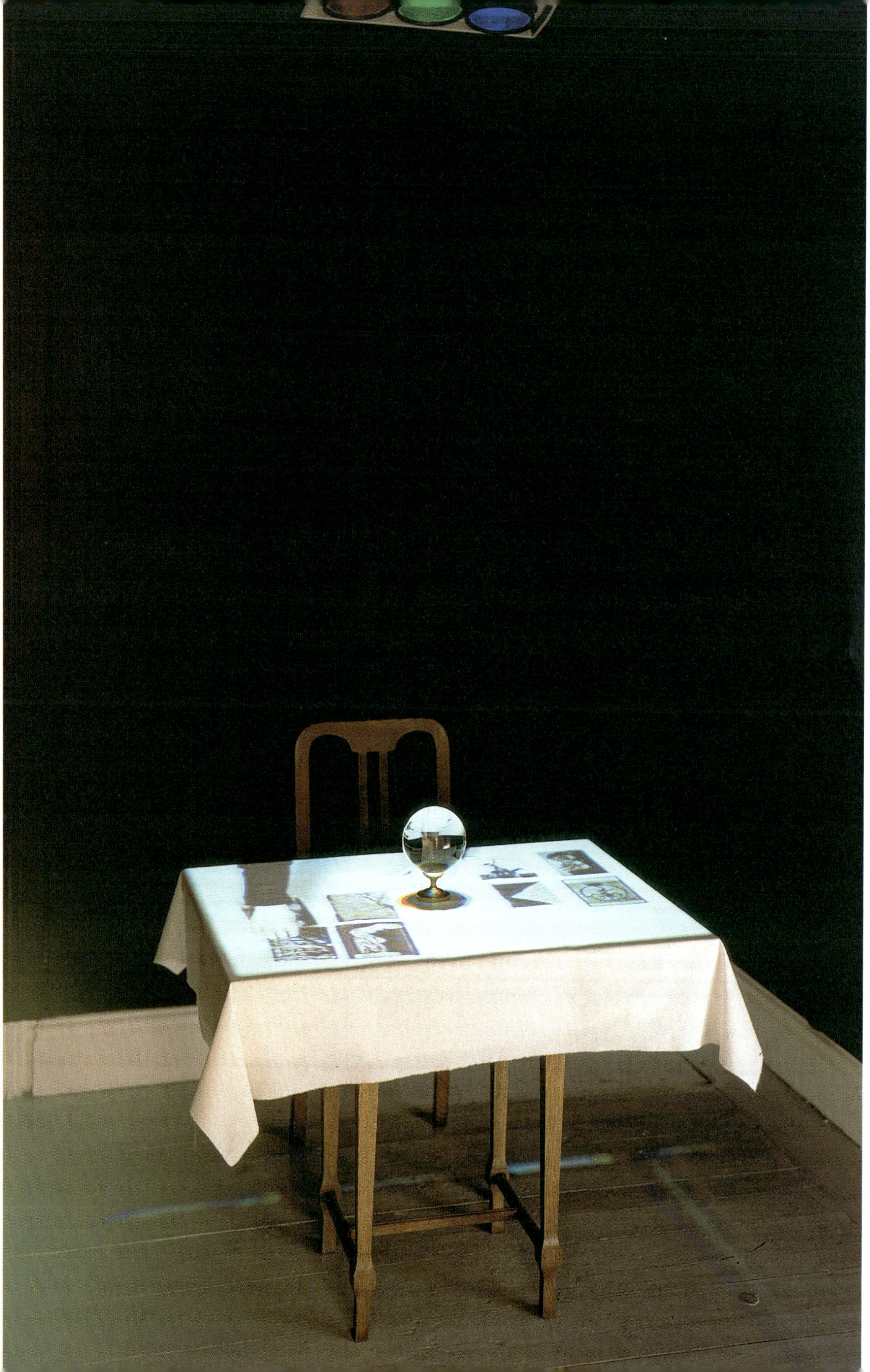

SILVIE DEFRAOUI, CARTOGRAPHIE DES CONTRÉES À VENIR, 1979, video installation / Videoinstallation.

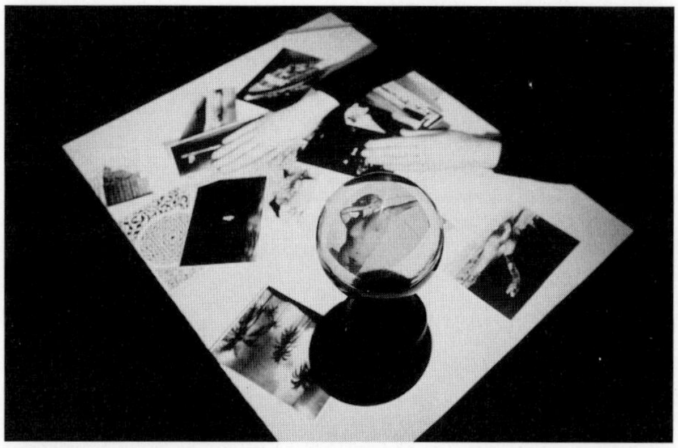

Im Inneren der Bilder erheben sich Wind und Feuer

DANIEL KURJAKOVIC

Ein abgedunkelter Raum, irgendwo ein erleuchteter Tisch. Hände, die körperlos aus dem Dunkel erscheinen, verteilen schwarzweisse und farbige Photographien, als wären es Tarotkarten: die Aufnahme einer über dem Sand aufspringenden Kobra; ein die Wasser durchpflügender Liniendampfer aus der Vogelperspektive; ein weisser Wolf; das Fragment einer Tempelanlage, deren Säulen von hartem Mittagslicht bestrahlt werden; eine aztekische Kultstätte... In der Mitte des Tisches liegt eine Kristallkugel. Als Prisma zerteilt sie das Licht (eines Dreilinsenprojektors) und wird so zur Chiffre für die Deutung von Wirklichkeit. Immer wieder verzerrt sie die Bildmotive und wölbt sie dem Betrachter entgegen. Für einen kurzen Moment stellt sich jeweils der Anschein von Lebendigkeit ein: Der Arm einer von Riefenstahl ins Bild gesetzten Athletin spannt sich! Die Schlange hebt ihren Körper vom Boden! Und Shiva tritt tanzend aus dem Feuerkreis! Bald liegen die Karten wieder ruhig und rätselhaft da, bereit gelesen zu werden oder gar die Zukunft aufscheinen zu lassen, die Zukunft unserer Gesellschaft sicherlich. Doch welche geisterhafte Präsenz legt hier die Karten aus? Und gilt es ernst? Oder ist alles nur Budenzauber?

Die Videoinstallation CARTOGRAPHIE DES CONTRÉES À VENIR (Vermessung der zu erwartenden Szenerien, 1979) ist die bekannteste frühe Arbeit von Silvie Defraoui. (Sie hat sie zusammen mit ihrem Partner Chérif Defraoui gemacht, mit dem sie von 1975 bis zu seinem Tod, 1994, alle Werke gemeinsam signierte.) CARTOGRAPHIE gehört – wie andere Arbeiten der Defraouis auch – zu einem generellen Projekt, das sich als Versuch lesen lässt, Welt zu «entbergen», das heisst unter dem visuellen Geröll der medialen Gesellschaft etwas sichtbar zu machen,

DANIEL KURJAKOVIC, Kunsthistoriker und Kurator, lehrt zurzeit an der Hochschule für Gestaltung und Kunst in Zürich.

was vielleicht den Lauf der Dinge erahnen liesse. Den Begriff Versuch kann man durchaus wörtlich nehmen, denn oft machen die Arbeiten allerlei Schwierigkeiten des Entbergens fühlbar. Vielleicht bleiben diese Schwierigkeiten aus dem klaren Bewusstsein darüber erhalten, dass auch immer etwas verborgen bleiben muss, wenn die Arbeit des Entbergens sinnfällig, wirksam und, vielleicht könnte man sagen, vertrauenswürdig sein soll. Wer weiss…

Trotz allem «Willen zur Wahrheit» glaubt Silvie Defraoui also nicht, man könne die Dinge ein für allemal entblössen, um zu einer verborgenen Logik derselben vorzudringen. Doch ebenso wenig scheint die Wirklichkeit für sie lediglich ein unentwirrbarer und zusammenhangsloser Knäuel von Phänomenen zu sein, der nicht von tiefer liegenden Strukturen und Mechanismen reguliert ist. Vielleicht werden deshalb in der Photoserie *Indices de variations* (Zeichen der Veränderung, 2002) erst auf den zweiten Blick jene merkwürdigen Falten sichtbar, welche die Landschafts- und Stadtansichten durchziehen: den Titicacasee, ein Haus in der Nähe von Delhi, die Gegend bei *Minas de plata* in Bolivien, Gerza in Ägypten oder die Terrassendächer von Kairo. Was zunächst lediglich wie postkartenartige Ansichten von diversen Reisen aussieht, verwandelt sich durch diese eindeutig nicht geologischen Verwerfungen in unsichere Zonen, affiziert von dem, was man einen «katastrophischen Effekt» nennen könnte. Defraoui: «Es geht darum, die Zeit anzuhalten, den Augenblick zu fixieren, in dem alles verschwinden wird, weil man sich einfach abwendet oder weil vielleicht die Welt einstürzt.»[1] Worum es bei den Landschaften von *Zeichen der Veränderung* sonst auch immer gehen mag, sicher stehen sie hier stellvertretend für eine «Ferne». Es sind Orte der Sehnsucht und zugleich der Bedrohung. Doch allzu viel Sentimentalität wird unterbunden. Denn die Ferne der Landschaften erweist sich als Illusion, wie sie aus gewissen Urformen des Theaters überliefert ist: Die Bilder sind «lediglich» Licht von bestimmten Diapositiven, das auf einige Falten in den unmittelbaren körperlichen Vorraum der Betrachter geworfen wurde, genauer: auf die Falten heller Stoffe, auf welche die Landschaften projiziert wurden – und eben nicht Fenster zur äusseren Welt. *Zeichen der Veränderung* zeigt modellhaft, mit anderen Worten, auf verletzliche und etwas machtlose Weise (aber was sonst vermag Kunst?), wie abhängig unser Verstehen von der Art und Weise ist, wie uns etwas näher oder ferner erscheint. Dies wiederum kann ein ziemlich erschreckendes, bitter ernstes Spiel werden, wenn man die eher vagen Begriffe Ferne und Nähe ersetzt durch Wortpaare wie: das Unwahrscheinliche und das Wahrscheinliche, das Unvernünftige und das Vernünftige, das Hirngespinst und der gesunde Menschenverstand.

Aber um Politik oder Moral geht es nicht auf offensichtliche Weise. Dafür ist die Arbeit von Silvie Defraoui erstens viel zu sehr mit magischen Spielen und verführerischem Bühnenzauber beschäftigt und zweitens von einem Zweifel geprägt, der sich an den sogenannten «Schwierigkeiten des Entbergens» entzündet. Weisen wir auf drei jüngere Videoarbeiten und eine grosse Serie von Photographien hin. (Seit Mitte der 70er Jahre hat Defraoui eine ganze Reihe von wichtigen Installationen mit Videos und Photographien geschaffen, was ihr, dies nur nebenbei, den etwas zweifelhaften Titel einer «Pionierin der Medienkunst» eingebracht hat.)

In BRUITS DE SURFACE (Oberflächengeräusche, 1995) sehen wir, eng kadriert, einen mit einem Wachstuch bedeckten Tisch, der mit Blumen und Früchten gemustert ist. Dämmriges Licht. Von oben stellt eine schwarz behandschuhte Hand leere Gläser auf den Tisch. Dann lässt sie Milch hineinfliessen – und während die Flüssigkeit hörbar zum Rand emporsteigt, werden langsam farbige, projizierte Bilder sichtbar, verzerrt durch die Wölbung des Glases: eine menschliche Figur im Gegenlicht, Schatten von herumtollenden Katzen, ein abendlicher Strand, an dem eine Figur entlanggeht, Fassaden von Häusern… Kaum haben sich die Bilder materialisiert, wischt die Hand die Gläser vom Tisch, in den Realraum hinein, wo sie laut und unsichtbar zerbersten. Das Tischtuch wird weggezogen, darunter erscheint das nächste. Der Zyklus beginnt erneut. Auch wenn die Bilder oft an ein privates Photographiealbum denken lassen, ist BRUITS DE SURFACE nichts für Voyeure, weil die fragmentierten, verzerrten Bilder von Orten, Personen, Pflanzen und Tieren namenlos bleiben. Umso eindrücklicher ist es aber, dass wir ins

Innere der Bilder vorzudringen scheinen, als wären wir Zeugen dafür, wie sie auf eine «wahre Empfindung» abgehört werden; diese ist jedoch ungefähr so real wie das undeutliche Echo einer unwiederbringlich verlorenen Tonquelle.

Wo Bilder zyklisch erscheinen und vergehen, ist die Vorstellung einer von Metamorphosen geprägten Kommunikation wirksam: Etwas wird bedeutsam erst im Übergang von einem Ort zum anderen, von einem Aggregatzustand zum anderen. In PLIS ET REPLIS (Falten und Gegenfalten, 2002) zum Beispiel fällt aus dem Off jeweils ein zerknittertes Stück Papier ins Bild, ein Paar Hände falten es auseinander und streichen es glatt, wobei allmählich Zeitungsbilder sichtbar werden: ein brennender Kahn, rauchende Industrieschlote, ein Karnevalszug, afrikanische Elefanten, die in unheimlicher und zugleich absurder Pose in einer Zirkusmanege sitzen. Nie zeigen die Bilder ein einzelnes Ding, immer sind es grössere Gruppen und Massen, als würde eine elementare Welt betont, die an den Rändern und Bruchlinien von Kultur, Technik, Geschichte und Natur lesbar wird. Kehrt Defraoui diesen Bereich deshalb heraus, weil erst darin Kräfte sichtbar werden, die mit der «Tiefenstruktur» der Gesellschaft zusammenhängen (wobei Tiefenstruktur nur der et-

SILVIE DEFRAOUI, BRUITS DE SURFACE, 1995, video installation / Videoinstallation.

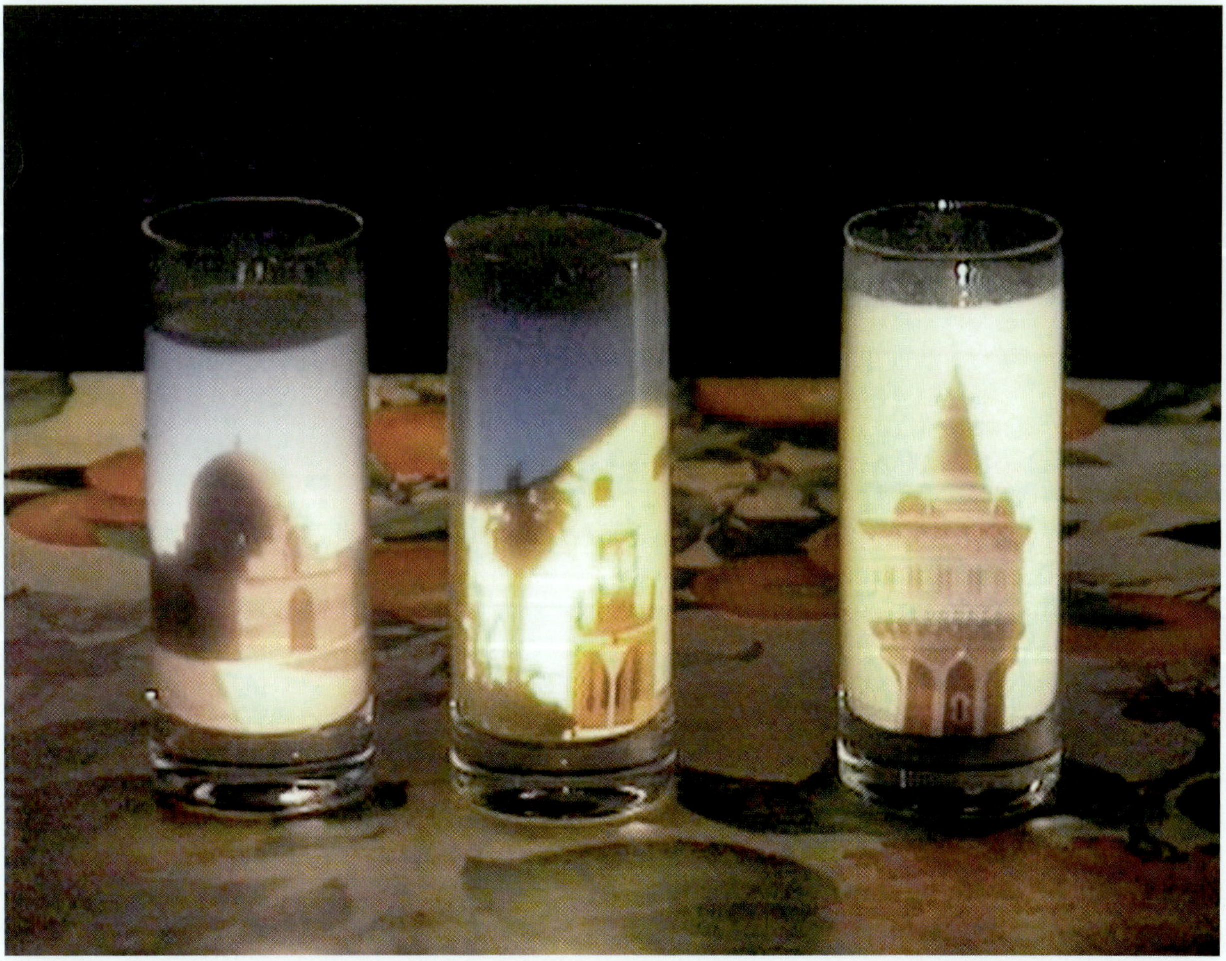

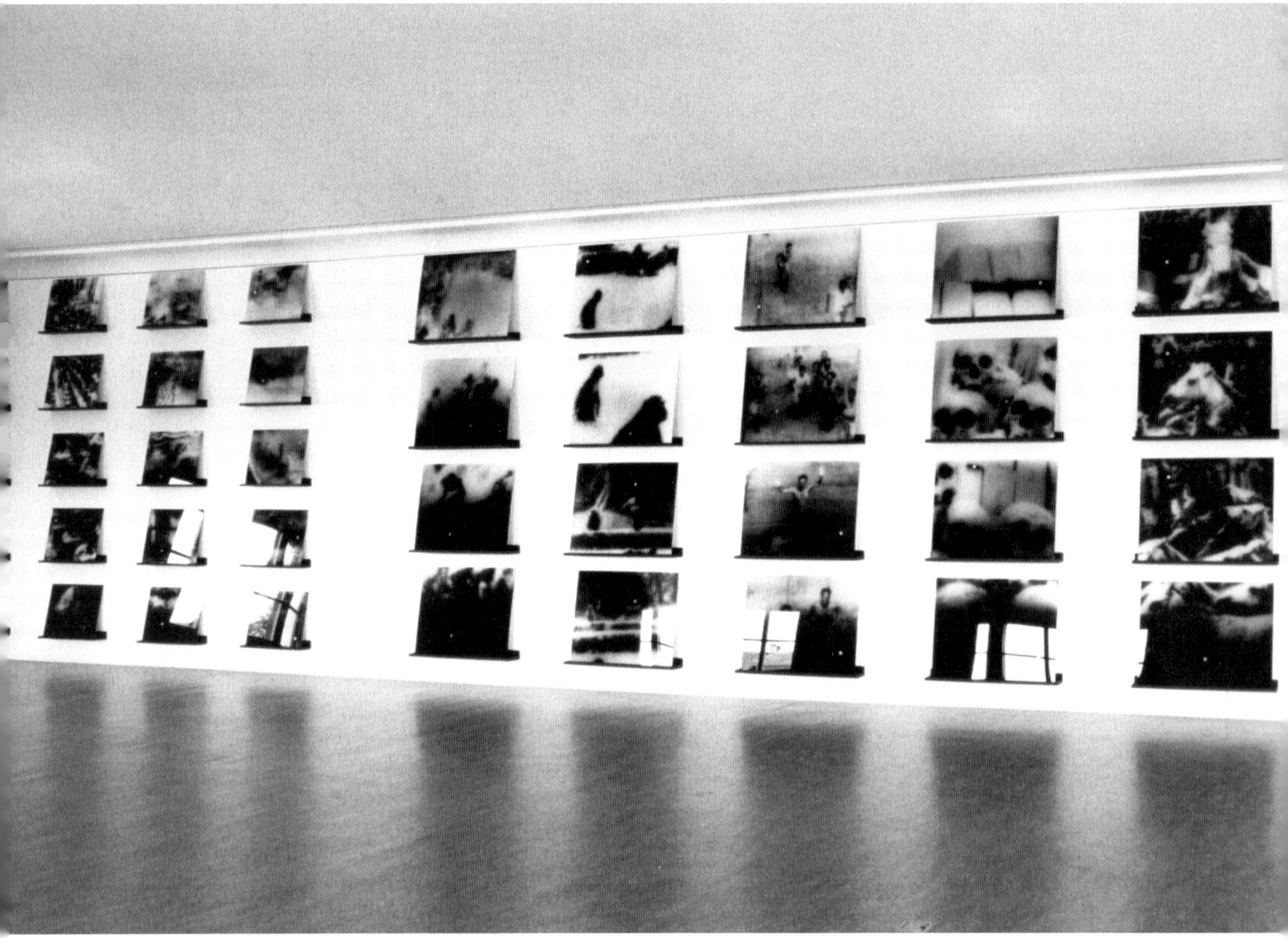

was gelehrte Name für die entgrenzten und deshalb für Katastrophen und mächtige Veränderungen anfälligen Bereiche der Gesellschaft ist)? Irgendwann erfasst ein Windstoss das Papier und das Bild erlischt. Manchmal fängt das Papier gar Feuer, so dass das Bild knisternd vergeht – aber schon fällt ein weiteres zerknülltes Papier ins Bildfeld...

Das Wesen der Umwälzung (der Revolution? der Katastrophe?) liegt eben nicht im Spektakel, sondern im entscheidenden kleinen Detail, was so ähnlich auch in den gross angelegten photographischen Serien *Passages* (Passagen, 1990 und 2000) verhandelt wird. Hier legt Defraoui eine Welt der Dinge offen, die sich unterhalb der historisch-politischen, aber noch oberhalb der mythisch-archetypischen Realitäten befindet. Ein dunkles visuelles Labyrinth wird in Form einer grossen vielteiligen Schautafel vor uns aufgebaut, die gezeichnet ist von etwas Diffusem und Formlosem. Diesem nähert sich das Auge und entdeckt Elementargewalten, von denen die Gesellschaft nicht unberührt und geschützt bleiben kann. Erstaunlicherweise entdeckt man als Betrachter diese Gewalten genau in jenen Bildern, die doch gegenüber dem «Drängen» anderer Zeiten und ent-

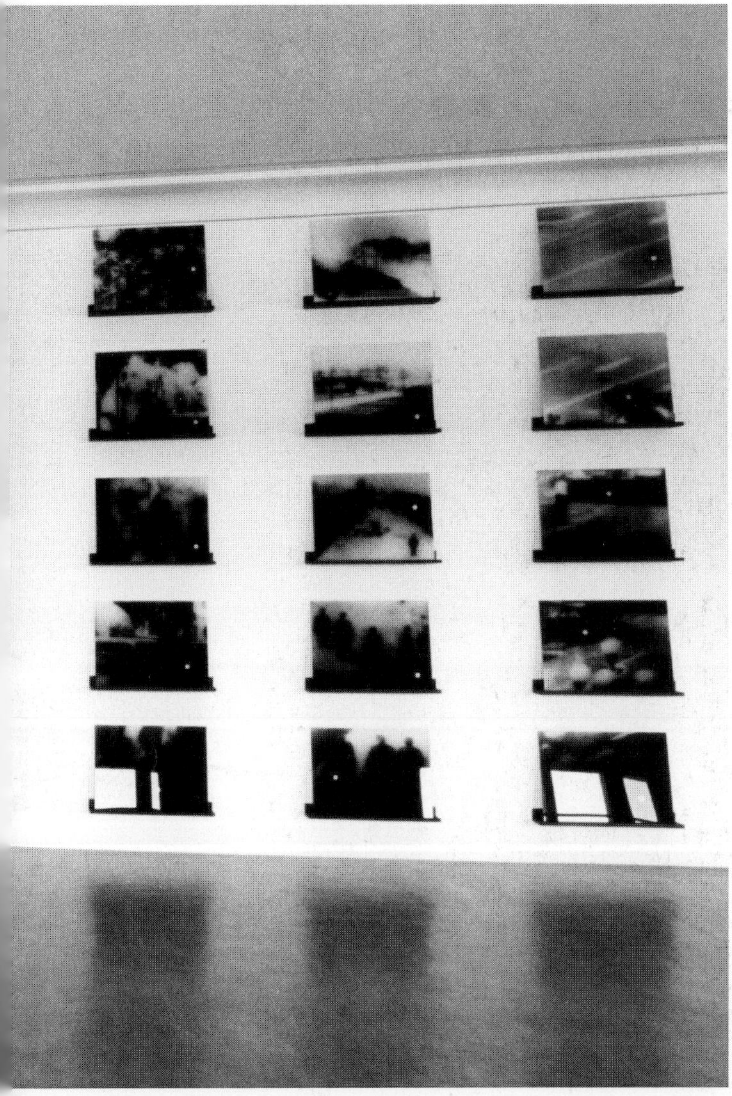

SILVIE DEFRAOUI, PASSAGES, 2000, exhibition view / Ausstellungsansicht, Helmhaus Zürich.

fernter Realitäten in Vergangenheit und Zukunft immun sein sollten – nämlich den Bildern des «aktuellen» Zeitgeschehens (erneut dienen ausgewählte Zeitungsbilder als konstruktive Basis).

Die Qualität von Silvie Defraouis Arbeit besteht darin, dass sie das Ferne und Verborgene in der nächsten Umgebung aufdeckt, auf verführerische Weise und manchmal so, dass das Ungenügen an der (westlichen?) Kultur virulent wird. In der jüngsten Videoinstallation EXORCISMUS (2004) gelingt ihr dies mit anarchischer Energie. Es herrscht ein kratzendes, trockenes Geräusch, das an- und abschwillt, als würde «trockene Haut gegen trockene Haut reiben» (Defraoui). An der Wand hängt ein kleiner Monitor: Der Blick dringt in ein Gewirr von Pflanzen vor. Die Kamera tastet sich voran und trifft dabei auf den Widerstand von starren, kaum zurückweichenden Palmblättern und einem harten kakteenartigen Gewächs. Erst nach und nach und nur selten gerät etwa in Form oranger oder blauvioletter Farbflecken inmitten des verschatteten Grüns eine Blüte oder eine Frucht, denen sich die Kamera umständlich nähern muss, in den Blick. Doch auch wenn die Kamera ihr «Ziel» erreicht, verflüchtigt sich das widersprüchliche Gefühl nicht: Auch die Frucht und die Blüte klingen, einmal berührt, nicht anders als das widrige Gewebe der hölzernen Blätter und Stängel. Sie wirken nur so lange nicht unnachgiebig und fremd, als die Distanz nicht aufgehoben wird und das Auge in Bewegung bleibt.

1) Kurzeintrag von Silvie Defraoui zu *Zeichen der Veränderung,* in: *Defraoui, Archives du futur, 1975–2004,* Ausstellungskatalog, Kunstmuseum St. Gallen / Musée d'art moderne et contemporain, Genf / Macedonian Museum of Contemporary Art, Thessaloniki, 2004, S. 216: *Il s'agit d'arrêter le temps, de fixer cet instant où tout va disparaître, simplement parce que l'on se détourne ou parce que le monde peut s'écrouler.* (Deutsche Übersetzung hier: *Parkett.*)

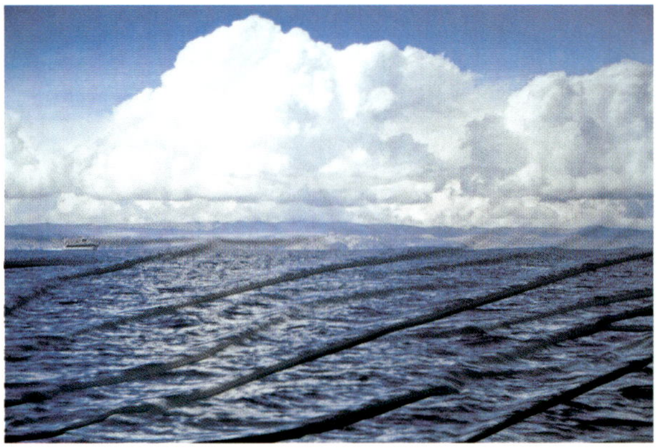

SILVIE DEFRAOUI,
INDICES DE VARIATIONS:
LAGO TITICACA, 2002.

Wind and Fire Rising Within

DANIEL KURJAKOVIC

A darkened room, somewhere an illuminated table. In the darkness, bodiless hands are seen laying out black-and-white and color photographs as if they were taro cards: a shot of a cobra leaping up out of the sand; a bird's eye view of a lake steamer plying the waters; a white wolf; a fragment of a temple, its columns bathed in the searing midday sun; an Aztec cult site... In the middle of the table, a crystal ball. As a prism, it breaks the light (a projector with three lenses) and thus becomes a cipher for the interpretation of reality. It keeps distorting the picture motifs and curves them towards the viewer. For a fleeting moment, an impression of live animation sets in. The arm of a woman athlete, (com)posed by Riefenstahl, begins stretching! The snake lifts its body off the ground! Shiva, dancing, steps out of the circle of fire! Soon the cards come to rest again, lying still and enigmatic, ready to be read or to predict the future, surely the future of our civilization. But which ghostly presence is laying out the cards? And is it serious? Or just street magic?

The video installation CARTOGRAPHIE DES CONTRÉES À VENIR (Surveying Anticipated Scenarios, 1979) is the earliest known work by Silvie Defraoui. (She created it with her partner Chérif Defraoui, with whom she signed all of her work from 1975 until his death in 1994.) Like other works by Defraoui, CARTOGRAPHIE is part of an overall project that can be interpreted as an attempt to uncover the world, to bring to light from under the visual screen of medial society something that might hint at the course of things. The term "attempt" may be taken literally because Defraoui's work often makes the difficulties of

DANIEL KURJAKOVIC, art historian and curator, is currently a lecturer at the University of Art and Design in Zürich.

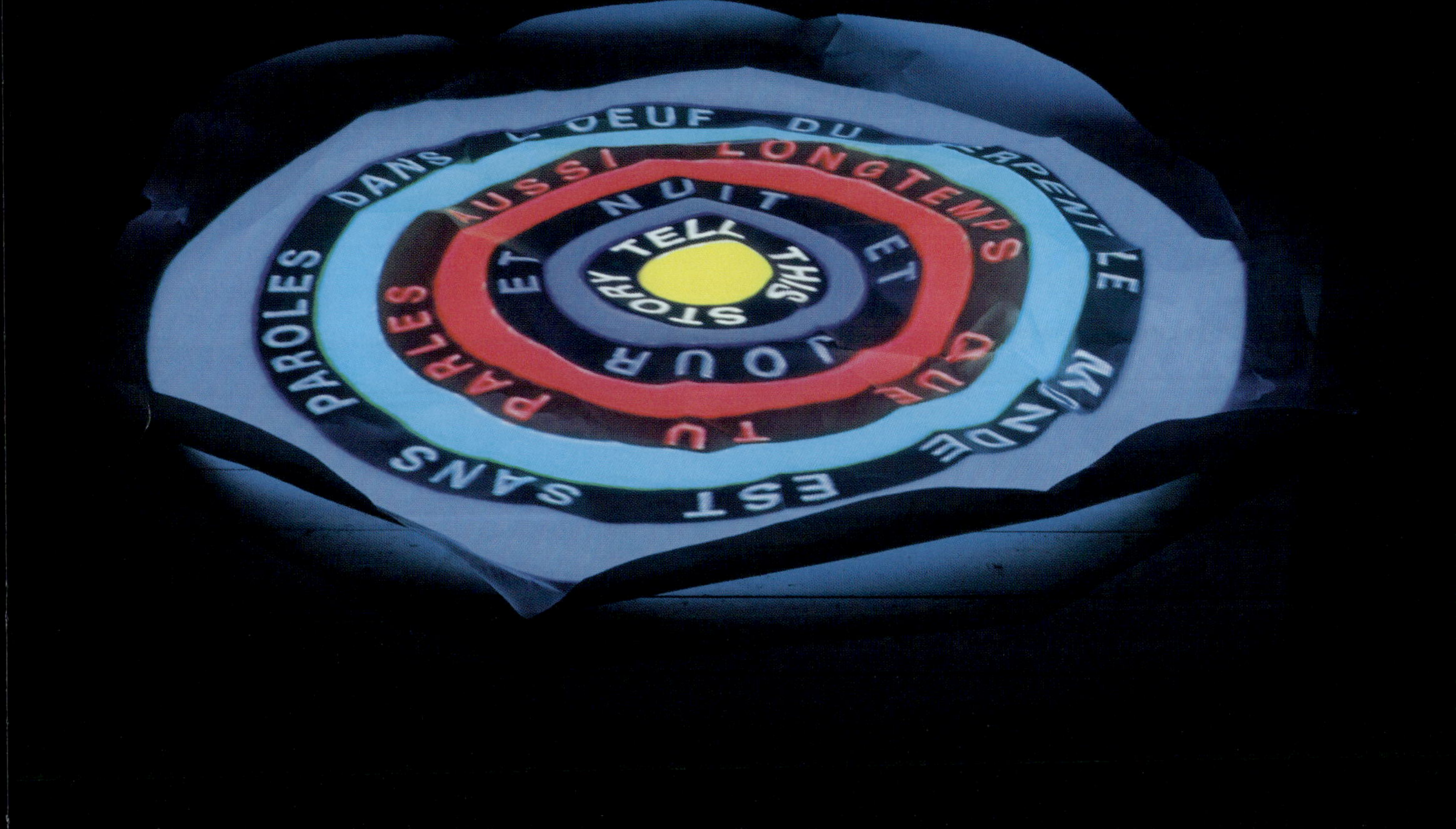

SILVIE DEFRAOUI, TELL THIS STORY, 2004, installation.

"uncovery" quite tangible. These difficulties possibly also prevail out of the certain realization that something must inevitably remain hidden for uncovery to be apparent, effective, and, we might even say, trustworthy. Who knows …

Despite her will to truth, Defraoui does not believe that things can be definitively uncovered in order to plumb their hidden logic. Nor does she treat reality as a hopelessly inexplicable tangle of phenomena unaffected by the regulatory influence of deeper structures and mechanisms. That may explain why, in the photo series *Indices de variations* (Signs of Change, 2002), it is only on second sight that we notice the strange faults that pass through the land- and cityscapes: Lake Titicaca, a house near Delhi, the *minas de plata* in Bolivia, Gerza in Egypt, or the terrace roofs of Cairo. Such images, perhaps initially perceived as postcard views from various trips, are transformed by these obviously nongeological faults into uncertain zones marked by what might be

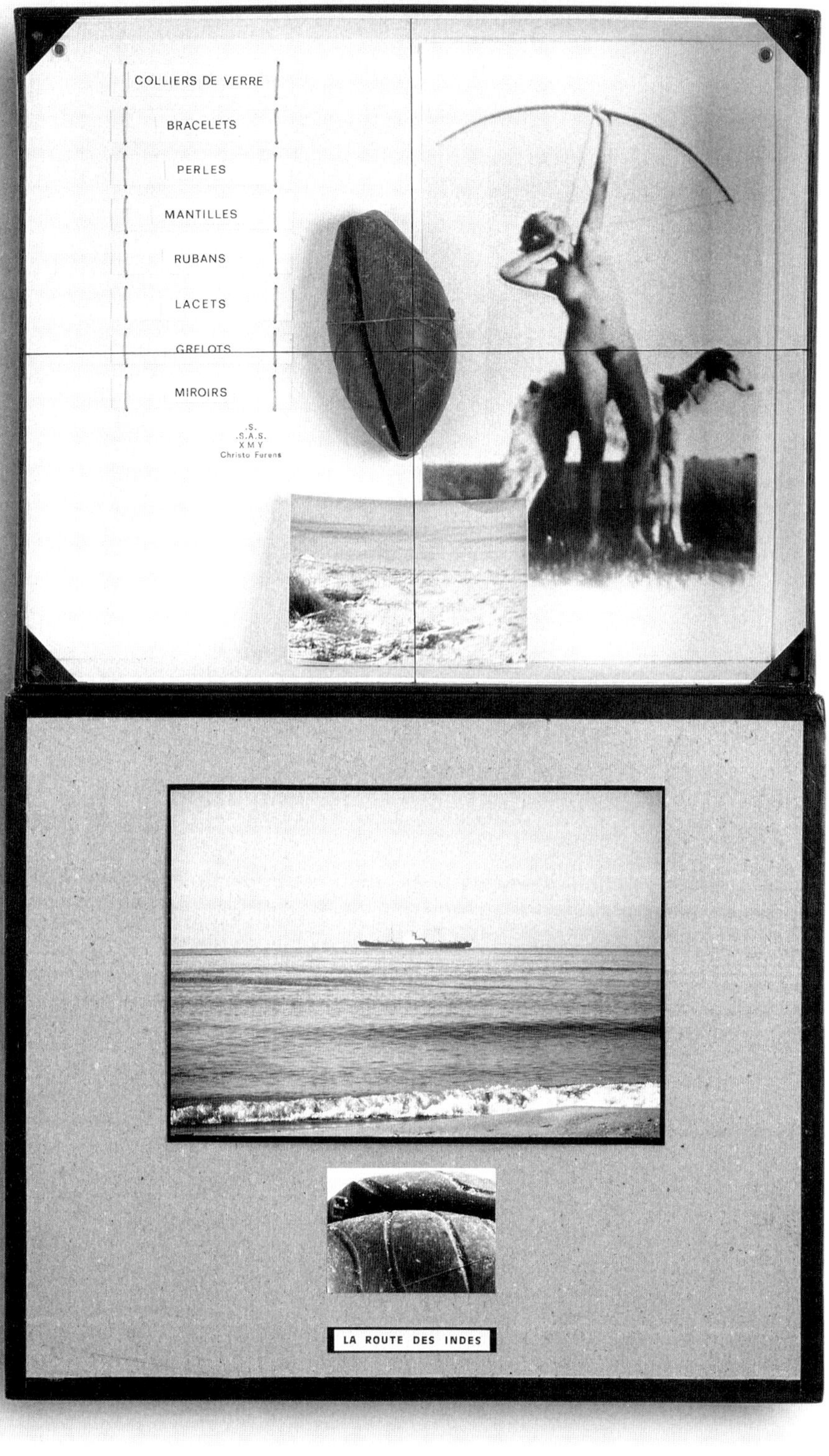

SILVIE DEFRAOUI, LA ROUTE DES INDES, 1978 , one of 14 cardboard boxes with hinged lids, objects, photographs, texts, 12 5/8 x 16 1/2 x 4 3/4" each, plus 6 boxes of 14 3/16 x 28 3/8 x 4 3/4" each / eine von 14 Kartonboxen mit aufklappbarem Deckel, Objekte, Photographien, Texte, je 32 x 42 x 12 cm, sowie 6 grösseren Boxen zu je 36 x 72 x 12 cm.

called a catastrophic effect. Defraoui: "It's like arresting time, capturing the instant when everything vanishes simply because we have turned our backs or because the world has collapsed." [1] But whatever else the landscapes in *Signs of Change* might be about, they undoubtedly function as an ersatz for remoteness. They are places that convey both longing and menace. Even so, sentimental excesses are avoided, for the remoteness of the landscapes proves to be illusion, as in certain early forms of theater. The pictures are not windows to the outside world; they are "only" light from specific slides that has been cast on a few folds in the viewer's immediate physical anteroom—more precisely, on the folds of light-colored fabrics on which landscapes have been projected. In other words, *Signs of Change* excellently demonstrates—albeit with a certain vulnerability and helplessness (what else can art do?)—how very much our understanding depends on the way in which something is made to appear closer or farther away.

SILVIE DEFRAOUI, DANS LE CADRE DES HISTOIRES... D'UNE ANNÉE EXCEPTIONNELLE, 1996, black-and-white photographs, Ilfochrome prints, 2 parts, 33 7/8 x 59" overall / Schwarzweiss-photographien, Ilfochromeabzüge, zweiteilig, insgesamt 86 x 150 cm.

That relationship can also become a disturbing and deadly serious game, for instance, when the somewhat vague terms, "remoteness" and "closeness," are replaced with such pairs as the improbable and the probable, the unreasonable and the reasonable, or figment and common sense.

However, politics or morals do not figure overtly in Silvie Defraoui's work. It is too concerned with playful enchantment and seductive theatricality while also marked by doubts ignited by the "difficulties of uncovery." Evidence is provided in three recent video works and a large series of photographs. (Since the mid-seventies Defraoui has produced a substantial number of important installations with videos and photographs, which have incidentally led critics to miscast her as a pioneer of media art.)

In BRUITS DE SURFACE (Surface Noises, 1995), we see, narrowly framed, a table under an oilcloth with a pattern of flowers and fruit on it. Poorly illuminated. A hand wearing a black glove places glasses on the table from above. Then it pours milk into them, and while the liquid audibly rises to the brim, projected images in color gradually become visible, distorted by the curvature of the glass: a backlit human figure,

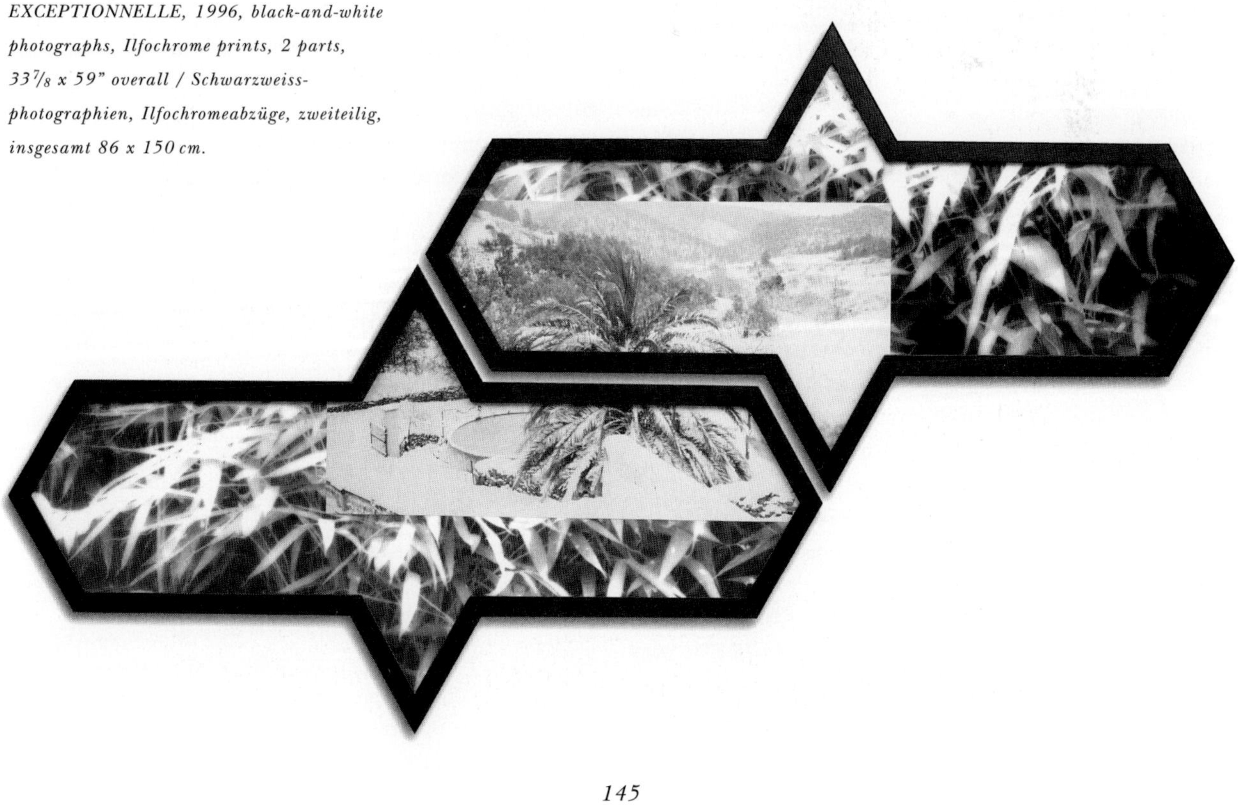

shadows of romping kittens, a figure walking along the beach in the evening, the façades of buildings... The pictures have barely materialized when the hand sweeps the glasses off the table into the room where they shatter loudly and invisibly. The tablecloth is pulled off and another appears underneath. The cycle begins all over again. Although the pictures often recall personal photograph albums, BRUITS DE SURFACE holds no frisson for the voyeur because the fragmented, distorted images of places, people, plants, and animals remain nameless—a namelessness that merely serves to enhance the impact of seeming to penetrate inside the pictures, of being witnesses to their eavesdropping on a "true" feeling that is about as real as the blurred echo of an irrevocably lost audio recording.

When pictures come and go in cycles, the idea of communication marked by metamorphosis comes into play: meaning is generated in the process of transition from one place to another, from one aggregate state to another. In PLIS ET REPLIS (Folds and Counterfolds, 2002), for example, a crumpled piece of paper falls into the picture from out of frame, a pair of hands opens it up and smoothes it out so that gradually newspaper pictures become visible: a burning barge, a smoking industrial chimney, a carnival parade, or African elephants sitting in uncanny and absurd positions in a circus ring. The pictures never show one thing in isolation but always larger groups and masses as if to emphasize an elementary world that surfaces on the margins and in the cracks of culture, technology, history, and nature. Does Defraoui unearth these areas because they reveal forces that are related to the deep structure of society (whereby deep structure is only the somewhat academic term for those unbounded areas of society that are susceptible to catastrophe and radical change)? At some point a gust of wind lifts the paper and the image evaporates. Sometimes the paper catches fire so that the picture crackles while fading—and immediately gives way to the next piece of crumpled paper dropping into the picture frame...

The essence of upheaval (revolution? catastrophe?) does not lie in the spectacle but rather in the small decisive detail, which is similarly addressed in the large-scale photographic series *Passages* (1990 and 2000). Here Defraoui exposes a universe of things situated beneath historical and political realities but still above mythical and archetypal realities. A dark visual labyrinth emerges before our eyes in the form of a large, multipartite wall chart covered with things diffuse and shapeless. We move closer and discover elementary forces from which society cannot escape. Astonishingly, the viewer discovers these forces in precisely those pictures that ought to be immune to the pressures of other ages and the distant realities of past and future—namely pictures of current events (once again, construction is based on selected newspaper images).

The quality of Silvie Defraoui's work lies in a seductive ability to comb her immediate surroundings for things remote and covert, such that the insufficiencies of (Western?) civilization become virulent. In her most recent video installation, EXORCISMUS (Exorcism, 2004), this agenda succeeds with anarchist energy. A scratching, dry noise dominates, swelling and receding as if "dry skin were rubbing against dry skin" (Defraoui). A small monitor is mounted on the wall revealing a tangle of plants. The camera gropes its way among them and meets with the resistance of stiff, unyielding palm leaves and hard cactus-like vegetation. Only rarely do blossoms or fruit come into view in the form of orange or bluish purple patches of color in the midst of the shady greenery; the camera approaches them slowly, laboriously, and with great circumspection. Even when the camera has finally reached its target, our contradictory feelings do not evaporate: fruit and blossoms, once they've been touched, sound no different from the stand-offish texture of the woody leaves and stems. Nonetheless, it is only as long as the distance is not negated and the eye remains in motion that they are protected from striking us as unyielding and alien.

(Translation: Catherine Schelbert)

1) Silvie Defraoui on *Signs of Change* in: *Defraoui, Archives du futur, 1975–2004,* exh. cat., Kunstmuseum St. Gallen / Musée d'art moderne et contemporain, Geneva / Macedonian Museum of Contemporary Art, Thessaloniki, 2004, p. 216. (*Il s'agit d'arrêter le temps, de fixer cet instant où tout va disparaître, simplement parce que l'on se détourne ou parce que le monde peut s'écrouler.*)

VARIATIONEN ÜBER EIN THEMA

DIE FILMISCHEN ETÜDEN VON CHRISTIAN JANKOWSKI

MARC GLÖDE

Betrachtet man die filmischen Arbeiten von Christian Jankowski, so kann man sich eines Schmunzelns in der Regel nicht erwehren. Seit seinen frühen Arbeiten durchzieht immer ein manchmal unterschwelliger, manchmal eher offensiver Humor die Werke des Künstlers. In seinem frühen Video DIE JAGD (1992) bewaffnet er sich beispielsweise mit Pfeil und Bogen, zieht in den Supermarkt und beginnt dort in «bester männlicher Tradition» Nahrung zu erlegen. Derselbe Humor kennzeichnet auch seine vielleicht bekannteste Arbeit, TELEMYSTIC (1999), für die Biennale in Venedig. Darin zeigt er Videoaufnahmen von seinen Anrufen in bekannten italienischen TV-Astrologieshows, in denen er die Astrologen unter anderem fragt, ob seine nächste Arbeit ein Erfolg werde und ob seine Idee die richtige sei. Jankowski spielt in diesen Arbeiten immer mit einem Humor, der sich aus der Verstrickung verschiedenster sozialer Umfelder wie Kunst, Familie und Beziehung ergibt, oder auch aus seiner eigenen Rolle innerhalb derselben als Künstler, Mann oder Freund.

MARC GLÖDE ist Filmwissenschaftler und seit 2002 als wissenschaftlicher Mitarbeiter am Sonderforschungsbereich «Kulturen des Performativen» der Freien Universität Berlin tätig. Er leitete diverse Filmfestivals zum Thema «Film und Architektur», u. a. in Berlin, Los Angeles und London.

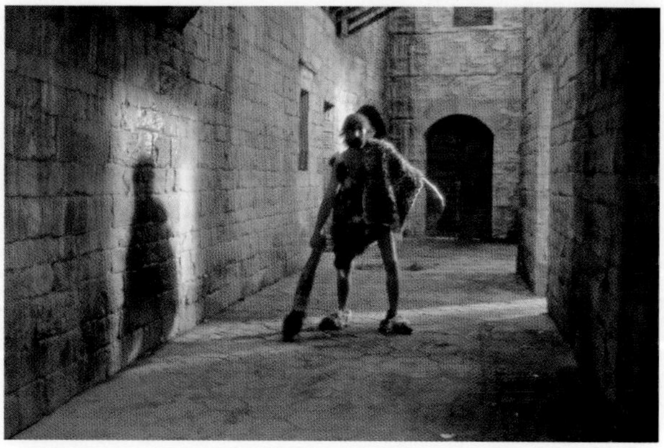

CHRISTIAN JANKOWSKI, THIS I PLAYED TOMORROW, 2003, film still / Szene aus dem Film.

Ungefähr seit TELEMYSTIC zeichnet sich in den Arbeiten von Jankowski aber eine Verschiebung ab, die aus filmwissenschaftlicher Perspektive besonders interessant ist. Hatte bis dahin vorwiegend seine eigene Person oder der Kunstkontext als Bezugsrahmen für seine Arbeiten gedient, begann Jankowski

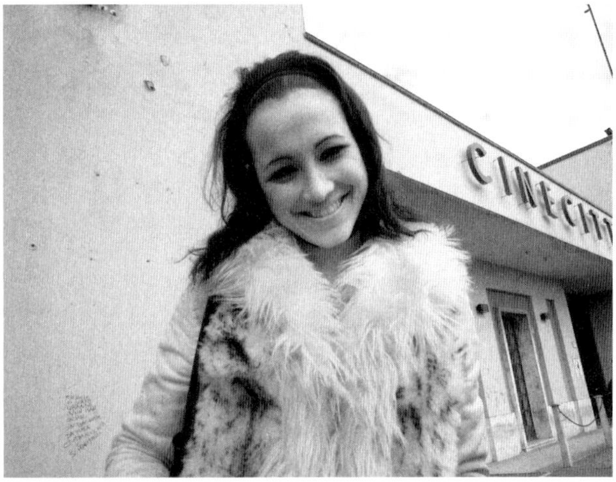

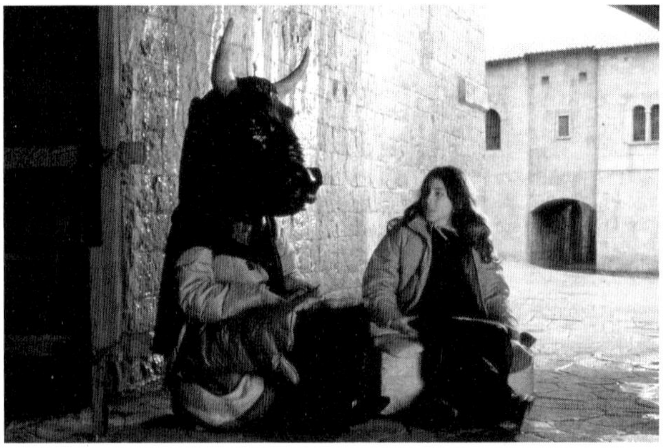

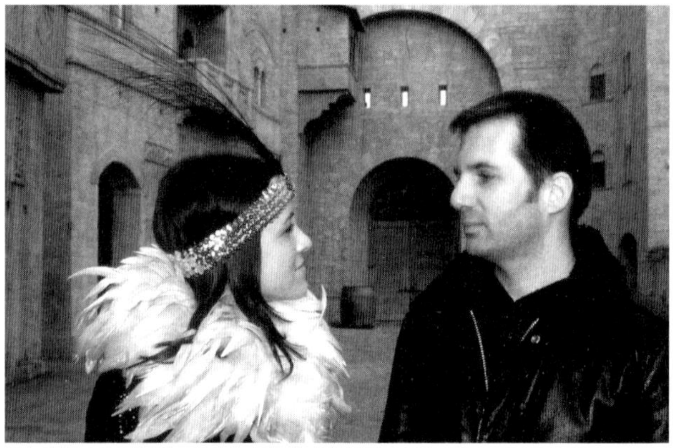

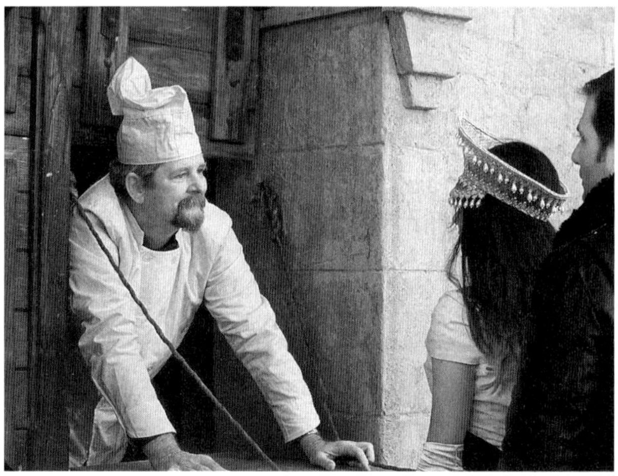

sich nun intensiver mit dem Medium Film und Video sowie dessen sozialen, aber auch formalen Bedingungen zu beschäftigen.

Bereits an der Arbeit CREATE PROBLEMS (Probleme schaffen, 1999) lässt sich das gut erkennen. Hierfür lud Jankowski zunächst fünf Paare in die Dolly-Buster-Studios in Dortmund ein und liess sie vor laufender Kamera die Anfänge von bereits existierenden Pornofilmen nachspielen. Noch bevor es zum Punkt der körperlichen «Action» kam, sollten die Paare jedoch abbrechen und mit einer Improvisation über ein eigenes Beziehungsproblem beginnen. Die so entstandenen Aufnahmen legte der Künstler einem Paar- und Familientherapeuten vor, der diese Szenen ebenfalls vor laufender Kamera kommentierte. Beide Aufnahmen, die der Paare und die des Therapeuten, führte Jankowski schliesslich in seiner Arbeit zusammen und stellte die beiden Seiten einander gegenüber. So werden dem Betrachter

CHRISTIAN JANKOWSKI, THIS I PLAYED TOMORROW, 2003, stills from the film shot in and around Cinecittà / Szenen aus dem in Cinecittà und dessen nächster Umgebung gedrehten Farbfilm.

von Jankowskis Film zunehmend mehr kleinbürgerliche Aspekte und vor allem eine damit verbundene Praxis der Zuweisung und Abgrenzung vor Augen geführt. Doch es ist weder das Reihenhausambiente der Pornosets, noch sind es die darin ausgetragenen Beziehungsprobleme der Protagonisten, die unangenehm berühren: Vor allen Dingen wirken die Kommentare und Haltungen des Psychologen in ihrer Kleinbürgerlichkeit entlarvend. Der Film wird hierbei für Jankowski explizit zu einem Mittel der Kritik. Wobei der nicht nur diesem Film von Jankowski innewohnende, kritische Gestus an ein Moment rührt, das fast so alt ist wie der Film selbst beziehungsweise wie das Erzählkino Hollywoods. Es ist ein Gestus, mit dem Kunst und Kino einander interessanterweise immer wieder gegenübertreten. So, als sei es das erste Mal, dass die Analyse des Kinos durch die Kunst und umgekehrt überhaupt geleistet würde. Gerade dies aber – Jankowskis jugendlich energische Geste des «Einer muss es schliesslich mal sagen...» – vermischt sich mit den verhandelten Inhalten und wird zu einem bestechenden Aspekt seiner Arbeit.

Das gilt auch für die neusten Filme des Künstlers, bei denen es sich um Reflexionen über den Film handelt. Es sind Annäherungen an den Kosmos des bewegten Bildes, dessen unterschiedliche Formen und Potenziale, und vor allem auch an sein Publikum. In WHAT REMAINS (Was bleibt, 2004) sehen wir beispielsweise eine Reihe von Porträtaufnahmen. Es sind Zuschauer, die gerade im Kino waren und uns kurz mitteilen, was der bleibende Eindruck ihres Kinoerlebnisses ist. Aus den erzählten Geschichten ergibt sich innerhalb kürzester Zeit ein Bild davon, was Film sein und wovon er handeln kann, und das umfasst die gesamte Bandbreite menschlicher Emotionen: Liebe, Hass, Langeweile, Angst, Freude... Sehr schnell beginnen sich aber in Jankowskis Arbeit diese äusserst unterschiedlichen Reaktionen und Beschreibungen mit den Personen und ihrer Selbstinszenierung kurzzuschliessen. Als Betrachter beginnt man sofort eigenartige Rückschlüsse zu ziehen, und zwar nicht nur in Bezug auf die gesehenen Filme, deren Titel nicht genannt werden, sondern auch in Bezug auf die Kinogänger. Es ist, als müsse man ganz unwillkürlich mit der Konstruktion einer zweifachen Typologie beginnen, die sich aus Erzähltem, Mimik, Gestik, Kleidung und so weiter zusammensetzt: zum einen eine Typologie der Kinogänger und zum anderen eine Typologie der Filme, deren Impression sich in den Betrachtern festgeschrieben hat. So verführerisch leicht und witzig dieses Zuordnen zunächst daherkommt, so bedenklich wird es, wenn nach kurzer Zeit diese Typologien schon gleich nach dem ersten Eindruck entstehen. Insofern gibt sich in Jankowskis Film der Film selbst als potenziell vorurteilsbildendes Feld zu erkennen.

In der Arbeit THIS I PLAYED TOMORROW (Das spielte ich morgen, 2003) sprechen Menschen ebenfalls über das Kino. Anders als in WHAT REMAINS geht es hier aber nicht um die Filmerfahrung der Interviewten, sondern vielmehr um Film und Kino als Projektionsfläche von Sehnsüchten und Wünschen. An einem mythisch aufgeladenen Ort, vor dem Eingang zu Cinecittà, jener legendären Produktionsstätte unzähliger italienischer und europäischer Filme, stellt Jankowski verschiedenen Personen eine Reihe von Fragen wie: «Würden Sie in einem Kinofilm mitspielen, auch wenn man Sie nicht bezahlen würde?», «Was für eine Rolle würden Sie spielen wollen?», oder: «Was kann das Kino erreichen?». Die Antworten der Befragten fügen sich zu einem sehr speziellen Spannungsverhältnis aus Wünschen und Realitäten der Interviewten zusammen. Zwar möchten die meisten immer eine Person jenes Geschlechts und Alters spielen, das sie in Wirklichkeit haben, die Charaktere und das Setting weichen in der Regel jedoch von ihrer persönlichen Realität ab. Man wünscht sich, eine Prinzessin zu verkörpern, oder dass das Drama in einer anderen Zeit spielen möge. Auch der Wunsch, seine eigenen Charaktereigenschaften ungebremster auszuleben, ist von den interviewten Personen immer wieder zu hören. Man phantasiert von einer aggressiven, einer heroischen oder einer dramatischen Rolle. Der Film entpuppt sich hier mehr und mehr als ein Raum, in dem zwei Projektionsmaschinen gleichzeitig agieren: zum einen die Bildfabrik, die Bildwelten herstellt und so Phantasien und Sehnsüchte in uns und durch uns erzeugt; zum anderen wir selbst, die Kinogänger, die, angereichert mit eigenen Bildwelten, Phantasien an das Kino und dessen Industrie herantragen. Dieser Wunsch nach einer Rolle innerhalb der repräsentati-

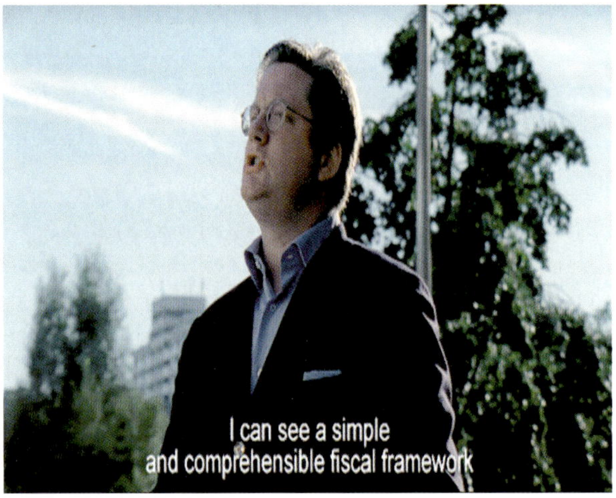

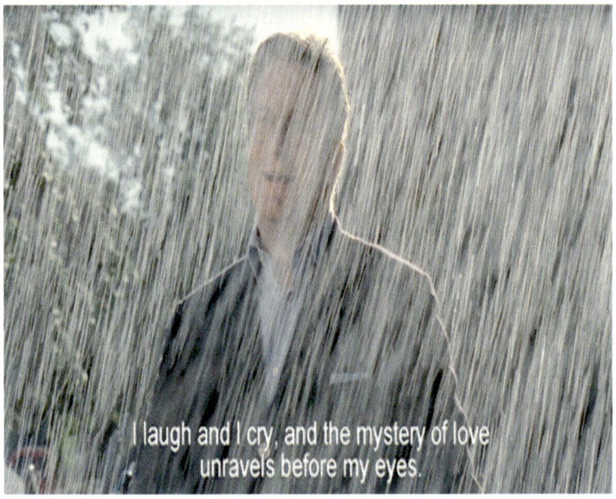

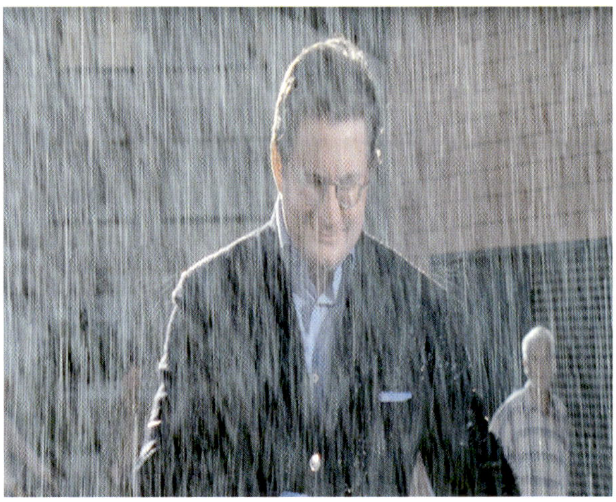

CHRISTIAN JANKOWSKI, HOLLYWOODSCHNEE, 2004, sequence from the film featuring Gronewold / Filmsequenz mit Gronewold.

ven Produktionsseite des Kinos lenkt den Blick unmittelbar auf eine dritte Arbeit Jankowskis mit dem Titel HOLLYWOODSCHNEE (2004). Denn hier sind nicht mehr die Rezipienten des Kinos im Blickfeld von Jankowskis Kamera, sondern Menschen, die an der Produktion und Vermarktung von Filmen beteiligt sind. Auch sie sprechen darüber, was das Kino für sie bedeutet. Dabei gibt es jedoch drei entscheidend andere Aspekte: 1. Alle Szenen sind nicht spontan aus Interviews entstanden, sondern klar strukturiert und aufwändig in Szene gesetzt. 2. Pro Szene wird jeweils ein klassischer Filmtrick (künstlicher Schnee, Filmexplosion etcetera) demonstriert, was ebenso wie die auswendig gesprochenen Texte den Eindruck grosser Künstlichkeit vermittelt. 3. Neben der persönlichen Erfahrung von Film, welche die vorherigen Arbeiten Jankowskis immer am Beispiel der Kinogänger zeigten, werden hier auch ökonomische und soziale Gesichtspunkte zur Sprache gebracht. Jankowski vollzieht hierbei eine interessante Überkreuzung. Denn während er die Phantasien der Zuschauer eher in einem essayistisch-dokumentarischen Stil zu erfassen sucht, wechselt er in dem Augenblick, wo er den Fokus auf die nüchterne Seite der Produktion und der daran beteiligten Personen richtet, zu einer eher hollywoodesken Sprache. Mittels dieser Gegenläufigkeit gewinnt er nicht nur dem Thema «Wunsch und Realität des Kinos» interessante Aspekte ab, sondern auch der eigenen Filmform. Dieser letzte Punkt ist ein durchgehendes Thema in den Filmen von Christian Jankowski, denn sie alle legen jeweils eine interessante Seite des filmischen Kosmos frei und thematisieren damit immer auch sich selbst. Dabei kann durchaus der Eindruck von Etüden entstehen – Übungen also, die nicht nur versuchen ein technisches Problem in den Griff zu bekommen, sondern auch eine eigene, anspruchsvolle Virtuosität aufweisen. Mehr noch: Wenn sie zusammen präsentiert werden, wie derzeit in der Galerie Martin Klosterfelde in Berlin, beginnen sie sich gegenseitig zu ergänzen und zu kommentieren. Es sind Denkbewegungen über ein Thema, die sich zusammenschliessen und so einen bestechend neuen Blick auf den Film entwickeln.

In seinem neusten Film 16MM MYSTERY (2004) schliesslich spitzt Christian Jankowski seine Fragen

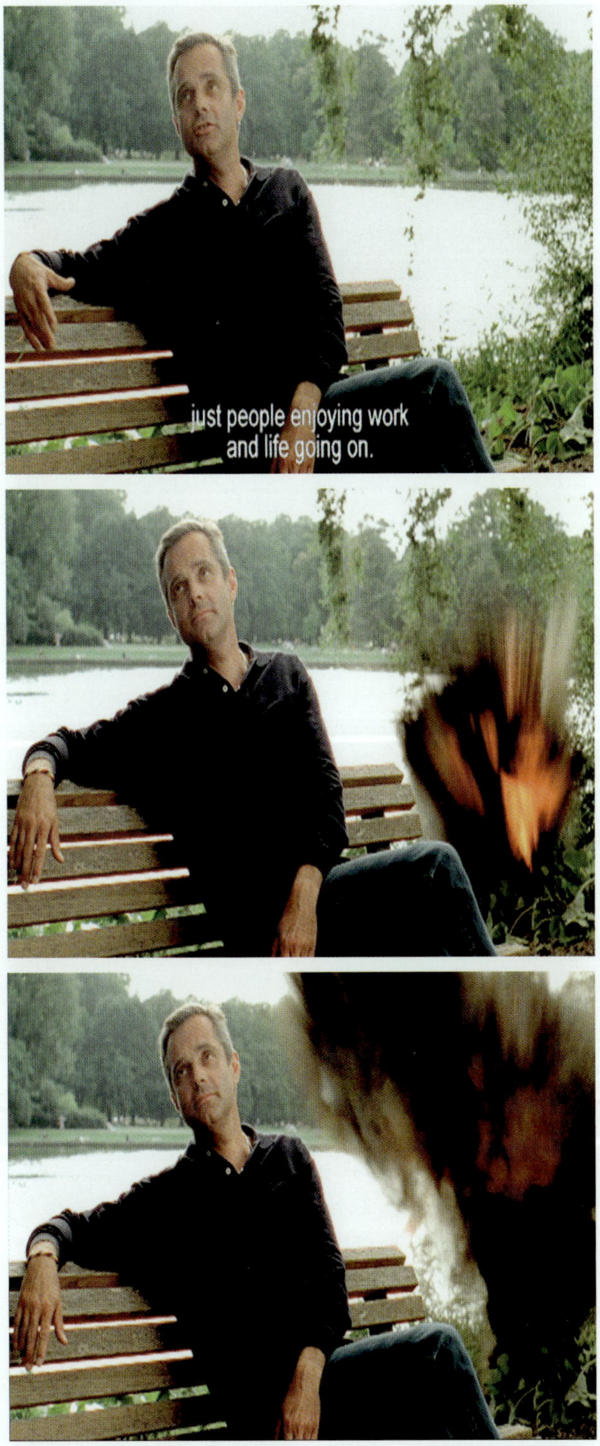

CHRISTIAN JANKOWSKI, HOLLYWOODSCHNEE, 2004, sequence from the film featuring Boje / Filmsequenz mit Boje.

nach dem komplexen Feld von Kunst, Kino und Film zu. Dabei gerät er wie in seinen früheren Arbeiten auch selbst wieder vor die Kamera. Er setzt sich selbst als Protagonist seines Films in Szene und demonstriert, wie sich Kunst- und Filmgeschichte ineinander weben lassen, um gemeinsam eine nachhaltige Irritation zu erzeugen. Ausgestattet mit einem Koffer und einer an eine Gewehrtasche erinnernden Verpackung geht Jankowski in diesem Film durch eine nicht näher definierte städtische Szenerie. Die kühlen Bilder, verbunden mit einem monotonen Elektrosound, erinnern durchaus an die präzisen Stadtinszenierungen eines David Fincher. Zielstrebig verfolgt der Protagonist seinen Weg und erinnert uns, wenn er etwa beginnt das Dach eines Hauses zu erklimmen, an Sniperszenen, die wir aus klassischen Hollywoodthrillern der 70er Jahre kennen. Auf dem Dach angekommen entpuppt sich das verpackte «Gewehr» jedoch als Filmleinwand, die Jankowski gegenüber einem Projektor aufstellt. Diesen setzt er in Gang und verlässt das Bild: Zurück bleibt nur der Schuss des Projektors auf die Leinwand vor einer Hochhauskulisse. Würde der Film hier enden, wäre es nicht mehr als eine unangenehm didaktische Inszenierung der filmischen Mittel – doch der Film geht weiter: Völlig unvermittelt bricht nach einigen Sekunden plötzlich eines der im Hintergrund sichtbaren Hochhäuser zusammen. Ein im wahrsten Sinn schockierender Moment. Nicht so sehr, weil in zusammenstürzenden Hochhäusern mittlerweile immer auch die Bilder vom 11. September 2001 mitschwingen. Vielmehr ist es schockierend, zu erleben, dass, trotz der über hundertjährigen Geschichte des Films und trotz des Wissens um das Lügen der Bilder, unser Glaube an das Mimetische des Bildes weiter besteht. Mit der unmittelbar auftauchenden Frage, ob das, was wir sehen, denn sein kann, führt uns der Film direkt an einen Abgrund. Indem wir aber das Potenzial des rechnerisch erzeugten Bildes so unmittelbar erleben, werden nicht nur die Bildformen von Kino und Kunst in Frage gestellt, sondern auch ihre getrennte Verhandlung. Und indem Christian Jankowski diese beiden Welten mit seinen Arbeiten wieder aufeinander zu bewegt, zeigen sich im Oszillieren der Bereiche Möglichkeiten zu einem neuen Bilddiskurs.

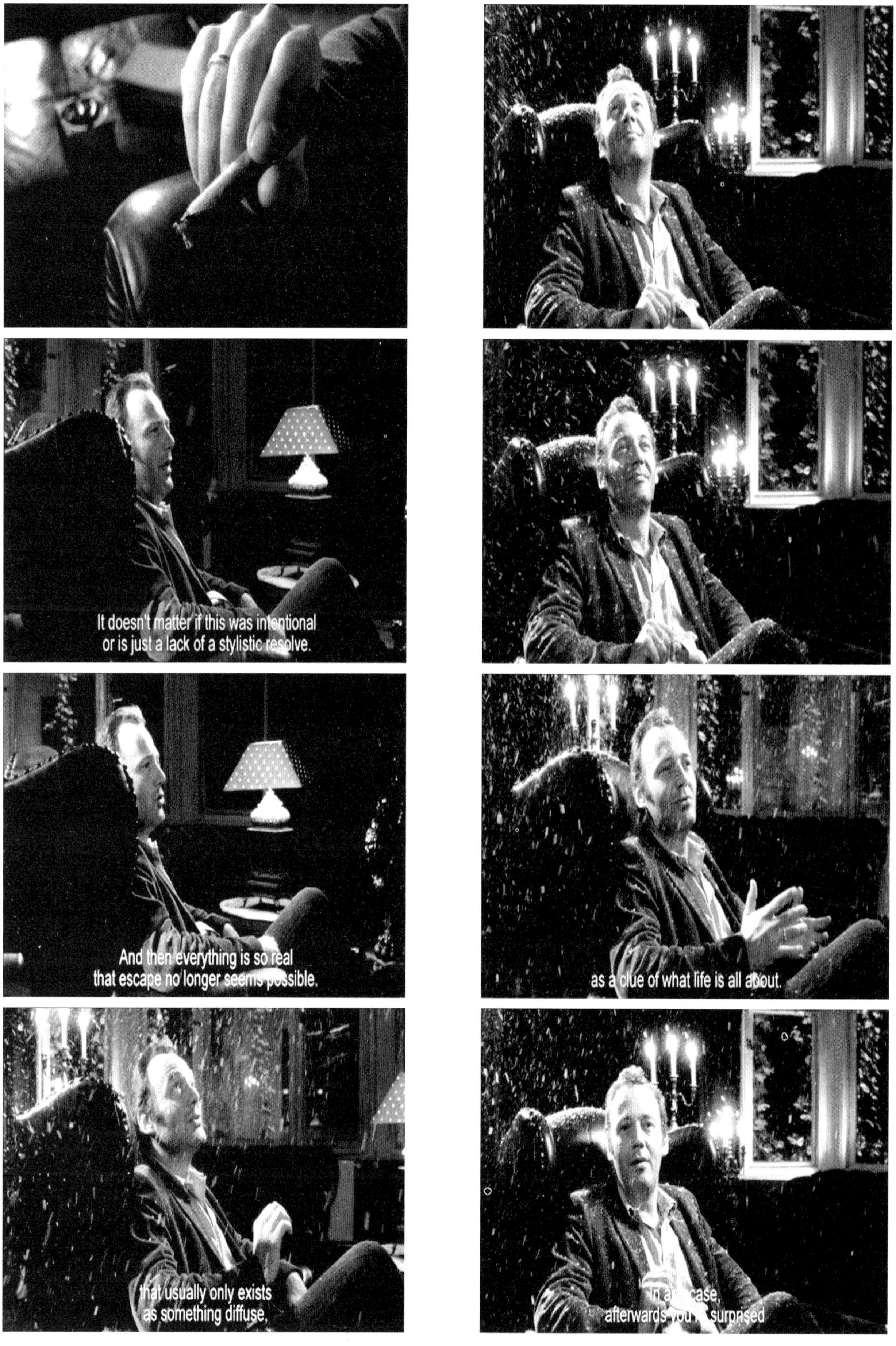

CHRISTIAN JANKOWSKI, HOLLYWOODSCHNEE, 2004, film sequence featuring Althen / Filmsequenz mit Althen.

VARIATIONS ON A THEME

THE FILM ETUDES OF CHRISTIAN JANKOWSKI

MARC GLÖDE

Often, when you watch the films that Christian Jankowski makes, you can't help smiling. There is a current of humor—sometimes low-key, sometimes more aggressive—that runs through all of his work. In an early video, DIE JAGD (The Chase, 1992), he marches off to a supermarket armed with bow and arrow and begins hunting foodstuffs in the "best manly tradition." The same humor characterizes one of his best-known works, TELEMYSTIC (1999), which he created for the Venice Biennale. The video shows him telephoning popular Italian TV astrologers, asking them, for example, whether his next piece will be a success and whether or not he is on the right track.

MARC GLÖDE is a film scholar and, since 2002, on a research team specializing in "Performative Culture" at the Freie Universität Berlin. He has organized several film festivals devoted to "Film and Architecture" in such places as Berlin, Los Angeles, and London.

Jankowski's humor plays on the complex interaction of various social contexts such as art, family, and relationships, as well as his own role as artist, man, or friend within those contexts.

However, since TELEMYSTIC's completion, his work has undergone a shift that is of particular interest when put in cinematic terms. Initially, Jankowski's frame of reference had been defined largely by his own person or in the context of art, but then he began directing his attention toward the medium of film and video as such, that is, the social and formal parameters. This can be observed as early as 1999 when he produced CREATE PROBLEMS. In this work Jankowski invited five couples to the Dolly Buster Studios in Dortmund and had them reenact the beginnings of existing porno movies. But just before the "climax" of the action, they were instructed to break off and begin improvising on problems in their own relationships. The artist presented the results to a marriage counselor, who analyzed the scenes, also on camera. By juxtaposing the two films—those of the couples and those of the therapist—in his final installation, Jankowski tips the scales toward the petit bourgeois revelations of his protagonists, in particular the practice of classification and dissociation. But the rowhouse atmosphere of porno stage sets peopled by protagonists with marital problems slugging it out is actually less objectionable than the revealingly petit bourgeois remarks and attitudes of the psychologists. Explicitly using the film medium as a means of criticism, Jankowski exploits a critical gesture (and not only in this film) to address an issue that is almost as old as cinema itself, or rather the narrative movies of Hollywood. It is a gesture in which art and film are, interestingly enough, frequently juxtaposed—as if it were the first time that art had ever undertaken to analyze movies or vice versa. But Jankowski's youthfully energetic gesture of "somebody's gotta say it" is exactly what enters into the subject matter he chooses to process, thereby becoming a striking aspect of his work.

CHRISTIAN JANKOWSKI, 16MM MYSTERY, film stills / Szenen aus dem Film.

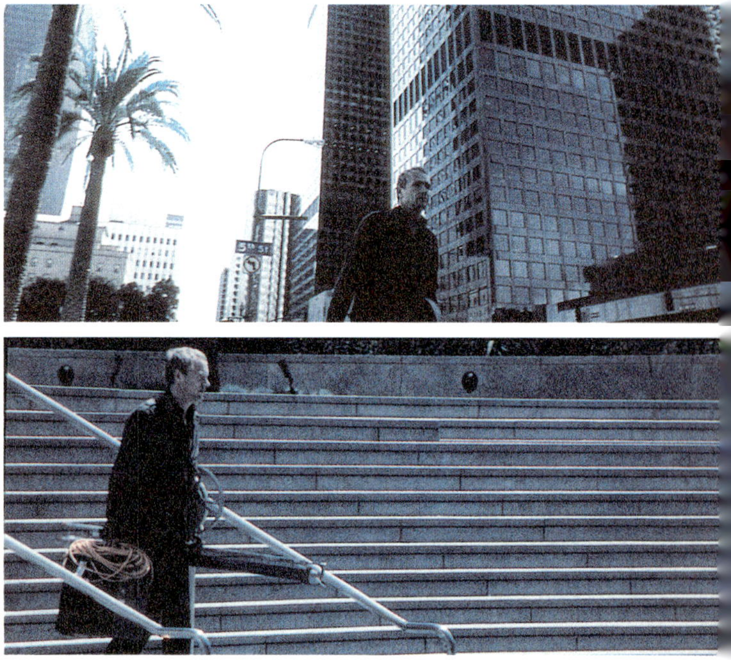

This also applies to the artist's most recent films, in which he reflects on film in general. He explores the universe of the moving image, its different forms, its potential, and above all, its audience. In WHAT REMAINS (2004), we see a series of portraits: pictures of spectators who have just been to the movies and give us a brief account of their impressions. The stories they tell coalesce into an image of what film can be and what it can be about, namely, nothing less than the entire spectrum of human emotions: love, hate, boredom, fear, joy… Very soon, however, the spectators' extremely varied reactions and descriptions begin to sync with the way they present themselves. We immediately begin to make curious assumptions not only about the films they have seen, whose titles are not mentioned, but also about the moviegoers themselves. Quite involuntarily, we find ourselves compelled to construct a twofold typology: on one hand, a typology of narrated material, facial expression, gesture, clothing, and so on; on the other, a typology of the films, whose impressions are so firmly inscribed in the viewers' minds. Seductively lighthearted and witty as this classification initially seems to be, it does provoke second thoughts to realize that the typologies emerge instantly following the first impression. Jankowski's piece therefore demonstrates the potential for film to generate prejudice.

People also talk about movies in THIS I PLAYED TOMORROW (2003), but unlike WHAT REMAINS, Jankowski does not inquire into their reactions to a film, but rather into the nature of film and movies as a surface for the projection of longings and desires. At the entrance to Cinecittà, the legendary studios that produced countless Italian and European films, and hence a site charged with myth, Jankowski asked

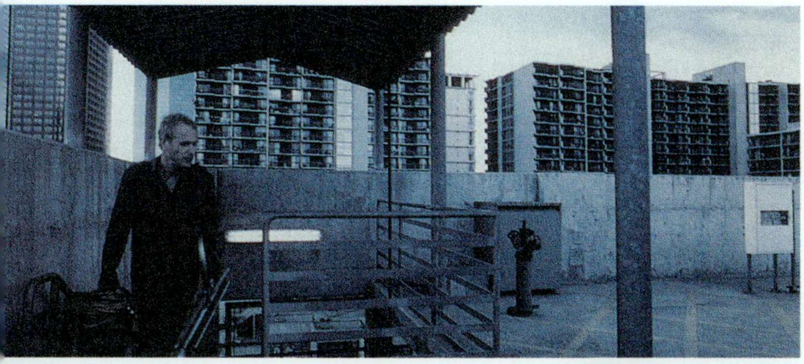

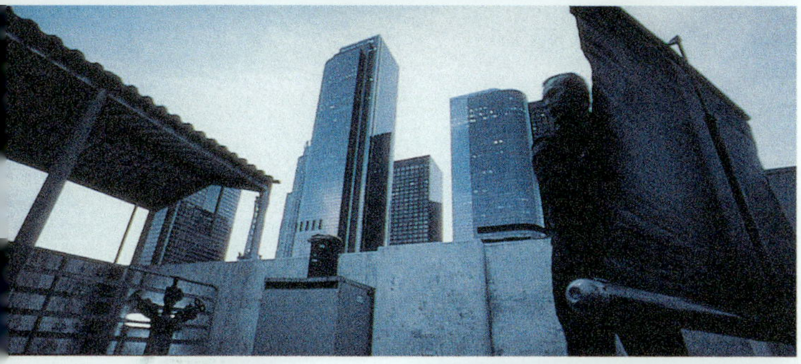

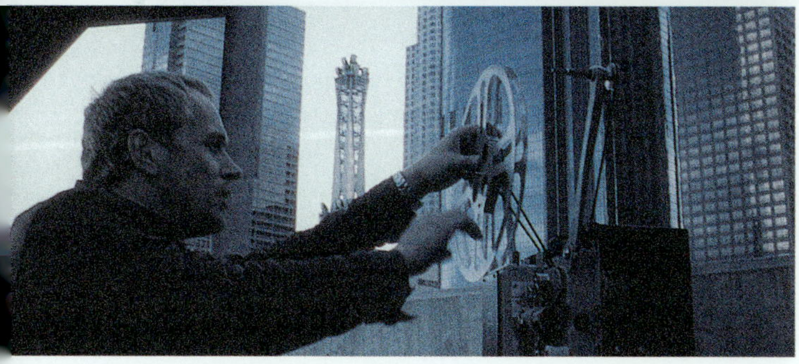

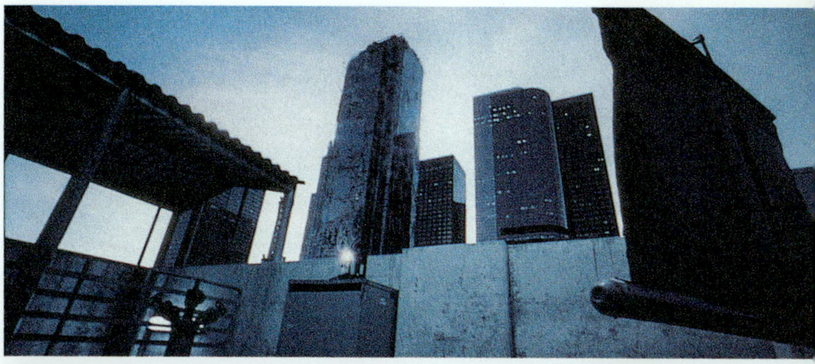

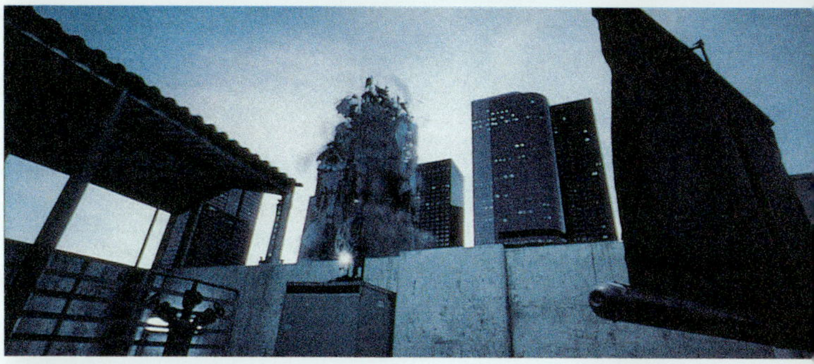

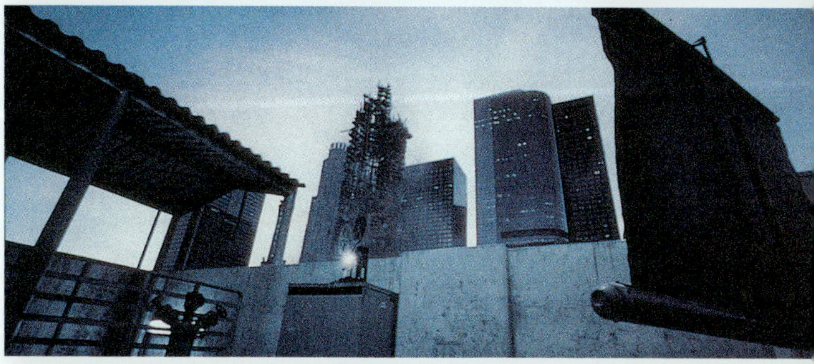

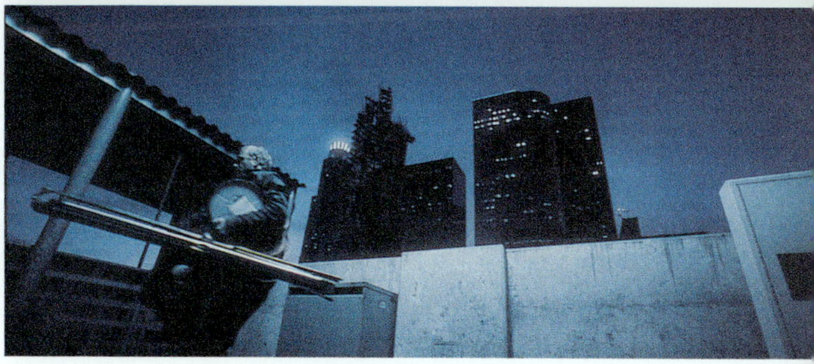

several people a number of questions including: Would you act in a movie for free? What kind of part would you like to play? What can cinema achieve? The responses of the interviewees reveal a telling relationship between their wishes and their realities. As a rule, they want to play a person of their own age and sex, but the characters and the settings they choose do not generally coincide with their own lives. One person wants to be a princess; another wants the action to take place in a different period. Many express the desire to be able to act out their own character traits uninhibitedly, while others have fantasies of playing an aggressive, a heroic, or a dramatic role. It becomes increasingly evident that movies allow two projection "machines" to be operative at the same time: on one hand, the image factory in which worlds of imagery are produced that evoke fantasies and longings in and through us; on the other hand, we ourselves, the moviegoers, who project the enriching potential of our own images and fantasies on to movies and the movie industry.

The desire to be participants in the movie industry takes us to another of Jankowski's projects, titled HOLLYWOODSCHNEE (Hollywood Snow, 2004). This time the artist's camera is not directed at the audience, but rather at people involved in the production and marketing of movies. They also talk about what movies mean to them, but there are three salient differences from the preceding films. 1) The scenes are not spontaneous interviews but clearly structured and elaborately staged scenarios. 2) Each scene demonstrates a classical cinematic trick (fake snow, an explosion, etcetera), which, like the memorized spoken texts, gives an impression of extreme artificiality. 3) In contrast to moviegoers' personal experiences of films expressed in the previous projects, the new protagonists additionally address their economic and social aspects. Jankowski intersects the two types of film, producing interesting composites. He uses an essay-like, documentary style when filming the fantasies of the spectators, but the moment he focuses on the less thrilling aspect of production, his protagonists adopt the theatrical language of Hollywood. This chiasmic technique yields illuminating insight not only into the subject of "desire and reality in movies," but also into the artist's own filmmaking. All of Christian Jankowski's films are essentially self-referential inasmuch as they uncover a singular aspect of the filmmaking universe. One can certainly think of them as etudes—exercises that attempt to come to terms with a technical problem and also display a distinctive, challenging virtuosity. Not only that: when presented together, as recently seen at Galerie Martin Klosterfelde in Berlin, they begin to complement and impact each other. Thoughts-in-motion on a specific subject matter converge and regroup to form a startling new vision of cinema.

Christian Jankowski's investigation of the complex field of art, cinema, and film comes to a head in his most recent production, 16MM MYSTERY (2004). As before, he appears on camera; he plays his own protagonist and demonstrates how the history of art and the history of film can be interwoven to enduringly unsettling effect. Armed with a suitcase and an item that resembles a gun case, Jankowski walks through an undefined urban location. The cool pictures in combination with monotonous electro sound easily compare with the precise urban scenarios of a filmmaker like David Fincher. The protagonist moves with single-minded purpose and when, for instance, he starts climbing up to the roof of a building, he reminds us of sniper scenes from classic seventies Hollywood thrillers. On the rooftop, we discover that he has not been toting a gun in his gun case but rather a portable screen, which he sets up opposite a projector. Jankowski turns the projector on and moves out of the frame. All that is left is the projector aimed at a screen against the backdrop of high-rise buildings. If the film were to end here, it would be little more than a mildly irksome educational display of cinematic devices—but the film goes on: after a few seconds and completely without warning, one of the high-rise buildings visible in the background suddenly collapses. A literally shattering moment: not so much because buildings collapsing in themselves inevitably evoke memories of 9/11, but because, despite the 100-year history of film and despite our knowledge of the ability of pictures to lie, our faith in the mimetic faculty of the image is still intact. By instantly making us wonder whether what we see is for real, the film leads us directly into the abyss. However, the immediacy of the experience of the digitally generated image not only calls into question the visual forms of cinema and art, but also their separate treatment. And by exploiting the potential of these two worlds in the act of oscillating convergence, Christian Jankowski demonstrates the possibilities of a new pictorial discourse.

(Translation: Catherine Schelbert)

INSERT LOREDANA SPERINI

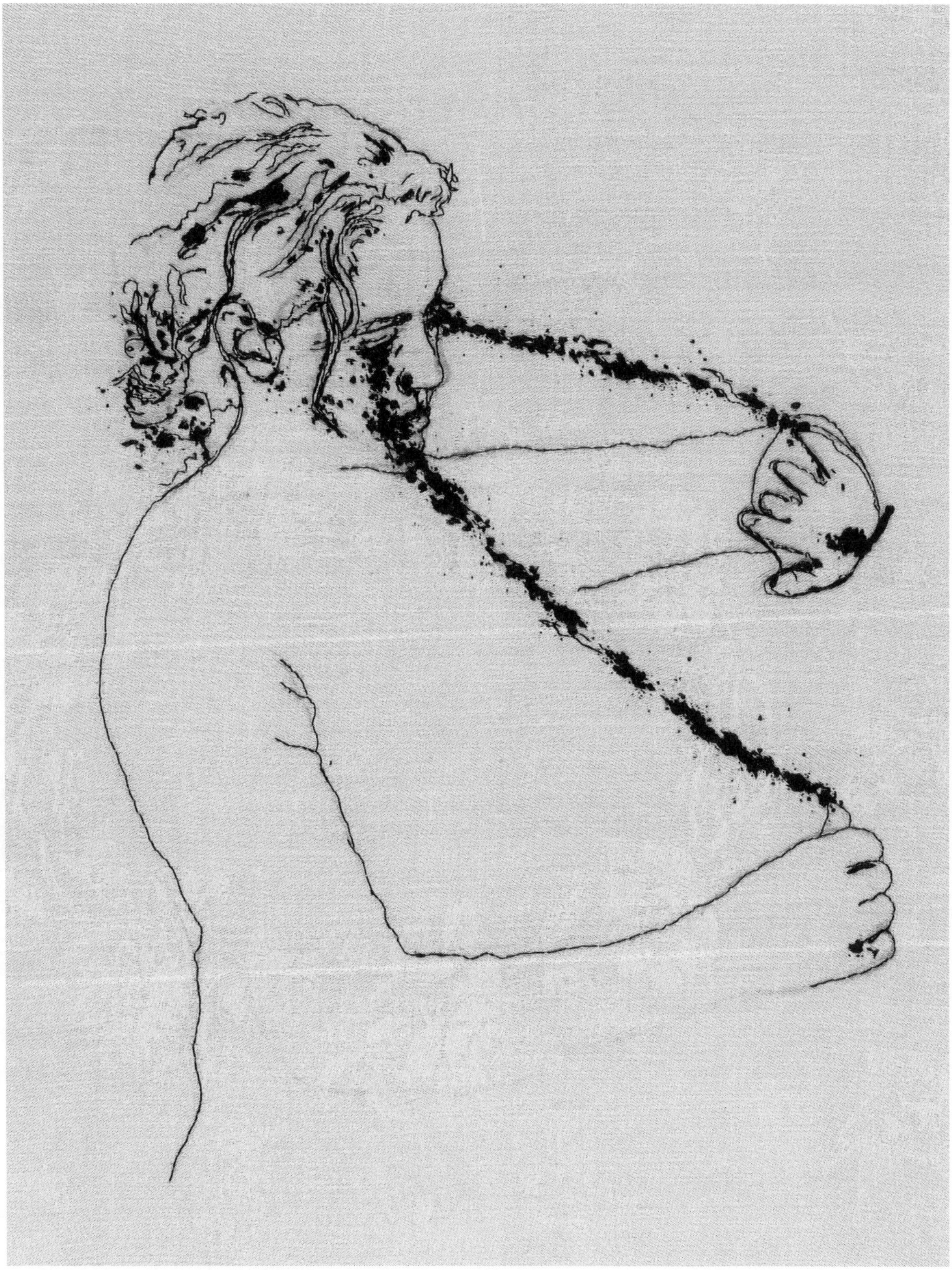

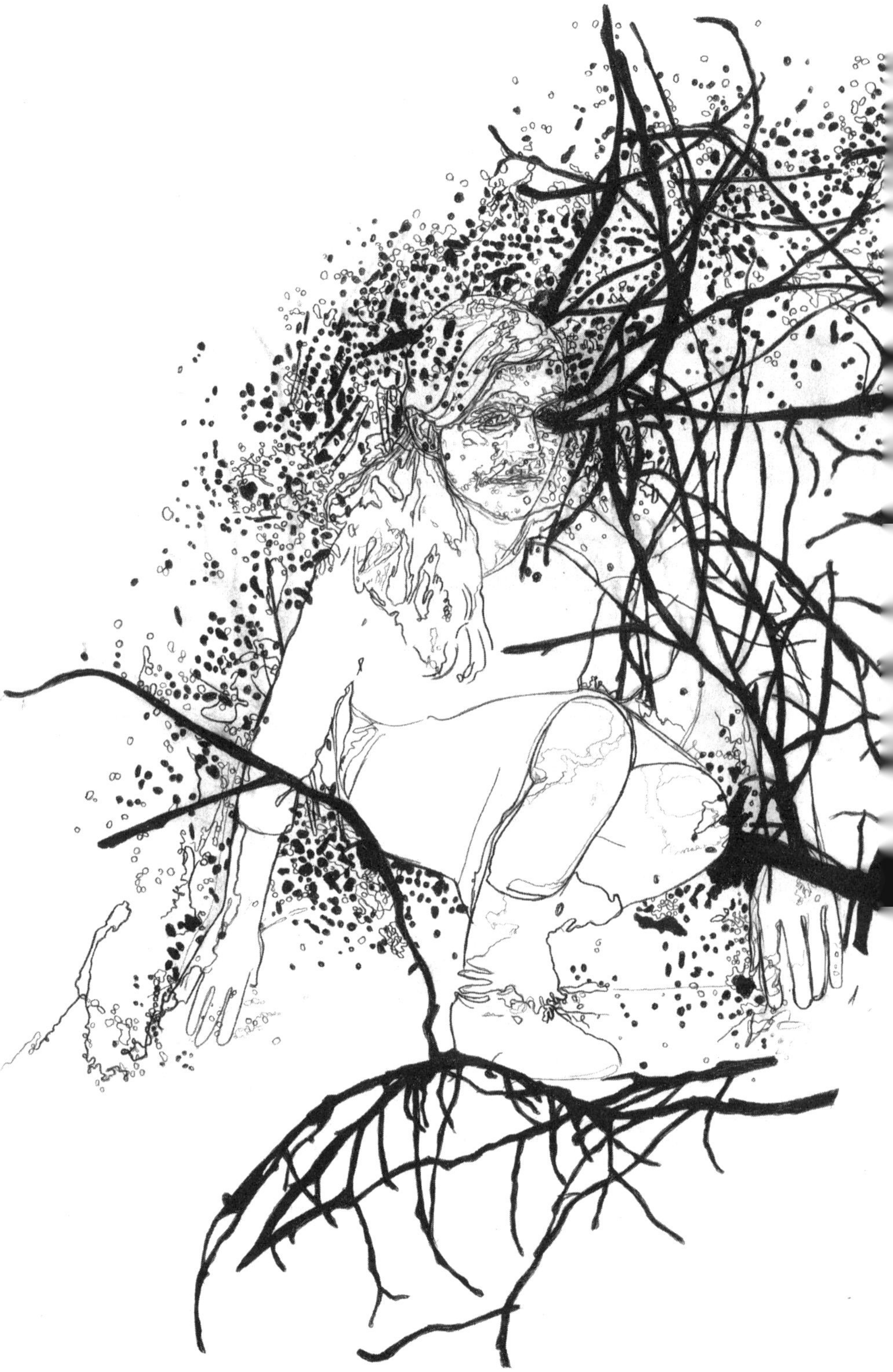

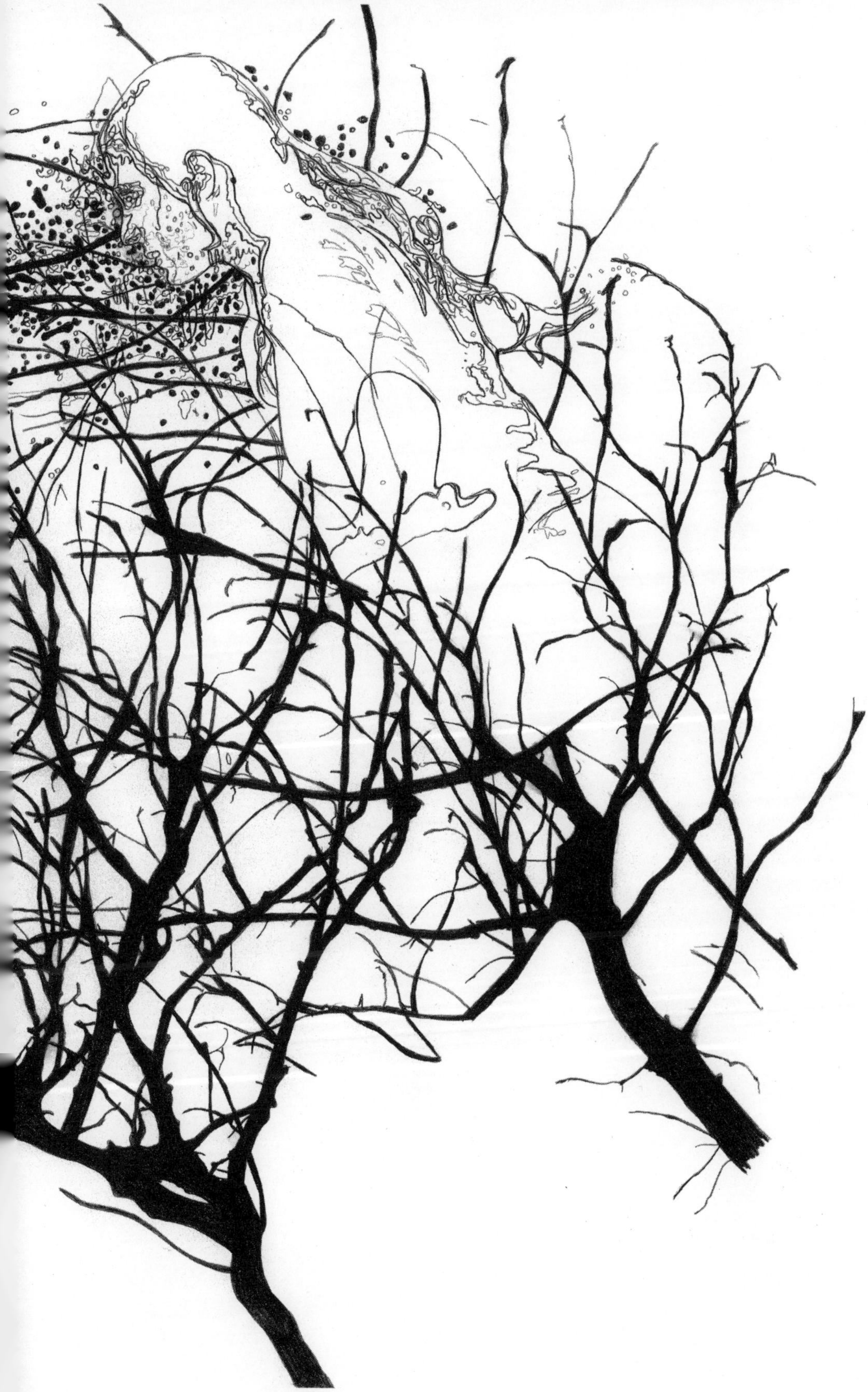

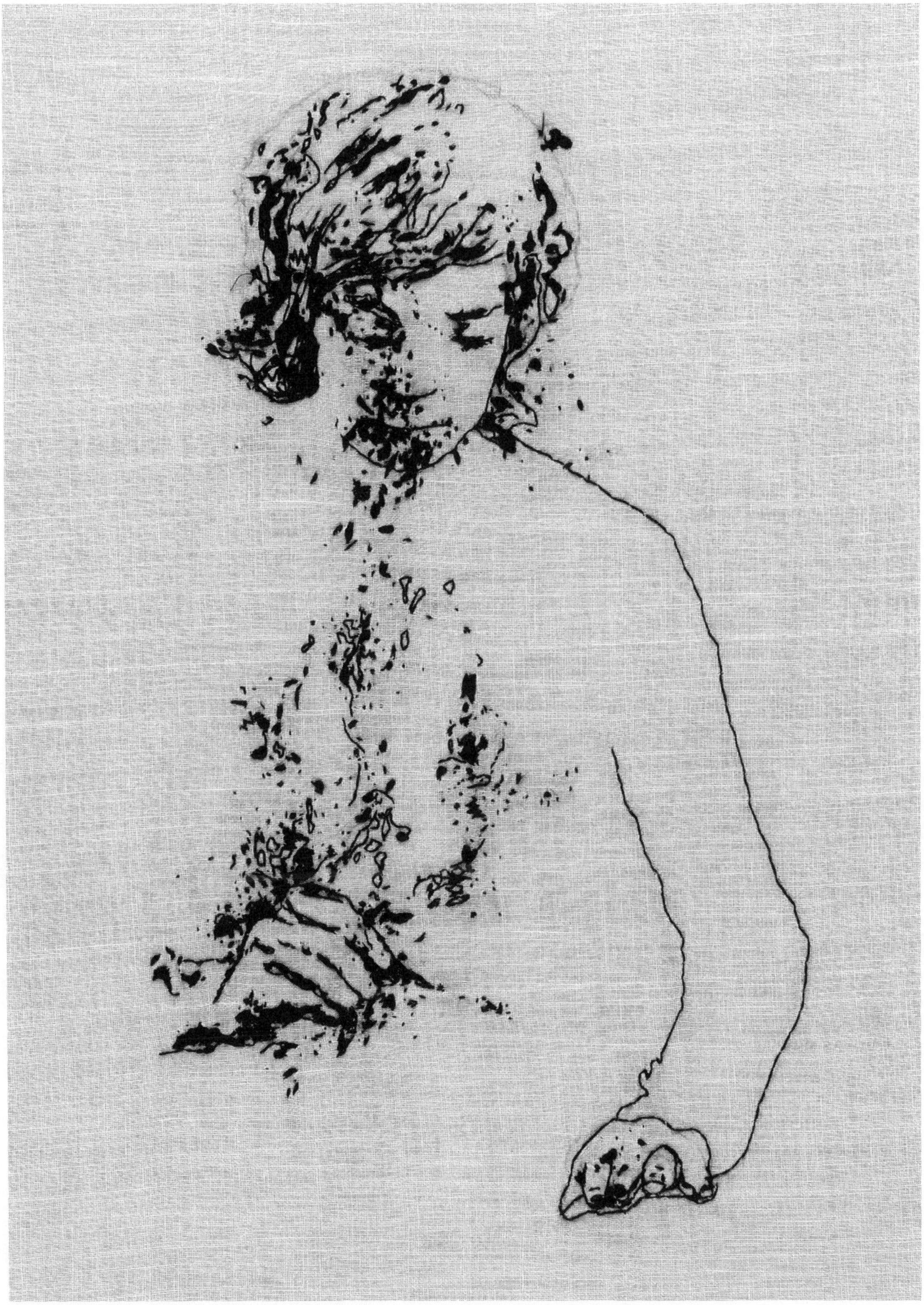

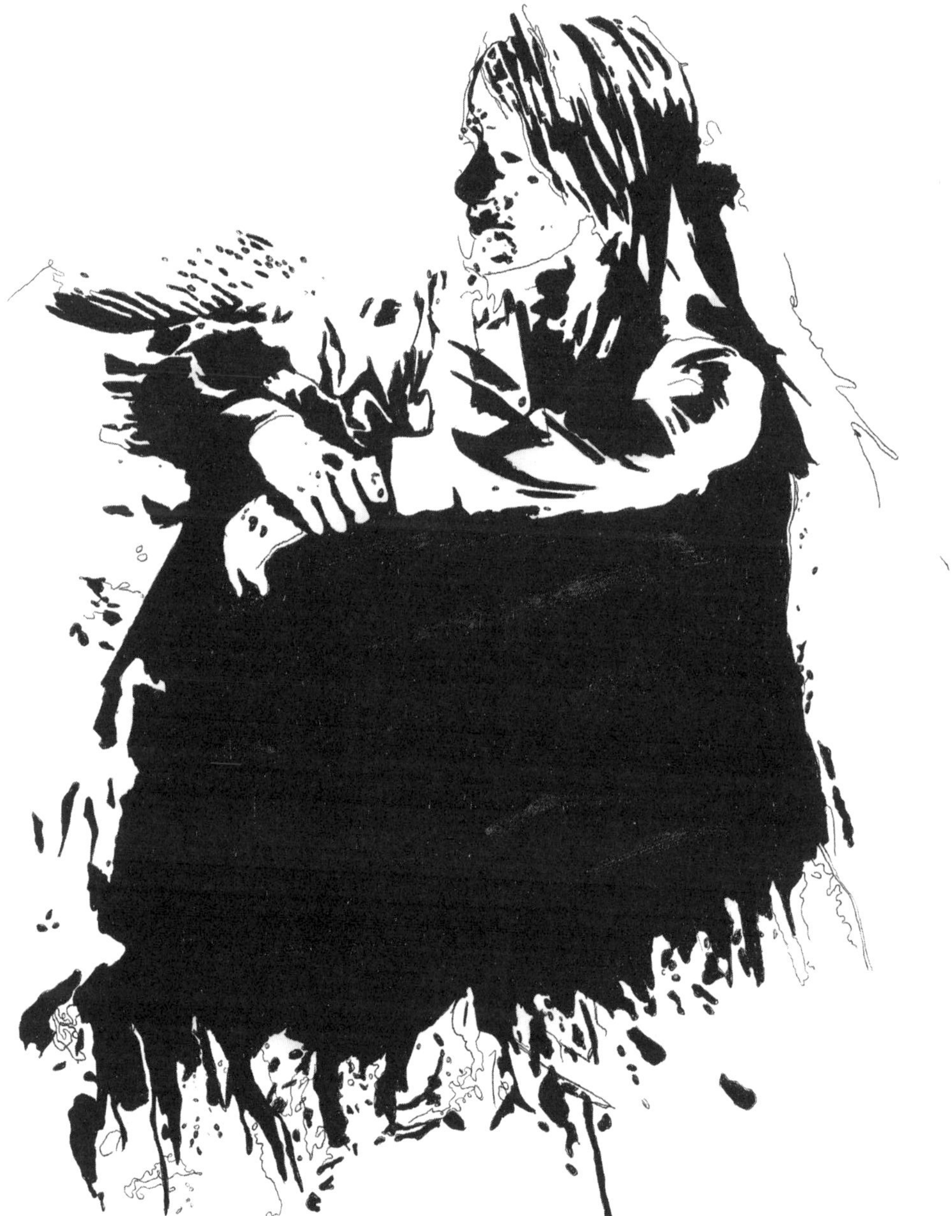

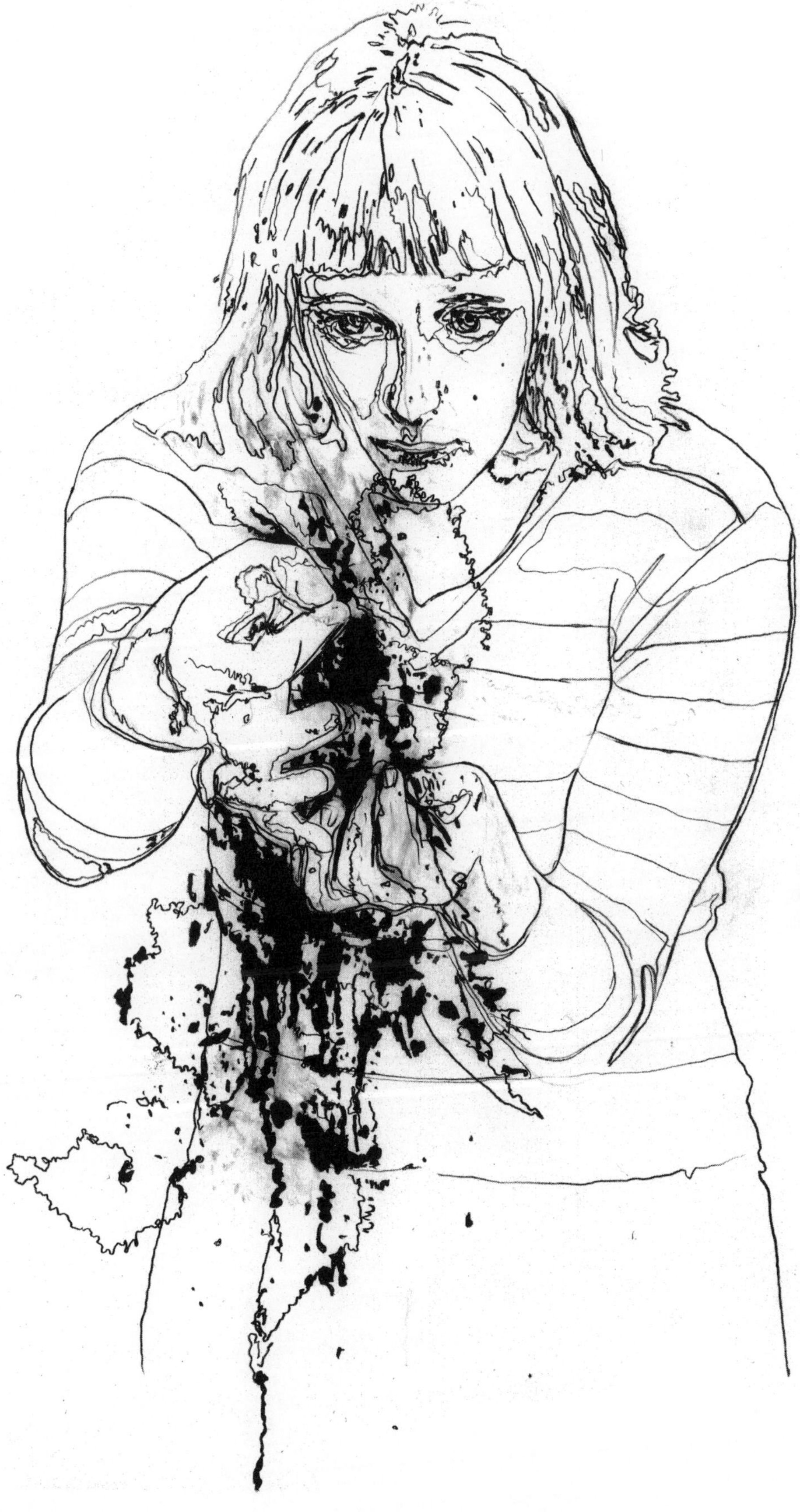

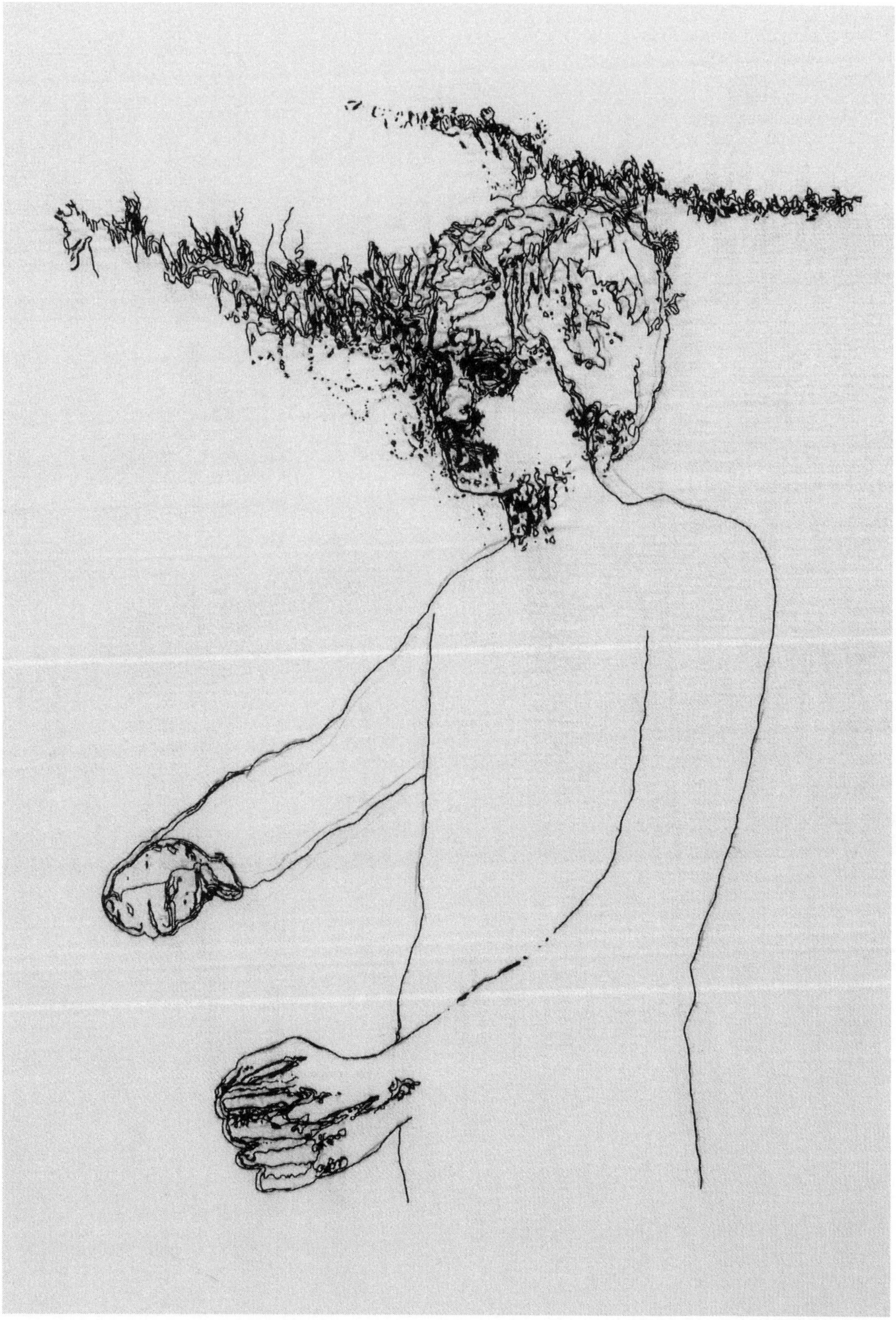

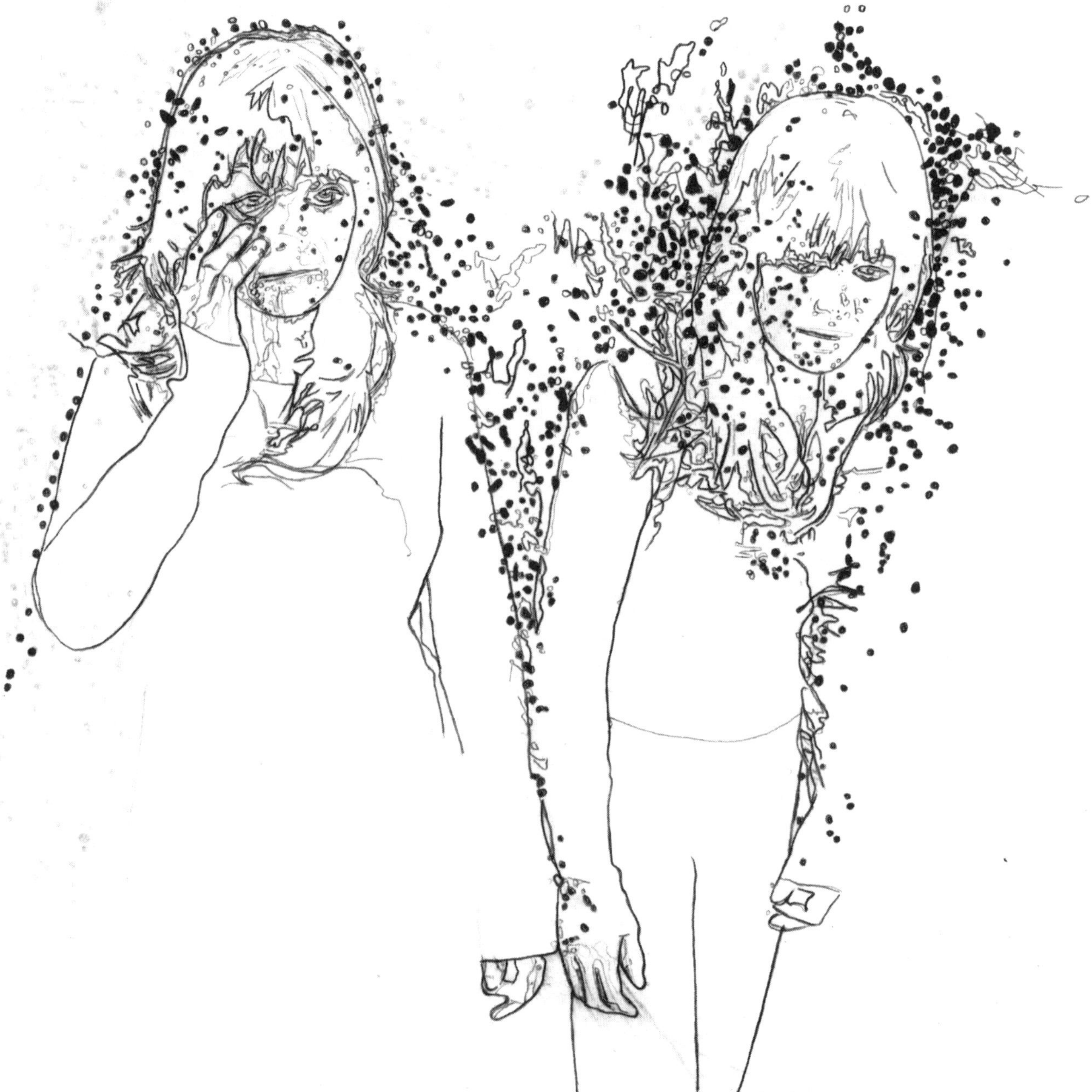

LOREDANA SPERINI, INSERT FOR PARKETT 72, 2004

CUMULUS

From America

IN EVERY EDITION OF PARKETT, TWO CUMULUS CLOUDS, ONE FROM AMERICA, THE OTHER FROM EUROPE, FLOAT OUT TO AN INTERESTED PUBLIC. THEY CONVEY INDIVIDUAL OPINIONS, ASSESSMENTS, AND MEMORABLE ENCOUNTERS—AS ENTIRELY PERSONAL PRESENTATIONS OF PROFESSIONAL ISSUES.

OUR CONTRIBUTORS TO THIS ISSUE ARE STEPHANIE SMITH, CURATOR OF THE SMART MUSEUM OF ART AT THE UNIVERSITY OF CHICAGO, AND HANS RUDOLF REUST, A CURATOR AND TEACHER AT THE UNIVERSITY OF ART, BERN, SWITZERLAND.

STEPHANIE SMITH

PROMISE PIECES

I recently picked up a copy of a sexy little book called *Cradle to Cradle: Remaking the Way We Make Things* by architect William McDonough and chemist Michael Braungart. By "picked up" I mean not only purchasing and reading the text but also the physical act of touching the object. It's a pleasant thing to hold, small but solid, with a satisfying heft and a sleek texture derived from its unusual substance: a paper-like material made from chemicals rather than the usual organic pulp. For the authors, this material represents a new mode of environmentally conscious design. The synthetic materials that comprise this *Waterproof Durabook*—note the trademark on the front cover—can be recycled or even reformulated into a useful new substance much more easily than other materials that might at first seem more environmentally friendly. (Unbleached recycled paper, for instance, may not be reusable or even biodegradable when bound using synthetic glues.)[1] In a parallel move, the cover uses clever typography and fresh acidic hues rather than more familiar, earth-tone eco-aesthetics. These choices exemplify McDonough's and Braungart's optimistic approach to design: the text offers ways that individuals and corporations can adopt in order to make and use things more effectively, and the book embodies that conceptual substance.

Although I don't have the technical expertise to know whether their propositions are practical or effective, I'm a sucker for this book. Like so many, I worry that my patterns of consumption are contributing to the death of the planet, and although I've changed some day-to-day habits I still pursue scores of eco-insensitive pleasures. I

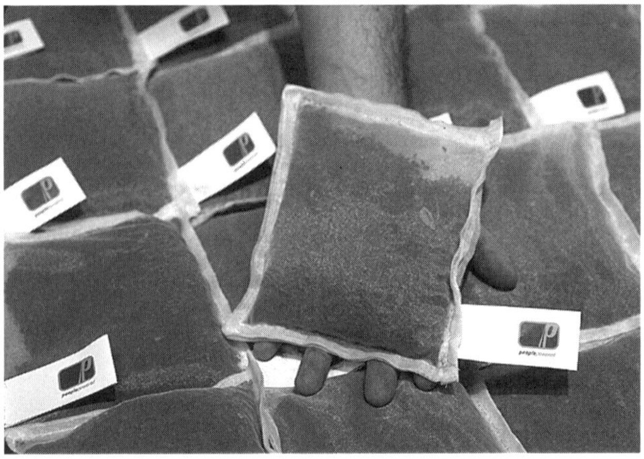

peoplepowered

PEOPLE POWERED (KEVIN KAEMPF), SOIL STARTER, 2003–ongoing, composted organic matter, fabric, and People Powered tag / kompostierte organische Materialien, Stoff und People-Powered-Etikette.

adore my lipstick and my iPod; I walk the city but will hop in my car for a gas-guzzling road-trip at the slightest provocation. So, though wary, I'm lured by the promise that some of these pleasures might be made environmentally palatable if produced through sustainable design, which takes a big-picture approach by considering the entire lifespan of an object or structure and by integrating not only environmental issues, but also social, economic, and aesthetic concerns. As articulated by Braungart/McDonough and others,[2] this doesn't require a puritan rejection of the pleasures afforded by objects—books, for instance—or a narrow approach to materials and aesthetics. Design historian Victor Margolin has described such approaches as part of an emerging "culture of sustainability" which he sees as a necessary development within design.[3]

Over the past few years I've been noticing what might be the beginnings of a parallel "culture of sustainability" among artists of my generation. This work offers a counterpoint to more established forms of environmentally conscious art. I'm thinking of projects like Robert Smithson's proposed sculptural interventions into mining sites in the early seventies, but perhaps even more, of projects in the eighties and nineties that drew on emerging notions of the artist as an interdisciplinary researcher and developed in tandem with the new modes of collaborative, process-oriented, and sometimes community-based "new genre public art."[4] Now, rather than working within specific built or natural sites or imagining global-scaled interventions, some artists are playing with the notion of "sustainability" at a more modest level. They make smaller, portable objects that combine some of the aesthetic qualities that make *Cradle to Cradle* such an enticing object—witty design, high-tech materials—with attention to the ways that objects fit into larger systems that include but are not limited to environmental impact. They often work collaboratively and make objects that function as triggers for speculation when presented within art contexts but have to be animated/activated by use outside the museum. They leaven serious social aims with a dash of playful, off-the-grid spark, updating Bauhaus form-meets-functionality or Beuysian social sculpture. Artworks that function in this manner include N55's portable PUBLIC THINGS (1999–ongoing), Superflex's SUPERGAS projects (1997–ongoing), Nils Norman's GEOCRUISER (2001), Andrea Zittel's *AZ Advanced Technologies* (2002–ongoing), Michael Rakowitz's inflatable homeless shelters (*ParaSITE*, 1998–ongoing), and Dan Peterman's sculptures made from post-consumer reprocessed plastic. With a nod to one trend in sustainable design—attention to local products—I'll focus here on just a few examples from my own city, Chicago.

Under the name *People Powered*, artist Kevin Kaempf has developed an ongoing series of projects that reinvigorate social sculpture, in part through modesty of scale and in part by adopting corporate eco-marketing tactics and a hip aesthetic. For his first *People Powered* project, SOIL STARTER (2002–ongoing), Kaempf gave instructions and a small green composting container to friends and acquaintances living in his neighborhood. He regularly cycles to the participating households to gather accumulated yard waste and kitchen scraps, and then composts this would-be trash into "teabags" full of composted matter that release nutrients when watered (ideal for malnourished urban house plants). He provides the participants with these teabags, which then become part of a new cycle of use, decay, and re-use.

SOIL STARTER serves several environmentally conscious social functions: raising awareness and changing daily habits among the participants, reducing waste by transforming it into actual food—nutrients—for another need, and providing an organic alternative to chemical fertilizers. Because of this functionality you might be tempted to lump this project with other activist, process-oriented art practices, especially those that intervene within relatively small communities. A few things, however, make Kaempf's project especially fresh. First, unlike many community-based art projects, SOIL STARTER takes place among Kaempf's peers. While the outsider position of crossing economic and/or cultural divides can be useful, it has its dangers as well—for instance, the trap of aesthetic evangelism, to use Grant Kester's phrase—and in this case it seems fitting that a project about sustainability would embed environmentalism within a relatively intimate social network. Second, note the aesthetic sensibility of those teabags, especially the bags' clean lines and the tags' sleek logos. When massed, the SOIL STARTER packets have sensual appeal—they could be post-minimal, even Hesse-ian sculptures—and each translucent square packet bears the *People Powered* logo with its energetically off-key colors and offset "P." Kaempf uses that logo on all the *People Powered* projects. He has consciously adopted a small-business model for his art practice and uses corporate marketing tactics to create a widely recognized brand identity that he hopes will eventually entice wider participation in projects like his current SHARED: CHICAGO BLUE BIKES (2004–ongoing).

The collaborative JAM (Jane Palmer and Marianne Fairbanks) creates projects that offer similarly poetic and practical ways of embedding sustainable habits within daily life. Palmer and Fairbanks have been working together since 2000, and in 2003 they combined their training in fiber arts with their interest in sustainable practices in a series that was originally titled *Personal Power* (2003–2004, no connection to Kaempf's project). This series includes prototypes for garments and bags equipped with lightweight, flexible solar panels that collect and store enough energy to power small-scale electric devices like cell phones. JAM is currently exploring partnerships that would allow their technology to be incorporated into mass-produced, high fashion bags under the name *Noon Solar* (2004–ongoing) so if all goes well their initial speculative project will soon be enveloped within a commercial sphere of production and distribution.

This shift in name and context makes the solar accessories more interesting to me than if JAM were only pursuing these ideas within their art production, for it suggests ways that these objects can carry multiple identities as they move among different contexts. *Personal Power* grew out of JAM's Iraq-heightened awareness of the political consequences of dependence on oil and other fossil fuels, but Palmer and Fairbanks decided that in a commercial context it made sense to downplay a "crunchy" sensibility in favor of a more open-ended and contemporary-sounding name. This fits with the nature of the works, which aren't about dropping out but rather about stepping free of the power grid while retaining the ability to hook into communication networks, to be fashionable, or simply to enjoy a little music. The name "Noon Solar" thus provides a bit of camouflage for JAM's utopian aims, and the hip eco-conscious or trendy consumers who will likely be the first users of the *Noon Solar* products will be participants in a work of social sculpture, though they might not be

JAM (JANE PALMER & MARIANNE FAIRBANKS), NOON SOLAR, 2004–ongoing, solar panels, rechargeable batteries, copper wire, clear vinyl, and variable fabrics, cell phone / Solarzellen, wiederaufladbare Batterien, Kupferdraht, transparentes Vinyl und Stoff, Mobiltelefon.

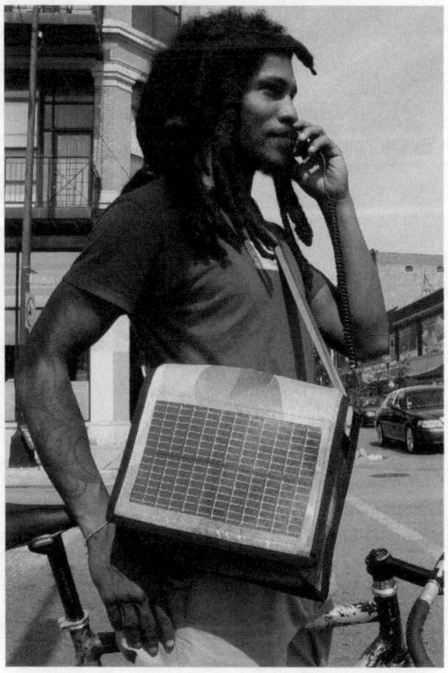

aware of or interested in JAM's larger project of making personal solar technology desirable, affordable, and widely available. The artists eventually hope, through collaborations with other designers and distributors, to "offer the technology to many different kinds of markets and potential users. This way it can become about a convenience that people want, and is not associated with a brand or consumer identity."[5] In the meantime, JAM will show *Noon Solar* in exhibitions and will produce and sell limited-edition products in a Chicago boutique.[6]

One final example takes such practices in a slightly different direction. The artists' group Temporary Services asked artist Brennan McGaffey to develop a small-scale, portable CD player that could contain all the necessary supplies for an audio "exhibition." In response he designed and constructed AUDIO RELAY (2003), with the crucial addition of a radio transmitter. Its glossy, bright yellow case, which can be carried with a shoulder strap, unpacks to reveal a set of solar panels with its own kickstand, a tray for CDs, a CD player, speakers, a folding chair, a radio transmitter, and all the relevant wiring. Temporary Services then curated a series of audio art works for AUDIO RELAY, which they sent out into the airwaves as an unofficial radio broadcast in Chicago. The broadcast audio program has changed as the piece has traveled to cities from Baltimore to Leipzig, for those who host the project are invited to curate and collect new CDs for the project. The work takes the private-museum-in-a-box premise of Marcel Duchamp's BOÎTE-EN-VALISE (1941–42) and makes it generous by including not only other artists but also a community of listeners.

As with the works by Kevin Kaempf and JAM, McGaffey's design for AUDIO RELAY is functional, sleek, and incorporates sustainable technologies but, unlike those works, environmental sustainability is not at the heart of the work's content. Solar power is used here both to allow the work to function in a variety of remote sites (a car battery can also be used to power the piece) and also as a visible marker of a nomadic, self-sustaining approach to producing and disseminating art. In this, as well as through the use of the radio transmitter, it extends McGaffey's *Intermod* series (2001–ongoing), which has explored metaphoric and actual interference through temporary interventions into urban spaces.

These works produced by Kaempf, JAM, and McGaffey and Temporary Services draw on global trends in contemporary art production and sustainable design, but are also made possible by specific local circumstances. Though separate from official civic projects, their works resonate with the various ways that Chicago has been wrapping a verdant mantle around its big shoulders through splashy public efforts like the city's new Center for Green Technology. Chicago also holds a growing community of architects, engineers, and designers engaged with green and sustainable practices. More important to artists like Kaempf, though, have been the development and continuation of socially engaged, critical strategies by artists who have chosen to base their practices here in Chicago and who have, in some key cases, chosen to address environmental sustainability within their work, and to share these practices not only through exhibitions and publications but also through teaching and mentoring.

In my role as a curator at the University of Chicago's Smart Museum of Art, I aim to sustain this strand of art practice by commissioning new projects and mounting an exhibition. Because I have become increasingly aware of the environmental excesses of exhibition design (So much drywall! So much paint!), as part of that project we'll be exploring ways that sustainable design might intersect not only with the production of art, but also with its presentation, as well as practical ways to make better use of (fiscal, aesthetic, social, environmental, and personal) resources.

1) William McDonough and Michael Braungart, *Cradle to Cradle: Remaking the Way We Make Things* (New York: North Point Press, 2002). Regarding their plans for the book design see especially the introduction, "This Book is Not a Tree," and the first few pages of chapter 3, "Eco-Effectiveness."

2) For instance, Paul Hawkin, Armory Lovins, and L. Hunter Lovins, *Natural Capitalism: Creating the Next Industrial Revolution* (Boston: Little, Brown, and Co., 1999).

3) Victor Margolin, *The Politics of the Artificial* (Chicago: University of Chicago Press, 2002), p. 102.

4) Examples include Helen and Newton Harrison's watershed projects (1980s and 1990s); Mel Chin's *Revival Field* (1990–93); Platform's *Delta* (1993); Peter Fend and Ocean Earth's bio-gas and hydro-power proposals (1990s–present); Buster Simpson's *Growing Vine Street* (1997–present), and Suzanne Lacy and Susan Leibovitz Steinman's *Landed: A Project for Elkhorn City* (2001–present). "New genre public art" is Lacy's term, taken from her influential book *Mapping the Terrain: New Genre Public Art* (Seattle: Bay Press, 1992).

5) E-mail from Jane Palmer to author, October 28, 2004.

6) They briefly sold limited-edition bags at this boutique under the name "Helia" which turned out to already be in use for another product.

STEPHANIE SMITH

ARBEITEN MIT ZUKUNFT

Neulich fiel mir ein sexy Bändchen in die Hände, das den Titel *Cradle to Cradle: Remaking the Way We Make Things* trug und von Architekt William McDonough und Chemiker Michael Braungart verfasst war. Mit «in die Hände fallen» meine ich nicht nur, dass ich das Buch kaufte und las, sondern auch den physischen Akt der Berührung. Der kleine, aber solide Band ist wohltuend schwer, liegt angenehm in der Hand und fühlt sich seidig an, was von dem ungewöhnlichen Grundstoff herrührt: einem papierähnlichen Material, das statt aus dem üblichen organischen Brei aus Chemikalien hergestellt ist. Aus Sicht der beiden Autoren verkörpert dieses Material ein neues Prinzip umweltbewussten Designs. Die Kunststoffe, aus denen sich dieses *Waterproof Durabook* zusammensetzt – man beachte das Markenzeichen auf der Umschlagvorderseite –, lassen sich wesentlich leichter als andere, zunächst umweltfreundlicher erscheinende Materialien wieder verwerten oder sogar in einen nützlichen neuen Grundstoff umsetzen. (Ungebleichtes Recyclingpapier etwa ist unter Umständen nicht wieder verwendbar, ja nicht einmal biologisch abbaubar, wenn synthetische Leimstoffe als Bindemittel verwendet werden.)[1] In einem entsprechenden Schritt wurde für die Umschlaggestaltung statt auf eine eher vertraute erdfarbene Ökoästhetik auf raffinierte Typographie und frische ätzende Farben zurückgegriffen. Diese Entscheidungen machen das optimistische Designverständnis anschaulich, das McDonough und Braungart vertreten: In dem Buch geht es darum, wie Einzelne und Unternehmen sich effektivere Methoden der Produktion und des Gebrauchs von Dingen aneignen können, und der Band selbst verleiht diesem Konzept konkrete Gestalt.

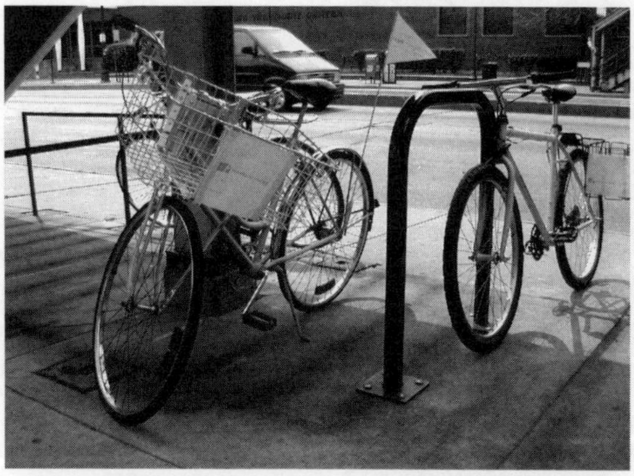

PEOPLE POWERED (KEVIN KAEMPF), SHARE: CHICAGO BLUE BIKES, 2004–ongoing, electric-blue paint, salvaged bicycles, wire baskets, and People Powered signs / blaue Farbe, wiederverwertete Fahrräder, Gitterkörbe und Schilder mit dem People-Powered-Logo.

Obwohl ich nicht das technische Fachwissen besitze, um beurteilen zu können, ob ihre Vorschläge praktisch oder effektiv sind, hat das Buch es mir angetan. Ebenso wie viele andere mache auch ich mir Sorgen, dass meine Konsumgewohnheiten dem Tod des Planeten Vorschub leisten, und obwohl ich in meinem Alltag einige alte Angewohnheiten abgelegt habe, gehe ich nach wie vor reichlich umweltschädlichen Vergnügungen nach. Ich liebe meinen Lippenstift und meinen iPod über alles, ich gehe zwar zu Fuss in der Stadt, schwinge mich aber beim geringsten Anlass in den Wagen für eine Kraftstoff verschleudernde Autofahrt. Bei aller Vorsicht reizt mich also das Versprechen, dass sich manche dieser Vergnügungen umweltverträglicher gestalten liessen, wenn die entsprechenden Produkte nach dem Prinzip eines nachhaltigen Designs hergestellt würden, das übergreifende Zusammenhänge berücksichtigt, indem es den gesamten Lebenszyklus eines Objekts oder eines Bauwerks unter Berücksichtigung von Umweltfragen, aber auch von gesellschaftlichen, wirtschaftlichen und ästhetischen Faktoren in den Blick

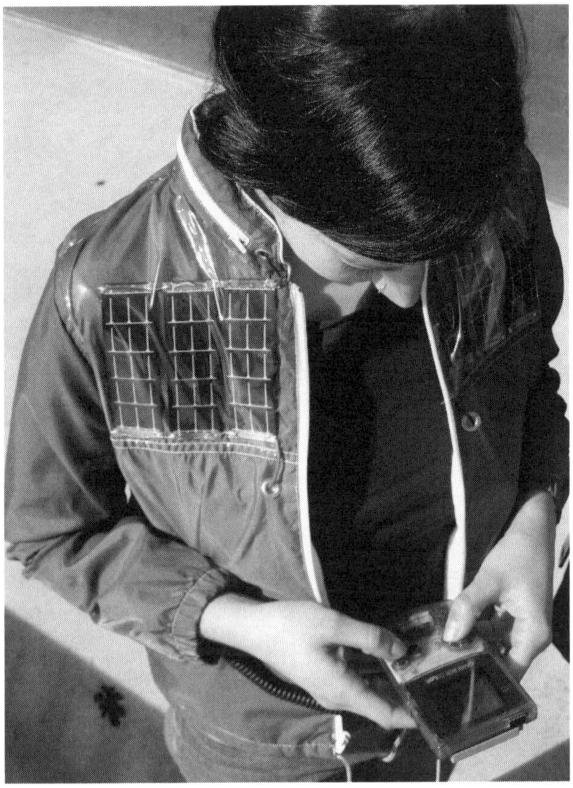

JAM (JANE PALMER & MARIANNE FAIRBANKS), NOON SOLAR, 2004–ongoing, solar panels, rechargeable batteries, copper wire, clear vinyl, and variable fabrics, Gameboy / Solarzellen, wiederaufladbare Batterien, Kupferdraht, transparentes Vinyl und Stoff, Gameboy.

nimmt. Wie Braungart/McDonough und andere deutlich machen,[2] erfordert dies weder eine puritanische Verleugnung der Freuden, die Objekte – etwa Bücher – bereiten, noch ein schmalspuriges Material- und Ästhetikverständnis. Der Designhistoriker Victor Margolin hat Vorstellungen dieser Art unter dem Oberbegriff einer sich herauskristallisierenden «Kultur der Nachhaltigkeit» beschrieben, welche er als zwangsläufige Entwicklung innerhalb des Designs versteht.[3]

Seit einigen Jahren beobachte ich etwas, was man als die Anfänge einer entsprechenden «Kultur der Nachhaltigkeit» im Kreis der Künstlerinnen und Künstler meiner Generation bezeichnen könnte. Diese künstlerische Praxis bildet einen Gegenpol zu etablierteren Formen umweltbewusster Kunst. Ich denke an Projekte wie die von Robert Smithson vorgeschlagenen Eingriffe in Tagebauanlagen aus der ersten Hälfte der 70er Jahre, aber vielleicht noch mehr an Arbeiten der 80er und 90er Jahre, die unter dem Einfluss eines sich neu herausbildenden Verständnisses des Künstlers als interdisziplinärer Forscher parallel zu den neuen Formen einer *new genre public art* (öffentlichen, als Gemeinschaftsprojekte angelegten Aktionen, zum Teil unter Bürgerbeteiligung) aufkamen.[4] Heute gibt es Künstlerinnen und Künstler, die, statt ihre Arbeit an bestimmten von Menschenhand geschaffenen oder natürlichen Orten anzusiedeln oder sich Eingriffe globalen Ausmasses auszumalen, auf einem bescheideneren Niveau mit dem Begriff der «Nachhaltigkeit» spielen. Sie machen kleinere, handlichere Objekte, die zum Teil dieselben ästhetischen Eigenschaften, die *Cradle to Cradle* zu einem derart reizvollen Objekt machen – witziges Design, Hightechmaterialien –, mit einem Sinn dafür vereinen, wie sich Objekte in grössere Zusammenhänge einfügen, was auch, aber nicht nur, die Auswirkung auf die Umwelt mit einschliesst. Sie machen, vielfach in Gemeinschaftsarbeit, Objekte, die, wenn im Kunstrahmen präsentiert, als Denkanstösse fungieren, aber durch den Gebrauch ausserhalb des Museums aktiviert oder zum Leben erweckt werden wollen. Sie durchsetzen ernsthafte soziale Ziele mit einer Prise spielerischer, ausgefallener Phantasie und geben dem Bauhausideal der Einheit von Form und Funktion oder Beuys' Begriff der Sozialen Plastik eine zeitgemässe Wendung. Zu den Kunstwerken, die in dieser Art und Weise funktionieren, zählen die tragbaren PUBLIC THINGS von N55 (seit 1999), die SUPERGAS-Projekte von Superflex (seit 1997), Nils Normans GEOCRUISER (2001), Andrea Zittels *AZ Advanced Technologies* (seit 2002), die aufblasbaren Obdachlosenunterkünfte von Michael Rakowitz (*ParaSITE,* seit 1998) und die aus rezykliertem Plastik hergestellten Skulpturen von Dan Peterman. An einen Trend des nachhaltigen Designs, nämlich die Berücksichtigung dessen, was vor Ort produziert wird, anknüpfend, werde ich mich hier auf einige wenige Beispiele aus meiner eigenen Heimatstadt Chicago konzentrieren.

Unter der Bezeichnung *People Powered* hat der Künstler Kevin Kaempf eine laufende Serie von Projekten entwickelt, die teils auf Grund ihres bescheidenen Rahmens, teils auf Grund der Aneignung einer an Wirtschaftsunternehmen angelehnten Ökomarketingstrategie und einer hippen Ästhetik die soziale Plastik neu beleben. Für sein erstes *People-Powered*-Projekt mit dem Titel SOIL STARTER (seit 2002) gab er Freunden und Bekannten aus seiner Nachbarschaft Anweisungen und eine kleine grüne Biotonne. Er fährt regelmässig mit dem Fahrrad die beteiligten Haushalte ab, um die angesammelten Garten- und Küchenabfälle abzuholen. Diesen potenziellen Müll füllt er daraufhin in «Teebeutel» ab, die, voller kompostierter Stoffe, bei Wässerung Nährstoffe freisetzen (ideal für unterernährte Zimmerpflanzen in der Stadt). Die Teebeutel überlässt er den Beteiligten, womit für sie ein neuer Zyklus von Gebrauch, Zersetzung und Wiederverwendung einsetzt. SOIL STARTER erfüllt mehrere umweltbewusste soziale Funktionen: die Bewusstmachung und Umstellung von Alltagsgewohnheiten in den Reihen der Beteiligten, Müllverringerung durch die Umwandlung von Müll in tatsächliche Nahrung – Nährstoffe – für einen anderen Bedarf, sowie die Bereitstellung einer organischen Alternative zu chemischen Düngemitteln. Auf Grund dieser Funktionalität mag man versucht sein, das Projekt mit anderen Beispielen einer aktivistischen, prozesshaften Kunstpraxis, insbesondere Aktionen in eher begrenztem gesellschaftlichem Rahmen, in einen Topf zu werfen. Manches an Kaempfs Projekt aber macht dieses besonders erfrischend. Erstens spielt sich SOIL STARTER anders als zahlreiche auf Bürgerbeteiligung gestützte Kunstaktionen im Bekanntenkreis von Kaempf ab, also unter seinesgleichen. Die Aussenseiterposition des Brückenschlags über wirtschaftliche und/oder kulturelle Grenzen kann zwar sinnvoll sein, sie birgt aber auch Gefahren – etwa die Falle des ästhetischen Bekehrungseifers, wie Grant Kester es nennt –, und in diesem Fall erscheint es angemessen, dass ein Projekt, welches sich um Nachhaltigkeit dreht, Engagement für die Umwelt in einem verhältnismässig engen gesellschaftlichen Rahmen verankert. Zweitens sei auf die feinsinnige Ästhetik der Teebeutel hingewiesen, insbesondere auf die klaren Linien der Beutel und die eleganten Logos auf den Schildchen. Gehäuft verströmen die SOIL STARTER-Päckchen einen sinnlichen Reiz – sie wirken fast wie postminimalistische, ja an Eva Hesse gemahnende Skulpturen – und jedes durchscheinende quadratische Päckchen trägt das *People-Powered*-Logo mit seinen entschieden schrillen Farben und dem versetzten «P.» Kaempf verwendet dieses Logo bei sämtlichen *People-Powered*-Projekten. Er hat für seine künstlerische Tätigkeit ganz bewusst das Geschäftsmodell eines Kleinunternehmens übernommen und bedient sich einer privatwirtschaftlichen

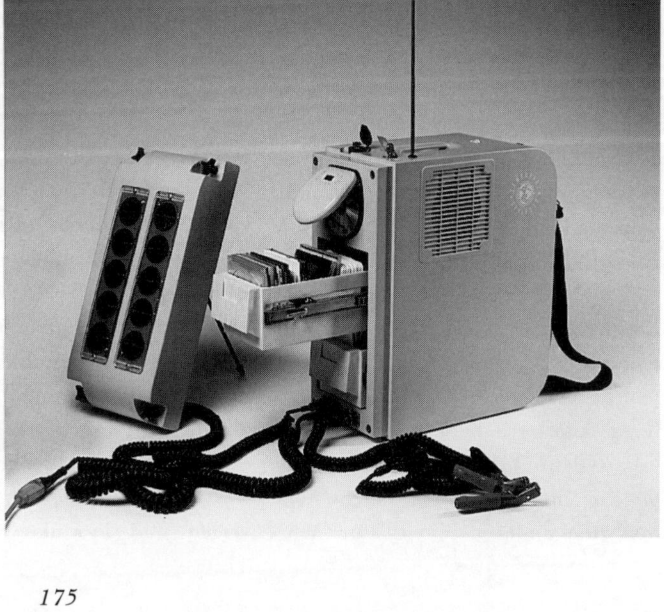

BRENNAN McGAFFEY AND TEMPORARY SERVICES, AUDIO RELAY, 2003, wood, paint, electrical components and cables, CD player, radio transmitter, folding chair, CD trays, and changing collection of audio works. Solar panels power unofficial broadcasts of changing, non-commercial audio exhibitions. / Holz, Farbe, Elektrokomponenten und -kabel, CD-Spieler, Radiosender, Klappstuhl, CD-Schubladen mit wechselnder CD-Sammlung. Solarzellen speisen die inoffizielle Ausstrahlung nicht kommerzieller Radiosendungen. (PHOTO: TOM VAN EYNDE)

Marketingstrategie, um eine weithin bekannte Markenzeichenidentität zu schaffen, die eines Tages, so hofft er, eine grössere Beteiligung an Projekten wie der aktuellen Initiative SHARED: CHICAGO BLUE BIKES (seit 2004) anlocken wird.

Das Künstlerduo JAM (Jane Palmer und Marianne Fairbanks) entwickelt Projekte, bei denen es um ähnlich poetische und praktische Methoden der Verankerung nachhaltiger Gewohnheiten im Alltag geht. Palmer und Fairbanks arbeiten seit 2000 zusammen und im Jahr 2003 starteten sie, zunächst unter dem Titel *Personal Power* (2003–2004; zu Kaempfs Projekt besteht keine Beziehung), eine Projektreihe, in der sich ihre Ausbildung in Faserstofftechnik mit dem Interesse an einer nachhaltigen Alltagspraxis verbindet. Zu dieser Serie gehören unter anderem Prototypen für Kleidungsstücke und Taschen, die mit leichten, biegsamen Sonnenkollektoren ausgestattet sind, die hinreichend Energie für den Betrieb kleiner Elektrogeräte wie Handys sammeln und speichern können. JAM prüft gegenwärtig potenzielle Partnerschaften, die die Integration ihrer Technologie in serienmässig produzierte Haute-Couture-Handtaschen unter dem Namen *Noon Solar* (seit 2004) ermöglichen würden. Wenn also alles gut geht, wird sich über ihr ursprüngliches spekulatives Projekt bald die kommerzielle Dimension von Produktion und Vertrieb stülpen.

Diese Namens- und Kontextänderung macht die Solaraccessoires in meinen Augen interessanter, als wenn JAM besagte Ideen lediglich innerhalb ihres künstlerischen Schaffens verfolgte, denn sie deutet an, wie diese Objekte im Wechsel von einem Kontext zum anderen jeweils eine neue Identität annehmen können. JAMs *Personal Power* entwickelte sich aus einer durch den Krieg im Irak verschärften Sensibilität für die politischen Folgen der Abhängigkeit von Öl und anderen fossilen Brennstoffen heraus, doch Palmer und Fairbanks beschlossen, dass es in einem kommerziellen Rahmen sinnvoll sei, ihr kritisches Bewusstsein zugunsten eines offeneren und zeitgemässer wirkenden Namens zurückzustellen. Dies entspricht dem Charakter der Arbeiten, bei denen es nicht um Verweigerung geht, sondern vielmehr um Befreiung vom Energienetz unter gleichzeitiger Wahrung der Möglichkeit, Verbindung zu Kommunikationsnetzen herzustellen, modisch zu sein oder einfach ein wenig Musik zu hören. Der Name *Noon Solar* kaschiert also bis zu einem gewissen Grad die utopischen Ziele von JAM, und die hippen umwelt- oder trendbewussten Verbraucher, welche die ersten Nutzer der *Noon-Solar*-Produkte sein dürften, werden zu Beteiligten an einem Werk der sozialen Plastik – obwohl das übergreifende Bestreben von JAM, individuelle Solartechnik attraktiv, erschwinglich und einer breiten Käuferschicht zugänglich zu machen, ihnen unter Umständen nicht einmal bewusst ist beziehungsweise sie kalt lässt. Letztlich erhoffen sich die Künstlerinnen, durch Zusammenarbeit mit anderen Designern und Vertreibern «die Technik einer breiten Vielfalt von Märkten und potenziellen Verbrauchern anzubieten. Auf diese Weise lässt sich bewirken, dass es um etwas Praktisches geht, nach dem tatsächlich Bedarf besteht und das nicht mit einer bestimmten Marke oder einem bestimmten Verbrauchertypus verbunden ist.»[5] In der Zwischenzeit wird JAM *Noon Solar* in Ausstellungen zeigen und Produkte in limitierter Auflage herstellen sowie über eine Boutique in Chicago verkaufen.[6]

Ein letztes Beispiel führt entsprechende künstlerische Bemühungen in eine etwas andere Richtung. Das Künstlerkollektiv Temporary Services bat den Künstler Brennan McGaffey einen kleinen tragbaren CD-Spieler zu entwickeln, auf dem sämtliches erforderliche Material für eine «Audio-Ausstellung» Platz hätte. Er entwarf und baute daraufhin AUDIO RELAY (2003) mit dem entscheidenden Zusatz eines Funkgeräts. Im Innern der hellgelben Hochglanztasche, die sich mit einem Tragriemen geschultert tragen lässt, finden sich ein Satz Sonnenkollektoren mit eigenem faltbarem Ständer, eine CD-Ablage, ein CD-Spieler, Lautsprecher, ein Klappstuhl, das Funkgerät sowie alle erforderlichen Verkabelungen. Temporary Services kuratierte daraufhin eine Reihe von Audioarbeiten für AUDIO RELAY, die das Kollektiv als inoffizielle Rundfunksendung in den Chicagoer Äther hinausschickte. Auf ihrer Reise durch verschiedene Städte von Baltimore bis Leipzig änderte sich immer wieder der Sendeinhalt der Arbeit, da diejenigen, die der Arbeit Aufnahme gewähren, aufgefordert sind, für das Projekt neue CDs zu kuratieren und zu sammeln. Die Arbeit greift das Prinzip des Privatmuseums in einer Schachtel auf, das Duchamp mit seiner BOÎTE-EN-VALISE (Schachtel im Koffer, 1941/42) vorexerziert hatte, und gibt ihm eine grosszügige Wendung, indem sie nicht nur andere Künstler, sondern auch eine Zuhörergemeinschaft einbezieht.

Wie bei den Arbeiten von *People Powered* und JAM ist auch McGaffeys Entwurf für AUDIO RELAY funktional, formschön und setzt nachhaltige Technologien ein, aber die umweltschonende Nachhaltigkeit macht nicht den Kern des Werks aus. Sonnenenergie ermöglicht hier einerseits, dass die Arbeit (die auch mit einer Autobatterie betrieben werden kann) auch an entlegeneren Orten funktioniert, steht aber gleichzeitig für ein nomadisches, sich selbst tragendes Prinzip der Produktion und Verbreitung von Kunst. In dieser Hinsicht wie auch durch die Verwendung des Funkgeräts knüpft AUDIO RELAY an McGaffeys *Intermod*-Serie an, eine Erkundung der metaphorischen und realen Einmischung durch zeitlich begrenzte Eingriffe im urbanen Raum.

Diese Arbeiten von *People Powered,* JAM und McGaffey und Temporary Services stützen sich auf globale Trends der zeitgenössischen Kunst und des nachhaltigen Designs, werden gleichzeitig aber erst durch bestimmte lokale Rahmenbedingungen möglich. Obwohl keinerlei Verbindung zu offiziellen Projekten der Stadt Chicago besteht, gibt es unübersehbare Parallelen zu neueren Bemühungen der Stadt, sich durch Aufsehen erregende öffentliche Projekte, wie etwa das neue städtische *Center for Green Technology,* einen grünen Mantel über den breiten Rücken zu streifen. Chicago beherbergt zudem eine wachsende Gemeinde von Architekten, Ingenieuren und Designern, die an grünen und nachhaltigen Lösungen interessiert sind. Noch wichtiger für Künstler wie Kaempf ist jedoch die Entwicklung und das konsequente Festhalten an gesellschaftlich engagierten, kritischen Positionen durch Künstlerinnen und Künstler, die Chicago zu ihrem Arbeitsort gemacht und sich in einigen wichtigen Fällen auch entschlossen haben, die umweltschonende Nachhaltigkeit zu thematisieren und dies dem Publikum nicht nur durch Ausstellungen und Veröffentlichungen nahe zu bringen, sondern auch durch ihre Lehr- und Mentorentätigkeit.

In meiner Eigenschaft als Kuratorin am Smart Museum of Art der University of Chicago beabsichtige ich, diese Kunstrichtung durch Aufträge für neue Projekte und mit der Organisation einer Ausstellung zu fördern. Weil ich mir der umweltbelastenden Exzesse des Ausstellungsdesigns (all die Gipsplatten! all die Farbe!) immer mehr bewusst wurde, werden wir im Rahmen dieses Projekts den Einsatz von nachhaltigem Design nicht nur in der Kunstproduktion selbst, sondern auch in ihrer Präsentation erproben und die praktischen Möglichkeiten einer besseren Nutzung der (finanziellen, ästhetischen, sozialen, individuellen und umweltbezogenen) Reserven prüfen.

(Übersetzung: Bram Opstelten)

1) William McDonough und Michael Braungart, *Cradle to Cradle: Remaking the Way We Make Things,* North Point Press, New York 2002 (dt. *Einfach intelligent produzieren. Cradle to Cradle: Die Natur zeigt, wie wir die Dinge besser machen können,* Berliner Taschenbuch Verlag, Berlin 2003). Zu Fragen der Buchgestaltung, siehe insbesondere die Einführung, «This Book Is Not a Tree», und die ersten Seiten von Kap. 3, «Eco-Effectiveness».

2) Victor Margolin, *The Politics of the Artificial,* University of Chicago Press, Chicago 2002, S. 102.

3) Zum Beispiel: Paul Hawkin, Armory Lovins und L. Hunter Lovins, *Natural Capitalism: Creating the Next Industrial Revolution,* Little, Brown & Co., Boston 1999.

4) Als Beispiele zu nennen wären die Wasserscheidenprojekte von Helen und Newton Harrison (80er und 90er Jahre), Mel Chins *Revival Field* (1990–93), Platforms *Delta* (1993), die Biogas- und Wasserkraftprojekte von Peter Fend und Ocean Earth (90er Jahre bis heute), Buster Simpsons *Growing Vine Street* (1997 bis heute) sowie *Landed: A Project for Elkhorn City* von Suzanne Lacy und Susan Leibovitz Steinman (2001 bis heute). Der Begriff *new genre public art* (neue Formen öffentlicher Kunst) stammt von Suzanne Lacy und ist dem Titel ihres einflussreichen Bandes *Mapping the Terrain: New Genre Public Art* (Bay Press, Seattle 1992) entlehnt.

5) E-Mail von Jane Palmer an die Autorin, 28. Oktober 2004.

6) JAM verkaufte für kurze Zeit exklusive Handtaschen unter dem Markennamen «Helia», der, wie sich herausstellen sollte, bereits für ein anderes Produkt in Gebrauch war.

JAM (JANE PALMER & MARIANNE FAIRBANKS), NOON SOLAR, 2004–ongoing, solar panels, rechargeable batteries, copper wire, clear vinyl, and variable fabrics, MP3 player / Solarzellen, wiederaufladbare Batterien, Kupferdraht, transparentes Vinyl und andere Materialien, MP3-Player.

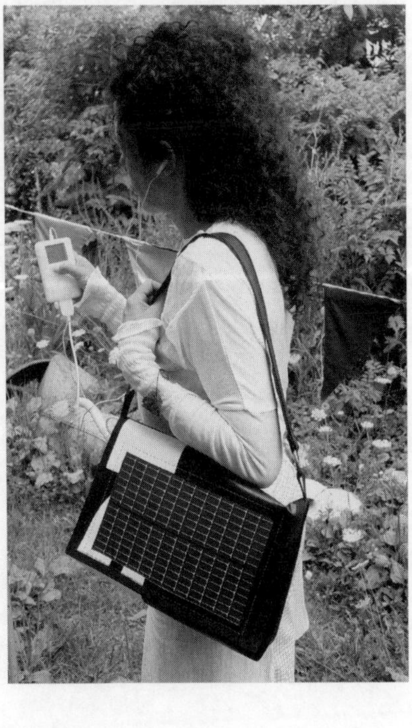

CUMULUS

Aus Europa

IN JEDER AUSGABE VON PARKETT PEILT EINE CUMULUS-WOLKE AUS AMERIKA UND EINE AUS EUROPA DIE INTERESSIERTEN KUNSTFREUNDE AN. SIE TRÄGT PERSÖNLICHE RÜCKBLICKE, BEURTEILUNGEN UND DENKWÜRDIGE BEGEGNUNGEN MIT SICH – ALS JEWEILS GANZ EIGENE DARSTELLUNG EINER BERUFLICHEN AUSEINANDERSETZUNG.

IN DIESEM BAND ÄUSSERN SICH HANS RUDOLF REUST, KURATOR UND DOZENT AN DER HOCHSCHULE DER KÜNSTE BERN, UND STEPHANIE SMITH, KURATORIN AM SMART MUSEUM OF ART DER UNIVERSITY OF CHICAGO.

GLOBAL SCRABBLE

HANS RUDOLF REUST

Die fünfundsechzig Kühe der Familie Gonzalez bewegen sich wie gewohnt auf einer Ranch in Buyeros. Jeder Kuh, ob schwarz oder braun, wurde auf beide Flanken gross ein weisser Buchstabe gemalt, so dass sich durch wechselnde Nachbarschaften in der Herde bewegliche Silben, allenfalls Worte auf Zeit ergeben. Wer die Gewohnheiten der Tiere kennt, könnte Sätze bilden. In trägem Rhythmus lösen sich Sinneinheiten auf und formen sich neue: CATTLE SCRABBLE (REALITY HACKING Nr. 156, 23. Mai 1999). Nicht der reine Zufall, nur codefremde Wesen scrabbeln hier. Erster und privilegierter Leser in der Einöde bleibt der hohe blaue Himmel über New Mexico. Als Dank an die Familie hat Peter Regli auf der Gonzalez-Ranch bei der *Rain Prayer-Butte* eine rote, freistehende Leiter errichtet: eine Lesehilfe und ein markantes Stück Vertikalität in der flachen Graslandschaft (RH Nr. 158, Mai 1999).

Seit 1995 verfolgt Regli seine Strategien des *Reality Hacking*. Dabei bedient er sich der unterschiedlichsten Materialien und Medien. Oft schaffen die Interventionen nur kleinste Abweichungen an der Schwelle zur Wahrnehmbarkeit. Anders als Roman Signer lädt Regli sein Publikum nicht ein und tritt selber kaum je auf. Seine Eingriffe bleiben weitgehend anonym, oft nur für Passantinnen und Passanten unvermittelt und wie beiläufig erkennbar.

Vielleicht wird ein Mann, der vom Rauchen auf dem Balkon zurück ins Zimmer trat, seiner Partnerin erzählt haben, dass er soeben doch etwas Sonderbares gesehen habe: einen Zug, den legendären Roten Pfeil, der leer und grellgrün erleuchtet am Haus vorbei durch die Nacht gefahren sei (RH Nr. 195, 24. August 2002, 20:12 – 23:45). Dieses kleine, unmerkliche Staunen mag auch jene Menschen bewegt haben, die zwischen dem 26. November und dem 16.

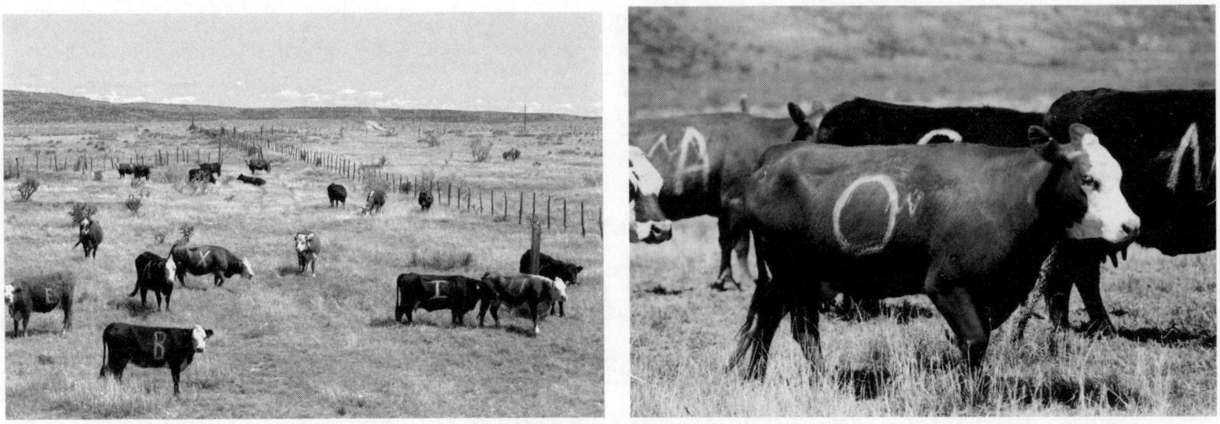

PETER REGLI, REALITY HACKING No. 156, Buyeros, New Mexico, USA, 1999.

Dezember 1999 (RH Nr. 172) eine der fünfhundert Uhren gesehen haben, die an verschiedenen Stellen in Manhattan verteilt, auf Lokalzeit eingestellt und sich selbst überlassen wurden. Uhren, die mit der Zeit die Zeit verloren; ähnlich jenen zwei Schweizer Bahnhofsuhren, die in der Ausstellung «Tempo» im MoMA Queens spiegelbildlich in entgegensetzter Richtung liefen und den Lauf der Zeit fortwährend zu Null addierten. (RH Nr. 147, 2002).

REALITY HACKING Nr. 177 (Erlenbach am Zürichsee, 18. Mai 2000): Eine Privatparty am See. Es wird Nacht. Auf einmal, völlig unerwartet, taucht aus der Finsternis ein Verkehrsschiff auf und wirft mit einem Schlag sämtliche Lichter an. Nukleargrün erstrahlend, zieht es zwei enge Kreise und eine Acht, fährt auf das Haus zu, hält zwanzig Meter vor dem Ufer, grüsst mit Signal- und Nebelhorn. Ebenso plötzlich erlöschen die Lichter wieder. Nur das Rauschen und das leise Brummen des Motors sind zu hören, während das Schiff in der Dunkelheit verschwindet. Eine Erscheinung? Ein Mirakel? Das plötzliche Geschehen ist real und unfassbar zugleich. Auch dies ist ein Moment von *Reality Hacking:* Der untrügliche Auftritt des Gewöhnlichsten, das für Augenblicke zum Wunder wird. Reales «hackt» den Zauber und kriegt etwas von ihm ab.

Bei jeder Arbeit geht Peter Regli vom genauen Studium einer bestimmten Situation aus, ohne schliesslich in einem strengen Sinn ortsspezifisch zu werden. Viele Vorkommnisse oder Einfügungen könnten sich auch an anderer Stelle ereignen – jedenfalls bleibt stets offen, ob sie es nicht unbemerkt tun. Erst ein Überblick über die inzwischen mehr als zweihundert Ereignisse und Projekte von Peter Regli zeigt, dass sich einzelne Elemente wiederholen: die Farbe Rot, Licht, Uhren, gefundene Objekte, Steine, Gletscher, Glas – Sprache. In jüngster Zeit hat Regli auch mehrfach mit Musikern zusammengearbeitet:

REALITY HACKING Nr. 212 (12. August 2004): Zur Eröffnung des 25. Zürcher Theaterspektakels spricht der Verkehrsminister auf der kleinen Bühne am See knapp und in feinsten Anspielungen über das Theaterspektakel als durchaus würdigen Anlass für einen Politiker, während hinter dem Redner lautlos sieben Passagierschiffe in Position fahren. Auftritt der Musiker des Ensembles für Neue Musik Zürich. In Winddrift und Regen folgt das kurze Konzert mit Kammerensemble, Schiffssirenen und Nebelhörnern. Ein Moment der Stille vor dem Applaus, unter dem sich die Schiffe in verschiedene Richtungen wieder über den See verziehen.

Diesem Live-Act steht das virtuelle Ereignis zum grossen Festakt anlässlich von «125 Jahre Kunstmuseum Bern» gegenüber (RH Nr. 226, Bern, 27. August 2004): drei Reden und zwei musikalische Zwischenspiele im übervollen Seitenlichtsaal. Dann «Apéro und sommerliches Festbuffet». Auf der anderen Seite der Strasse gleichzeitig der leere, nur für eine Kamera ausgeleuchtete Festsaal für die virtuelle Feier, da, wo einmal die lang umstrittene Abteilung für Gegenwartskunst einziehen soll. Ganz ohne Publikum spielt das Ensemble für Neue Musik Zürich eine «gehackte» Passage aus der *Lustigen Witwe,* schleust eigene Töne ein, küsst seine Instrumente, wirft sie weg. Zum Fest-programm für das grosse Publikum am kommenden Tag entsteht über Nacht eine DVD mit den alten Reden und den neuen Interludes. Reglis virtueller «live act» ist eine Geburtstagsüberraschung der Hochschule der Künste Bern für das Kunstmuseum.

Meistens jedoch befragt Regli den Rahmen der Kunst ausserhalb der Museen und Galerien, aber auch jenseits der bekannten Parameter von Kunst im öffentlichen Raum. Er hält seine Person zurück, um die Codes der Kunst nicht vorschnell einzuführen und die verschiedensten Assoziationsfelder gleichzeitig offen zu halten. Wie ein Hacker ins Netz, bricht Regli an ausgewählten Stellen in reale Systeme ein, um mit leiseren oder härteren Eingriffen die Wahrnehmungsgrenze auszuloten, jene Differenz, die Kunst in den Alltagskontext einführt. Durch ästhetische Differenzen in wirklichen Situationen wird die Kritik am «Betriebssystem Kunst», wie sie vom Readymade an den Institutionen geübt wurde, unmittelbar in einen breiteren politischen Rahmen zurückgeführt. Wo beginnt in einem durch verschiedenste Deutungsmuster besetzten öffentlichen Raum die Sichtbarkeit, wo die Unverwechselbarkeit von Kunst? Wenn die primären Indikatoren von Sockel, Rahmen, Beschriftung und Autorschaft entfallen, führt die Reflexion auf das Subjekt der Wahrnehmung zurück. Die *Miranda-Rights* umfassen jene sechs Bestimmungen, über die jeder US-Bürger bei seiner Festnahme aufgeklärt werden muss: *«1. You have the right to remain silent and refuse to answer questions. (...)»* Diese sechs Sätze sollten in TRUCKING FOR CIVIL RIGHTS (RH Nr. 168, Oktober 1998, pendentes Projekt) einzeln auf Planen von Trucks durch das Land fahren.

Klar verortet besteht Reglis Werk zugleich nur in einem imaginären Archiv von Spuren, welches weltweit über das Netz abrufbar ist unter www.realityhacking.com. Von allen Interventionen bleibt letztlich der Eintrag in einer im Labyrinth des Web kursierenden Datei. CATTLE-SCRABBLE ist eine Form des Schweigens in Buchstaben. Regli untersucht die Grenze zur Wahrnehmbarkeit, den Radius von Bedeutung in minuziös recherchierten Situationen an unterschiedlichsten Stellen der Welt. Er hackt die Mikrocodes im Alltag und verweist damit auch auf die Sprachlosigkeit zwischen den Kulturen und innerhalb politischer Machtstrukturen. Ein aktuelles Beispiel solchen Schweigens im globalen Austausch bietet die Biennale in São Paulo:

Bekanntlich hat São Paulo schon lange vor Venedig und Kassel Kunst aus allen Gegenden der Welt, vor allem auch aus der sogenannten Dritten Welt unter einem Dach versammelt. Das Interesse an dieser Ausstellung ist unter den Kunstinteressierten Europas und der USA heute entsprechend gross. Schliesslich begleitet die Rede von der Globalisierung inzwischen die alte Suche nach frischen Impulsen für das westliche Kunstsystem, das den globalisierten Markt regelt.

(...) Ein Markt ist, wo Samarkand Johannesburg / heimsucht und, wenn die Läden schliessen, / ohne Bedauern und spurlos wieder verschwindet / bis zur nächsten Reinkarnation. Ein Markt ist, / wo Londons Portobello wie Caracas und Yoruba, / Katalane und Chorasan buchstabiert wird, / und obwohl hier harte Währung von Hand zu Hand geht, / treibt er dich in Strömungskanäle, wo / Sinneswahrnehmungen im Tauschgeschäft florieren. (...)

– Wole Soyinka [1)]

PETER REGLI, REALITY HACKING No. 172, 500 wall clocks for New York City, USA, 1999 / 500 Wanduhren für New York.

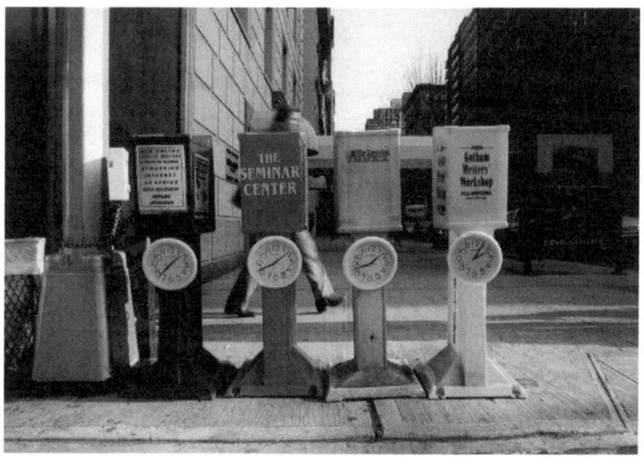

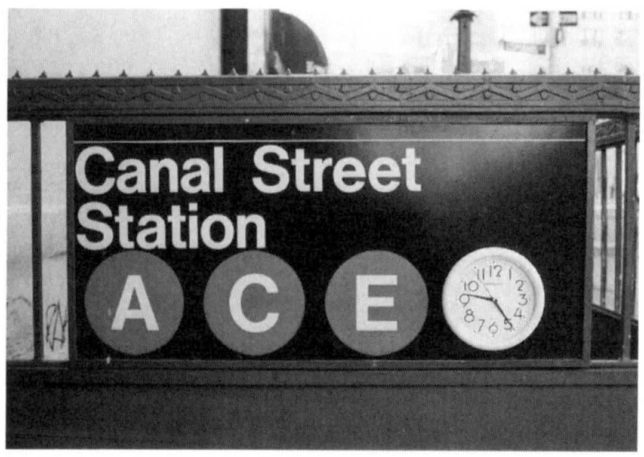

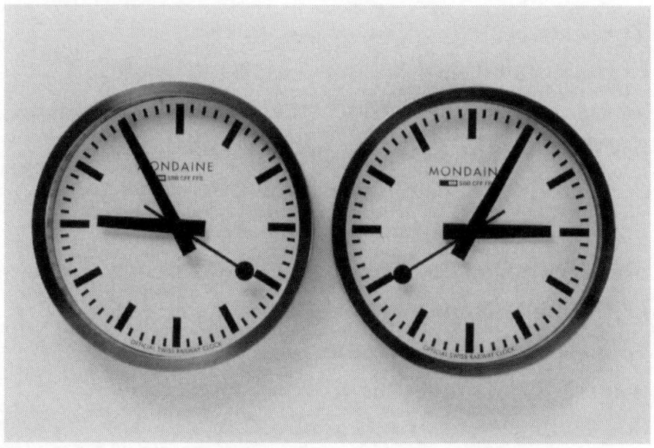

PETER REGLI, REALITY HACKING No. 147 A,
MoMA Queens, USA, 2002.

Dass die einzelnen, klar umrissenen Positionen in Oscar Niemeyers ausserordentlichem Bau grosszügig und doch in Sichtweite zueinander präsentiert sind, bedeutet nicht, dass sie auch untereinander in einen Dialog treten. Den verhindert nicht nur die schlicht nach Medien segmentierte Ausstellungsdramaturgie – die Halle für raumgreifende Installationen, ein Multiplex für Projektionen und Tageslichträume für Bilder und Objekte. Der globale Diskurs findet grundsätzlich über, nicht zwischen Kunst statt. Die gleichzeitige Anwesenheit von Werken verschiedenster Herkunft ist ebenso wenig ein Moment der Auseinandersetzung, wie die Anwesenheit von Entscheidungsträgern bei der Eröffnung ein Dialog ist. Die Zeit zwischen Ankunft und Weiterflug ist streng bemessen, der Diskurs mag sich fortsetzen in Pittsburgh oder an der Messe in London. Im Langhaus dehnt sich derweilen die Sprachlosigkeit zwischen den Kunstwerken aus.

Dabei will die aktuelle Biennale explizit auf Ästhetik vertrauen, sich nicht der Soziologisierung unterwerfen und die Kunst gegenüber den ökonomischen und politischen Fakten wieder zum «herrschaftsfreien Raum» erklären: *Das Niemandsland der Ästhetik beginnt dort, wo die gewöhnliche Welt aufhört. Es bezeichnet jenen Raum, in dem Wirklichkeit und Imagination miteinander im Widerstreit liegen. Künstler sind Grenzwächter eines Reichs, das jenseits der verwalteten Welt liegt und wo die Deutungshoheit von Politik und Wirtschaft nicht mehr hinreicht. Kunst ist das eigentliche, klassische «Movimento sem Terra». Während alle Welt sich ständig über die Frage streitet, wem was gehört, klärt die Kunst die Besitzverhältnisse auf ihre Weise: Im Reich der Ästhetik gehört allen alles.*

(...) Da Kunstwerke mehr sind als blosse Fakten, wird eine künstlerische Verdichtung von Phänomenen der Realität immer mehrdeutiger und komplexer sein als simple Reportage.[2)]

Dass in der Kunst «allen alles gehört», bleibt eine jener «kontrafaktischen Annahmen», auf die schon Jürgen Habermas seinen herrschaftsfreien Diskurs gegründet hat. Der kürzlich erschienene Atlas der Globalisierung von *Le Monde diplomatique* beschreibt dagegen mit seinen Karten, Diagrammen und sachlich knappen Kommentaren einen weltpolitischen Zustand, dem sich die «Grenzwächter» der Ästhetik auch mit Imagination nicht entziehen können.

Globale Ängste stören selbst die Wahrnehmung der Lokaltradition. Wie brüchig der interkulturelle Diskurs ist, hat eine kleine Intervention in der Schweiz gezeigt, REALITY HACKING Nr. 197 (10.–15.9.02): Am Kirchturm in Willisau werden in den vier Himmelsrichtungen vier Stadionlautsprecher angebracht, aus denen bei Sonnenuntergang der traditionelle Betruf erklingt. Die Installation wurde nach vier Tagen ohne Wissen des Künstlers gestoppt, weil der Ruf heftige Reaktionen auslöste. Im aktuellen Klima der Islamangst, hält man den Hirtenruf aus den Innerschweizer Bergen für den Ruf eines Muezzin. Der Kunst bleibt eine geschärfte Bezeichnung von Differenzen. Reglis Begleitprojekt zur Biennale in Havanna 2003 (RH Nr. 208) weist durch die Poesie nächtlicher Lichter die ökonomische Differenz auf: Fünfzig der zahllosen *Bicitaxis* in der Stadt versieht er an den Heckrädern mit zwei Signallampen, die zumindest für eine Nacht wirbelnd durch die Stadt leuchten, bis sie in privaten Besitz übergehen und vermutlich einer anderen Verwendung zugeführt werden.

1) Aus dem Gedicht «Samarkand und andere Märkte», im gleichnamigen, englisch-deutschen Gedichtband von Wole Soyinka, Ammann Verlag, Zürich 2004, S. 91.

2) Chefkurator Alfons Hug, «Bilderschmuggler im Niemandsland der Kunst», in der Presseinformation zur 26. Biennale von São Paulo, Juli 2004.

GLOBAL SCRABBLE

HANS RUDOLF REUST

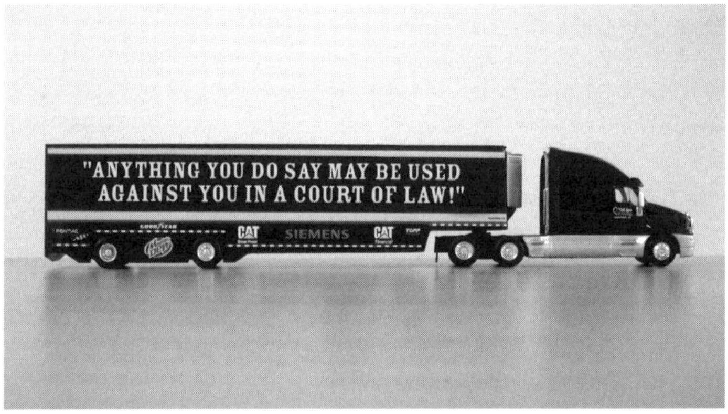

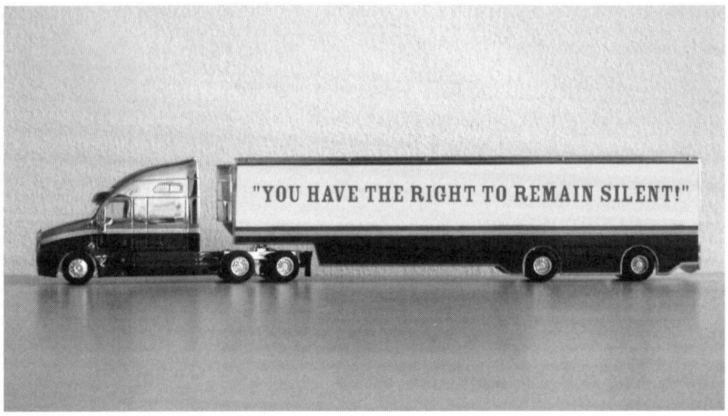

PETER REGLI, REALITY HACKING No. 168, TRUCKING FOR CIVIL RIGHTS, USA, 1998 (project pending/hängiges Projekt).

The sixty-five cows that belong to the Gonzalez family are grazing as usual on a ranch in Buyeros. A large white letter has been painted on both flanks of each cow, whether black or brown, so that moveable syllables, and even words, emerge and dissolve as positions in the herd change. If one knew the animals' habits, one could form sentences. To a languorous rhythm, units of meaning dissolve and re-form: CATTLE SCRABBLE (REALITY HACKING No. 156, 23 May 1999). In this case, it is not pure chance but only creatures foreign to the code that dictate the scrabbling. The first and privileged readers, in their solitude, are left with the blue skies high above New Mexico. In gratitude to the family, Peter Regli has put up a red, free-standing ladder on the Gonzalez Ranch near Rain Prayer Butte: a reading aid and a distinctively vertical accent on the flat grazing lands (RH No. 158, May 1999).

Since 1995, Regli has pursued his strategies of reality hacking, exploiting a diversity of materials and media. His interventions often create miniscule deviations on the threshold of perception. Unlike Roman Signer, Regli never invites his audience and rarely appears in his work himself. What he does remains largely anonymous, perceived unexpectedly and almost casually by people in passing. A man, who has walked back into the room after smoking a cigarette on the balcony, might tell his partner that he has just seen something peculiar: a train, the legendary Red Arrow, slipping through the night, empty and glowing green (REALITY HACKING No. 195, 24 August 2002, 8:12–11:45 pm). A slight, barely perceptible astonishment may also have affected those who saw one of the five hundred clocks scattered through-

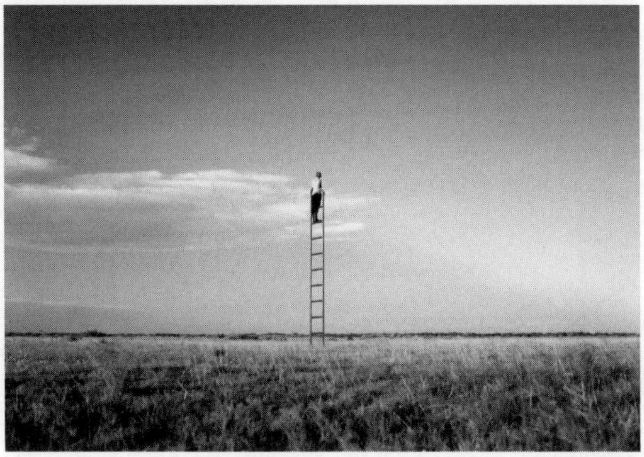

PETER REGLI, REALITY HACKING No. 158, Buyeros, New Mexico, USA, 1999.

out Manhattan between 26 November and 16 December 1999 (RH No. 172), set to the local time and abandoned: clocks, which, in time, lost time, like the two Swiss railroad clocks at the MoMA Queens "Tempo" exhibition. They both started out reading the same time, but ran in opposite directions so that the course of time consistently added up to zero (RH No. 147, 2002).

RH No. 177 (Erlenbach am Zürichsee, 18 May 2000): a private party at the lake. Night is falling. Without warning, a commercial steamer looms up out of the darkness and suddenly turns on all of its lights at once. Radiating a nuclear green, it sails two tight circles and a figure eight, bears down on the house, stops twenty meters from the shore, and blasts a greeting with its signal and foghorn. Just as suddenly, all the lights go out again. Only the swishing water and soft humming of the engine can be heard as the ship vanishes into the darkness. A vision? A miracle? Its sudden appearance is both real and incomprehensible at once. This, too, is an exercise in reality hacking: the unmistakable appearance of something utterly ordinary that has, for a brief moment in time, turned into a miracle. Reality "hacks" the magic and gets a share of it.

In every project, Peter Regli begins with careful study of a specific situation but without becoming strictly site specific. Many of the artist's events or interventions could take place elsewhere—but wherever they are, one can never be quite sure whether they have been noticed. Only by looking back at the over two-hundred pieces and projects organized so far, does one realize that certain elements repeat themselves: the color red, light, clocks, found objects, stones, glaciers, glass—and language.

Recently, Regli has begun working with musicians, as in RH No 212, 12 August 2004. For the opening of the 25th Zürich Theater Spectacle, the Swiss Transportation Minister stood on a small stage at the lake, speaking briefly and with great delicacy about the value of the Theater Spectacle for politicians, while seven passenger boats silently sailed into position behind him. Performance: the musicians of the "ensemble for new music zürich." The chamber ensemble, the ship's sirens, and its foghorns presented their brief concert in driving wind and rain. A moment of silence preceded the applause while the ships slipped away across the lake in different directions.

This live act stands in contrast to the virtual event ancillary to the solemn ceremony celebrating "125 Years Kunstmuseum Bern" (RH No. 226, Bern, 27 August 2004): three speakers and two musical interludes in the overcrowded side gallery. Then: "Reception and Summer Buffet." Simultaneously, on the other side of the street, the virtual celebration for only one camera in the brightly illuminated, empty gallery, where the long-controversial department of contemporary art is meant to be housed some day. Entirely without an audience, the "ensemble for new music zürich" played a "hacked" passage from the *Merry Widow,* smuggling in a few notes, kissing their instruments, and throwing them away. Overnight and in time for the large public ceremony on the following day, a DVD was created with the old speeches and the new musical interludes. Regli's live act is Bern University of Art's surprise birthday present to the Bern Museum of Art.

Regli examines the framework of art not only outside museums and galleries but also beyond the familiar parameters of art in public spaces. He himself remains anonymous to avoid preempting the codes of art and prejudicing the viewer's associative potential. Like a hacker on the Net, Regli's subtle or in-your-face interventions break into real systems at selected spots in order to probe the limits of perception or the difference that art makes in the context of everyday life. Readymades once targeted institutions but Regli's enactment of aesthetic dif-

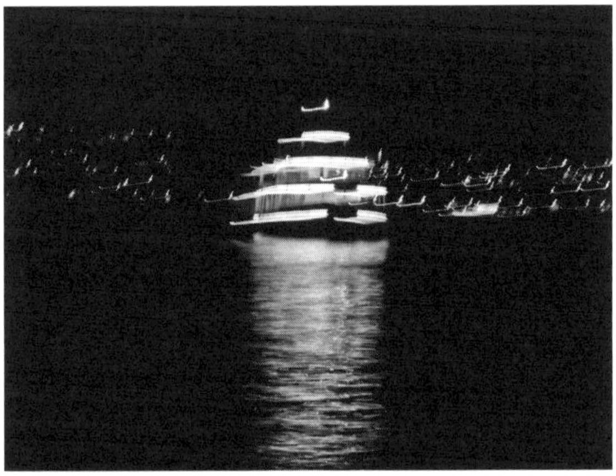

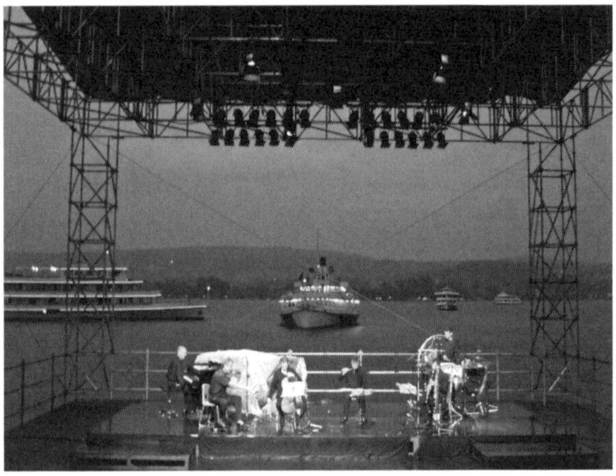

PETER REGLI, REALITY HACKING No. 177, GHOST SHIP, Lake Zurich, Switzerland, 2000.

ference in real situations thrusts the critique of the "operating system of art" directly into the broader political framework. In public space, which is subject to so many different interpretive patterns, where does visibility begin and where the inimitability of art? Without the primary indicators of base, frame, label, and authorship, reflection is thrown back on the subject of perception. The *Miranda Rights* comprise the six rights about which every US citizen must be advised upon arrest. The first one reads "You have the right to remain silent and refuse to answer questions." The project titled TRUCKING FOR CIVIL RIGHTS (RH No. 168, October 1998, project pending) calls for trucks that would drive around the country with one of the six rights painted on their sides.

There is only one place in which Regli's work can be specifically located: in an imaginary archive of traces accessible worldwide at www.realityhacking.com. Ultimately, all that is left of each project is its existence as a document circulating in the labyrinth of the Web. CATTLE SCRABBLE is a form of silence in letters. Regli examines the limits of perception—the radius of meaning—in meticulously researched situations in various places throughout the world. He hacks the microcodes of everyday life and draws attention to the speechlessness that prevails between

cultures and political power structures. The current São Paulo Biennial tellingly illustrates such silence in the context of global exchange.

Long before Venice and Kassel, São Paulo brought together art from all regions of the world, especially from the so-called Third World, so it is only natural that interest in this exhibition, particularly among art professionals in Europe and the United States, is substantial. The ongoing quest for impulses that will revitalize the art system of the West, which regulates the global market, has, of course, now joined forces with the discourse on globalization.

A market is where Samarkand invades / Johannesburg, and, as the shutters close,/ Departs without regrets or trace / Until its next reincarnation. A market is / Where London's Portobello spells / Caracas and Yoruba, Catalan or Khourassan, / And though hard currency is what changes hands, / It lets you drift in fluid channels where / Sensations thrive on trade by barter.
– Wole Soyinka [1]

The fact that the single, clearly outlined elements in Oscar Niemeyer's extraordinary Biennial Foundation building are expansive and yet still within sight of each other, does not mean that they also enter into a mutual dialogue. And dialogue is obstructed not only by the straightforward segmentation of the exhibition according to medium—the large gallery for installations, a multiplex for projections, and daylight spaces for pictures and objects. Essentially, the global discourse takes place not between but rather about artistic agendas and the art that results. The simultaneous presence of works from many different cultures does not lead to fruitful exchange, just as the presence of decision makers at the opening does not lead to dialogue. The time between arrival and onward flight is tightly scheduled; the discourse will continue in Pittsburgh or at a fair in London. In the meantime, in the long-house, speechlessness spreads among the works of art.

The current São Paulo Biennial explicitly intends to foreground aesthetics, to avoid a sociological bias, and to provide a "power-free zone" where art is not subject to economic and political strategies:

The no-man's-land of aesthetics begins where the normal world ends. It describes the space in which reality and imagination are in conflict with each another. Artists are the border guards of a realm that lies beyond the administered world, where politics and economics have no more jurisdiction over interpretation. While the whole world is constantly arguing about what belongs to whom, art clarifies the ownership issue in its own way: in the realm of aesthetics everything belongs to everyone.

(...) Since works of art are more than bare facts, an artistic condensing of the phenomena of reality will always be more ambiguous and more complex than simple reporting.[2)]

The idea that "everything belongs to everyone" is not new; it is one of those "counterfactual assumptions," on which Jürgen Habermas based his power-free discourse. In contrast, maps, diagrams, and brief, objective commentaries in the *Atlas of Globalization,* recently published by *Le Monde diplomatique,* describe a world which the "border guards" of aesthetics can not ignore, not even by any stretch of the imagination.

Global anxieties even intrude on the perception of local traditions. The following project illustrates just how fragile intercultural discourse is. RH No. 197 (10–15 Sept. 2002): four stadium loudspeakers were mounted in four directions on the steeple of the church in Willisau. At sunset, they broadcast the traditional Alpine blessing. The authorities terminated the project after four days without advising the artist because the broadcast message met with great opposition. In the current climate of fear, the shepherd's call, still heard on rare occasions among Alpine farmers in Central Switzerland, was thought to be a Muezzin's call to prayer. All art can do is offer a heightened designation of difference. In the poetry of nocturnal illumination that marks Regli's ancillary project at the Havana Biennial 2003 (RH No. 208), the designation of difference is economic: he mounted two signal lamps on the rear wheels of fifty of the countless *Bicitaxis* in the city so that they were seen twirling through the darkness, at least for the duration of one night, until they were transferred to private ownership and presumably used for another purpose.

(Translation: Catherine Schelbert)

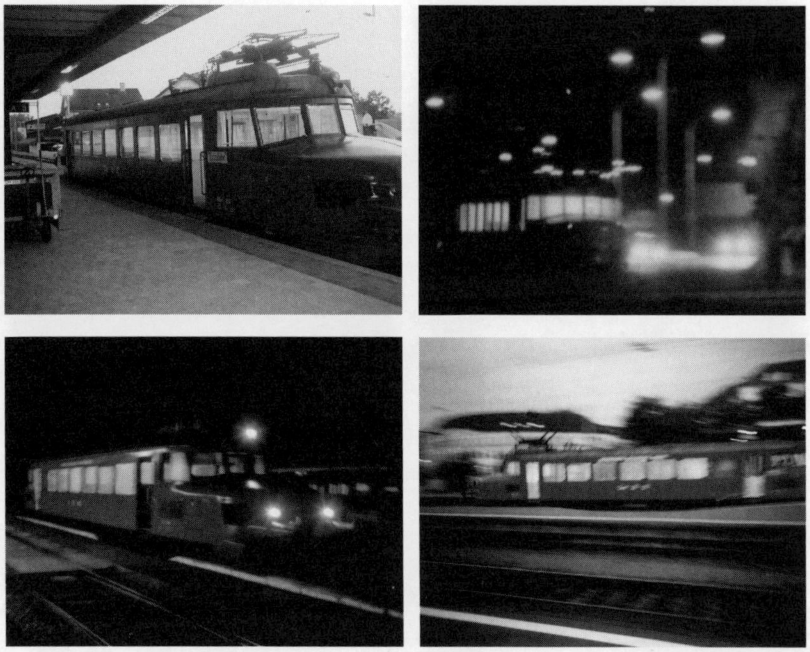

PETER REGLI, REALITY HACKING No. 195, RUNAWAY TRAIN ACROSS SWITZERLAND, 2002.

1) From the poem "Samarkand and Other Markets" in: Wole Soyinka, *Samarkand and Other Markets I Have Known* (London, Methuen, 2002), p. 49.

2) Chief curator Alfons Hug, "Território Livre," press information, 26th São Paulo Biennial, July 2004.

20 YEARS OF PARKETT – KUNSTHAUS ZÜRICH

EXHIBITION 26 NOV. – 13 FEB. 2005, OPENING NIGHT

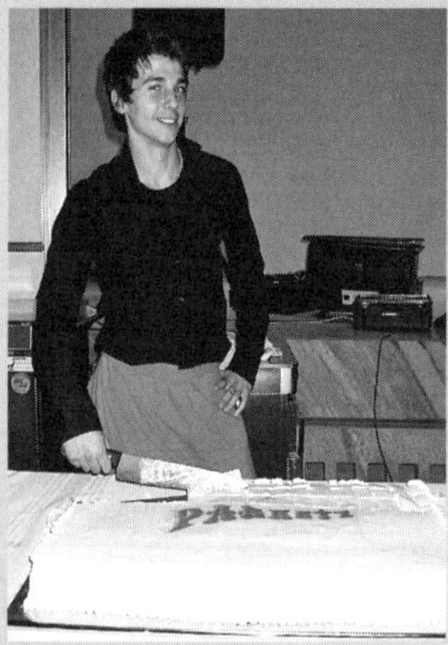

The Birthday Cake / Die Geburtstagstorte.

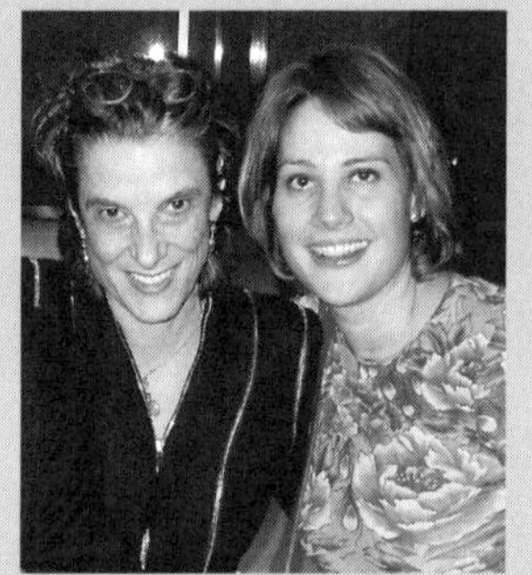

Jacqueline Burckhardt mit Kuratorin / with Kunsthaus curator Mirjam Varadinis.

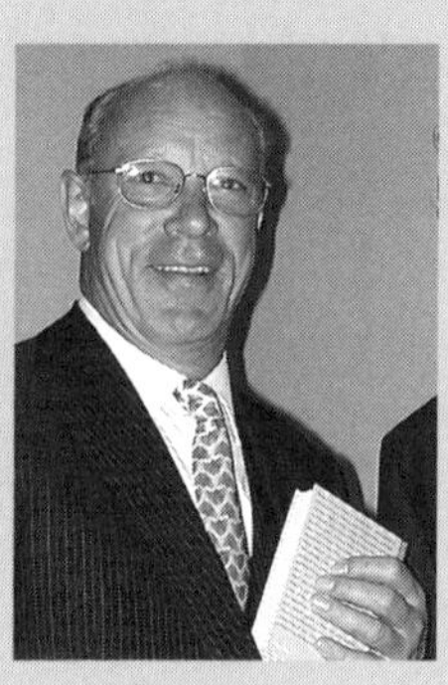

Franz Wassmer, collector & patron / Sammler & Mäzen.

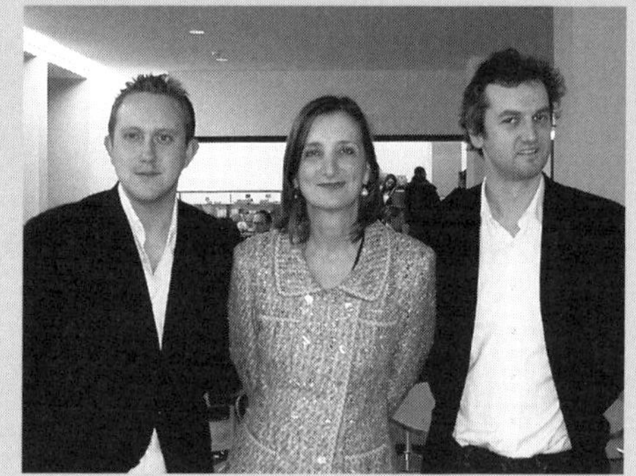

Simon Grant, editor of "Tate Etc.," Bice Curiger, and Matt Watkins, publisher of "Tate Etc."

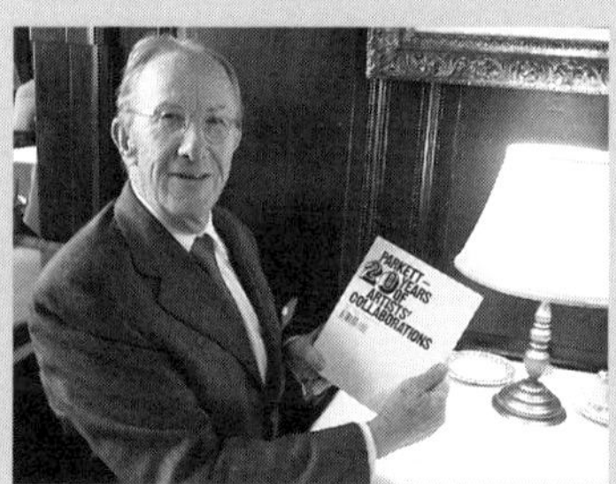

Beat Curti, collector, with hot-off-the-press catalogue at Restaurant Kronenhalle, Zurich / Sammler, mit druckfrischem Katalog.

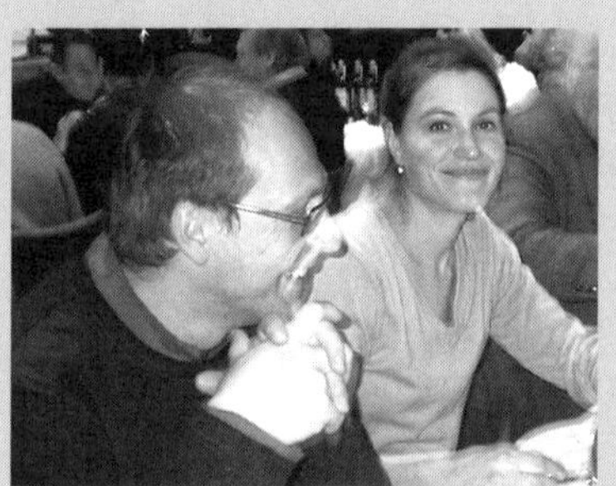

Mathias Arnold (Parkett subscriptions) and Alice Cantaluppi (assistant editions).

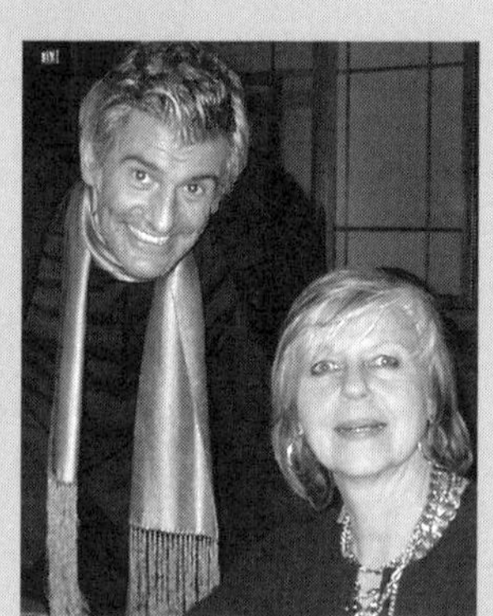

Alfredo Häberli, designer of the Zurich exhibition, and Trix Wetter, Parkett's founding designer.

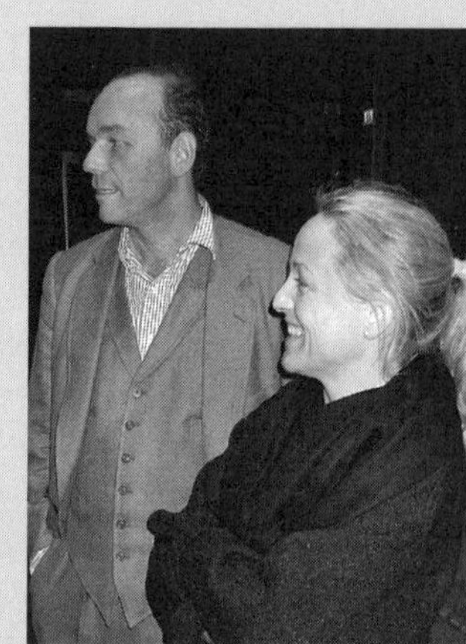

Publisher Dieter von Graffenried and his wife, art dealer Carolina Nitsch.

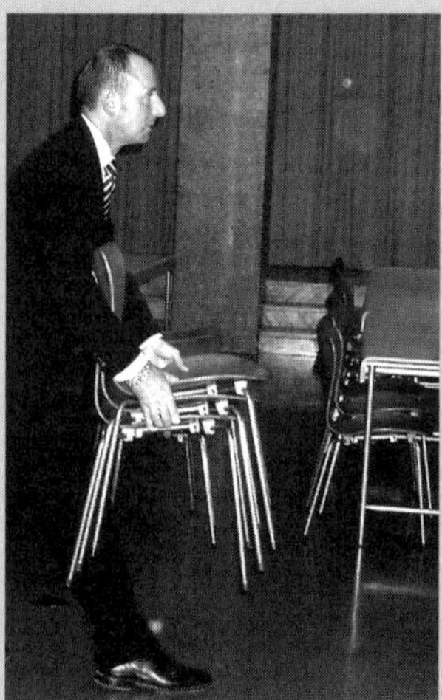

Kunsthausdirektor Christoph Becker legt nach der Eröffnungsrede bei der Festbestuhlung Hand an. / Christoph Becker, director of the Kunsthaus, lending a hand with the dinner seating.

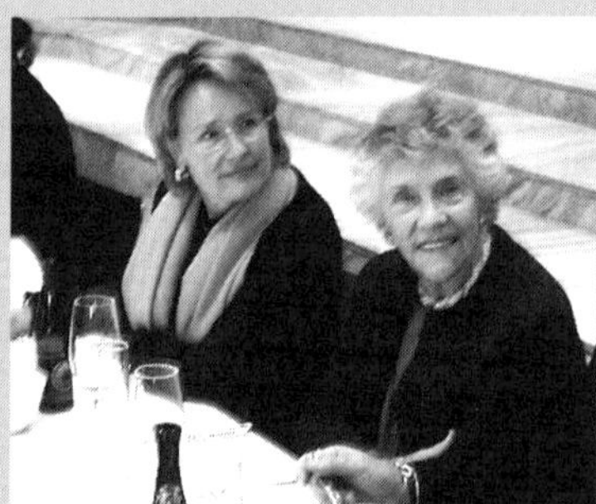

Eleonore & Marlies von Graffenried.

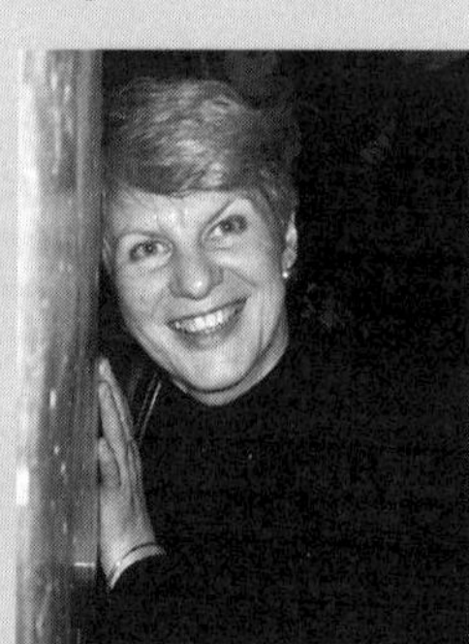

Beatrice Fässler, responsible for Parkett's editions since 1994.

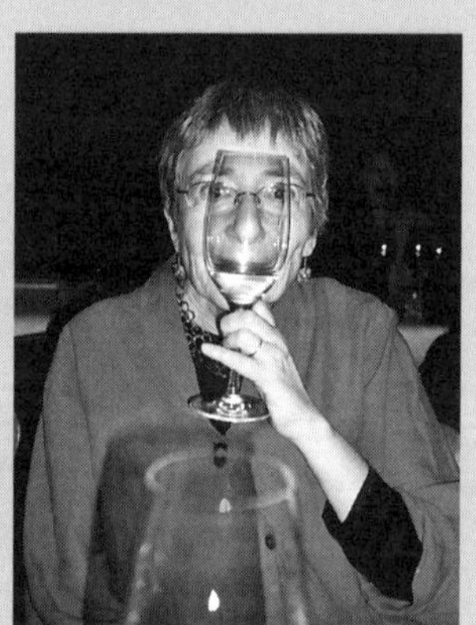

Catherine Schelbert, English translator & editorial allrounder with Parkett since No. 1.

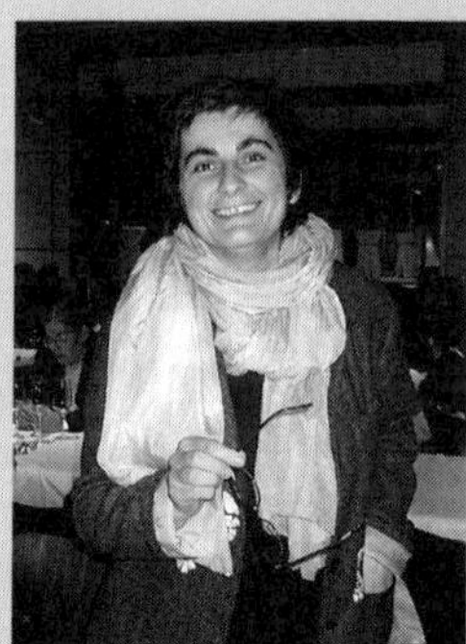

Marica Gojevic, assistant editions.

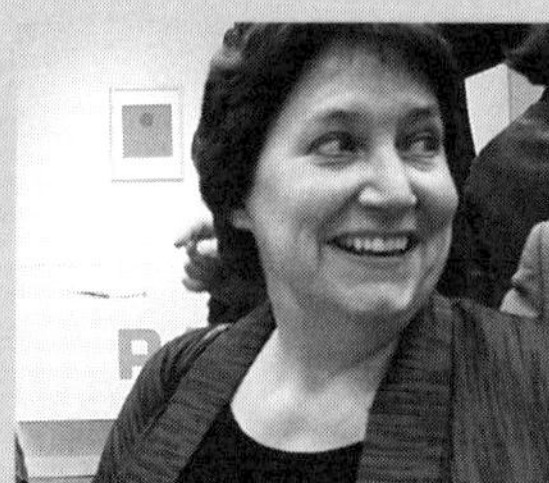

Suzanne Schmidt, Parkett editor & production manager since 1994.

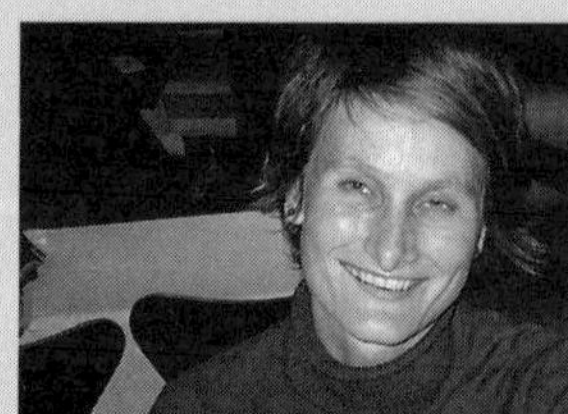

Nicole Stotzer, Parkett administration & distribution.

PHOTO: K. F. PICKERT)

Garderobe

'gär-ˌdrōb

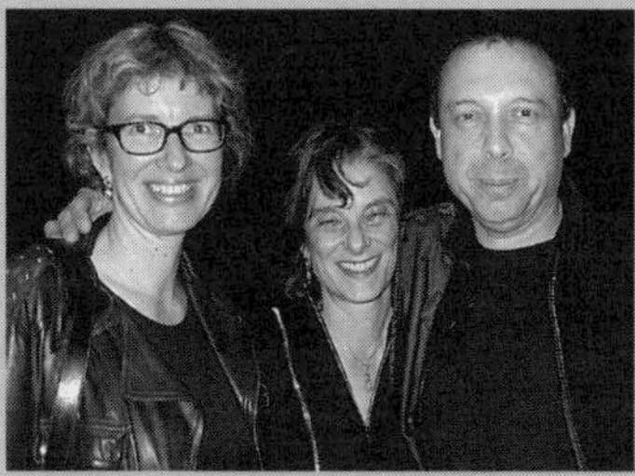

Photographers Franziska Bodmer & Bruno Mancia with Parkett co-founder Jacqueline Burckhardt.

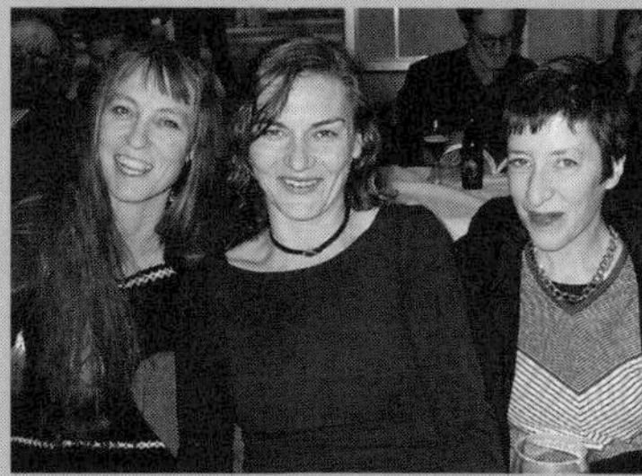

Parkett designers Simone Eggstein & Hanna Koller, artist Bessie Nager.

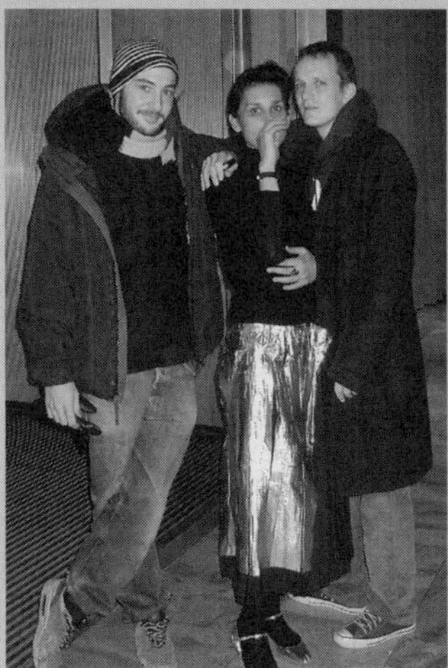

Louise Neri, Parkett's former N.Y. editor, with Laurenz Brunner & Cornel Windlin, designers of "Tate Etc."

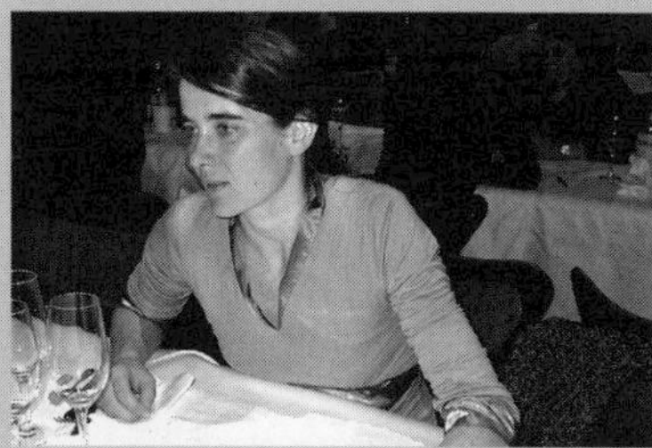

Katja Schenker, artist and responsible for Parkett's web index.

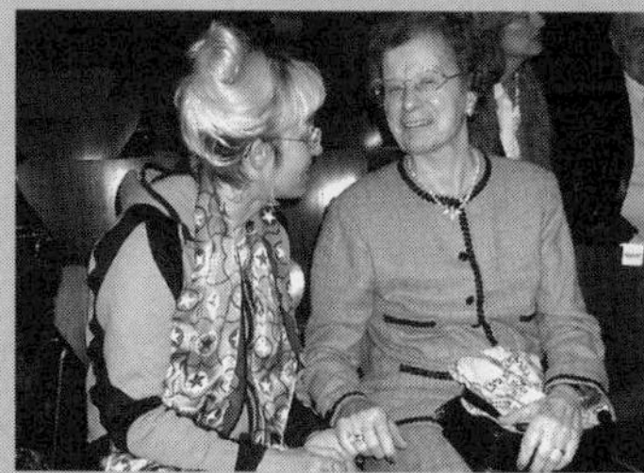

Pipilotti Rist & Livia Curiger, Stickerin des Parkett-Logos / maker of Parkett's embroidered logo.

(PHOTOS: JAKOBETT)

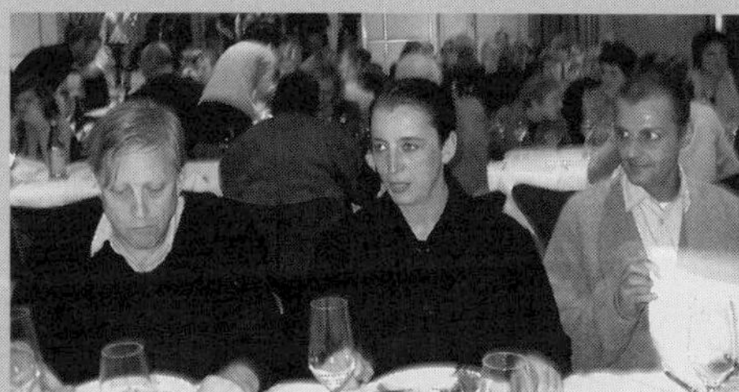

Artist David Weiss, Beatrix Ruf, director of the Kunsthalle Zürich, and artist Ugo Rondinone.

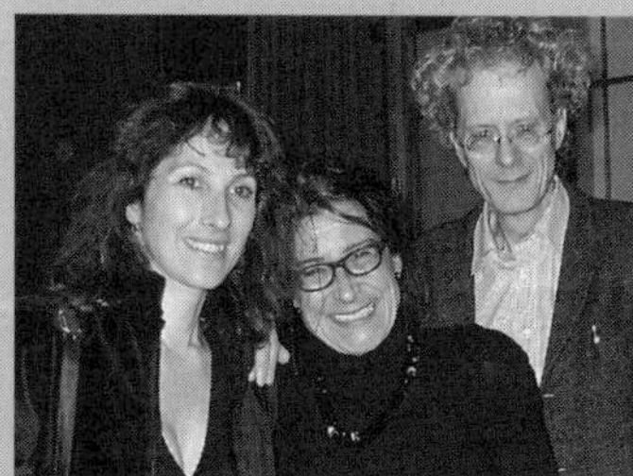

Franca Comalini, Grazia Conti Rossini, and Parkett co-founder, Walter Keller.

WHITECHAPEL ART GALLERY, LONDON

A celebration of Parkett's 20th Anniversary at the Whitechapel, co-hosted by Haunch of Venison and supported by Swiss Embassy, London, Black Bush and Lettice. The Sotheby's auction at the event raised funds for the Whitechapel's Education Programme. / 20 Jahre Parkett: Geburtstagsfeier in der Whitechapel Gallery, London.

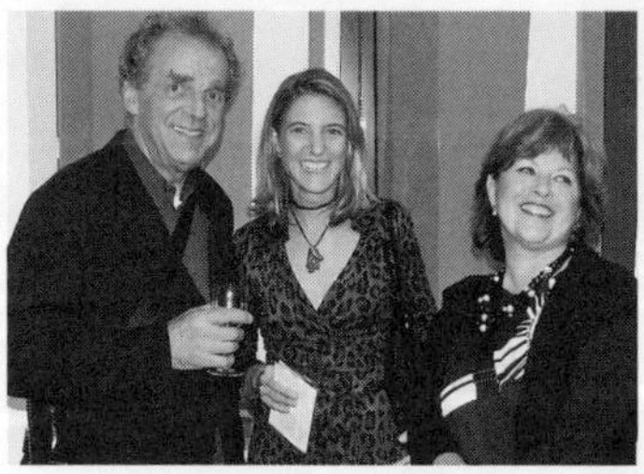

Gijs van Tuyl, Pilar Corrias, Enake van Tuyl.

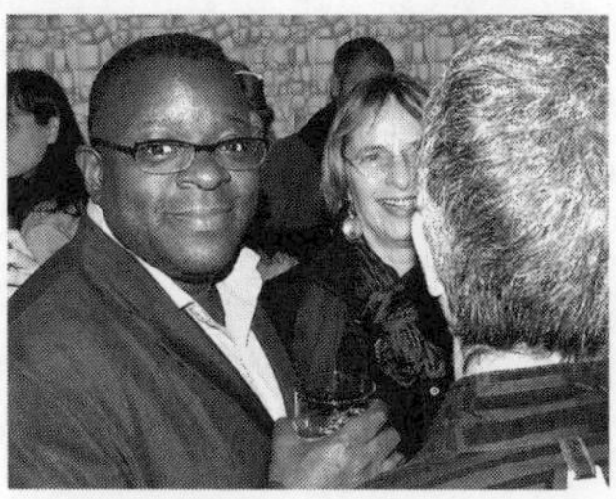

Isaac Julien.

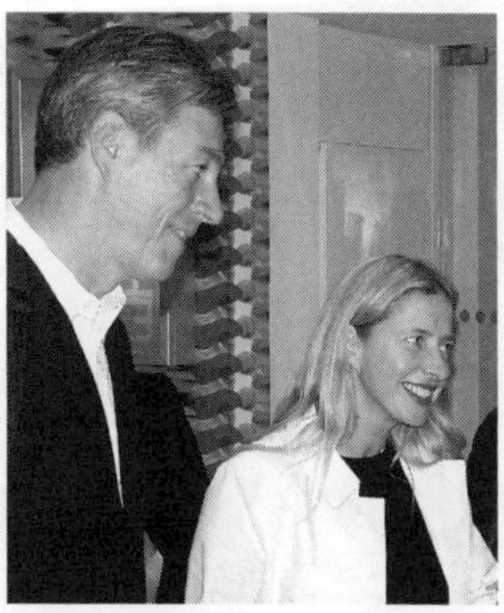

Richard Noble & Iwona Blazwick.

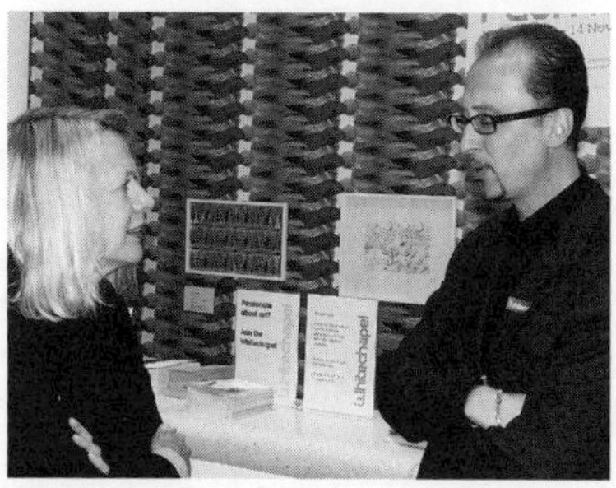

Lynne Cooke & Andrea Tarsia.

(PHOTOS: ZOE PANTING)

Anzeigenbedingungen: Kauf eines Abonnements bzw. eines Geschenkabonnements bei Platzierung eines Inserates. / Advertising rates: Order of one (gift) subscription per ad.

COMPLETE YOUR PARKETT LIBRARY
VERVOLLSTÄNDIGEN SIE IHRE PARKETT-BIBLIOTHEK

OUT OF PRINT / VERGRIFFEN: **NO. 1** ENZO CUCCHI, **2** SIGMAR POLKE, **3** MARTIN DISLER, **4** MERET OPPENHEIM, **5** ERIC FISCHL, **6** JANNIS KOUNELLIS, **7** BRICE MARDEN, **8** MARKUS RAETZ, **9** FRANCESCO CLEMENTE, **10** BRUCE NAUMAN, **12** ANDY WARHOL, **13** REBECCA HORN, **16** ROBERT WILSON, **17** FISCHLI/WEISS, **19** JEFF KOONS, MARTIN KIPPENBERGER, **20** TIM ROLLINS&K.O.S., **22** CHRISTIAN BOLTANSKI, JEFF WALL, **25** KATHARINA FRITSCH, **26** GÜNTHER FÖRG, PHILIP TAAFFE, JAMES TURRELL, **27** LOUISE BOURGEOIS, ROBERT GOBER, **29** CINDY SHERMAN, JOHN BALDESSARI, **30** SIGMAR POLKE, **31** DAVID HAMMONS, MIKE KELLEY, **35** GERHARD RICHTER, **38** ROSS BLECKNER, MARLENE DUMAS, **45** MATTHEW BARNEY, SARAH LUCAS, ROMAN SIGNER

For out-of-print issues you can register your name and address with Parkett and you will be notified, if your issue(s) become(s) available on the secondary market / Für vergriffene Bände nimmt der Verlag gerne Ihren Suchauftrag entgegen und macht Ihnen bei allfälliger Verfügbarkeit im Handel ein Angebot.

COLLABORATIONS

PARKETT – 20 YEARS OF ARTISTS' COLLABORATIONS
MIRJAM VARADINIS, ED.
KUNSTHAUS ZÜRICH
"A RARE BEHIND-THE-SCENES LOOK AT ONE OF THE ART WOLRD'S MOST RESPECTED ART MAGAZINES"
(D.A.P., NEW YORK)
248 PAGES, 22 COLOR PAGES, 1 COLOR POSTER
248 SEITEN, DAVON 22 IN FARBE
1 FARBPOSTER
€ 32 / USA: **$ 39** / **CHF 45**
PLUS POSTAGE / ZZGL. VERSANDKOSTEN

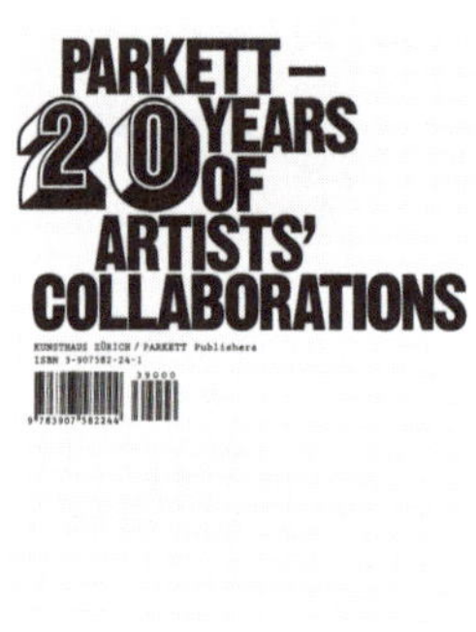

ISBN 3-907582-24-1

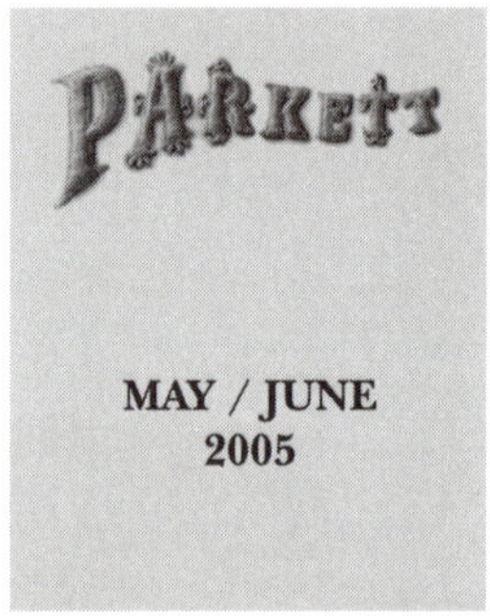

No. 73 - ISBN 3-907582-33-0

ELLEN GALLAGHER
PAUL McCARTHY
ANRI SALA

MONICA BONVICINI
URS FISCHER
RICHARD PRINCE
REBENTISCH, LERUP, HEISER
RICHARDSON, RUF, WEISSMAN
BLAIR, FOGLE, GINGERAS, PÉCOIL
INSERT: **LOREDANA SPERINI**
A. FRANKE: **MATTHEW BUCKINGHAM**
D. KURJAKOVIC: **SILVIE DEFRAOUI**
M. GLÖDE: **CHRISTIAN JANKOWSKI**
CUMULUS: S. SMITH, H. R. REUST
20 YEARS OF PARKETT: ESSAY BY BORIS GROYS
ARTISTS' PAGES, SPECIAL COLLABORATION: **ALEX KATZ** IN CONVERSATION WITH ENA SWANSEA & BRUCE HAINLEY

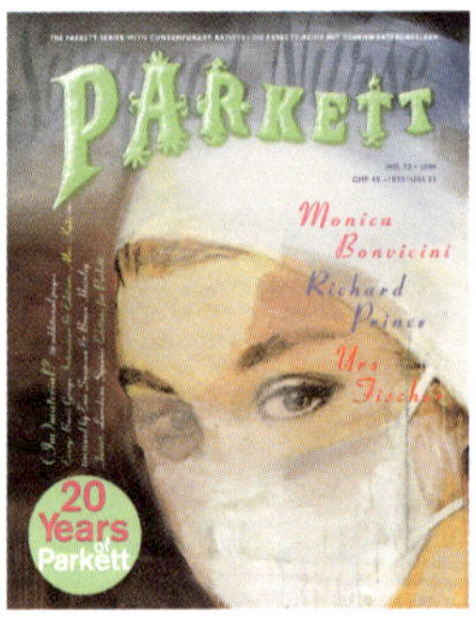

No. 72 - ISBN 3-907582-32-2

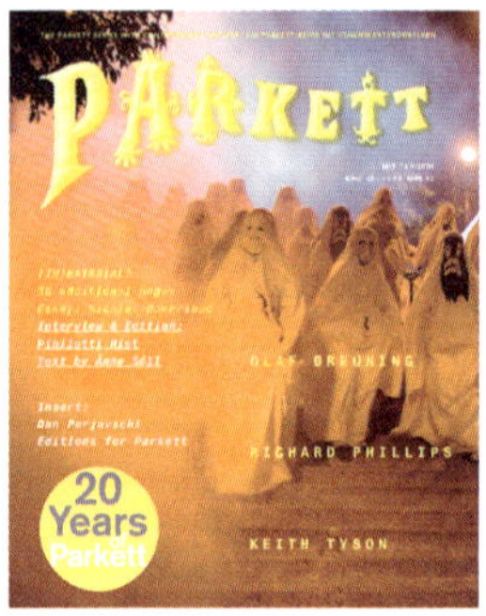

No. 71 - ISBN 3-907582-31-4

OLAF BREUNING
RICHARD PHILLIPS
KEITH TYSON
WAHLER, RODRIGUEZ, JETZER
DIEDERICHSEN, KOETHER, RATTEMEYER
ARCHER, WAGNER/TYSON, REUST
INSERT: **DAN PERJOVSCHI**
V. KATZ: **KIKI SMITH**, M. NICOL: **WALTER PFEIFFER**, F. McKEE: **FIONA BANNER**
CUMULUS: P. BIANCHI, W. BAERWALDT
BALKON: KLAUS THEWELEIT
20 YEARS OF PARKETT: ESSAY BY NICOLAS BOURRIAUD; ARTISTS' PAGES; SPECIAL COLLABORATION: **PIPILOTTI RIST**
ÄNNE SÖLL; CONVERSATION / GESPRÄCH

CHRISTIAN MARCLAY
WILHELM SASNAL
GILLIAN WEARING
SHERBURNE, SCHAFFNER, VERGNE
DAILEY, SZYMCZYK, JANSEN; CAMERON BURN, WEARING/RABINOWITZ
INSERT: **NIC HESS**
GREG HILTY: **REBECCA WARREN**
D. VAN DEN BOOGERD: **AERNAUT MIK**
LES INFOS: C. WOOD ON **MARK LECKEY**
CUMULUS: C. THEA, G. SCHOR
BALKON: TINEKE REIJNDERS
20 YEARS OF PARKETT: ESSAY BY JOHANNA BURTON, ARTISTS' PAGES
SPECIAL COLLABORATION: **FRANZ WEST**

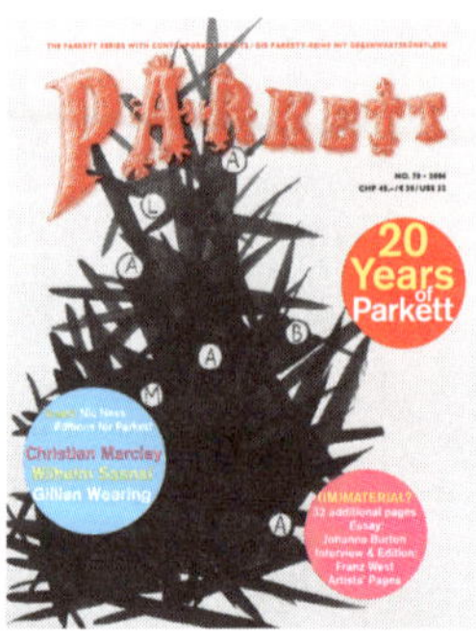

No. 70 - ISBN 3-907582-20-9

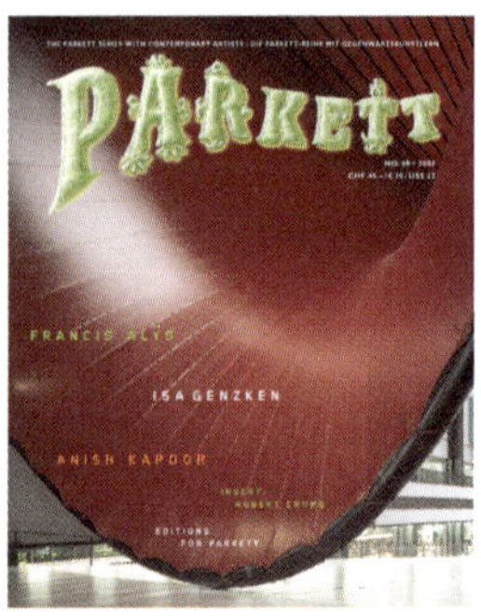

No. 69 - ISBN 3-907582-19-5

FRANCIS ALŸS
ISA GENZKEN
ANISH KAPOOR
SCOTT, ANTON, STORR, HEISER
LEE, KRAJEWSKI, BRYSON
FORSTER, WARNER
INSERT: **ROBERT CRUMB**
KAISER: **AMELIE VON WULFFEN**
COMER: **SWETLANA HEGER**
INQUIRY: CONSENSUS/KONSENS
CUMULUS AMERICA: J. PEARSON
CUMULUS EUROPE: E. TRONCY
BALKON: SERGIO RISALITI

FRANZ ACKERMANN
EIJA-LIISA AHTILA
DAN GRAHAM
FOGLE, DECTER, STANGE, ILES, ELFVING
KOCH, GUAGNINI/SCHNEIDER, MACDONALD
DI BARTOLOMEO, ROSENBERG MILLER
INSERT: **JONATHAN MONK**
D. KURJAKOVIC: **BOJAN SARCEVIC**
H. U. OBRIST: **BERNARD FRIZE**
G. JANSEN: **DIRK SKREBER**
LES INFOS: J. MURPHY
CUMULUS: C. RABINOWITZ, J. HOFFMANN
BALKON: HANS RUDOLF REUST

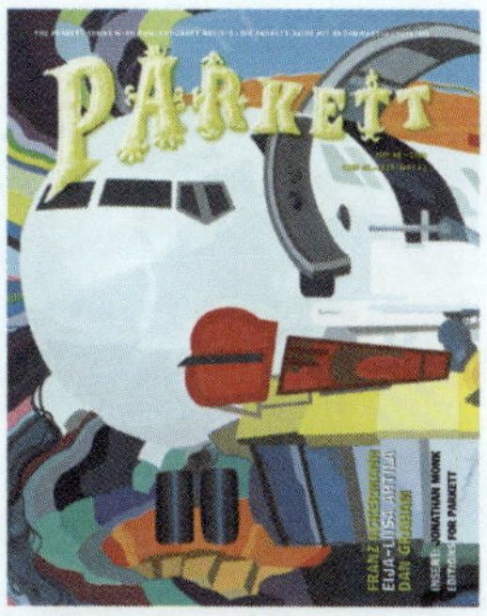

No. 68 - ISBN 3-907582-18-7

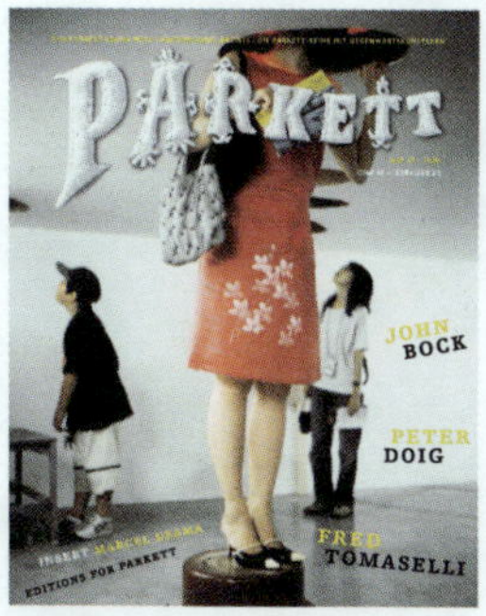

No. 67 - ISBN 3-907582-17-9

JOHN BOCK
PETER DOIG
FRED TOMASELLI
HOFFMANN, BIRNBAUM, AVGIKOS
BONAVENTURA, FUCHS, RUF
CAMERON, RONDEAU, PINCHBECK
INSERT: **MARCEL DZAMA**
T. SELVARATNAM: **SIMON STARLING**
S. OMLIN: **HANNE DARBOVEN**
VISCHER/HERZOG: SCHAULAGER BASEL
LES INFOS: H. BÖHME ON **WANG FU**
CUMULUS: FIRSTENBERG, KERSTING
BALKON: DANIELE MUSCIONICO

ANGELA BULLOCH
DANIEL BUREN
PIERRE HUYGHE
REBENTISCH, WILSON, PRINZHORN
RORIMER, GINGERAS, BUREN/HUYGHE
MILLAR, OBRIST, HOBBS
T. NICHOLS GOODEVE/G. BRUNO
E. DIMENDBERG: **ALLAN SEKULA**
LES INFOS: ROBERTO OHRT ON
MONICA BONVICINI
CUMULUS AMERICA: NATO THOMPSON
CUMULUS EUROPA: GREG HILTY

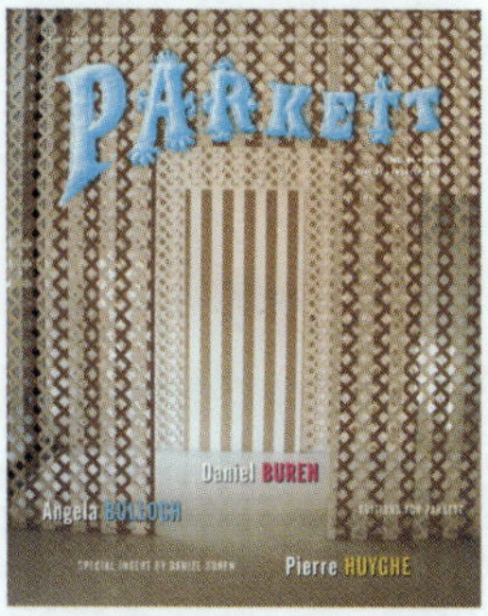

No. 66 - ISBN 3-907582-16-0

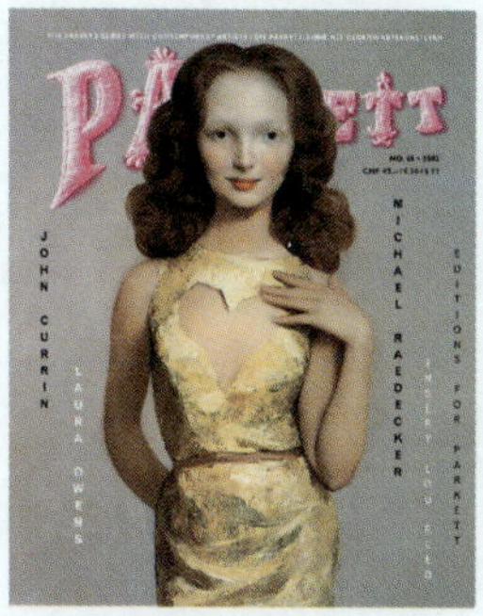

No. 65 - ISBN 3-907582-15-2

JOHN CURRIN
LAURA OWENS
MICHAEL RAEDECKER
SEWARD, VAN DE WALLE, BERG
FERGUSON, THOMSON, WEISSMAN
VERSCHAFFEL, MYERS, EGGERS
INSERT: **LOU REED**
KURT W. FORSTER: **JEFF WALL**
STORR: **DIETER ROTH & D. IANNONE**
K. BITTERLI: **HUBBARD/BIRCHLER**
LES INFOS: CHRISTINA VÉGH
CUMULUS: O. WESTPHALEN, T. HAHN
BALKON: SHEENA WAGSTAFF

OLAFUR ELIASSON
TOM FRIEDMAN
RODNEY GRAHAM
BLOM, MORGAN, CAMERON, MATSUI
WATERS/FRIEDMAN, COOKE, HALE
INSERT: **AMY SILLMAN**
VÉRONIQUE D'AUZAC:
XAVIER VEILHAN
INTERVIEW:
A.M. HOMES: **CHRIS VERENE**
HAKAN NILSSON: **ANNIKA LARSSON**
INQUIRY/UMFRAGE:
LEARNING FROM "DOCUMENTA"

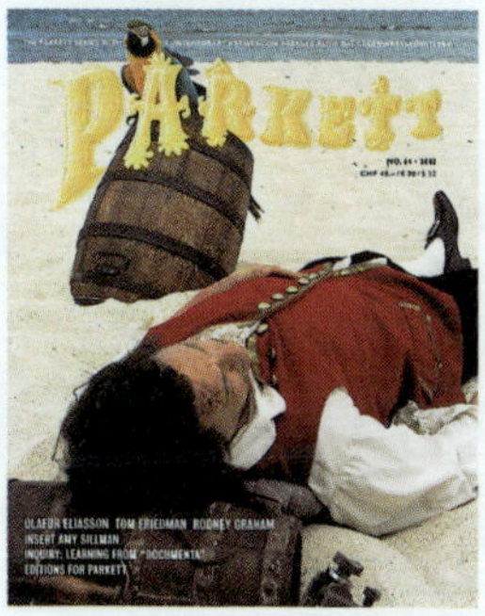

No. 64 - ISBN 3-907582-14-4

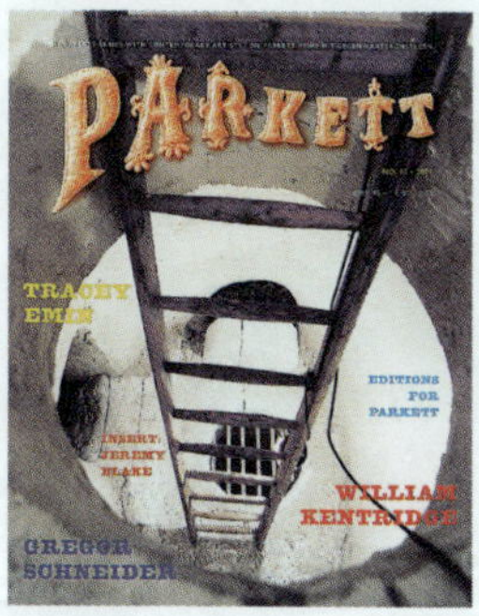

No. 63 - ISBN 3-907582-13-6

TRACEY EMIN
WILLIAM KENTRIDGE
GREGOR SCHNEIDER
BARBER, MUIR, PREECE
GUNNING, STEWART, GOLDBERG
PUVOGEL, LOOCK
INSERT: **JEREMY BLAKE**
CLAUDIA SPINELLI: **FABRICE GYGI**
RAINER FUCHS: **KATHARINA GROSSE**
ADRIAN DANNATT: **THE THREE**
CUMULUS: CHRISTIAN RATTEMEYER
DANIEL BIRNBAUM
BALKON: MICHAEL OPPITZ

JOHN WESLEY
TACITA DEAN
THOMAS DEMAND
MILLAR, CARABELL, SCHWARZ
NORDEN, KÖNIG/STOCKEBRAND
HAINLEY, SEARLE, RUBY, HEISER
INSERT: **G. STEINER & J. LENZLINGER**
PHILIP URSPRUNG: **ALLAN KAPROW**
RUSSELL FERGUSON: **GLEN WILSON**
EDWARD A. SCHEER: **MIKE PARR**
LES INFOS: DAVID GREENBERG
CUMULUS: G. CARMINE, S. DIETZ

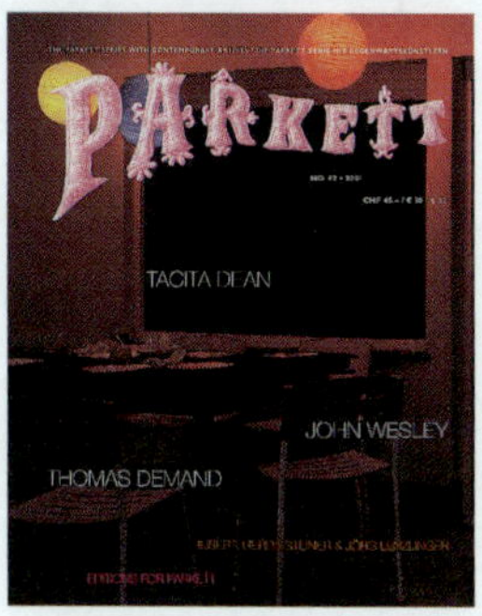

No. 62 - ISBN 3-907582-12-8

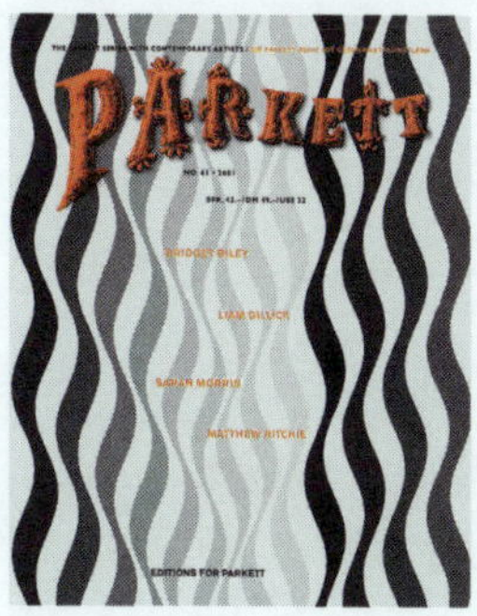

No. 61 - ISBN 3-907582-11-X

BRIDGET RILEY
LIAM GILLICK
SARAH MORRIS
MATTHEW RITCHIE
KUDIELKA, HICKEY
GILLICK, STEMMRICH, WOLLEN
NICHOLS GOODEVE, KLEIN
PRINZHORN, RABINOWITZ
GALISON/JONES, MARCUS
ELISABETH KLEY: **PAUL LINCOLN**
CUMULUS: O. ENWEZOR, M. WARNER
BALKON: STELLA ROLLIG

CHUCK CLOSE
DIANA THATER
LUC TUYMANS
PROSE, CLOSE/PEYTON, SHIFF
CLOSE/CURIGER, ARRHENIUS
HASLINGER, GILBERT-ROLFE
HOPTMAN, MOSQUERA, REUST
INSERT: **SHIRANA SHAHBAZI**
GREG HILTY: **JEREMY DELLER**
HOWARD SINGERMAN: **DAVID BUNN**
LES INFOS: T. DE DUVE—INTERVIEW
CUMULUS: F. WARD, H. U. RECK

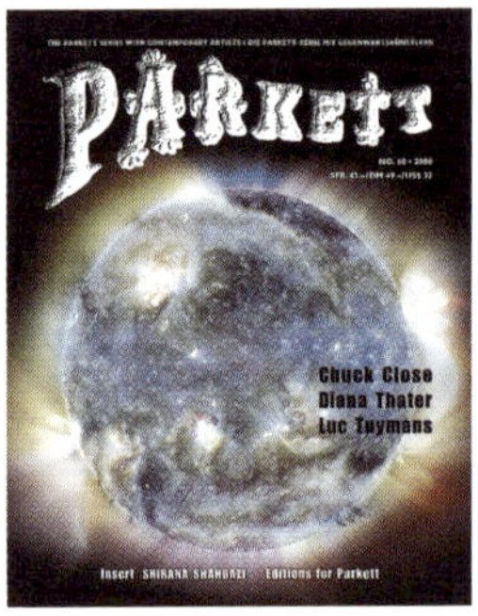

No. 60 - ISBN 3-907582-10-1

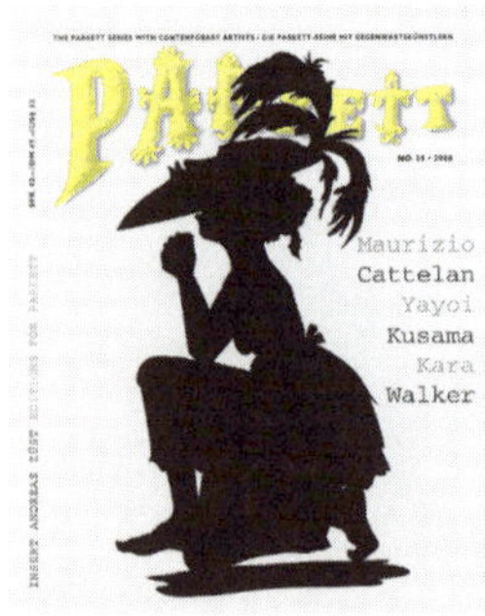

No. 59 - ISBN 3-907582-09-8

MAURIZIO CATTELAN
YAYOI KUSAMA
KARA WALKER
BOURRIAUD, GINGERAS, BONAMI
PANHANS-BÜHLER, MATSUI, POLLOCK
DUBOIS SHAW, JANUS, WALKER
INSERT: **ANDREAS ZÜST**
VINCENT KATZ
E. BRONFEN: **ANNETTE MESSAGER**
JAN AVGIKOS: **ANNA GASKELL**
LES INFOS: ALI SUBOTNICK
CUMULUS: M. ROWELL, L. FÖLDENYI
BALKON: MICHELLE NICOL

JAMES ROSENQUIST
SYLVIE FLEURY
JASON RHOADES
RUSSELL, KOONS/ROSENQUIST
HULTEN, FELIX, GLENN, LOBEL
DANNATT, RUF, KOETHER, FERGUSON
ORTH, SCHEIDEMANN/HERMANN
INSERT: **HENRY BOND**
G. WILLIAMS: **JANE & LOUISE WILSON**
S. ZIZEK, PAUL D. MILLER & CHRIS OFILI
LES INFOS: ANNA HELWING
CUMULUS: D. ROBBINS, H. TEERLINCK
BALKON: KNUT EBELING

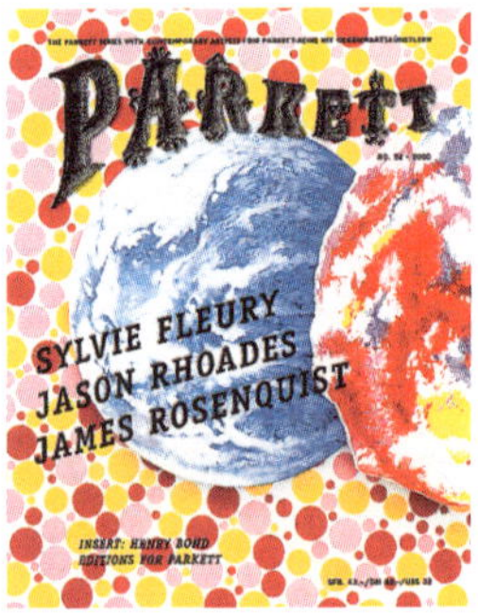

No. 58 - ISBN 3-907582-08-X

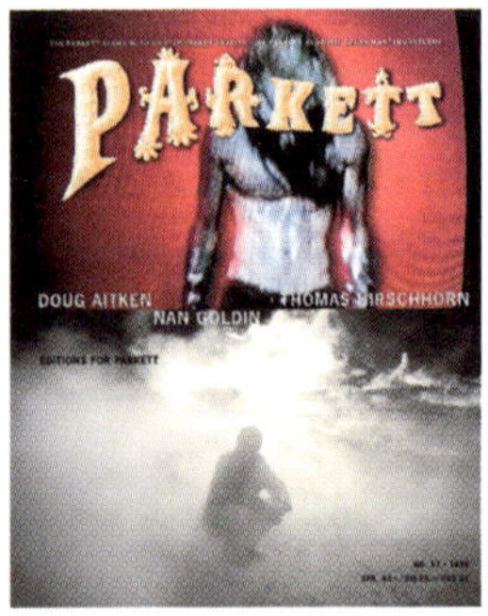

No. 57 - ISBN 3-907582-07-1

DOUG AITKEN
NAN GOLDIN
THOMAS HIRSCHHORN
ROBERTS, BONAMI, VAN ASSCHE
LEBOVICI, DANTO, LIEBMANN
FRIIS-HANSEN, HAKERT, EISENBERG
FLECK, GINGERAS, VERGNE, STEINWEG
D. GREENBERG: **DONALD BAECHLER**
ANDREA KROKSNES: **LOUISE LAWLER**
LIONEL BOVIER: **JOHN MILLER**
LES INFOS: RUDOLF SCHMITZ
CUMULUS: H.U. OBRIST, C. BUTLER
BALKON: J. STEINER/ANNELISE COSTE

ELLSWORTH KELLY
VANESSA BEECROFT
JORGE PARDO
KELLEIN, FER, MAURER, RIMANELLI
BRYSON, TAZZI, SEWARD, AVGIKOS
FERGUSON, VÉGH, VAN WINKEL
FRANGENBERG, BUSH
GREG HILTY: **CERITH WYN EVANS**
THOMAS Y. LEVIN: **CHRISTIAN MARCLAY**
LYNNE COOKE: **DIANA THATER**
LES INFOS: DIANE LEWIS
CUMULUS: A. DANNATT, P. NEDOMA

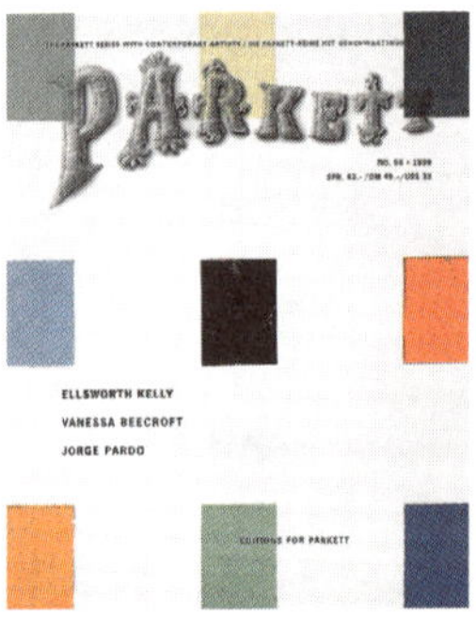

No. 56 - ISBN 3-907582-06-3

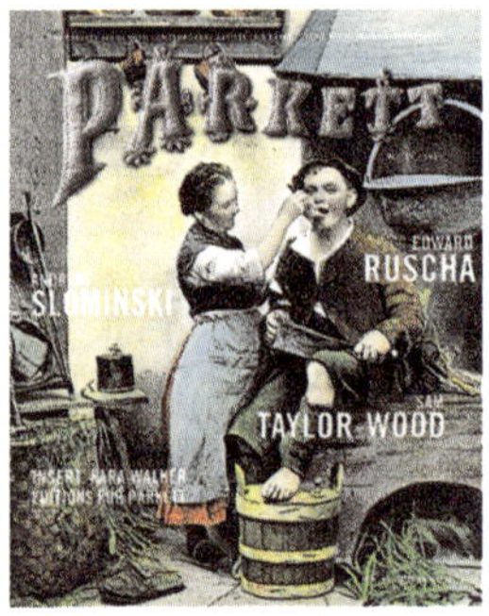

No. 55 - ISBN 3-907582-05-5

EDWARD RUSCHA
ANDREAS SLOMINSKI
SAM TAYLOR-WOOD
PERRONE, HIGGIE, SINGERMAN
SCHENKER, SCANLAN, SPECTOR, FREY
HEYNEN, GROYS/FUNCKE/HOFFMANN
BRONFEN, BONAMI, LAJER-BURCHARTH
INSERT: **KARA WALKER**
BORIS GROYS: **PAVEL PEPPERSTEIN**
RUDOLF SCHMITZ: **ALEXANDER KLUGE**
BEATRIX RUF: **EIJA-LIISA AHTILA**
CUMULUS: M. NICOL, S. ROLNIK

RONI HORN
MARIKO MORI
BEAT STREULI
SCHORR, GUNNARSSON, GOROVOY, LEWIS
SPECTOR, BRYSON, NAKAZAWA, NICHOLS
GOODEVE, STALS, DANTO, AMANO, SMITH
INSERT: **MATTHEW RITCHIE**
VINCENT KATZ: **ALEX KATZ**
H. BREDEKAMP: **STEPHAN VON HUENE**
PAUL D. MILLER: **SHIRIN NESHAT**
LES INFOS:
OKWUI ENWEZOR & WILLIAM KENTRIDGE
CUMULUS: VALÉRIA PICCOLI, MARIA LIND

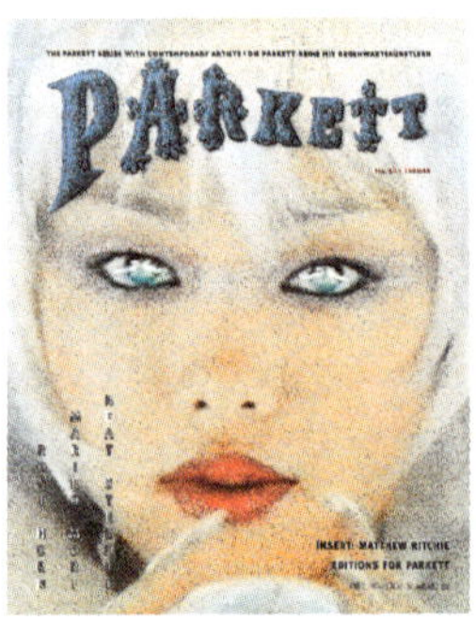

No. 54 - ISBN 3-907582-04-7

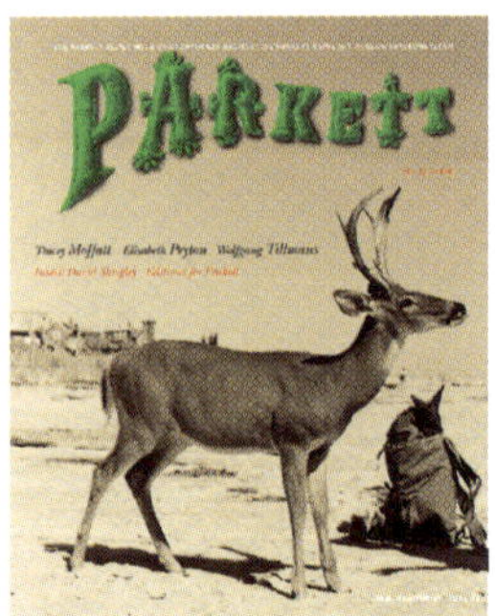

No. 53 - ISBN 3-907582-03-9

TRACEY MOFFATT
ELIZABETH PEYTON
WOLFGANG TILLMANS
MARTIN, LAJER-BURCHARTH, RIMANELLI
PILGRIM, URSPRUNG, LIEBMANN, MATSUI
WAKEFIELD, BUDNEY, NESBITT, ZIEGLER
INSERT: **DAVID SHRIGLEY**
C. BERNARD: **JOHAN GRIMONPREZ**
BERNARD MARCADÉ: **ROBERT GOBER**
LES INFOS DE L'ENFER: V. LIEBERMANN
CUMULUS: BLESSING, AUPETITALLOT
BALKON: STEINER/MAGNAGUAGNO

KAREN KILIMNIK
MALCOLM MORLEY
UGO RONDINONE
SCHORR, BÜRGI, JUNCOSA
MORLEY, LEBENSZTEJN, BONAMI
VERWOERT, HOPTMAN
INSERT: **THOMAS BAYRLE**
ED WHITE: **JEAN MICHEL OTHONIEL**
NEVILLE WAKEFIELD: **RICHARD SERRA**
GILDA WILLIAMS: **GILLIAN WEARING**
R. GRESKOVIC: **MERCE CUNNINGHAM**
CUMULUS: WALKER, KURZMEYER
BALKON: CECILIA VICUÑA

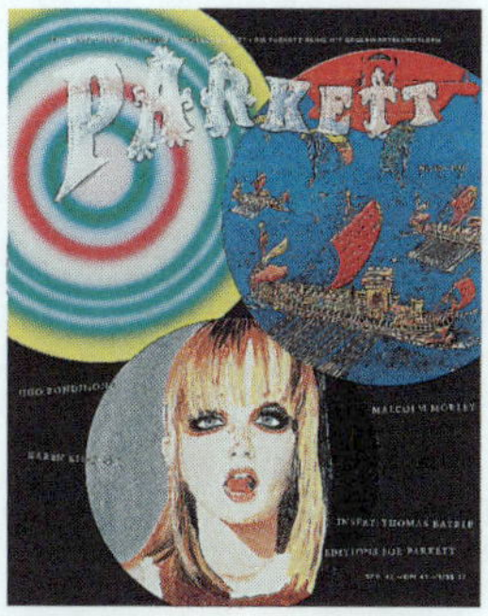

No. 52 - ISBN 3-907582-02-0

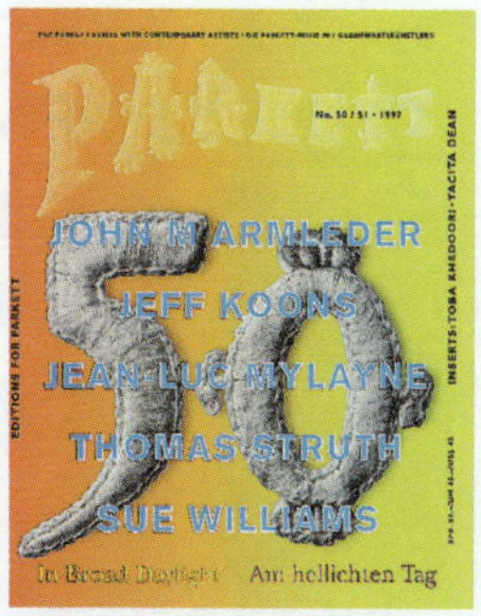

50/51 - ISBN 3-907582-00-4

JOHN M ARMLEDER, JEFF KOONS
JEAN-LUC MYLAYNE
THOMAS STRUTH, SUE WILLIAMS
DI PIETRANTONIO, BOVIER, MUNIZ
SEWARD, LOERS, NICHOLS GOODEVE
COOKE, DION, ARNAUDET, MYLAYNE
CURIGER, LINGWOOD,OKUTSU, BRYSON
SCHJELDAHL, NESBIT, DANNATT, CAMHI
INSERTS: **TOBA KHEDOORI, TACITA DEAN**
ONFRAY: **H. RIGAUD,** NICOL: **SAM SAMORE**
MURPHY, VAN DER WALLE, STEINER
KURT W. FORSTER: **FRANK GEHRY**
CUMULUS: COLEMAN, BIRNBAUM

LAURIE ANDERSON
DOUGLAS GORDON
JEFF WALL
FLOOD, BEZZOLA, FERGUSON
GILLICK/GORDON, BRYSON
PONTBRIAND, SCHORR, ANDERSON
BURCKHARDT, BUDNEY
INSERT: **SILVIA BÄCHLI**
COLIN DE LAND: **JOHN WATERS**
ROBERT STORR: **SEYDOU KEITA**
D. SALVIONI: **CLEGG & GUTTMANN**
CUMULUS: KITTELMANN, MEYER

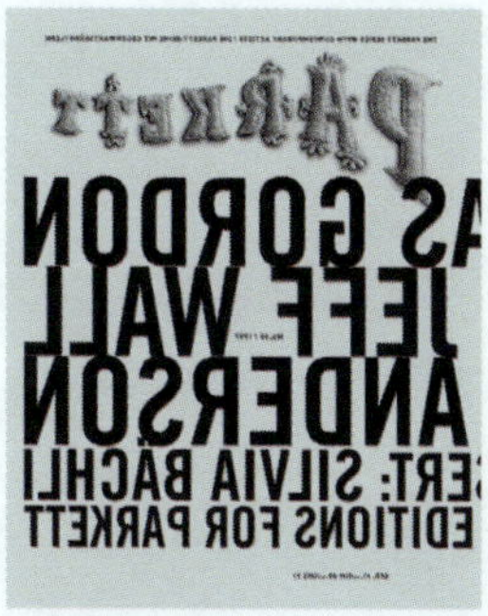

No. 49 - ISBN 3-907509-99-4

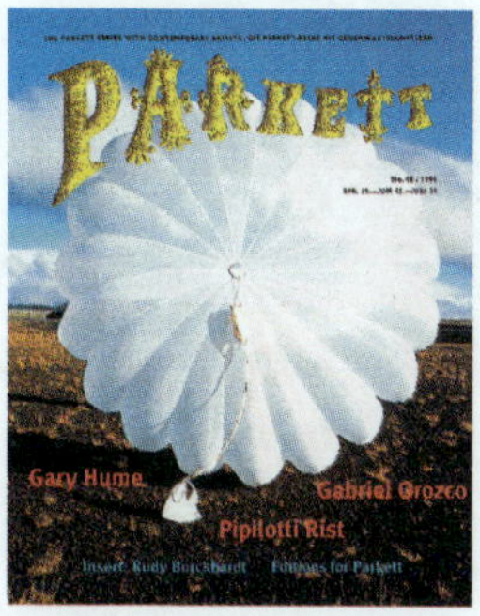

No. 48 - ISBN 3-907509-98-6

GARY HUME
GABRIEL OROZCO
PIPILOTTI RIST
BOVIER, MUIR, FOGLE, BONAMI
DE ZEGHER, SPECTOR, URSPRUNG
BABIAS, COLOMBO, ANDERSON
INSERT: **RUDY BURCKHARDT**
V. KATZ: **RUDY BURCKHARDT**
MARK VAN DER WALLE:
CHARLES LONG & STEREOLAB
FAYE HIRSCH: **BRUCE CONNER**
CH. DOSWALD: **IAN ANÜLL**
CUMULUS: LEGGAT, SCHNEIDER

TONY OURSLER
RAYMOND PETTIBON
THOMAS SCHÜTTE
COOKE, RICHARD, NERI
LEWIS, GROYS, ALS, RUGOFF
GOODEVE, SEARLE, MARI, REUST
WAKEFIELD, LOOCK, JANUS
INSERT: **ZOE LEONARD & CHERYL DUNYE**
JURI STEINER: **EMMA KUNZ**
M. WECHSLER: **CHRISTOPH RÜTIMANN**
SUSAN MORGAN: **DIANE ARBUS**
CUMULUS: PRINCENTHAL, BOVIER/CHERIX

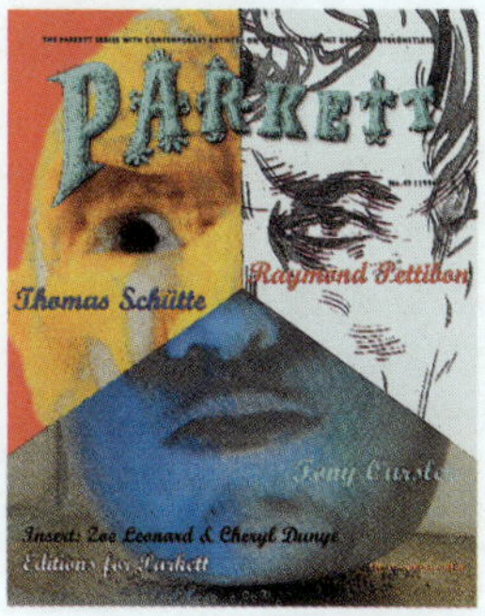

No. 47 - ISBN 3-907509-97-8

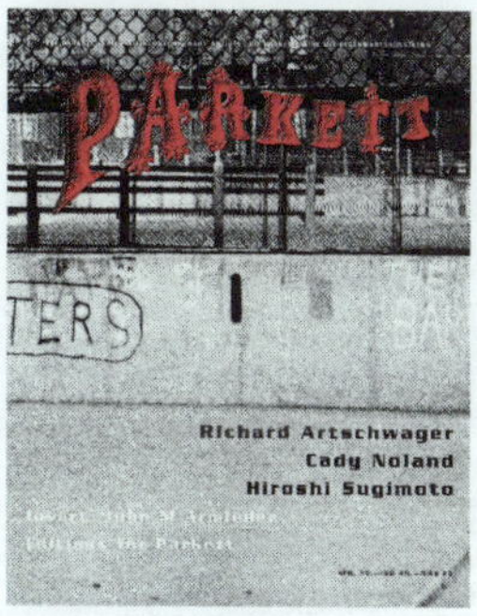

No. 46 - ISBN 3-907509-96-X

RICHARD ARTSCHWAGER
CADY NOLAND
HIROSHI SUGIMOTO
DEITCHER, SCHAFFNER, FORSTER
MUNIZ, ARMSTRONG, RELYEA
BOGDAN, GOODEVE, NICKAS
BRYSON, RUGOFF, DENSON
INSERT: **JOHN M ARMLEDER**
ROLAND WÄSPE: **ERWIN WURM**
D. BIRNBAUM: **ÖYVIND FAHLSTRÖM**
LES INFOS DU PARADIS: ROBERT FLECK
CUMULUS: MILLER, VETTESE
BALKON: MARTIN HELLER

VIJA CELMINS
ANDREAS GURSKY
RIRKRIT TIRAVANIJA
PRINCENTHAL, LEWIS, SILVERTHORNE
SHIFF, CRIQUI, BURCKHARDT, WAKEFIELD
SCHORR, MELO, GILLICK, FLOOD, STEINER
INSERT: **HANS DANUSER**
LES INFOS: LIAM GILLICK /DOUGLAS GORDON
LYNNE COOKE, DAVID DEITCHER
DANIEL KURJAKOVIC: **MARIE JOSÉ BURKI**
NAN GOLDIN: **PETER HUJAR**
NOEMI SMOLIK: **ANDREAS SLOMINSKI**
JASON SIMON: **MARK DION**
LUK LAMBRECHT: **MARK LUYTEN**

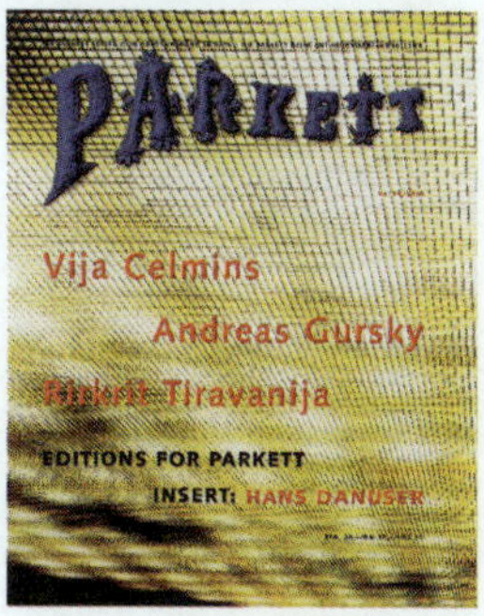

No. 44 - ISBN 3-907509-94-3

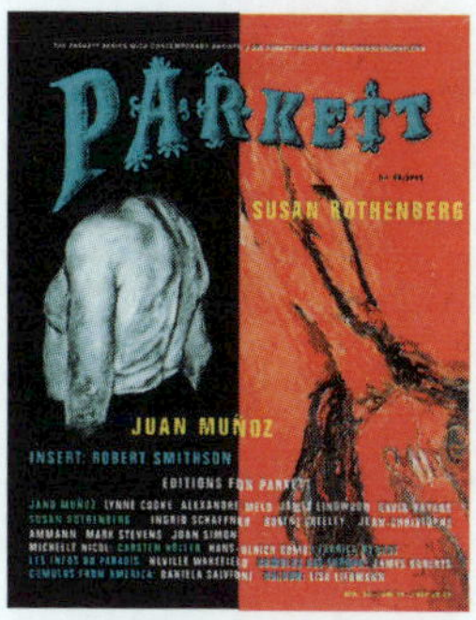

No. 43 - ISBN 3-907509-93-5

JUAN MUÑOZ
SUSAN ROTHENBERG
LYNNE COOKE, ALEXANDRE MELO
JAMES LINGWOOD, GAVIN BRYARS
ROBERT CREELEY, INGRID SCHAFFNER
JEAN-CHRISTOPHE AMMANN
MARK STEVENS, JOAN SIMON
INSERT: **ROBERT SMITHSON**
NEVILLE WAKEFIELD
MICHELLE NICOL: **CARSTEN HÖLLER**
H.U. OBRIST: **FABRICE HYBERT**

LAWRENCE WEINER
RACHEL WHITEREAD
B. ADAMS, F. RICHARD
D. SCHWARZ, D. SALVIONI
E. LEFFINGWELL, L. RELYEA
N. WAKEFIELD, R. SCHMITZ
T. FAIRBROTHER, S. WATNEY
INSERT: **NAN GOLDIN**
VINCE LEO: **ROBERT FRANK**
C. RITSCHARD: **MARKUS RAETZ**

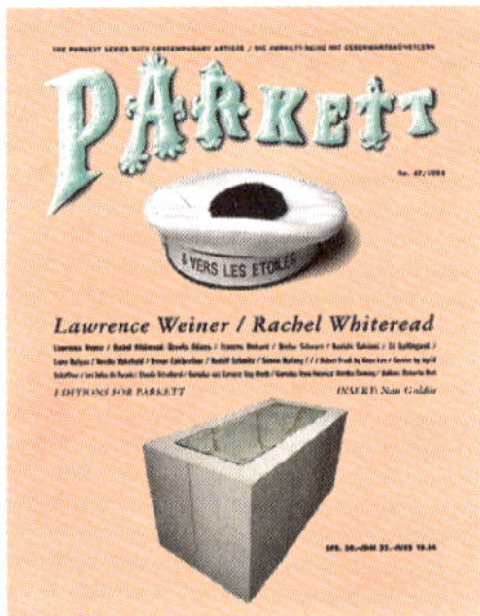

No. 42 - ISBN 3-907509-92-7

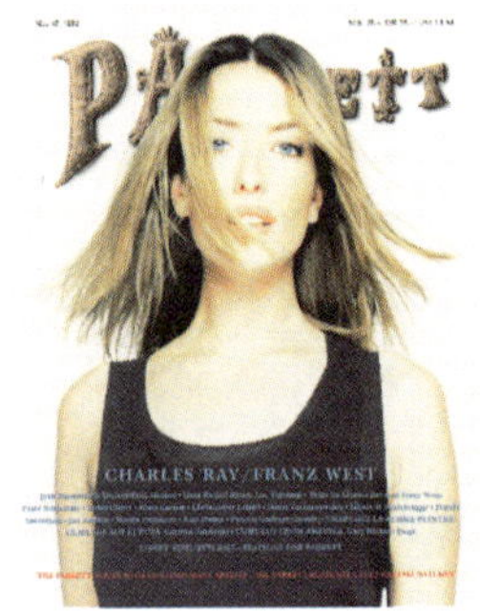

No. 37 - ISBN 3-907509-87-0

CHARLES RAY
FRANZ WEST
K. KERTESS, CH. KNIGHT
P. SCHJELDAHL, R. STORR
J. AVGIKOS, A. HUBER
M. PRINZHORN, E. SCHLEBRÜGGE
HARALD SZEEMANN
D. ZACHAROPOULOS
INSERT: **PIPILOTTI RIST**
JEAN BAUDRILLARD
HANS RUDOLF REUST: **LUC TUYMANS**
PARKETT INQUIRY:
CHERCHEZ LA FEMME PEINTRE

ILYA KABAKOV
RICHARD PRINCE
BORIS GROYS, ROBERT STORR
JAN THORN-PRIKKER
CLAUDIA JOLLES, EDMUND WHITE
SUSAN TALLMAN, DANIELA
SALVIONI, KATHY ACKER
INSERT: **TATSUO MIYAJIMA**
GUDRUN INBODEN: **ASTA GRÖTING**
LYNNE COOKE: **GARY HILL**
PATRICK McGRATH: **STEPHEN ELLIS**

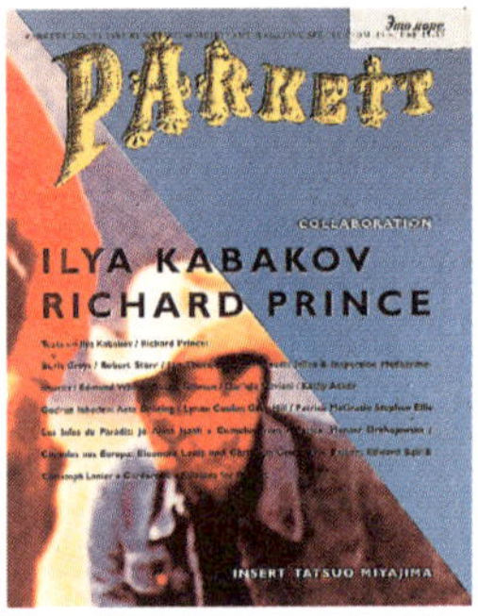

No. 34 - ISBN 3-907509-84-6

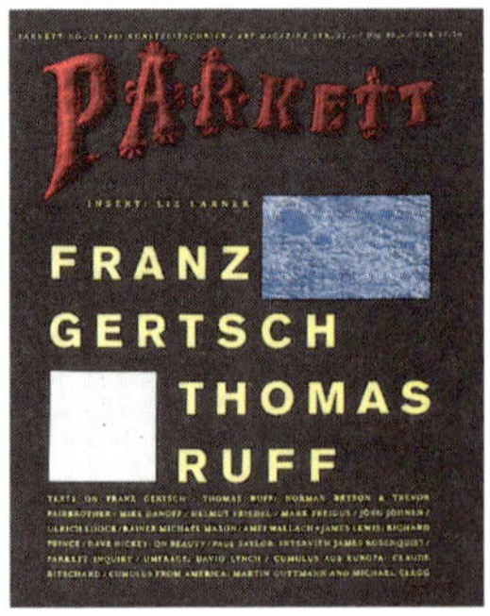

No. 28 - ISBN 3-907509-78-1

FRANZ GERTSCH
THOMAS RUFF
H. FRIEDEL, U. LOOCK
I. MICHAEL DANOFF
A. WALLACH. R. M. MASON
M. FREIDUS, J. JOHNEN
T. FAIRBROTHER/N. BRYSON
INSERT: **LIZ LARNER**
JAMES LEWIS: **RICHARD PRINCE**
DAVID HICKEY: **THE INVISIBLE DRAGON/DER UNSICHTBARE DRACHEN**
P. TAYLOR: **JAMES ROSENQUIST**

ALEX KATZ
JOHN RUSSELL, BROOKS ADAMS
DAVID RIMANELLI, FRANCESCO
CLEMENTE, MICHAEL KRÜGER
RICHARD FLOOD, PATRICK FREY
CARL STIGLIANO, BICE CURIGER
GLENN O'BRIEN
INSERT: **WILLIAM WEGMAN**
LISA LIEBMAN: **ROBERT GOBER**
JACQUELINE BURCKHARDT:
GIULIO ROMANO

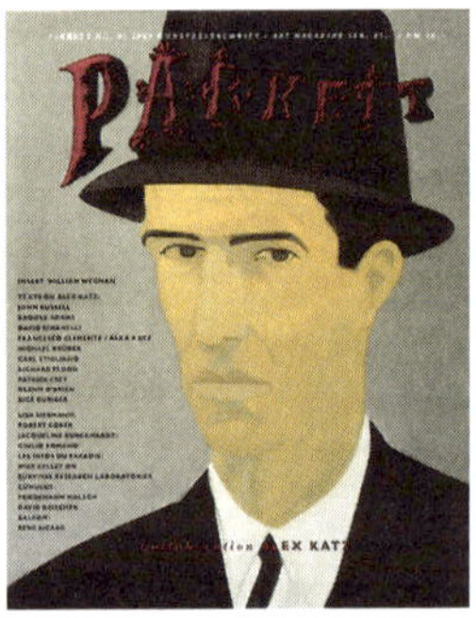

No. 21 - ISBN 3-907509-71-4

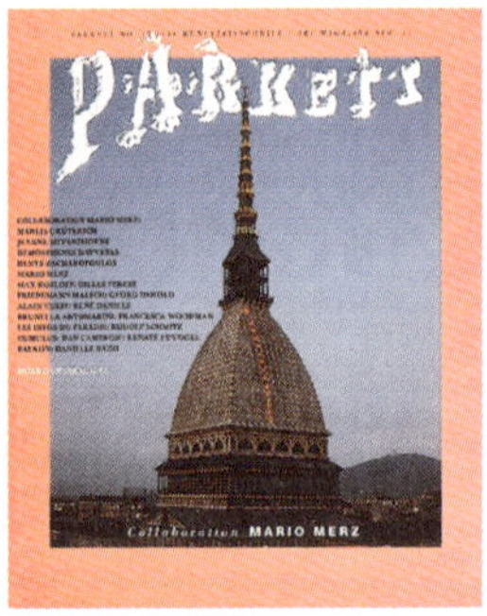

No. 15 - ISBN 3-907509-65-X

MARIO MERZ
MARLIS GRÜTERICH, JEANNE
SILVERTHORNE, DEMOSTHENES
DAVVETAS, HARALD SZEEMANN
DENYS ZACHAROPOULOS
INSERT: **GENERAL IDEA**
MAX KOZLOFF: **GILLES PERESS**
FRIEDEMANN MALSCH:
GEORG HEROLD
BRUNELLA ANTOMARINI:
FRANCESCA WOODMAN

GILBERT & GEORGE
DUNCAN FALLOWELL
MARIO CODOGNATO
JEREMY COOPER
DEMOSTHENES DAVVETAS
WOLF JAHN
INSERT: **ROSEMARIE TROCKEL**
ROBERT STORR: **NANCY SPERO**
HAIM STEINBACH: **MANIFESTO**
JÖRG ZUTTER: **THOMAS HUBER**

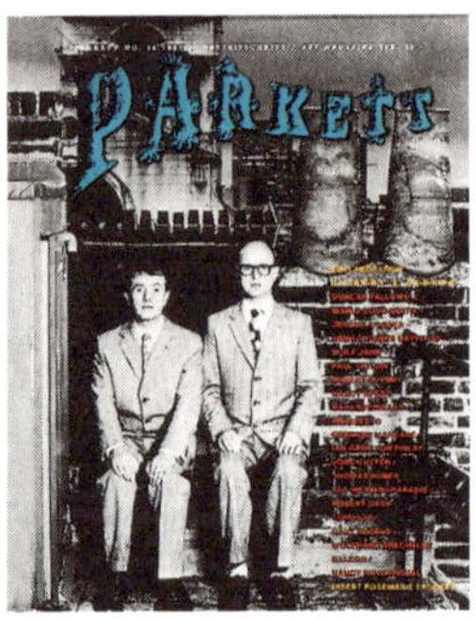

No. 14 - ISBN 3-907509-64-1

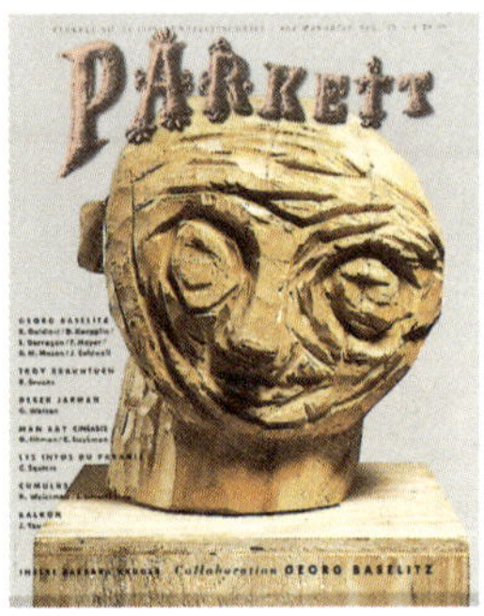

No. 11 - ISBN 3-907509-61-7

GEORG BASELITZ
REMO GUIDIERI
DIETER KOEPPLIN
ERIC DARRAGON
RAINER MICHAEL MASON
FRANZ MEYER, JOHN CALDWELL
INSERT: **BARBARA KRUGER**
GRAY WATSON: **DEREK JARMAN**
CAROL SQUIERS:
PHOTO OPPORTUNITY
ROSETTA BROOKS:
TROY BRAUNTUCH

PARKETT

ARTISTS' EDITIONS FOR PARKETT SUBSCRIBERS
WWW.PARKETTART.COM

The PARKETT Series is created in collaboration with artists, who contribute an original work available exclusively to the subscribers in the form of a signed limited SPECIAL EDITION. The available works are also reproduced in each PARKETT issue.

Each SPECIAL EDITION is available by order from any one of our offices in New York or Zurich. Just fill in the details below and send this card to the office nearest you. Once your order has been processed, you will be issued with an invoice and your personal edition number. Upon receipt of payment, you will receive the SPECIAL EDITION. (Please note that supply is subject to availability. PARKETT does not assume responsibility for any delays in production of SPECIAL EDITIONS. Postage is not included.)

☐ **As a subscriber to PARKETT, I would like to order the following Special Edition(s), signed and numbered by the artist.**

PARKETT No. ARTIST ____ NAME: ____

PARKETT No. ARTIST ____ ADDRESS: ____

PARKETT No. ARTIST ____ CITY: ____

PARKETT No. ARTIST ____ STATE/ZIP: ____

PARKETT No. ARTIST ____ COUNTRY: ____

PARKETT No. ARTIST ____ PHONE: ____

☐ **I have indicated my way of payment on the reverse side of this form.**

Send this form to the PARKETT office nearest you:

PARKETT PUBLISHERS 155 AV. OF THE AMERICAS NEW YORK, NY 10013 PHONE (212) 673-2660 FAX (212) 271-0704

PARKETT VERLAG QUELLENSTRASSE 27 CH-8031 ZÜRICH TELEFON +41-1-271 81 40 FAX +41-1-272 43 01

Visit our website: www.parkettart.com

PARKETT

KÜNSTLEREDITIONEN FÜR PARKETT-ABONNENTEN
WWW.PARKETTART.COM

Die PARKETT-Buchreihe entsteht in Zusammenarbeit mit Künstlern, die eigens für die Abonnenten einen Originalbeitrag in Form einer limitierten und signierten EDITION gestalten. Diese Editionen sind auch in der Zeitschrift abgebildet und können mit dieser Bestellkarte in jedem unserer Büros in Zürich, Frankfurt oder New York bestellt werden. Sie erhalten dann Ihre persönliche Editionsnummer und eine Rechnung. Sobald wir Ihre Zahlung erhalten haben, schicken wir Ihnen Ihre Edition(en). Lieferung solange Vorrat. PARKETT übernimmt keine Verantwortung für allfällige Verzögerungen bei der Herstellung der Vorzugsausgaben. Versandkosten und MwSt (Schweiz) nicht inbegriffen.

☐ **Ich bin PARKETT-Abonnent(in) und bestelle folgende EDITION(EN), nummeriert und vom Künstler signiert:**

PARKETT Nr. KÜNSTLER/IN ____ NAME: ____

PARKETT Nr. KÜNSTLER/IN ____ STRASSE: ____

PARKETT Nr. KÜNSTLER/IN ____ PLZ/STADT: ____

PARKETT Nr. KÜNSTLER/IN ____ LAND: ____

PARKETT Nr. KÜNSTLER/IN ____ TEL.: ____

☐ **Meine Zahlungsweise habe ich auf der Rückseite angegeben.**

Senden Sie die Bestellkarte an das PARKETT-Büro in Ihrer Nähe:

PARKETT VERLAG QUELLENSTRASSE 27 CH-8031 ZÜRICH TELEFON +41-1-271 81 40 FAX +41-1-272 43 01

PARKETT PUBLISHERS 155 AV. OF THE AMERICAS NEW YORK, NY 10013 PHONE (212) 673-2660 FAX (212) 271-0704

Besuchen Sie unsere Website: www.parkettart.com

Each volume of PARKETT is created in collaboration with artists, who contribute an original work specially made for the readers of PARKETT. The works are available in a signed and numbered Special Edition. Prices are subject to change. Postage is not included.

EDITIONS FOR PARKETT

Jeder PARKETT-Band entsteht in Collaboration mit Künstlern, die eigens für die Leser von PARKETT Originalbeiträge gestalten. Diese Vorzugsausgaben sind als nummerierte und signierte Editionen erhältlich. Preisänderungen vorbehalten. Versandkosten und MwSt. (Schweiz) nicht inbegriffen.

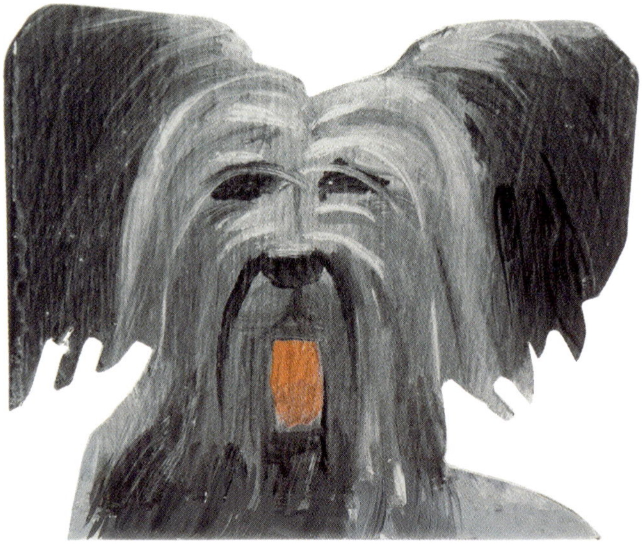

ANNIVERSARY EDITION PARKETT 72

ALEX KATZ

SUNNY, 2004

Silkscreen on aluminum, 5 1/8 x 5 7/8 x 2".

Printed by Atelier für Siebdruck Lorenz Boegli, Zürich.

Edition of 70/XXX, signed numbered,

$ 1400 / € 1100

THE HELP, 2004

Siebdruck auf Aluminium, 13 x 15 x 5cm.

Druck; Atelier für Siebdruck Lorenz Boegli, Zürich.

Auflage: 70/XXX, signiert und nummeriert,

CHF 1600 / € 1100

I HAD A DOG, HIS NAME WAS SUNNY.
WAS THAT A DOG, WAS THAT A DOG.
THAT'S WHAT PEOPLE KEEP ASKING.

ICH HATTE EINEN HUND, ER HIESS SUNNY.
WAR DAS EIN HUND, WAR DAS EIN HUND.
DAS FRAGEN MICH DIE LEUTE IMMER.

PARKETT 72

MONICA BONVICINI

DRILL 4 CHASTITY, 2004

2-part cast, bronze and resin, 4 1/8 x 5 7/8 x 3 1/2".

Edition of 35/XX, signed and numbered,

$ 2300 / € 1700

2-teiliger Guss, Bronze und Kunstharz, 10,5 x 15 x 9cm.

Auflage: 35/XX, signiert und nummeriert,

CHF 2600 / € 1700

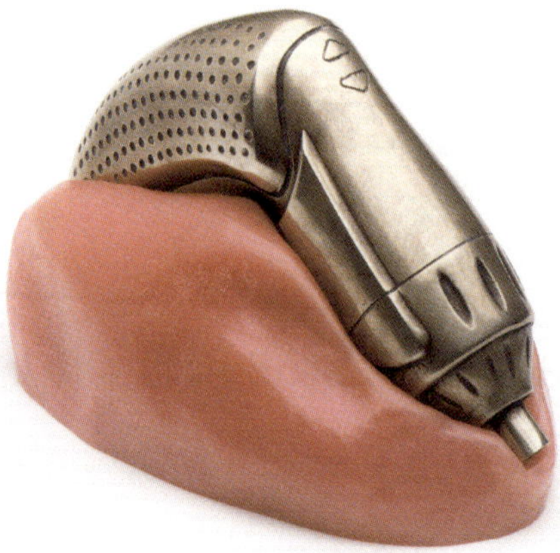

EROTIK DES WIDERSPRUCHS: DAS UNVEREINBARE WIRD EINS, WIRD FORM UND FETISCH.

THE EROTICISM OF IRRECONCILABLE OPPOSITES UNITED IN THE COOL EMBRACE OF FORM AND FETISH.

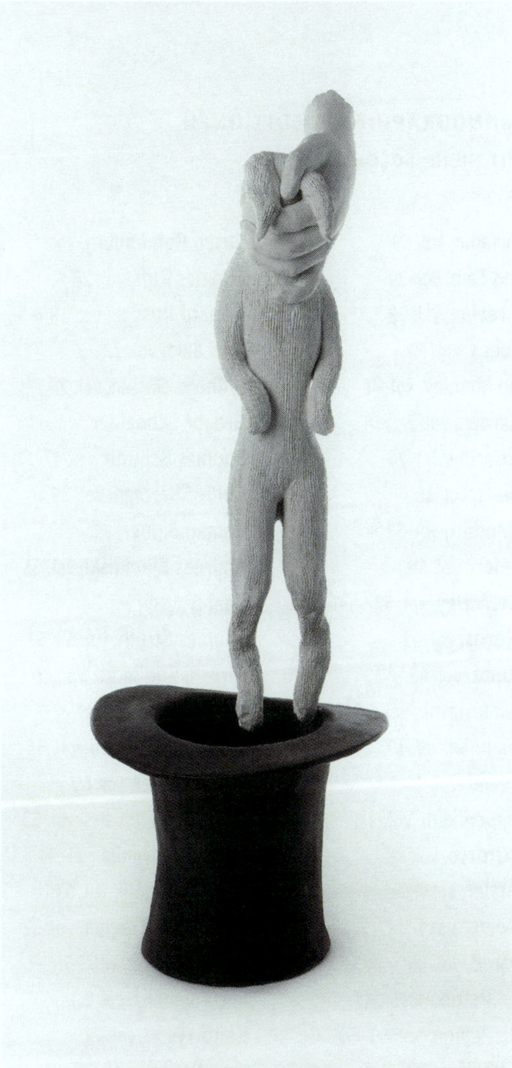

AUS DUNKLEM GRUND ANS ROHE LICHT GEZOGEN: SCHICKSAL ALLER KREATUR.

SIGH NO MORE, LADIES, SIGH NO MORE; MEN WERE DECEIVERS EVER...

PARKETT 72
URS FISCHER
SIGH, SIGH, SHERLOCK! 2004
Fiberglass reinforced plaster cast, partially painted, 36 1/4 x 12 5/8 x 12 5/8.
Cast by Kunstgiesserei Felix Lehner, St. Gall, Switzerland.
Edition of 45/XXV, signed and numbered,
$ 3000 / € 2300

Glasfaserverstärkter Hartformgips, teilweise bemalt,
92 x 32 x 32cm.
Guss: Kunstgiesserei Felix Lehner, St. Gallen.
Auflage: 45/XXV, signiert und nummeriert,
CHF 3500 / € 2300

WOODSTOCK REVISITED, WHERE MEMORY RESIDES IN THE BACKLIT DARKNESS OF INVENTED MYTHOLOGY.

DURCH DIE LINSE KOLLEKTIVER ERINNERUNG BLICKEN WIR AUF DEN ZUM MYTHOS GERONNENEN MOMENT.

PARKETT 72
RICHARD PRINCE
IT'S A FREE CONCERT FROM NOW ON, 2004
Ektacolor Print,
paper size 30 x 40", image size 30 x 33 1/2".
Edition of 66/XXVI, signed and numbered,
$ 2400 / € 1800

Farbphotographie,
Blattformat: 76,2 x 101,6cm; Bildformat: 76,2 x 85,1cm.
Auflage: 66/XXVI, signiert und nummeriert,
CHF 2700 / € 1800

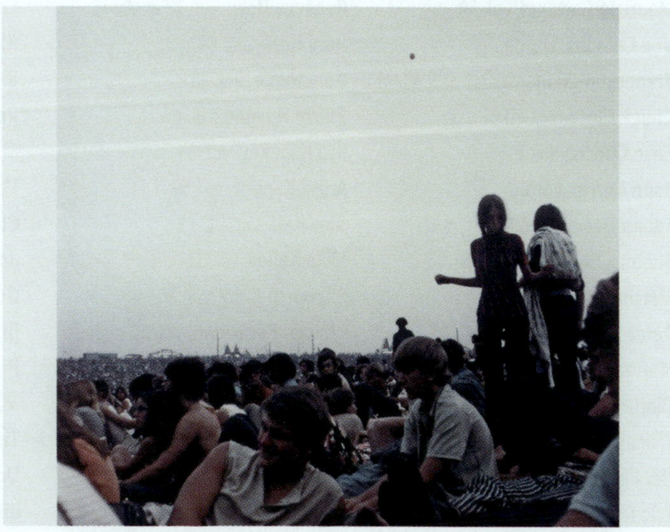

PARKETT

ARTISTS' MONOGRAPHS & EDITIONS / KÜNSTLERMONOGRAPHIEN & EDITIONEN

FOR AVAILABILITY SEE NEXT PAGE / LIEFERBARKEIT SIEHE FOLGENDE SEITE

Franz Ackermann, vol. 68
Eija-Liisa Ahtila, vol. 68
Doug Aitken, vol. 57
Francis Alÿs, vol. 69
Laurie Anderson, vol. 49
John Armleder, vol. 50/51
Richard Artschwager, vol. 23, vol. 46
John Baldessari, vol. 29
Stephan Balkenhol, vol. 36
Matthew Barney, vol. 45
Georg Baselitz, vol. 11
Vanessa Beecroft, vol. 56
Ross Bleckner, vol. 38
John Bock, vol. 67
Alighiero e Boetti, vol. 24
Christian Boltanski, vol. 22
Monica Bonvicini, vol. 72
Louise Bourgeois, vol. 27
Olaf Breuning, vol. 71
Angela Bulloch, vol. 66
Daniel Buren, vol. 66
Sophie Calle, vol. 36
Maurizio Cattelan, vol. 59
Vija Celmins, vol. 44
Francesco Clemente, vol. 9 & 40/41
Chuck Close, vol. 60
Enzo Cucchi, vol. 1
John Currin, vol. 65
Tacita Dean, vol. 62
Thomas Demand, vol. 62
Martin Disler, vol. 3
Peter Doig, vol. 67
Marlene Dumas, vol. 38
Olafur Eliasson, vol. 64
Tracey Emin, vol. 63
Urs Fischer, vol. 72
Eric Fischl, vol. 5
Peter Fischli /
David Weiss, vol.17, 40/41
Sylvie Fleury, vol. 58
Günther Förg, vol. 26 & 40/41
Tom Friedman, vol. 64
Katharina Fritsch, vol. 25
Ellen Gallagher, vol. 73
Isa Genzken, vol. 69
Franz Gertsch, vol. 28
Gilbert & George, vol. 14
Liam Gillick, vol. 61
Robert Gober, vol. 27
Nan Goldin, vol. 57
Felix Gonzalez-Torres, vol. 39
Douglas Gordon, vol. 49
Dan Graham, vol. 68
Rodney Graham, vol. 64
Andreas Gursky, vol. 44
David Hammons, vol. 31
Thomas Hirschhorn, vol. 57
Damien Hirst, vol. 40/41
Jenny Holzer, vol. 40/41
Rebecca Horn, vol. 13 & 40/41
Roni Horn, vol. 54
Gary Hume, vol. 48
Pierre Huyghe, vol. 66
Ilya Kabakov, vol. 34
Anish Kapoor, vol. 69
Alex Katz, vol. 21, 72
Mike Kelley, vol. 31
Ellsworth Kelly, vol. 56
William Kentridge, vol. 63
Karen Kilimnik, vol. 52
Martin Kippenberger, vol. 19
Imi Knoebel, vol. 32
Jeff Koons, vol. 19, 50/51
Jannis Kounellis, vol. 6
Yayoi Kusama, vol. 59
Wolfgang Laib, vol. 39
Sherrie Levine, vol. 32
Sarah Lucas, vol. 45
Christian Marclay, vol. 70
Brice Marden, vol. 7
Paul McCarthy, vol. 73
Mario Merz, vol. 15
Tracey Moffatt, vol. 53
Mariko Mori, vol. 54
Malcolm Morley, vol. 52
Sarah Morris, vol. 61
Juan Muñoz, vol. 43
Jean-Luc Mylayne, vol. 50/51
Bruce Nauman, vol. 10
Cady Noland, vol. 46
Meret Oppenheim, vol. 4
Gabriel Orozco, vol. 48
Tony Oursler, vol. 47
Laura Owens, vol. 65
Jorge Pardo, vol. 56
Raymond Pettibon, vol. 47
Elizabeth Peyton, vol. 53
Richard Phillips, vol. 71
Sigmar Polke, vol. 2, 30 & 40/41
Richard Prince, vol. 34, 72
Michael Raedecker, vol. 65
Markus Raetz, vol. 8
Charles Ray, vol. 37
Jason Rhoades, vol. 58
Gerhard Richter, vol. 35
Bridget Riley, vol. 61
Pipilotti Rist, vol. 48, 71
Matthew Ritchie, vol. 61
Tim Rollins & K.O.S., vol. 20
Ugo Rondinone, vol. 52
James Rosenquist, vol. 58
Susan Rothenberg, vol. 43
Thomas Ruff, vol. 28
Edward Ruscha, vol. 18 & 55
Anri Sala, vol. 73
Wilhelm Sasnal, vol. 70
Gregor Schneider, vol. 63
Thomas Schütte, vol. 47
Cindy Sherman, vol. 29
Roman Signer, vol. 45
Andreas Slominski, vol. 55
Beat Streuli, vol. 54
Thomas Struth, vol. 50/51
Hiroshi Sugimoto, vol. 46
Philip Taaffe, vol. 26
Sam Taylor-Wood, vol. 55
Diana Thater, vol. 60
Wolfgang Tillmans, vol. 53
Rirkrit Tiravanija, vol. 44
Fred Tomaselli, vol. 67
Rosemarie Trockel, vol. 33
James Turrell, vol. 25
Luc Tuymans, vol. 60
Keith Tyson, vol. 71
Kara Walker, vol. 59
Jeff Wall, vol. 22 & 49
Andy Warhol, vol. 12
Gillian Wearing, vol. 70
Lawrence Weiner, vol. 42
John Wesley, vol. 62
Franz West, vol. 37, 70
Rachel Whiteread, vol. 42
Sue Williams, vol 50/51
Robert Wilson, vol. 16
Christopher Wool, vol. 33

vol.	Collaboration		
73	Ellen Gallagher		
	Paul McCarthy		
	Anri Sala		
72	Monica Bonvicini	m	e
	Urs Fischer	m	e
	Richard Prince	m	e
71	Olaf Breuning	m	e
	Richard Phillips	m	e
	Keith Tyson	m	e
70	Christian Marclay	m	e
	Wilhelm Sasnal	m	e
	Gillian Wearing	m	e
69	Francis Alÿs	m	
	Isa Gentzken	m	e
	Anish Kapoor	m	
68	Franz Ackermann	m	e
	Eija-Liisa Ahtila	m	e
	Dan Graham	m	e
67	John Bock	m	e
	Peter Doig	m	e
	Fred Tomaselli	m	
66	Angela Bulloch	m	e
	Daniel Buren	m	e
	Pierre Huyghe	m	e
65	John Currin	m	
	Laura Owens	m	e
	Michael Raedecker	m	e
64	Olafur Eliasson	m	
	Tom Friedman	m	
	Rodney Graham	m	
63	Tracey Emin	m	e
	William Kentridge	m	
	Gregor Schneider	m	
62	Tacita Dean	m	e
	Thomas Demand	m	
	John Wesley	m	e
61	Liam Gillick	m	
	Sarah Morris	m	e
	Bridget Riley	m	
	Matthew Ritchie	m	e
60	Chuck Close	m	
	Diana Thater	m	e
	Luc Tuymans	m	e
59	Maurizio Cattelan	m	
	Yayoi Kusama	m	e
	Kara Walker	m	
58	Sylvie Fleury	m	
	Jason Rhoades	m	
	James Rosenquist	m	
57	Doug Aitken	m	e
	Nan Goldin	m	
	Thomas Hirschhorn	m	

vol.	Collaboration		
56	Vanessa Beecroft	m	
	Ellsworth Kelly	m	
	Jorge Pardo	m	e
55	Edward Ruscha	m	
	Andreas Slominski	m	
	Sam Taylor-Wood	m	
54	Roni Horn	m	e
	Mariko Mori	m	
	Beat Streuli	m	
53	Tracey Moffatt	m	
	Elizabeth Peyton	m	
	Wolfgang Tillmans	m	
52	Karen Kilimnik	m	e
	Malcolm Morley	m	e
	Ugo Rondinone	m	e
50/51	John Armleder	m	
	Jeff Koons	m	e
	Jean-Luc Mylayne	m	
	Thomas Struth	m	
	Sue Williams	m	
49	Laurie Anderson	m	e
	Douglas Gordon	m	
	Jeff Wall	m	
48	Gary Hume	m	
	Gabriel Orozco	m	
	Pipilotti Rist	m	
47	Tony Oursler	m	
	Raymond Pettibon	m	
	Thomas Schütte	m	e
46	Richard Artschwager	m	
	Cady Noland	m	
	Hiroshi Sugimoto	m	
45	Matthew Barney		
	Sarah Lucas		
	Roman Signer		e
44	Vija Celmins	m	
	Andreas Gursky	m	
	Rirkrit Tiravanija	m	e
43	Juan Muñoz	m	
	Susan Rothenberg	m	
42	Lawrence Weiner	m	e
	Rachel Whiteread	m	
40/41	Francesco Clemente	m	
	Fischli/Weiss	m	
	Günther Förg	m	
	Damien Hirst	m	
	Jenny Holzer	m	
	Rebecca Horn	m	
	Sigmar Polke	m	
39	Felix Gonzalez-Torres	m	
	Wolfgang Laib	m	
38	Ross Bleckner		

vol.	Collaboration		
38	Marlene Dumas		
37	Charles Ray	m	
	Franz West	m	e
36	Stephan Balkenhol		
	Sophie Calle		
35	Gerhard Richter		
34	Ilya Kabakov	m	
	Richard Prince	m	
33	Rosemarie Trockel	m	
	Christopher Wool	m	
32	Imi Knoebel	m	
	Sherrie Levine	m	
31	David Hammons		
	Mike Kelley		
30	Sigmar Polke		
29	John Baldessari		
	Cindy Sherman		
28	Franz Gertsch	m	
	Thomas Ruff	m	
27	Louise Bourgeois		
	Robert Gober		
26	Günther Förg		
	Philip Taaffe		
25	Katharina Fritsch		e
	James Turrell		
24	Alighiero e Boetti	m	
23	Richard Artschwager	m	
22	Christian Boltanski		
	Jeff Wall		
21	Alex Katz	m	
20	Tim Rollins + K.O.S.	m	
19	Martin Kippenberger		
	Jeff Koons		
18	Ed Ruscha	m	
17	Fischli/Weiss		
16	Robert Wilson		
15	Mario Merz	m	
14	Gilbert & George	m	
13	Rebecca Horn		
12	Andy Warhol		
11	Georg Baselitz	m	
10	Bruce Nauman		
9	Francesco Clemente		
8	Markus Raetz		
7	Brice Marden		
6	Jannis Kounellis		
5	Eric Fischl		
4	Meret Oppenheim		
3	Martin Disler		
2	Sigmar Polke		
1	Enzo Cucchi		

m = available monograph / erhältliche Monographie, e = available edition / erhältliche Edition
Delivery subject to availability at time of order / Lieferung solange Vorrat

PARKETT IN BOOKSHOPS (Selection)

PARKETT IS AVAILABLE IN 500 LEADING ART BOOKSHOPS AROUND THE WORLD. FOR FURTHER INFORMATION CONTACT:

PARKETT GIBT ES IN 500 FÜHRENDEN KUNSTBUCHHANDLUNGEN AUF DER GANZEN WELT. FÜR WEITERE INFORMATIONEN WENDEN SIE SICH BITTE AN:

PARKETT VERLAG, QUELLENSTRASSE 27, CH-8031 ZÜRICH, TEL. +41-1 271 81 40, FAX 272 43 01, WWW.PARKETTART.COM;

PARKETT, *155, AVENUE OF THE AMERICAS, 2ND FLOOR, NEW YORK, N.Y. 10013, PHONE +1 (212) 673-2660, FAX 271-0704, WWW.PARKETTART.COM*

NORTH & SOUTH AMERICA, ASIA, AUSTRALIA

DISTRIBUTOR / VERTRIEB
D.A.P. (DISTRIBUTED ART PUBLISHERS)
155 AVENUE OF THE AMERICAS, 2ND FLOOR,
NEW YORK, NY 10013

USA

AUSTIN, TX
BOOK PEOPLE
603 N. LAMAR

BERKELEY, CA
BERKELEY ART MUSEUM
2625 DURANT AVENUE
CODY'S BOOKS
2454 TELEGRAPHE AVENUE

BEVERLY HILLS, CA
RIZZOLI
9501 WILSHIRE BOULEVARD

BOSTON, MA
INSTITUTE OF CONTEMPORARY ART
955 BOYLSTON STREET
TRIDENT BOOKSELLERS
338 NEWBURY STREET

BUFFALO, NY
TALKING LEAVES
3158 MAIN STREET

CAMBRIDGE, MA
MIT PRESS BOOKSTORE
292 MAIN STREET

CHICAGO, IL
ART INSTITUTE OF CHICAGO
104 S. MICHIGAN
MUSEUM OF CONTEMPORARY ART
220 EAST CHICAGO AVENUE
QUIMBY'S
1854 W. NORTH AVENUE
SMART MUSEUM OF ART
5550 S. GREENWOOD AVENUE

CINCINNATI, OH
CONTEMPORARY ARTS CENTER
115 E. 5TH STREET

COLUMBUS, OH
COLUMBUS MUSEUM OF ART
372 COMMONS MALL
WEXNER CENTER BOOKSTORE
30 W. 15TH STREET

CORAL GABLES, FL
BOOKS & BOOKS
296 ARAGON ROAD

HOUSTON, TX
BRAZOS BOOKSTORE
2421 BISSONNET
CONTEMPORARY ARTS MUSEUM
5216 MONTROSE BOULEVARD
MENIL COLLECTION
1520 SUL ROSS

HUNTINGTON, WV
HUNTINGTON MUSEUM OF ART
2033 MCCOY ROAD

LOS ANGELES, CA
BOOKSOUP
8818 SUNSET BOULEVARD
MUSEUM OF CONTEMPORARY ART
250, S. GRAND
UCLA / ARMAND HAMMER MUSEUM OF ART
10899 WILSHIRE BOULEVARD

MIAMI, FL
BOOKS & BOOKS
296 ARAGON AVENUE, CORAL GABLES
MUSEUM OF CONTEMPORARY ART
770 N.E. 125TH STREET NORTH MIAMI

MINNEAPOLIS, MN
THE WALKER ART CENTER BOOKSTORE
VINELAND PLACE

NEW YORK, NY
GUGGENHEIM DOWNTOWN MUSEUM
575 BROADWAY
MUSEUM OF MODERN ART
11 W. 53RD STREET
NEW MUSEUM OF CONTEMPORARY ART
583 BROADWAY
RIZZOLI
454 WEST BROADWAY
SAINT MARK'S BOOKSTORE
31 3RD AVENUE

OAKLAND, CA
DIESEL, A BOOKSTORE
5433 COLLEGE AVENUE

OAK PARK, MI
BOOK BEAT LTD.
26010 GREENFIELD

OMAHA, NE
JOSLYN ART MUSEUM
2200 DODGE STREET

PHILADELPHIA, PA
AVRIL 50
3406 SANSOM STREET
WATERSTONE BOOKSELLERS
2191 HORNIG ROAD

PITTSBURGH, PA
CARNEGIE INSTITUTE
4400 FORBES AVENUE

PORTLAND, OR
POWELL'S BOOKS
7 NW 9TH STREET

PROVIDENCE, NY
ACCIDENT OR DESIGN
128 N. MAIN STREET
RHODE ISLAND SCHOOL OF DESIGN
2 COLLEGE STREET, 1765

SAN ANTONIO, TX
SLOAN / HALL SAN ANTONIO
5930 BROADWAY

SAN FRANCISCO, CA
A CLEAN WELL LIGHTED PLACE
601 VAN NESS AVENUE
CITY LIGHTS BOOKSHOP
261 COLUMBUS AVENUE
SAN FRANCISCO MUSEUM OF MODERN ART,
MUSEUMBOOKS
151 3RD STREET, 1ST FLOOR

ST. LOUIS, MO
LEFT BANK BOOKS
399 NORTH EUCLID

SANTA MONICA, CA
ARCANA
1229 3RD STREET PROMENADE
HENNESSEY & INGALLS BOOKS
1254 3RD STREET PROMENADE

ST. PAUL, MN
HUNGRY MIND BOOKSTORE
1648 GRAND AVENUE

SEATTLE, WA
UNIVERSITY BOOKSTORE
4326 UNIVERSITY WAY

WASHINGTON D.C.
NATIONAL GALLERY OF ART
6TH STREET & CONSTITUTION AVENUE, NW

CANADA / KANADA

CALGARY
TREPANIER BAER GALLERY
105 999 8TH STREET SW

MONTREAL
ARTEXTE
3575 STREET LAURENT
OLIVIERI LIBRAIRIE BOOKSTORE
185 STREET CATHERINE WEST

TORONTO
ART GALLERY OF ONTARIO
317 DUNDAS STREET WEST
ART METROPOLE
788 KING STREET WEST
DAVID MIRVISH BOOKS ON ART
596 MARKHAM STREET

VANCOUVER
VANCOUVER ART GALLERY
750 HORNBY STREET

AUSTRALIA / AUSTRALIEN

DARLINGHURST
EAST SYDNEY BOOKSTORE
THE DOME, THE ELAN BUILDING
1 KINGS CROSS ROAD

SYDNEY
MUSEUM OF CONTEMPORARY ART
140 GEORGE STREET, CIRCULAR QUAY NORTH
GLEE BOOKS
191 GLEBE POINT ROAD, GLEBE

NEW ZEALAND / NEUSEELAND

AUCKLAND
PROPAGANDA
2 CARR ROAD, MT ROSKILL

ASIA / ASIEN

JAPAN

TOKYO
AOYAMA BOOK CENTRE, SHIBUYA-KU
COSMOS AOYAMA GARDEN FLOOR B2F
5-53-97, JINGUMAE
ART & BOOKS
2-1-13-307
TAKANAWA, MINATO-KU
WATARI MUSEUM OF CONTEMPORARY ART,
ON SUNDAYS BOOKSHOP
376 JINGUMAE SHIBUYA-KU

SINGAPORE / SINGAPUR
PAGE ONE BOOKSTORE
20 KAKI BUKIT VIEW TECHPARK

GREAT BRITAIN / GROSSBRITANNIEN

DISTRIBUTOR / VERTRIEB
CENTRAL BOOKS
99, WALLIS ROAD
LONDON E9 5LN

BRISTOL
ARNOLFINI BOOKSHOP
16 NARROW QUAY

LONDON
BORDERS BOOKSHOP
120 CHARING CROSS ROAD

BORDERS BOOKSHOP
203–207 OXFORD STREET
CAMDEN ARTS CENTRE
ARKWRIGHT ROAD
HAYWARD GALLERY
SOUTH BANK
IAN SHIPLEY BOOKSHOP
70 CHARING CROSS ROAD
INSTITUTE OF CONTEMPORARY ARTS
12 CARLTON HOUSE TERRACE
THE MALL
SERPENTINE GALLERY
KENSINGTON GARDENS
TATE MODERN
BANKSIDE
ZWEMMER LTD. ART BOOKS
24 LITCHFIELD STREET

IRELAND / IRLAND

DUBLIN
DOUGLAS HYDE GALLERY
TRINITY COLLEGE

GERMANY / DEUTSCHLAND

DISTRIBUTOR / VERTRIEB
GVA VERLAGSSERVICE GÖTTINGEN
PF 2021
D-37010 GÖTTINGEN

BERLIN
BÜCHERBOGEN AM SAVIGNYPLATZ
STADTBAHNBOGEN 593
GALERIE 2000 KUNSTBUCHHANDLUNG
KNESEBECKSTRASSE 56/58
WALTHER KÖNIG BUCHHANDLUNG, MUSEUM FÜR GEGENWARTSKUNST
IM HAMBURGER BAHNHOF INVALIDENSTRASSE 50–51
WIENS LADEN & VERLAG
LINIENSTRASSE 158 (HOF)
WASMUTH GMBH & CO.
PFALZBURGERSTRASSE 43–44

BREMEN
BEIM STEINERNEN KREUZ GMBH
BEIM STEINERNEN KREUZ 1

DÜSSELDORF
LITERATUR BEI RUDOLF MÜLLER
NEUSTRASSE 38
WALTHER KÖNIG BUCHHANDLUNG
HEINRICH-HEINE-ALLEE 15

FRANKFURT
KUNST-BUCH, KUNSTHALLE SCHIRN
RÖMERBERG 7
WALTHER KÖNIG BUCHHANDLUNG
DOMSTRASSE 6

HAMBURG
HELMUT VON DER HÖH BUCHHANDLUNG
GROSSE BLEICHEN 21
SAUTTER + LACKMANN BUCHHANDLUNG
ADMIRALITÄTSTRASSE 71/72

HANNOVER
MERZ KUNSTBUCHHANDLUNG
KURT-SCHWITTERS-PLATZ

KARLSRUHE
HANS MENDE BUCHHANDLUNG
KARLSTRASSE 76

KÖLN
SCHADEN.COM BUCHHANDEL
BURGMAUER 10
WALTHER KÖNIG BUCHHANDLUNG
EHRENSTRASSE 4
KIOSK-BUCH-EVENT GMBH
IM MEDIAPARK 7

MÜNCHEN
HANS GOLTZ BUCHHANDLUNG FÜR BILDENDE KUNST
TÜRKENSTRASSE 54
ILKA KÖNIG BUCHHANDLUNG
MAXIMILIANSTRASSE 35
L. WERNER BUCHHANDLUNG
RESIDENZSTRASSE 18

NÜRNBERG
WALTHER KÖNIG BUCHHANDLUNG
LUITPOLDSTRASSE 5

STUTTGART
LIMACHER BUCHHANDLUNG
KÖNIGSTRASSE 28 / KÖNIGSBAU

SPAIN / SPANIEN

BARCELONA
LAIE – CAIXAFÒRUM
MARQUES DE COMILLAS 6–8
LAIE – CCCB (CENTRE DE CULTURA CONTEMPORÀNIA DE BARCELONA)
MONTALEGRE 5

MADRID
MUSEO NACIONAL REINA SOFIA
C/ SANTA ISABEL, 52

FRANCE / FRANKREICH

PARIS
CENTRE POMPIDOU, FLAMMARION 4
26, RUE JACOB
GALERIE NATIONALE DU JEU DE PAUME
1, PLACE DE LA CONCORDE
LIBRAIRIE DU MUSÉE D'ART MODERNE
9, RUE GASTON DE SAINT-PAUL
CHRISTOPH DAVIET-THERY, LIVRES & EDITIONS D'ARTISTES
10, RUE DUCHEFDELAVILLE
COLETTE
213, RUE SAINT-HONORÉ

ITALY / ITALIEN

MILANO
A&M BOOKSTORE
30, VIA TADINO

ROMA
GALLERIA NAZIONALE D'ARTE MODERNA
131, VIA DELLE BELLE ARTI
GALLERIA PRIMO PIANO
203, VIA PANISPERNA

NORWAY / NORWEGEN

OSLO
THE NATIONAL MUSEUM OF CONTEMPORARY ART
BANKPLASSEN 4 / SKATTEFOG

PORTUGAL

LISBOA
MODULO CENTRO DIFUSOR DE ARTE
CALÇADA DOS MESTRES 34 A–B

PORTO
MODULO CENTRO DIFUSOR DE ARTE
AV. BOAVISTA 854

SWEDEN / SCHWEDEN

STOCKHOLM
KULTURHUSET KONSTIG
MEDIA & KONSTBOKHANDEL
SERGELS TORG 3
MODERNA MUSEET
SKEPPSHOLMEN

GÖTEBORG
GÖTEBORGS KONSTMUSEUM
GÖTAPLATSEN / AVENYN

TURKEY / TÜRKEI

ISTANBUL
ROBINSON CRUSOE BOOKS PUSULA PRODUCTIONS
389 ISTIKAL CADDESI BEYOGLU

NETHERLANDS, BELGIUM AND LUXEMBURG

DISTRIBUTOR / VERTRIEB
IDEA BOOKS
NIEUWE HERENGRACHT 11
NL-1011 RK AMSTERDAM

NETHERLANDS / NIEDERLANDE

AMSTERDAM
ART BOOK
VAN BAERLESTRAAT 126
ATHENAEUM NIEUWSCENTRUM
SPUI 14–16
ROBERT PREMSELA BOOKSHOP
VAN BAERLESTRAAT 78

GRONINGEN
SCHOLTENS / WRISTERS BOOKSHOP
FULDENSTRAAT 20

ROTTERDAM
DONNER BOOKSHOP
LIJNBAAN 150

BELGIUM / BELGIEN

ANTWERPEN
F.N.A.C.
GROENPLAATS

BRUXELLES
TROPISMES LIBRAIRIES
GALERIE DES PRINCES 11

GENT
COPYRIGHT BOOKSHOP
JACOBIJNENSTRAAT 8

LUXEMBOURG / LUXEMBURG

LUXEMBOURG
CASINO LUXEMBOURG
41, RUE NOTRE-DAME

SWITZERLAND / SCHWEIZ

DISTRIBUTOR / VERTRIEB
SCHEIDEGGER & CO. C/O AVA
CENTRALWEG 16
CH-8910 AFFOLTERN A. A.

BASEL
FONDATION BEYELER
BASELSTRASSE 77, RIEHEN
GALERIE STAMPA
SPALENBERG 2
JÄGGI BUCHHANDLUNG
FREIE STRASSE 32
KUNSTHALLE BASEL
KLOSTERGASSE 5

BERN
STAUFFACHER BUCHHANDLUNG
IM KUNSTMUSEUM
HODLERSTR. 12

LUZERN
RÄBER BÜCHER AG
FRANKENSTRASSE 7-9

GENÈVE
LIBRAIRIE PAYOT
5, RUE DE CHANTEPOULET

MENDRISIO
GABRIELE CAPELLI LIBRERIA ARCHITETTURA
4, VIA NOBILI BOSIA

ST. GALLEN
RÖSSLITOR BÜCHER
WEBERGASSE 5

ZÜRICH
CALLIGRAMME BUCHHANDLUNG
HÄRINGSTRASSE 4
HOWEG BUCHHANDLUNG
WAFFENPLATZ 1
KUNSTGRIFF BUCHHANDLUNG
LIMMATSTRASSE 270
KUNSTHAUS ZÜRICH
HEIMPLATZ 1
KUNSTKIOSK
LIMMATQUAI 31
ORELL FÜSSLI KRAUTHAMMER
MARKTGASSE 12
ORELL FÜSSLI BUCHHANDLUNG
FÜSSLISTRASSE 4
SCALO BOOKS & LOOKS
LIMMATQUAI 18
SEC 52 BUCHHANDLUNG
JOSEFSTRASSE 52

E X H I B I T I O N S

ZÜRICH

ARS FUTURA GALERIE AG	Bleicherweg 45 8002 Zürich Tel. 01 201 88 10 www.arsfutura.com info@arsfutura.com	OLAF BREUNING – Home	**4.2.–30.4.2005**
ELISABETH KAUFMANN	Müllerstrasse 57 8004 Zürich Tel./Fax 043 322 01 15 info@elisabethkaufmann.com	GEORGES ADÉAGBO Le Dieu-créateur dans la création	**14.1.–26.2.2005**
		JAMES HYDE	**11.3.–23.4.2005**
GALERIE LELONG	Predigerplatz 10–12 8001 Zürich Tel. 01 251 11 20 www.galerie-lelong.com galerie.lelong@dplanet.ch	IMI KNOEBEL	**bis 29.1.2005**
		Focus Norway: METTE STAUSLAND – Paintings BÅRD BREIVIK – Sculptures	**30.10.–3.2.2005** **3.2.–2.4.2005**
MAI 36 GALERIE	Rämistrasse 37 8001 Zürich Tel. 01 261 68 80 www.mai36.artgalleries.ch mai36@artgalleries.ch	STEFAN THIEL	**21.1.–26.2.2005**
		PEDRO CABRITA REIS	**4.3.–16.4.2005**
		Arco Madrid	**10.–14.2.2005**
		Armory New York	**11.–14.3.2005**
MARK MÜLLER	Gessnerallee 36 8001 Zürich Tel. 01 211 81 55 www.markmueller.ch mark.mueller@dplanet.ch	PATRICK ROHNER «Begehungen und Malerei» Guestroom: JÜRG ALTHERR «Skulpturen»	**15.1.–26.2.2005**
		Malerei – CHRISTINE STREULI, JESSICA STOCKHOLDER, KATHARINA GROSSE u.a.	**12.3.–23.4.2005**
SEMINA RERUM IRÈNE PREISWERK	Cäcilienstrasse 3 8032 Zürich Tel. 01 251 26 39 www.seminarerum.ch ipreiswerk@bluewin.ch	NIVES WIDAUER	**2.12.2004–29.2.2005**
		DUNJA EVERS	**5.2.–9.4.2005**
		ERIK STEFFENSEN	**16.4.–4.6.2005**
GALERIE PROARTA	Bleicherweg 20 8002 Zürich Tel. 01 202 02 02 www.proarta.ch proarta@proarta.ch	KEITH SONNIER	**18.11.2004–26.2.2005**
		nächste Ausstellung: TRAUTE KLINGHAMMER	

E X H I B I T I O N S

BOB VAN ORSOUW	Limmatstrasse 270 Tel. 01 273 11 00 www.bobvanorsouw.ch mail@bobvanorsouw.ch	DAIDO MORIYAMA	**22.1.–12.3.2005**
		SHIRANA SHAHBAZI	**19.3.–14.5.2005**
		DAVID REED	**21.5.–23.6.2005**
ANNEMARIE VERNA	Neptunstrasse 45 8032 Zürich Tel. 01 262 38 20 www.annemarie-verna.ch office@annemarie-verna.ch	JOSEPH EGAN & RICHARD FRANCISCO	**bis 5.2.2005**
		ANDREAS CHRISTEN	**10.2.–16.4.2005**
JAMILEH WEBER	Waldmannstrasse 6 8001 Zürich Tel. 01 252 10 66 www.jamilehweber.com info@jamilehweber.com	30th gallery anniversary show: 1974–2004	**Januar 2005**
		ANNA KEEL	**4.2.–19.3.2005**
BRIGITTE WEISS	Müllerstrasse 67 8004 Zürich Tel. 01 241 83 35 www.likeyou.com/brigitteweiss brigitteweiss@bluewin.ch	MARCO GANZ	**14.1.–26.2.2005**
		Preview VI – Group Show	**März/April 2005**

BASEL

NICOLAS KRUPP	Erlenstrasse 15 4058 Basel Tel. 061 683 32 65 www.nicolaskrupp.com nic@nicolaskrupp.com	GABRIELLA GEROSA	**16.12.2004–29.1.2005**
		RENEE LEVI	**4.2.–26.3.2005**
		JOANNE GREENBAUM	**1.4.–21.5.2005**

ST. GALLEN

WILMA LOCK	Schmiedgasse 15 9000 St. Gallen Tel. 071 222 62 52 wilmalock@freesurf.ch	BERNARD FRIZE | IMI KNOEBEL	**15.2.–12.3.2005**
		STEPHEN WESTFALL – Painting	**16.3.–7.5.2005**
		FRANZ ERHARD WALTHER	**Ab Mitte Mai**

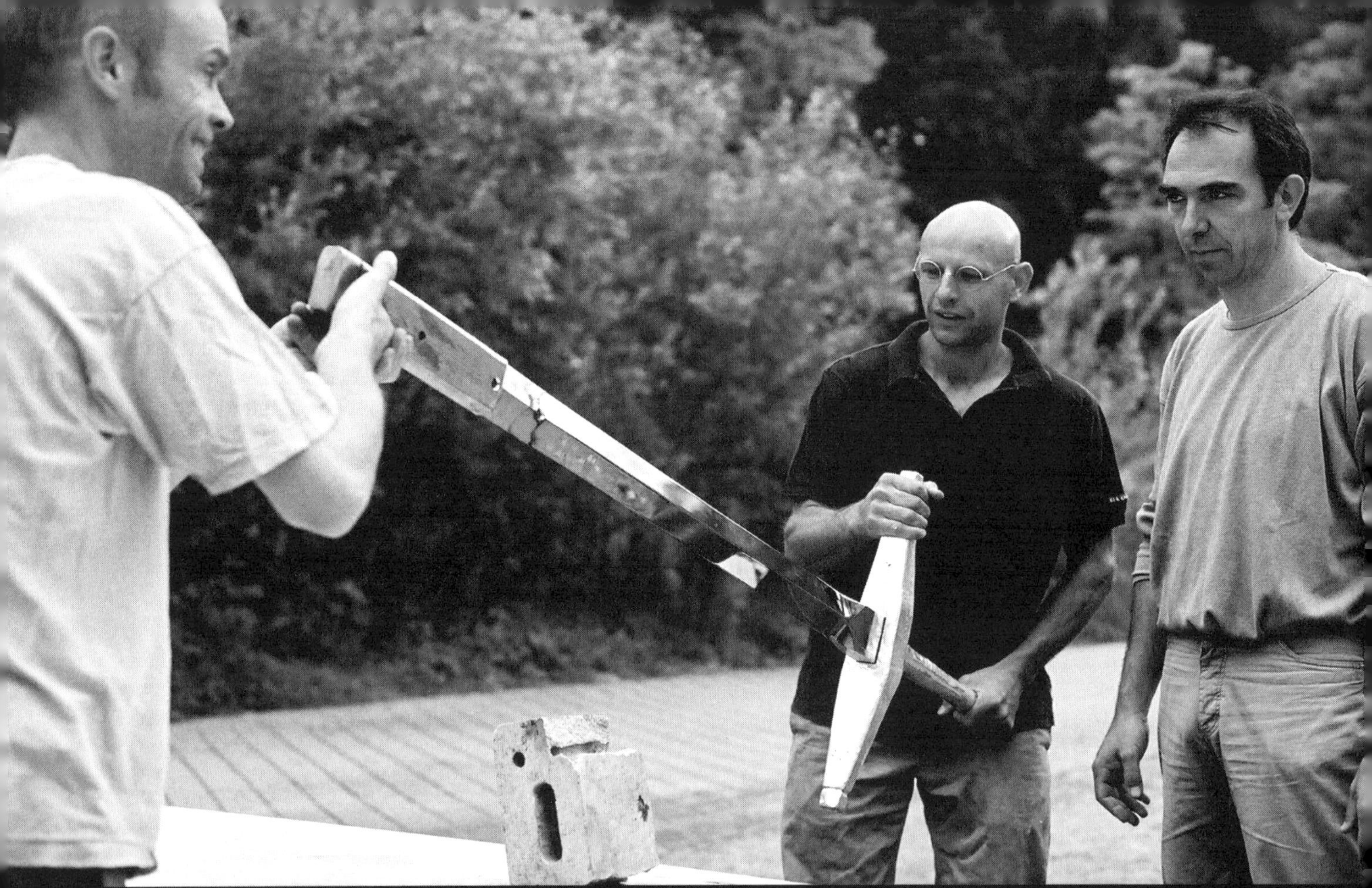

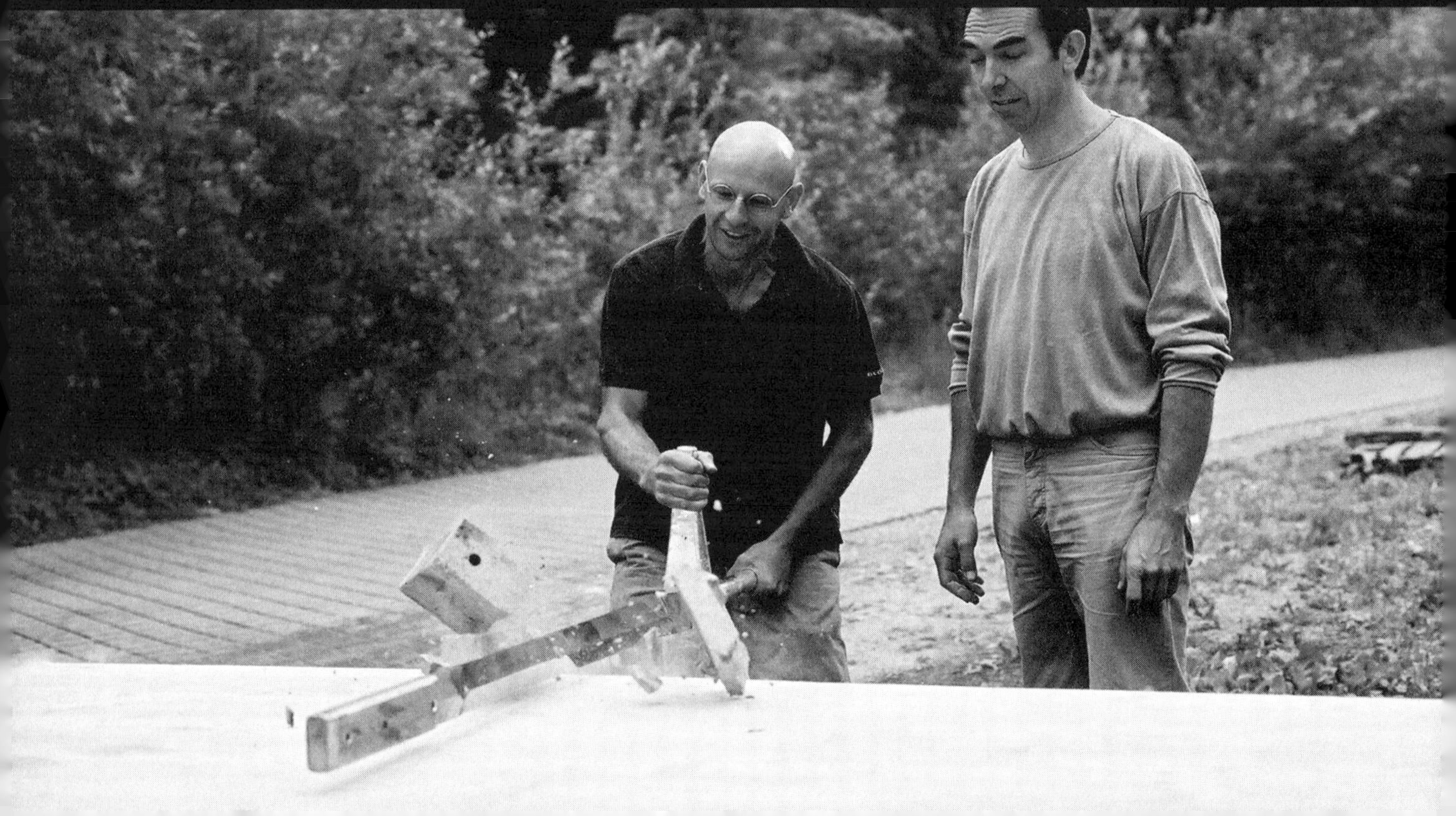

RICHARD PRINCE

GLADSTONE GALLERY

PAULA COOPER GALLERY

Christian Marclay
Shake, Rattle and Roll (fluxmix)

January 8 - February 7

Rudolf Stingel

February 12 - March 12

John Tremblay

March 5 - April 9

Wayne Gonzales

March 19 - April 16

Carl Andre / Anne Truitt

April 21 - May 27

Sophie Calle
Exquisite Pain

May 5 - June 30

534 WEST 21ST STREET NEW YORK 10011 T 212 255 1105 F 212 255 5156

and suddenly
there was a clash
of voices.

José Manuel **Ballester**

Merlin **Carpenter**

Naia **del Castillo**

Filipa **César**

José **Damasceno**

Richard **Deacon**

Pia **Fries**

Iñaki **Gracenea**

Alex **Hartley**

Guillermo **Kuitca**

Svetlana & Igor **Kopystiansky**

Abigail **Lane**

Jorge **Macchi**

Miquel **Mont**

Felicidad **Moreno**

Matthias **Müller**

Fernando **Renes**

James **Rielly**

Rui **Toscano**

Dario **Urzay**

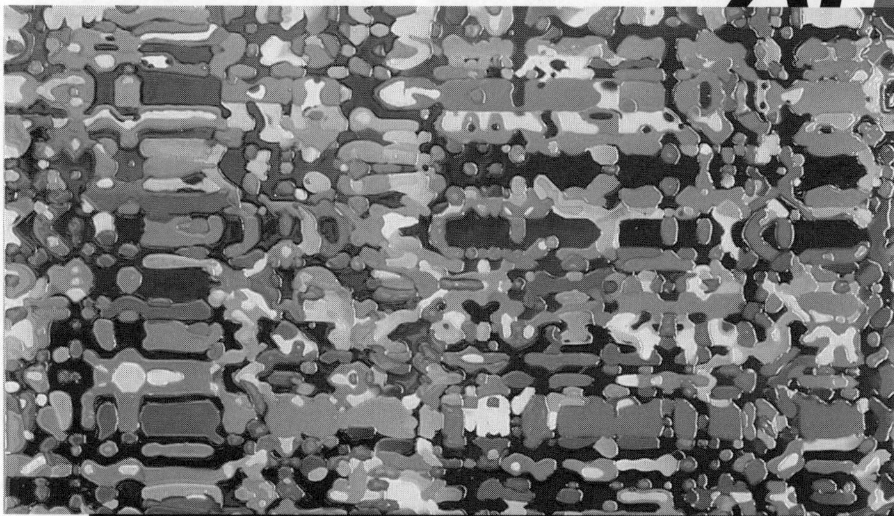

Peter Zimmermann: O.T., 2004 (Detail)
Kunstharz a. Lw.

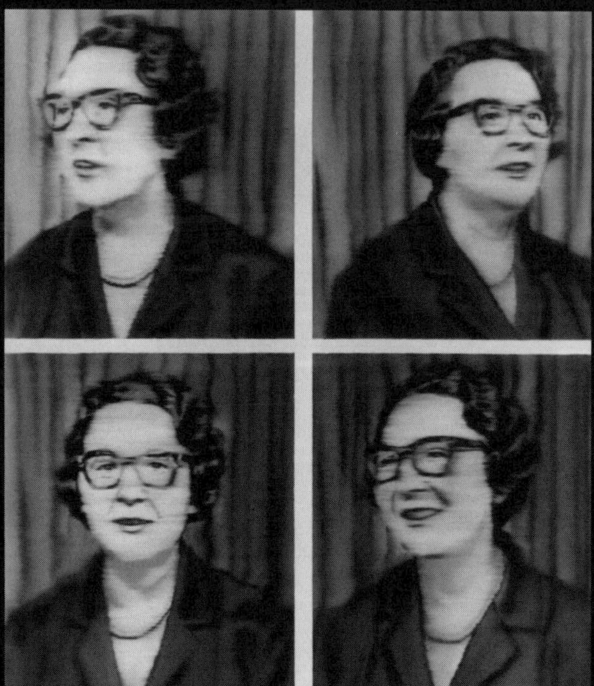

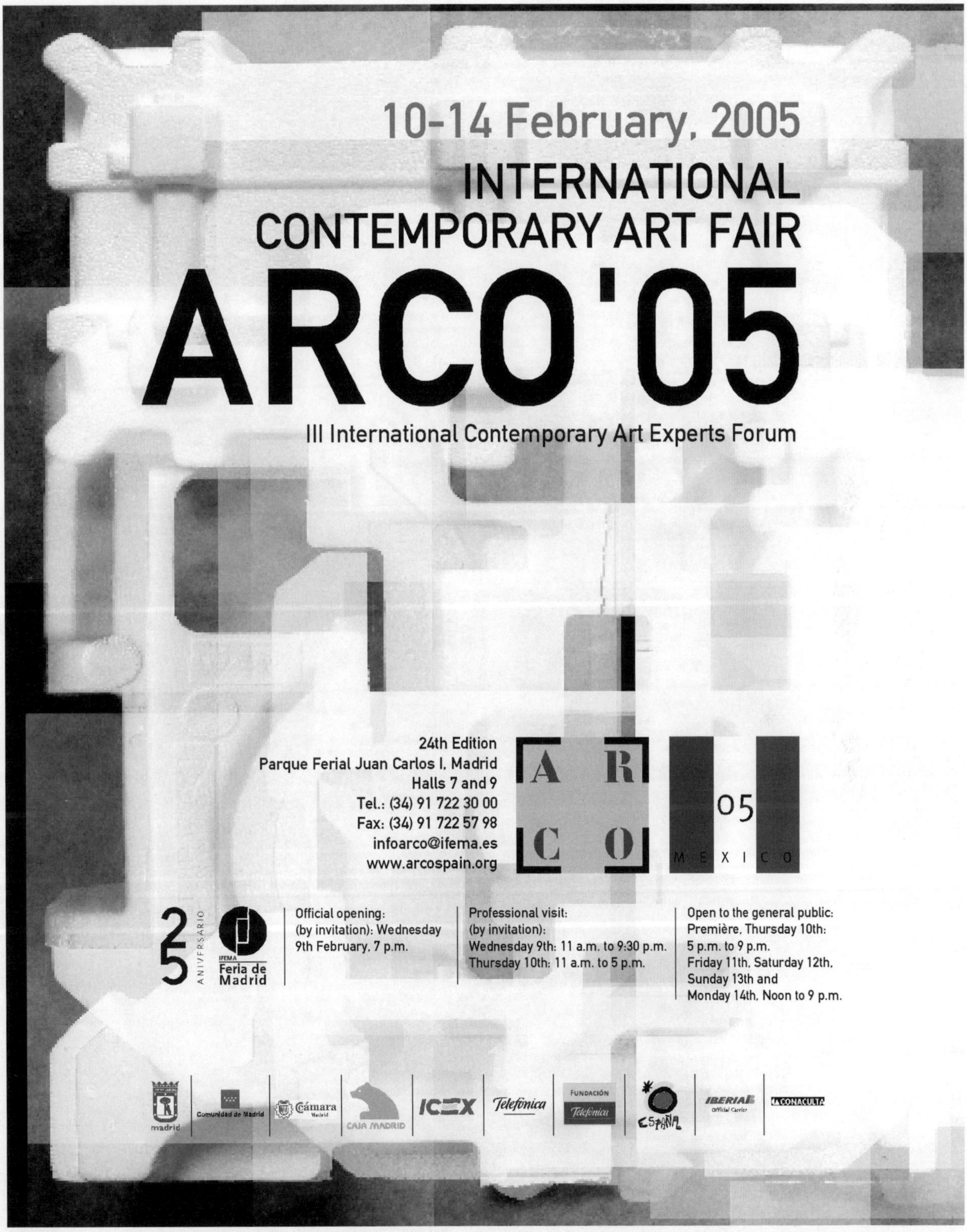

10-14 February, 2005
INTERNATIONAL
CONTEMPORARY ART FAIR
ARCO'05
III International Contemporary Art Experts Forum
24th Edition
Parque Ferial Juan Carlos I, Madrid
Halls 7 and 9
Tel.: (34) 91 722 30 00
Fax: (34) 91 722 57 98
infoarco@ifema.es
www.arcospain.org
ARCO 05
MEXICO
25 ANIVERSARIO
IFEMA Feria de Madrid
Official opening:
(by invitation): Wednesday
9th February, 7 p.m.
Professional visit:
(by invitation):
Wednesday 9th: 11 a.m. to 9:30 p.m.
Thursday 10th: 11 a.m. to 5 p.m.
Open to the general public:
Première, Thursday 10th:
5 p.m. to 9 p.m.
Friday 11th, Saturday 12th,
Sunday 13th and
Monday 14th, Noon to 9 p.m.
madrid
Comunidad de Madrid
Cámara Madrid
CAJA MADRID
ICEX
Telefónica
FUNDACIÓN Telefónica
ESPAÑA
IBERIA Official Carrier
CONACULTA

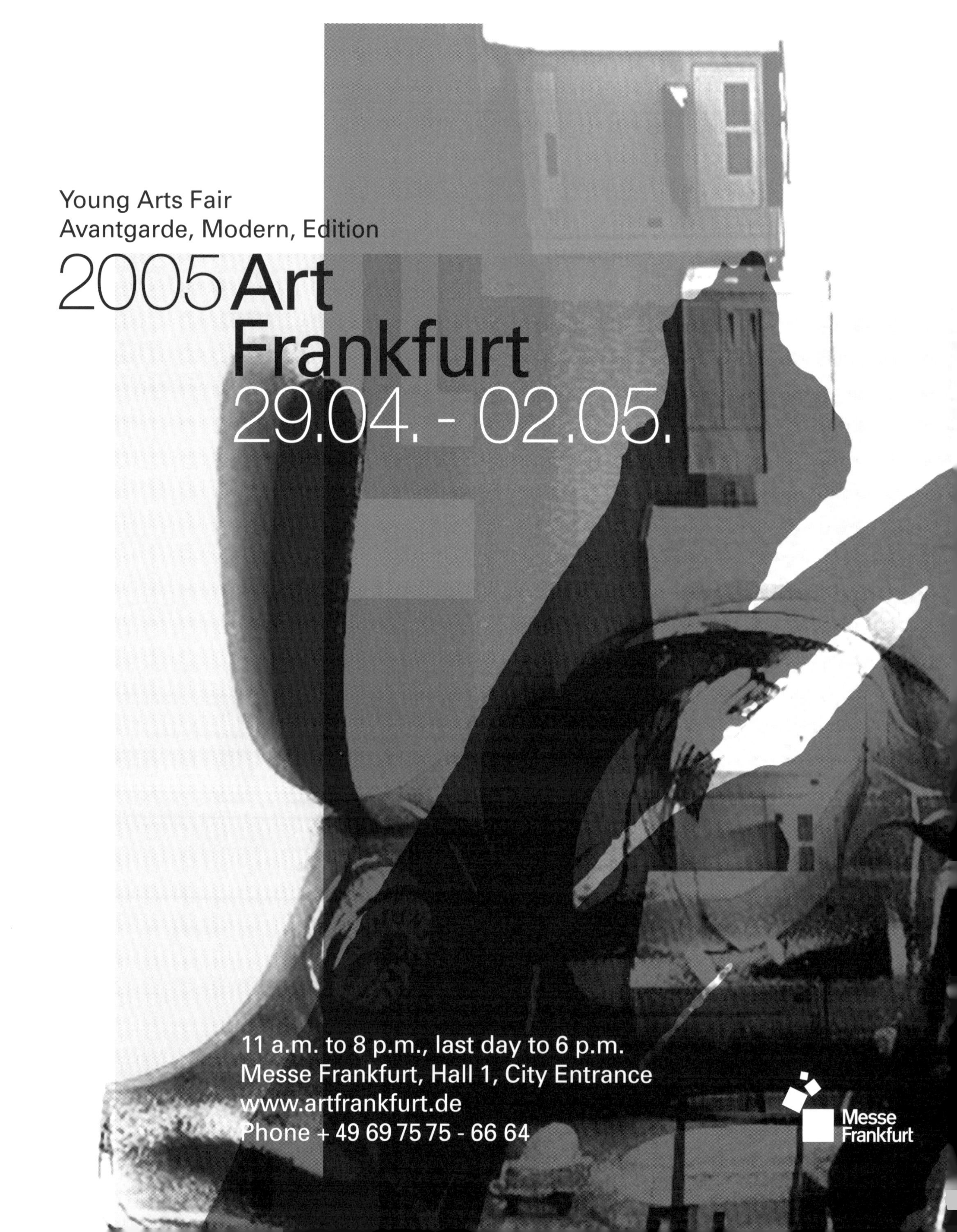

Young Arts Fair
Avantgarde, Modern, Edition
2005 Art
Frankfurt
29.04. - 02.05.
11 a.m. to 8 p.m., last day to 6 p.m.
Messe Frankfurt, Hall 1, City Entrance
www.artfrankfurt.de
Phone + 49 69 75 75 - 66 64
Messe
Frankfurt

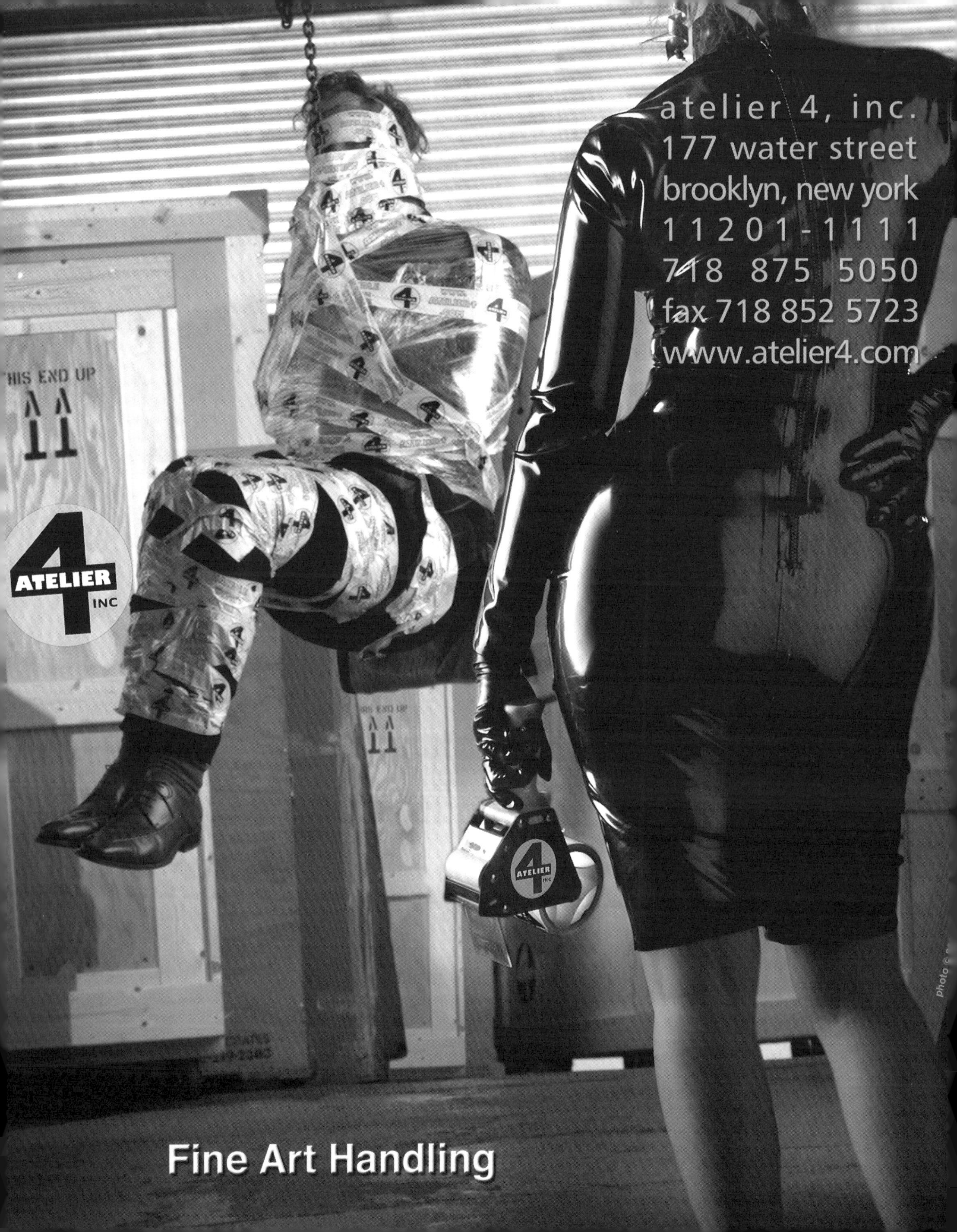
atelier 4, inc.
177 water street
brooklyn, new york
11201-1111
718 875 5050
fax 718 852 5723
www.atelier4.com
THIS END UP
4 ATELIER INC
Fine Art Handling

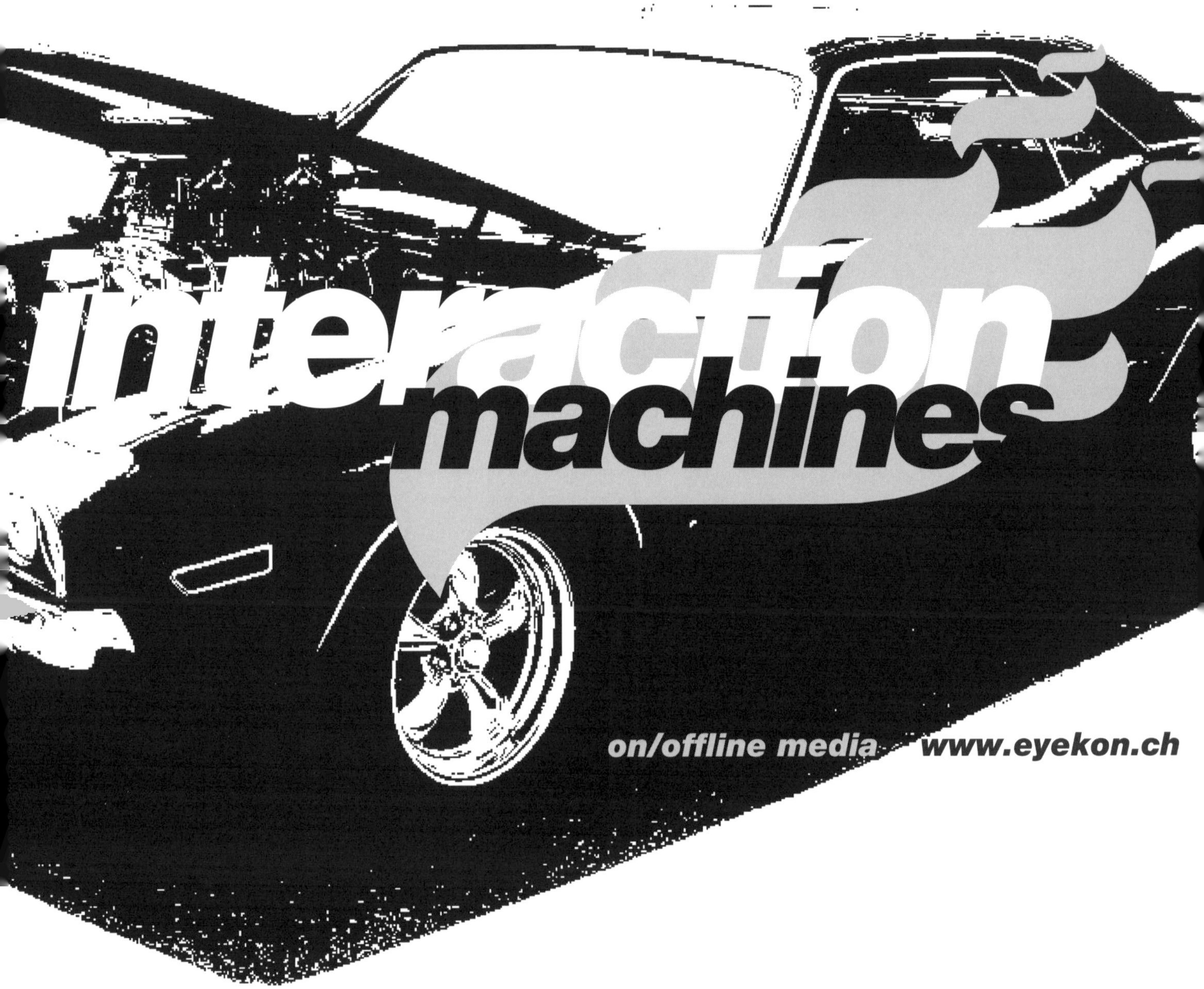
interaction
machines
on/offline media
www.eyekon.ch

e-flux video rental

september 2004 - february 2005

53
ludlow street
new york
10002

contact @e-flux.com

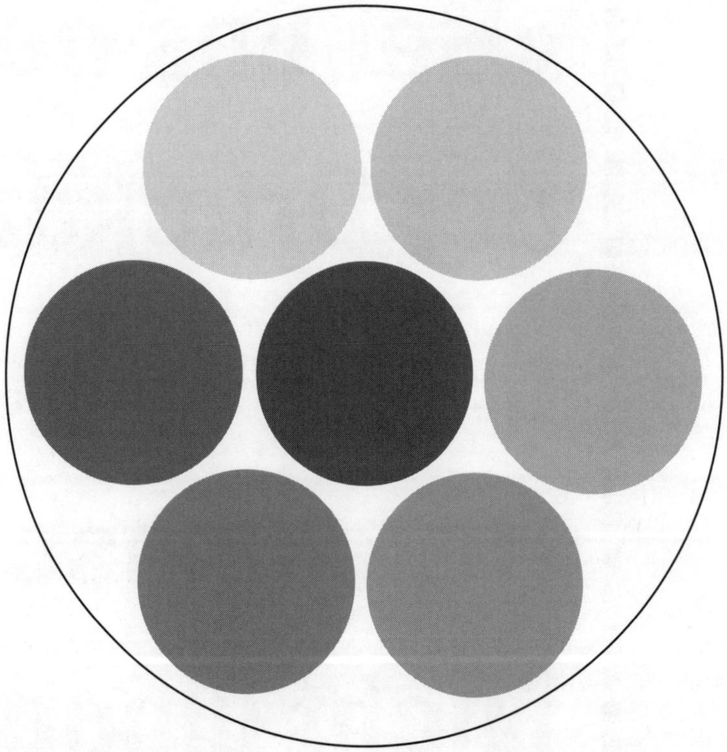

Selections by: Fernanda Arruda, Zdenka Badovinac, Regine Basha, Pablo Leon de la Barra, Gabriel Perez-Barreiro, Daniel Birnbaum, Thomas Boutoux, Adam Budak, Mariana David, Mai Abu ElDahab, Power Ekroth, Elena Filipovic, Lauri Firstenberg, Annie Fletcher, Gabrielle Giattino, Massimiliano Gioni, Julieta Gonzalez, Francesca Grassi, Sofia Hernandez, Jens Hoffmann, Anthony Huberman, Pierre Huyghe, Eungie Joo, Christoph Keller, Adam Klimczak, Vasif Kortun, Anders Kreuger, Fernando Llanos, Omar Lopez Chahoud, Viktor Misiano, Molly Nesbit, Hans Ulrich Obrist, November Paynter, Natasa Petresin, Karyn Riegel, Itala Schmelz, Henk Slager, Hanno Soans, Ali Subotnick, Barbara Vanderlinden, Gilbert Vicario, Florian Waldvogel and e-flux employees.

Participating artists (list in formation): 24/7, Lucas Ajemian, Nevin Aladag, Jennifer Allora & Guillermo Calzadilla, Adriana Arenas, Vasco Araujo, Viktor Alimpiev, Paulo Almeida, Eliu Almonte, Andre Amparo, Tiong Ang, Michel Auder, Assume Vivid Astro Focus, Miriam Backstrom, Lucas Bambozzi, Edson Barrus, Sarah Bennington, Roberto Berliner, Colectivo Bijari, John Bock, Mike Bouchet, Frank Boue, Andrea Bowers, Eriks Bozis, Ulla von Brandenburg, Mircea Cantor, Domenico Capello, Carolina Caycedo, Alejandro Cesarco, Paul Chan, Marcos Chaves, Loulou Cherinet, Olga Chernishova, Heman Chong, Coliseum, Alexander Costello, Roberto Cuoghi, Heavy Industries, Hubert Czerepok, Independent State, Jeremy Deller, Angela Detanico y Rafael Lain, Trisha Donnelly, Melissa Dubbin / Aaron Davidson, Ivan Edeza, Espacio La Culpable, Hector Falcon, Jeanne Faust, Jakup Ferri, Alicia Framis, Dara Friedman, Rene Gabri, Galeria Chilena, Gilbert & George, Jeremie Gindre, Andrea Geyer, Piero Golia, Loris Greaud, Nicolas Guagnini/Karin Schneider, Natascha Sadr Haghighian, Driton Hajredini, Sharon Hayes, Daniel Herskowitz, Shere Hite, Enrique Jezik, Tom Johnson, Spike Jonze / Rick Howard / Ty Evans / Vory Weincheque, Michael Joo, Ilya Kabakov, Tellervo Kalleinen, Leopold Kessler, Katarzyna Kozyra, Elke Krystufek, Korpys/Loffler, Tim Lee, Mark Leckey, Jesse Lerner, Erik van Liesthout, Daniel Lima, Fernando Llanos, Dora Longo Bahia, Polonca Lovsin, Maria Lusitano, Jorge Macchi, Teresa Margolles, Christopher Maner, Marepe, Marssares, Jonas Mekas, John Menick, Ohad Meromi, Simone Michellin, Sarah Minter, Aleksandra Mir, Melvin Motti, Argentino Neto, Filip Noterdaeme, Tuan Nguyen, Love Nordberg, Yoshua Okon, Annee Olofsson, Yoko Ono, The Otolith Group, Jenny Perlin, Diego Perrone, Alessandro Pessoli, John Pilson, Steven Pippin, Michelangelo Pistoletto, Shannon Plumb, Linda Post, Arturas Raila, Egle Rakauskaite, Nick Relph / Oliver Payne, Guy Richards-Smit, Jozef Robakowsk, Aida Ruilova, Alfredo Salomon, Markus Schinwald, Corinna Schnitt, Ene-liis Semper, Wael Shawky, Taro Shinoda, Santiago Sierra, Silverio, Michael Smith, Robert Smithson, Aaron Steffes, Hito Steyerl, A.L. Steiner, Tetine (Bruno Verner & Eliete Mejorado), Rirkrit Tiravanija, Jaan Toomik, Kerry Tribe, Manuela Viera Gallo, Jenny Vogel, Lawrence Weiner, Suara Welitoff, Jordan Wolfson, Erwin Wurm, Cerith Wyn Evans, Olivier Zabat, Akram Zaatari, Darius Ziura and others.

alessandro twombly

20_01_05–05_03_05

5 rue de la muse

EVERGREENE

Works on paper at Evergreene
Paintings at BFAS Blondeau Fine Art Services

Catalogue available

EVERGREENE

27/29 RUE DE LA COULOUVRENIÈRE 1204 GENÈVE
TEL + 41 22 321 3740 GREENGAL@IPROLINK.CH WWW.EVERGREENE.CH

BFAS
Blondeau Fine Art Services

5 rue de la Muse
1205 Geneva _ Switzerland
T +41 (0)22 544 95 95
F +41 (0)22 544 95 99

■ exhibition
TUE–FRI 14h–18h30
SAT 11h–17h
■ office
MON–FRI 9h–12h30 / 14h–18h30

SI

WINTER / SPRING PROGRAM 2004/05

NONE OF THE ABOVE

DAVE ALLEN, RICHARD ARTSCHWAGER, FIA BACKSTRÖM, MASSIMO BARTOLINI, FRANCIS BAUDEVIN, PATTERSON BECKWITH, MONICA BONVICINI, OLAF BREUNING, AA BRONSON, MAURIZIO CATTELAN, JAN CHRISTENSEN, MARTIN CREED, STÉPHANE DAFFLON, PHILIPPE DECRAUZAT, JASON DODGE, FISCHLI & WEISS, SYLVIE FLEURY, AMY GRANAT, TIMOTHY GREENFIELD-SANDERS, FABRICE GYGI, ALIX LAMBERT, BERTRAND LAVIER, BALTHAZAR LOVAY, CHRISTIAN MARCLAY, MATHIEU MERCIER, SIMON MORETTI, OLIVIER MOSSET, AMY O'NEILL, LAURENT PACHE, STEVEN PARRINO, MAI-THU PERRET, BREIER P-ORRIDGE, PETER PUMPLER, GERWALD ROCKENSCHAUB, MICHAEL ROSS, MARKUS SIXAY, HAIM STEIN-BACH, RUDOLF STINGEL, BLAIR THURMAN, JOHN TREMBLAY, PIERRE VADI, XAVIER VEILHAN, LAWRENCE WEINER, JORDAN WOLFSON

CURATED BY JOHN ARMLEDER

NOVEMBER 23 – JANUARY 15 2005

NORMA JEANE

FEBRUARY 8 – MARCH 19 2005

OK /OKAY

CHRISTIAN ANDERSSON, OLIVIER BLANCKART, VALENTIN CARRON, LAURENT GRASSO, BOB GRAMSMA, GRAHAM GUSSIN, LEOPOLD KESSLER, GABRIELE DI MATTEO, ADAM MCEWEN, GIANNI MOTTI, WERNER REITERER, NEDKO SOLAKOV, JEAN-LUC VERNA, BEN WOODESON (list in formation)

CURATED BY MARC-OLIVIER WAHLER

EXHIBITION AT THE SI AND THE GREY ART GALLERY NEW YORK

APRIL 18 – JULY 16 2005

SI

SWISS INSTITUTE - CONTEMPORARY ART,
495 BROADWAY 3RD FLOOR / NEW YORK NY 10012
TUESDAY – SATURDAY 11 A.M. – 6 P.M. / p 212 925 2035 / f 212 925 2040
www.swissinstitute.net / info@swissinstitute.net

Centre Culturel Suisse 38, rue des Francs-Bourgeois
75003 **Paris** France T +33 (0)1 42 71 44 50 F +33 (0)1 42 71 51 24
ccs@ccsparis.com www.ccsparis.com
pro helvetia - fondation suisse pour la culture

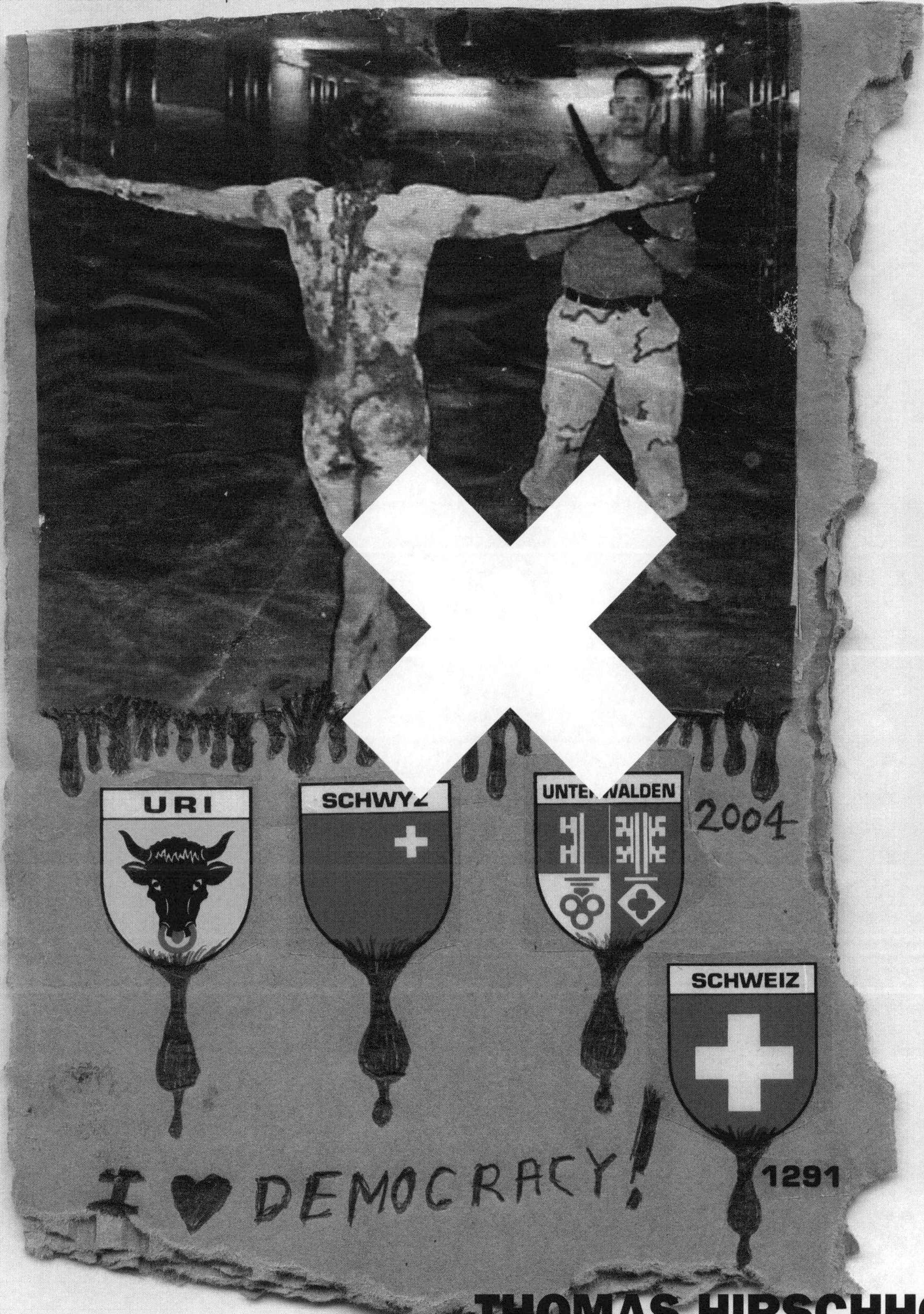

THOMAS HIRSCHHORN
SWISS-SWISS DEMOCRACY
04.12.04 - 30.01.05

OUVERTURE LE 04.12.04/11H00 à 21H00

HORAIRES SPÉCIAUX : DU MARDI AU DIMANCHE/11H00 à 21H00

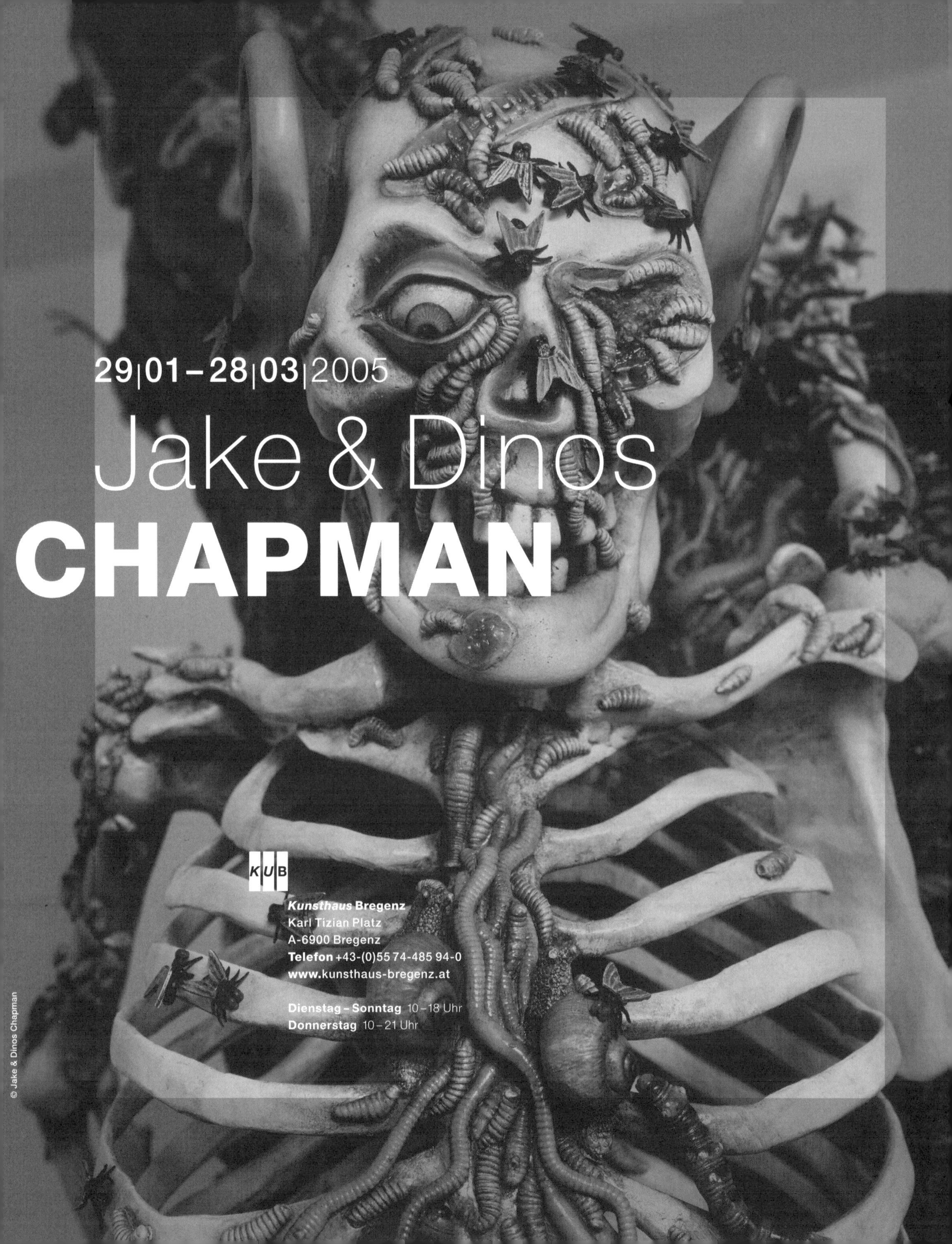
29|01 – 28|03|2005
Jake & Dinos
CHAPMAN
KUB
Kunsthaus Bregenz
Karl Tizian Platz
A-6900 Bregenz
Telefon +43-(0)55 74-485 94-0
www.kunsthaus-bregenz.at
Dienstag – Sonntag 10 – 18 Uhr
Donnerstag 10 – 21 Uhr
© Jake & Dinos Chapman

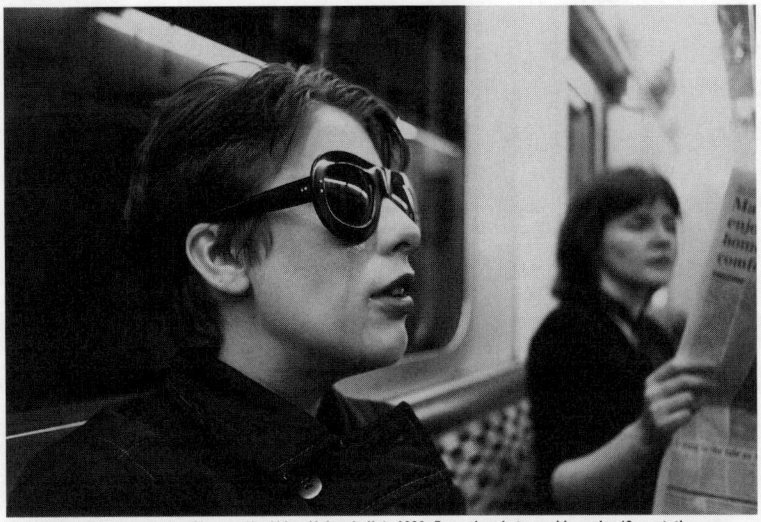

Hayley Newman, Crying Glasses (An Aid to Melancholia), 1998. From the photographic series 'Connotations: Performance Images, 1994–1998'. Courtesy the artist and Matt's Gallery, London. Photo: Casey Orr

16.2–30.4.2005

GALLERIAGOTTARDO

In collaboration with

Jean-Pascal Imsand

Fondation Jean-Pascal Imsand
Musée de l'Elysée, Lausanne
Fotostiftung Schweiz, Winterthur

Galleria Gottardo

una fondazione per la cultura della
eine Kulturstiftung der
a foundation for the promotion of cultural activities of

BANCADEL GOTTARDO

Institutional Patron of the
Solomon R. Guggenheim Foundation

Dienstag
14.00 - 17.00 Uhr
Mittwoch bis Samstag
11.00 - 17.00 Uhr
Sonntag, Montag und Feiertage geschlossen

Tuesday
2 p.m. - 5 p.m.
Wednesday - Saturday
11 a.m - 5 p.m.
Closed Sundays, Mondays, and public holidays

Viale Stefano Franscini 12
6900 Lugano, Switzerland

phone +41 808 1988
galleria@gottardo.com
www.galleria-gottardo.org

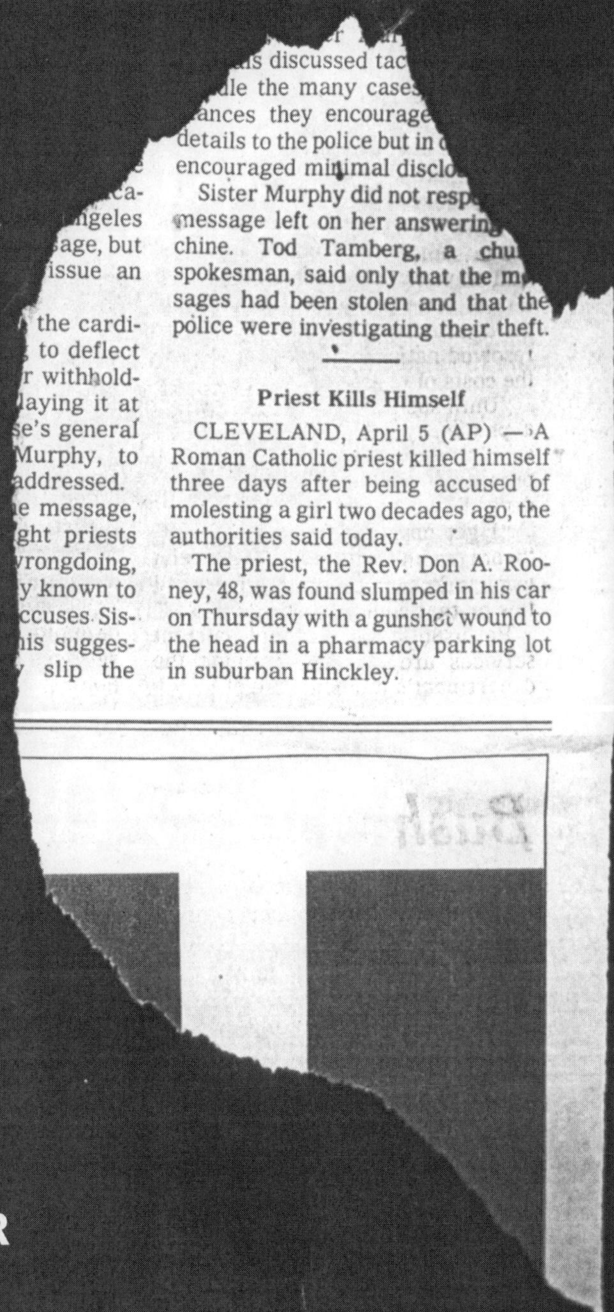

discussed tac
the many case
they encourage
details to the police but in
encouraged minimal disclo
Sister Murphy did not resp
message left on her answering
chine. Tod Tamberg, a chu
spokesman, said only that the m
sages had been stolen and that the
police were investigating their theft.
Priest Kills Himself
CLEVELAND, April 5 (AP) — A Roman Catholic priest killed himself three days after being accused of molesting a girl two decades ago, the authorities said today.
The priest, the Rev. Don A. Rooney, 48, was found slumped in his car on Thursday with a gunshot wound to the head in a pharmacy parking lot in suburban Hinckley.

Jonathan Lasker

february - march, 2005

Vik Muniz

april - may, 2005

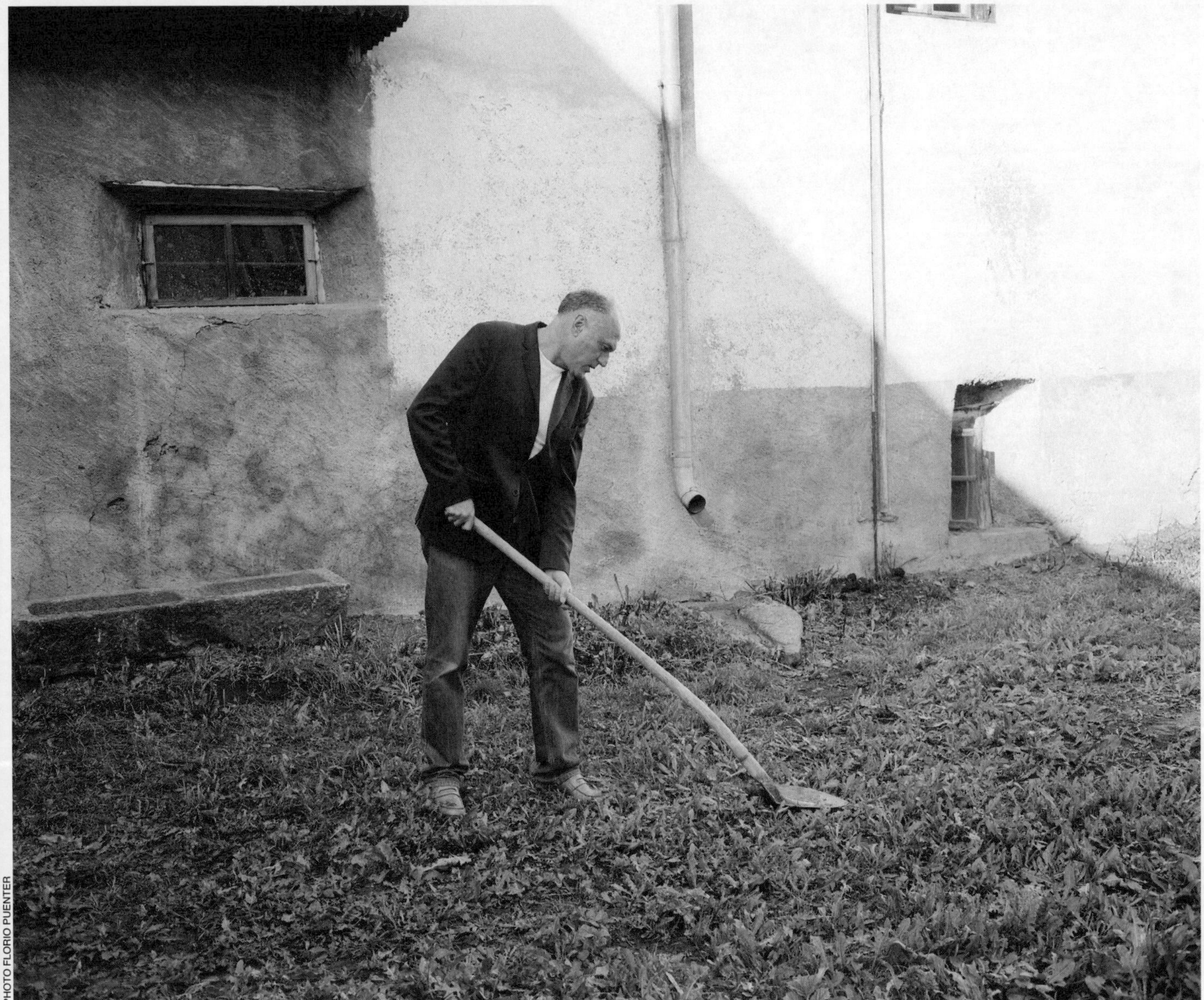

PHOTO FLORIO PUENTER

NOT VITAL

DECEMBER 2004 – FEBRUARY 2005

JOHN M ARMLEDER

MARCH – MAY 2005

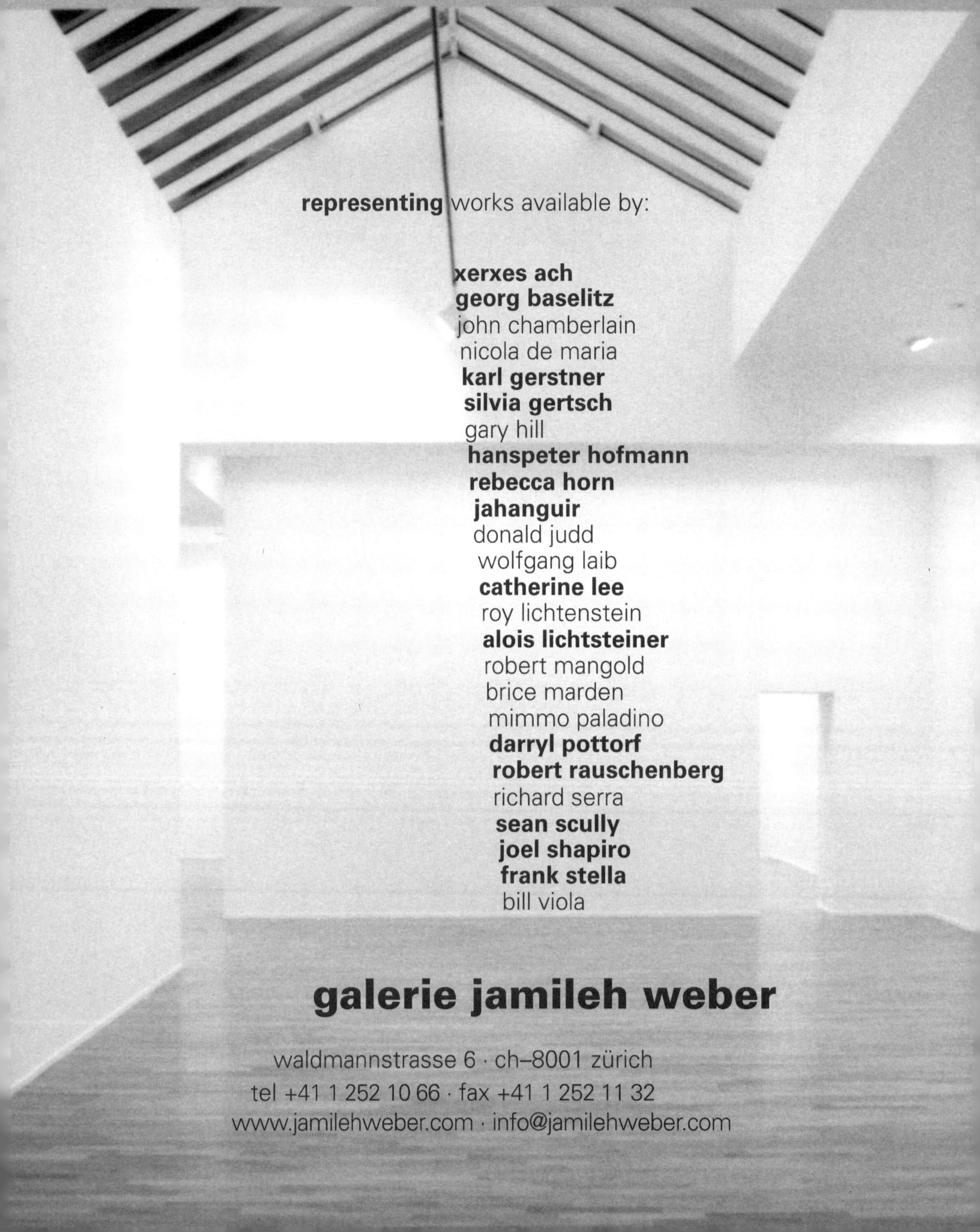
representing works available by:
xerxes ach
georg baselitz
john chamberlain
nicola de maria
karl gerstner
silvia gertsch
gary hill
hanspeter hofmann
rebecca horn
jahanguir
donald judd
wolfgang laib
catherine lee
roy lichtenstein
alois lichtsteiner
robert mangold
brice marden
mimmo paladino
darryl pottorf
robert rauschenberg
richard serra
sean scully
joel shapiro
frank stella
bill viola
galerie jamileh weber
waldmannstrasse 6 · ch–8001 zürich
tel +41 1 252 10 66 · fax +41 1 252 11 32
www.jamilehweber.com · info@jamilehweber.com